Australia

Dawn till Dusk

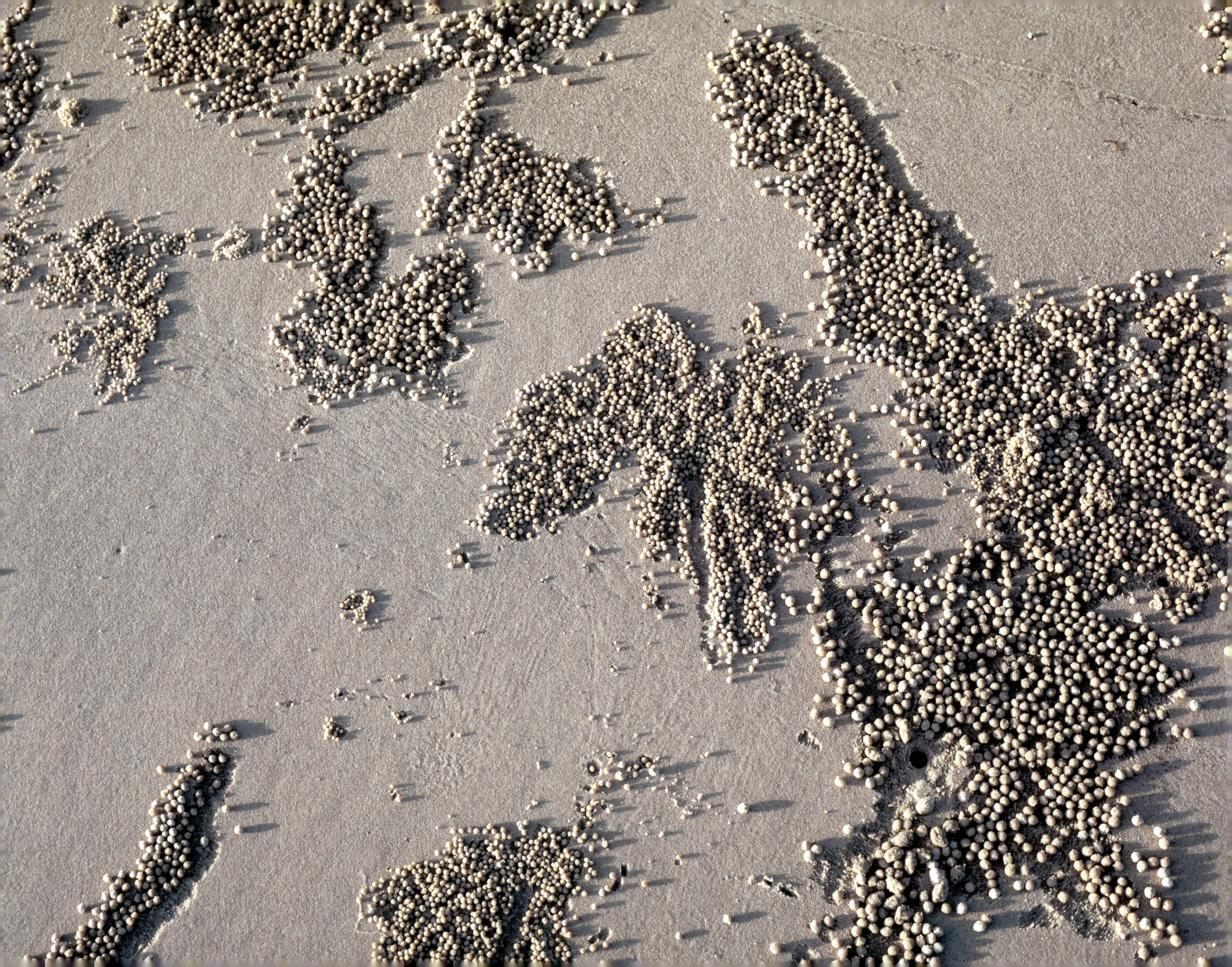

Australia

Dawn till Dusk

Rob Olver

DAWN TILL DUSK
Publications

First published in 2014 by
Dawn till Dusk Publications
3/149 Murwillumbah Street, Murwillumbah, NSW 2484

National Library of Australia
Cataloguing-in-Publication entry:

Olver, Rob (Robert), 1968 –

Australia, Dawn till Dusk/Rob Olver
ISBN number 978-0-9757627-2-1

Bibliography
Australia--Pictorial works.
Australia--Description and travel.

Front cover image: Boab tree near Windjana Gorge in the Kimberley, with the Napier Range behind.

Back cover images: Left to right – View to Mount Freycinet from Cape Tourville lookout, Tasmania; sandstone escarpment and ghost gum in the Keep River National Park, Northern Territory; a beautiful dawn over Dunk Island and South Mission Beach in Far North Queensland.

Page 2 image: Patriotic pattern created by sand bubbler crabs on a northern New South Wales beach. These small crabs strain beach sand in their hunt for worms and crustaceans during low tide, producing many tiny sand balls. They radiate out from their sand burrow and usually produce a roughly circular group of sand balls – but not in this case!

Editor Christina Houen

Designed by Ji Min energydesign.com.au, and Rosalie Okely

Printed by Everbest Printing Co Ltd, China

Acknowledgments and Photographic Notes
I would like to thank: my parents Des and Pat, family and friends including Stuart, Afroula, Con and John; Di, Nigel, Connor, Riley and Sam; Colleen, Chris, Jake and Liam; Anaïs Keller, Christina Houen, Jenni Hibbard, Marion Douglas, Stella Huttlestone, James Hill; Photo Continental, Mt Gravatt, QLD; Justin Moriarty from FujiFilm Australia.

I use FujiFilm Velvia exclusively for its vivid colours, sharpness and fine grain. Most images in this book were taken with a Pentax 67II medium format camera. I also use a Nikon F70 SLR camera and a Pentax Optio S5i digital camera.

www.robolver.com

Contents

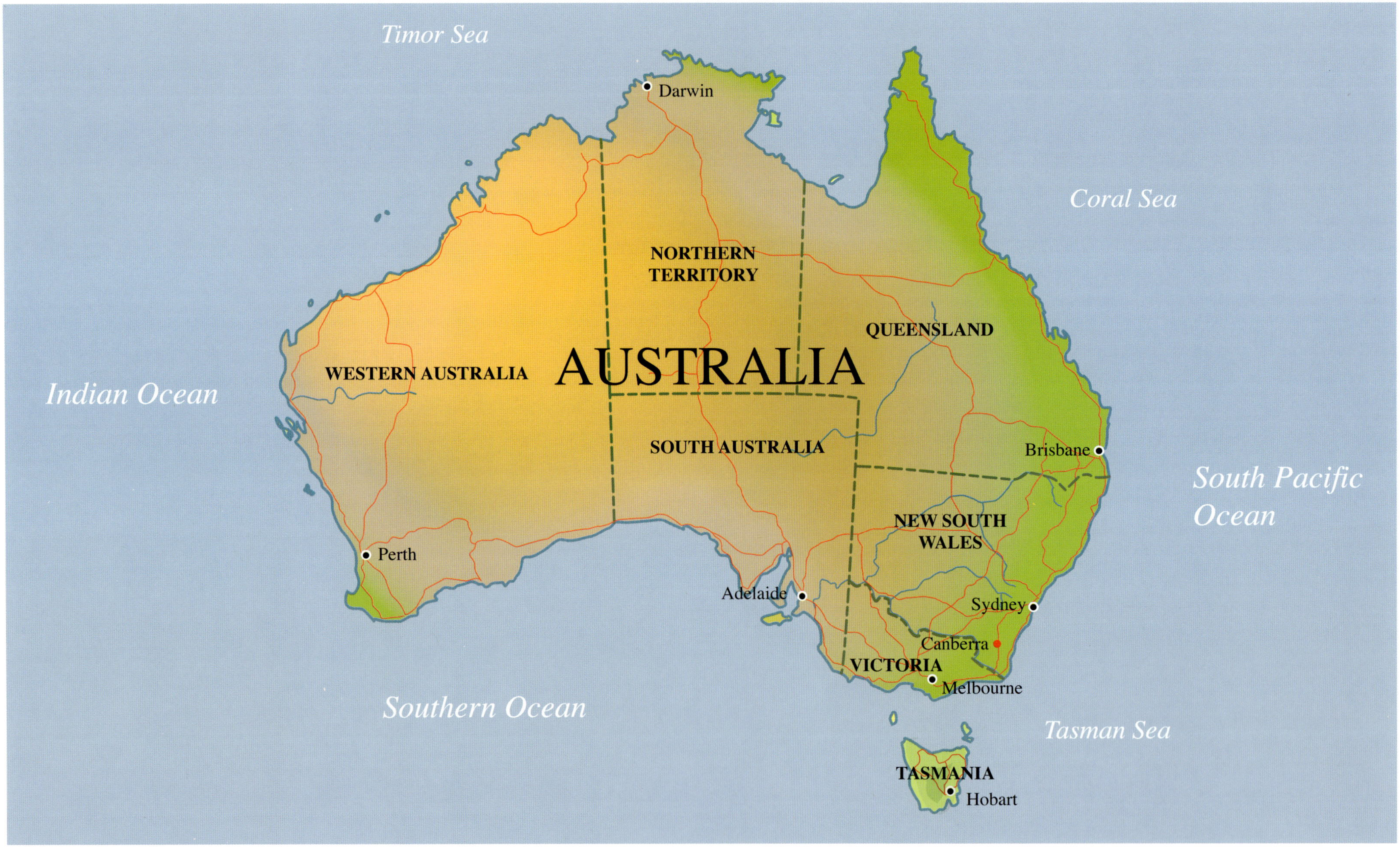
Timor Sea
Darwin
Coral Sea
NORTHERN TERRITORY
QUEENSLAND
AUSTRALIA
WESTERN AUSTRALIA
Indian Ocean
SOUTH AUSTRALIA
Brisbane
South Pacific Ocean
NEW SOUTH WALES
Perth
Adelaide
Sydney
Canberra
VICTORIA
Melbourne
Southern Ocean
Tasman Sea
TASMANIA
Hobart

Preface

I was not born in Australia. I emigrated in 1983 with my family when I was 14, from the land of my birth South Africa. We left that country because we didn't agree with its apartheid policies of that time and chose Australia because of its similar landscape and way of life. I became an Australian citizen in 1988.

Some of my earliest memories are of hiking and climbing in South Africa's Drakensberg Mountains, in Kwazulu-Natal Province, when I was only four or five. When we emigrated I received a black and white photographic book on these mountains from my parents. This book was to change my life. I have always felt a strong affinity with nature and for the first time I saw how an artist could capture this passion on film. I bought a cheap camera soon after and took my first pictures while on a bushwalk. I was hooked! Landscape photography has since become an absorbing and deeply fulfilling career for me.

How do you photograph a book about Australia? It is such a huge and beautiful country and a daunting prospect. Well, in my case I jumped in my car and started driving. I didn't have the funds to buy a big 4WD or a caravan and went in my Toyota Camry! I took along three cameras, two tripods, water, food and a tiny tent.

The next obvious question is, why do it? The photograph right may give you some insight as it captures one of the low points of my life. Here, I am preparing for a garage sale at my erstwhile dream home in the Porongurup Range of southern Western Australia. The house had been sold and I was moving out in a week or two. Everything had turned pear-shaped, and I had lost all of my usual passion and zest for life. I love those mountains (my first book, co-written with my brother Stuart, was on the Porongurup and Stirling Ranges) but you can't live on scenery. You have to have something to do! I decided to be bold, follow my own path and start being creative again. I have never desired a "normal" life of a house in the suburbs, a mortgage and 2.3 children, and I finally gave myself permission to follow my dreams of photographing Australia.

It was very hard at first. My first entry in my trip diary was: "*I said goodbye to the family and everyone gave me a big hug. I got in the car and beeped the horn a few times and then drove off. I immediately got very emotional and teary. This lasted about 20 minutes.*" I took about a month to unwind and relax during the trip, and even after that period had moments of reflection and sadness. I headed north from Perth, through the Pilbara and Kimberley to the Northern Territory and Queensland. I visited family and friends in Brisbane, Sydney and Melbourne, and from there travelled via South Australia back to Perth. The five month journey was wonderful, and I was able to reflect on my life and also on the difficult challenges facing humanity like peak oil and climate change. I saw some amazing sights and regained my love for myself and the world. It may have saved my life! Most of the images in this book are from this one long road-trip around Australia in 2011 and a second shorter trip through New South Wales, Victoria and Tasmania in 2013. I hope these words and images inspire you to experience more of this beautiful country for yourself.

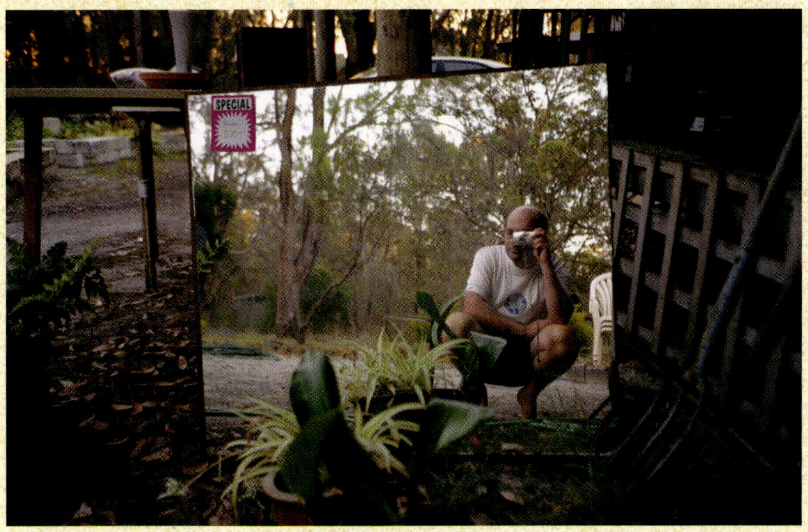

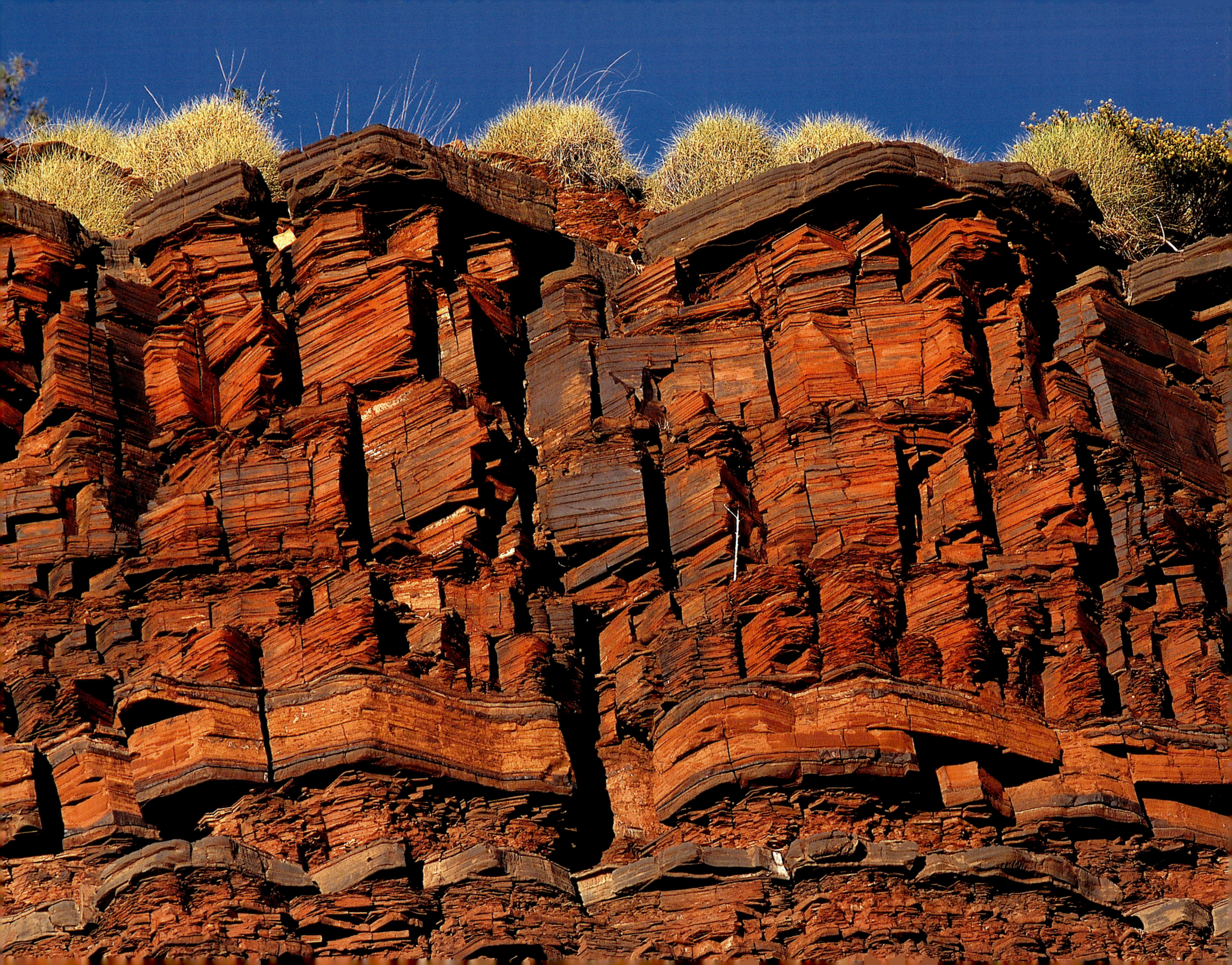

The Natural Landscape

Australia is a big and diverse country. The wet tropics of the far north is a different world to the alpine mountains of Tasmania or to the arid Nullabor Plain. As I roamed slowly around the country in my Camry, changes usually took place gradually and without drama. But after a while you would see a change in the quality of the light, a subtle change in the colour of the trees and grasses and a distant hill would suddenly be upon you. Occasionally there would be dramatic change, for example, descending the Great Dividing Range from the arid interior to the lush eastern coastal strip or driving into the rugged King Leopold Ranges in the Kimberley. The landscapes here are some of the most mesmerising in the world, and places like Uluru and Kata Tjuta, Arnhem Land, Kakadu and the Flinders Ranges have ancient spirituality imbued in their rocks and trees.

Australia is the sixth largest country on earth, covering an area of 7,692,024 square kilometres. It is as big as Europe, excluding Russia, and as large as the continental United States excluding Alaska. Some 70 per cent of the country is arid or semi-arid and generally low lying and flat. Australian landforms are usually ancient and the soils are poor, low in nutrients and high in salt, which has encouraged plant diversity, as no one species can dominate. The only exceptions to this are the few areas of comparatively recent volcanic activity, like the Tweed Caldera in northern New South Wales and the Atherton Tablelands in Far North Queensland. The climate varies from temperate to tropical and the rainfall from only 100-150 mm annually at Lake Eyre in South Australia to over 4000 mm each year in Far North Queensland near the towns of Tully and Babinda.

The main area of mountains is the long line of the Great Dividing Range on the mainland and the peaks of Tasmania, which were mostly formed by ancient volcanic activity. The most recent eruption was about 4,800 years ago. The volcanic activity was associated with the Pacific plate colliding with and descending below the Australian/Indian plate. Many of Australia's mountains are made of granite, which is intruded molten rock that cools slowly underground; for example, Mount Buffalo in Victoria and the Hazards on the Freycinet Peninsula in Tasmania. Sandstone rocks occur in other areas, producing striking landscapes like the Blue Mountains in New South Wales and Carnarvon Gorge in Queensland. Ancient folded mountains occur in central Australia and the Flinders and Mount Lofty Ranges of South Australia. Western Australia has high plateau country and gorges in the Kimberley and Pilbara and isolated small ranges, like the Stirling Range, near the south coast. Australia protects many of these mountainous landscapes, along with semi-desert, tropical savannahs and islands, in over 500 national parks.

Australia is unlike any other country or continent in the world in terms of its unique habitats and wildlife. The Great South Land finally separated from Antarctica about 50 million years ago and since then has drifted alone in the Southern Hemisphere, allowing the plants and animals to evolve in isolation. While other habitable continents have exchanged species and genetic material via land bridges, Australia's flora and fauna has gone on its own different evolutionary journey. Almost all Australian plants are evergreen and a high proportion are endemic or only found naturally here. Most are flowering plants, and where conifers occur they are generally not dominant in the landscape. The two most important and widespread genera here are Eucalyptus and Acacia. Eucalypts, also known as gum trees, are found throughout Australia, except for the desert regions. There are over 700 species here. Eucalypts are well adapted to fire, and indeed fire is necessary to recycle nutrients, as gum leaves do not decompose easily. The other important genus is Acacia, which are especially common in arid and semi-arid regions. There are around 800 species in Australia, and one of these, the golden wattle, a shrub or small tree with distinctive yellow flowers found in South Australia, Victoria and New South Wales, is the floral emblem of Australia. Acacias are drought tolerant and many have a symbiotic relationship with nitrogen-fixing bacteria on root nodules, which aids their survival in poor soils. Other important plant genera are banksias, casuarinas and melaleucas.

Opposite page: Iron rich, jointed rocks in Wittenoom Gorge, Pilbara, Western Australia.

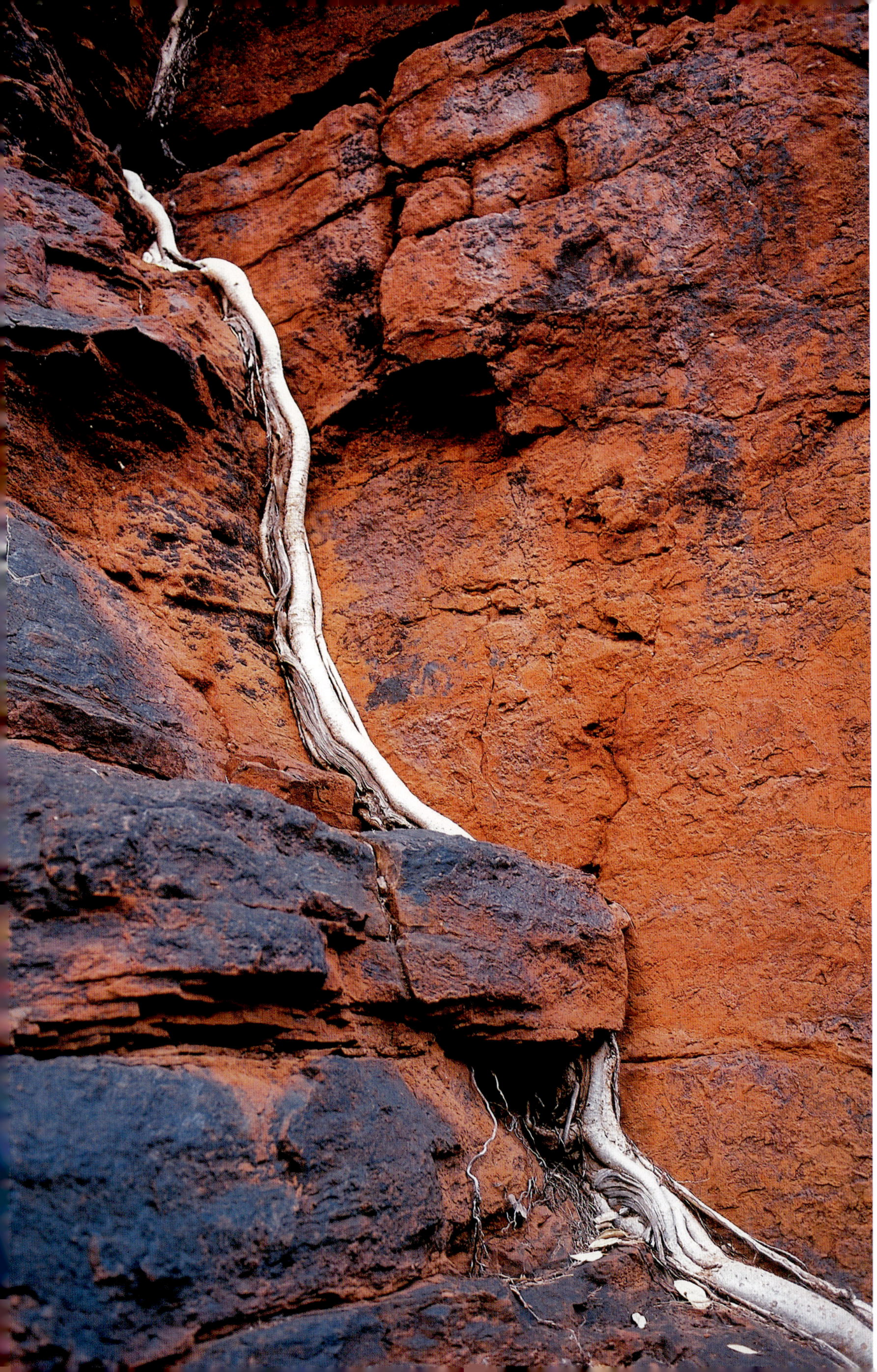

The most ancient flora in Australia occurs in small areas of rainforest along the Great Dividing Range; these are the surviving remnants of Gondwana flora that covered Australia when it was still connected to Antarctica 60 million years ago. A good example of this are Antarctic beech trees that still live in rainforests from Tasmania north to the Lamington plateau in southern Queensland. Some Gondwana conifers surviving in restricted areas include Queensland kauri, hoop and bunya pines. Another remarkable relict species, the Wollemi pine, was only recently discovered in 1994 in remote steep sided gorges in the Blue Mountains near Lithgow. Tropical, subtropical and temperate rainforests are extraordinarily rich in biodiversity, but altogether today they cover only 0.5 per cent of Australia's land surface. After the breakup of the continents Australia gradually drifted north and became progressively drier and hotter with more fires. This aided the spread of Eucalypts and Acacias, which are resistant to fire and drought.

Australia has some of the most amazing animals in the world, including marsupials like kangaroos, wombats, possums and koalas. Marsupials are primitive mammals that give birth to highly undeveloped young which are nurtured in a pouch on the lower abdomen. Animals like kangaroos are supremely adapted to Australia's harsh conditions, and their hopping motion is an energy efficient way of getting around. The largest native mammal in Australia is the red kangaroo, which can stand over 2 metres tall and weigh up to 82 kilograms. Echidnas and platypus are only found in Australia, and belong to an ancient mammalian order, the monotremes; they lay eggs to reproduce but are warm blooded and suckle their young. In all there are around 350 species of native mammal in Australia. Australia's birdlife is astonishingly rich; 770 species having been recorded in the country, including the famous kookaburra – the largest species of kingfisher in the world – emus, wedge-tailed eagles, cassowaries, and many species of parrot. Reptiles are well represented with 860 species, being especially suited to the hot, semi-arid areas of the continent, and Australia has 130 species of frog.

"Thirst for Life", a tree root in a Pilbara gorge searches for moisture.

Australia has ancient landforms and a rich and fascinating geology. The country is one of the world's treasure troves, with deposits of iron ore, coal, gold, bauxite, nickel and diamonds. Natural gas and oil are also found in some areas. At present the nation's economy relies heavily upon the exploitation of these resources, which are vulnerable to changes in the world economy and variation in demand and prices for raw materials.

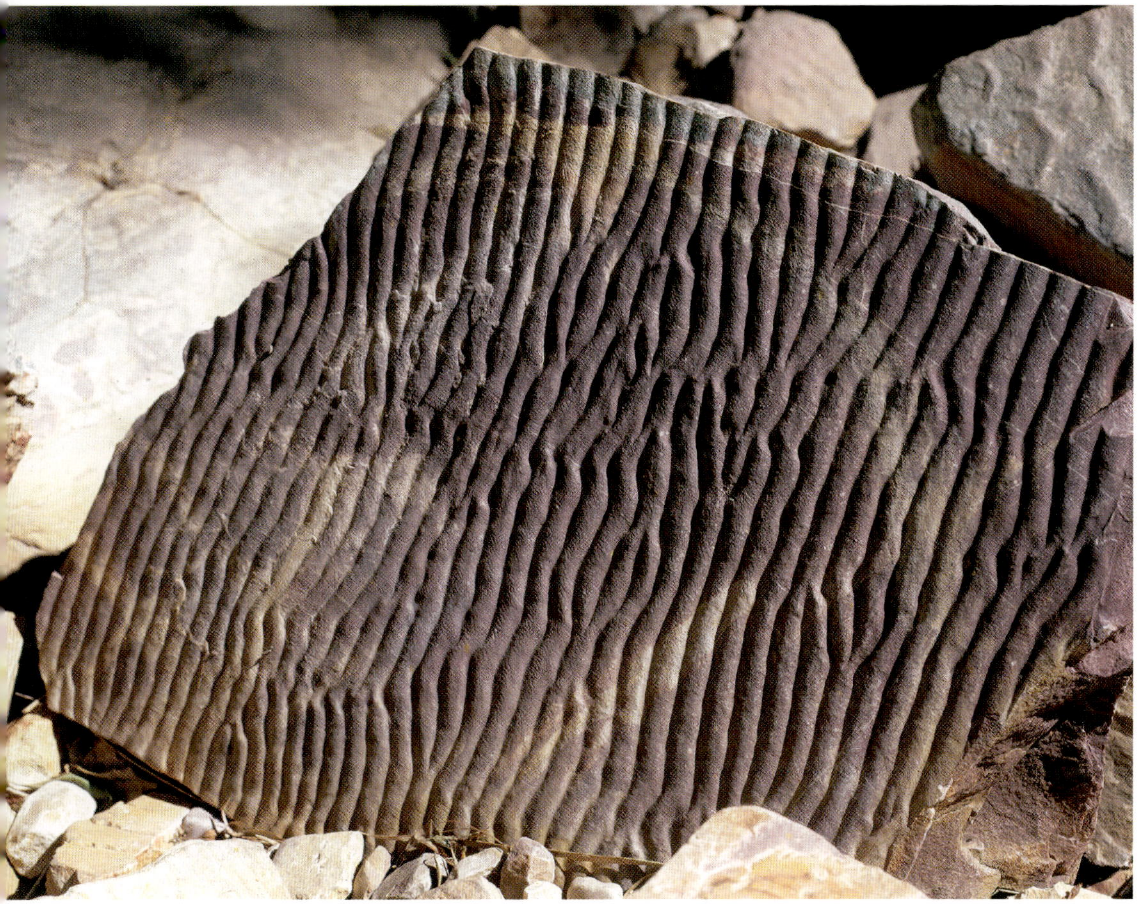

Ripple rocks at Emma Gorge in the Kimberley region of Western Australia betray their origin as sediments deposited in water.

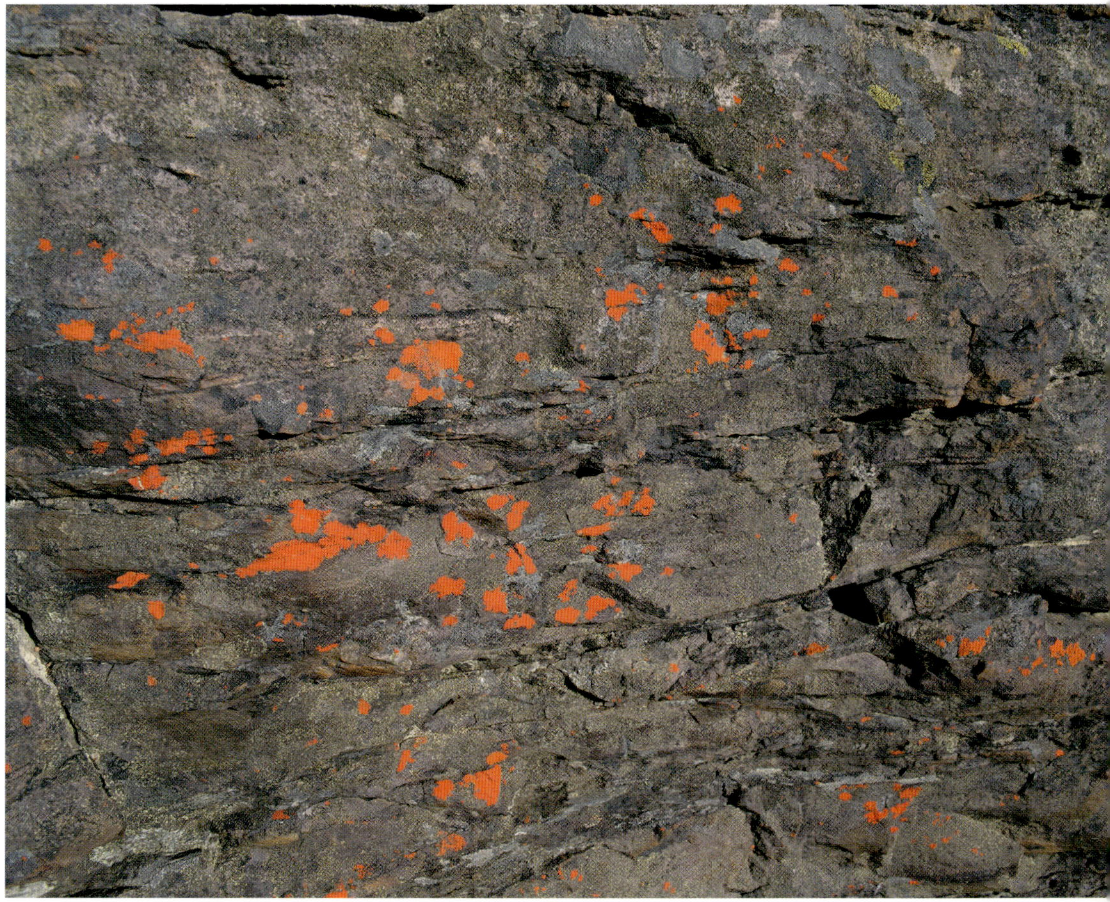

A lichen splashed sandstone rock on Talyuberlup Peak in the Stirling Range of southern Western Australia.

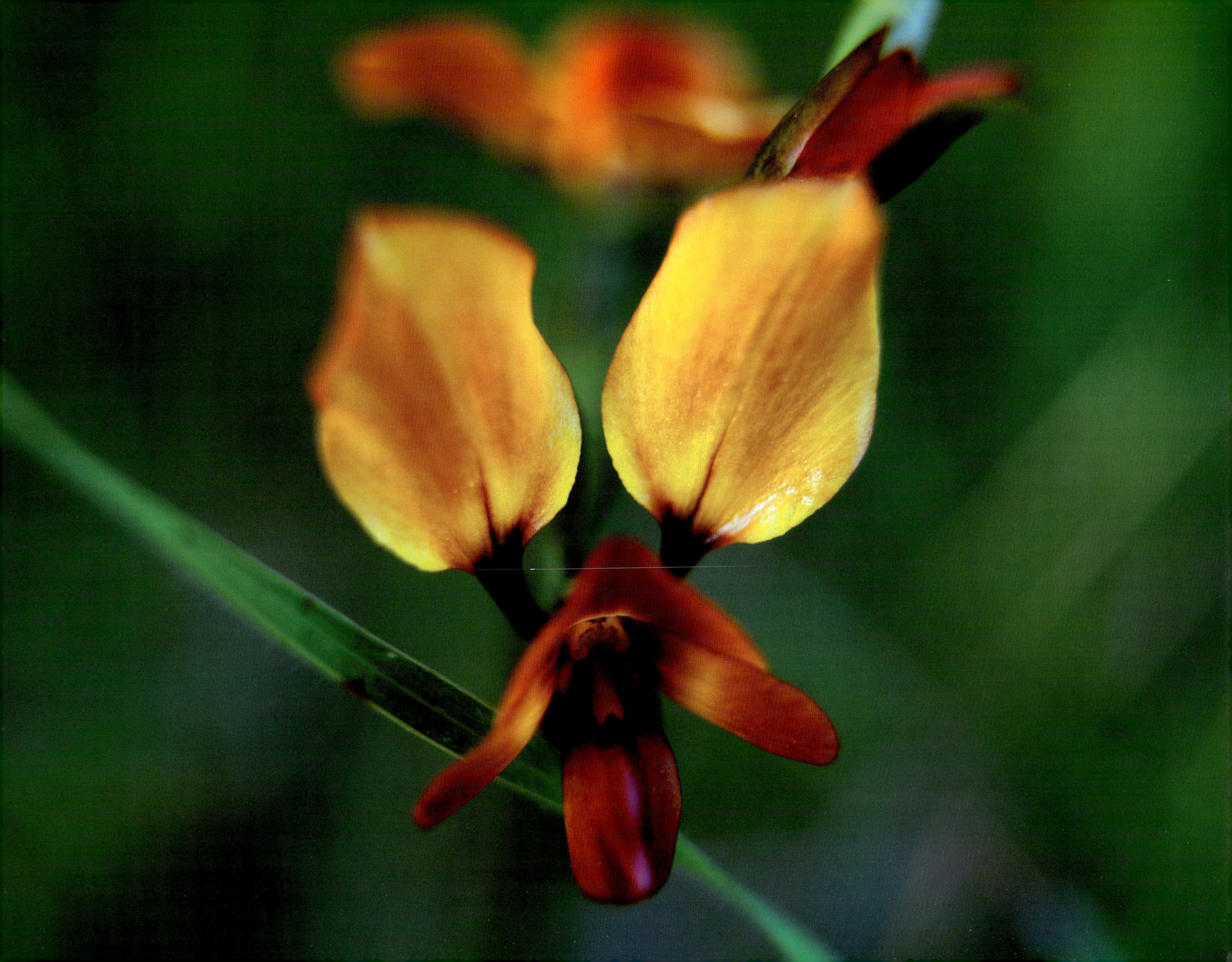

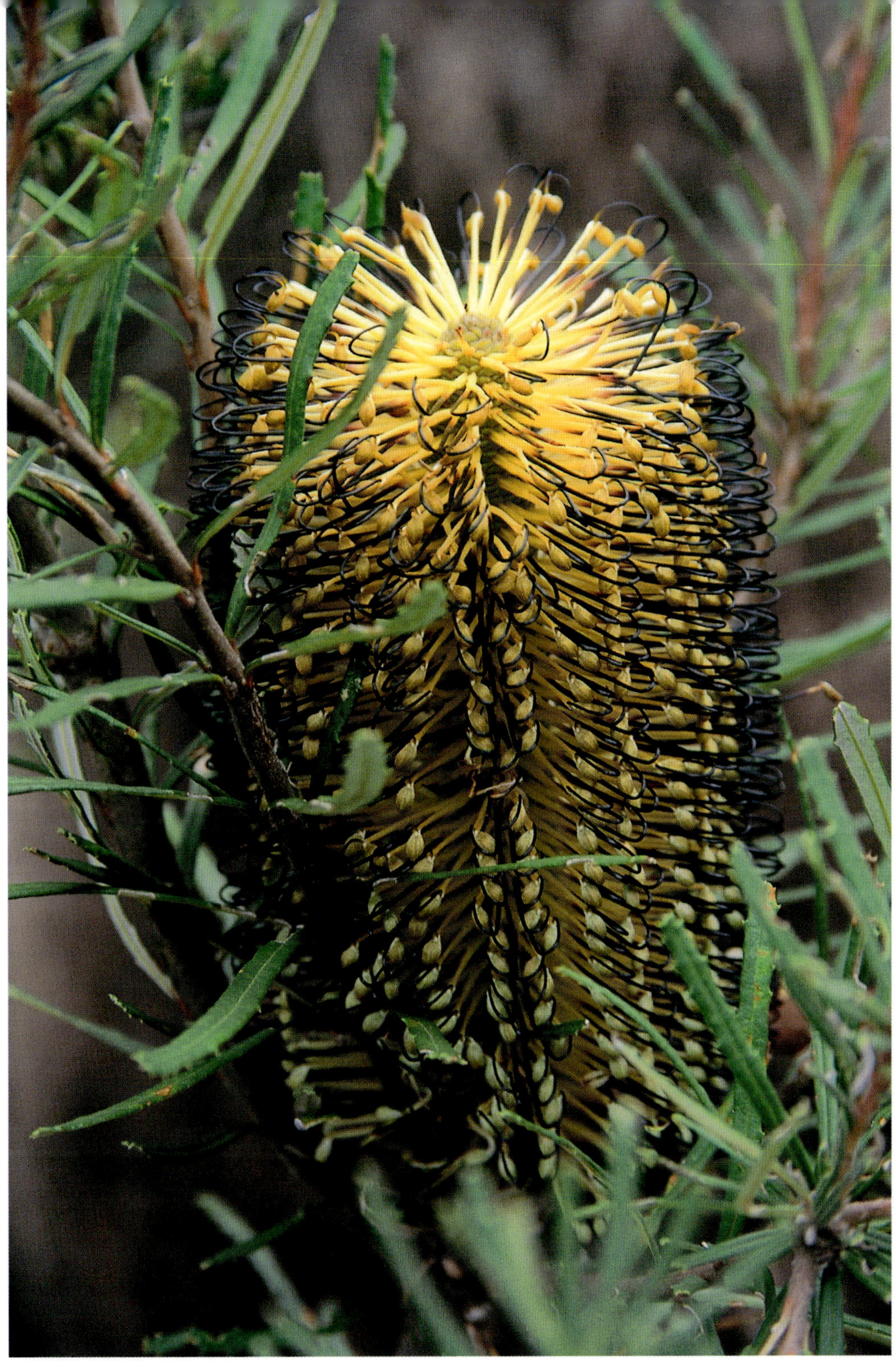

Top: *Flowering* banksia spinulosa, *Gibraltor Range NP, New South Wales.*

Opposite page: Common Donkey orchid, photographed in Perth bushland.

Australia is blessed with rich plant life and many wildflowers. Banksias and Dryandras are an important Australian genus and, of about 170 species, all except one are endemic or only found naturally here. Western Australia alone has over 450 species of native orchids. Overall, Australia has over 20,000 species of vascular plant and many more species of mosses, lichen and algae.

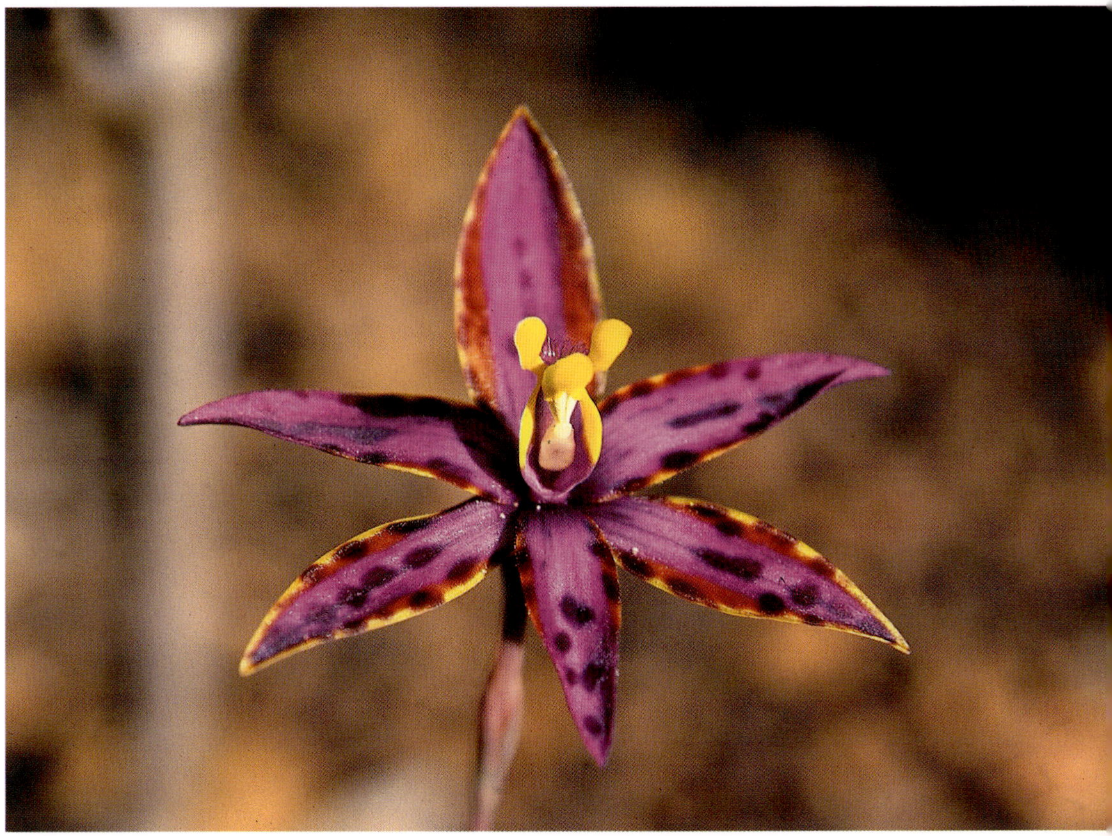

The beautiful Queen of Sheba orchid is a sun orchid and each flower opens only on sunny days in early spring for a brief time until it is pollinated; Stirling Range, Western Australia.

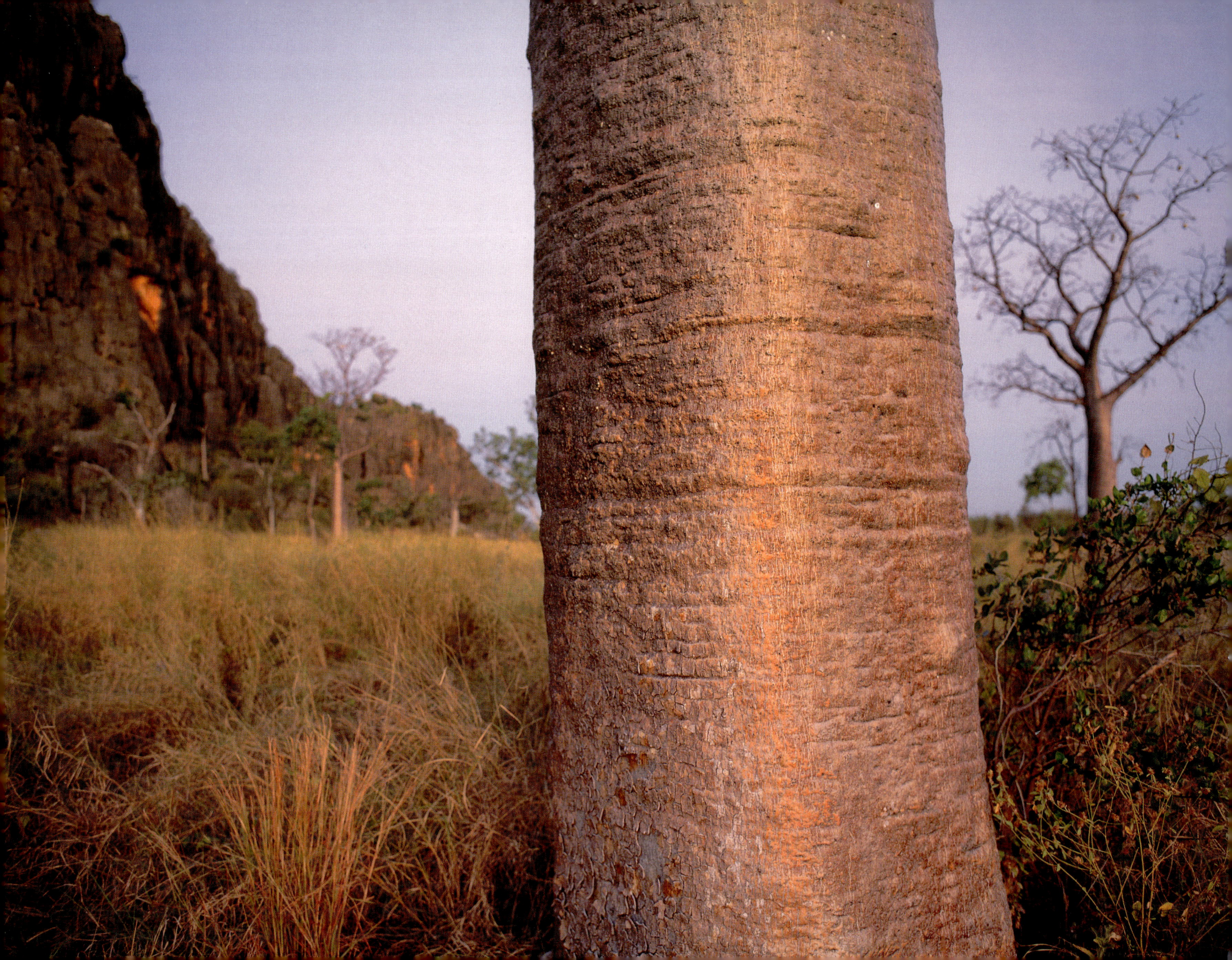

The outback areas of Australia have a distinctive flora adapted to the poor soils and low rainfall. Australia has extensive grasslands of spinifex in the west and tussock in the east. Some trees also do well in semi-desert areas, including ghost gums, desert oaks and the many species of acacia. The distinctive bulbous trunks of boabs are found in the rugged Kimberley region of Western Australia.

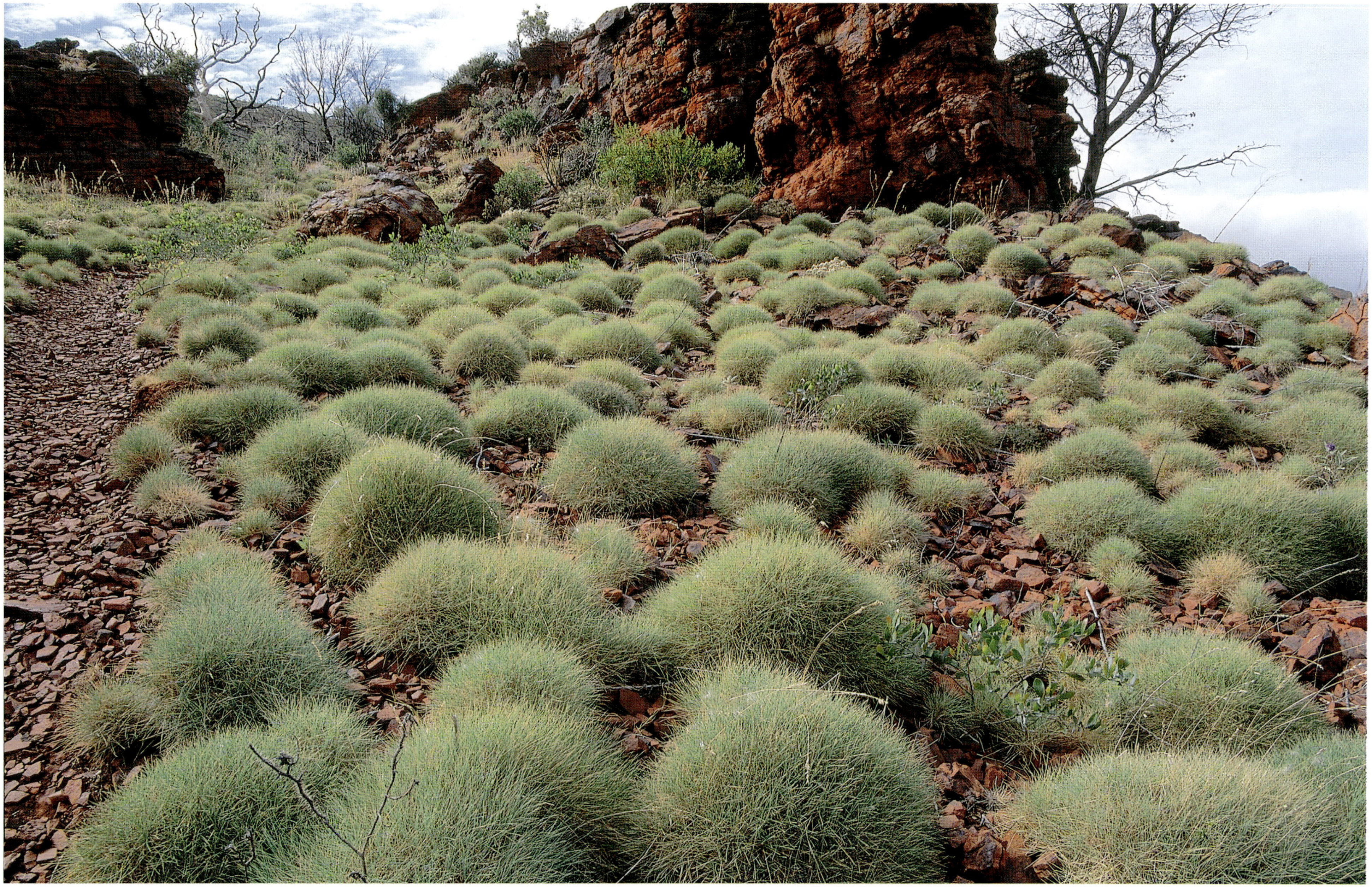

Spinifex occurs over large areas of arid Australia and is seen here on the Mount Bruce climb in Karijini National Park.

Opposite page: Boab tree near Windjana Gorge in the Kimberley, with the Napier Range behind.

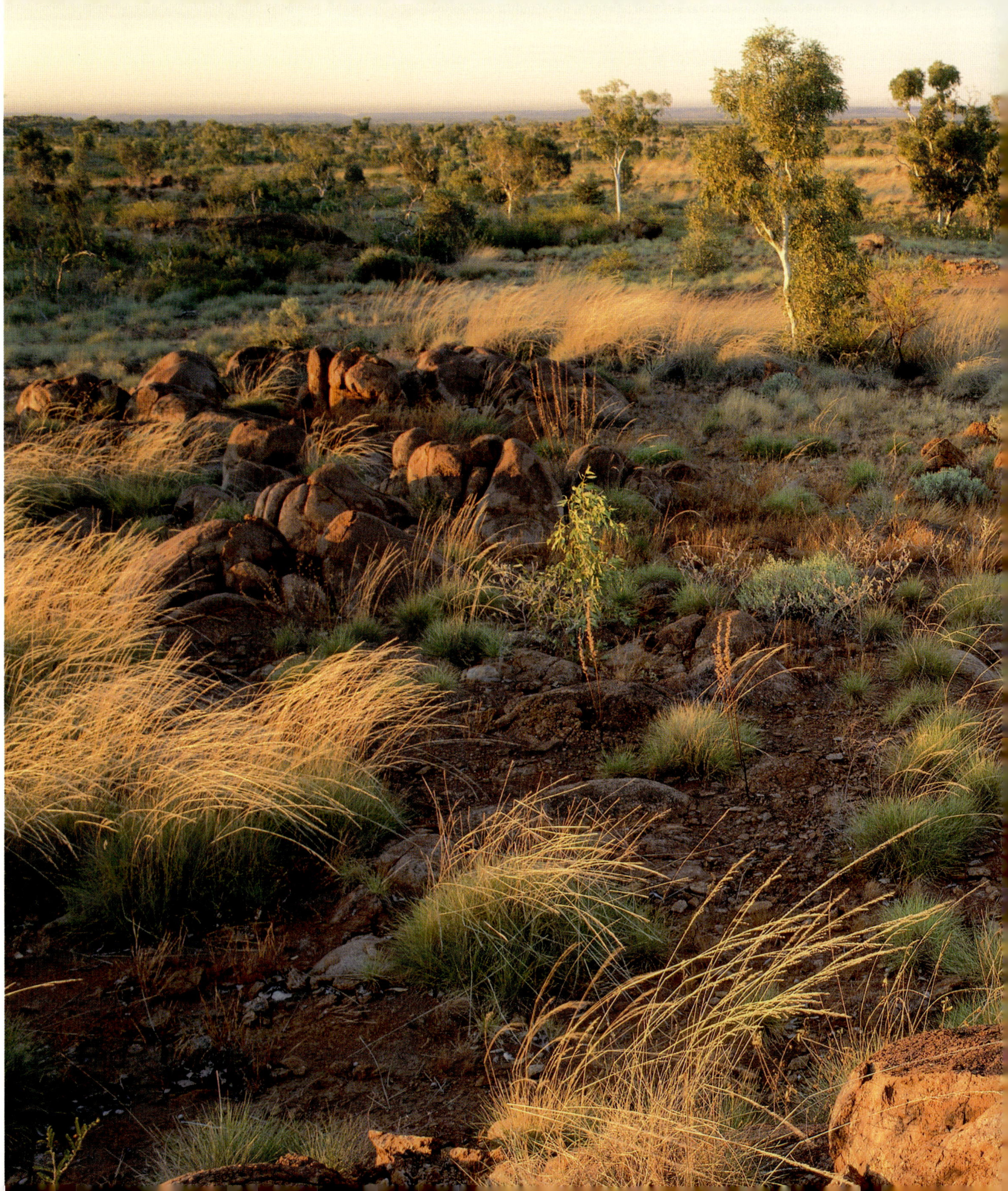

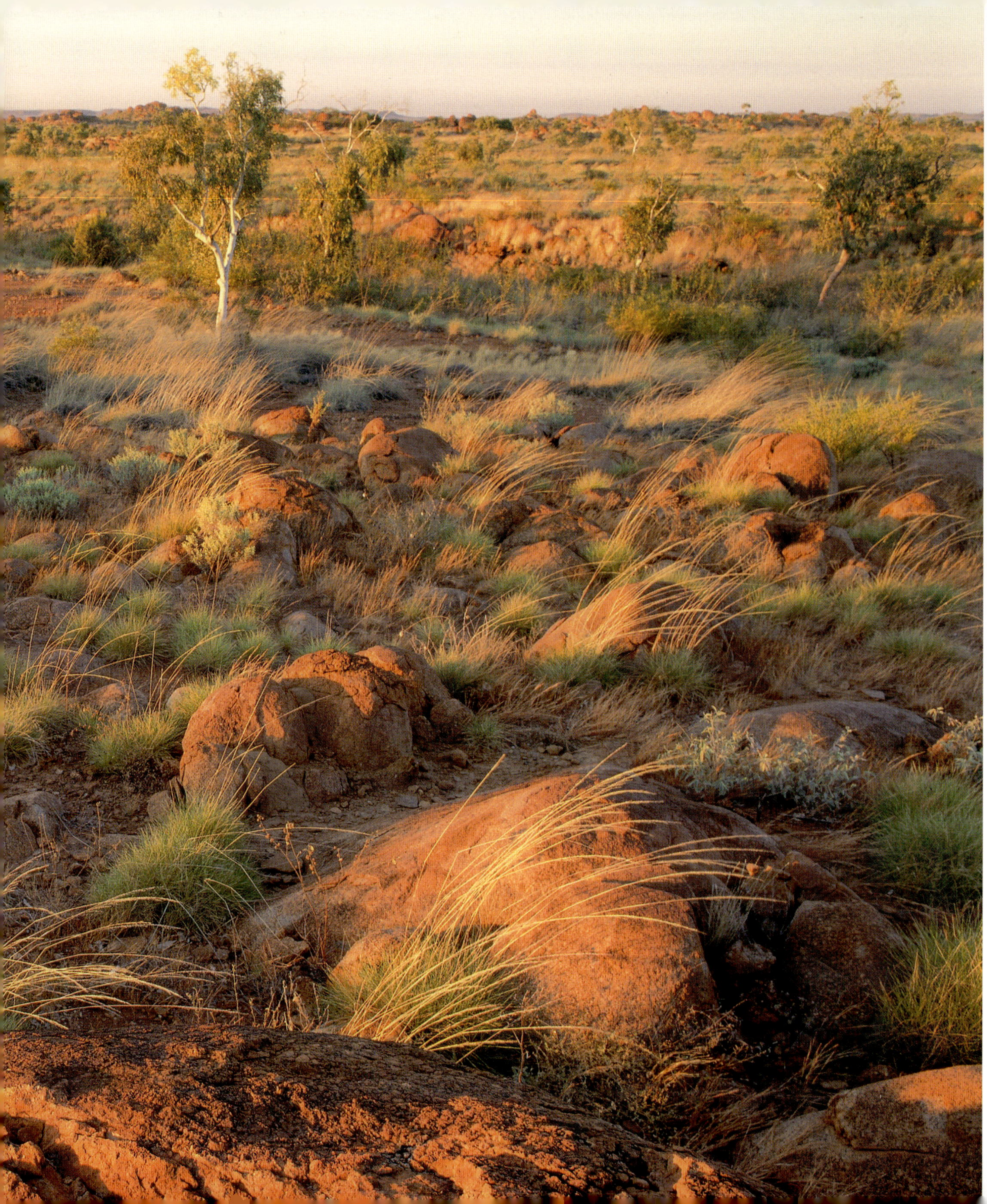

Typical outback semi-desert country at the Pebbles near Tennant Creek in the Northern Territory.

Australia has great diversity of vegetation types and habitats. Areas of rainforest survive in Tasmania and along the Great Dividing Range of mainland Australia wherever rainfall is high and soils are rich. There are also small remnant pockets of rainforest in the Kimberley region of Western Australia. In drier and more fire-prone areas, gum trees (eucalypts) dominate, along with other species like casuarinas and acacias. Melaleuca paperbarks are common around swamps and lakes.

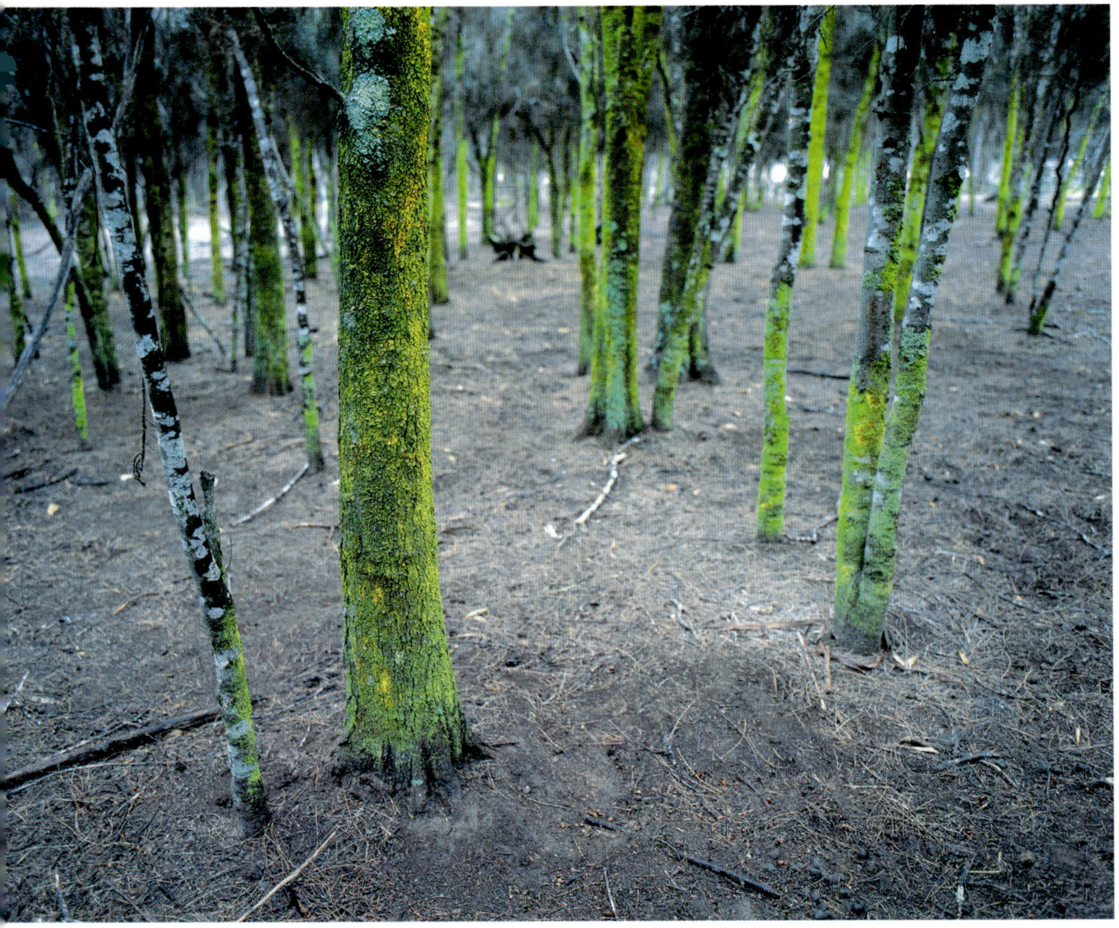

Moss and lichen encrusted she-oak (casuarina) trees near the Pallinup River in southern Western Australia.

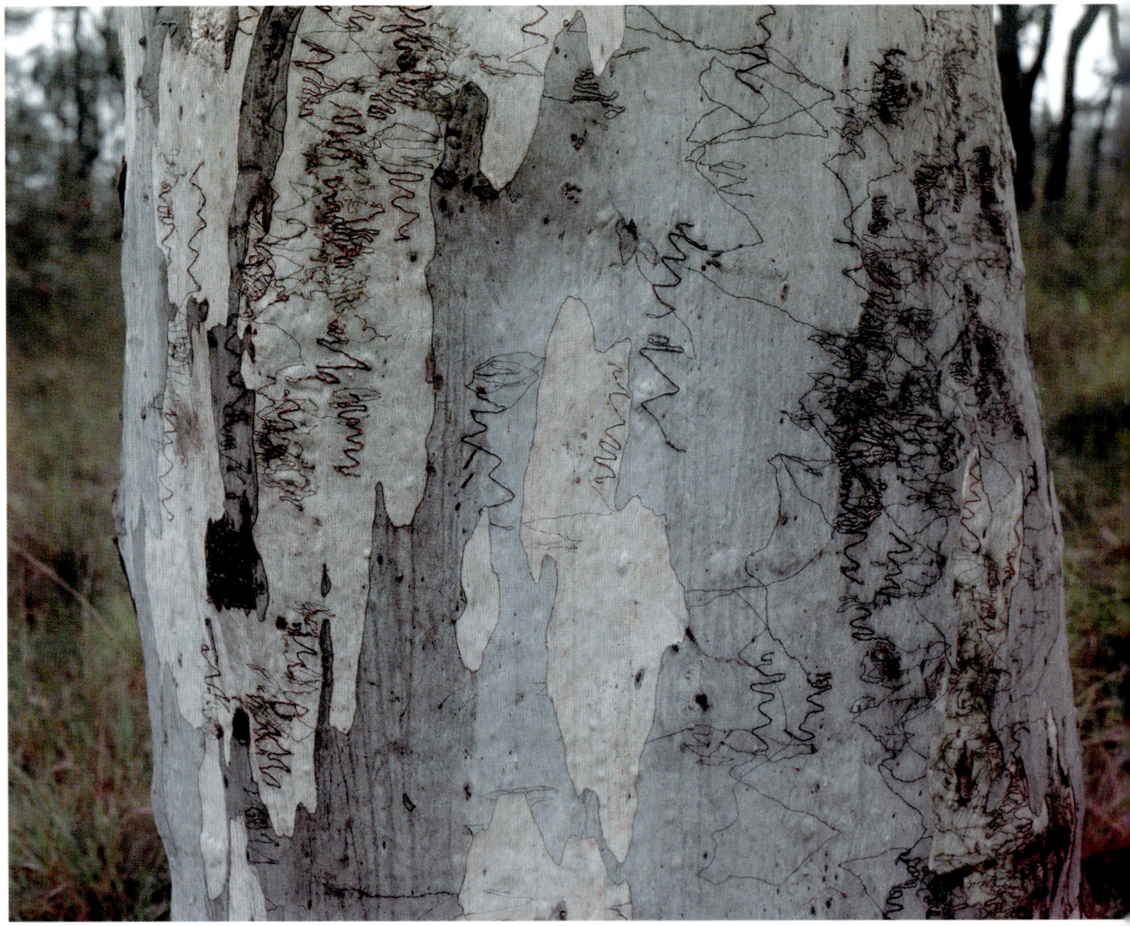

Scribbly gum near Umina Beach, New South Wales. The "scribbles" are zigzag tracks made by scribbly gum moth larvae.

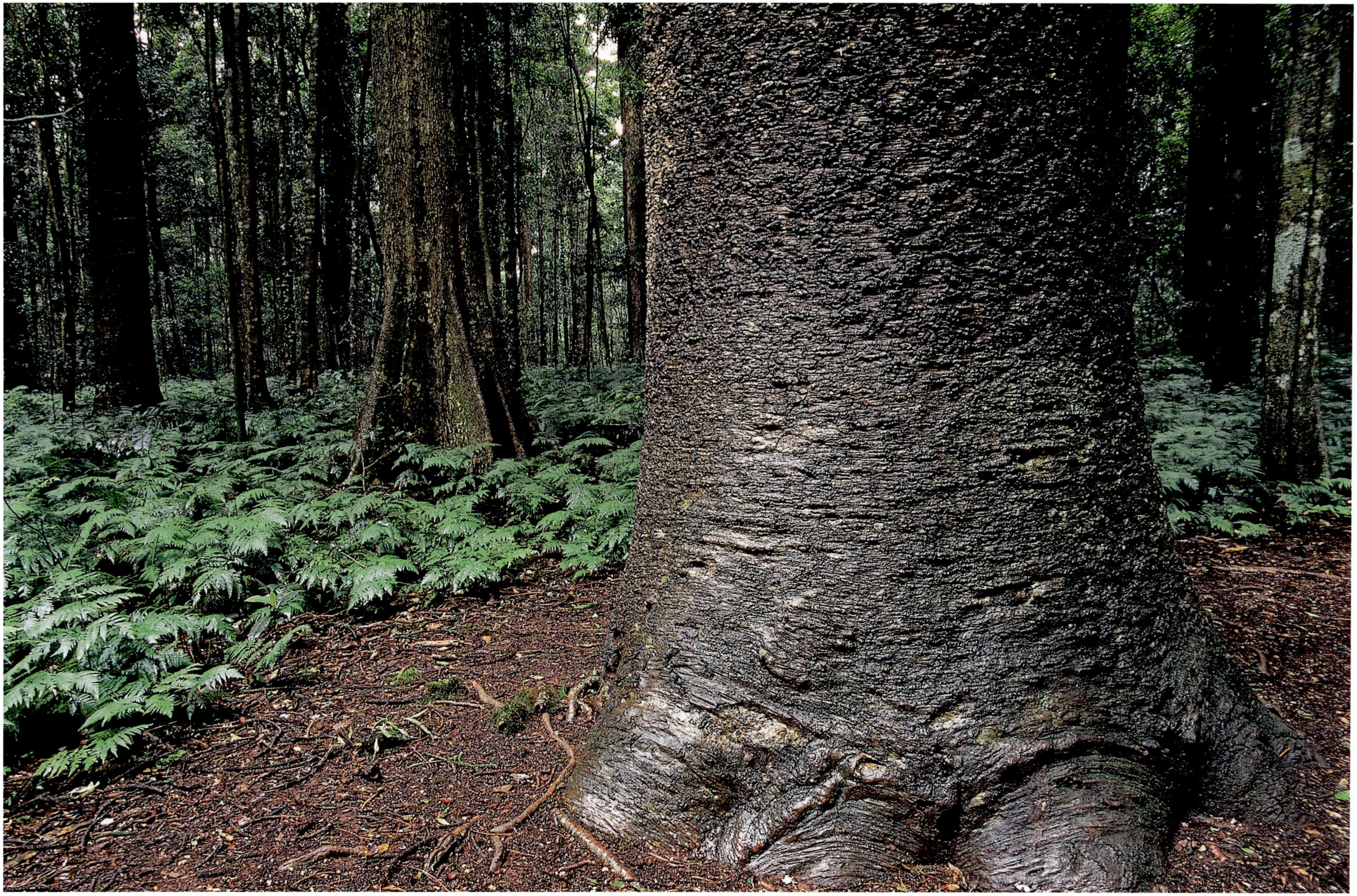

A "big footed" Hoop pine in ancient subtropical rainforest at the Bunya Mountains in Queensland.

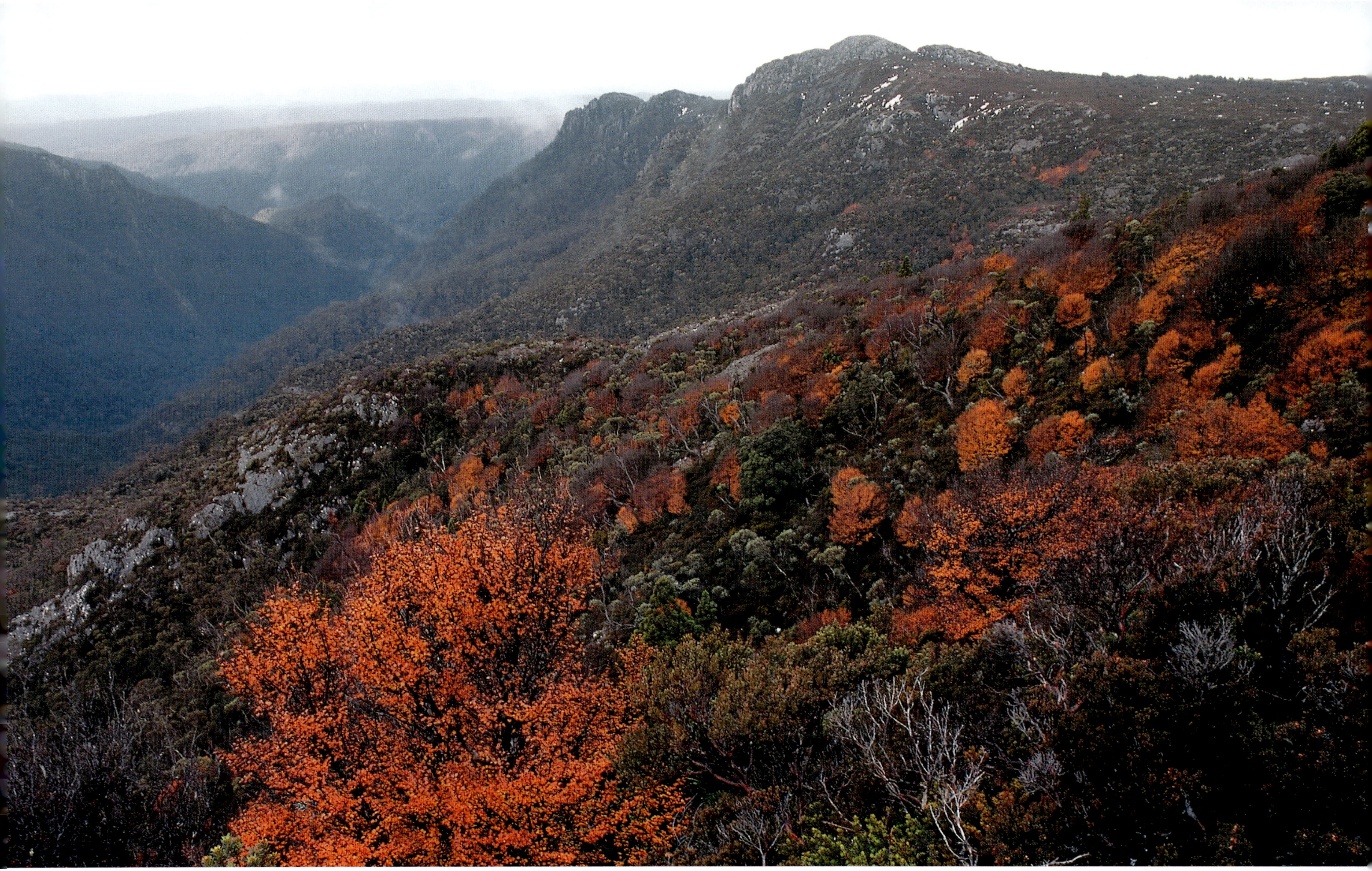

Deciduous beech or Fagus colours the mountains near Hansons Peak above Dove Lake in Tasmania.

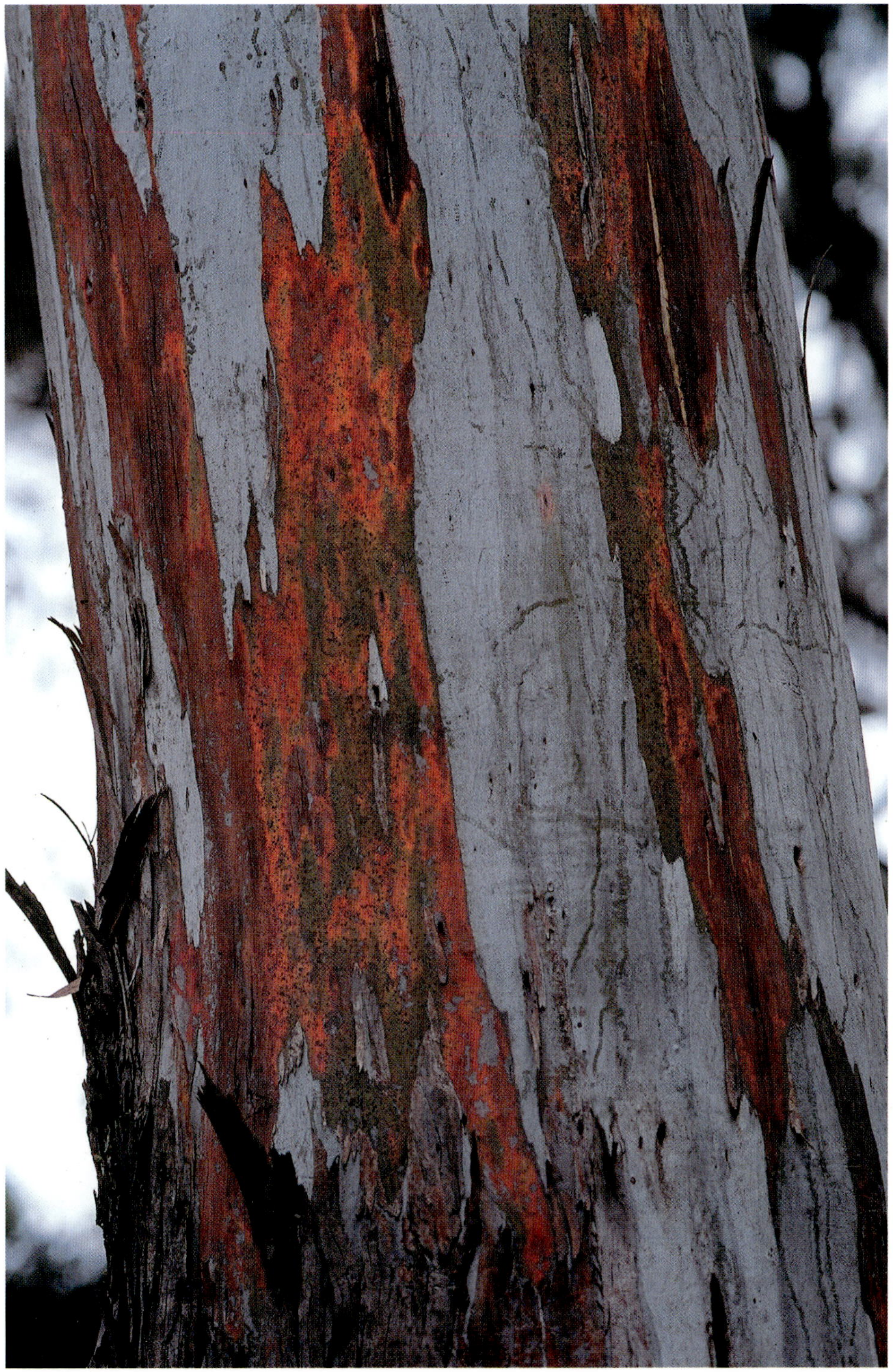

Tree bark near Point Lookout, New South Wales.

Most Australian trees are evergreen and often shed bark annually instead of leaves, revealing colourful new bark. A notable exception is Fagus or deciduous beech, found only on the mountains of Tasmania. The red and white cedars of the subtropical rainforests of Queensland and New South Wales are also deciduous. Xanthorrhoea are another distinctive Australian plant and are known colloquially as grasstrees.

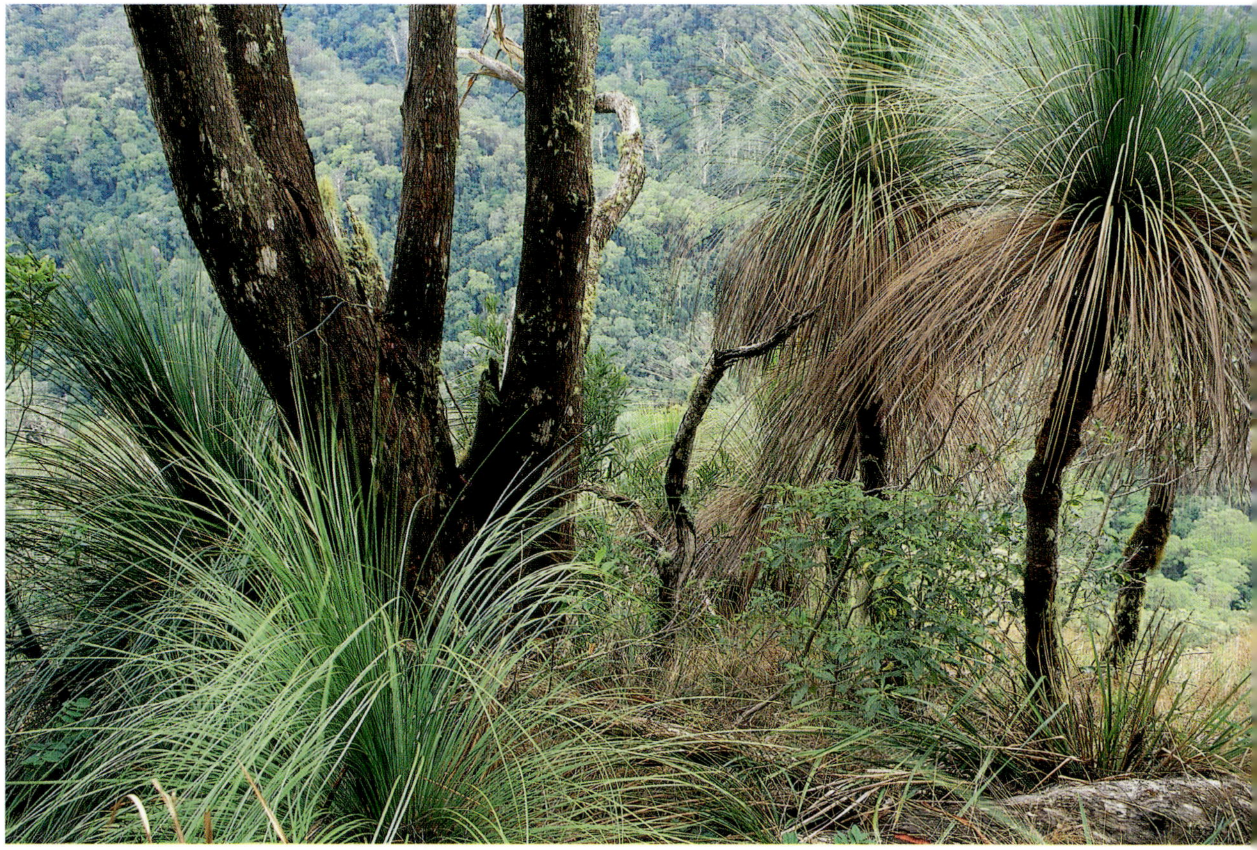

Grasstrees above dense subtropical vegetation at Brummies Lookout in northern New South Wales.

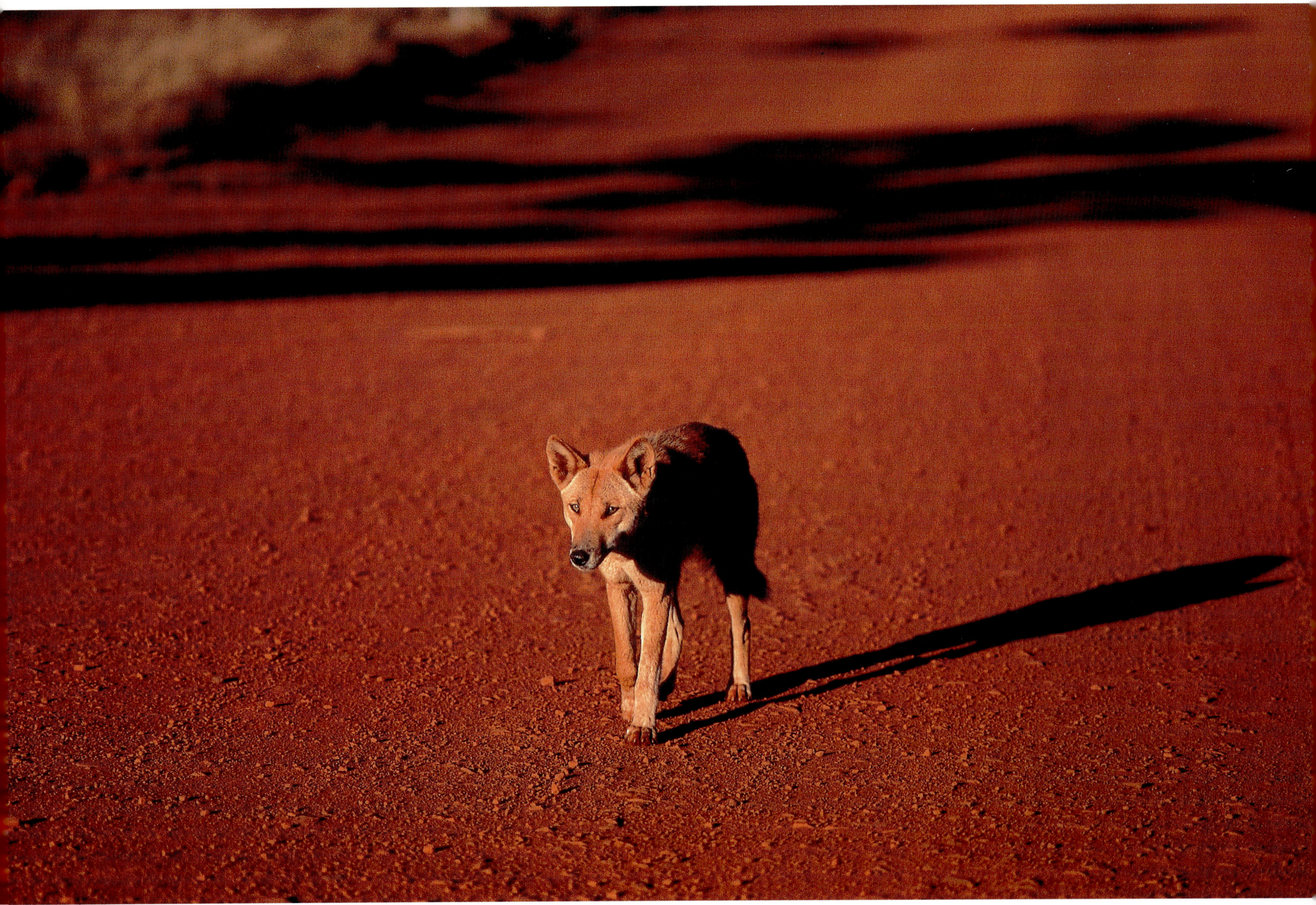

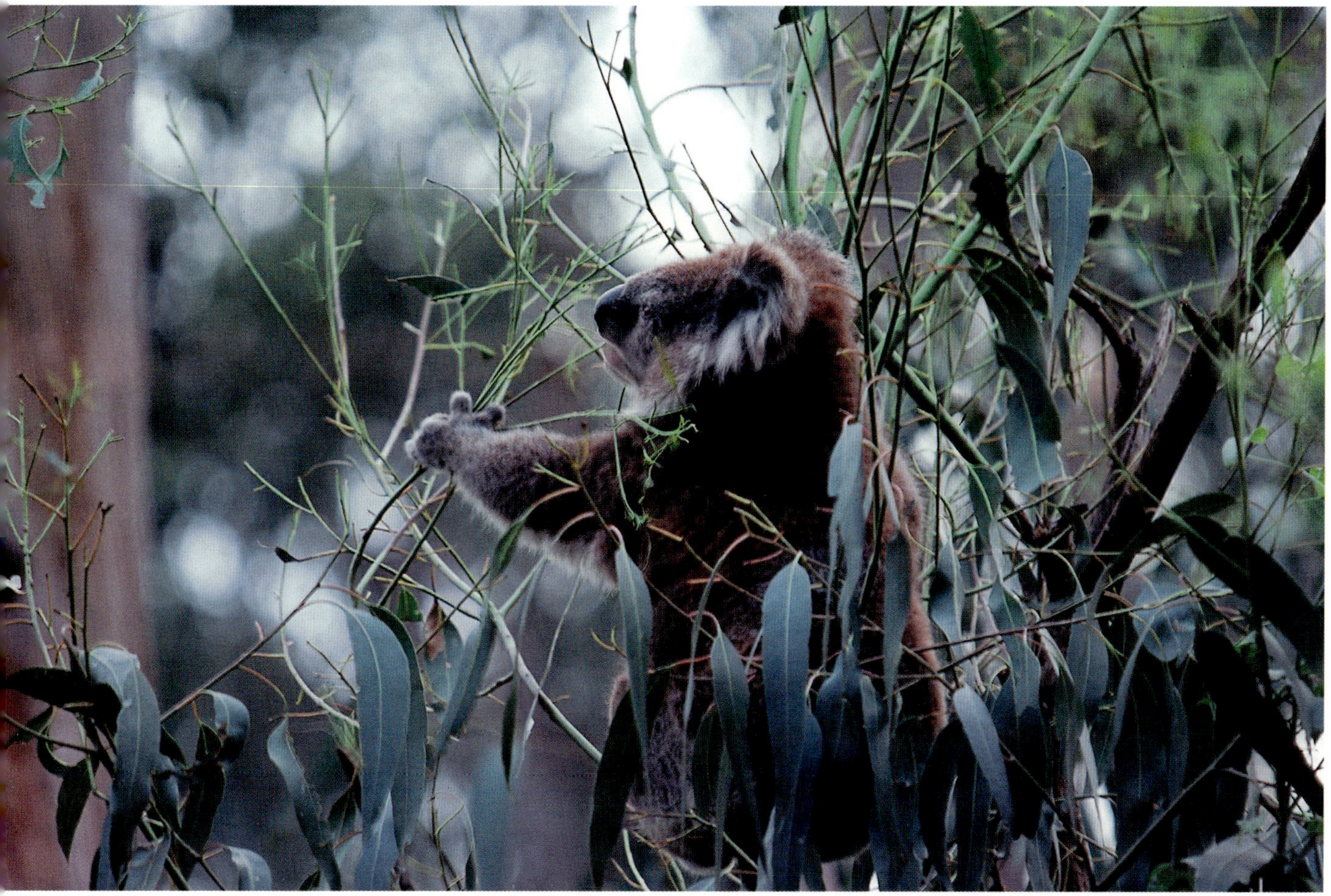

Iconic Australian animals include the koala, kangaroo, dingo and echidna. Koalas and kangaroos are marsupials, carrying and suckling their young in a pouch until they are independent. Echidnas lay eggs like reptiles but are warm blooded and feed the hatched young on milk. They belong to a primitive mammalian order, the monotremes. Dingos, a placental mammal, are a relatively new arrival and are thought to have been brought over by Asian seafarers around 4000 years ago.

Left: "I walked halfway around the waterhole at the White Woman camping area and had stopped to answer a 'call of nature', when I was startled by a sound behind me. I turned around and there was a large koala feeding in a small gum tree only about 10 metres away"; Gippsland, Victoria.

Below right: A western grey kangaroo joey peers out from his or her comfortable fur-lined pouch.

Right: An echidna on Broken Head Beach in Northern New South Wales.

Opposite page: A dingo on a road in Karijini National Park, Western Australia.

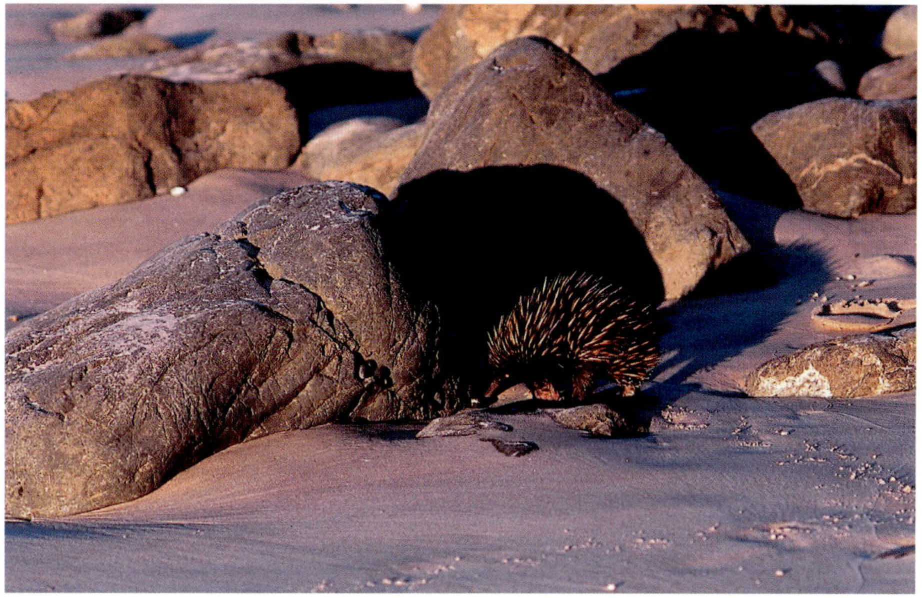

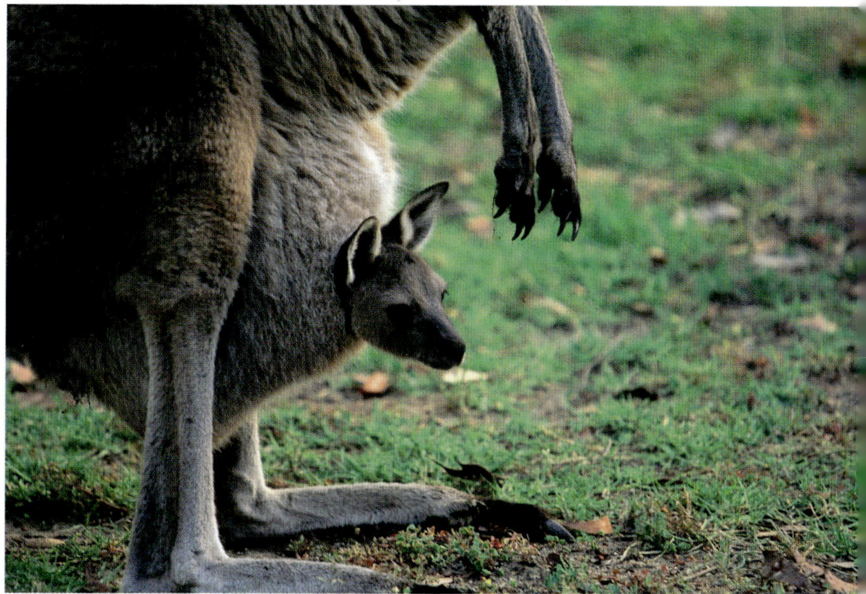

Australia is blessed with colourful and interesting birdlife, among which are about 50 species of parrots including galahs, rainbow lorikeets and corellas. The flightless emu can be 1.5 metres tall and is the second biggest bird in the world after the ostrich. The male emu does most of the incubation of the eggs and also looks after the chicks. The wedge-tailed eagle is the largest bird of prey in Australia, with a wingspan of over 2.5 metres, and occurs over the whole continent. Wedge-tails eat mainly carrion (dead animals), rabbits, birds and small native animals. Australia has many species of bush birds, including wrens, robins, finches, firetails and bellbirds.

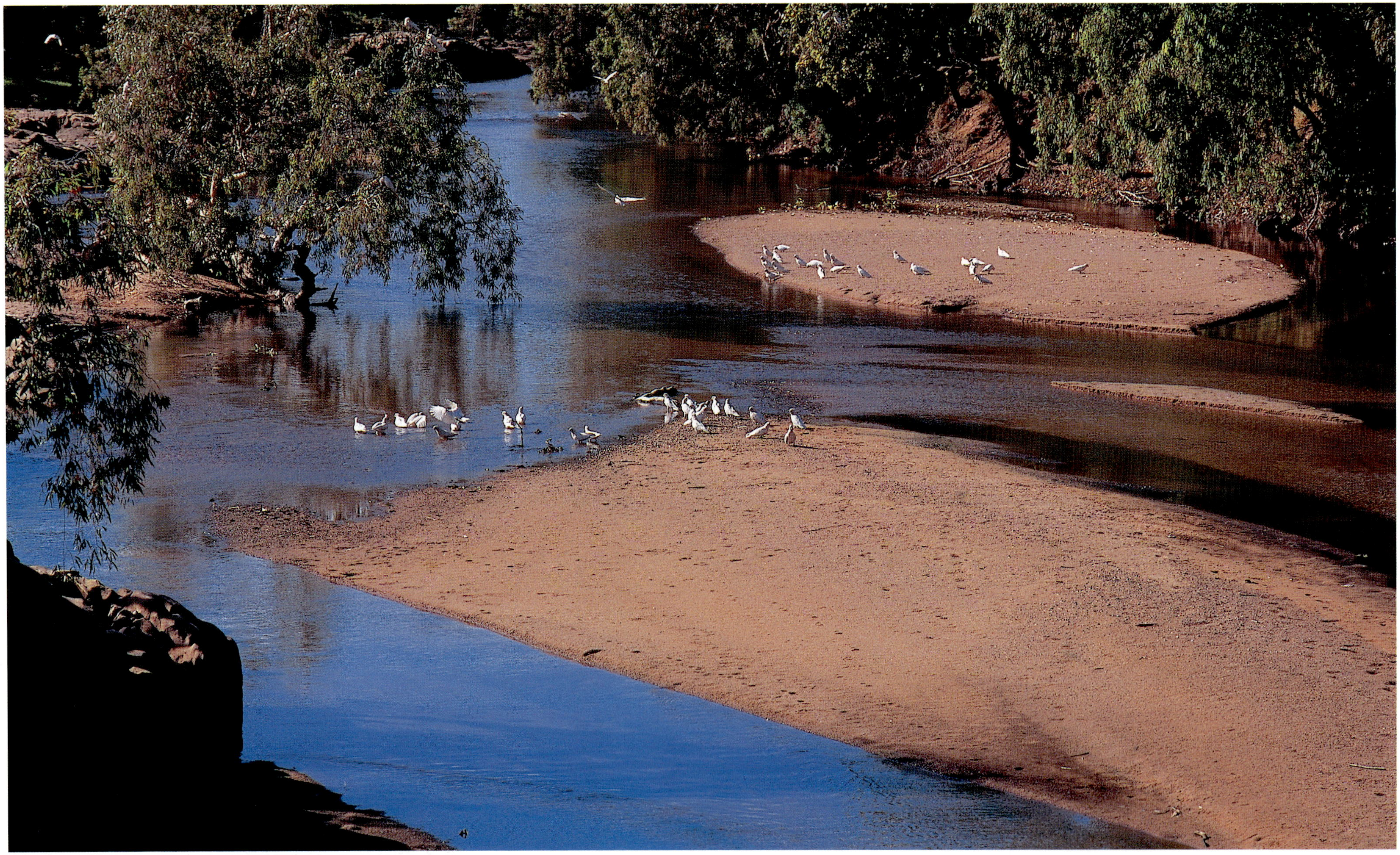

A flock of little corellas on the Lennard River, one of the wild rivers of the Kimberley.

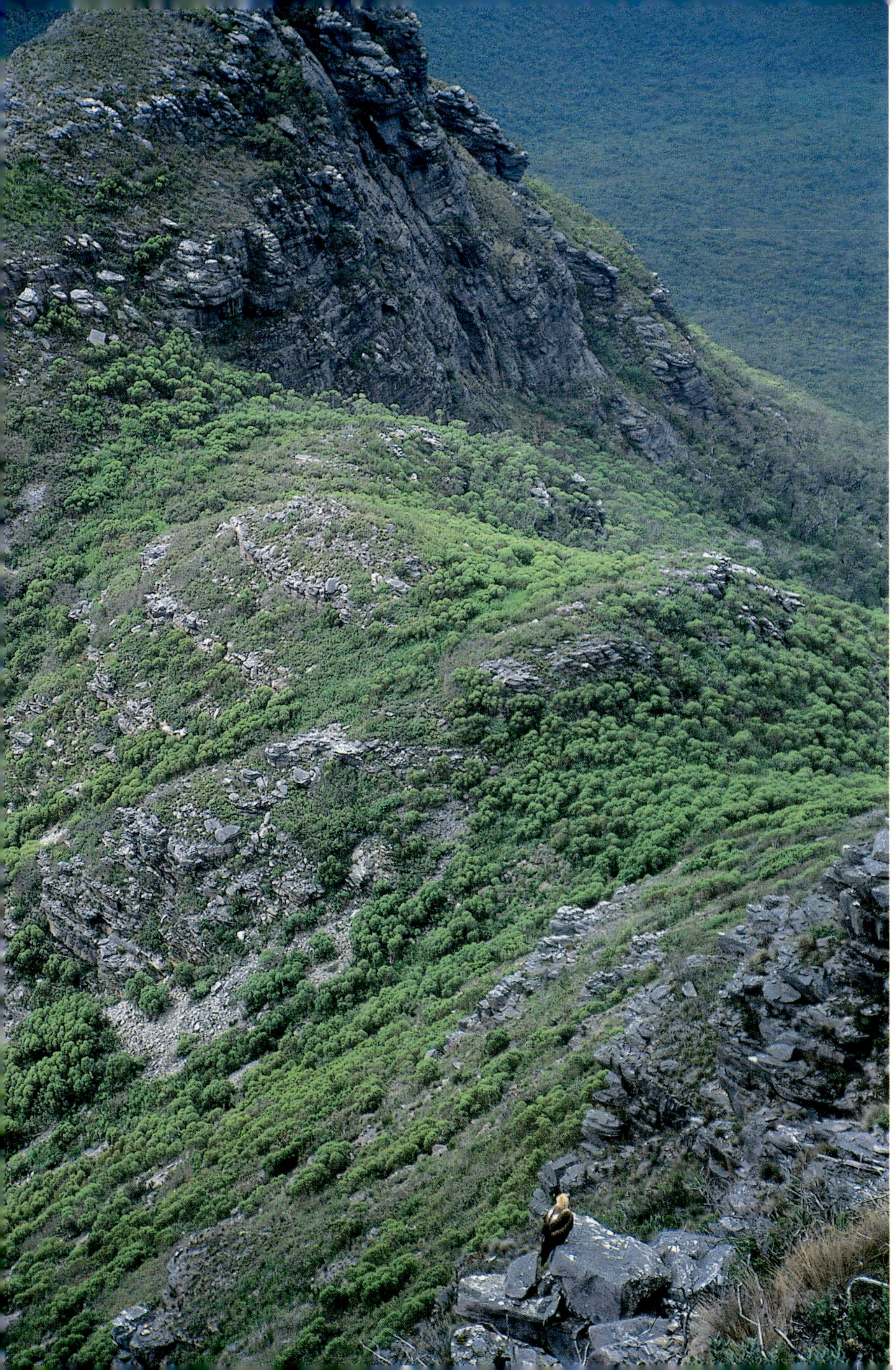

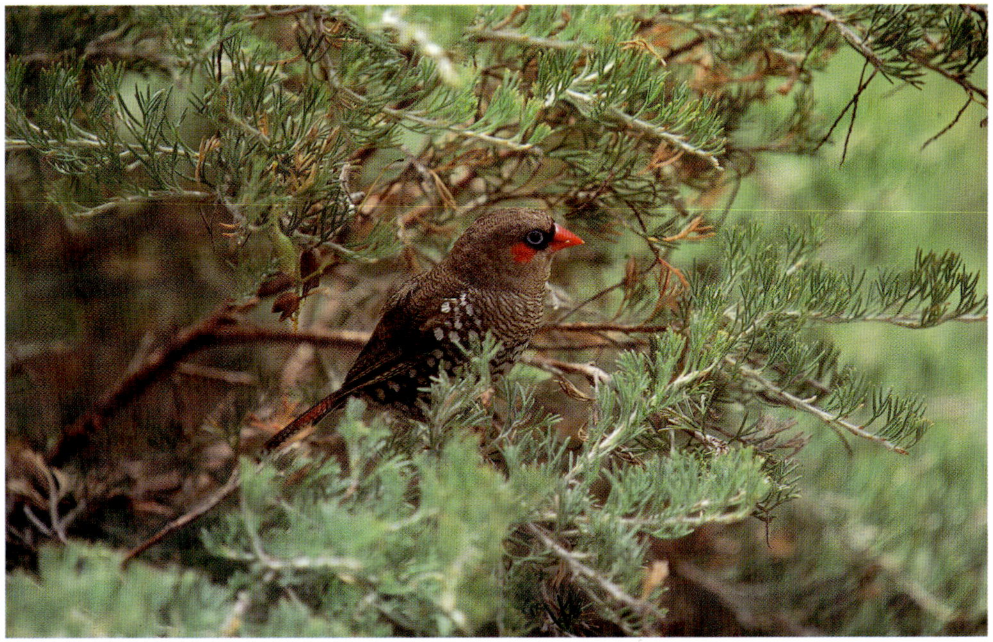

Red-eared firetail spotted in Albany, Western Australia.

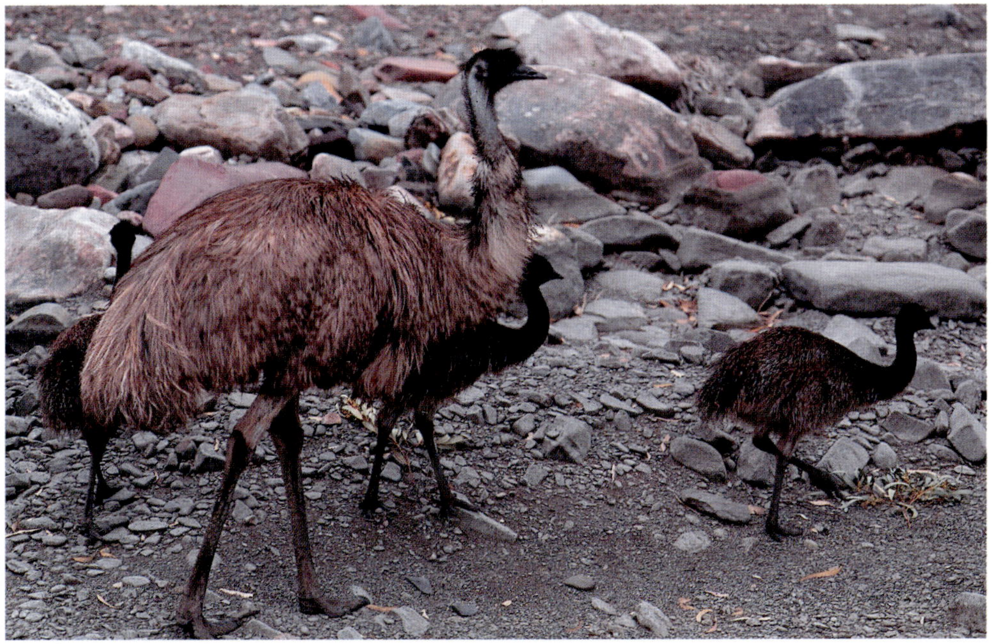

Emu and chicks in Branchina Gorge, Flinders Ranges, South Australia.

Left: A wedge-tailed eagle on the steep slopes of Toolbrunup Peak in the Stirling Range, Western Australia.

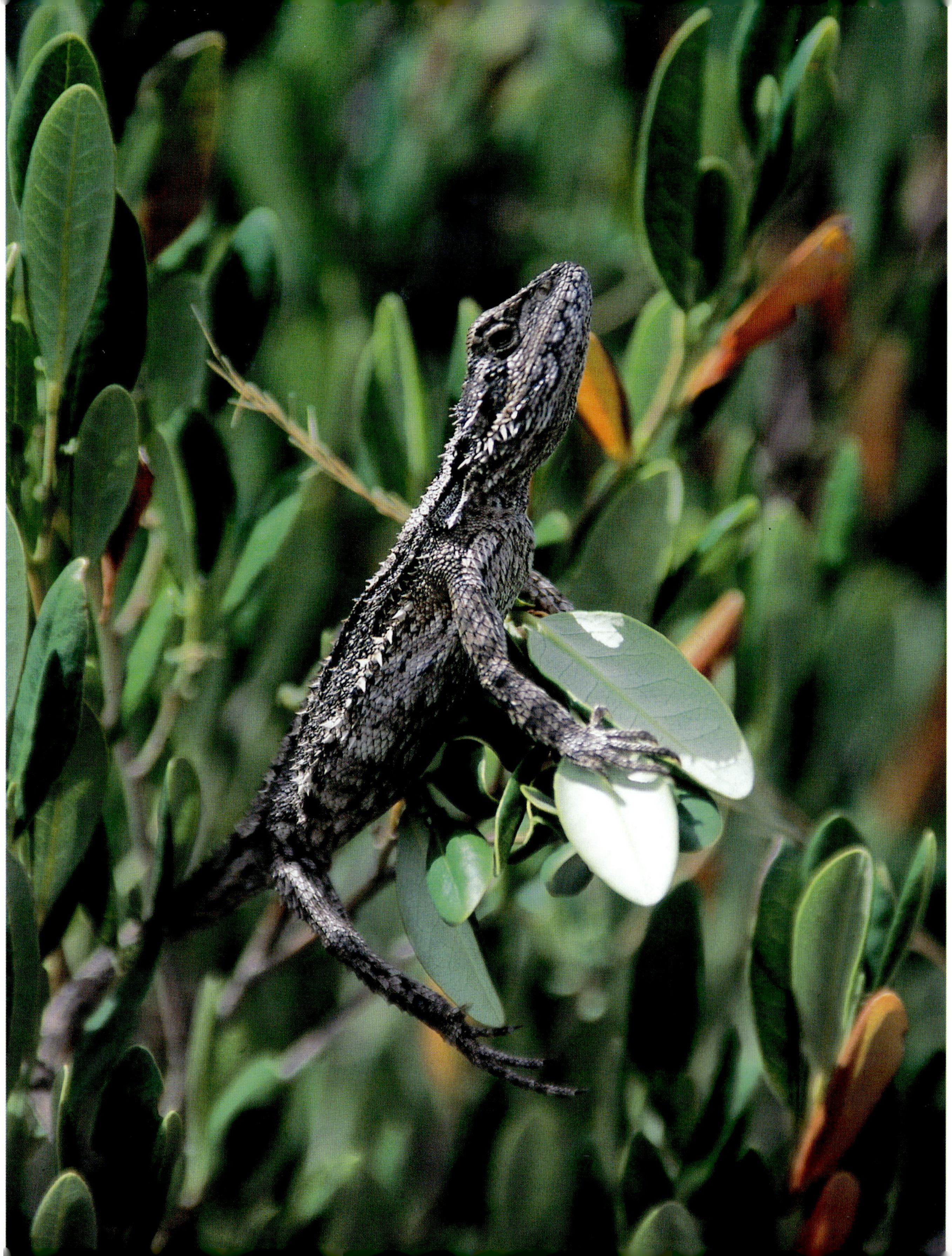

Reptiles are common in Australia and two crocodile species are present, the freshwater and the estuarine or saltwater. Both are common in Australia's north, and the saltwater crocodile, the largest living reptile in the world at up to 6.5 metres long, is considered very dangerous to people. There are many species of lizard, including goannas, skinks and bearded dragons. The 140 species of snakes are common but seldom seen, and Australia has the dubious distinction of having some of the most deadly venomous snakes in the world, including the taipan.

A western bearded dragon in the Leeuwin-Naturaliste NP of Western Australia.

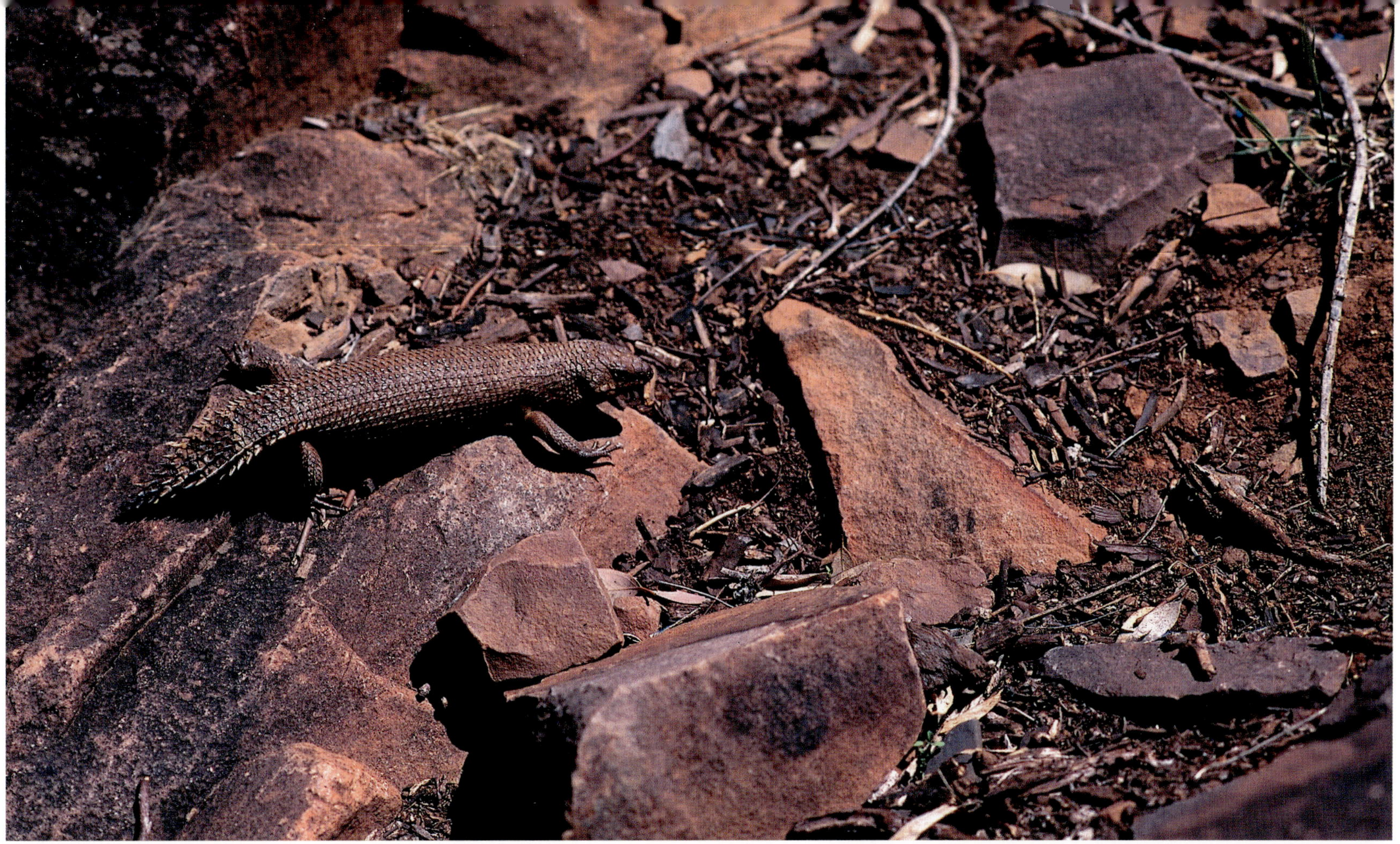

A sleepy lizard in the Flinders Ranges, South Australia.

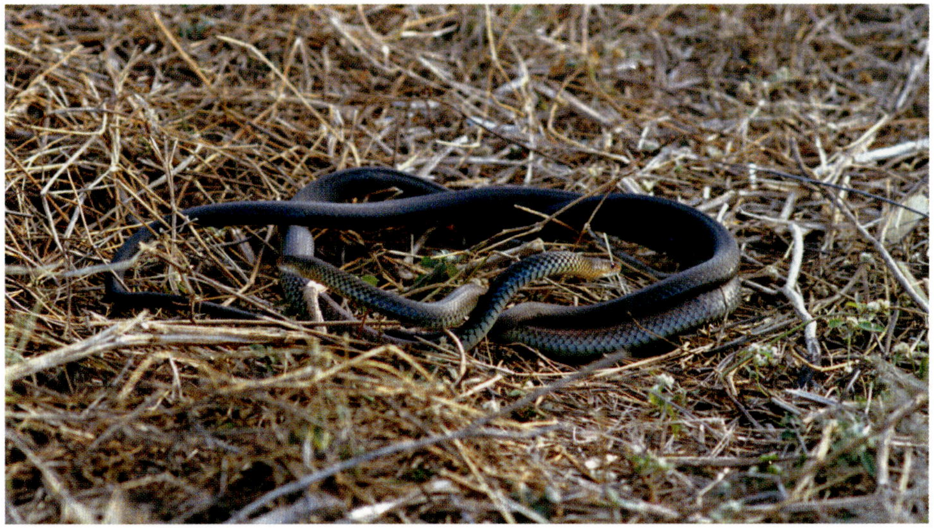

"All of a sudden I noticed two snakes 'going for it' (making love) on the sunlit path directly in front of me! They came together head to head to start with and then twined themselves together and went in a circle faster and faster." Mildly venomous lesser black whip snakes at a lake near Townsville.

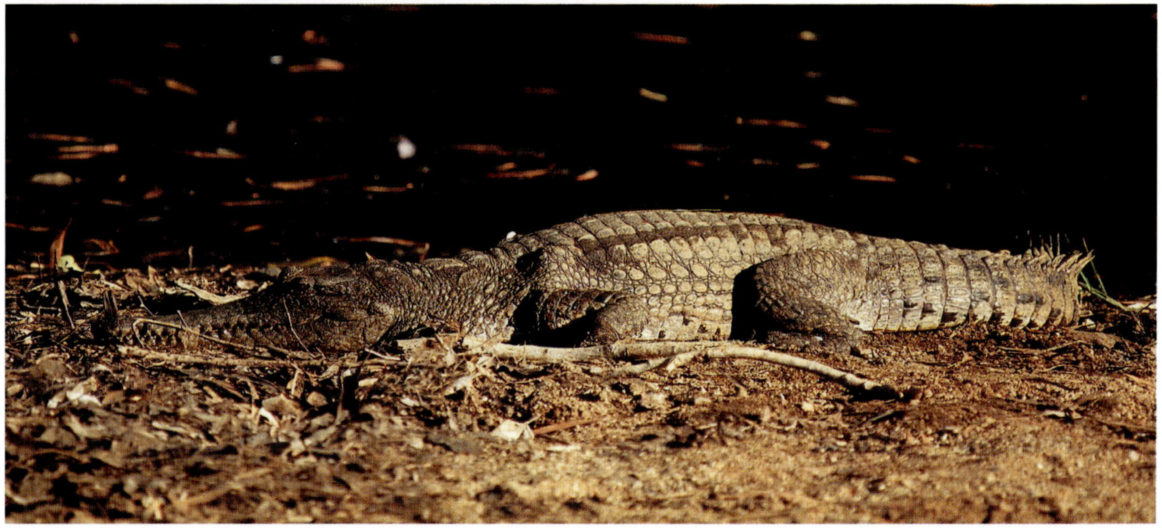

Freshwater crocodile sunbathing at Windjana Gorge in the Kimberley.

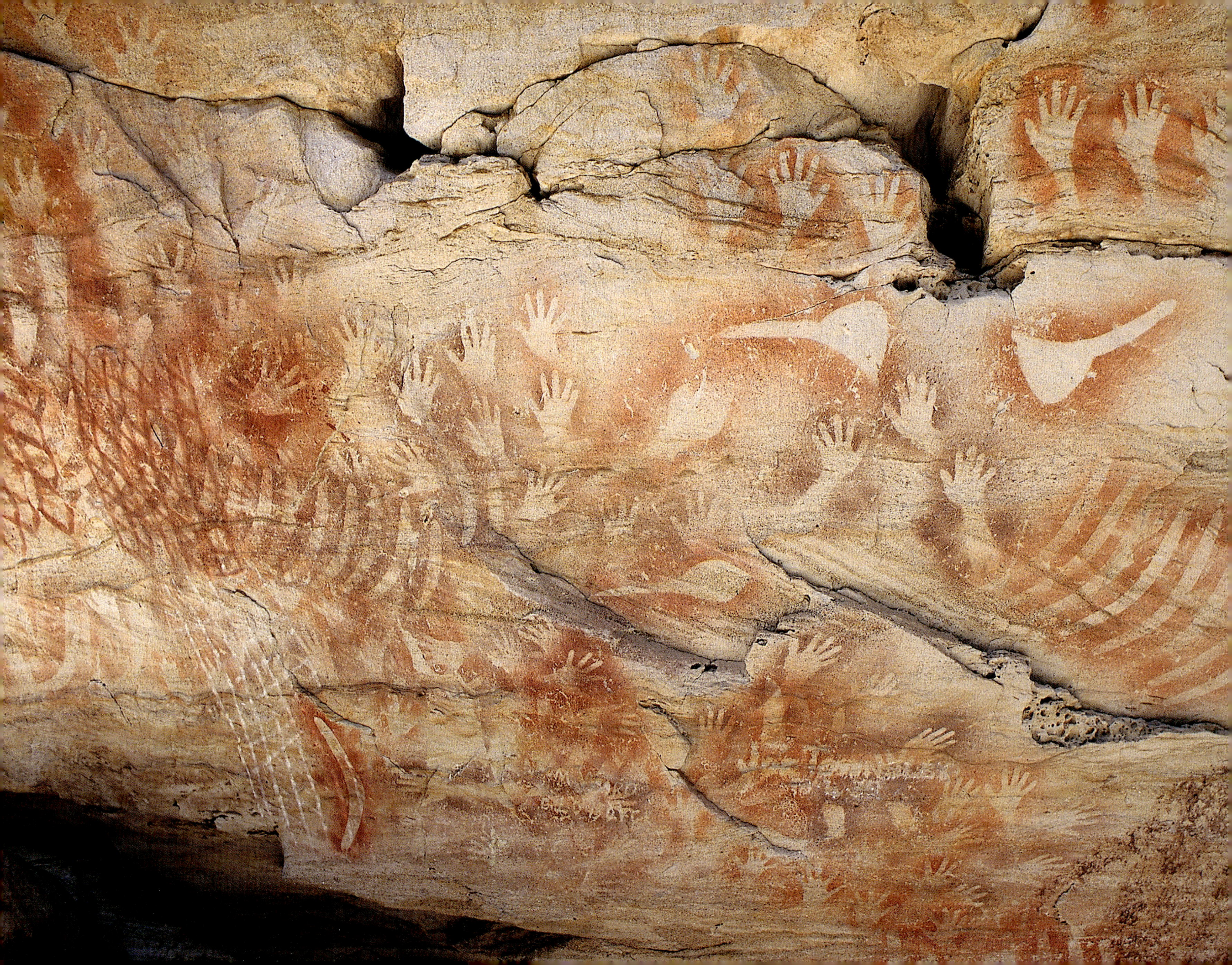

The Human Landscape

There is an ancient campsite in a remote corner of Kakadu National Park in the Northern Territory with remains dating back an estimated 55,000 to 60,000 years. This means that Australian Aborigines have perhaps the longest surviving continuous culture in the world. How they arrived on these shores is a mystery. They may have come from Timor in the Indonesian Archipelago to the Kimberley coast during an Ice Age, but even so there would have been about 70 kilometres of open sea to cross. Interestingly, the Bundjalung people of northern New South Wales have a dreamtime legend about three brothers, Birrung, Mamoon and Yarbirri, who came to this land after a massive catastrophe destroyed their ancestral island at the centre of the world. The brothers, along with their wives and children, travelled in a great canoe over the seas. A storm blew up as they neared the shore, breaking the canoe in pieces, but the occupants managed to swim ashore. A rock in the ocean at Goanna Headland in northern New South Wales is said to be a piece of this canoe.

After their arrival, Aboriginal people spread over the new continent; campsites have been dated at 45,000 years in the Nepean valley near Sydney, and 40,000 years at a site near Melbourne's Tullamarine Airport, and skeletal remains found in a cave near Hobart date back 35,000 years. For hundreds of generations, Aborigines passed on their intimate knowledge of the land, its wildlife, plants and seasons through songlines, dance and rock art. They were hunter/gatherers who lived on specified areas of land and who treasured knowledge and skill above material possessions. Aborigines belonged to the land and the land belonged to them and they managed to survive in even the harsh inland deserts. The country seen initially by Europeans was not, in fact, a wilderness. Almost all had been altered by the hand of man, particularly by the practice of "firestick farming". Aborigines would periodically fire parts of their country to clear thick undergrowth, promote the growth of new shoots and food plants, and flush out game animals like goannas and wallabies.

Among many achievements, Aborigines invented the boomerang, a curved piece of wood that returns to the thrower, and one of the world's most distinctive musical instruments, the didgeridoo. Australia's other indigenous people are the Torres Strait Islanders who came from Melanesia about 2000 years ago. They have unique cultures, different to Australian Aborigines or Papua New Guineans, and they traditionally inhabit about 17 islands in the Torres Strait. Malay seamen have also visited the Australian northern coastline for at least 400-500 years, fishing for trepang and shellfish and trading with Aborigines.

Over 2,000 years ago, Greek philosophers like Aristotle and Pythagoras hypothesised the existence of a Great Southern Land in the southern hemisphere to balance out the landmasses of the north. Over time this became known as "Terra Australis Incognita" or the unknown southern land. The Dutch were the first European nation to stumble on the shores of this new continent, today called Australia. In 1606 Willem Jansz and his crew aboard the Duyfken came ashore on the western coast of Cape York Peninsula, near the present day town of Weipa. Many other Dutch vessels encountered the Western Australian coast over the next hundred years and some of their ships came to grief on its treacherous islands and reefs. In 1642 Abel Tasman explored the south coast of Australia and discovered Tasmania. The Dutch never explored the fertile east coast and in 1644 they formally abandoned the search for riches in New Holland, as they called the continent. They never seriously considered a settlement and regarded most of the land as barren and useless.

Opposite page: Hand and boomerang stencils feature among other Aboriginal rock art and engravings at Cathedral Cave in Carnarvon Gorge, Queensland.

The first European to explore the eastern seaboard was Englishman Captain James Cook in the barque Endeavour, who sighted the south-eastern tip (near Cape Hicks) of the continent on 20 April 1770. He sailed north and chartered the east coast, finding it to be well watered and suitable for settlement. He took possession of the entire east coast for King George III on 2 August 1770 and called it "New South Wales". One of the bays he discovered had a profusion of strange plants and flowers, which excited the ship's naturalist Joseph Banks (after whom banksias are named); Cook called it Botany Bay. Cook alerted Europe to the possibilities of the Great Southern Land and the French now began to take an interest, with extensive expeditions by Bruni d'Entrecasteaux in 1792 and Nicolas Baudin in 1801-1803.

Before that, however, in 1786 the British Government had decided to found a penal colony in New South Wales, and the "First Fleet" of 11 small vessels under the command of Captain Arthur Phillip sailed into Botany Bay on 18 January 1788. The boats carried over 1000 people, three quarters of them convicts. Captain Phillip found the location unsuitable and relocated the colony to a small cove with good water and timber supplies in the protected harbour of Port Jackson on 26 January 1788. The cove lies in the traditional country of the Eora Aboriginal people. This date is known today as Australia Day and the settlement was named after the British Home Secretary, Lord Sydney.

Australia has come a long way from this inauspicious first European colonisation. Additional penal and free settlements gradually became established in six separate colonies; the first after Sydney was a Tasmanian colony on the Derwent River set up in 1803. Gold was discovered in 1851 in NSW, with further strikes in Victoria the same year. This brought prosperity and large numbers of new immigrants to these states. Queensland and Western Australia had their own gold rushes in the 1880s and 1890s respectively. In 1901 the six states came together to form the Federation of Australia. A constitution was drawn up and the new democratic nation became a Constitutional Monarchy. In 1902 women won the right to vote in Federal Elections, although most Aboriginal women (and men) were excluded as they were not considered citizens at that time. The nation has played its role on the world stage, including being involved in both World Wars and many other conflicts and peacekeeping activities. Australia's strategic and trade focus has shifted over the years away from England and Europe and more towards the United States and Asia.

The country today has a population of over 23 million from more than 200 nationalities. Since World War II, when Australia accepted thousands of immigrants from war-torn Europe, the country has welcomed people from all over the world, including Asia, the Middle East and Africa. Today Australia is a successful multicultural country. There are archetypes like wheatbelt farmers, outback graziers and miners, but most Aussies live in cities or coastal towns and come from a variety of ethnic backgrounds. Australians are generally unpretentious, friendly and willing to give others a "fair go". They love sport and outdoor activity and there is increasing appreciation of music, culture and the arts. A growing trend is the establishment of community gardens, farmer's markets, sustainability streets and transition town groups, which have been set up in many parts of the country in response to global economic and environmental problems, such as peak oil and climate change. These localisation movements aim to restore community living and promote more sustainable use of resources.

Australia is still a young country, but is slowly beginning to understand and value one of the oldest continuous cultures in the world – the indigenous Aboriginal culture. Most Aborigines and Torres Strait Islanders did not receive the vote until 1962 and were not regarded as full citizens in their own country until 1967. In June 1992, in what became known as the Mabo decision, the High Court of Australia overturned the principal of "terra nullius" or "no man's land", established when Captain Cook claimed Australia on behalf of the crown in 1770. This was an historic judgement that allowed for recognition of native title and Aboriginal land claims. In 2007, then Prime Minister Kevin Rudd issued a formal apology to Aboriginal people for the injustices they had suffered over the last two centuries. Aboriginal and Torres Strait Islanders have contributed greatly to modern Australia, and I hope their voice continues to gain in strength and that full reconciliation can be achieved with non-indigenous Australians.

Opposite page: Leaping into the Swan River at sunset from low cliffs along Blackwall Reach, Perth.

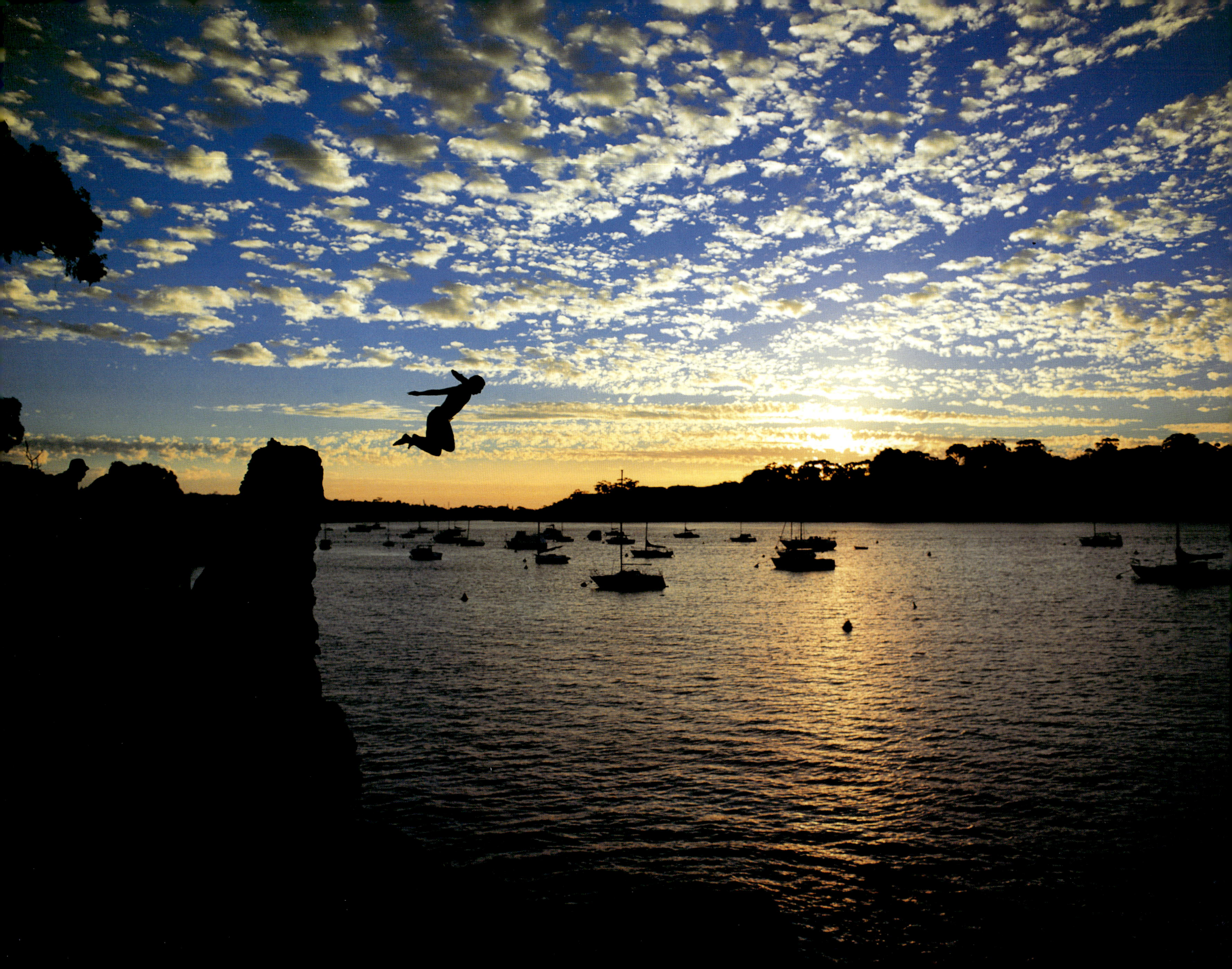

Aboriginal rock art and engravings are found throughout Australia and display tremendous skill and variety. The heritage of their rock art, stone tool manufacturing sites, fish traps and scarred trees is priceless. All of the painting and symbols have deep significance to local Aboriginal clans and are part of ongoing cultural practice. The meanings of the artworks are best given by the local custodians of each site.

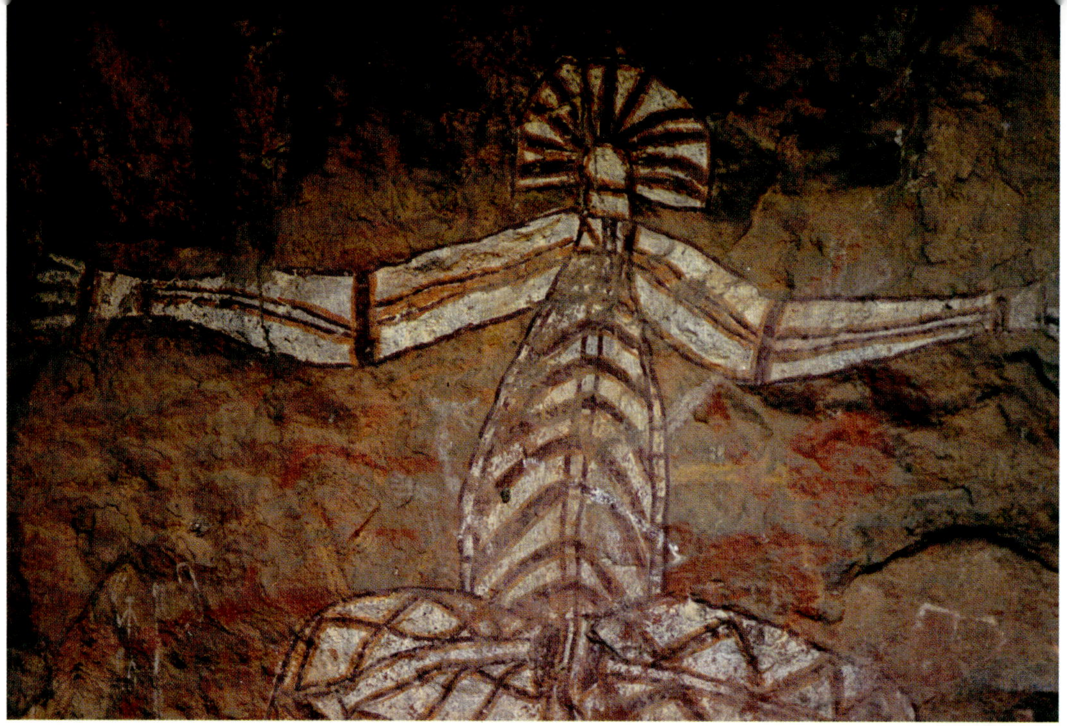

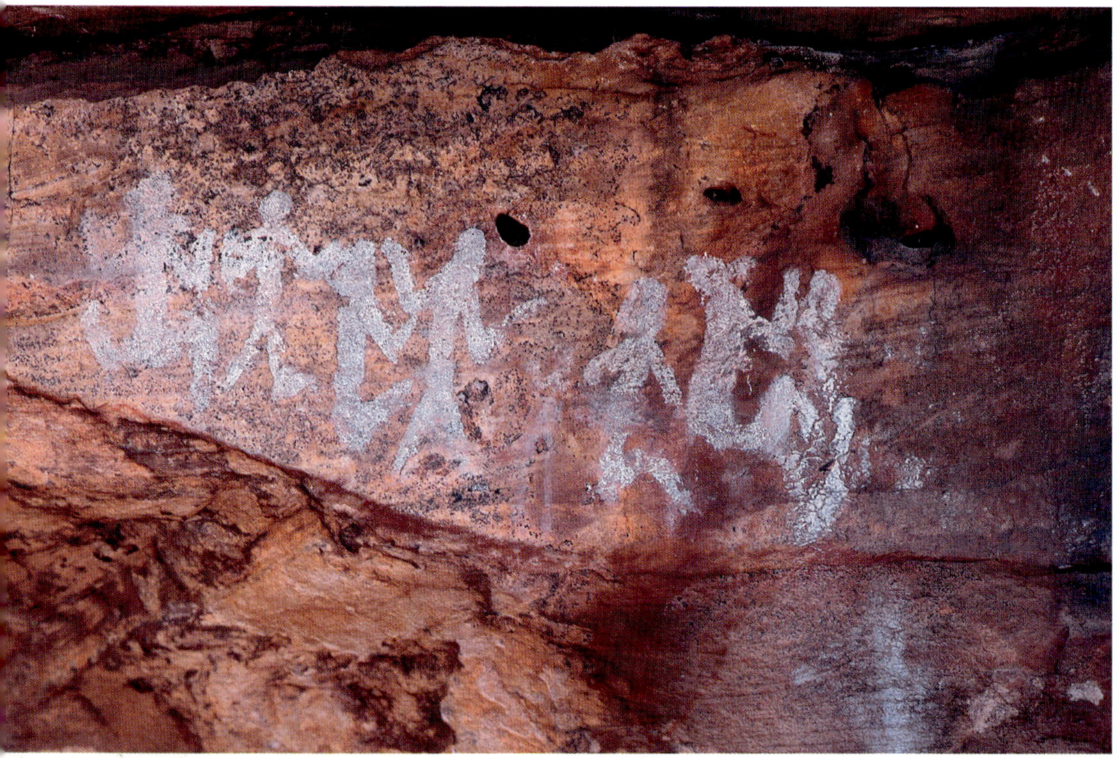

Aboriginal art at Ngamadjidj Shelter in the Grampians NP, Victoria.

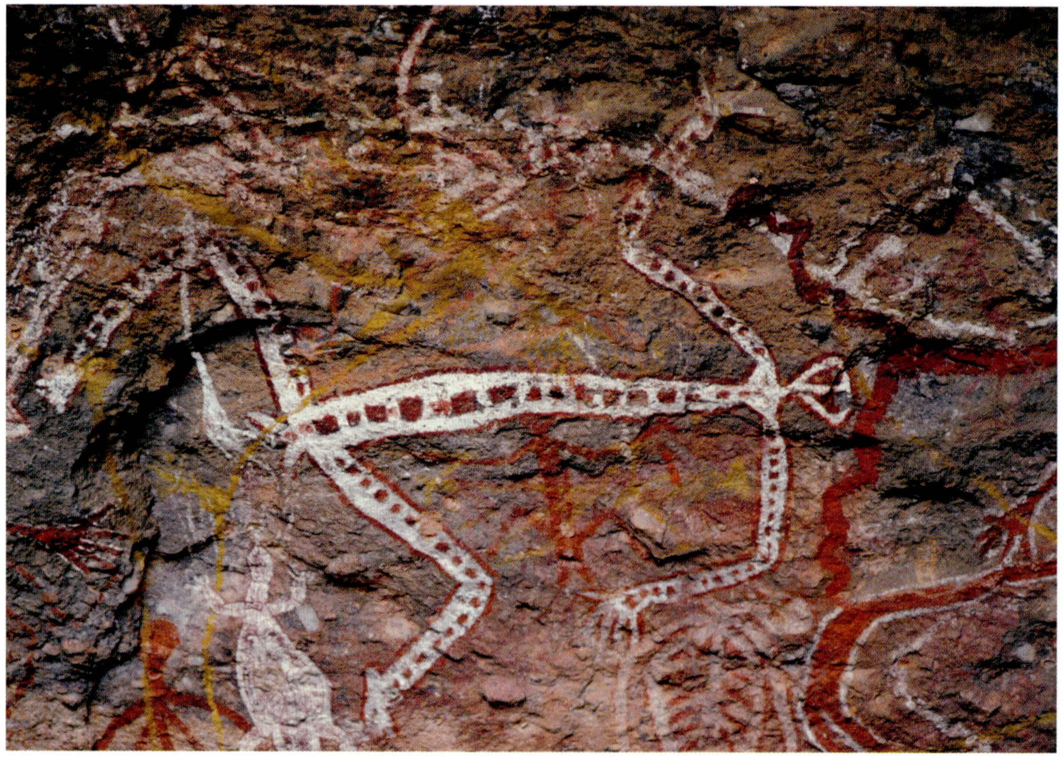

Two examples of rock paintings at the Anbangbang Shelter below Nourlangie Rock, Kakadu NP, Northern Territory. Kakadu rock walls feature at least 20 000 years of Aboriginal art.

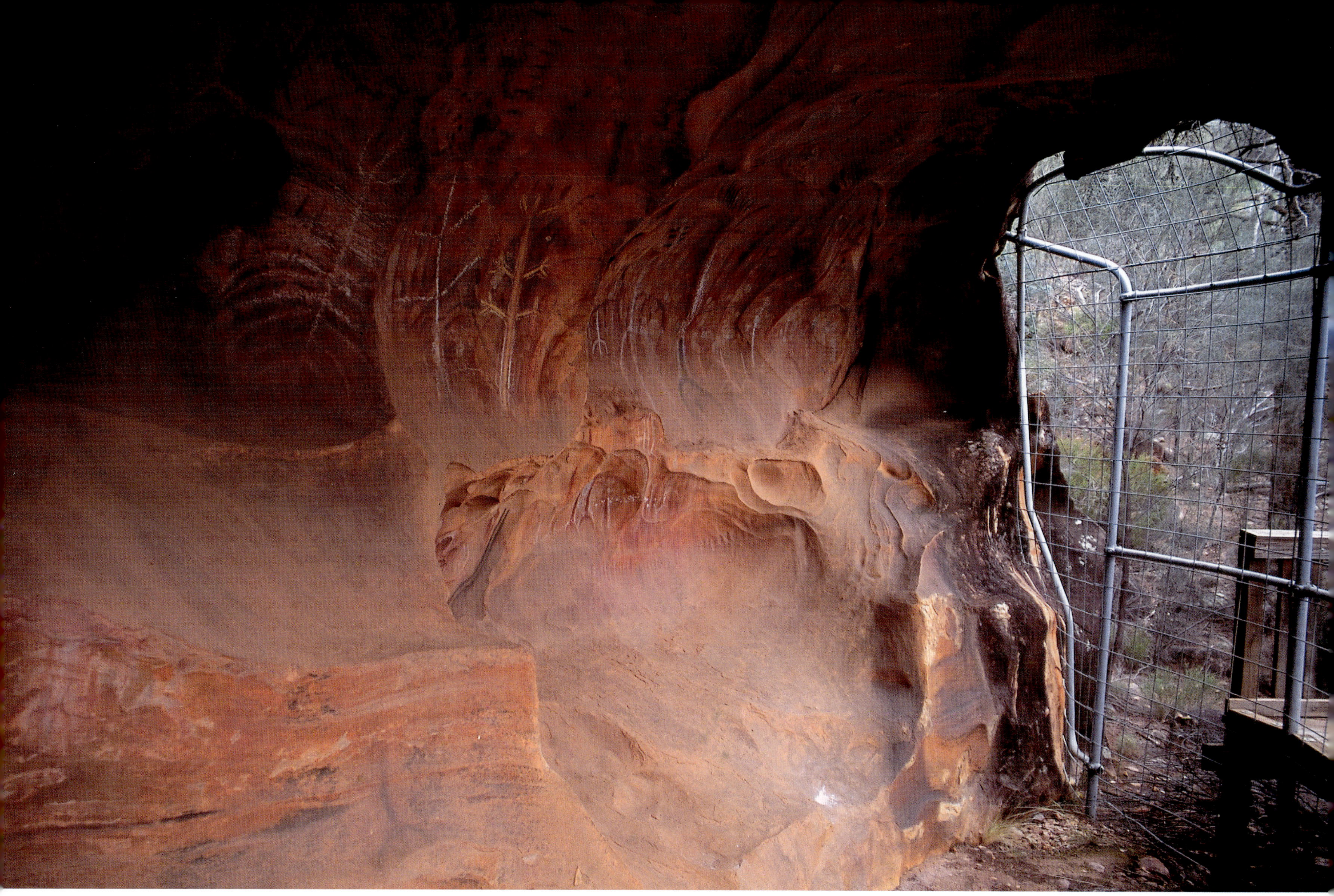

Ochre and charcoal images at Arkaroo Rock in the central Flinders Ranges, South Australia.

Australia is a young country architecturally compared to Europe, but even so there is a wealth of heritage to be seen. Its cities have historic buildings dating from colonial times, and many country towns have well preserved old buildings and streetscapes.

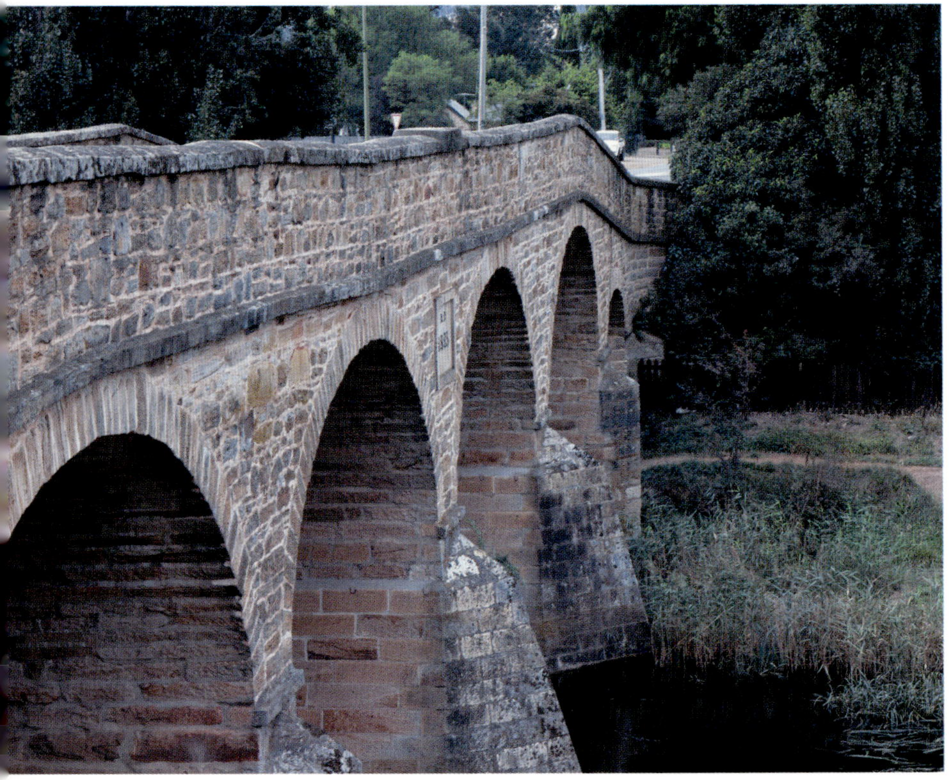

The oldest surviving bridge in Australia is the Richmond Bridge over the Coal River in southern Tasmania, included on the National Heritage List in 2005. It was begun in 1823 and completed in 1825 using convict labour and local sandstone.

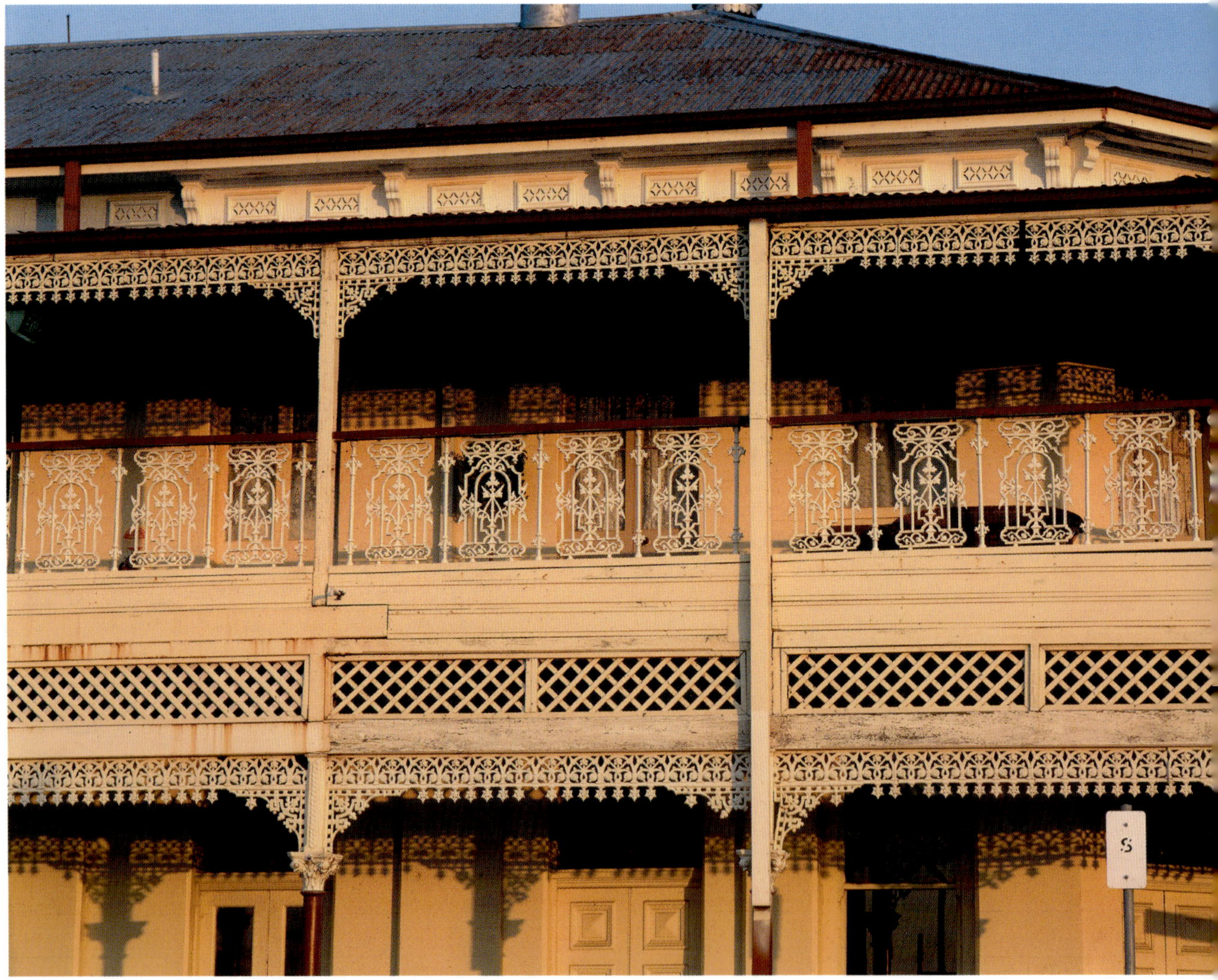

The elaborate wrought iron lacework of the Royal Private Hotel in Charters Towers, established in 1888. The town had its own stock exchange and a population of 30,000 during a gold rush in the 1880s and 1890s (today it is only 8000).

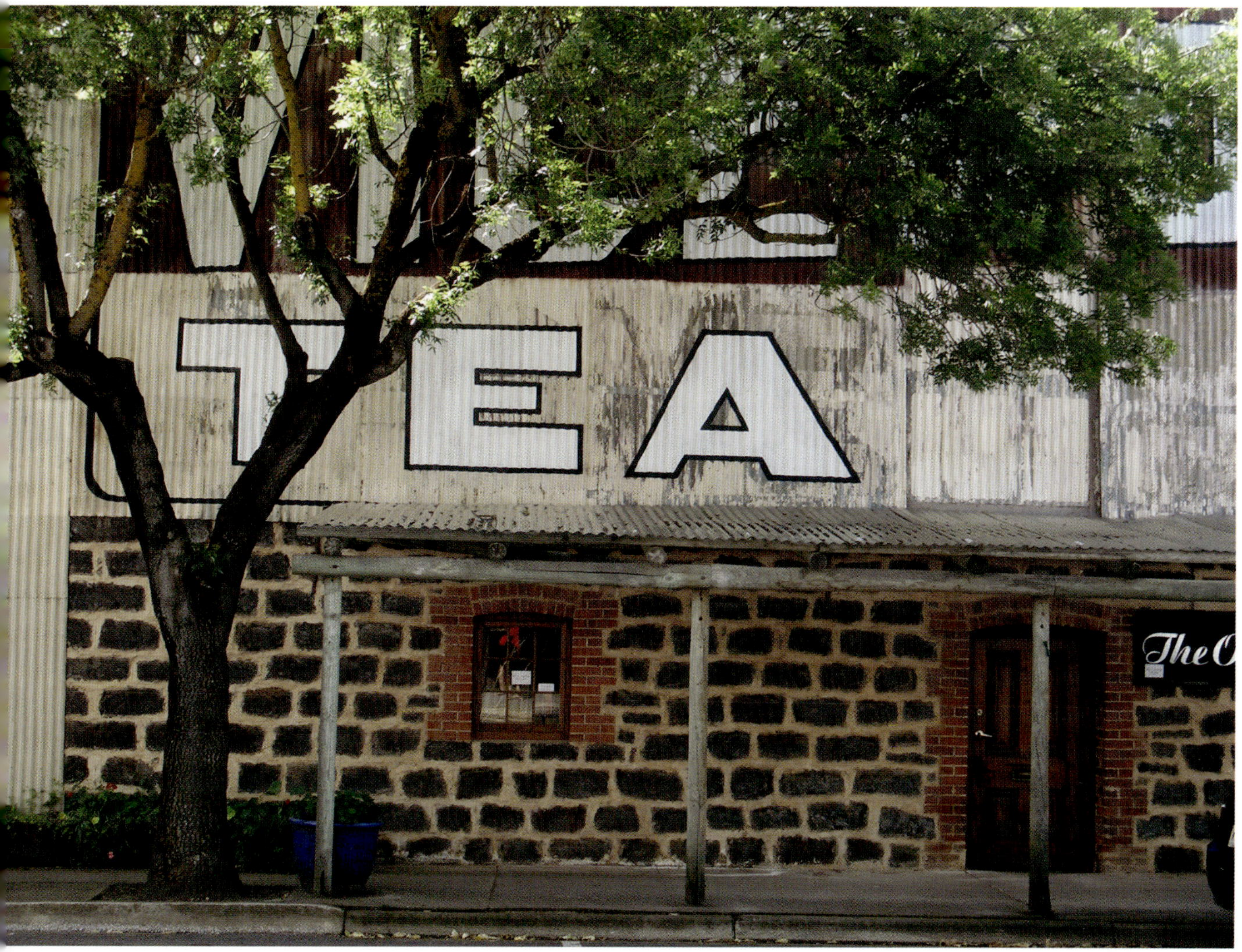

The heritage listed Old Mill at Tanunda in the Barossa Valley is now a gallery and a cafe.

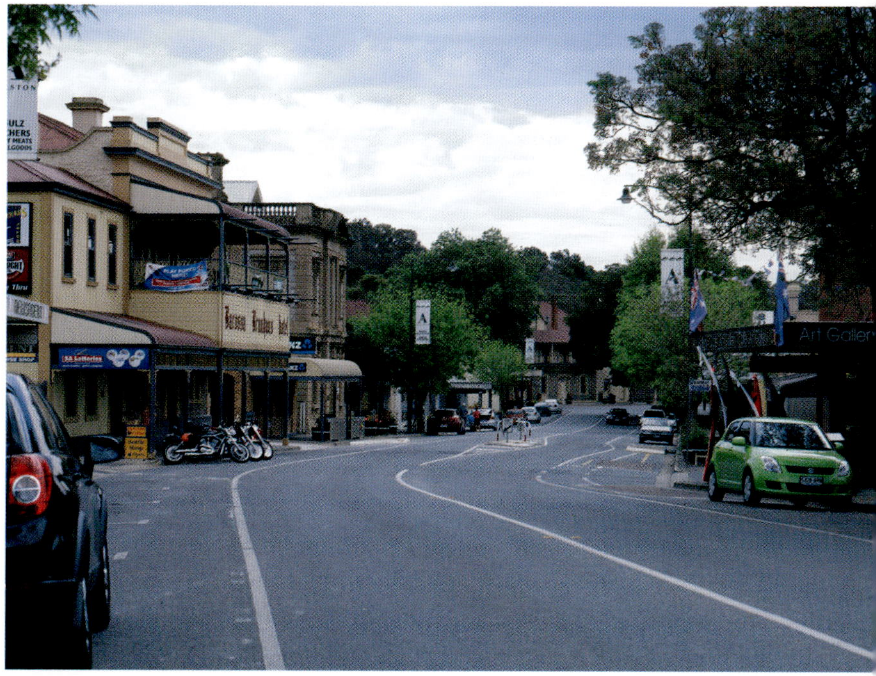

Angaston in the Barossa Valley of South Australia was settled by German Lutheran, English and Scottish pioneers. The town was originally called Angas Town after George Fife Angas, a businessman who played an important role in the settlement of South Australia.

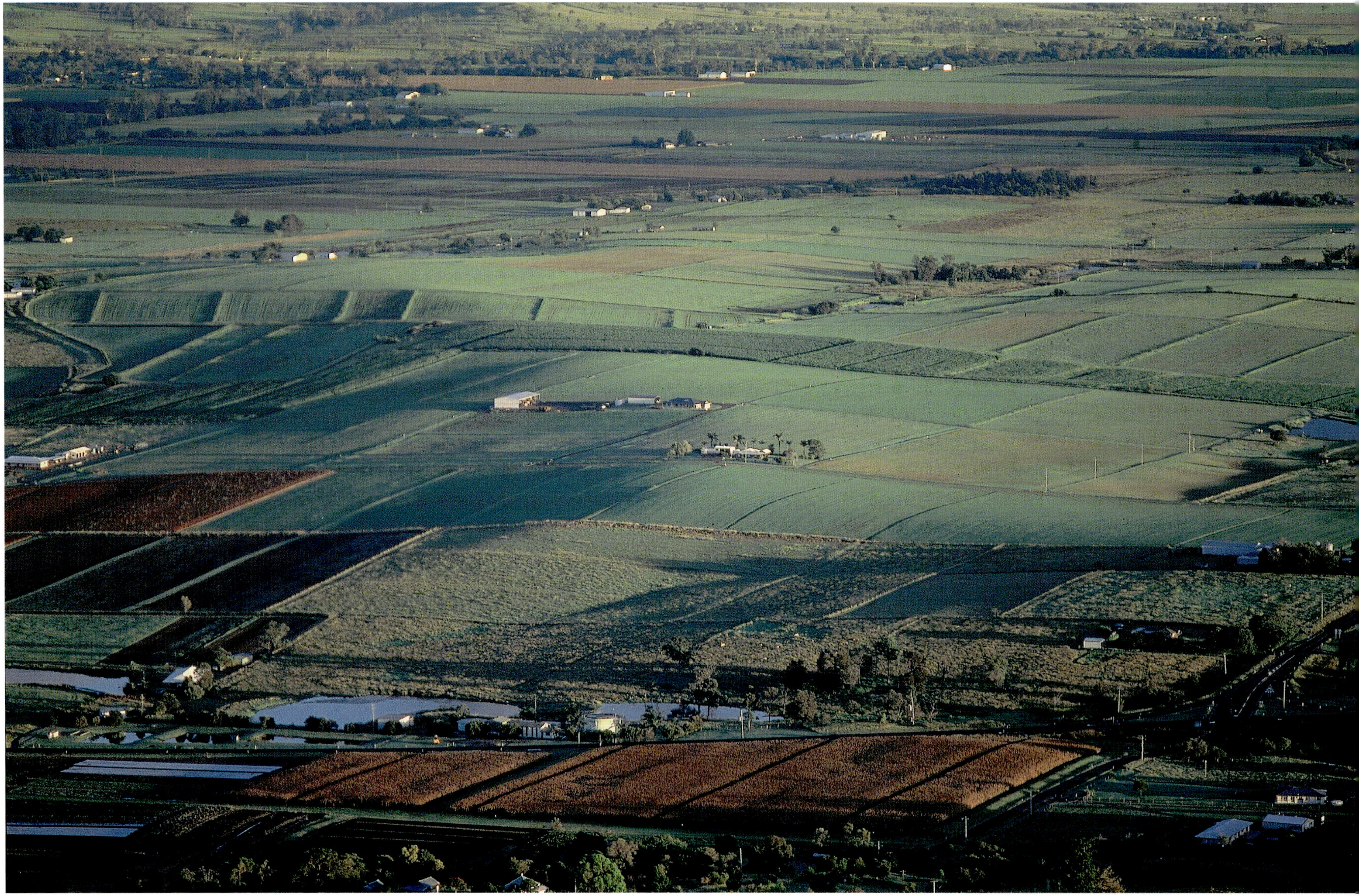

Fertile farmlands in the Fassifern Valley near Boonah, South East Queensland, supply vegetables to the city of Brisbane and beyond.

The Australian economy used to "ride on a sheep's back" and agriculture is still important today. Some agricultural areas unfortunately have issues with salinity and land degradation and there is a growing awareness of the need to care for the land and to move towards more sustainable farming practices.

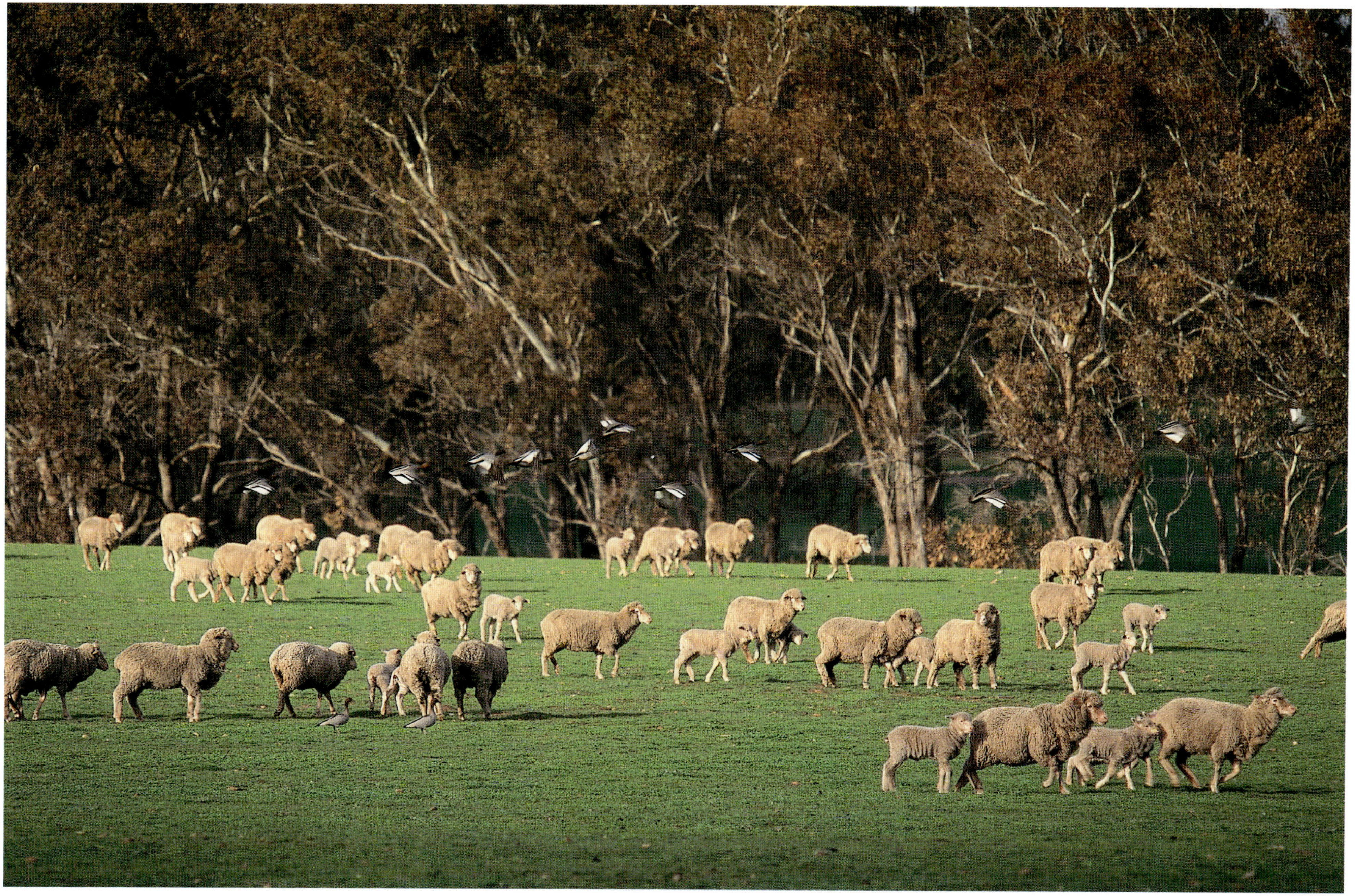

Maned duck and merinos in the Great Southern region of Western Australia.

Australians are famous for their laidback, laconic way of life. The sun-drenched climate allows for all manner of outdoor pursuits, and they are often followed religiously. Surfing, fishing, swimming, bushwalking and cycling are only a few of the options. Australians also love organised sport, either playing it or following their chosen team. Cricket and Soccer are the main games in summer and Australian Rules football, Rugby League and Rugby Union in winter.

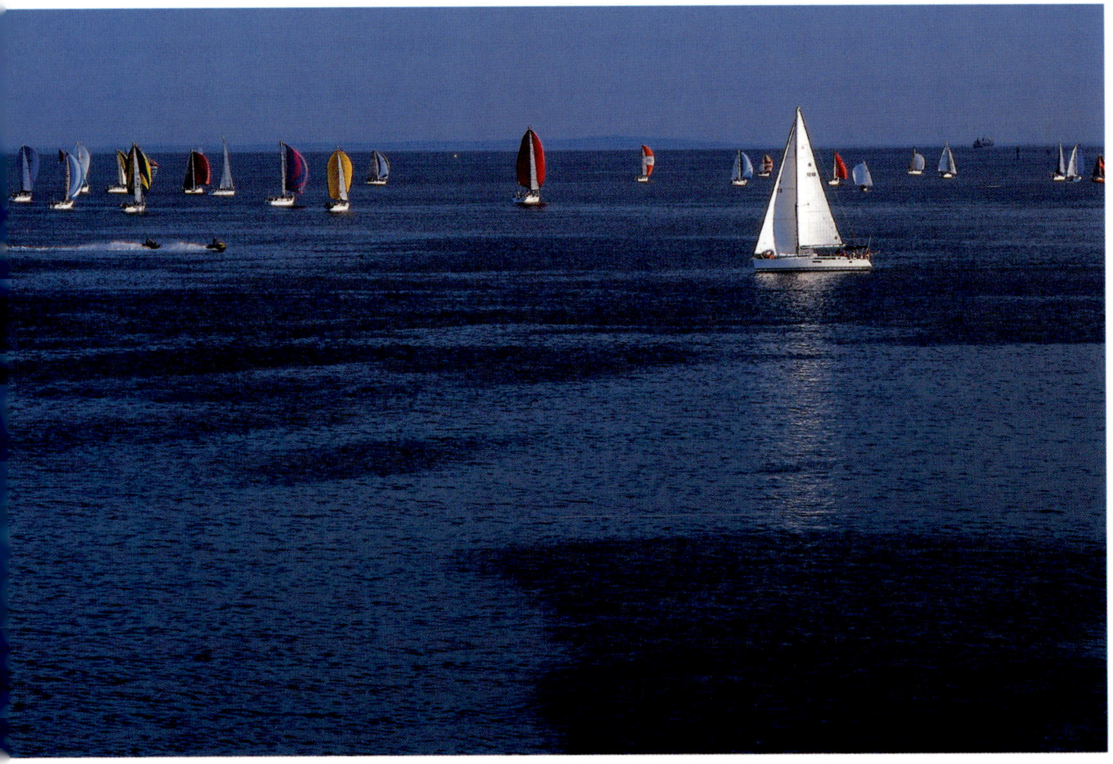

Yachts and jetskis on Port Phillip Bay on a hot summer afternoon, Melbourne.

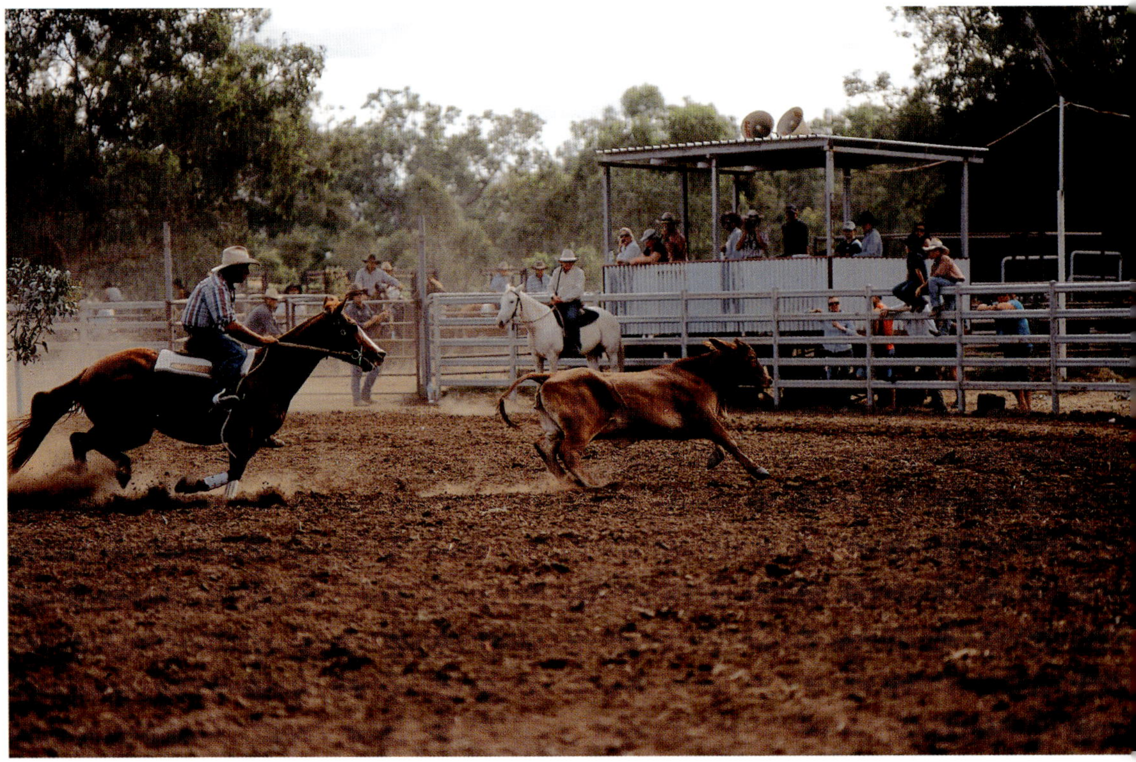

Camp drafting at the Fitzroy Crossing rodeo, Kimberley region.

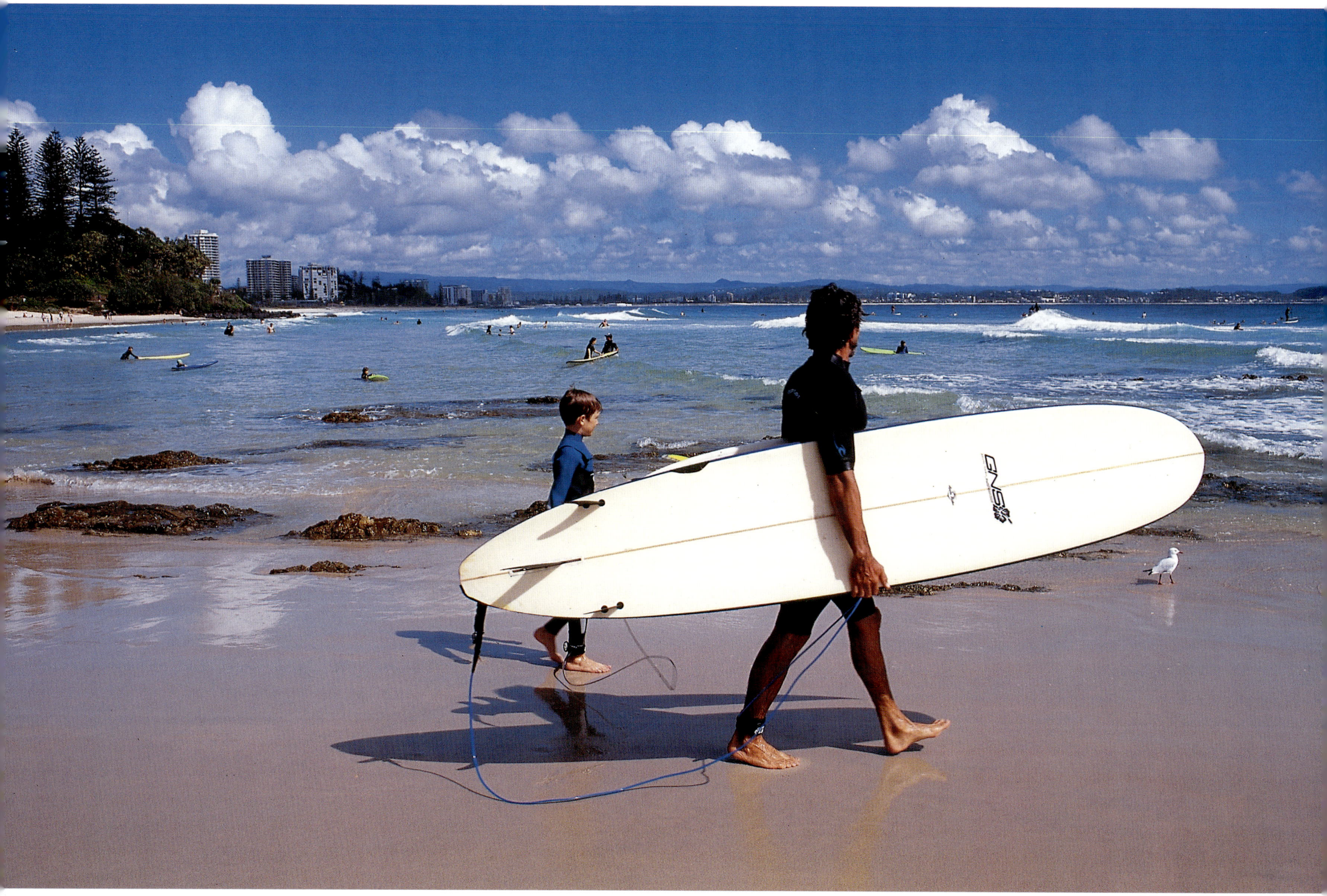

Surfing at Greenmount Beach, near Coolangatta on the Gold Coast of Queensland.

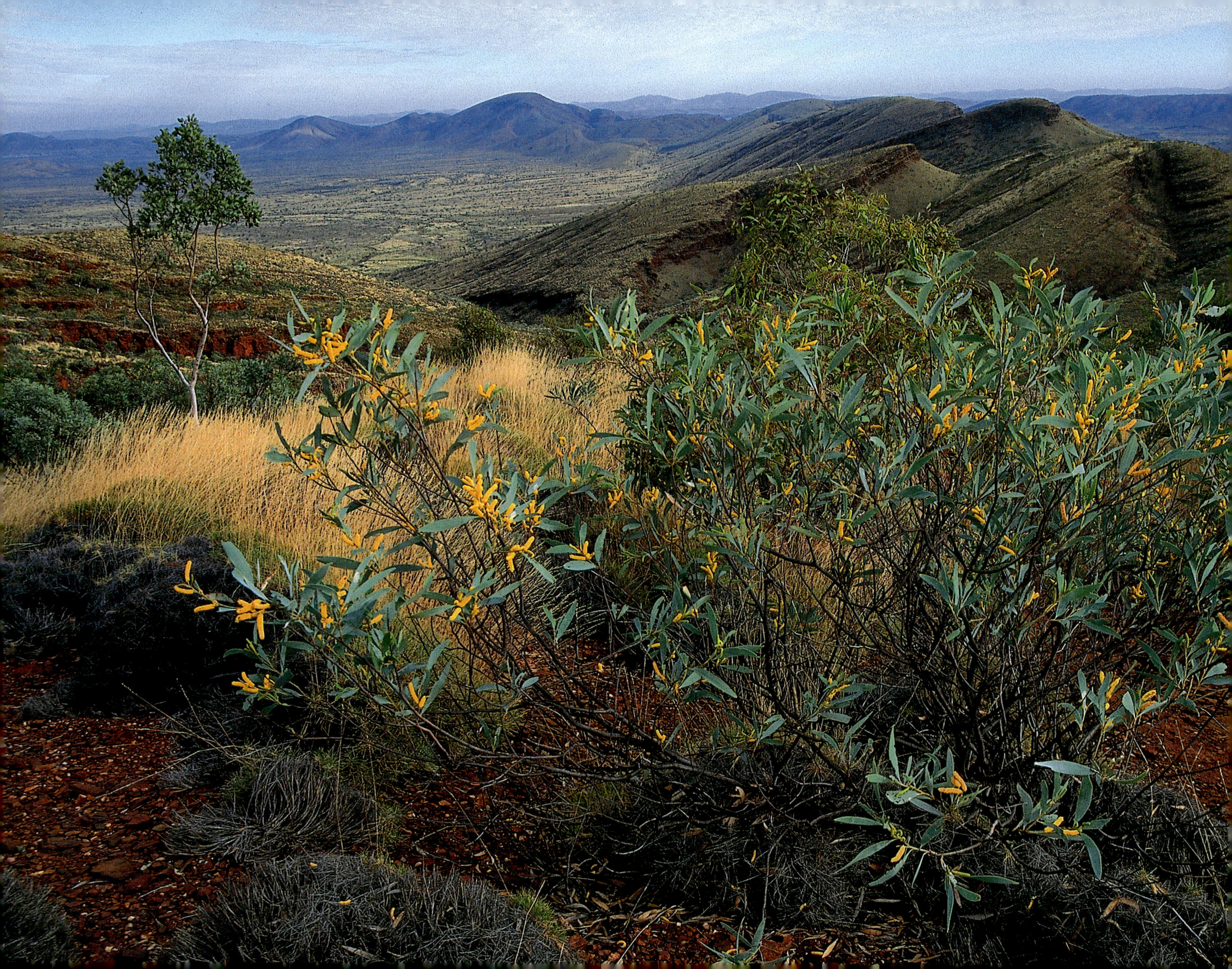

Western Australia

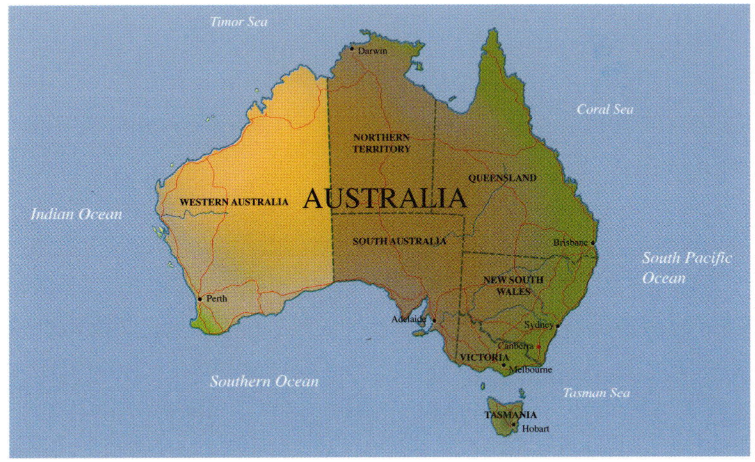

Western Australia is vast! Australia's largest state is almost one-third the size of the whole country, and covers an area of over 2.5 million square kilometres. It stretches from the cool temperate south coast, where it can snow on the Stirling Range near Albany, through the semi-arid Gascoyne and Pilbara regions to the tropical Kimberley. There are tall forests of jarrah and karri in the south-west corner, famous vineyards around Margaret River, Pemberton and Mount Barker, and stunning beaches along the south coast, including some of the finest in the country around Esperance. The capital of the state, Perth, lies on the Swan River and is a busy city of about 1.5 million people. To the north and east of the city lies an arable wheatbelt which eventually gives way to sheep and cattle station and desert country.

Western Australia is renowned for unique and beautiful natural landscapes and has extraordinary biodiversity. There are an estimated 7,000 – 9,000 species of flowering plants in the South West alone, extending south and west of a line drawn from Shark Bay to Israelite Bay. 80 per cent of these plants are endemic, only growing naturally here. The wildflower season starts after good winter rains, with everlastings blooming in June and July in the Gascoyne and Pilbara regions, and extends to October or November in the hills and mountains of the south coast around Albany and Denmark.

Aboriginal people have lived in Western Australia for at least 50,000 years. The first European settlement in Western Australia was at Albany in 1826, set up as an outpost of New South Wales to prevent possible French colonisation. The Swan River Colony (which became the city of Perth) was founded in 1829 by Captain James Stirling and was the first free European settlement on the continent. The colony struggled in the first few decades, so in 1850 the decision was made to accept convicts from England to increase the population and encourage development. In 1892, gold was discovered at Coolgardie, starting Western Australia's first economic boom. The state has huge mineral wealth with deposits of gold, bauxite, nickel, iron ore, diamonds, oil and natural gas.

Opposite page: Flowering wattles on Mount Nameless, near the town of Tom Price in the Pilbara.

The south coast of Western Australia is a stunning series of squeaky clean white beaches and rugged granite headlands and islands. I think the beaches at Cape Le Grand National Park near Esperance are the most visually stunning in the country, although the water tends to be rather cool – even in summer! There is wonderful bushwalking, surfing and fishing along this coast and much of it remains pristine and wild.

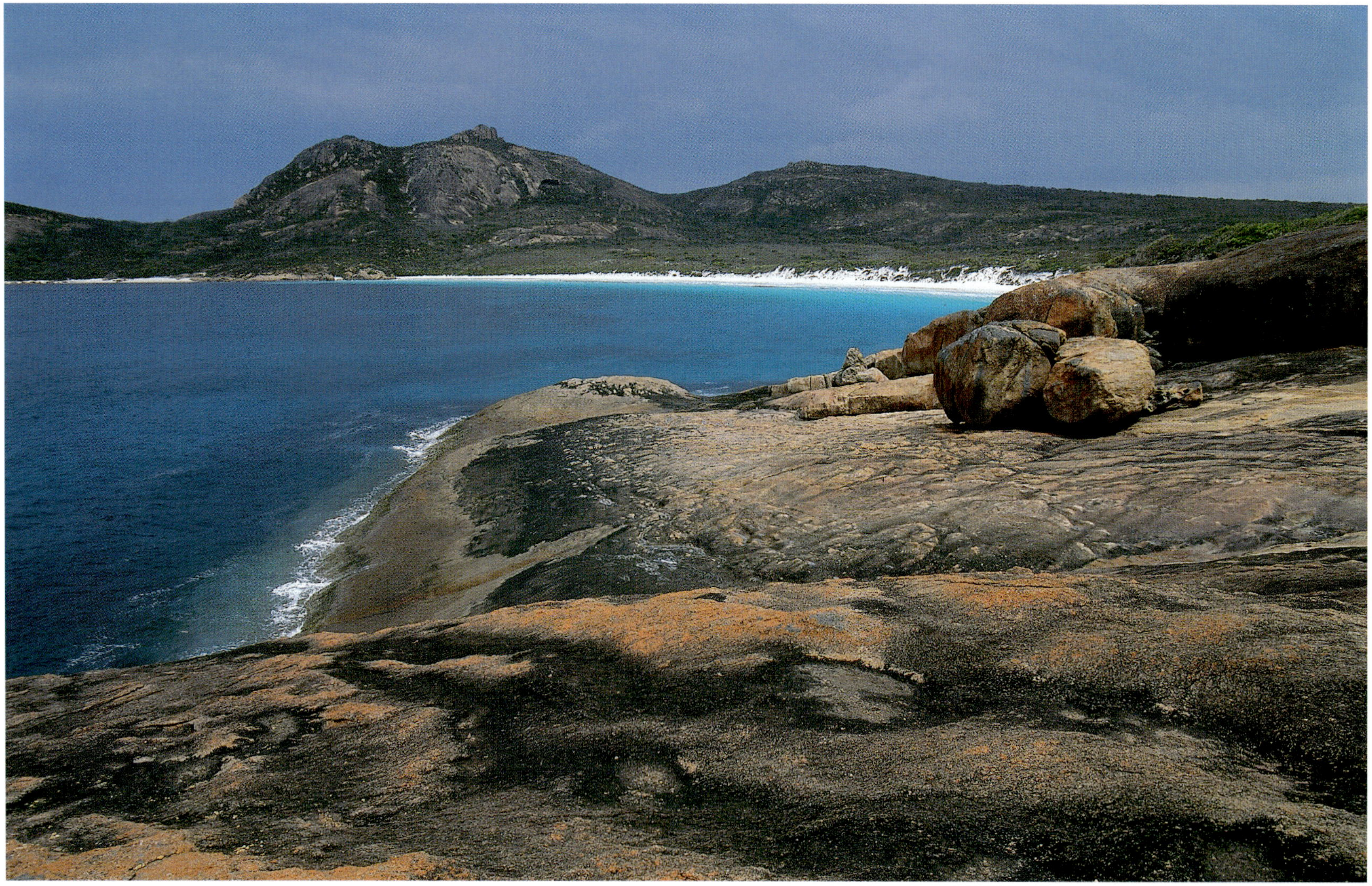

Top: Looking over granite rocks to Thistle Cove and Boulder Hill, Cape Le Grand NP.

Opposite page: A lone fisherman at Mutton Bird Island Beach, near Albany on the south coast.

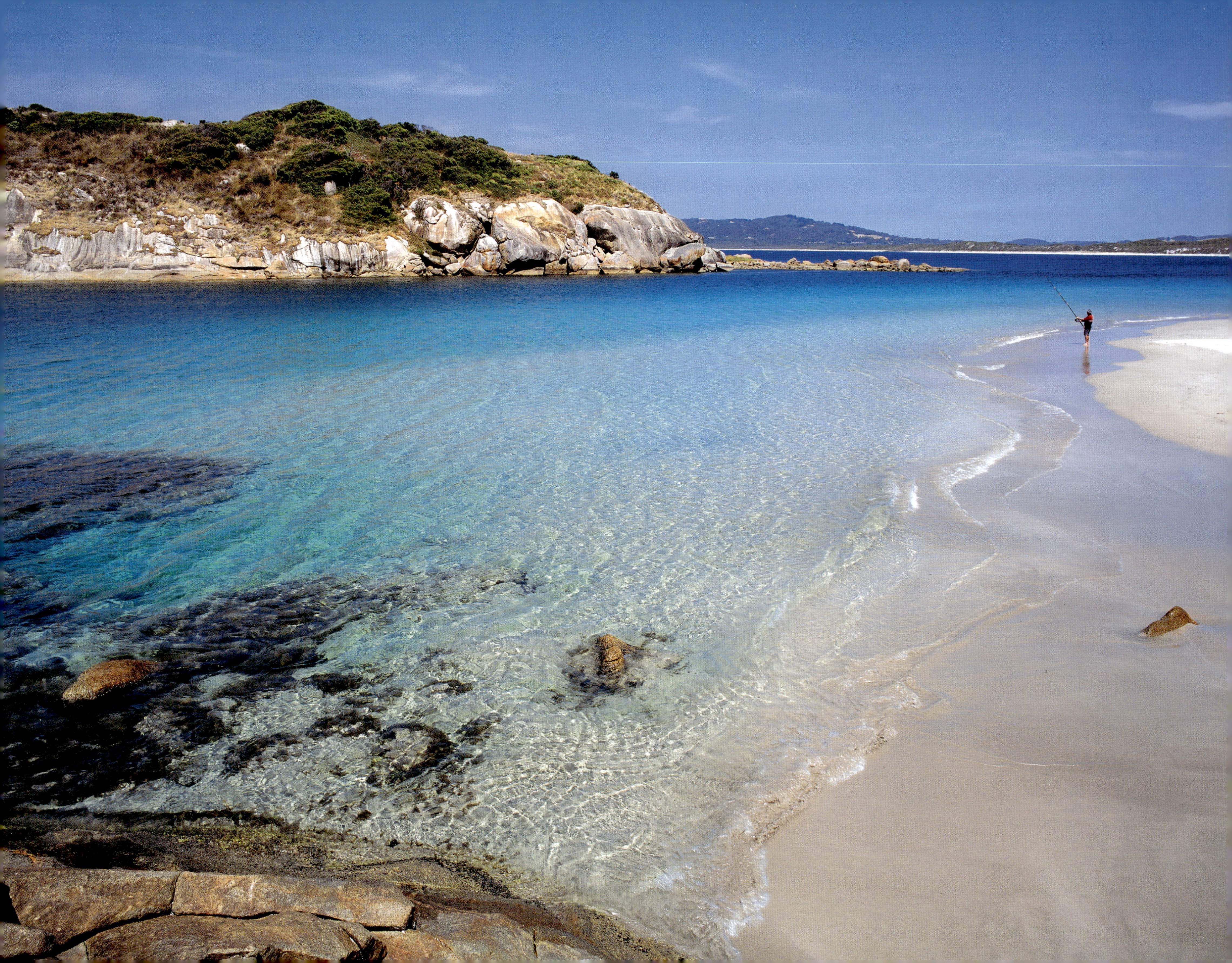

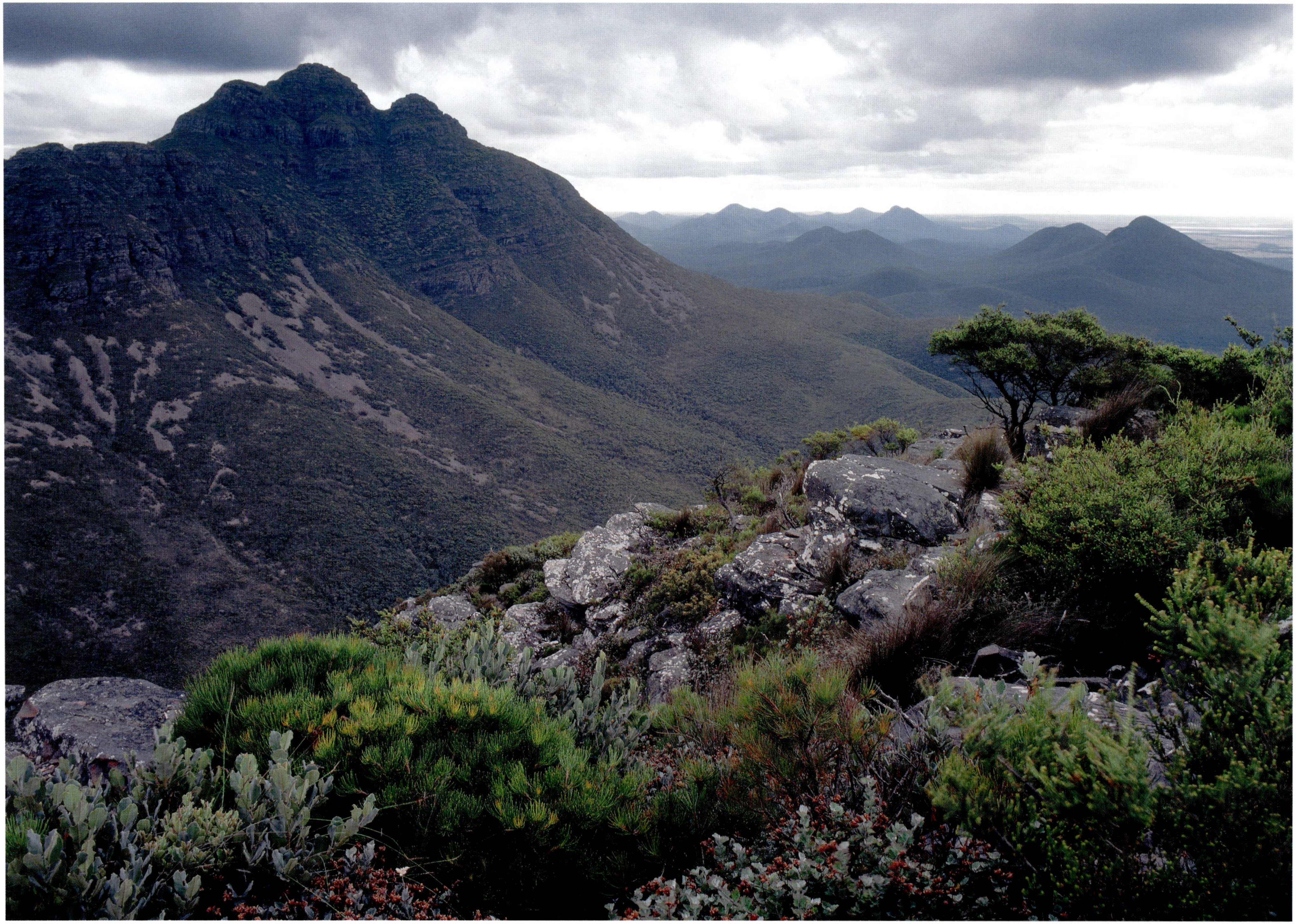

View from Mt Hassell to Toolbrunup Peak (1052m), the third highest summit in the range.

The Stirling Range National Park protects the entire 65 kilometre length of this rugged mountain range near Albany in the Great Southern, famed for its diversity of wildflowers. This is a special part of the world for my family and I, who have shared many wonderful holidays visiting these peaks. There are great mountain climbs here up many of the peaks and also a spectacular but tough two to three day ridge walk from Bluff Knoll to Ellen Peak. This is a rough track winding through dense bush up steep gullies and over precipitous peaks. The hike takes two to three days, with walkers sleeping in small camping caves in the cliffs or in occasional clearings suitable for tents.

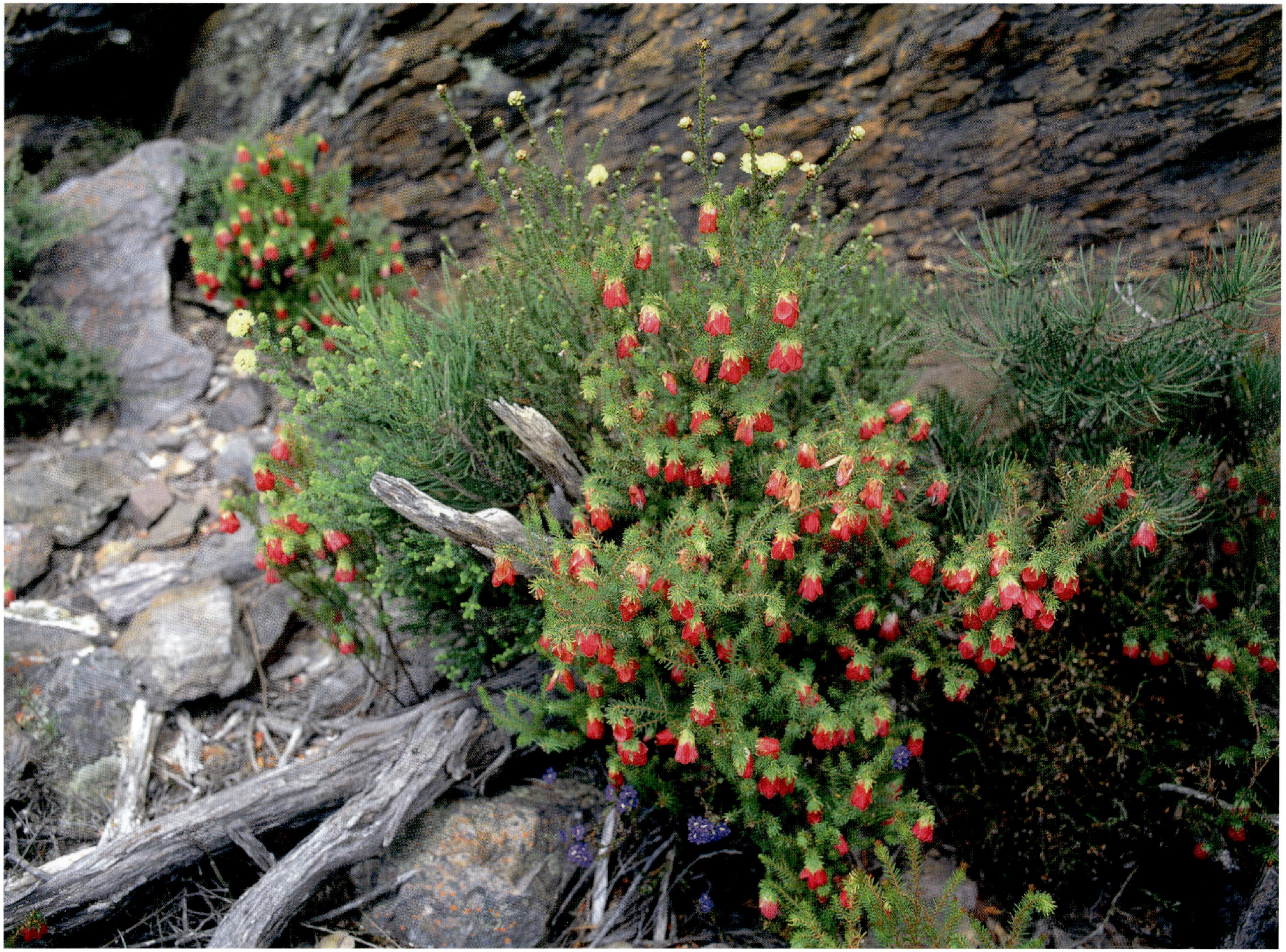

Common mountain bell on Mount Trio, Stirling Range.

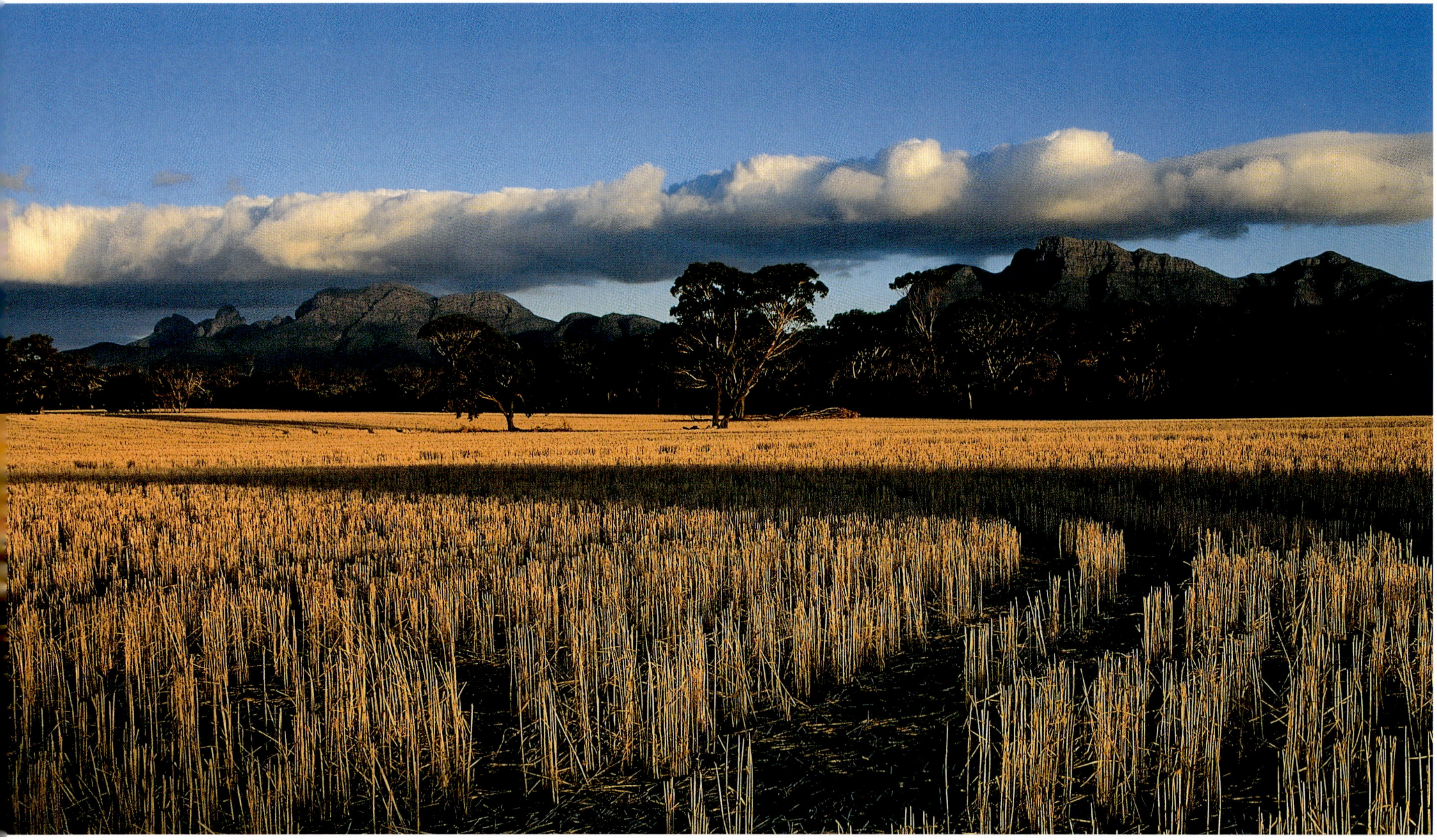

Top: Wheat stubble below the eastern Stirling Range with Bluff Knoll (1095m), the highest peak in the range, to the right.

Right: View at dawn from Bluff Knoll summit over a sea of clouds.

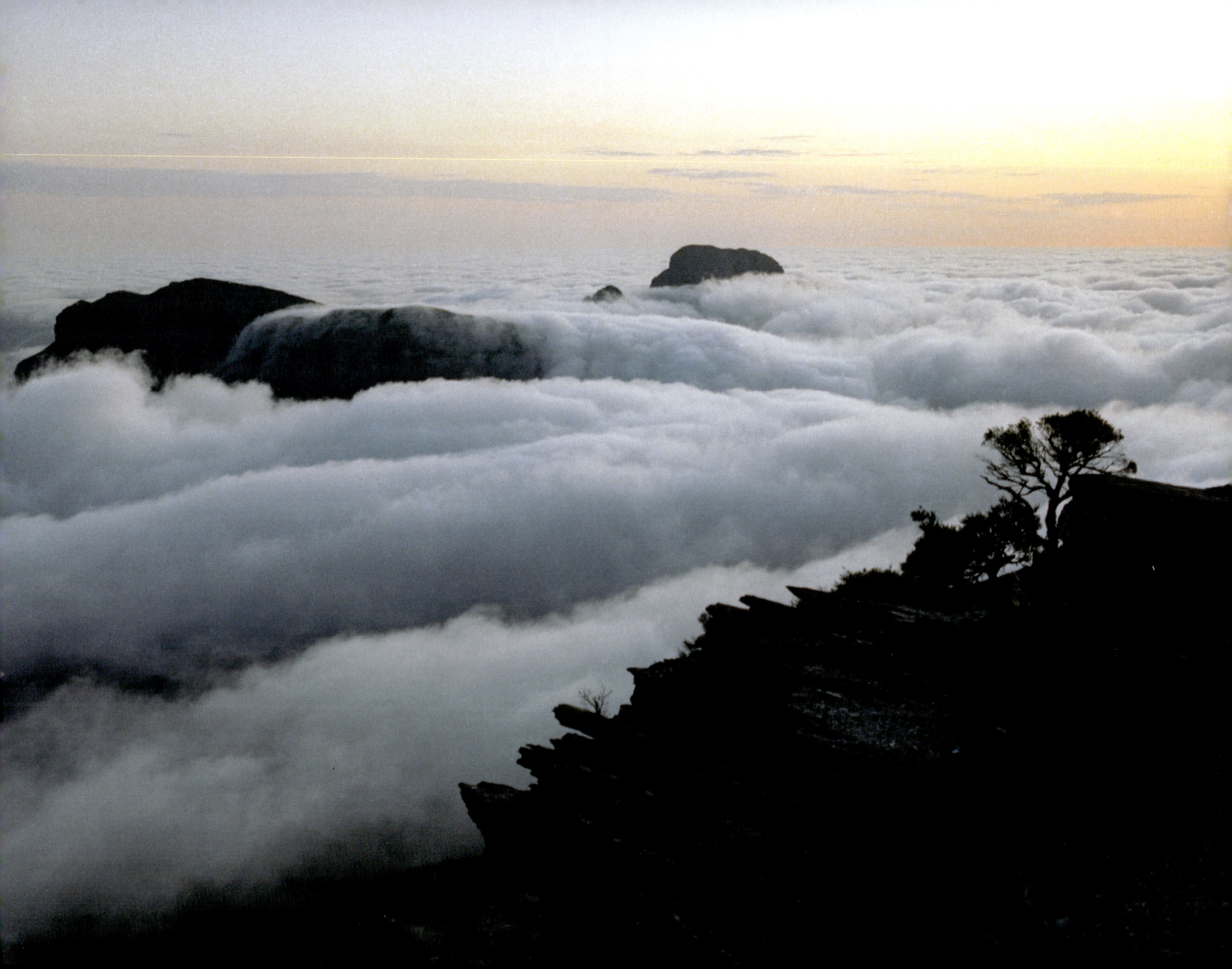

I lived beneath the Porongurup Range for three years, and it remains one of my favourite places in Australia. The granite rocks of Devils Slide, the highest peak, rise to 670 metres above verdant karri forests, heathlands and colourful wildflowers in spring. The range is only 12 kilometres long but is very scenic and has some of the best bushwalking in Western Australia. The surrounding lush farmland boasts many fine cool climate vineyards and wineries, some with cellar sales. The range even has a great Thai Restaurant, renowned as one of the best in Australia, located in a farm paddock with views to the Stirling Range.

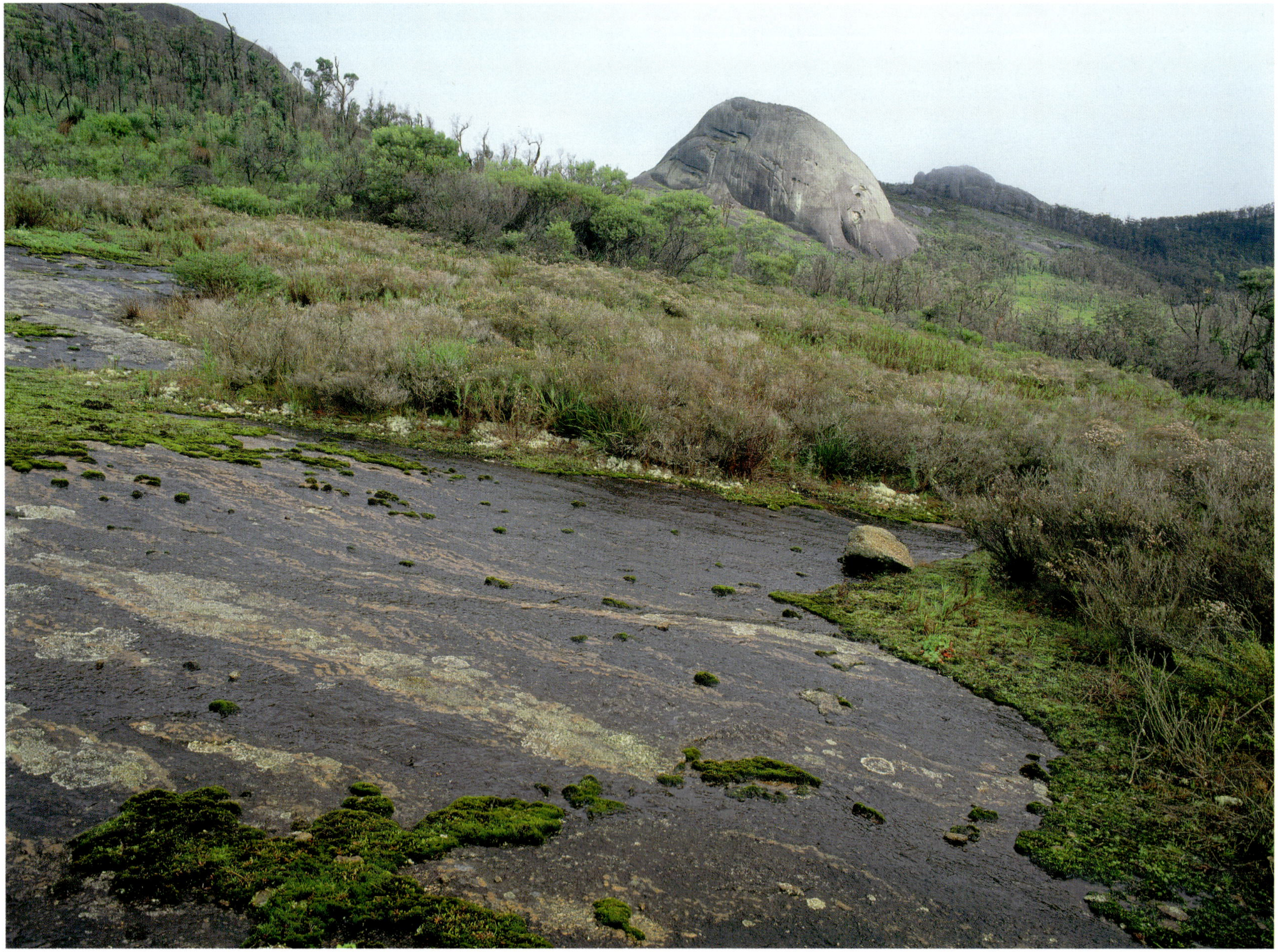

Looking from a mossy granite slab across to Gibraltor Rock (640m) in the Porongurup Range.

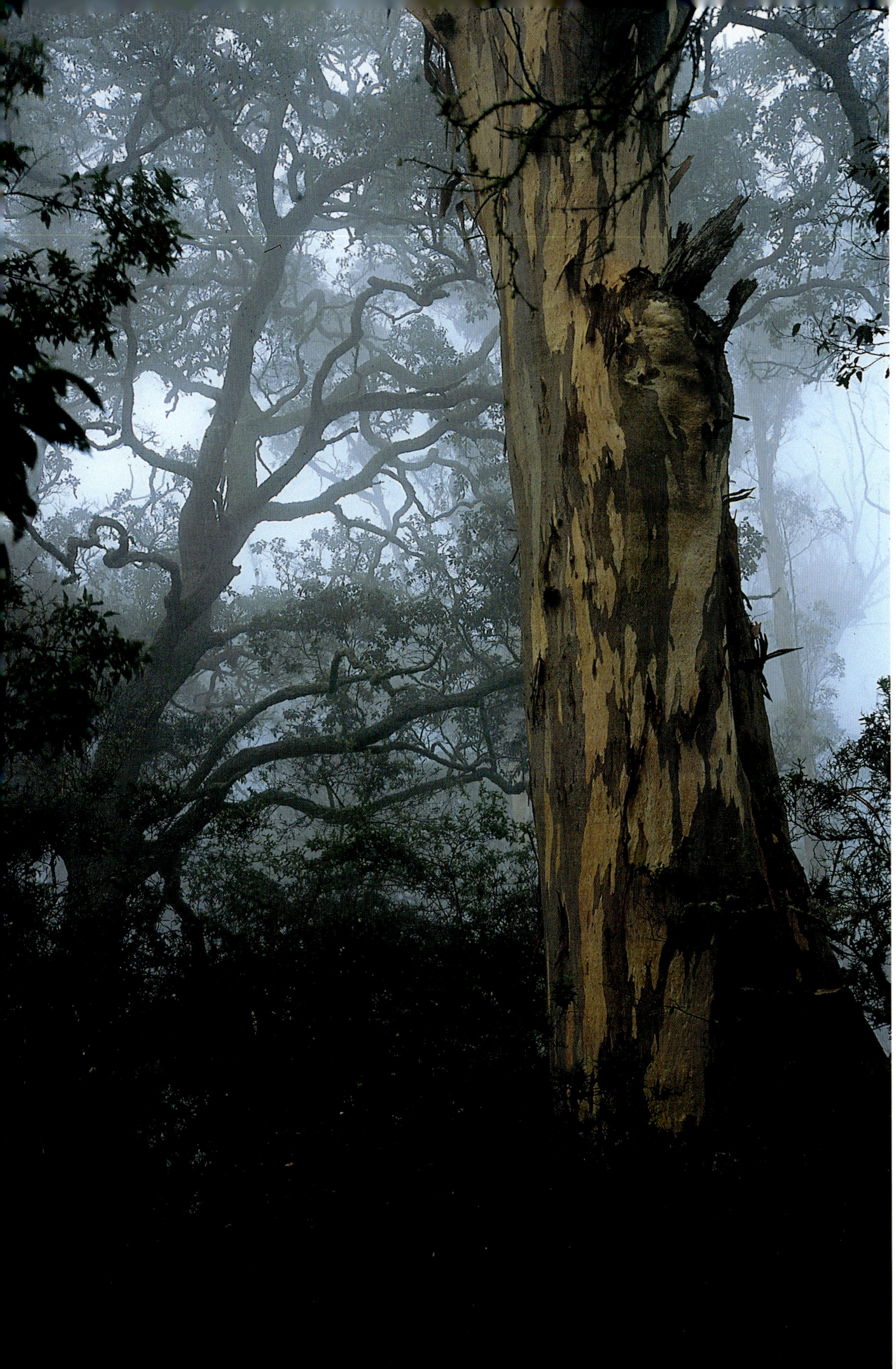

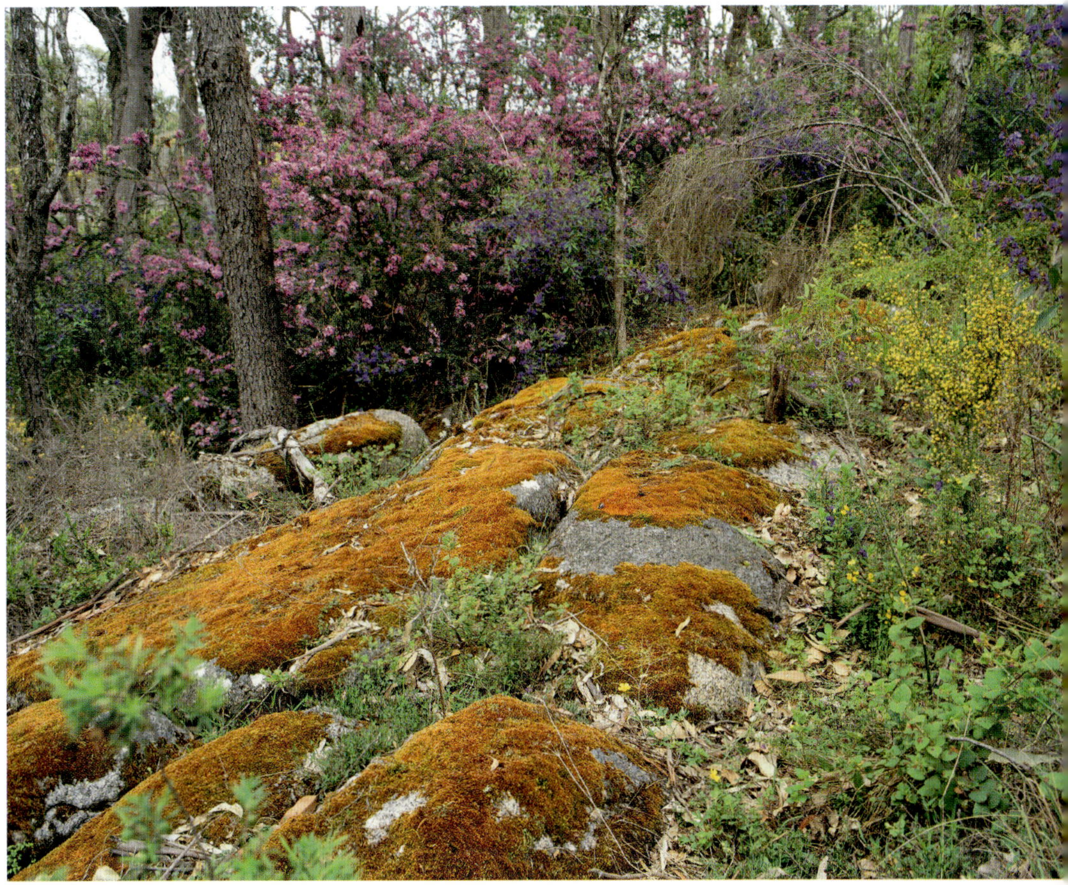

Top: A moss and wildflower garden high up in the Porongurup Range.

Left: Karri tree in mist, Porongurup Range.

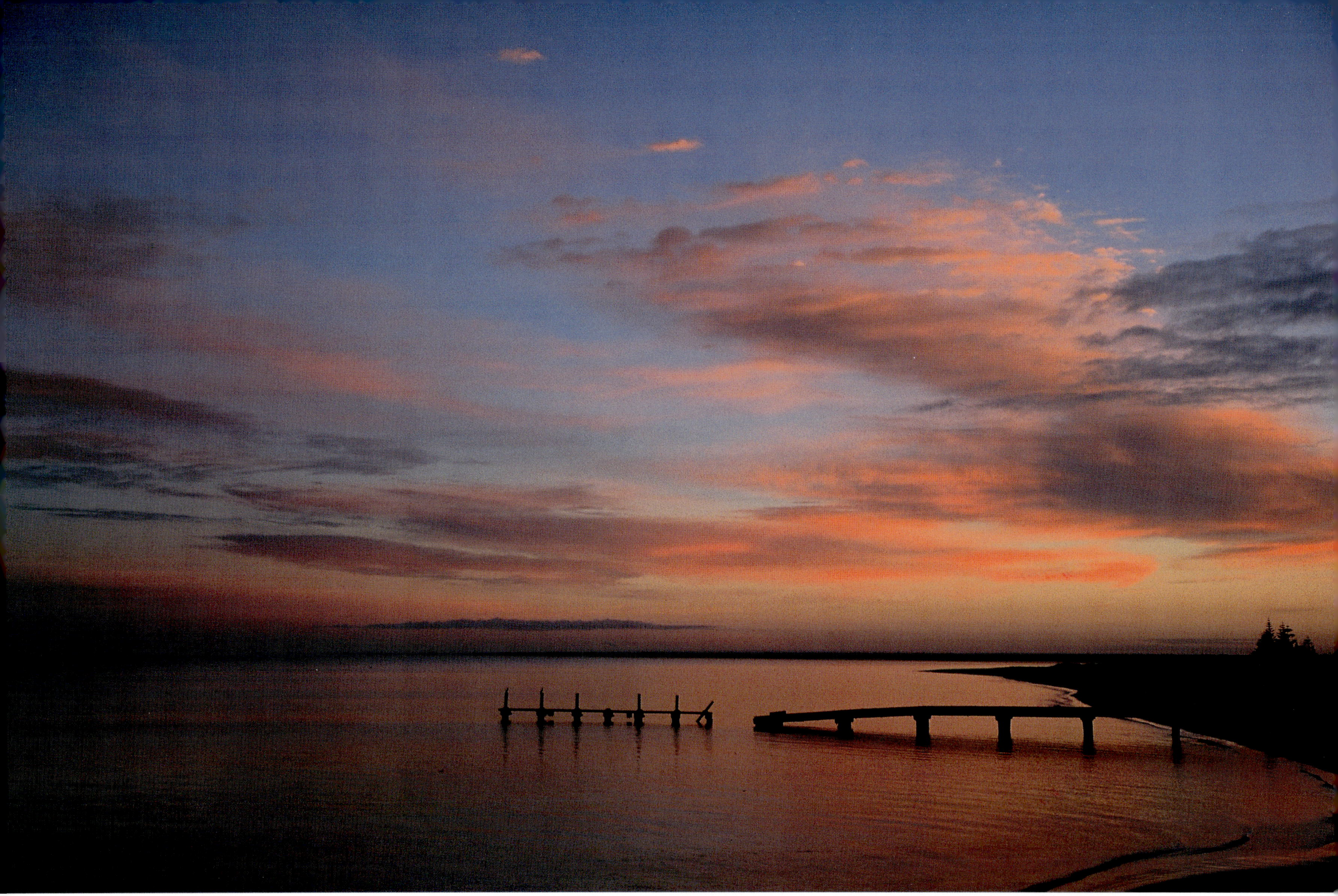

Sunrise over a small jetty at Busselton.

The south-west covers the area south of Perth from Mandurah to Albany, and is a diverse region of productive farmland, tall forests of karri, tingle and jarrah and spectacular coastal scenery. Many well-known and lesser-known boutique wineries, like Leeuwin Estate, Sandalford, Cape Mentelle, Salitage and Castle Rock Estate, can be found in the Margaret River, Pemberton and Great Southern areas. The south-west is one of the most popular tourist regions of Western Australia.

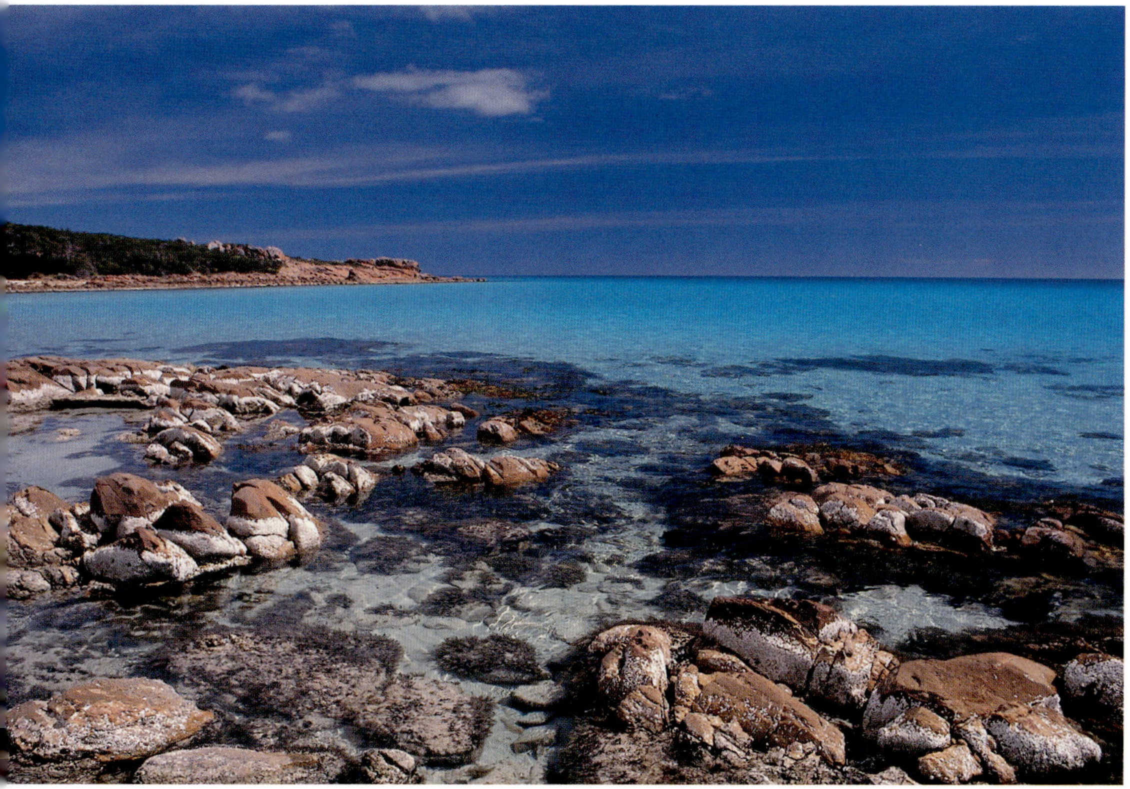

The stunning clear waters of Castle Rock Beach are near the town of Dunsborough on Geographe Bay.

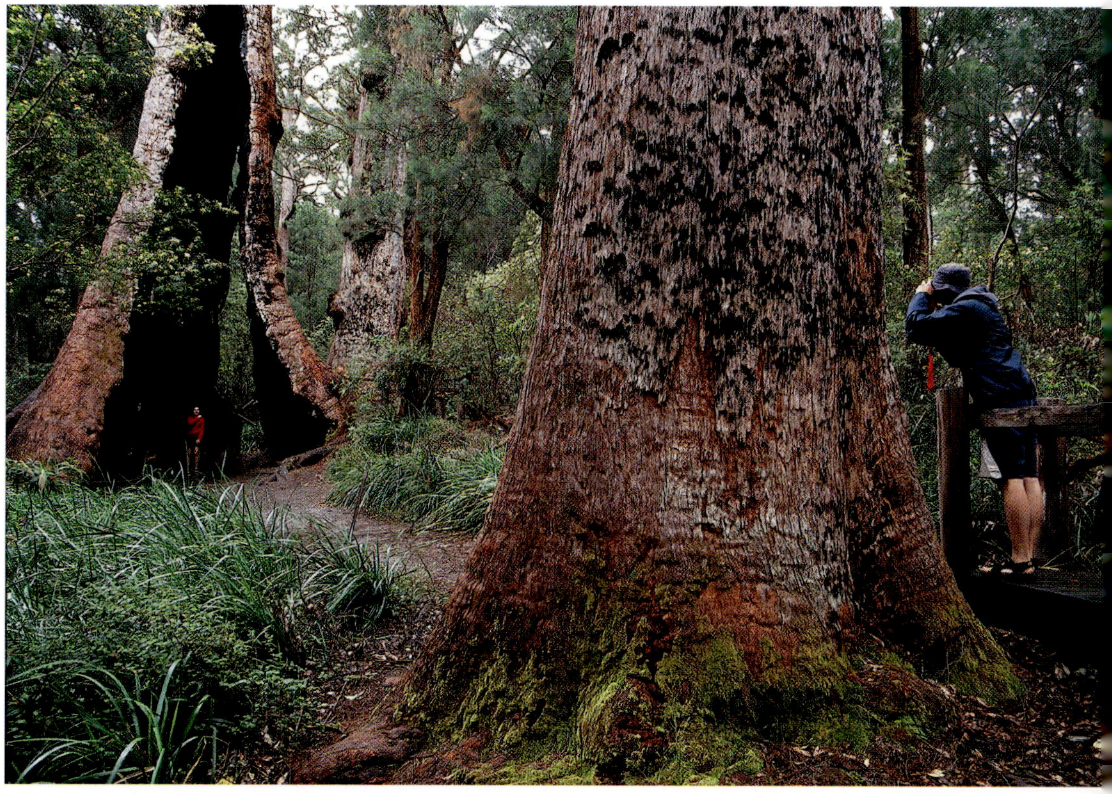

In amongst giant tingle trees, found naturally only in a small area near Walpole on the south coast of Western Australia.

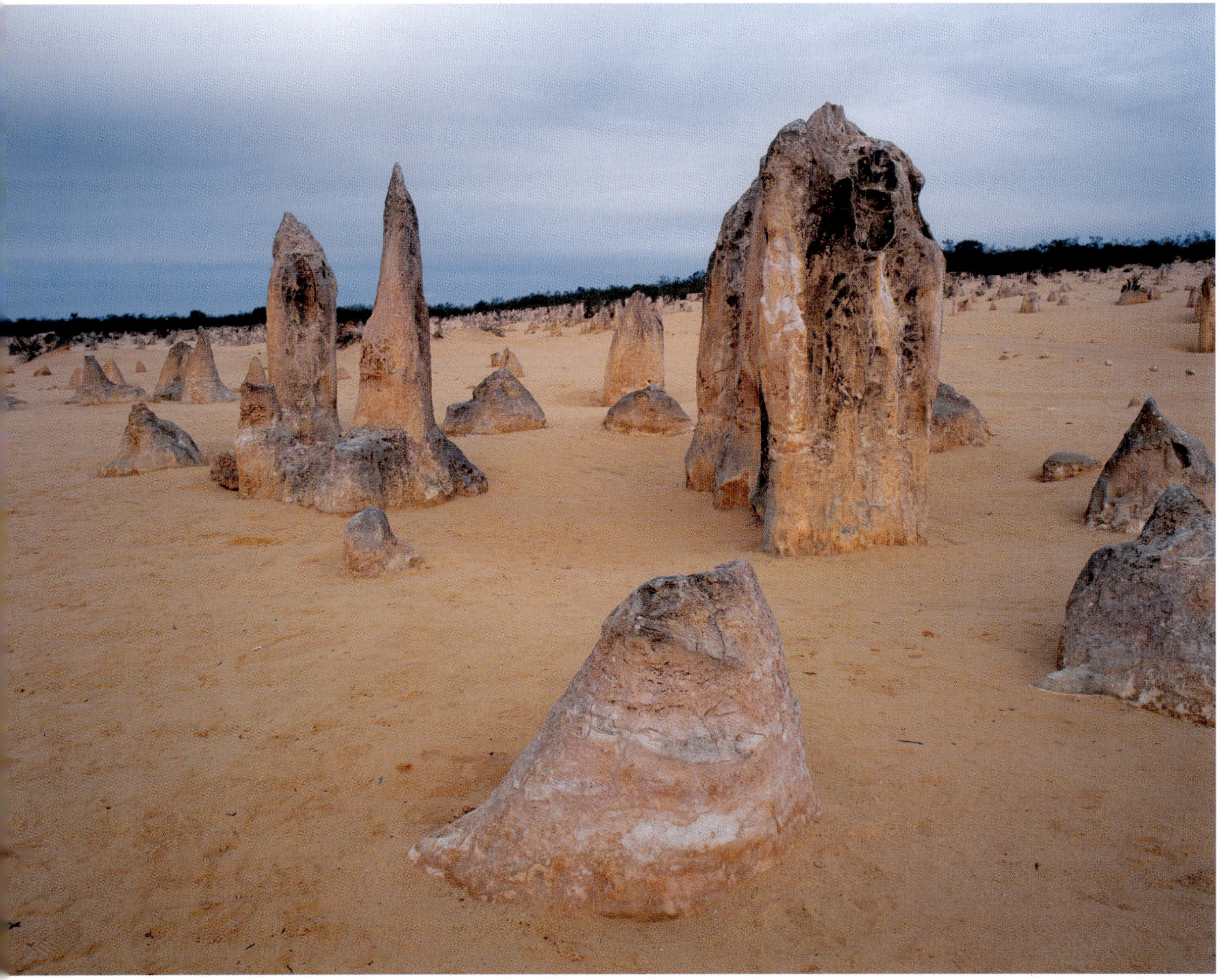

The Pinnacles near Cervantes is a famous Western Australian tourist attraction.

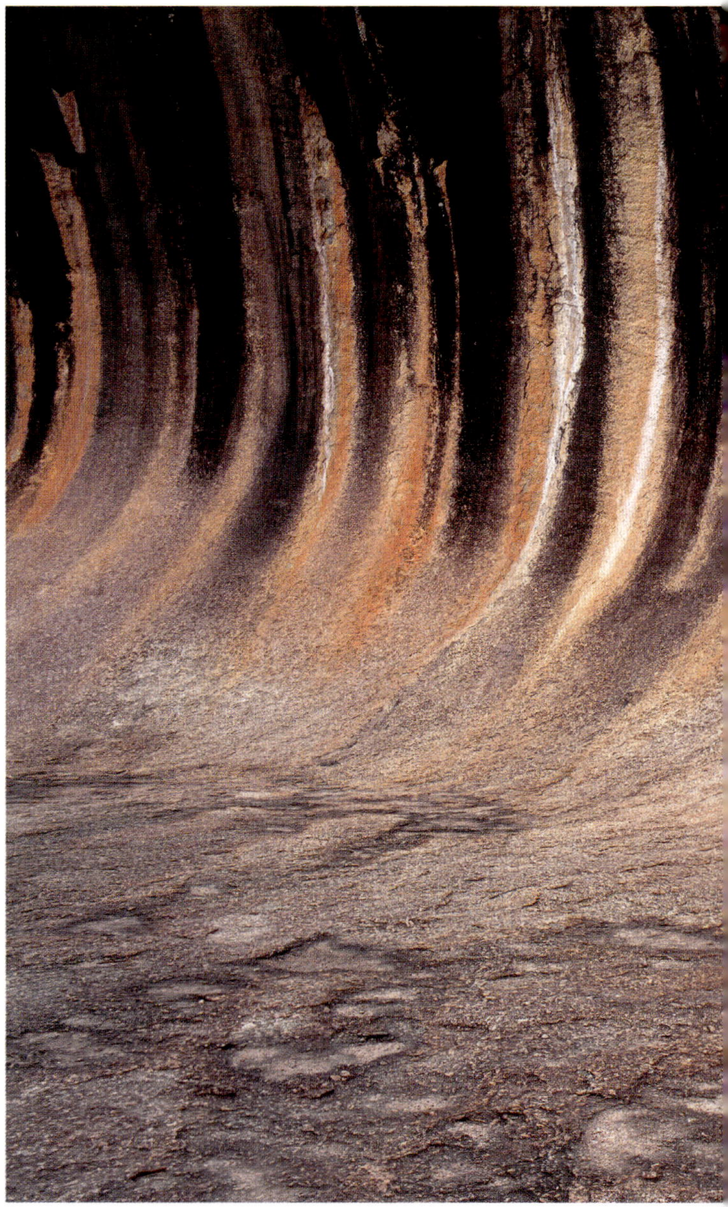

Rainwater patterns down the side of Wave Rock.

Western Australia also has quirky attractions like Wave Rock and the Pinnacles. Many ancient granite inselbergs – isolated rock hills rising from a flat plain – can be found in the vast area of the West Australian wheatbelt, including Elachbutting Rock near the town of Mukinbudin and Wave Rock, four hours east of Perth near Hyden. The Pinnacles lie 200 kilometres north of Perth and are limestone pillars, up to 5 metres high, exposed by wind erosion of coastal sand dunes.

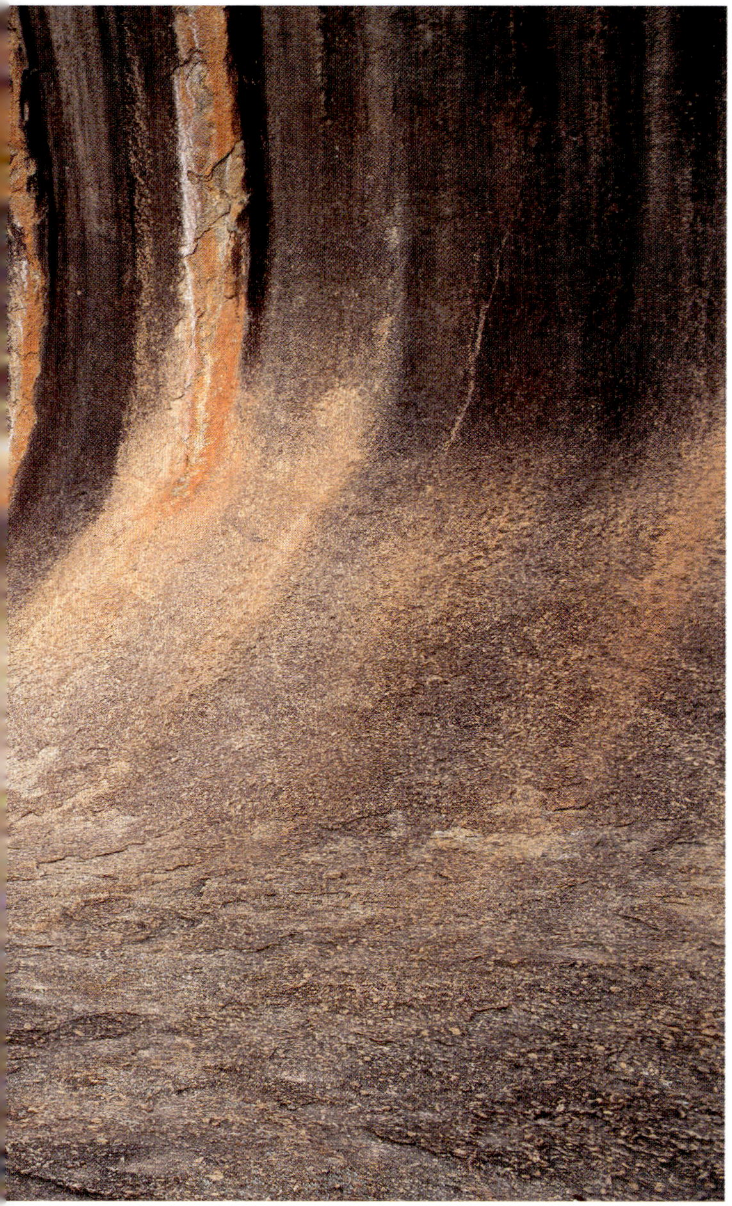

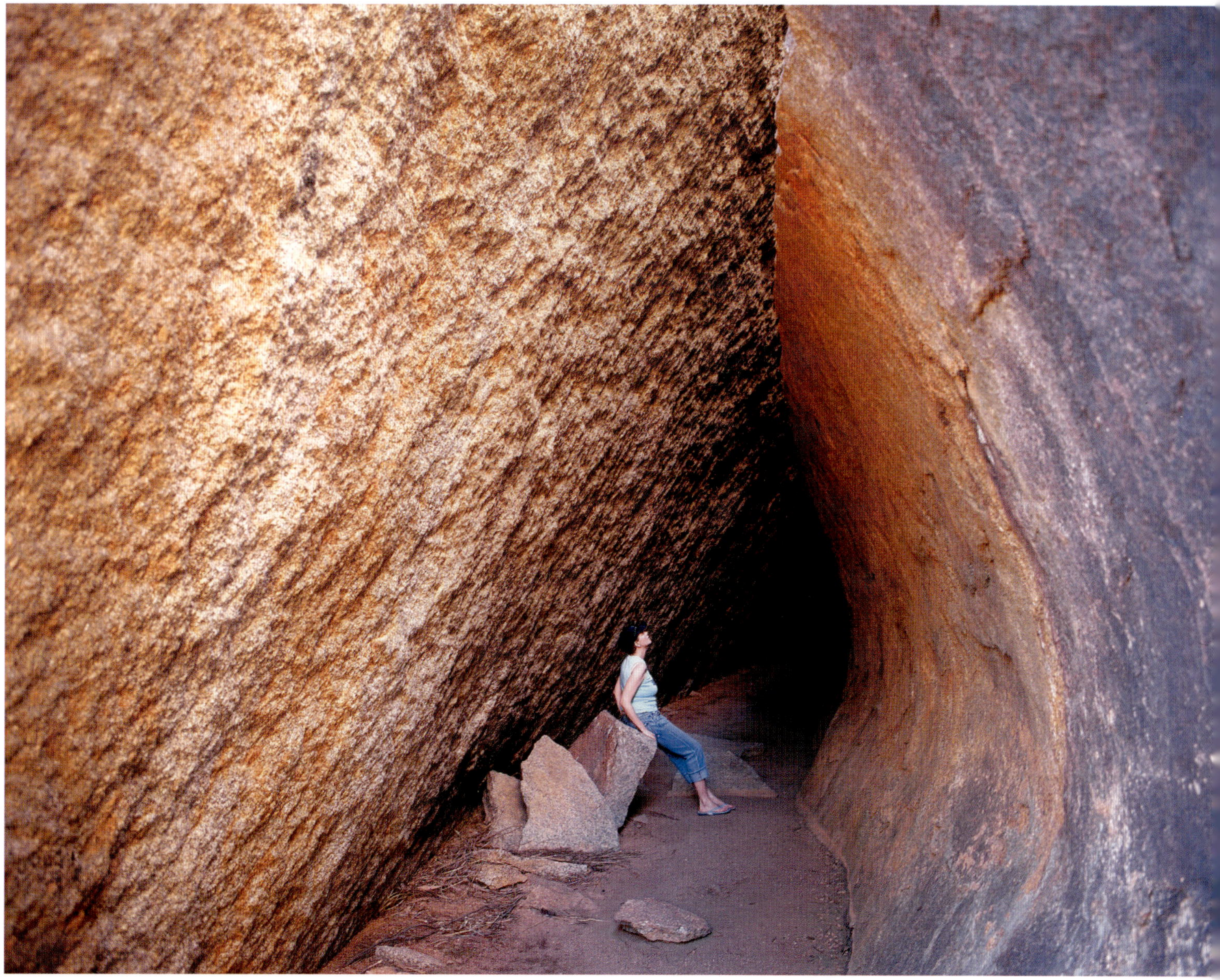

The 30 metre long crevice known as "Monty's Pass" cuts through Elachbutting Rock near Mukinbudin in the north eastern wheatbelt.

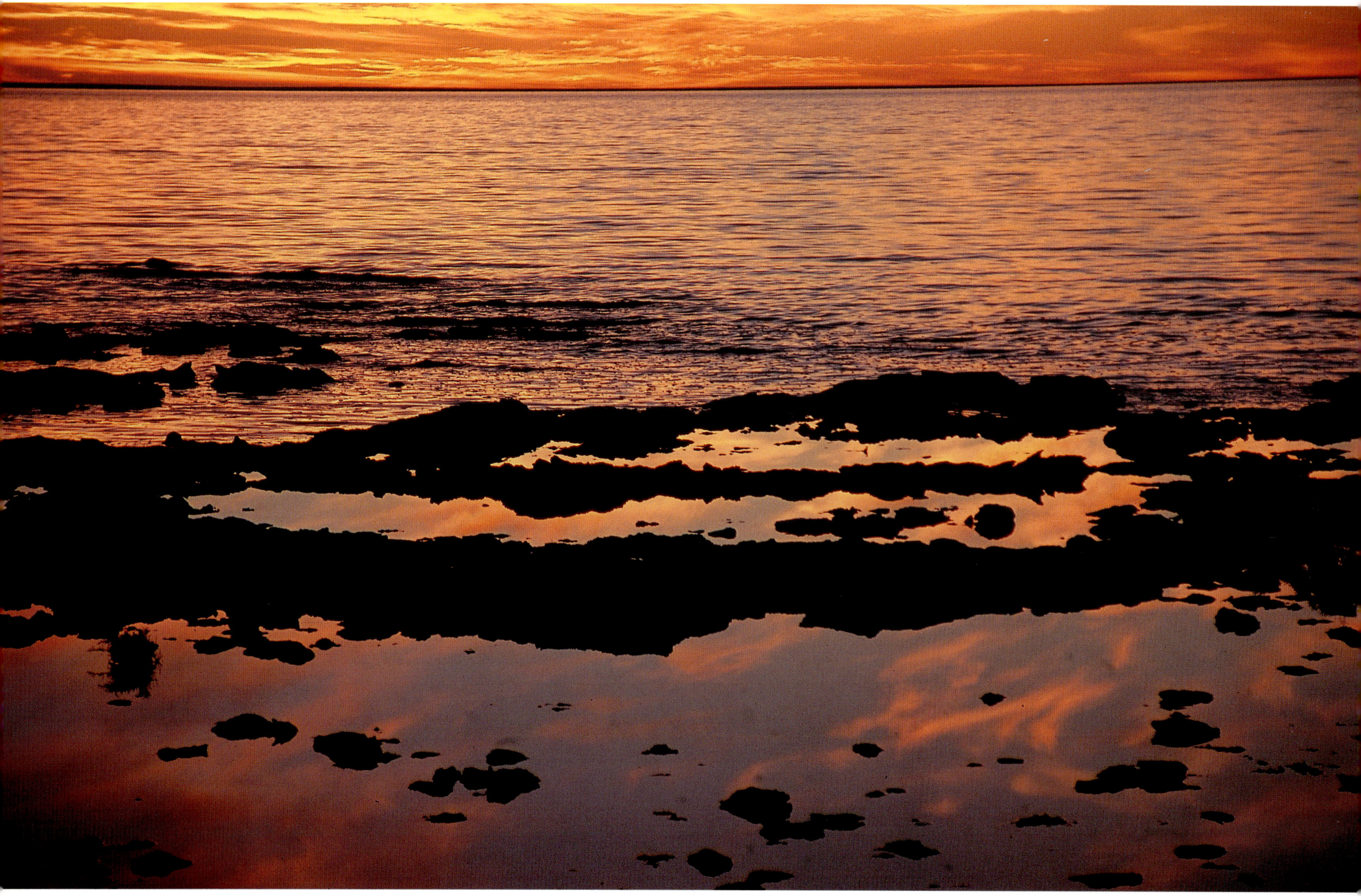

Hamelin Pool sunset, Shark Bay.

Heading north, Shark Bay is a World Heritage-listed wonderland of arid peninsulas, scenic bays, vast seagrass meadows and abundant sea life. The seagrass meadows are some of the most extensive in the world and provide an important habitat for endangered dugongs. The hypersaline Hamelin Pool contains stromatolites, living examples of one of the earliest known forms of life on the earth. Fossil stromatolites in the Marble Bar area of Western Australia are estimated to be over three billion years old.

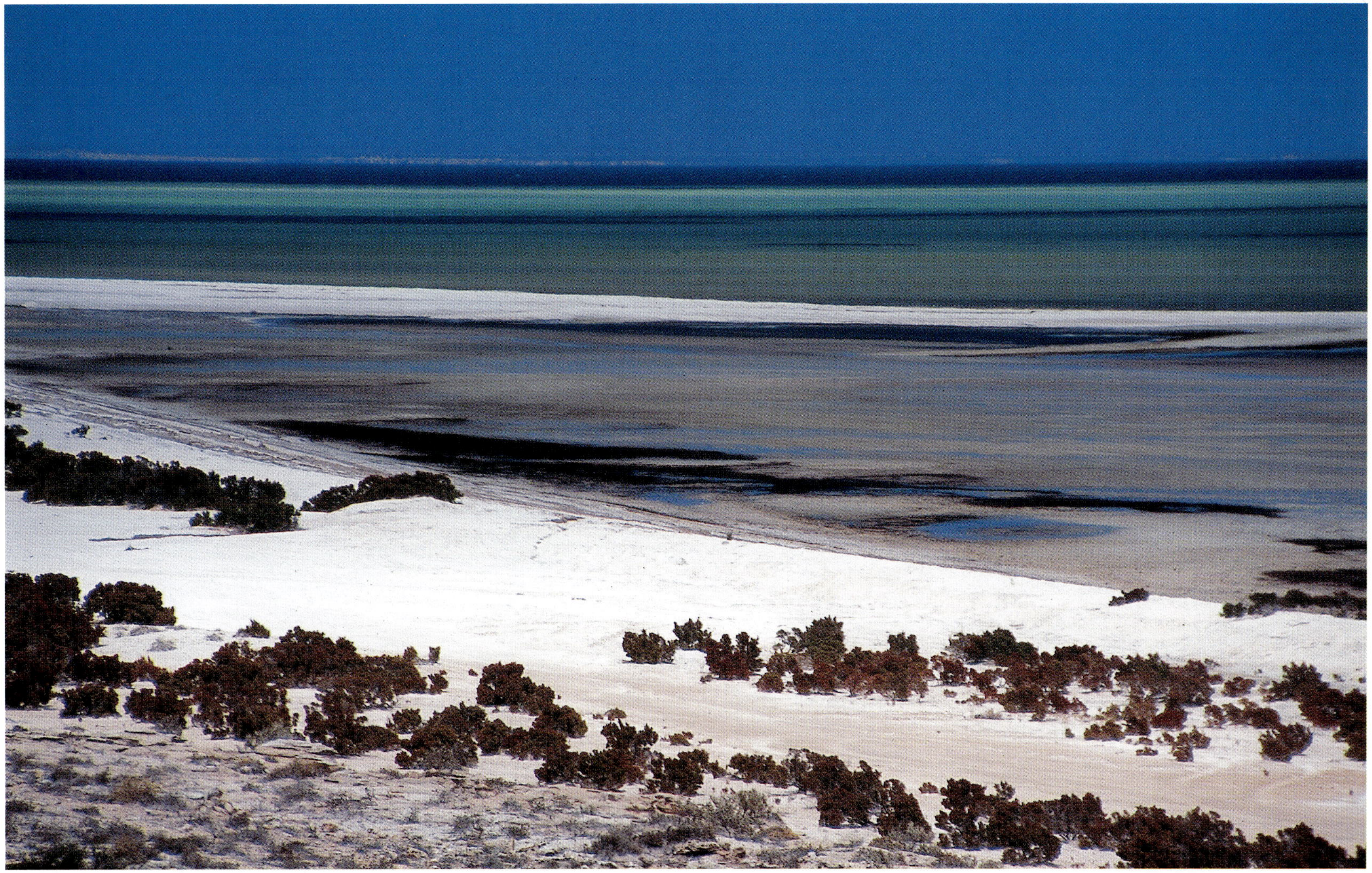

The amazing colours of Shark Bay.

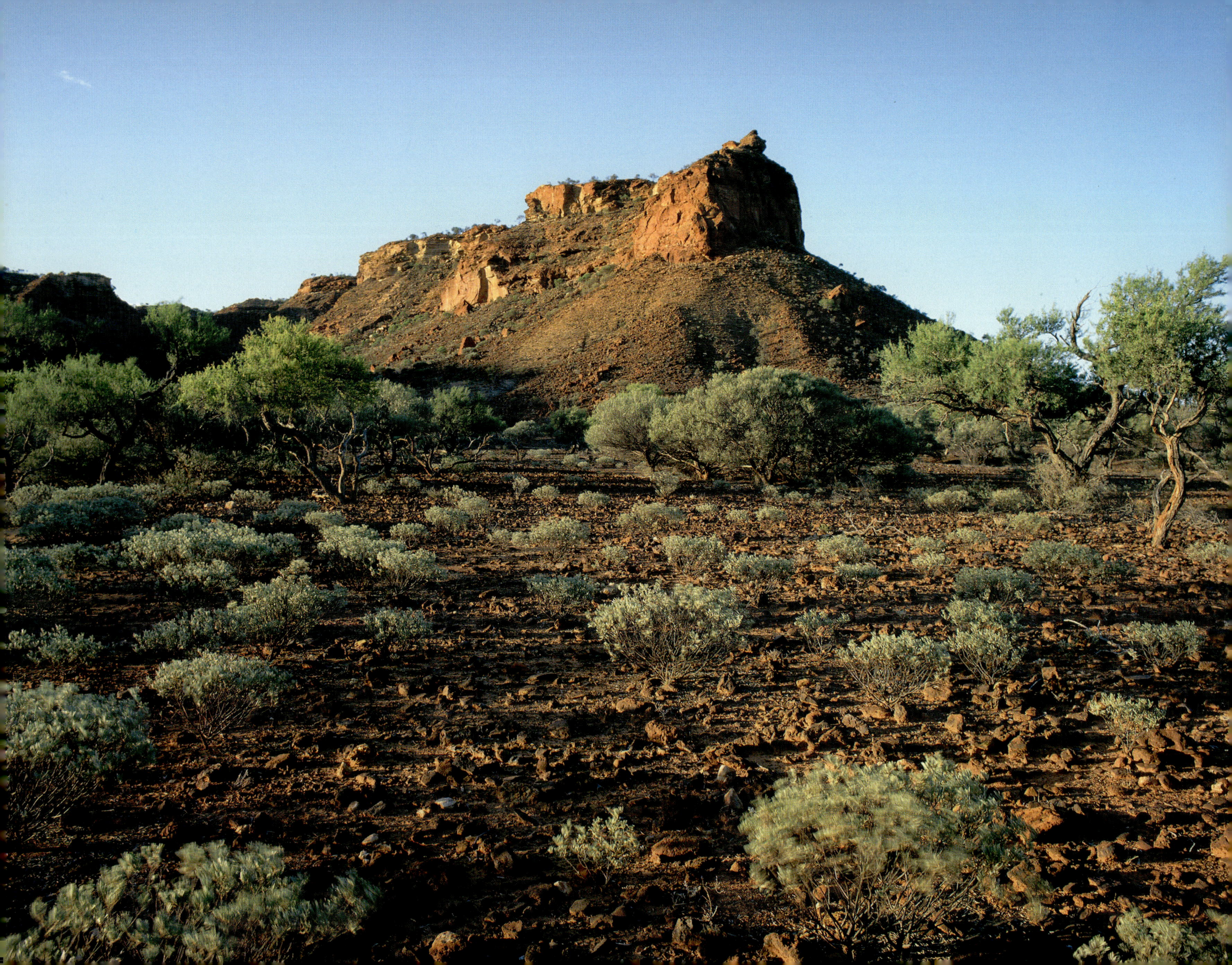

The Kennedy Range National Park lies 150 kilometres inland from Carnarvon in the Gascoyne region and protects an east-facing escarpment of sandstone rocks. The stark cliffs are cut by ravines and there is great adventurous hiking to rock caves and up the gorges. After good winter rains, the plains below the peaks are covered in everlastings and other wildflowers, especially around July and August. There is a bush campsite here with basic facilities for well equipped outback travellers.

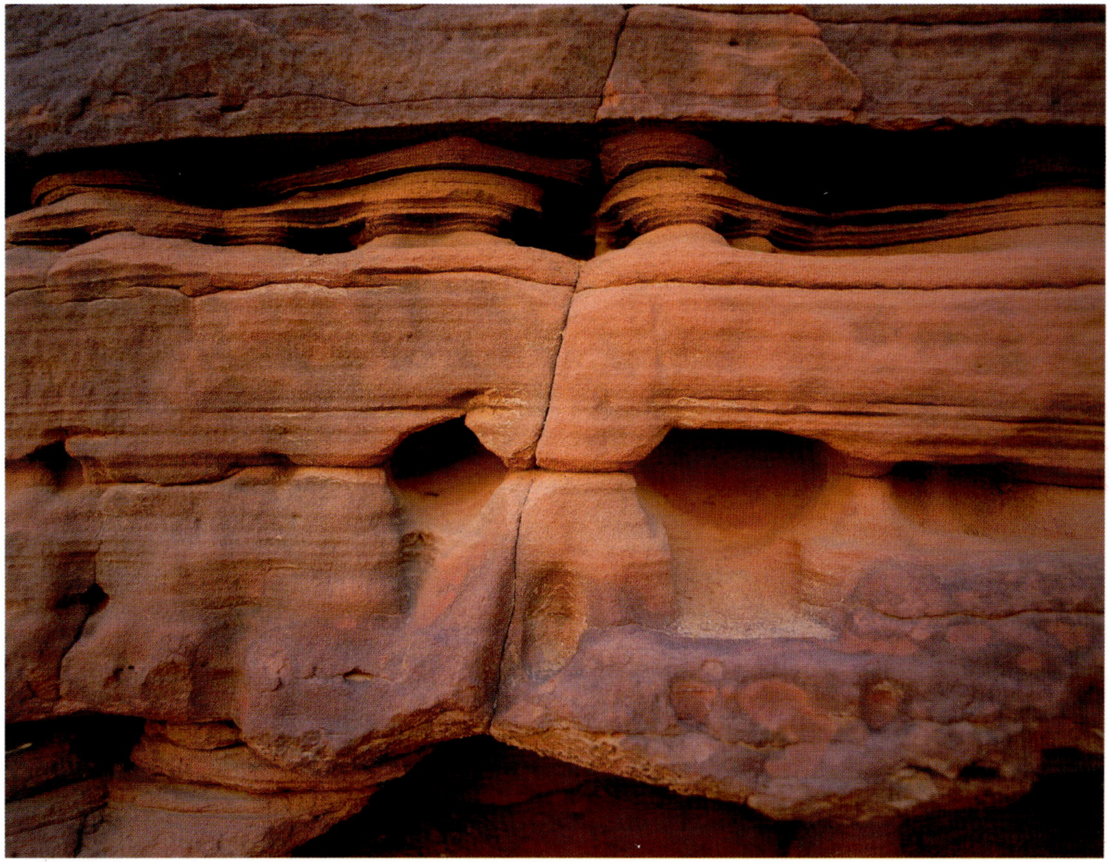

Top: Eroded rock wall in Temple Gorge, Kennedy Range.

Opposite page: Sparse mulga woodland below the escarpment of the Kennedy Range.

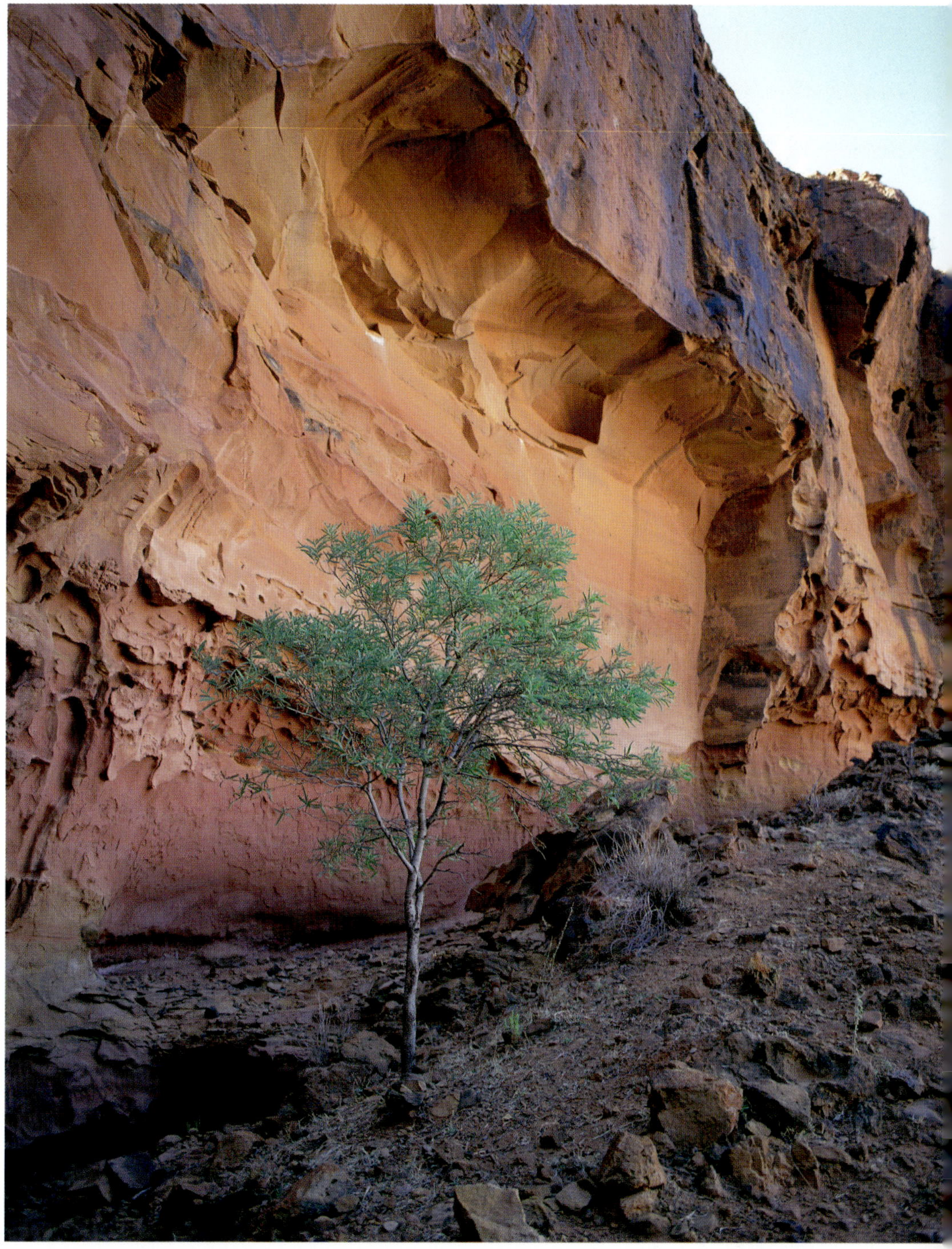

A small tree below the beautifully coloured sandstone of the Kennedy Range.

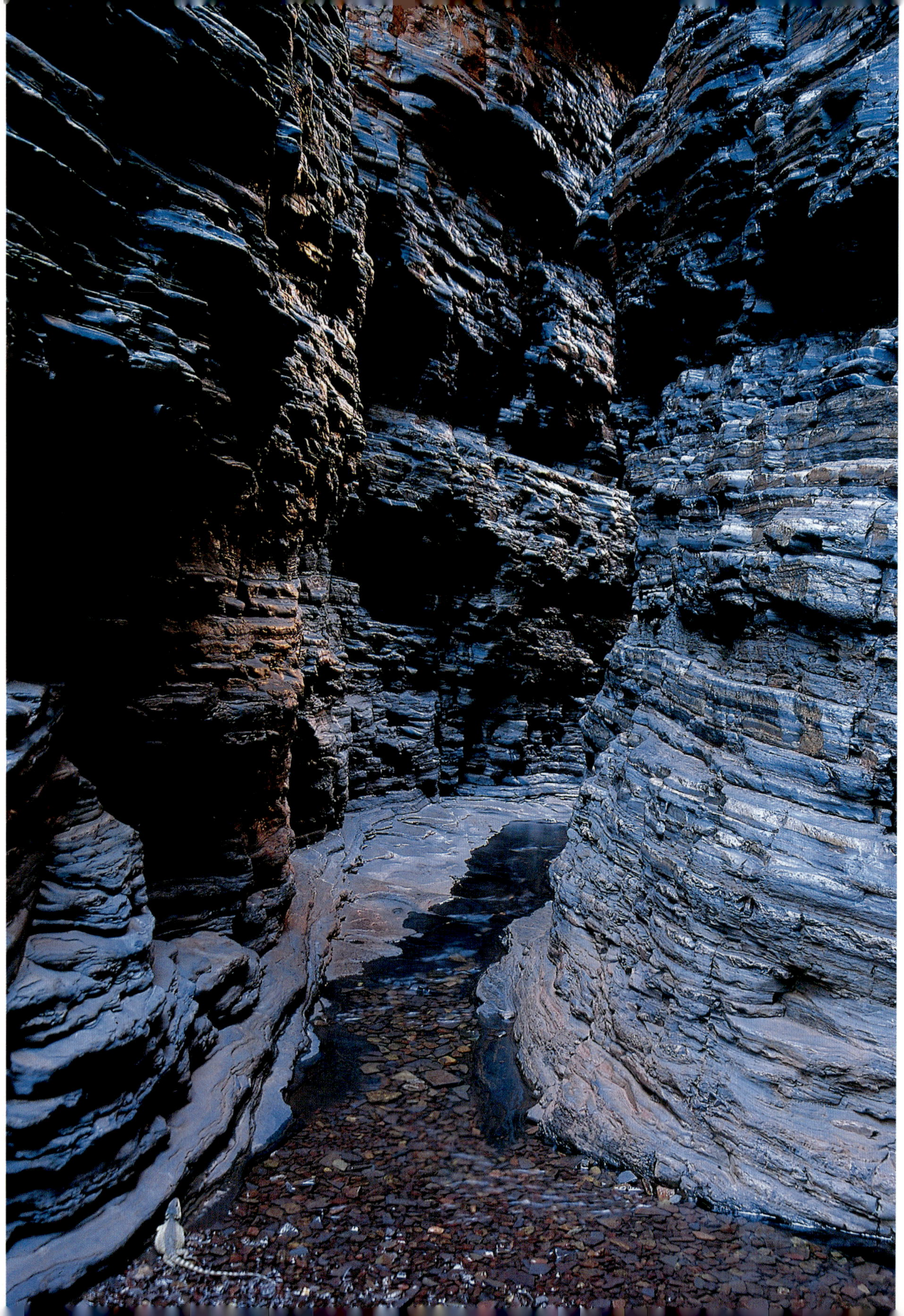

The rich red soils, spinifex-covered ranges and deep gorges make the Pilbara one of my favourite parts of Australia. The vast Karijini National Park covers an area of 627,445 hectares and protects most of the Hamersley Range, including Mt Meharry (1249m), the highest peak in Western Australia. I climbed the mountain during my trip around Australia, driving as far as I could along the rough access road. *"I grabbed my camera, water and food. After walking parallel to the mountain for an hour the track finally turned towards the peak. I was half-way up the steep ascent of the main peak when I saw a 4WD in the distance. I continued onwards and eventually they overtook me. I gave them the thumbs up and said I would meet them at the top! And I did (eventually). After taking some photos I caught a lift back down with them."*

Left: A western water dragon in Weano Gorge, Karijini NP.

Opposite page: The gorgeous Fern Pool is a great place for a cooling dip, although the water can be icy cold in winter.

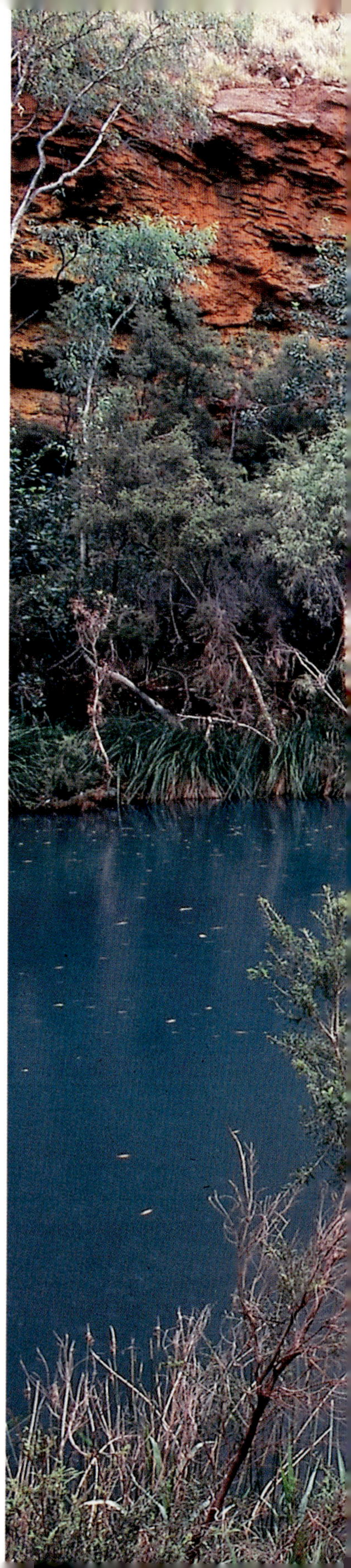

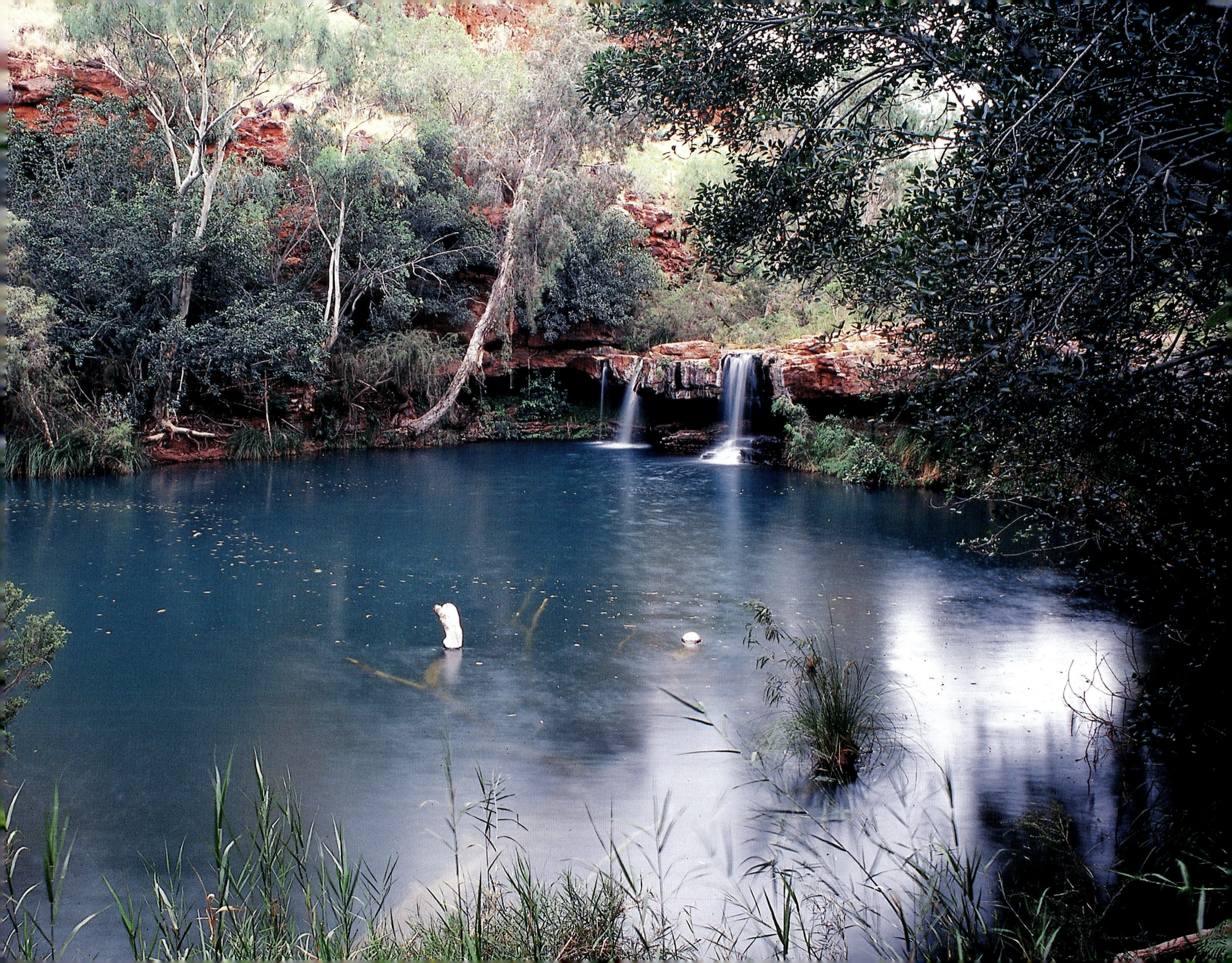

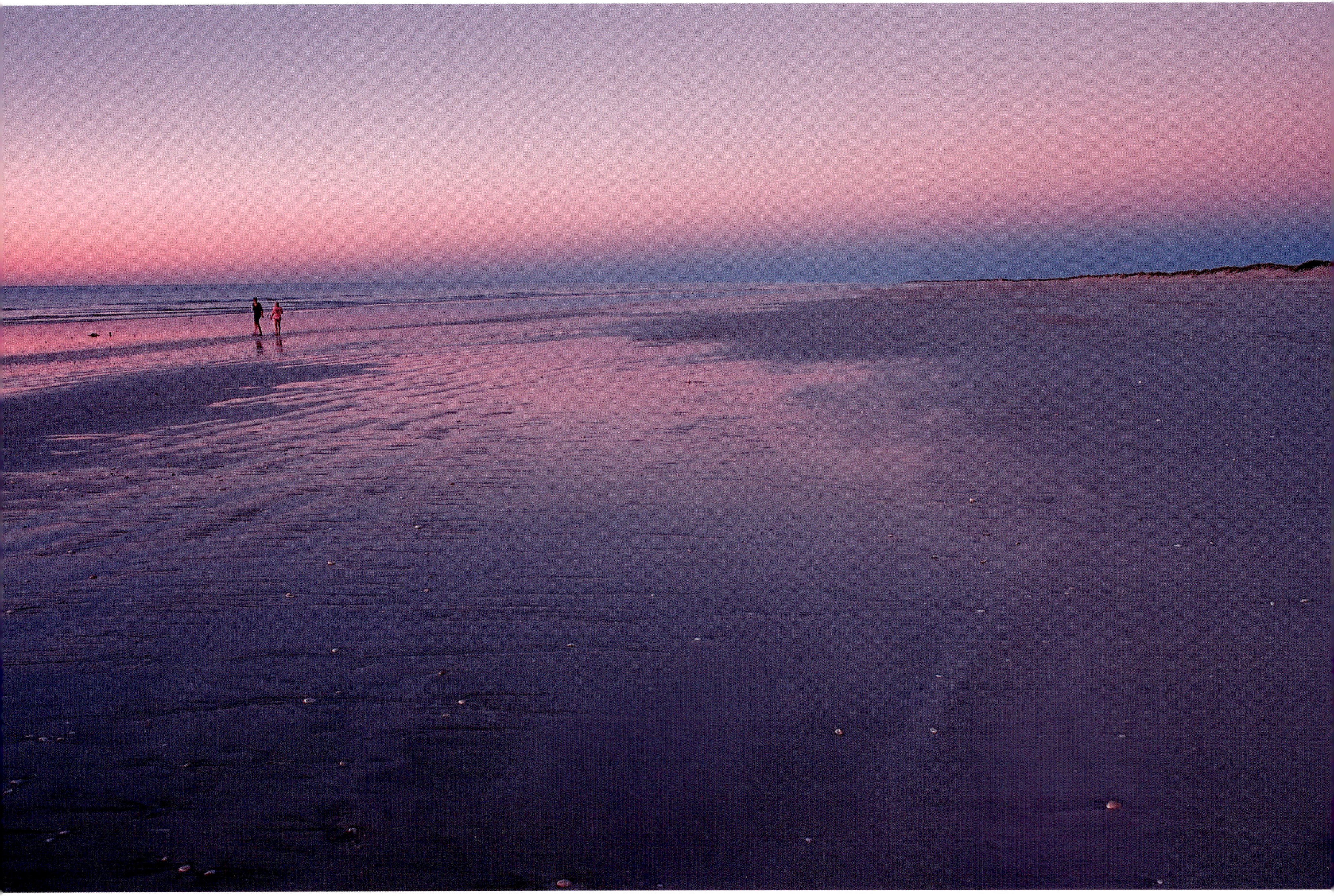

Dusk colours on 80 Mile Beach.

Broome is a popular destination year round, but especially so in winter when southern Australia is shivering, and is famous for camel rides along Cable Beach at sunset. The town is sited on the traditional lands of the Yawuru Aboriginal people, and was founded on the pearling industry. It suffered at least four bombing raids by Japanese aircraft in World War Two. I camped for a night at 80 Mile Beach which lies between Broome and Port Hedland: *"I popped the tent up and went to the beach to watch the sunset. It is a lovely wide beach and long! The light was beautiful so I took a lot of shots – there were some seagulls silhouetted against the light and lots of shells on the seashore. I came back and had an awesome shower – my first for days. I was covered in red dust from my time in the Pilbara."*

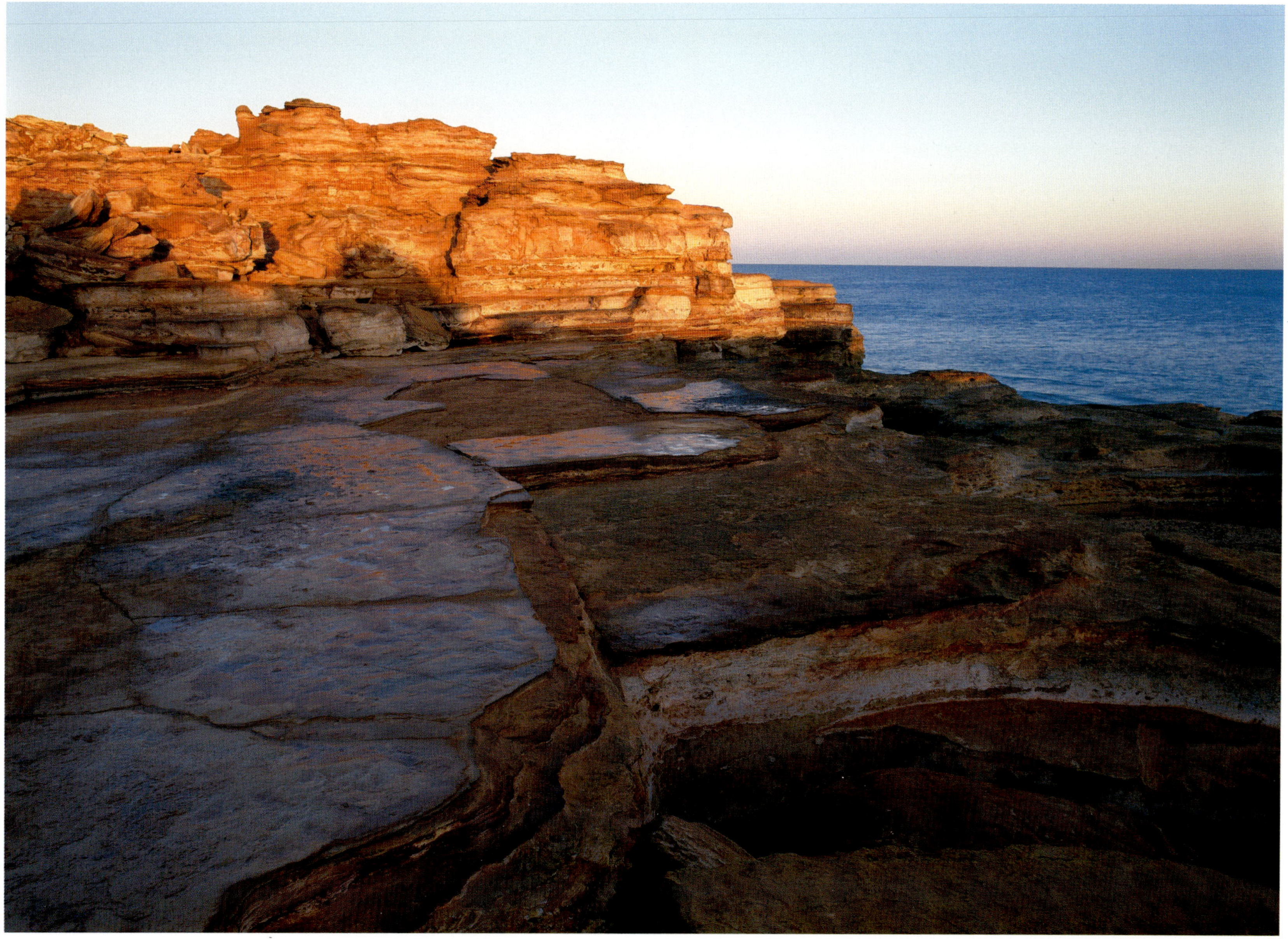

First light on pindan rocks at Gantheaume Point, Broome. There are some dinosaur prints here, dated at approximately 130 million years old.

The Kimberley region of Western Australia is a wild and rugged land of ranges, gorges and waterfalls. It is cattle station country, although much of it is protected in conservation reserves or national parks. I slept one night under the stars at a lookout near Warmun and wrote: *"it was lovely watching the moon and the stars and I remember wondering why we don't normally sleep like that – it felt so natural. During the night I again heard dingoes howling in the distance. I woke up and set off very early to the top of a small hill behind the carpark. When the sun came up there was beautiful light on the mountains all around me – I shot three rolls of film!"*

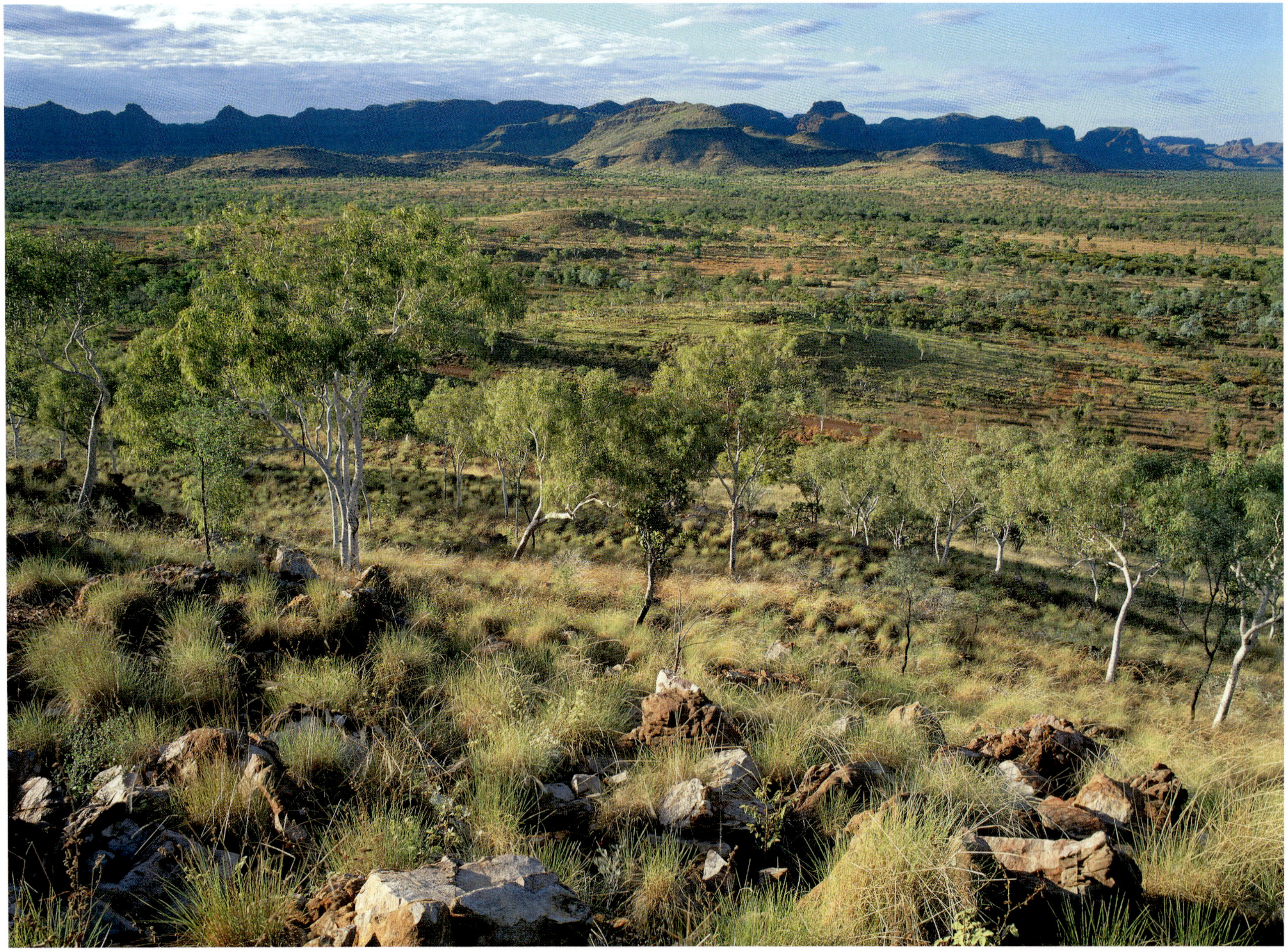

Top: Looking over savannah-covered plains to the Ragged Range in the East Kimberley.
Opposite page: Rugged Kimberley ranges from a lookout near Warmun.

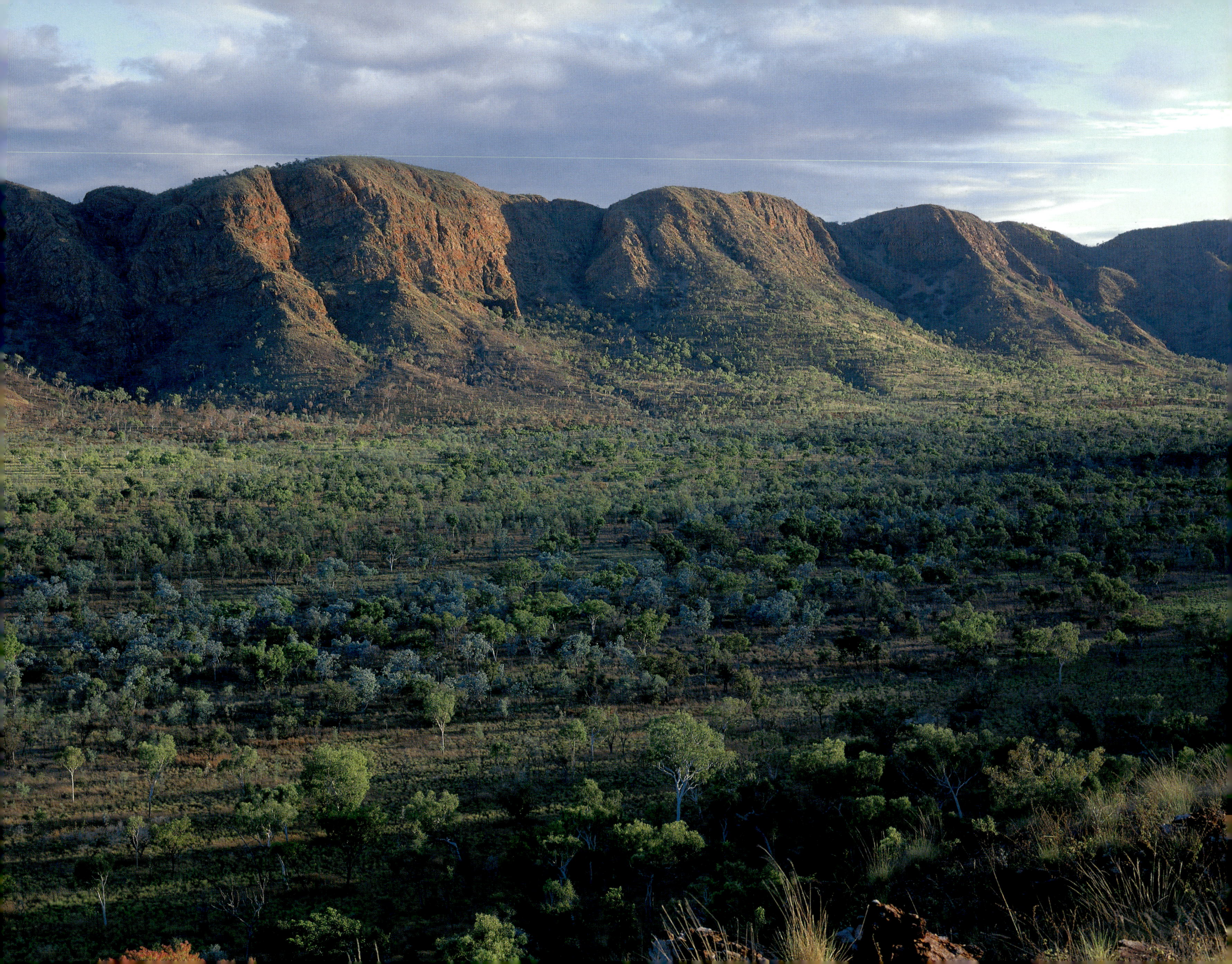

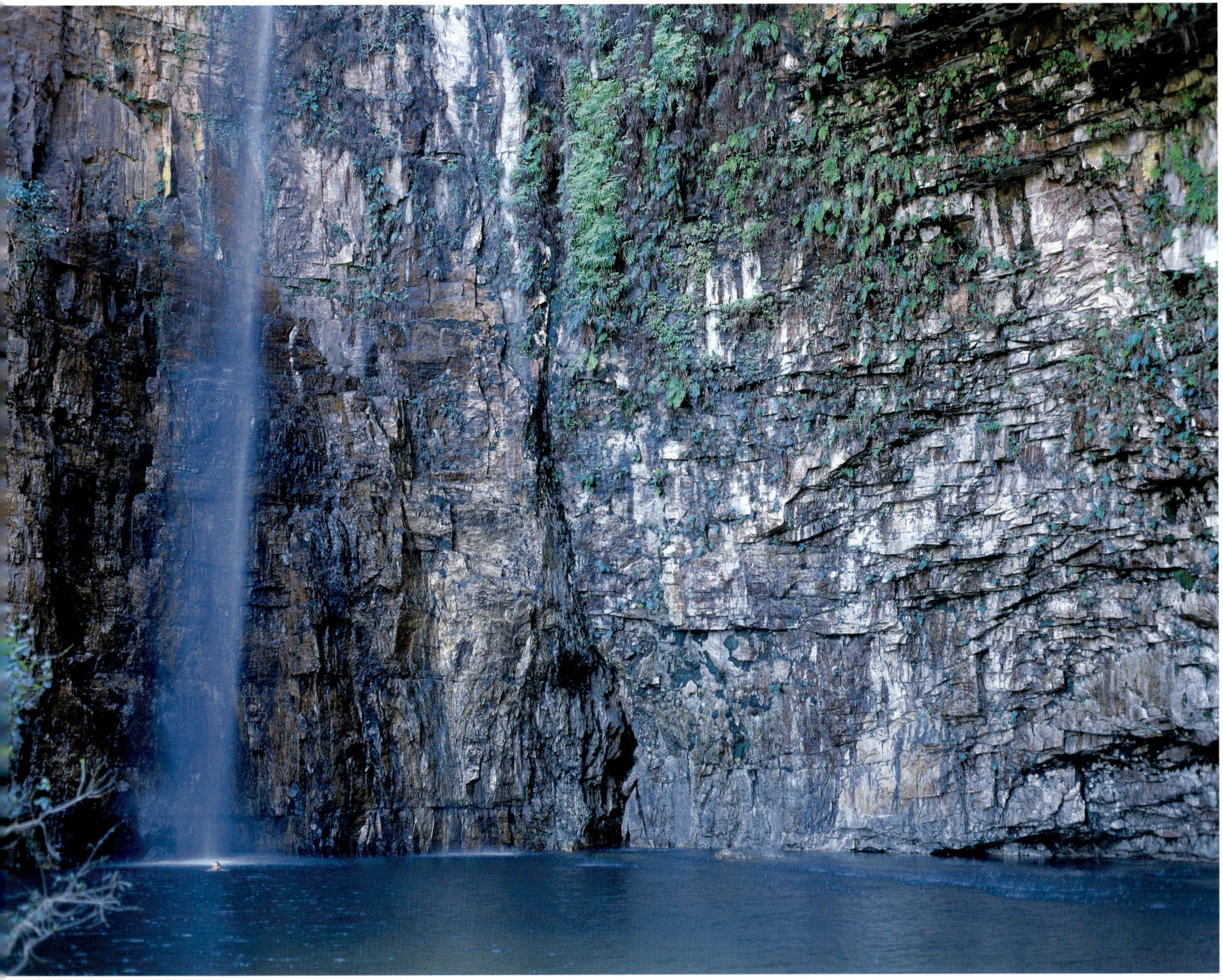

The Kimberley is famous for the many spectacular gorges which cut through the rugged landscape. I visited quite a few during my travels, including Lennard Gorge in the King Leopold Ranges, Geikie Gorge near Fitzroy Crossing and Emma Gorge in the Cockburn Range. I described the latter thus: *"the walk to the gorge itself was awesome and follows a crystal clear mountain stream. It ends in a canyon with a 60 metre high waterfall and small patches of rainforest. I jumped in the deep plunge pool and swam about, it was coldish but not as bad as some. On the right hand side a small thermal stream entered the pool with quite warm water."*

Left: Emma Gorge is a wonderful attraction in El Questro Wilderness Park in the east Kimberley.

Opposite page: The cliffs at Geikie Gorge show the high water mark of the wet season.

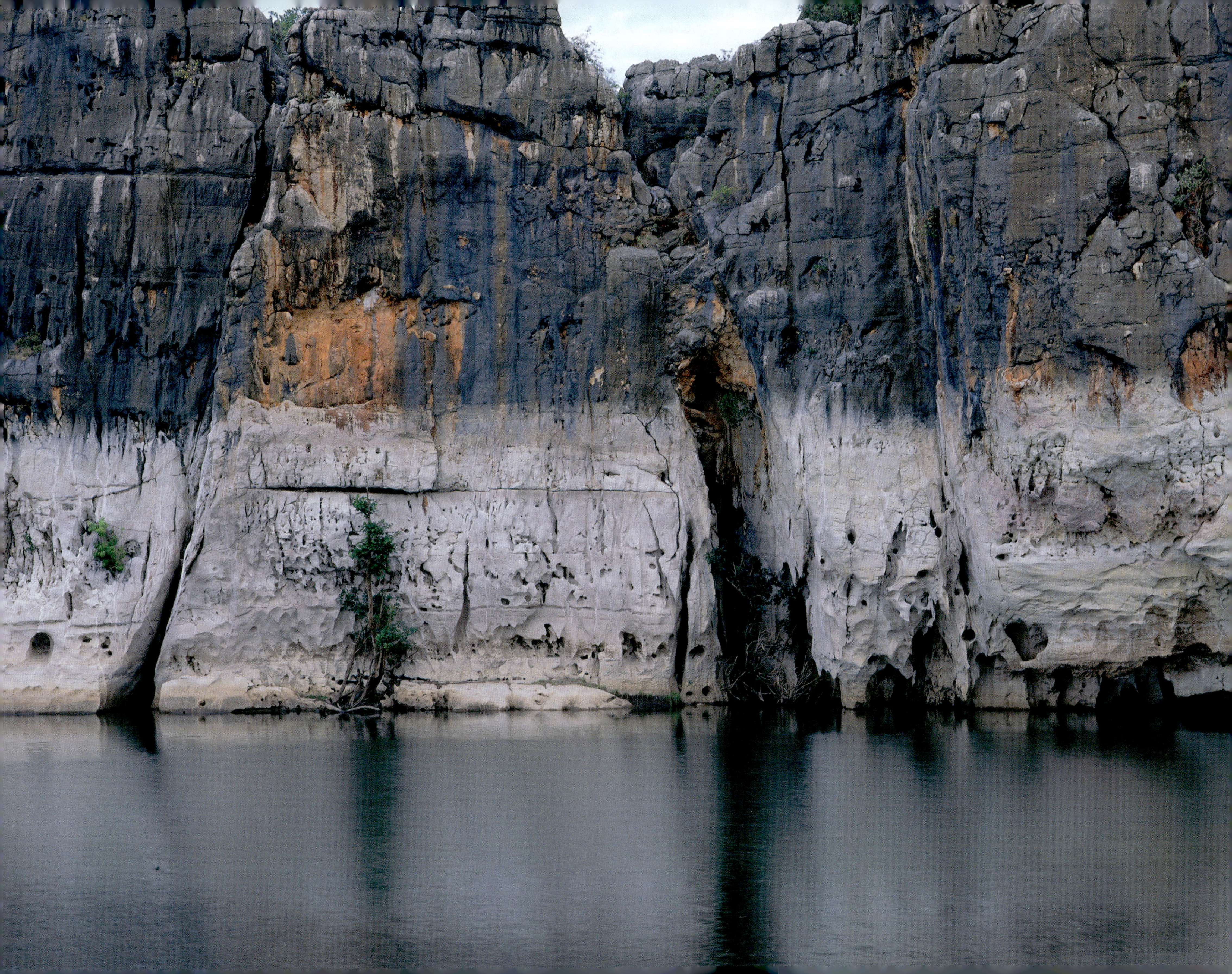

Two roads traverse the rugged country between Derby and Kununurra in the Kimberley region – the bitumen Great Northern Highway and the famous Gibb River Road, which is mainly a graded dirt and gravel road. Both are scenic, but the Gibb River Road is one of the most spectacular drives in the country, and a popular 4WD adventure. It provides access to many wilderness lodges, gorges and waterfalls. The "Gibb" is only open in the dry season from about May until October, depending on the season. I managed to do short sections of the road at both ends, although I don't necessarily recommend doing it in a Camry!

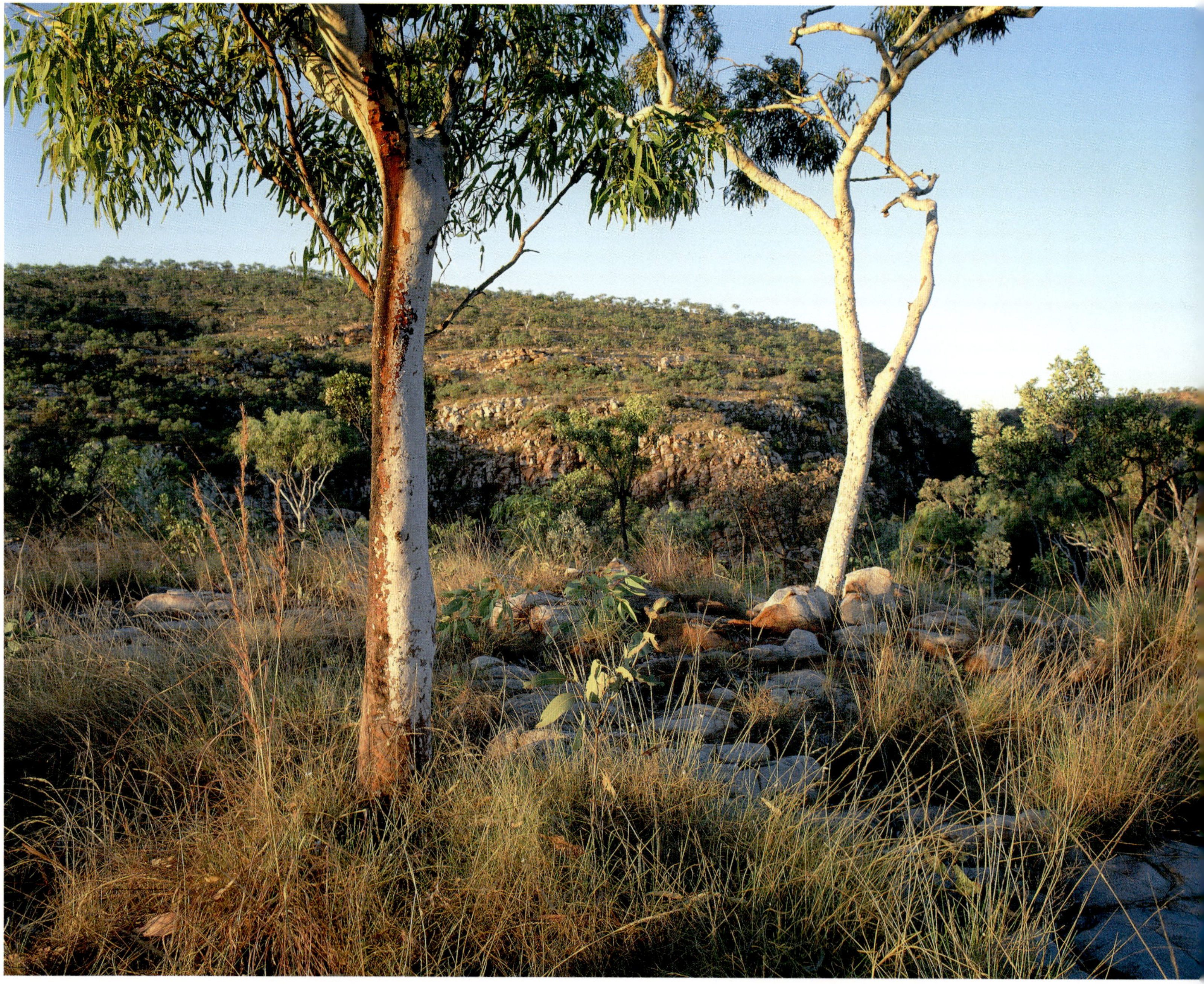

Right: Ghost gums on the edge of a Kimberley gorge near the March Fly Glen rest area, on the Gibb River Road.

Opposite page: The Ngumban Cliffs at sunset from the Great Northern Hwy.

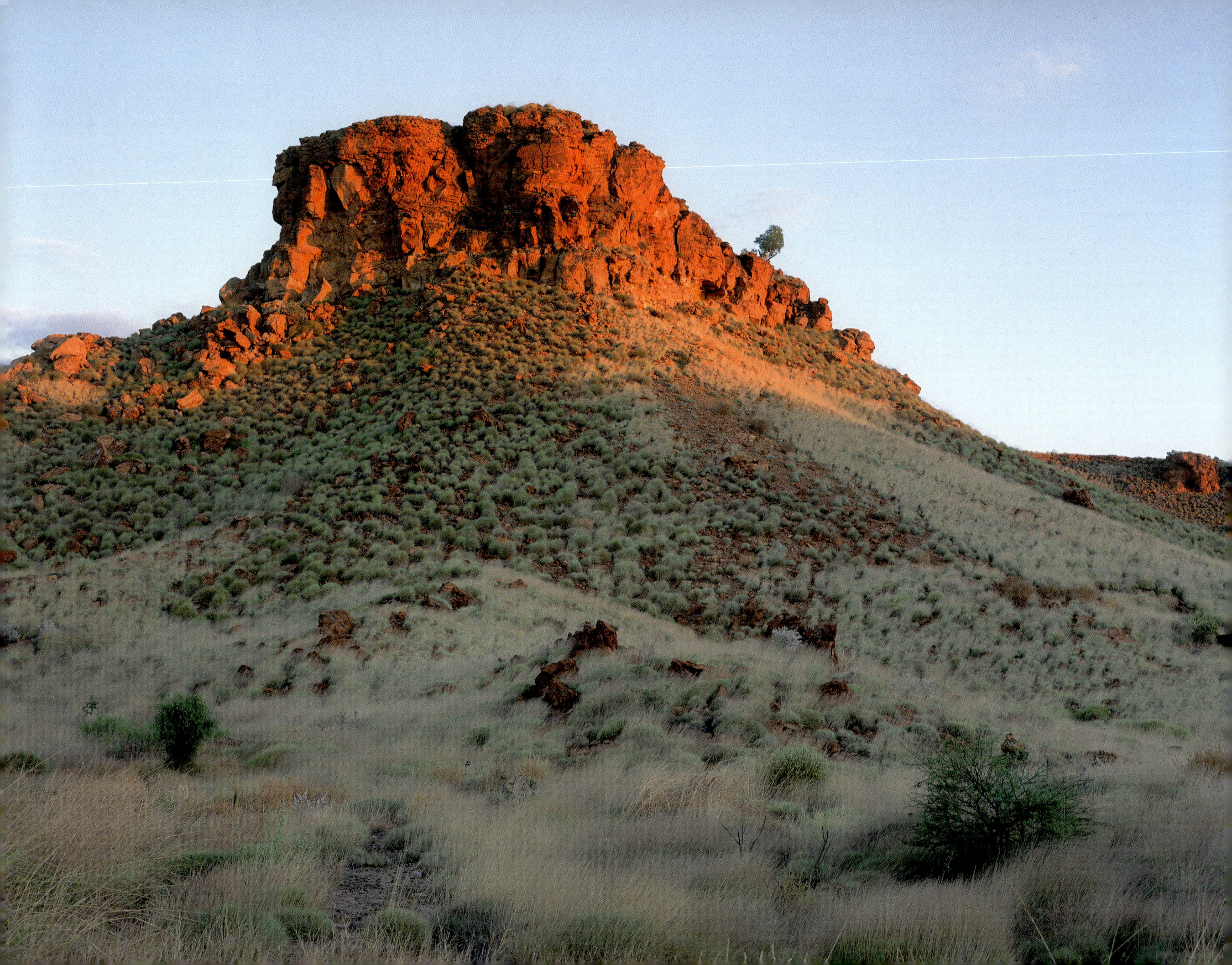

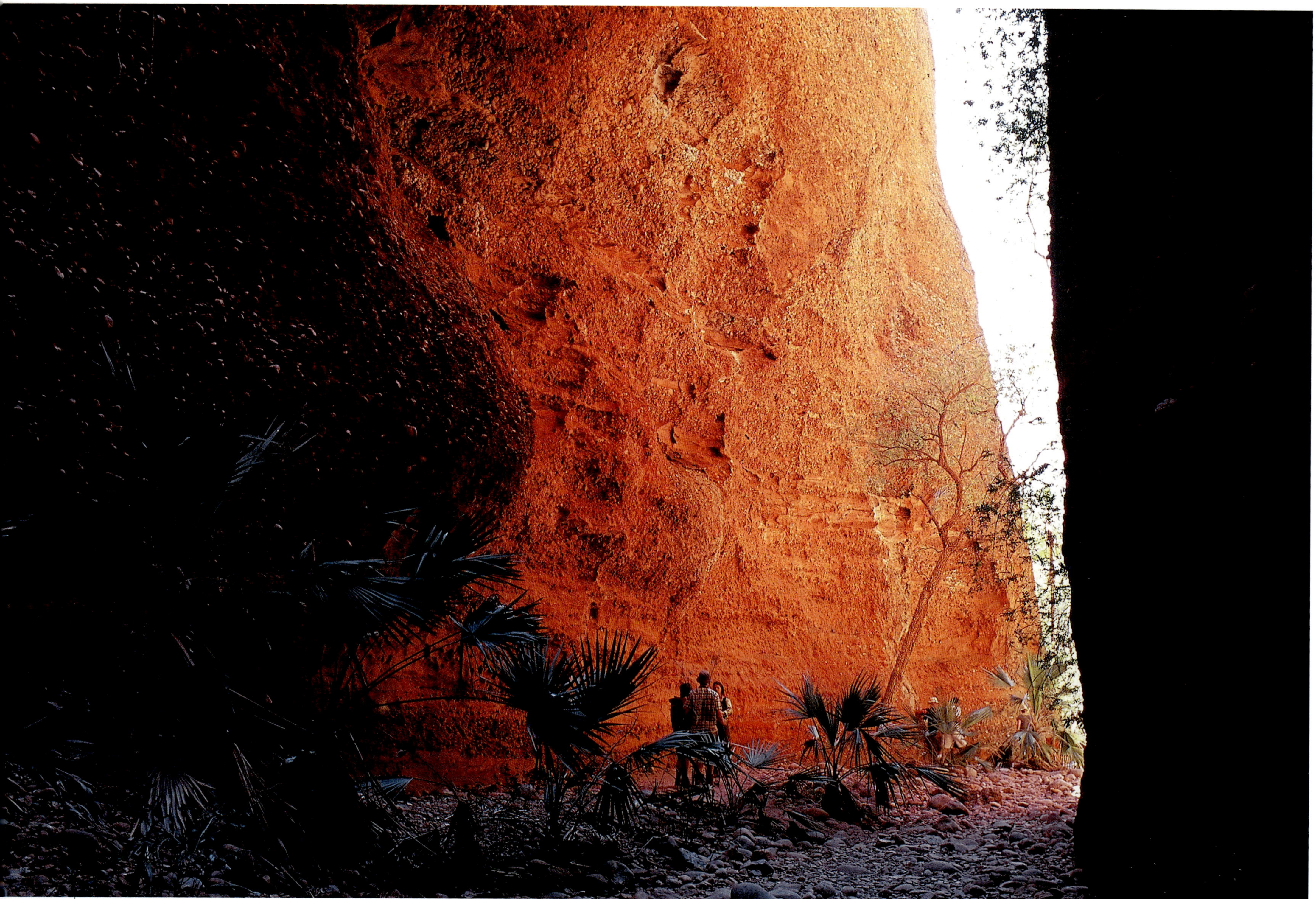

Purnululu National Park is one of the iconic parks of Australia, and is a World Heritage Area. Parts of the heavily eroded sandstone plateau are sacred to the Kija Aboriginal people. I flew there with a tour company and spent two wonderful days exploring the gorges and beehive formations with my cameras. I was deeply moved by what I saw. *"The astonishing thing about Echidna Chasm is how long it is – you wind for almost a kilometre into the deepness of the mountain like Jules Verne! Parts of the mountain high above you have a deep red glow."*

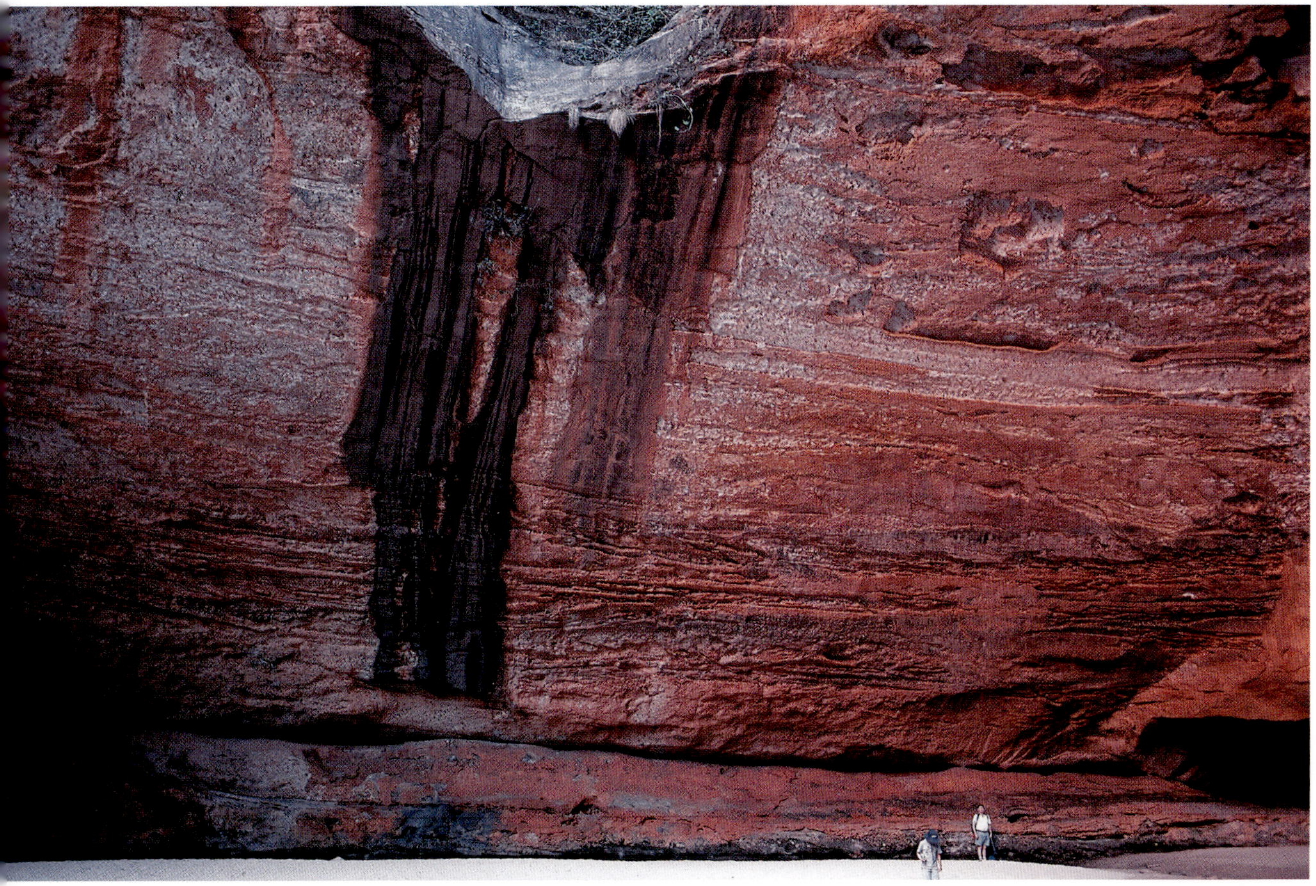

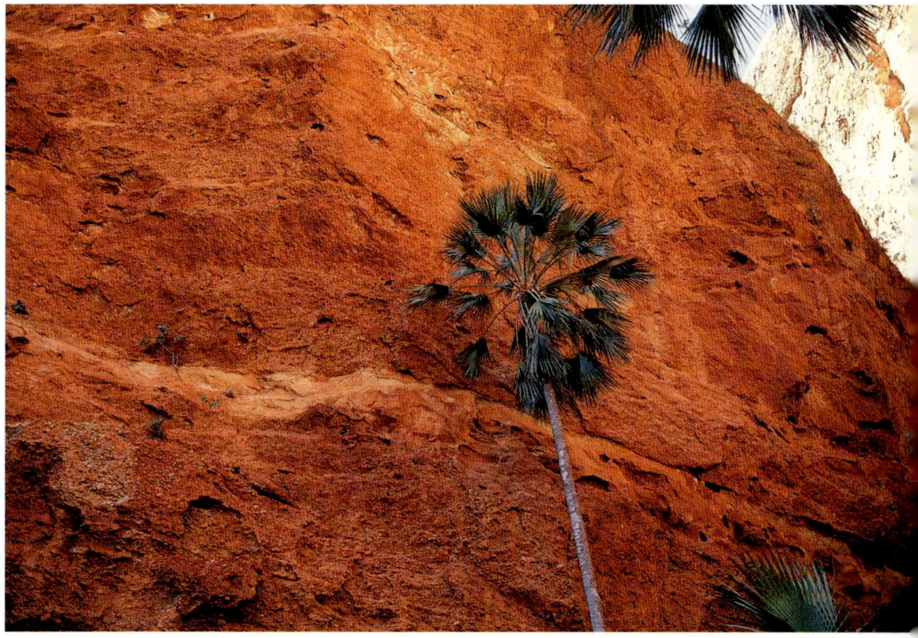

A livistona palm silhouetted against a red rock wall in Purnululu NP.

Top: A wet season waterfall has scoured out a natural rock chamber known as Cathedral Gorge.

Opposite page: The dramatic entrance to Echidna Chasm in Purnululu NP.

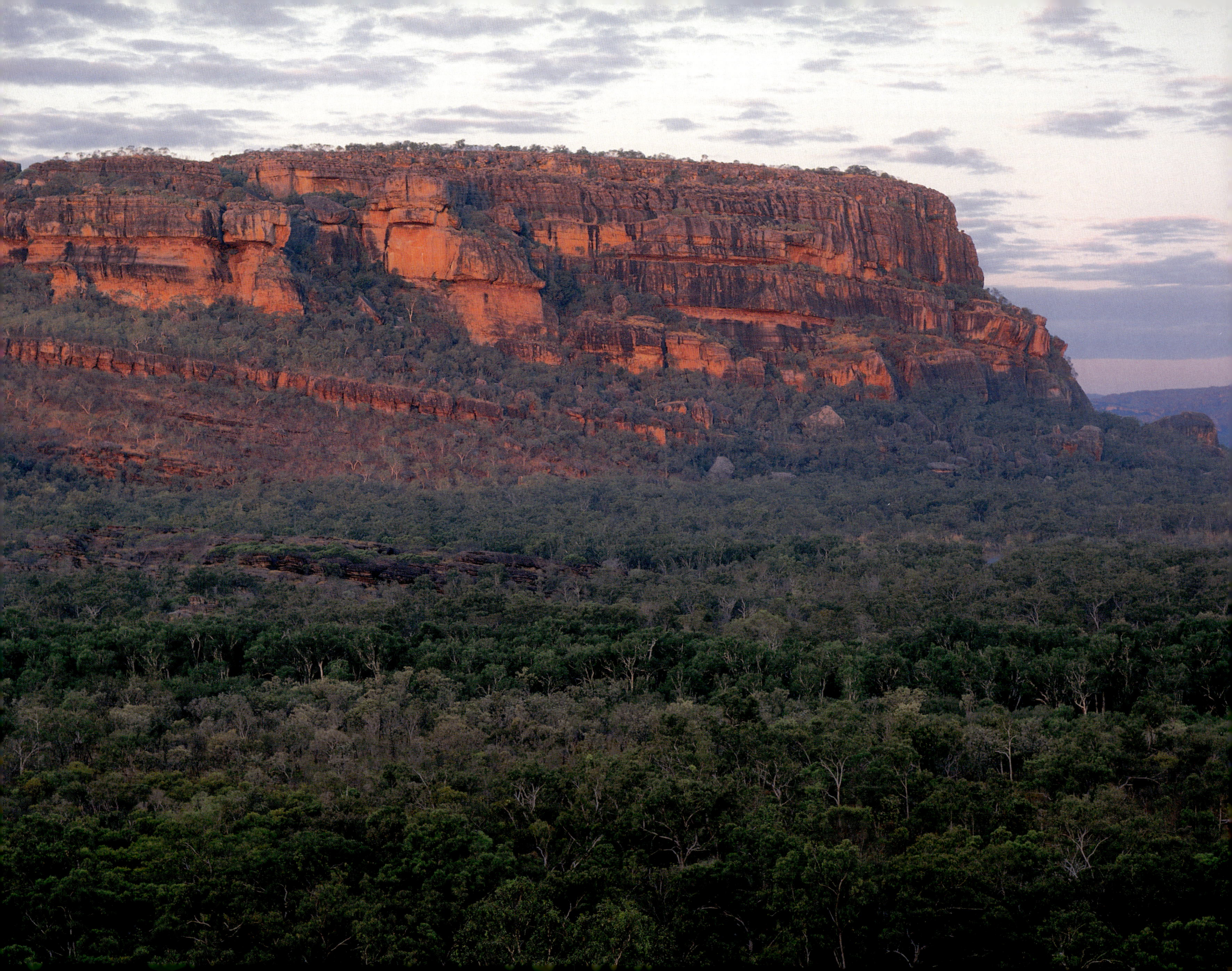

Northern Territory

The Northern Territory is true frontier country, six times the size of Great Britain. Its vast horizons include many of the iconic landscapes of Australia, like Uluru, Kakadu and the semi-arid mountains of the MacDonnell Ranges, famously featured in paintings by the Aboriginal artist Albert Namatjira. Aboriginal culture remains strong in many areas, including Arnhem Land, Melville Island and in communities throughout the Red Centre.

The Top End, covering the upper third of the territory, has a marked Wet and Dry season, and is an ancient landscape with bountiful wildlife. The billabongs and tidal rivers abound in barramundi and freshwater and estuarine (saltwater) crocodiles. As you head south, the rainfall falls away and you enter classic outback country with sandplains, dunes, saltpans and gibber expanses. At the very centre of the continent lie red sand dunes, ancient mountain ranges, and the astonishing exposed monoliths of Uluru and Kata Tjuta.

Aboriginal people have lived in the Territory for a very long time. An ancient campsite in a remote corner of Kakadu National Park has remains dating back an estimated 55,000 to 60,000 years. The first European settlement was attempted on Melville Island in 1824, but was unsuccessful. It was not until 1869 that Palmerston (later called Darwin) was established on the northern coast. Darwin today is a relaxed, modern town of some 130,000 people. Katherine and Alice Springs are other important towns in the territory, the latter lying nestled in amongst the MacDonnell Ranges near the geographical centre of the continent. Alice Springs is named after the wife of the former Postmaster General of South Australia, Sir Charles Todd, who also gives his name to the usually dry river which flows through the town. Originally part of New South Wales, the Northern Territory was annexed to South Australia for a period, came under Commonwealth control in 1911 and in July 1978 attained self-government. Its major industries are mining, beef cattle farming and tourism.

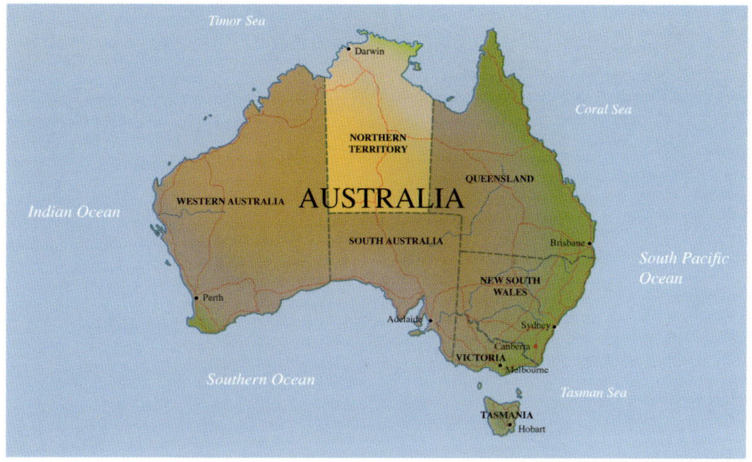

Opposite page: Nourlangie Rock, an outlier peak of the Arnhem Land Plateau, glows in the last light of day; view from Nawurlandja Lookout, Kakadu NP.

Uluru is an amazing place and is the world's greatest monolith. My first visit here was during the 1999/2000 New Year's Eve celebrations with a group of friends. I was deeply moved by the spirit of the country and the beauty of the rock. Uluru (863m) is the spiritual heart of Australia, and has deep significance to the local Anangu Aboriginal people. Anangu request that visitors do not climb Uluru as it is a highly sacred place of many Dreaming stories. A great alternative is the walk around the base of the rock, a distance of 9.4 kilometres taking three to four hours. Uluru-Kata Tjuta National Park is inscribed on the World Heritage List, and is jointly managed with Anangu traditional owners.

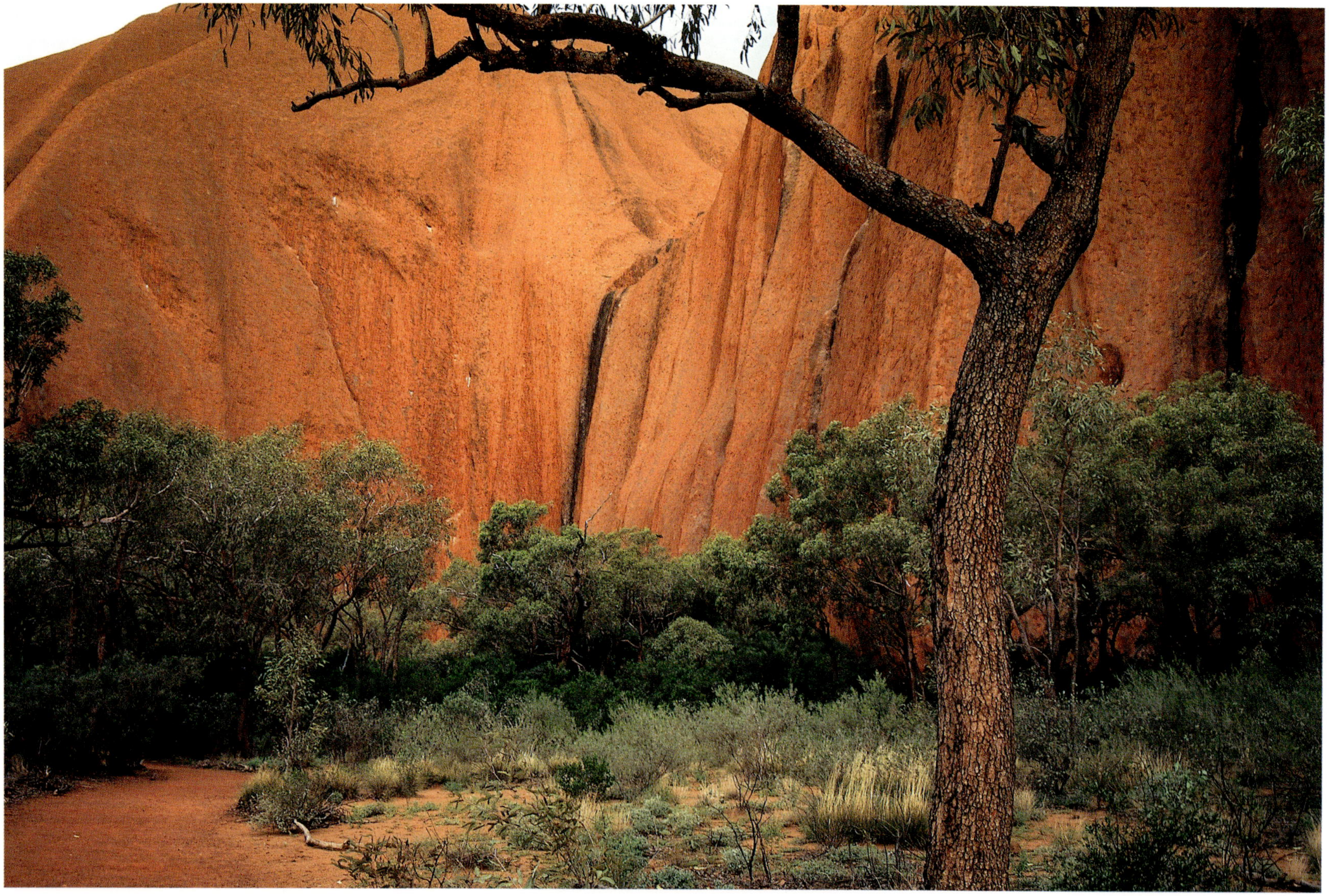

The dry waterfall known as Kantju Gorge can be seen on the walk around the base of Uluru.

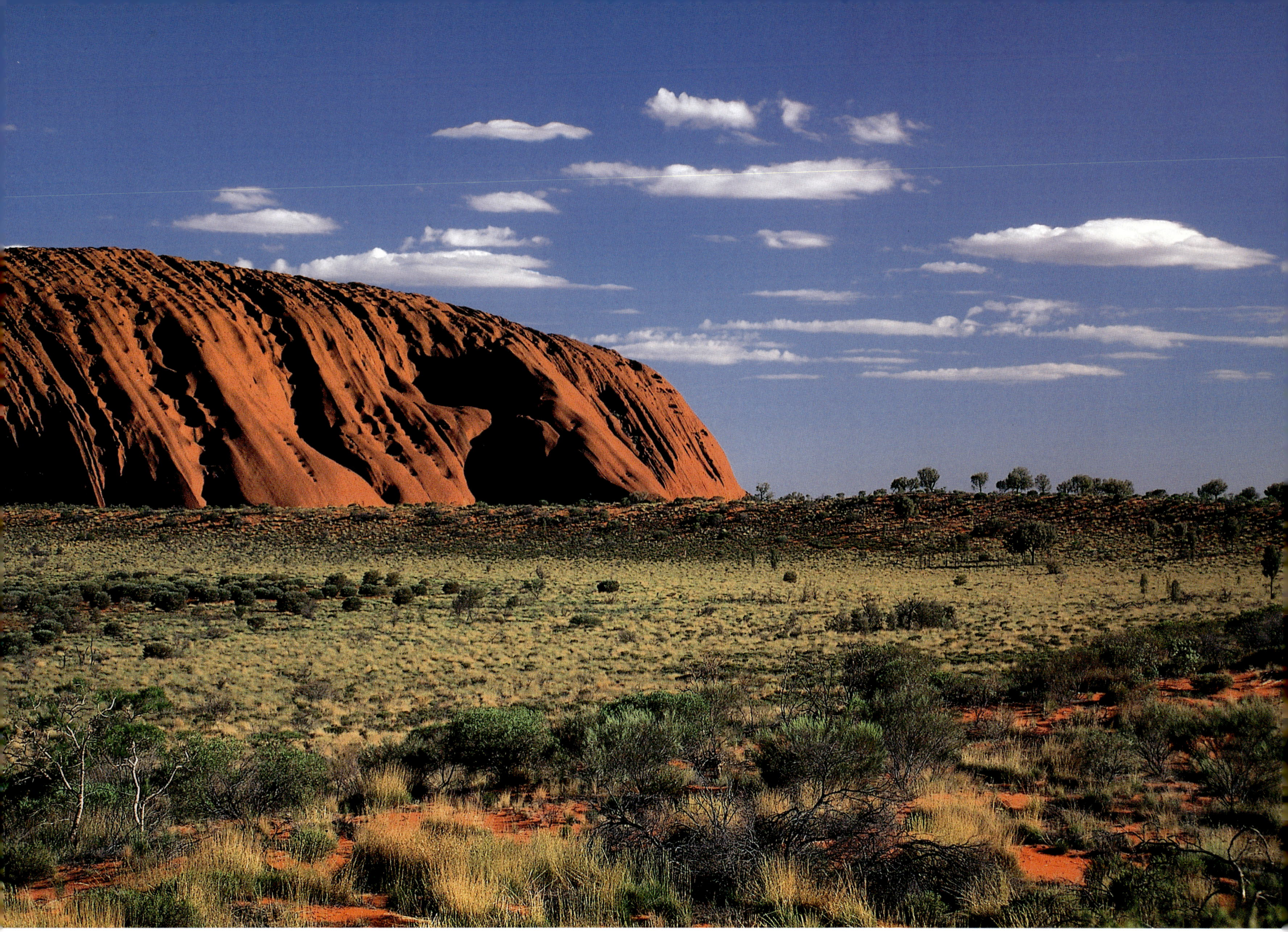

Uluru rises 348 metres above the endless red sand ridges of central Australia.

I found Kata Tjuta as awe-inspiring as Uluru. Kata Tjuta means "many heads" in the Pitjantjatjara language. There are 36 conglomerate domes in total, the highest being Mount Olga (1066m). A must do walk here is the "Valley of the Winds", a seven kilometre circuit which winds around and through the huge domes. Another attraction of the Red Centre is Kings Canyon, a deep chasm cut into the western edge of the George Gill Range, and protected by the Watarrka National Park.

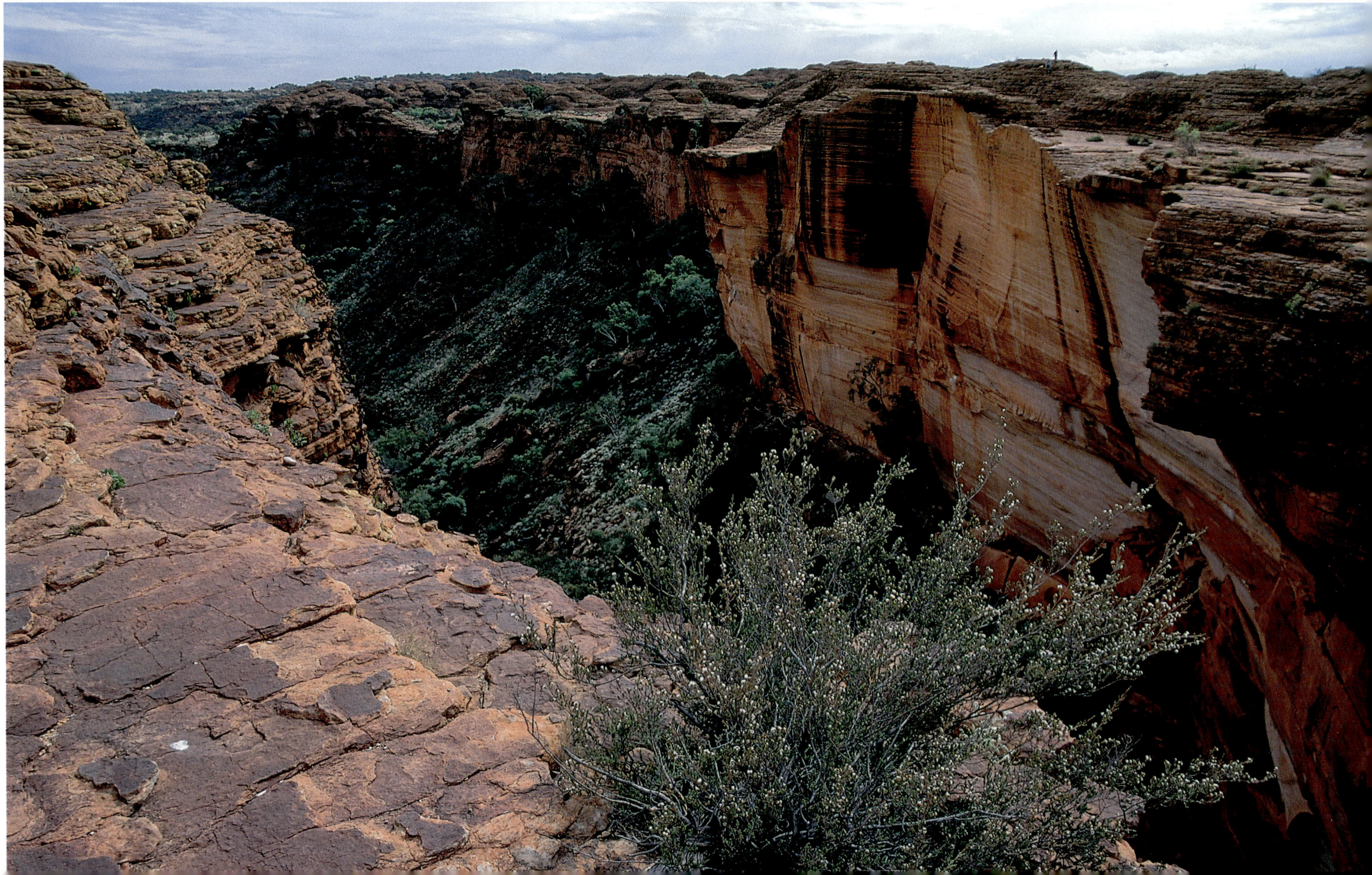

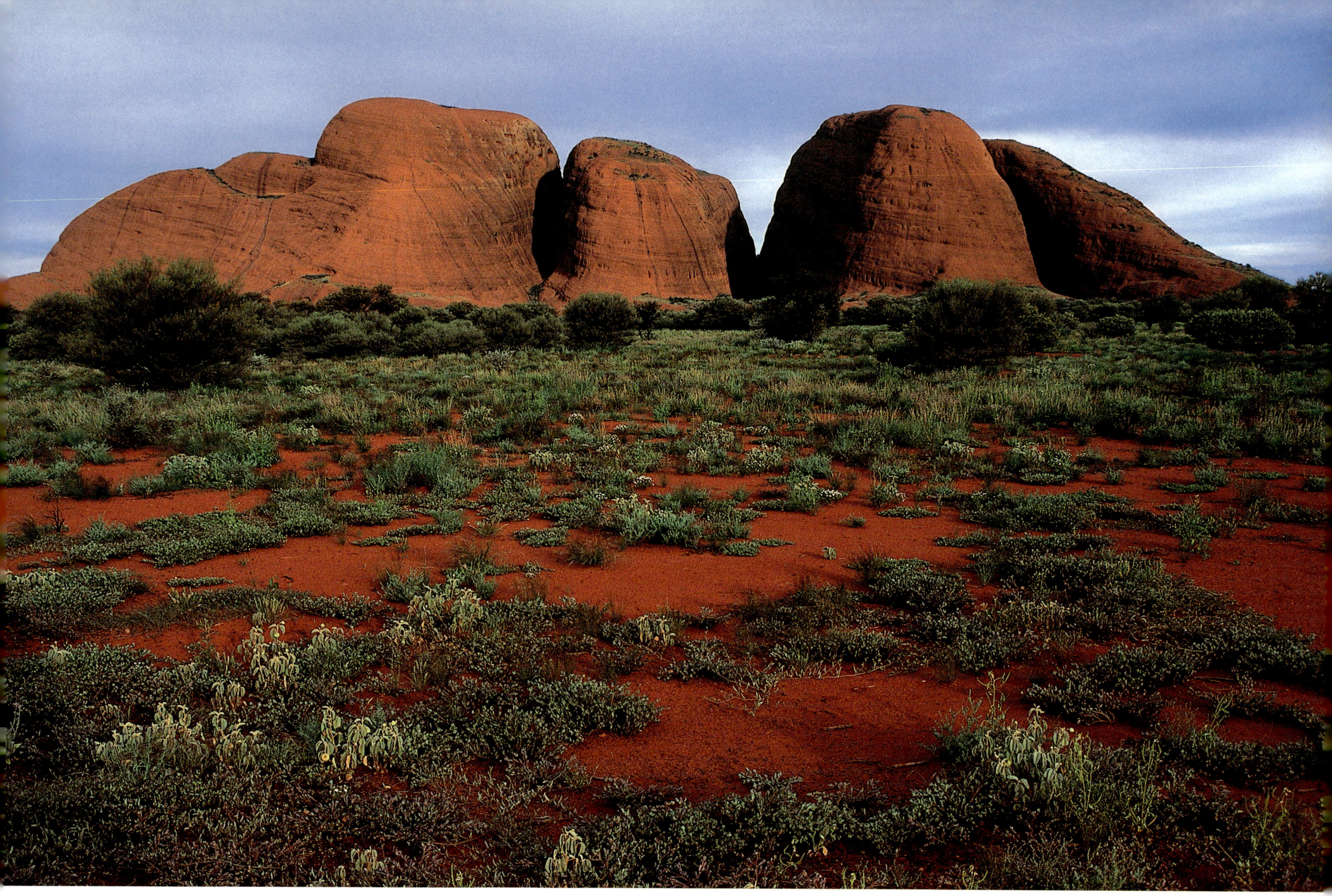

Top: Red sands and desert vegetation below the domes of Kata Tjuta.

Opposite page: A loop walk follows the rim of Kings Canyon and takes 3 to 4 hours over a distance of 6 kilometres. Note the figure on the skyline.

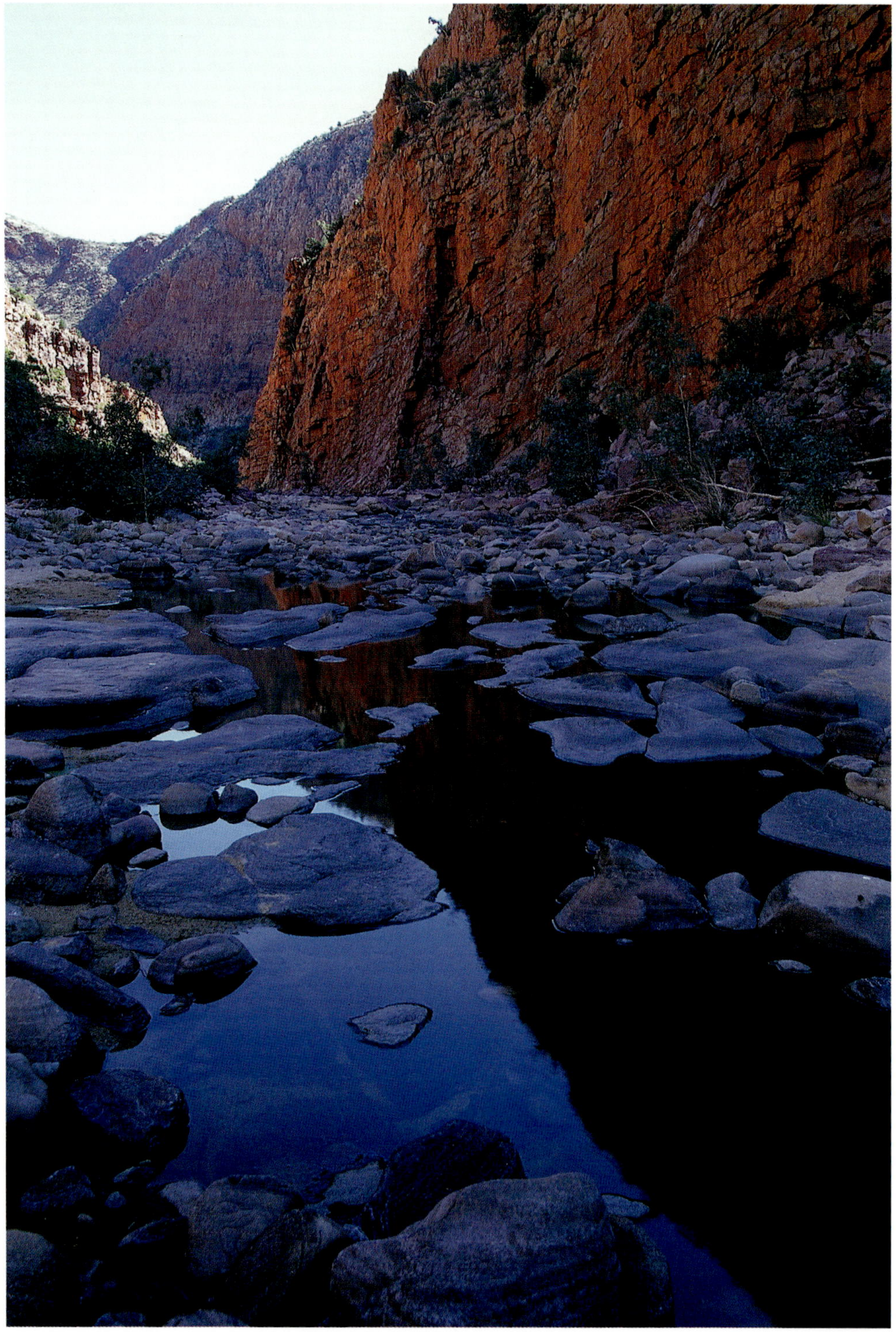

The boulder-strewn upper reaches of Ormiston Gorge.

The MacDonnell Range's ancient folds stretch from east to west for 400 kilometres and are split in many places by tremendous gorges and chasms. The ranges were formed 350 million years ago and originally may have been as high as the Himalaya. They still boast the highest peak in the Northern Territory, Mount Zeil (1531m). A popular long distance walk, the Larapinta Trail, covers the spine of the range for about 223 kilometres west of Alice Springs to Mount Sonder (1380m). One of my favourite walks in Australia is the Ormiston Pound walk, a seven kilometre circuit that climbs over the rocky walls of the pound to its flat floor and returns through the spectacular gorge.

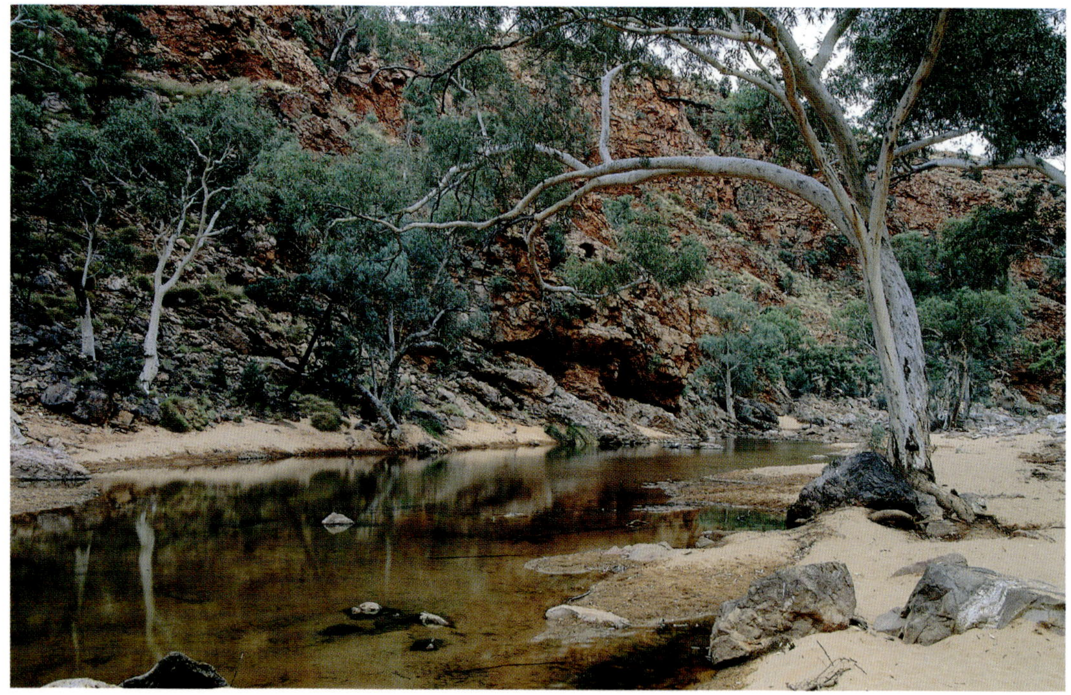

Tranquil tree lined pools at Redbank Gorge.

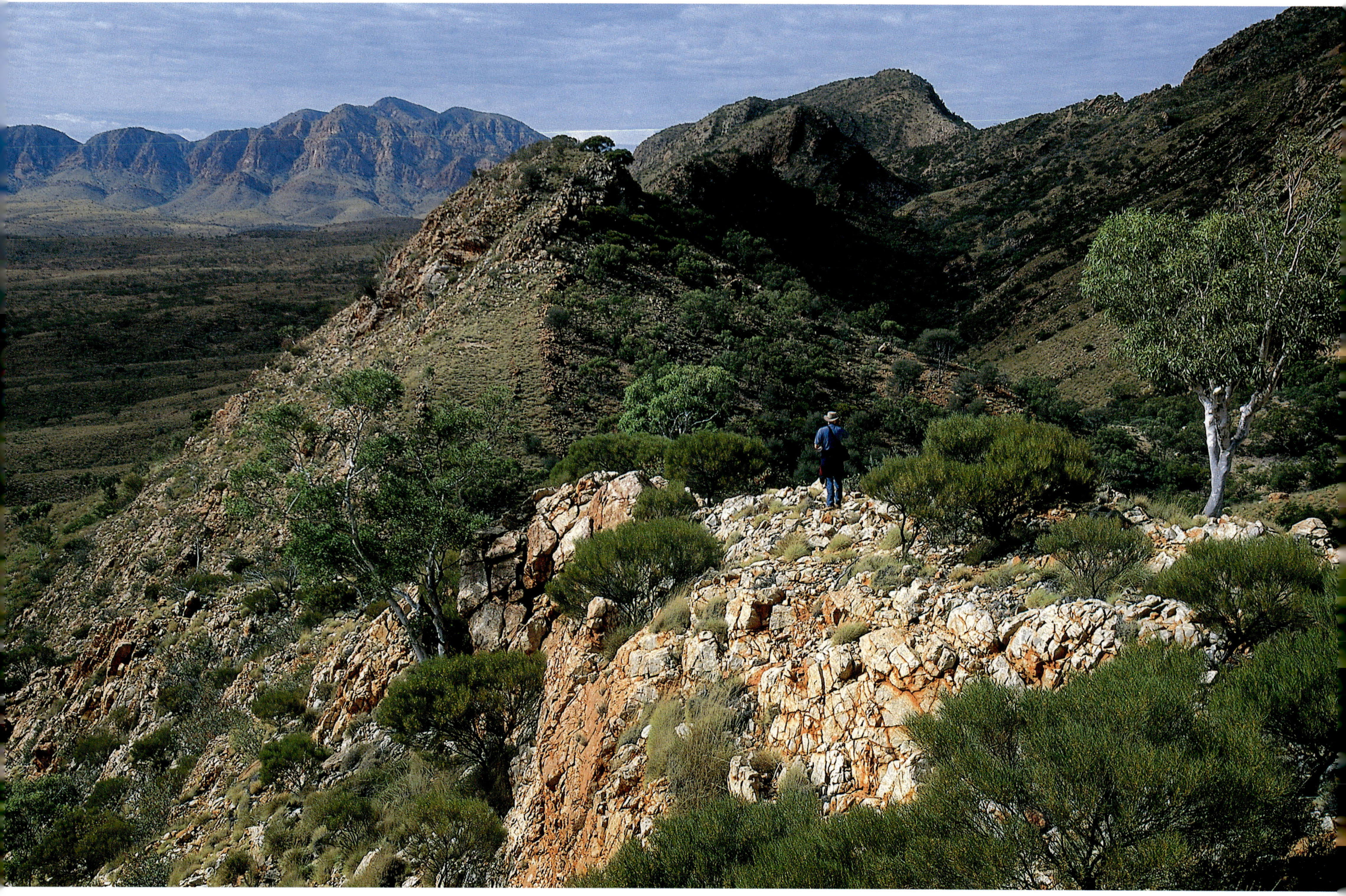

Looking over Ormiston Pound towards Mount Giles (1389m) in the distance.

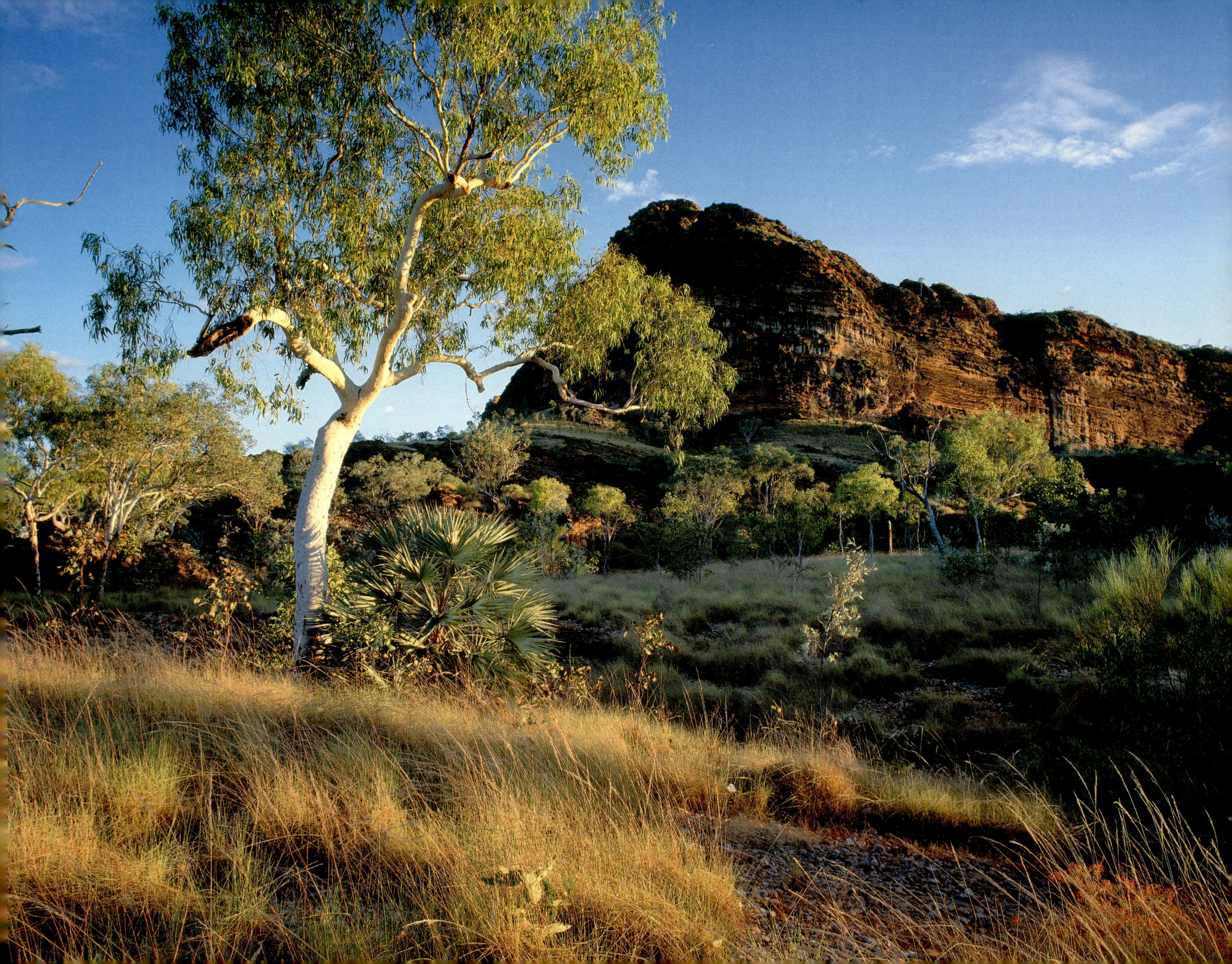

The entrance to Keep River National Park is close to the Western Australia border, and the park boasts seclusion and wonderful scenery and wildlife. It was my first night's stop after crossing into the Northern Territory. *"I left Kununurra and went briefly to Lake Argyle where I checked out the Durack Homestead, moved piece by piece when they flooded the lake. I headed back to the main highway and crossed the state line. No real emotion, but it is a significant milestone in my adventure. From there I went to the Gurrandalng campground in the Keep River National Park, a lovely spot below an impressive sandstone escarpment. I had a short walk before dinner and it is certainly a beautiful landscape. I decided to stay for two nights to see the area properly."*

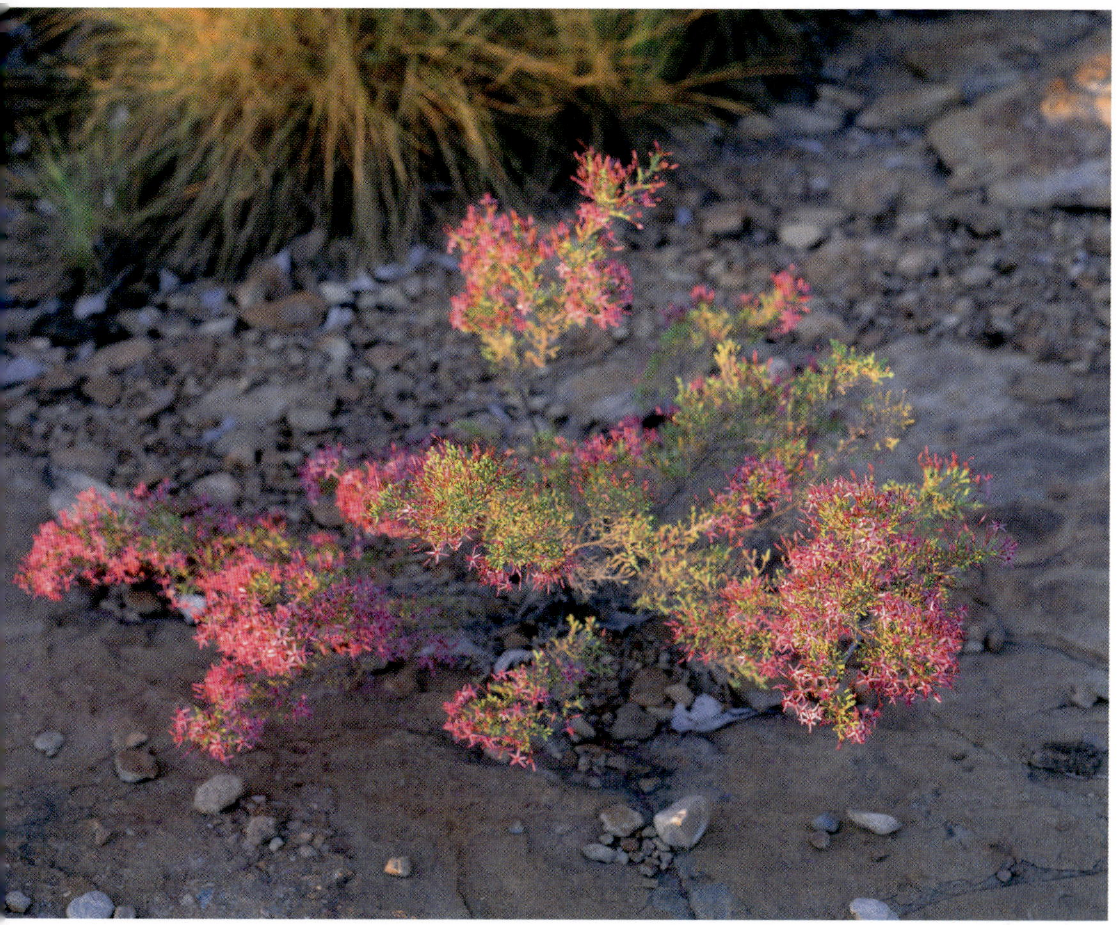

Top: The vivid pink starflowers of the Turkey bush are common in northern Australia.

Opposite page: Ghost gums and the sandstone escarpment near Gurrandalng campsite in the Keep River NP.

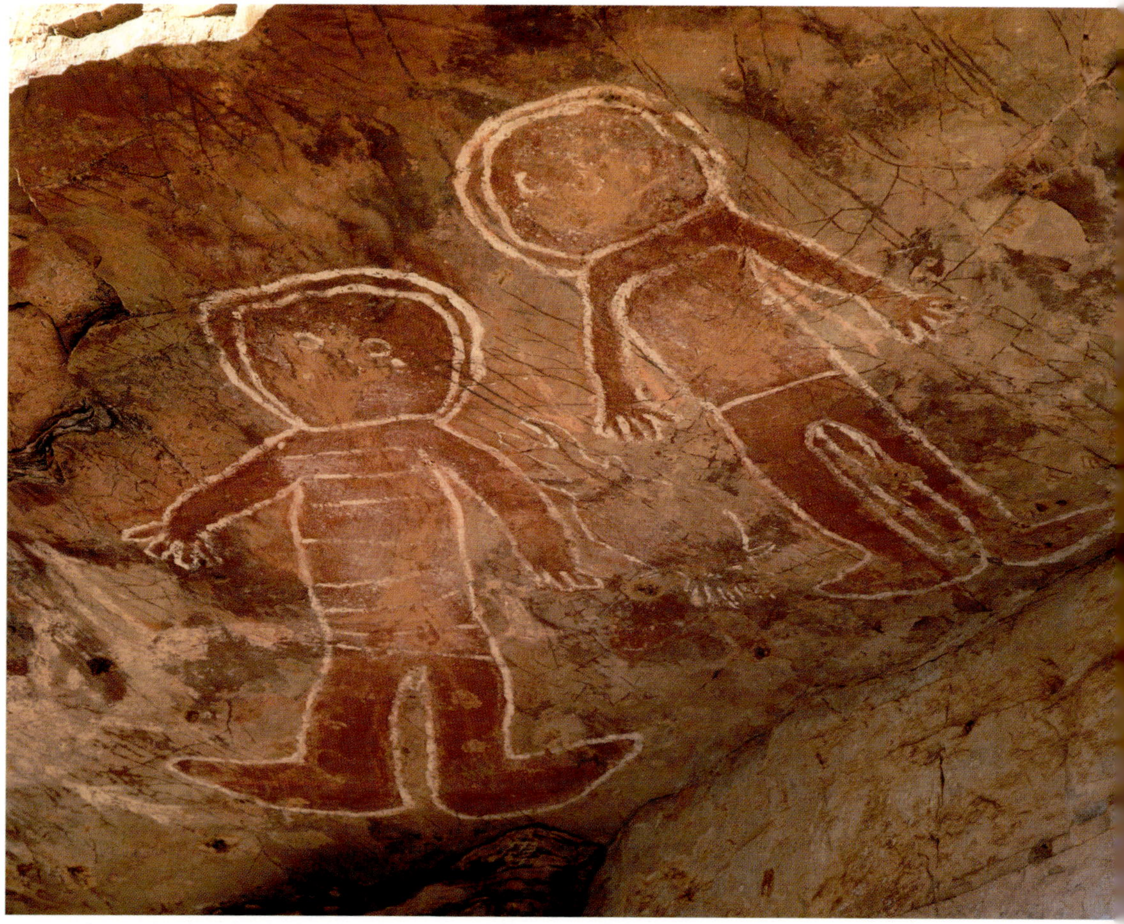

Aboriginal rock art in a cliff overhang alongside the Keep River Gorge, once used by the Miriwoong Aboriginal people as a wet season shelter.

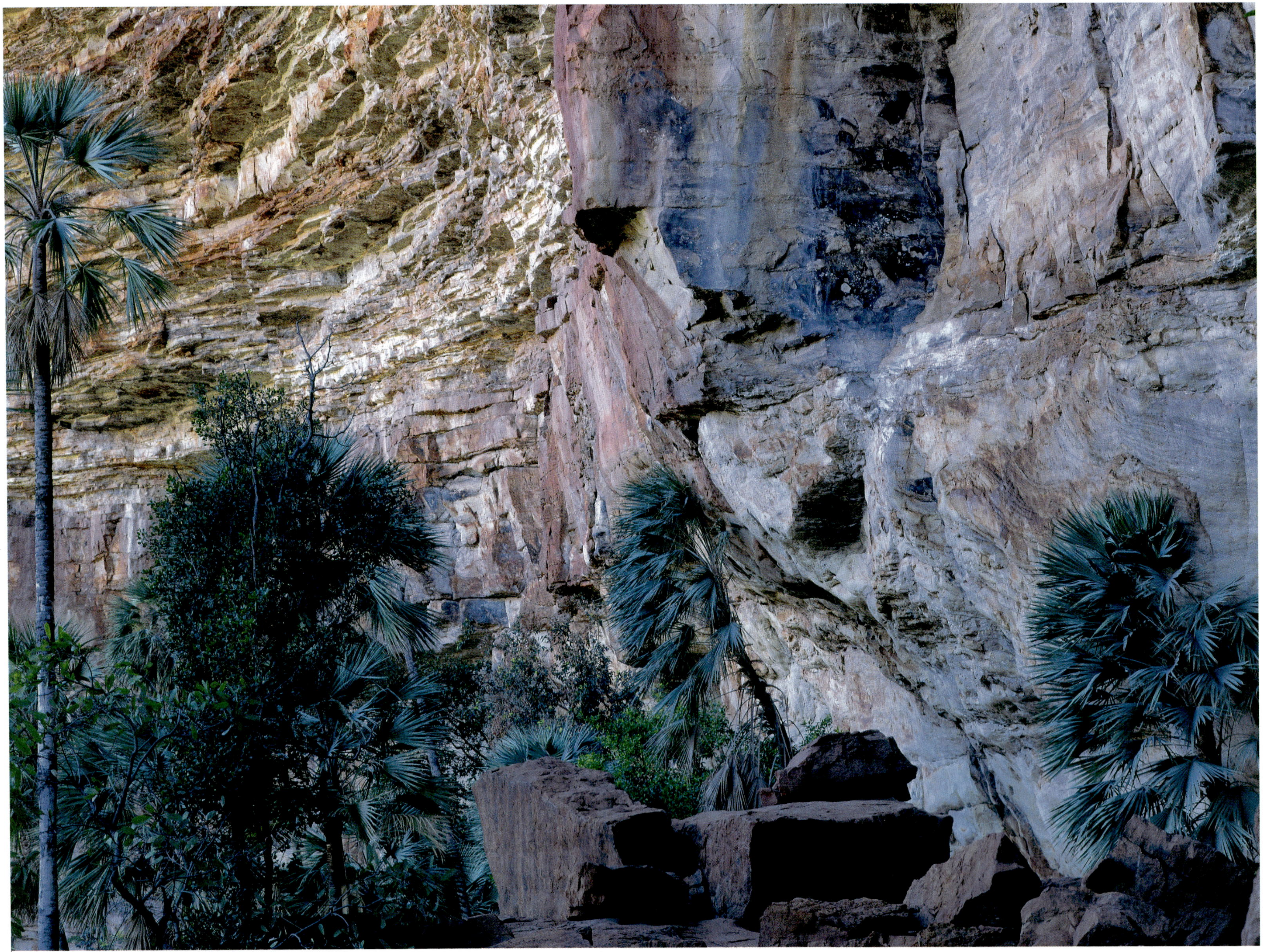

Judbarra or Gregory National Park in the north west of the Territory is the traditional country of the Nungali and Wardaman Aboriginal people and is jointly managed with the traditional owners. I camped at the Victoria River Roadhouse and the next morning *"headed to the Joe Creek Picnic Area to do the walk there. The path was steep in places but virtually the whole walk was shaded as you traverse along a westerly facing cliffline. The area is magnificent – a narrow gorge festooned with livistona palms and fig trees in places. Towards the end of the traverse you come across Aboriginal paintings of emus, frogs and spirit figures."*

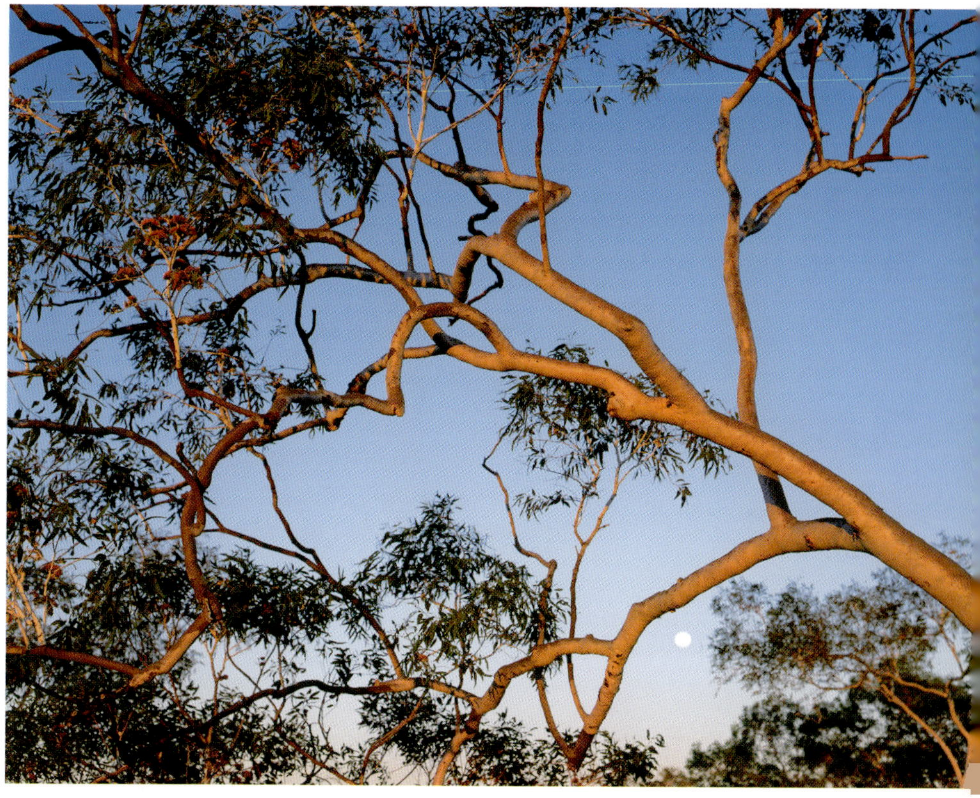

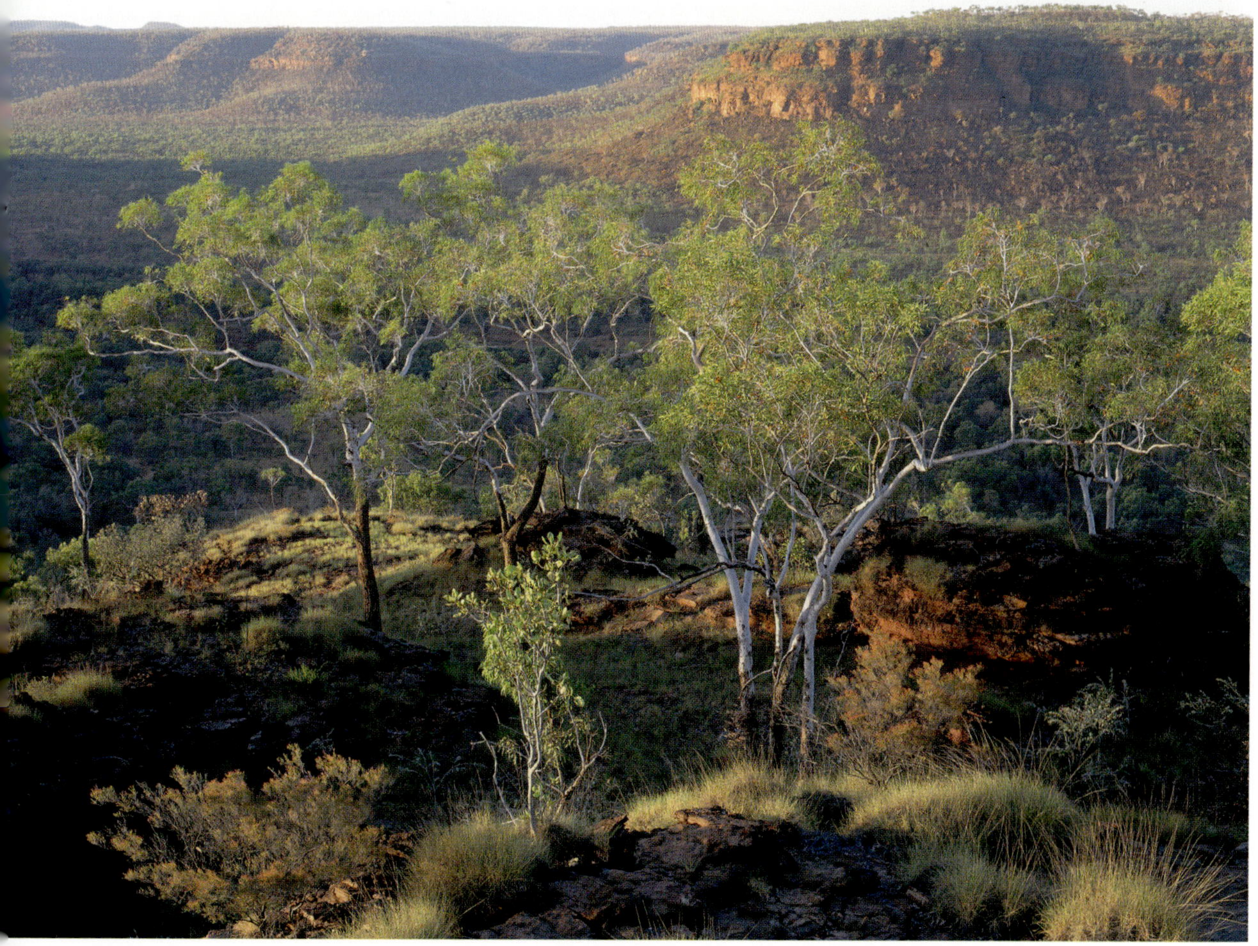

Top: Moonrise behind a eucalypt tree at dusk.

Left: Sunset view from the top of the escarpment looking down into the Victoria River valley.

Opposite page: Vividly coloured cliff face and livistona palms near the Joe Creek Picnic Area. The Nawulbinbin Walk here (1.7 kilometre loop) leads to an Aboriginal shelter and rock art gallery.

Leliyn, or Edith Falls, is part of Nitmiluk National park and is a great spot to camp, swim and bushwalk. I stayed here for a couple of nights on my way towards Darwin and Kakadu. I set up the tent and after lunch, *"I had a long swim in the lower pool. It is massive, 150 metres long, and I swam to the waterfall and jumped off some rocks into the water. After the swim I mooched around and read my book. Eventually at 5pm I wandered over to the falls to take photographs. I initially thought I would walk to a lookout on top of the escarpment but as soon as I got to the bridge over the Edith River I stopped. The wind had dropped and the reflections here were just amazing."*

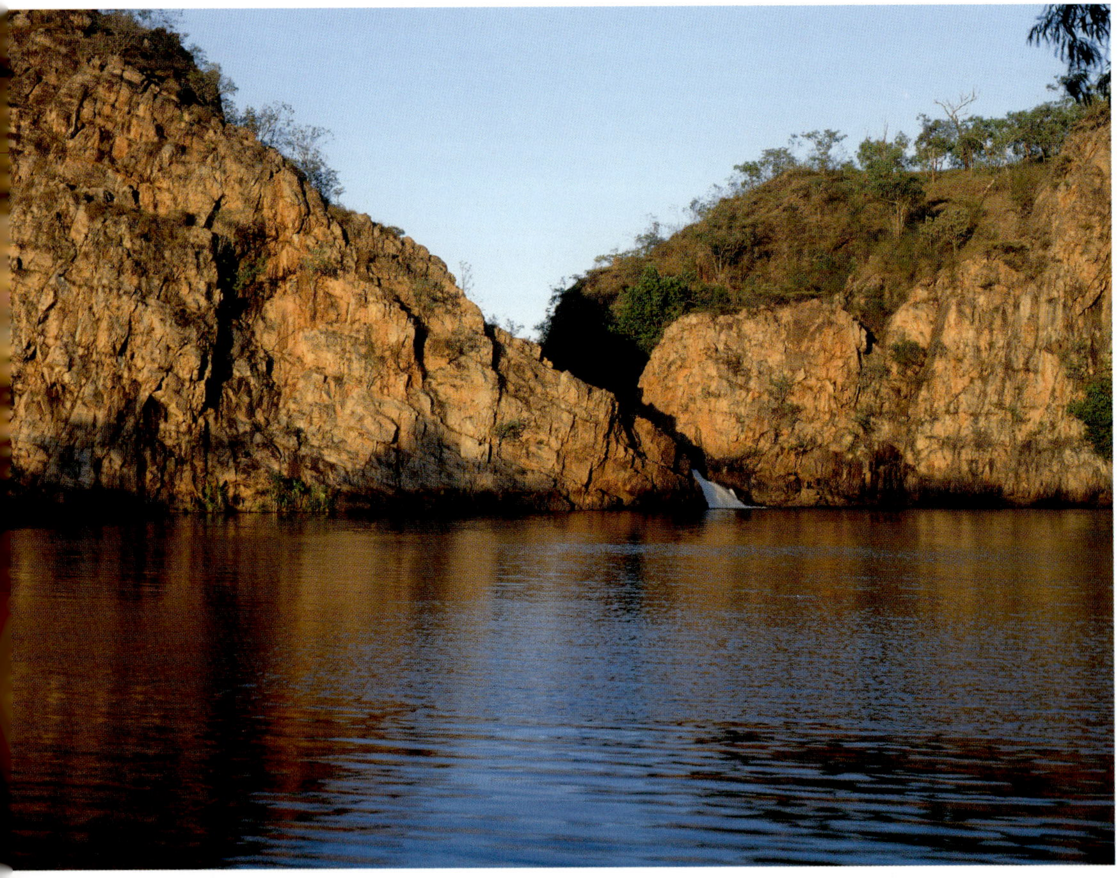

Leliyn or Edith Falls.

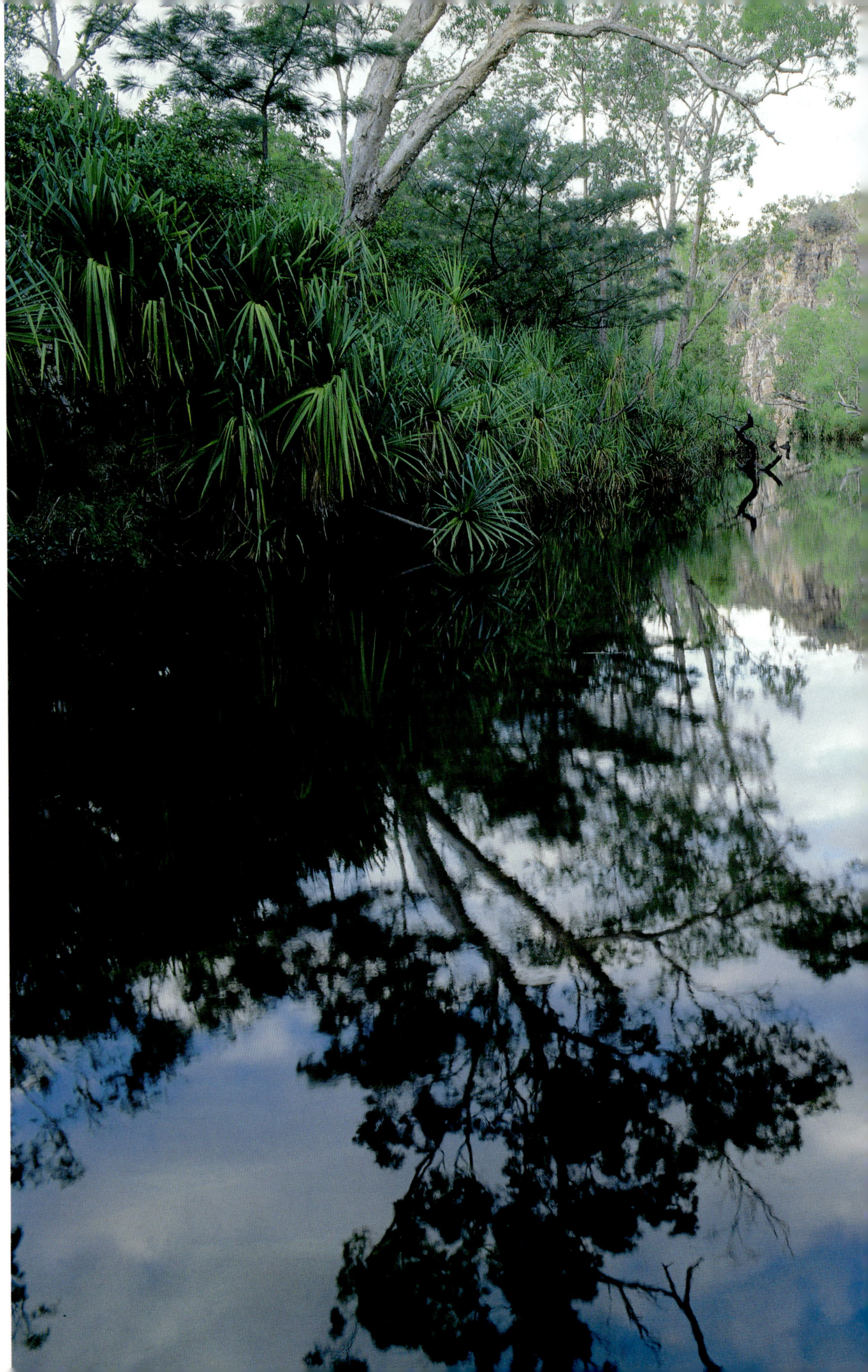

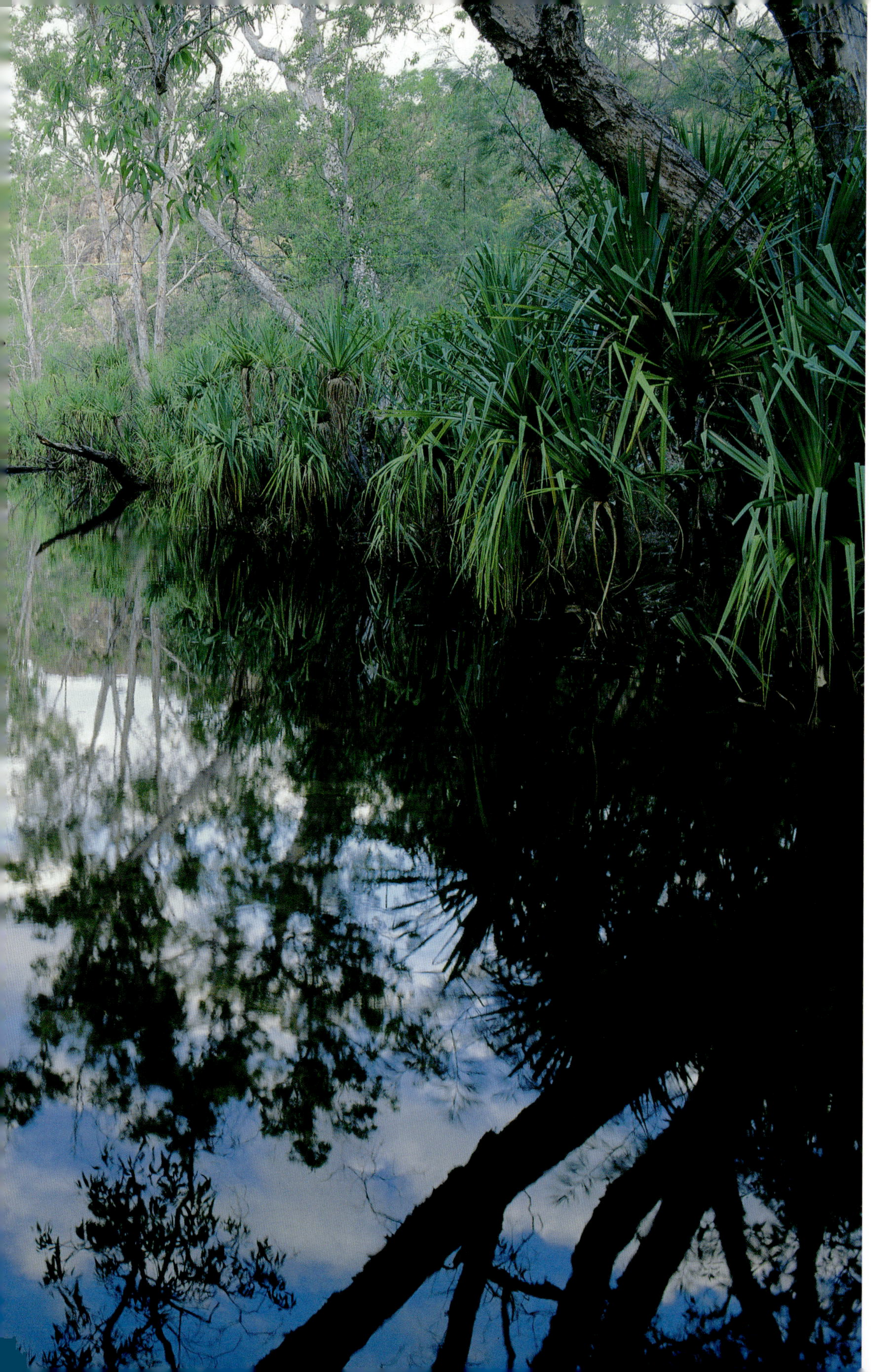

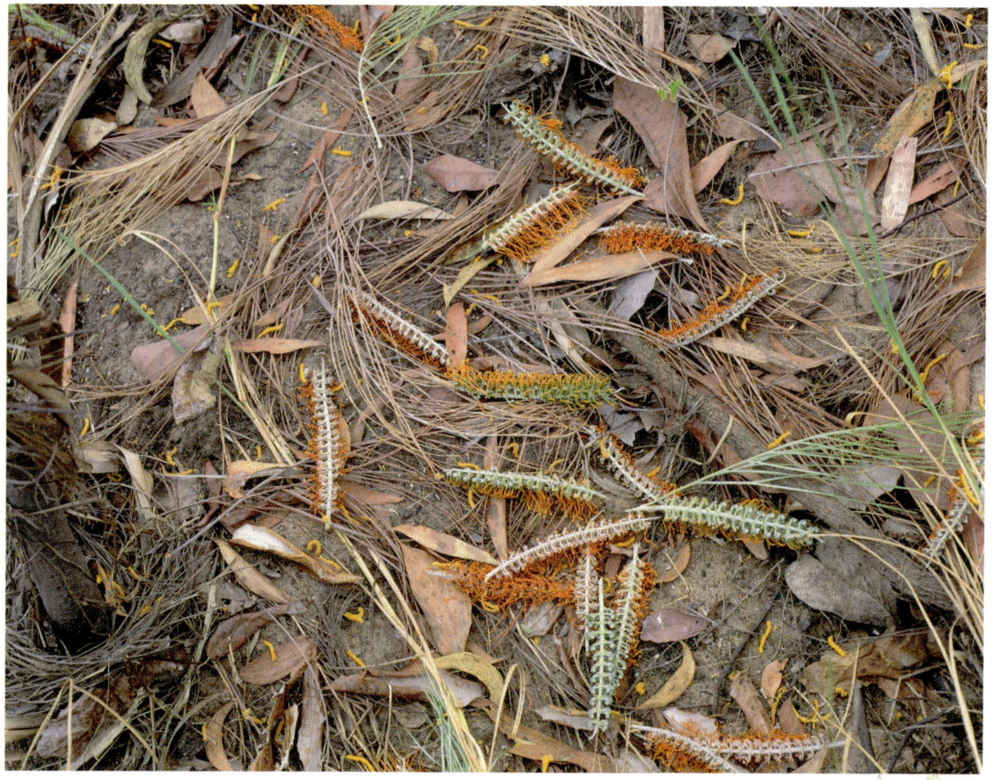

Top: Fallen grevillea flowers, Leliyn.

Left: Reflections in the Edith River below the falls.

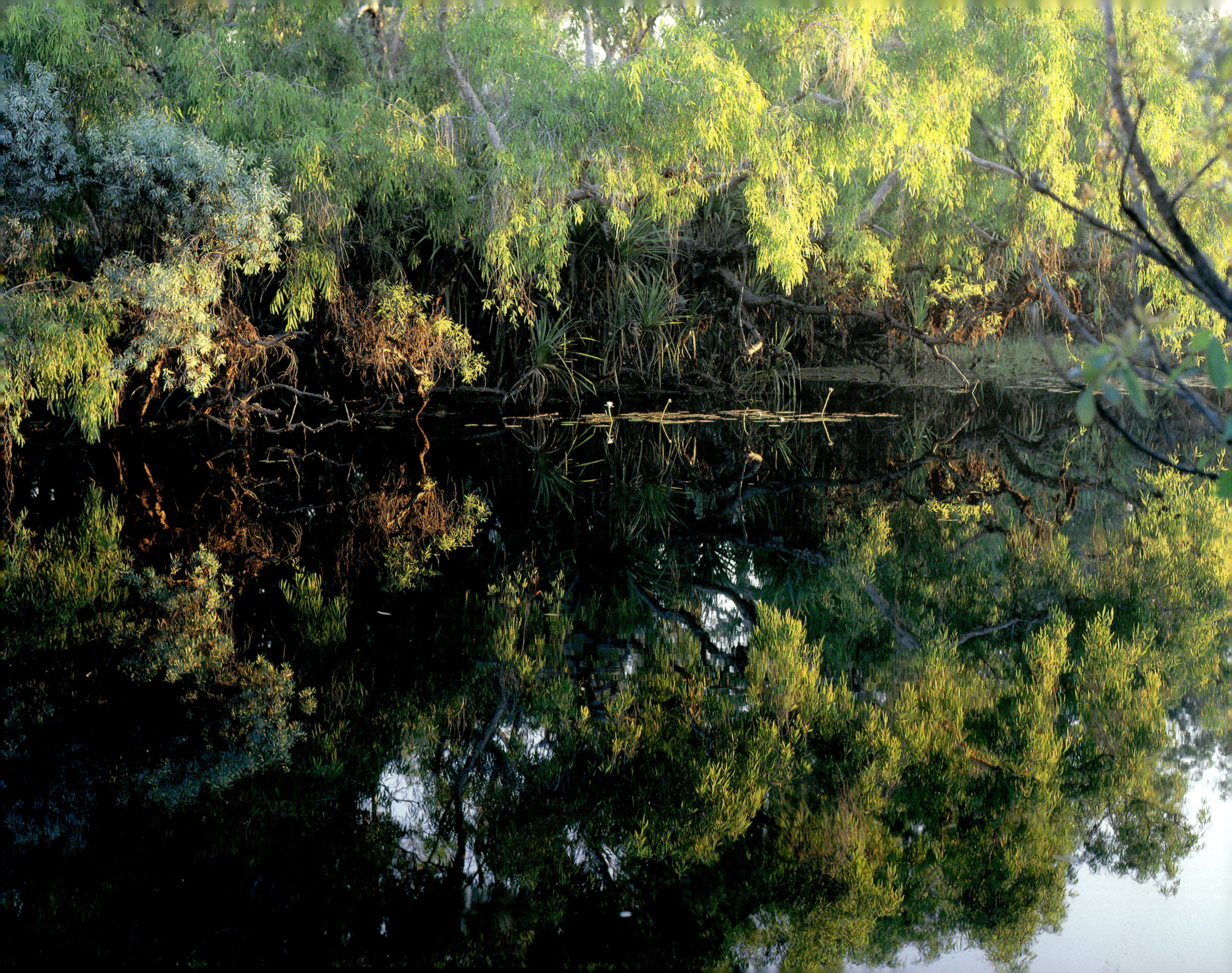

Kakadu National Park is a World Heritage area, listed for both its natural and cultural values, and is one of the great national parks of the world. It covers an area of 19,757 square kilometres. The word Kakadu is derived from an Aboriginal floodplain language called Gagudja. The traditional owners of the land are various clans of the Bininj and Mungguy Aboriginal peoples, who have a majority on the board of management of the national park. Kakadu boasts over 250 bird species, 25 frog species, fresh and saltwater crocodiles, and vast floodplains which cover a third of the park in the Wet season. In the south the stone country of the Arnhem Land Plateau has spectacular sandstone cliffs, waterfalls and Aboriginal rock art galleries.

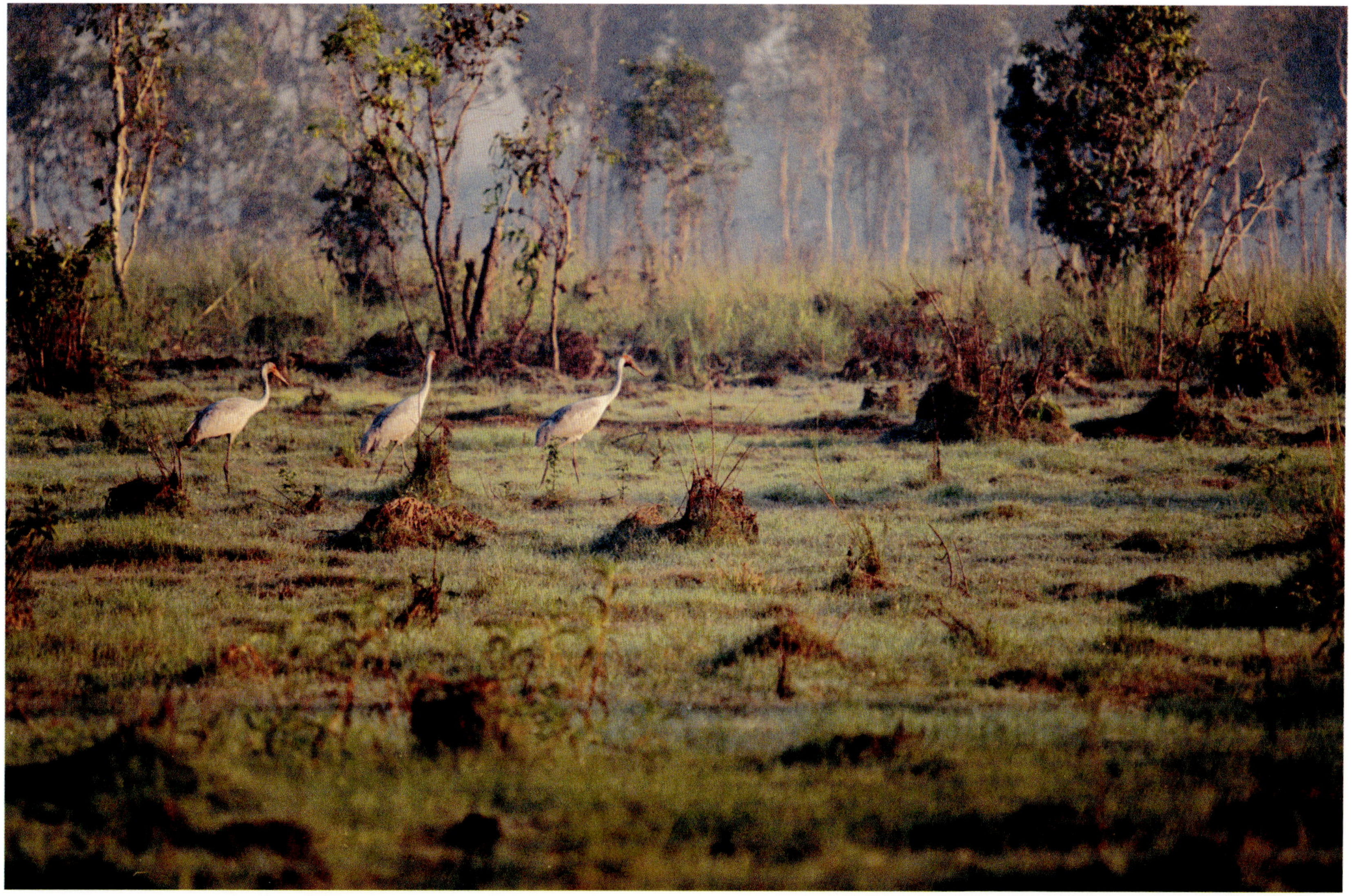

Top: During the wet season the floodplains support a population of an estimated 2.5 million birds, including these brolga.

Opposite page: Reflections in the Burdulba Billabong, south of the township of Jabiru.

Gunlom is a popular campsite in the south of Kakadu National Park. I wrote: *"I continued to Gunlom along a rough, corrugated road. There is a high waterfall and a deep plunge pool here which is lovely for swimming. I had a dip and then went back for the camera because there were awesome green colours in the pool waters where the sunlight caught it."* Gunlom is extensively surveyed for saltwater crocodiles at the beginning of each dry season and traps are placed, but swimming here is at your own risk. Another lovely pool can be found at the top of the cliffs and may be safer, because crocodiles can't rock climb!

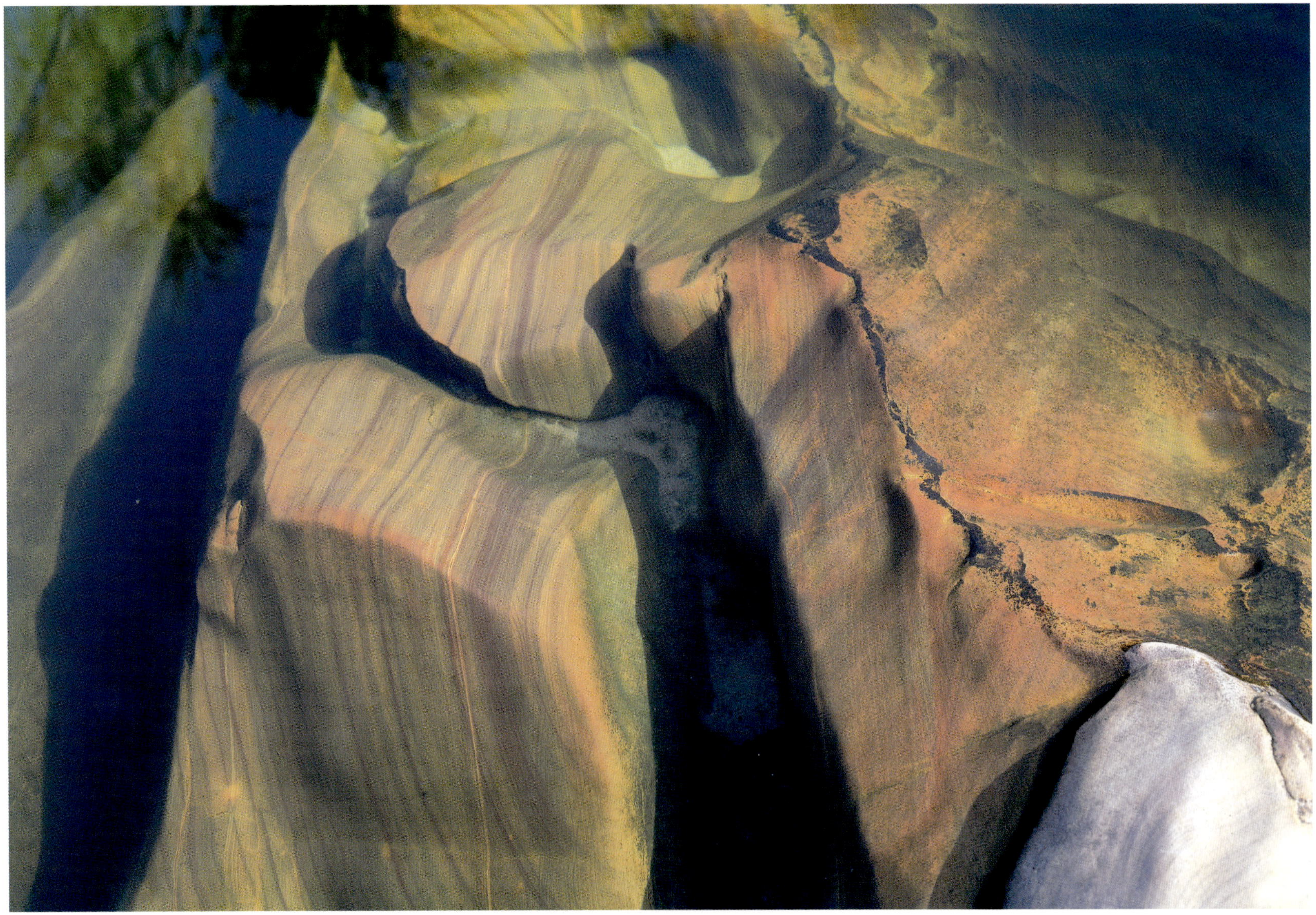

Top: Beautifully marked rocks in the upper pool at Gunlom.

Opposite page: The waterfall and plunge pool at Gunlom in Kakadu NP.

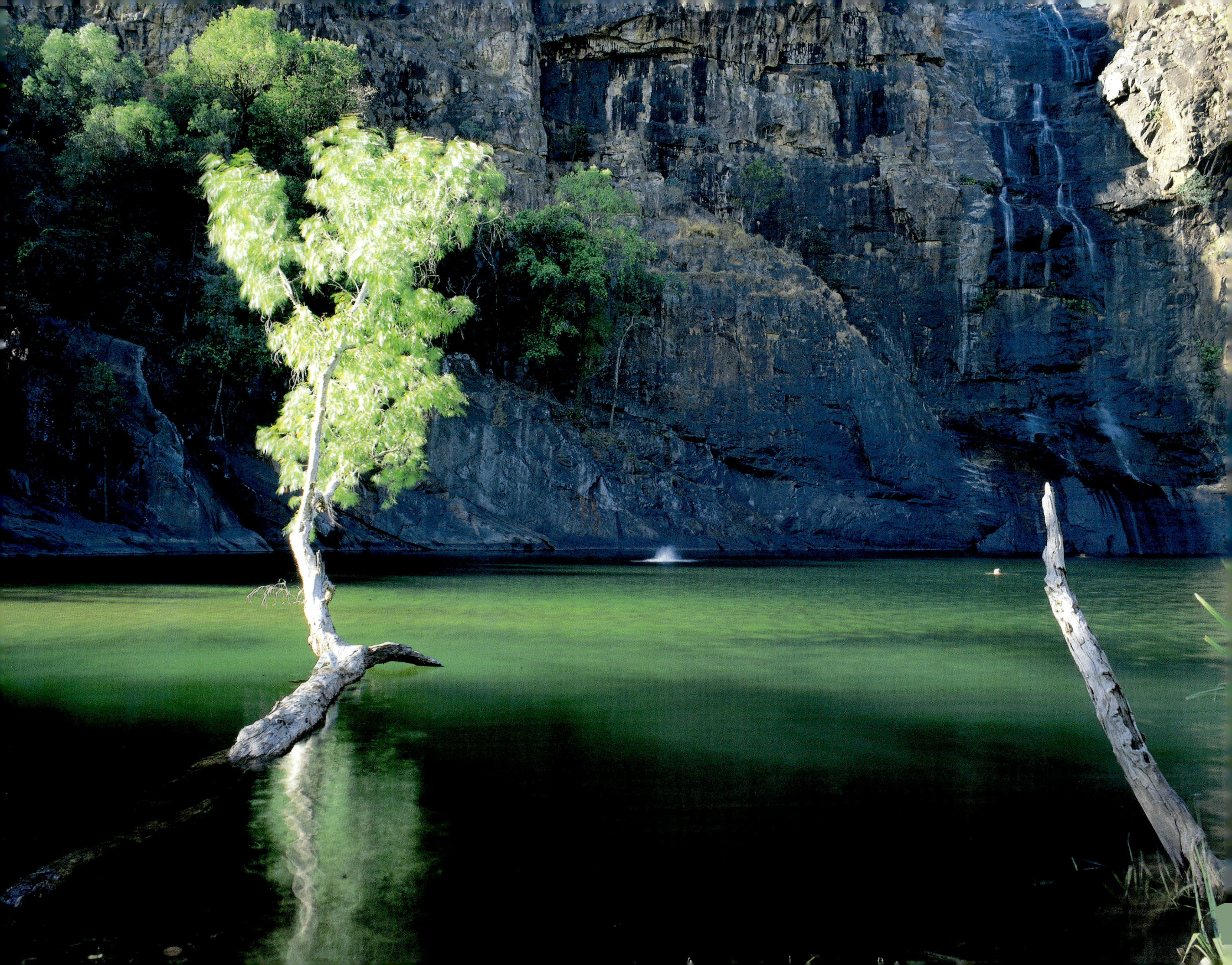

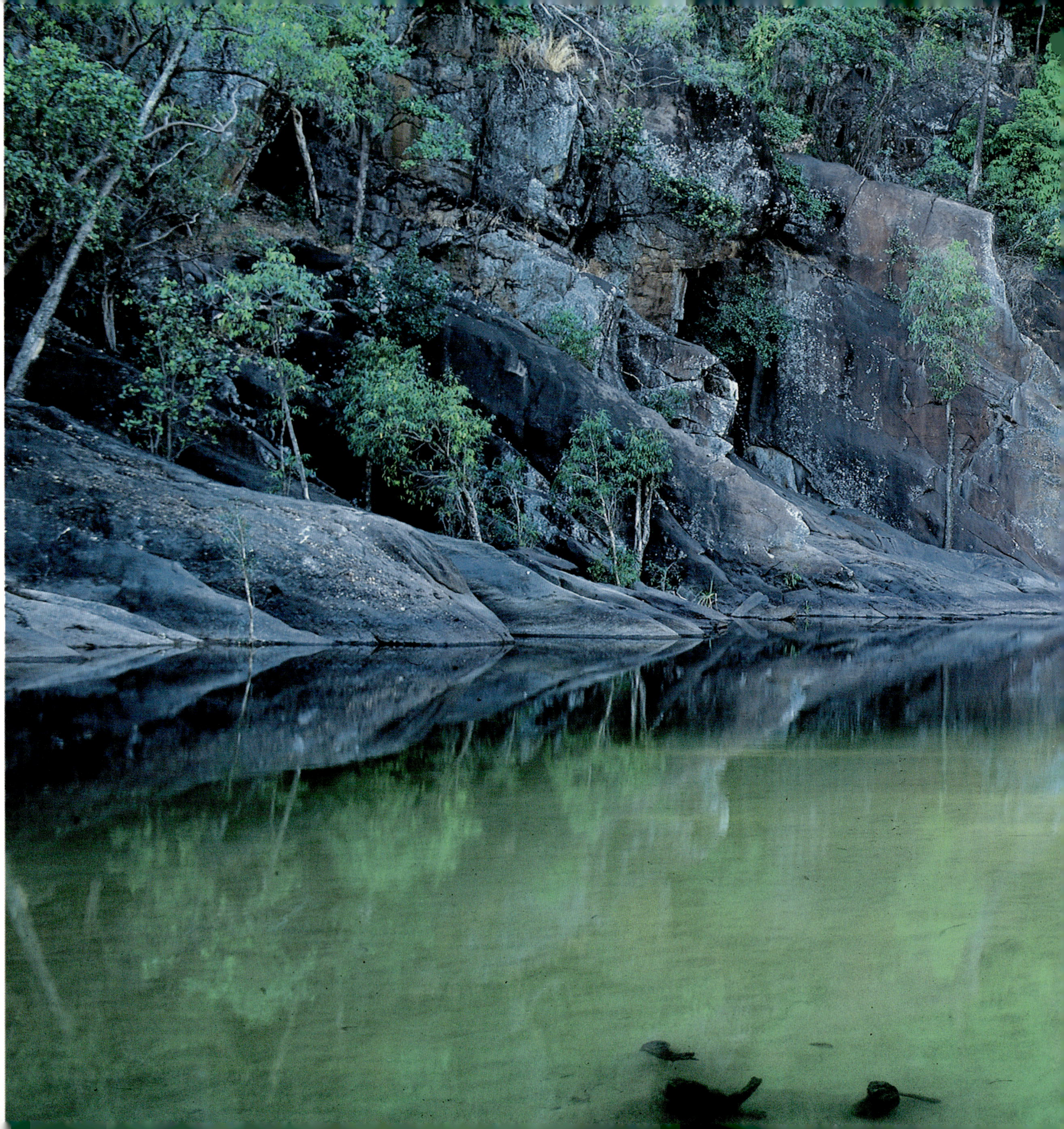

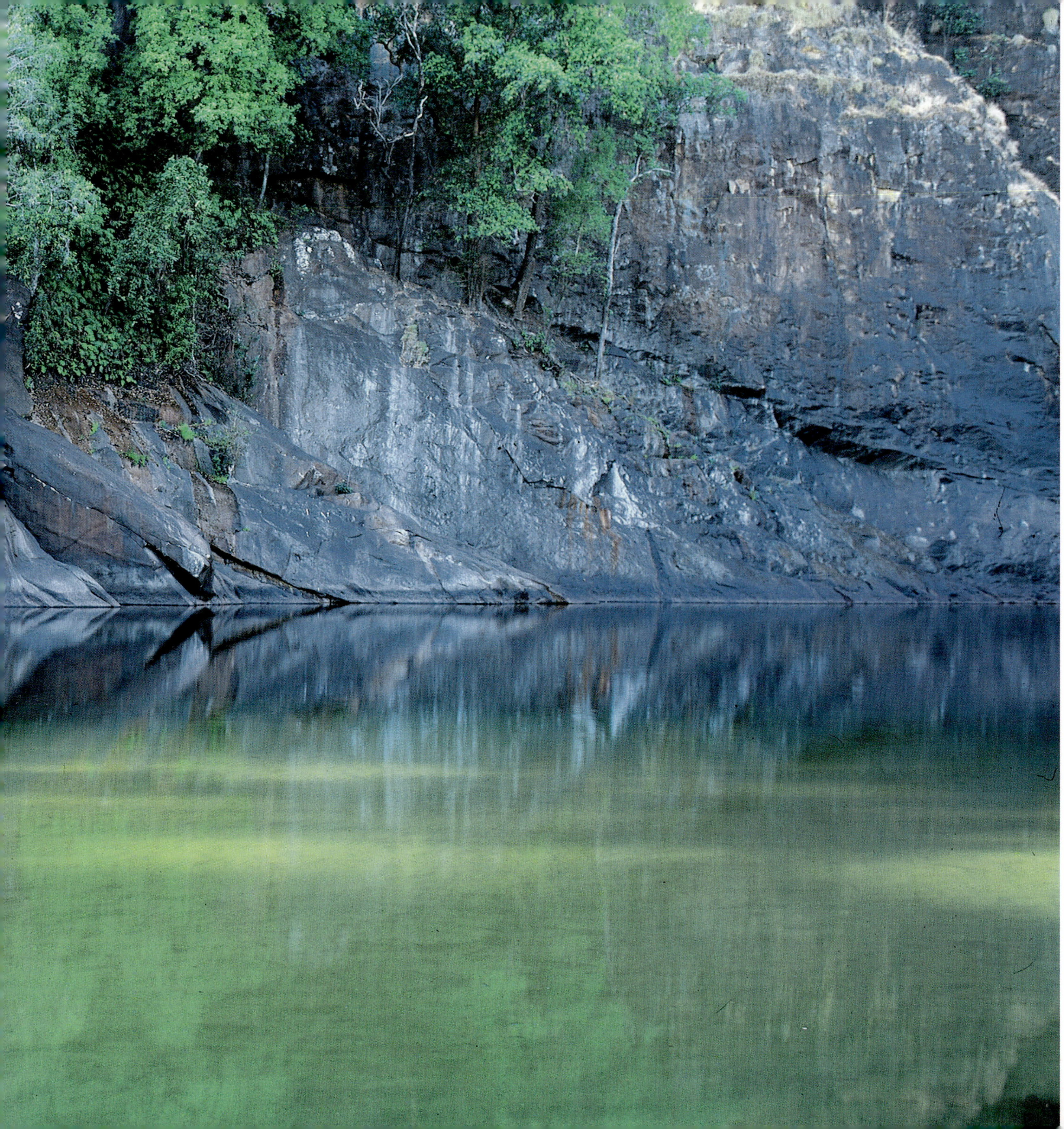

Magnificent colours in the plunge pool at Gunlom.

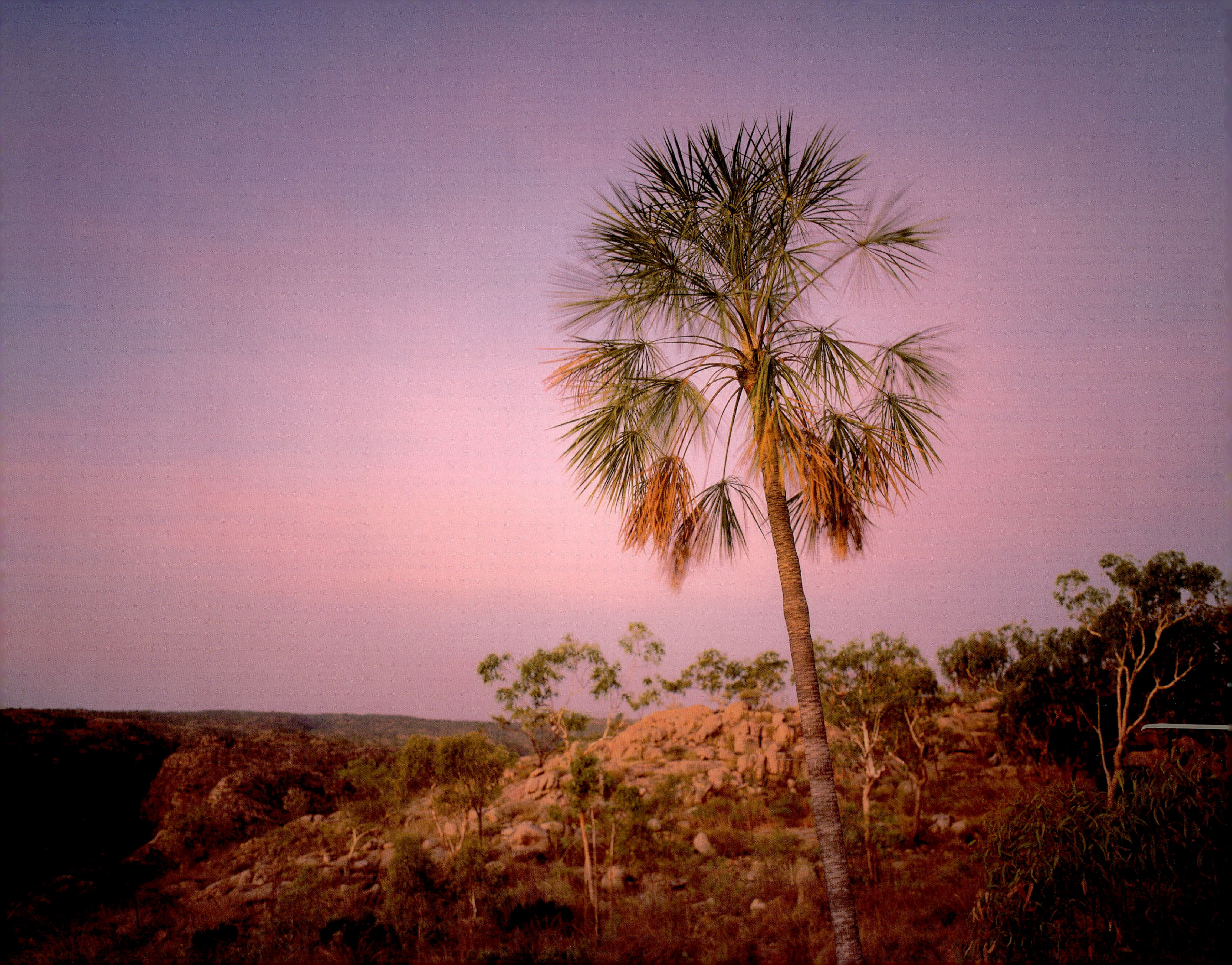

I headed south again to Nitmiluk National Park, which protects the remarkable Katherine Gorge, a complex series of gorges cut into a sandstone plateau. Bushwalking and canoeing are popular, or for the less active there are boat cruises in the lower gorges and helicopter flights available. For serious backpackers, the Katherine Gorge to Leliyn walk takes five days through remote and spectacular country along the gorge system.

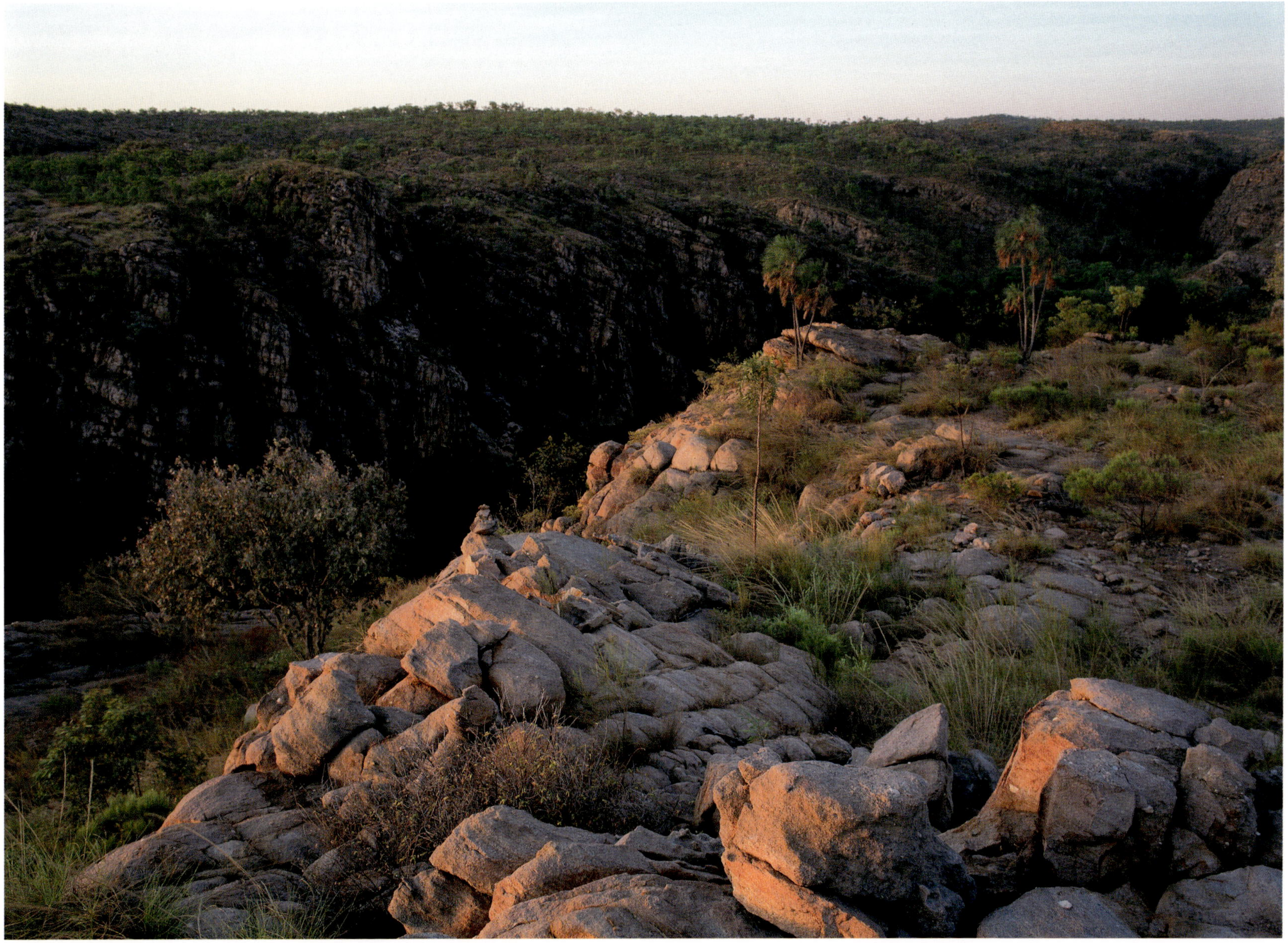

Top: Jumbled rocks on the escarpment high above the Katherine River.

Opposite page: Livistona palm on the plateau above Katherine Gorge at dusk, reached by following the Baruwei Loop Walk which takes about 2 hours.

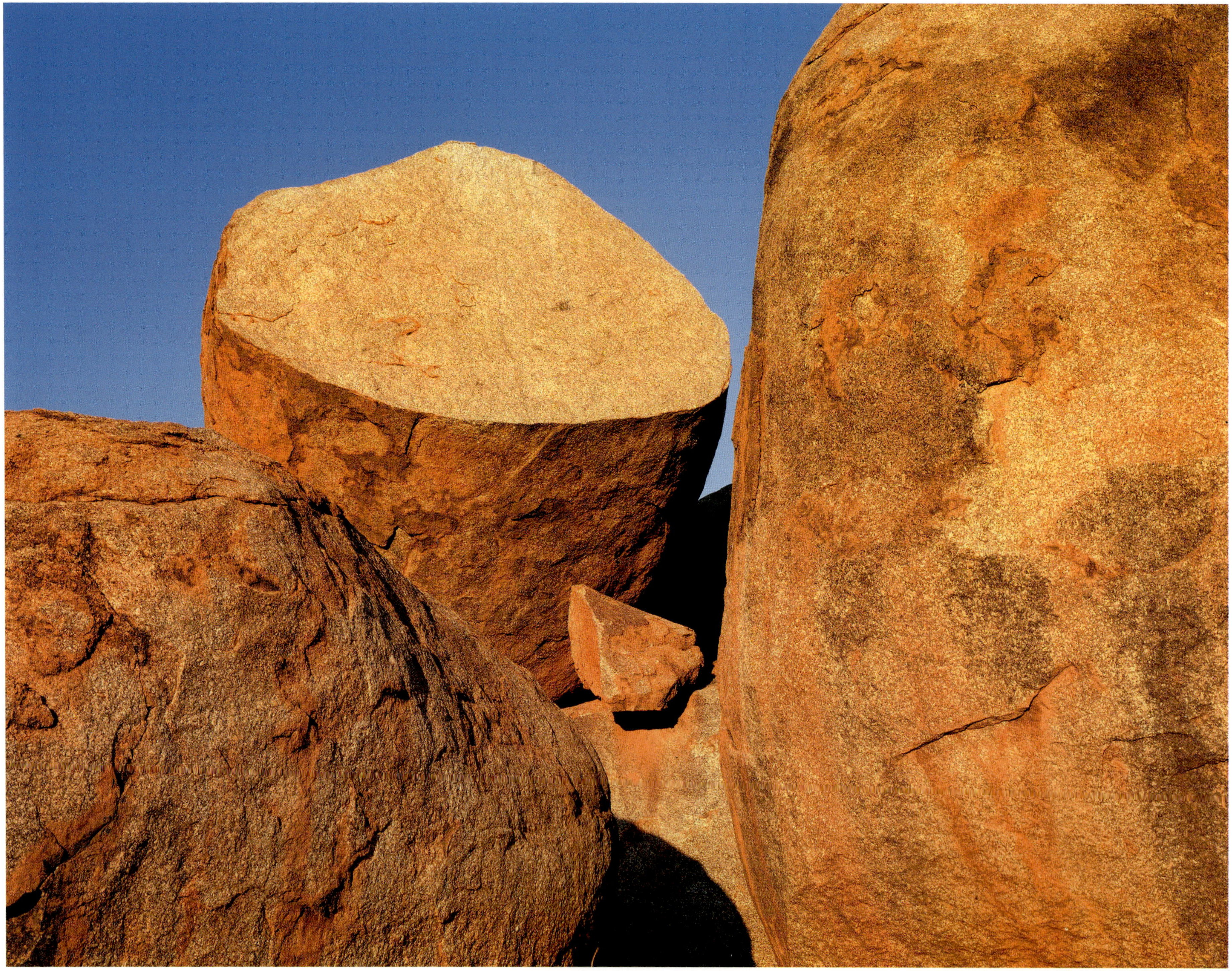

Not all of the Devils Marbles are round ... this one looks like a bread roll that has been sliced in half!

The Devils Marbles or Karlu Karlu lie nine kilometres north of the tiny settlement of Wauchope on the Stuart Highway, and are a sacred Aboriginal site. The "marbles" are rounded granite boulders left behind after extensive erosion of the ancient Davenport Range. An Aboriginal legend says that Karlu Karlu are eggs laid by the rainbow serpent. In 2008 the ownership of the conservation reserve was officially handed back to the traditional Aboriginal owners. They leased it back to the Northern Territory Government and the reserve is now jointly managed.

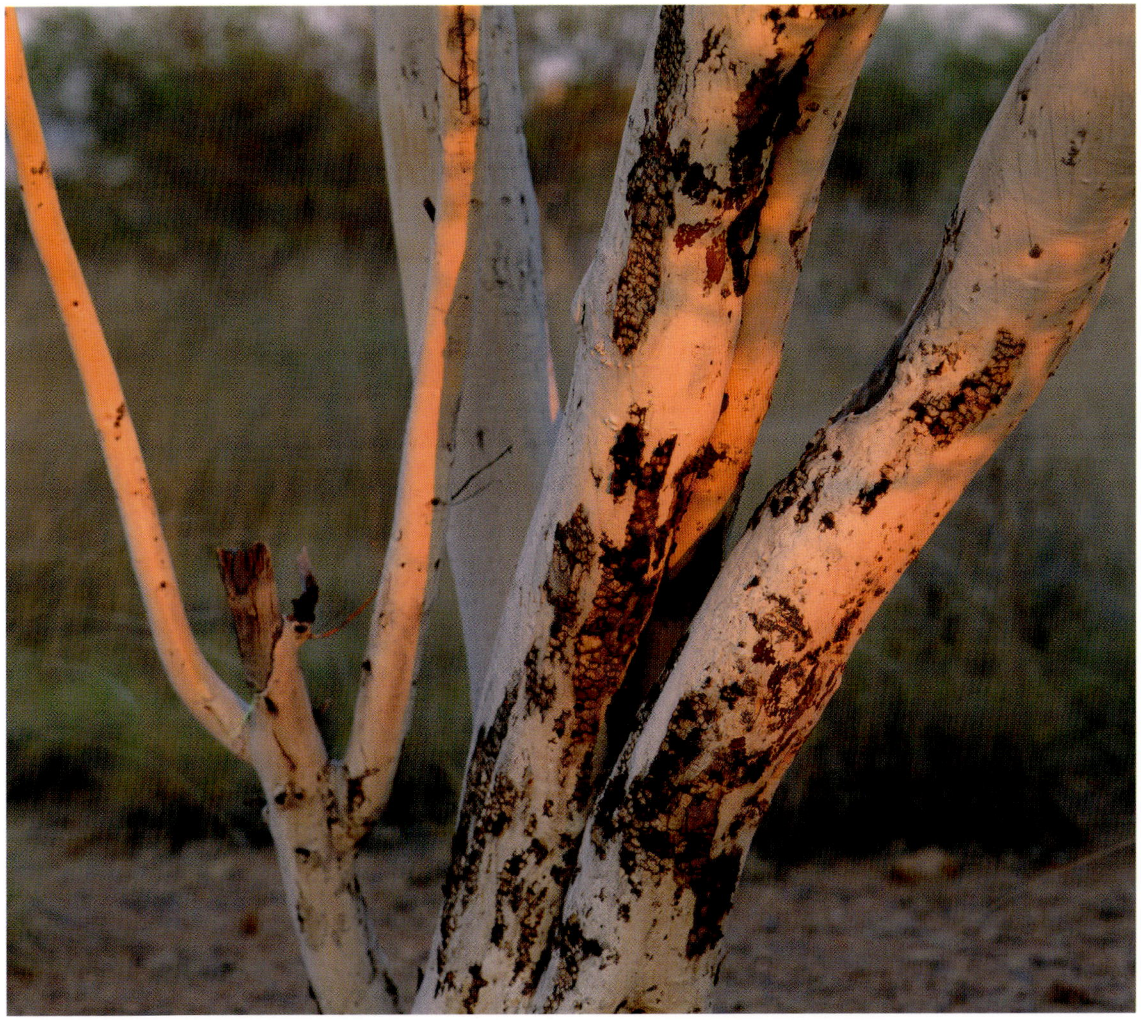

Ghost gums catch the last light of day at the Devils Marbles.

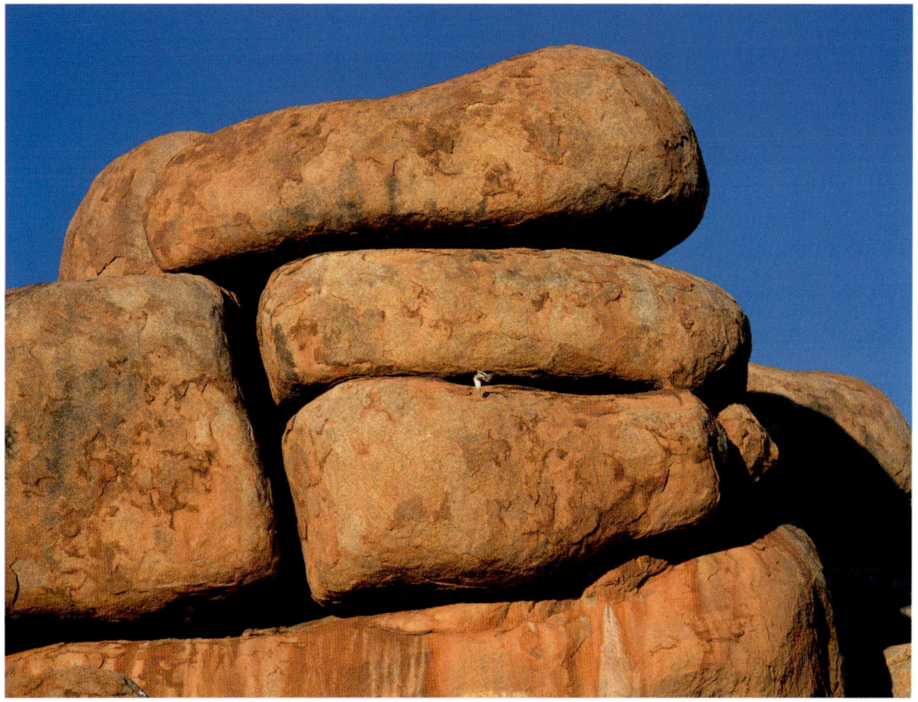

A nankeen kestrel takes flight from an impressive stack of Devils Marbles.

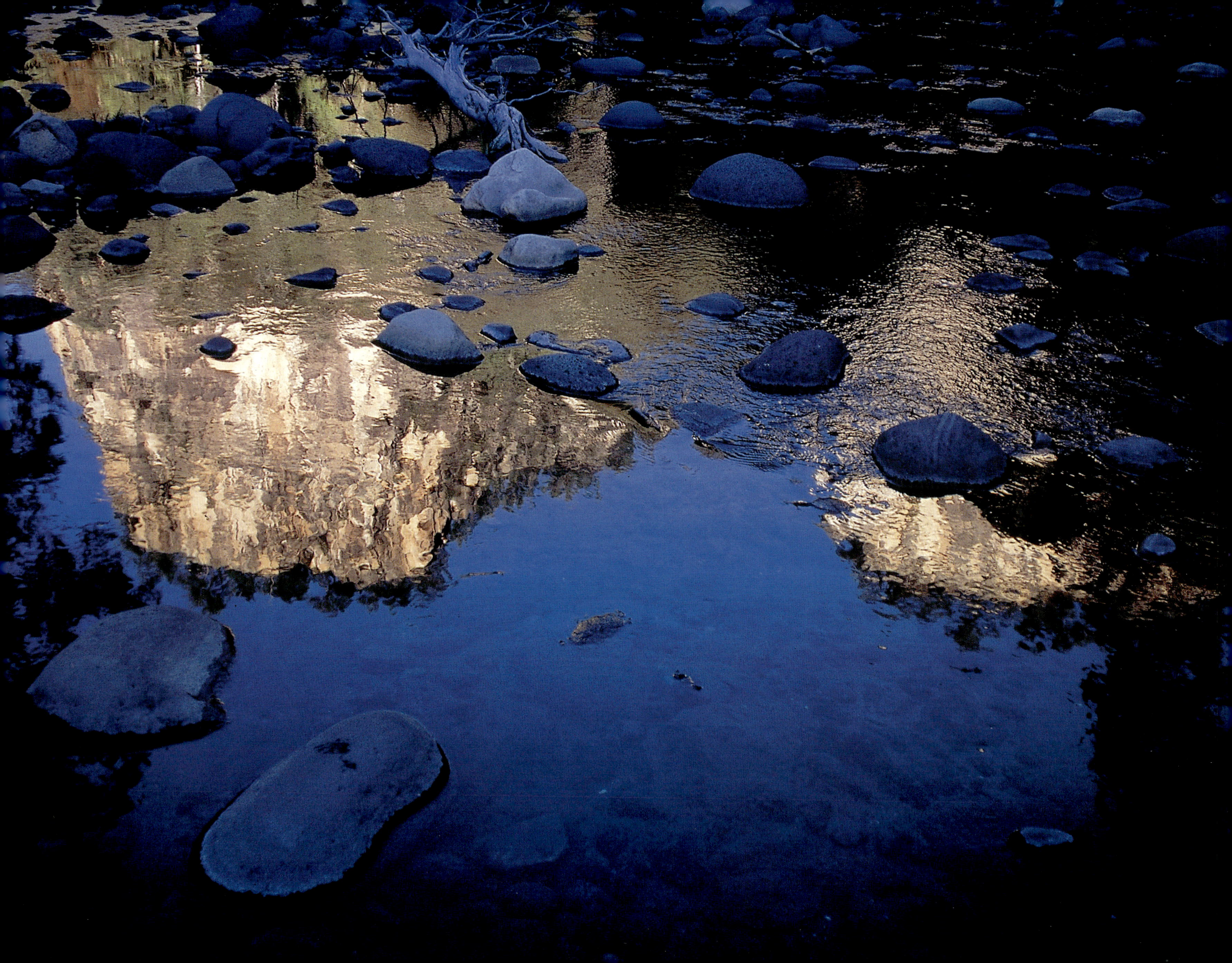

Queensland

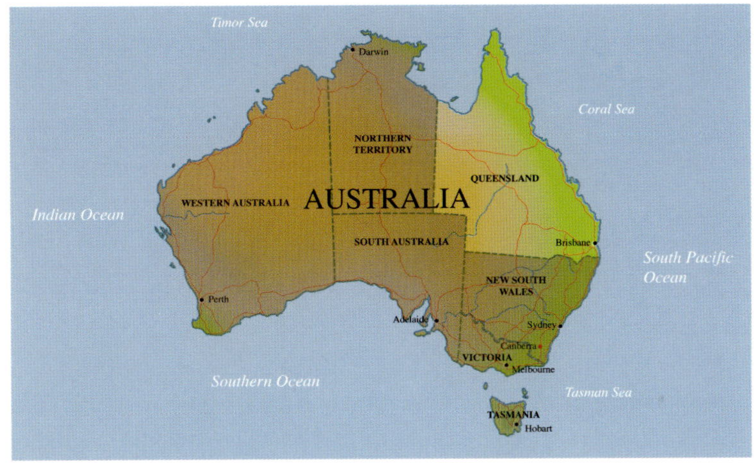

Queensland has a unique culture and sense of place. The people here, especially away from the big centres, are laconic and easy going, but also tough and resourceful. The landscape is vast and the usually benign climate can be challenging when cyclones, floods or droughts occur. The most northerly part of Queensland, Cape York Peninsula, is an important wilderness of tropical forests and woodlands, wild rivers, ranges and wetlands. The cattle station country of the gulf region extends inland to the outback towns of Mount Isa, Winton and Longreach. In Far North Queensland two World Heritage Areas sit side by side – the rain forested mountains of the Wet Tropics and the Great Barrier Reef, the largest coral formation in the world. In the southern half of the state other natural attractions include Carnarvon Gorge, Lamington National Park and Fraser Island, the largest sand island in the world.

Queensland has been occupied for tens of thousands of years by Aboriginal people, who developed a rich and complex culture. European settlement began after the Governor of New South Wales, Sir Thomas Brisbane, sent his Surveyor-General John Oxley to find a suitable site for a penal colony in the almost unknown northern parts of the east coast in 1821. In 1824 troops and convicts arrived at the area now called Redcliffe on Moreton Bay. The settlement was forced to move south to the present site of Brisbane in 1825 due to a lack of fresh water and hostility from local Aborigines. By 1859 the colony was well established and after agitation from its free settlers the State of Queensland separated from New South Wales.

Brisbane has an average of 7.5 hours of sunshine per day and a wonderful subtropical climate. Other important centres in Queensland include Cairns, Townsville, Rockhampton, Mount Isa and Toowoomba. Popular holiday playgrounds for local and overseas visitors include the Gold and Sunshine Coasts near Brisbane, the Whitsunday Islands off the coast near Airlie Beach, and the 2600 kilometre long stretch of the Great Barrier Reef.

Opposite page: The towering sandstone cliffs of Carnarvon Gorge reflect in Carnarvon Creek.

I entered Queensland near the small town of Camooweal, spent a few days in Mount Isa and Julia Creek and made my way to Porcupine Gorge National Park, 60 kilometres north of the town of Hughenden in Far North Queensland. The twenty kilometre long gorge system here cuts through thin, hard cap basalt, from a geologically recent lava flow, into softer sandstone rocks. I camped here, *"was up at dawn and soon headed to the gorge. There was great lighting at the lookout so I took some pics before descending to the river. I wandered downstream slowly past the Pyramid and found a cave and a deep pool with hundreds of fish … I was a bit hot on the way back and so jumped in another pool – the water was pretty cool but refreshing!"*

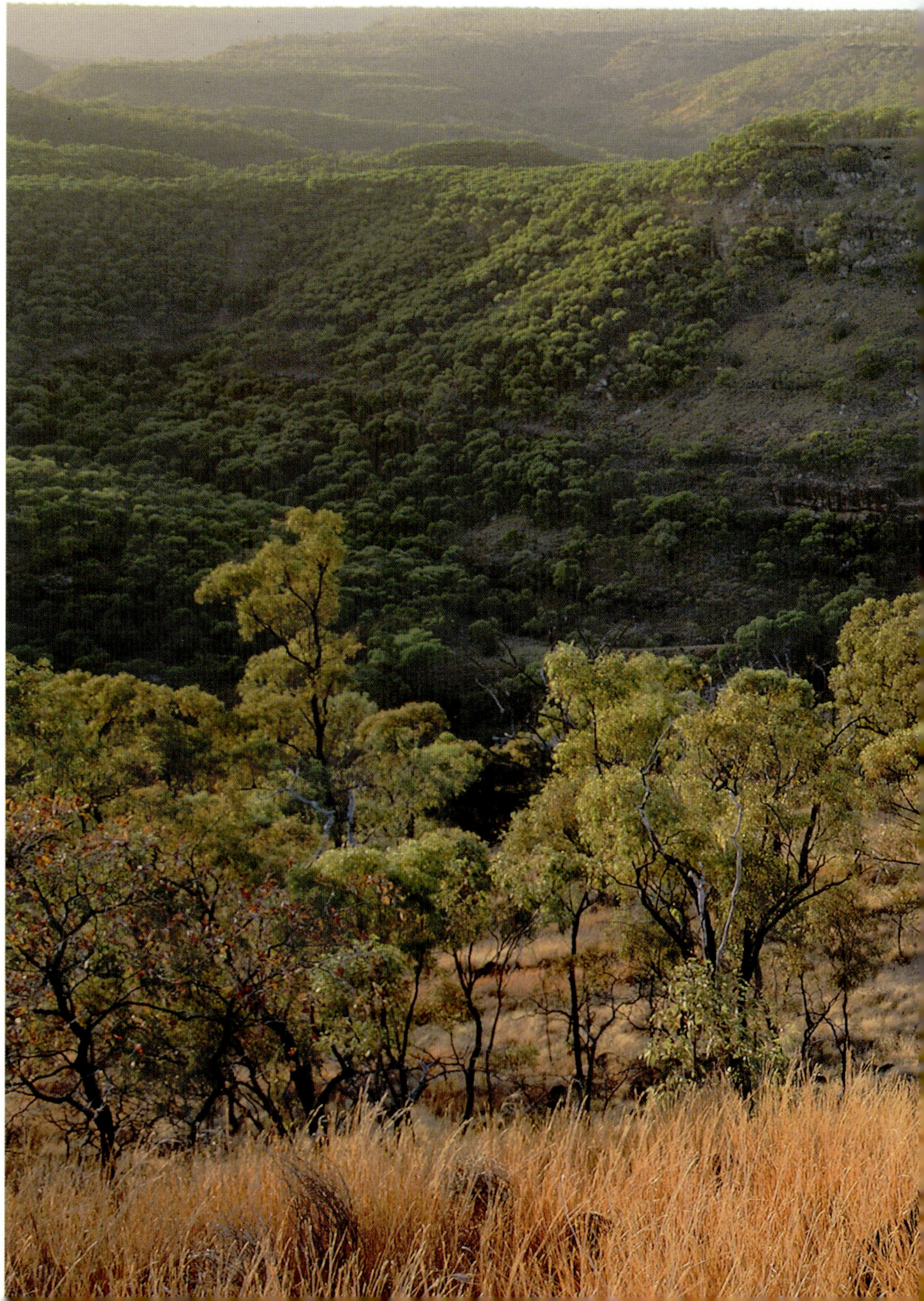

Dry savannah grasses on the edge of Porcupine Gorge.

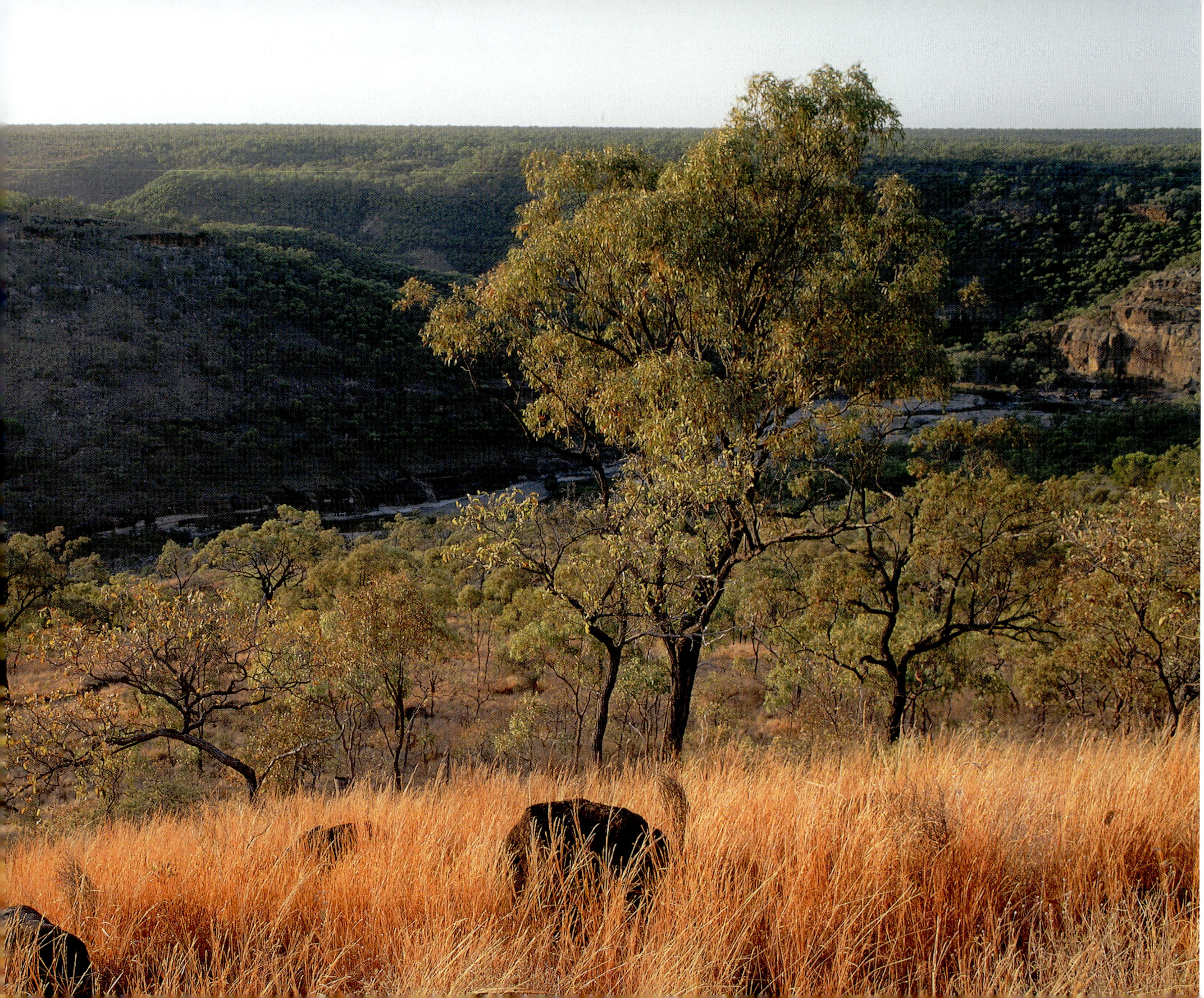

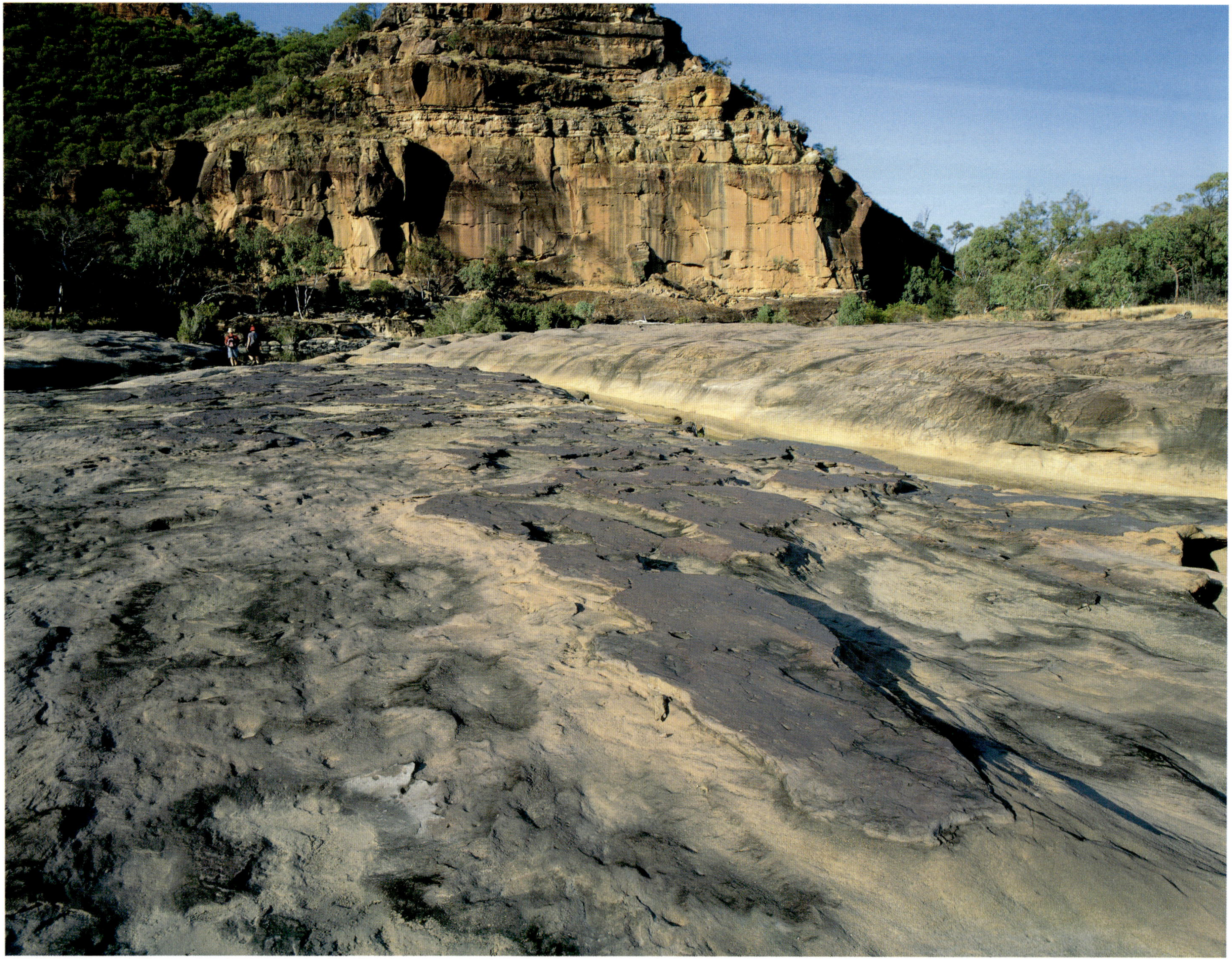

Flood worn rock slabs below the sandstone formation known as the Pyramid.

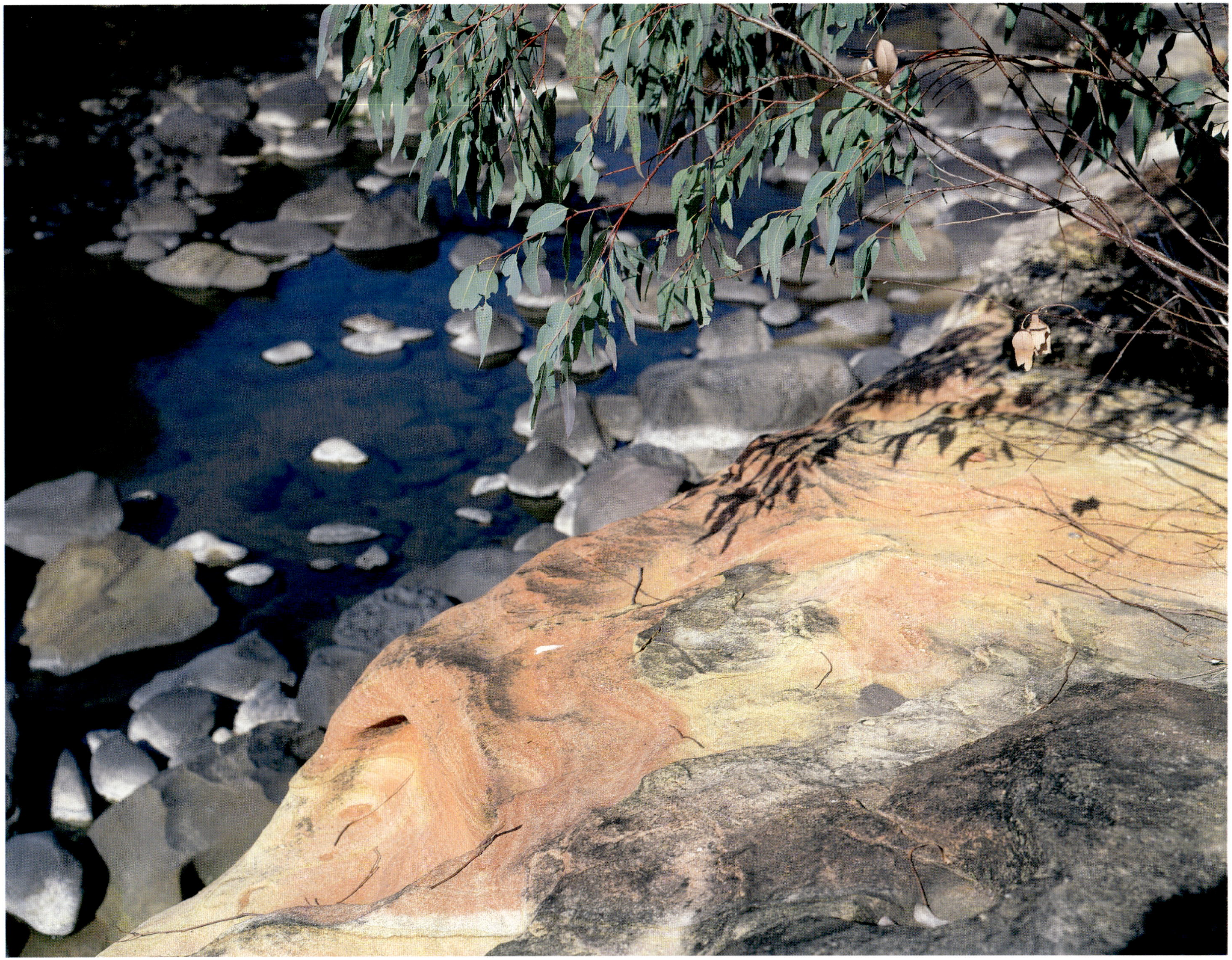

Colourful sandstone and gum leaves above Porcupine Creek.

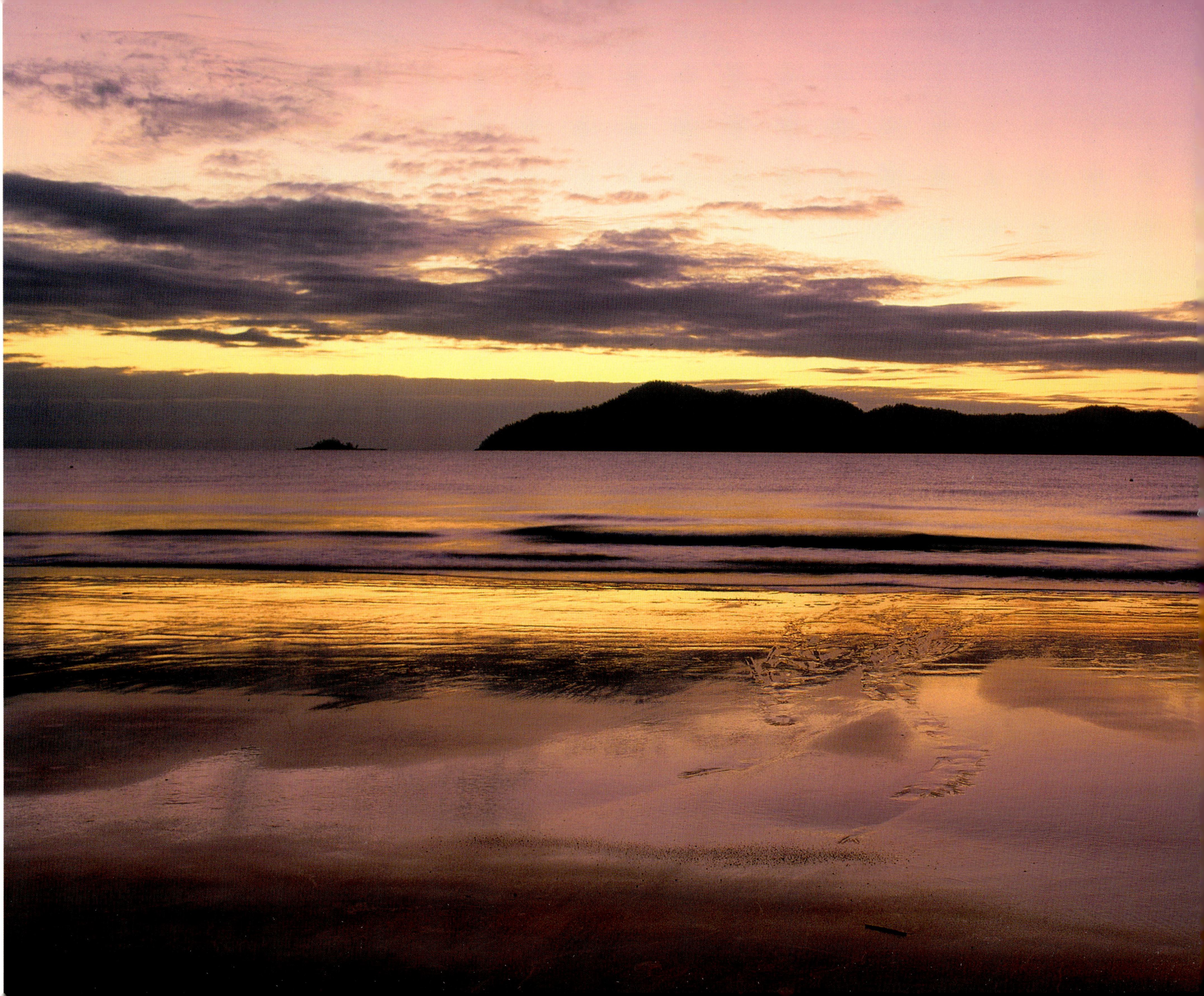

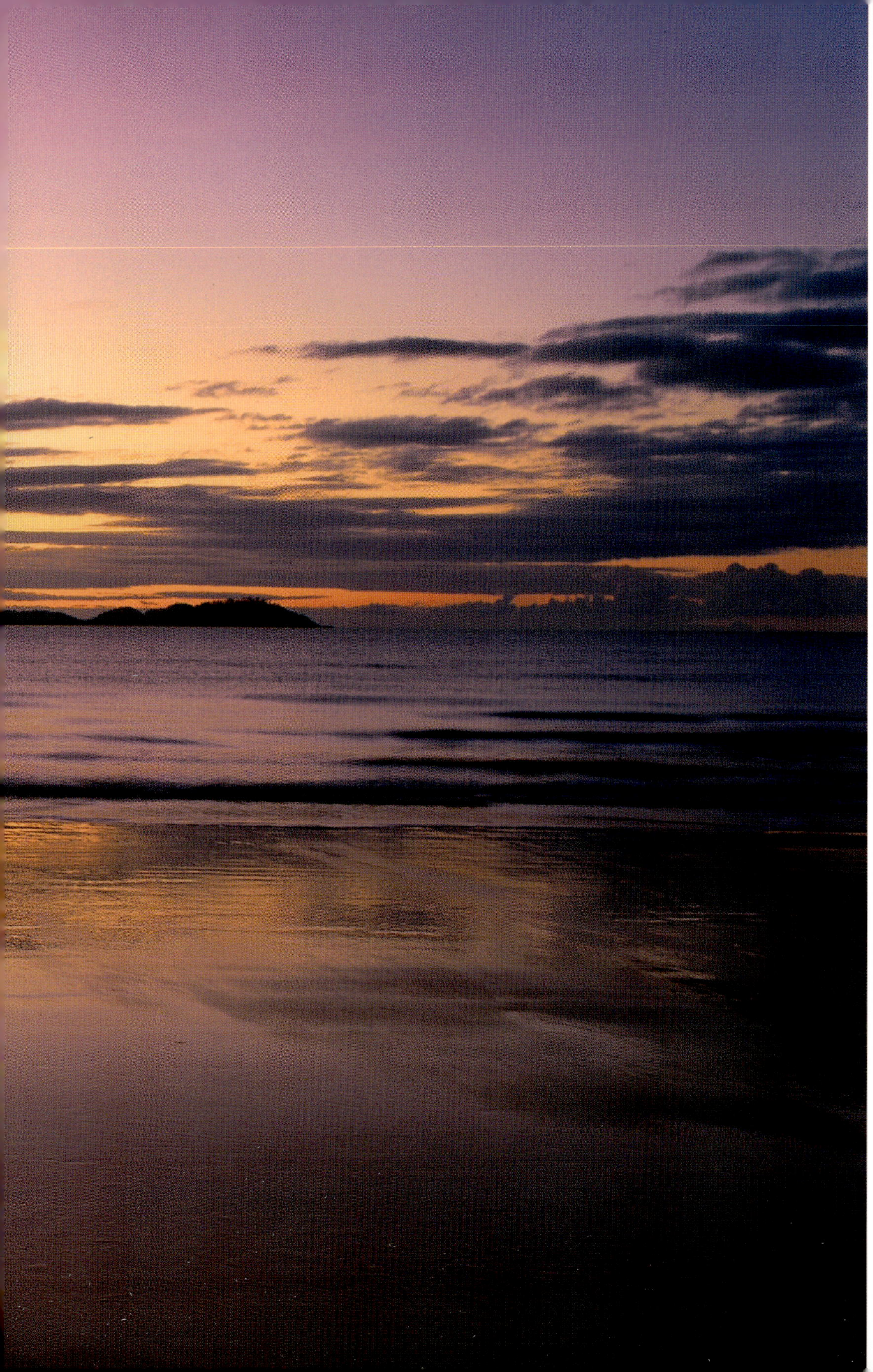

The Great Barrier Reef stretches for about 2600 kilometres in the Coral Sea, from near Gladstone to just south of Papua New Guinea. It is the most extensive reef system in the world and exists here because of the wide plateau of the continental shelf in Northern Queensland. The reef has about 4000 species of coral and 1500 species of fish; and has some 900 coral atolls and continental islands dotted along its length. A large part of the reef is protected in the Great Barrier Reef Marine Park, and virtually all of it is also a World Heritage Area.

A beautiful dawn at South Mission Beach looking out to Dunk Island which lies four kilometres offshore.

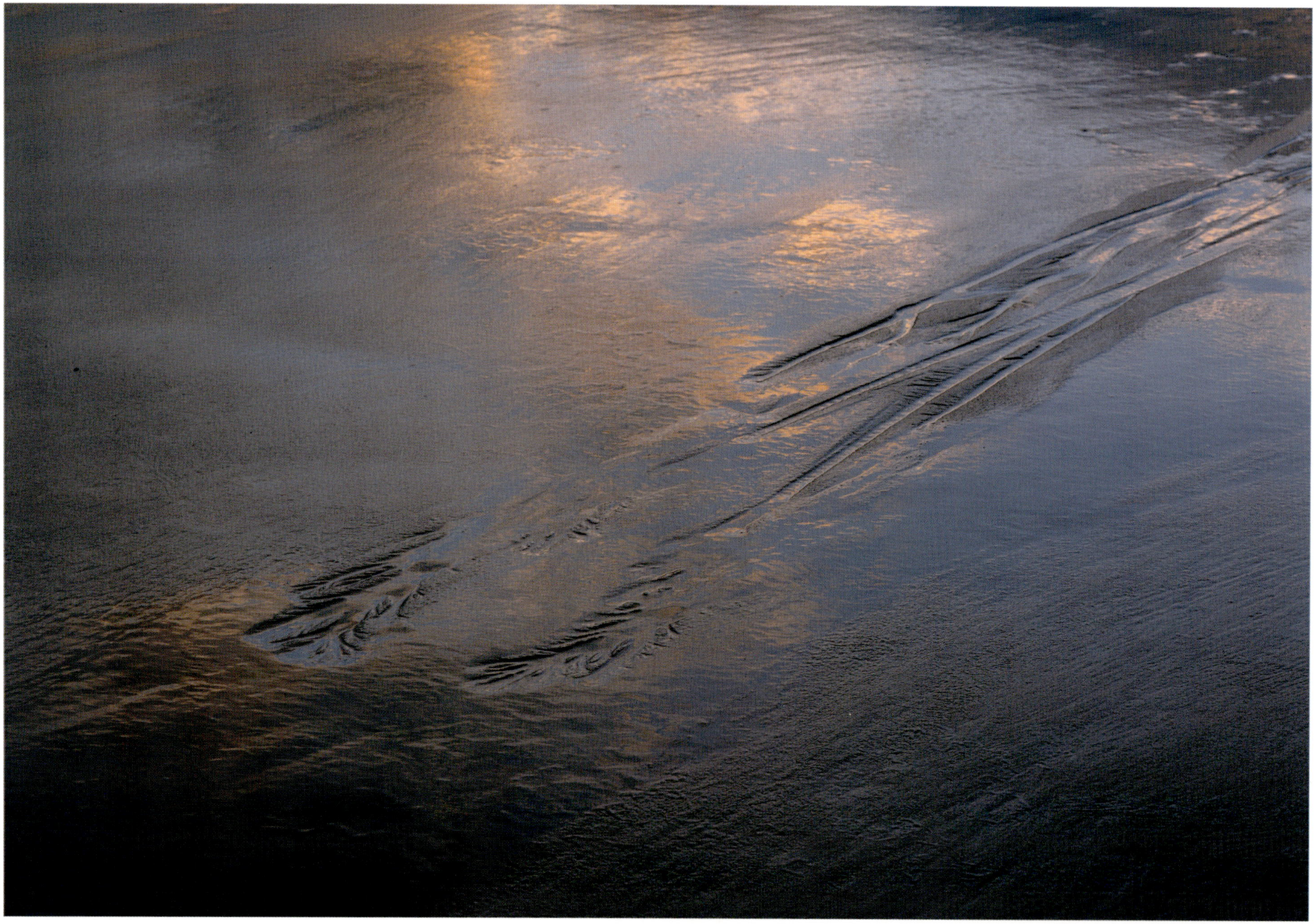

Top: Sunrise reflections on the sands of South Mission Beach.

Opposite page: The Great Barrier Reef off Cairns from the air.

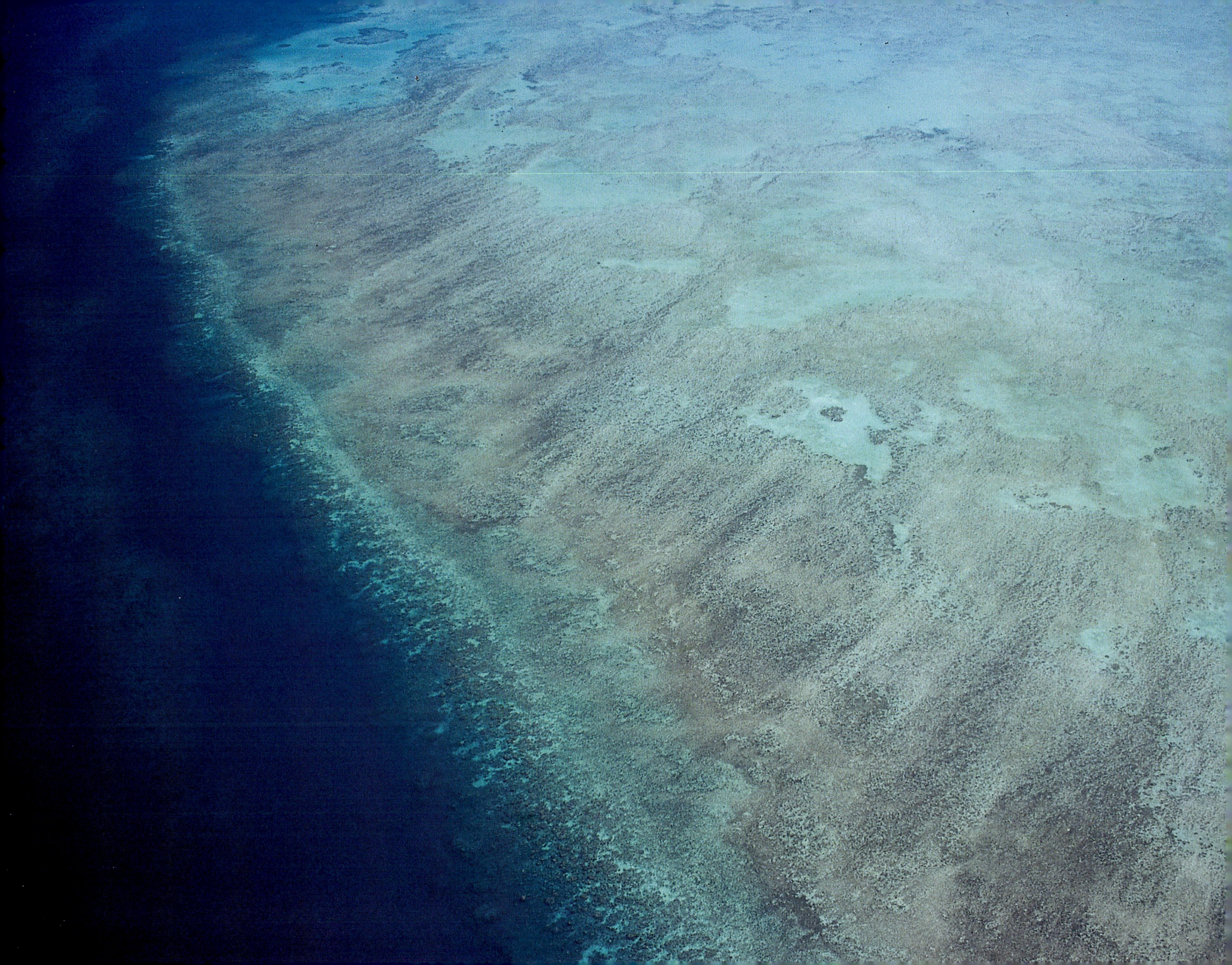

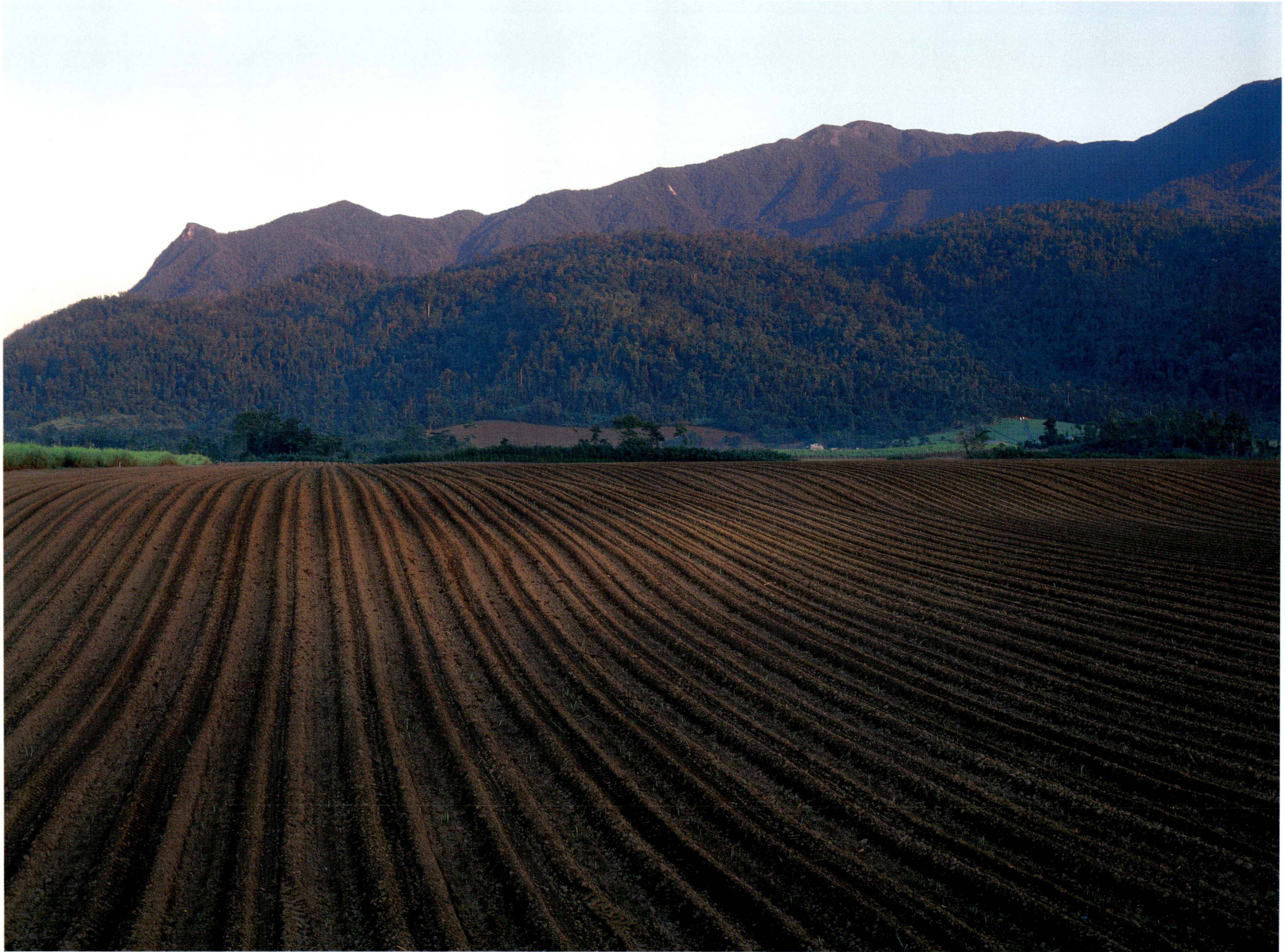

Ploughed cane fields below Mount Bartle Frere.

Mount Bartle Frere (1611m) is the highest mountain in Queensland and is part of the Wet Tropics of Queensland World Heritage Area. I decided to climb the mountain in August 2011. *"I couldn't sleep most of last night because I was hyped up about the climb today. I got up at 6am and drove across, stopping to take dawn pics of the mountain over a ploughed field. It was a brilliantly clear and cold morning with mist in the valleys. I headed to the carpark, threw stuff in the backpack and started out. The first part of the track was ok and eventually you come to a crossroads with one path to Broken Nose and the other to the summit – you can guess which path I chose! It was exceptionally steep in places ... and I did it although it took 11 hours up and back."*

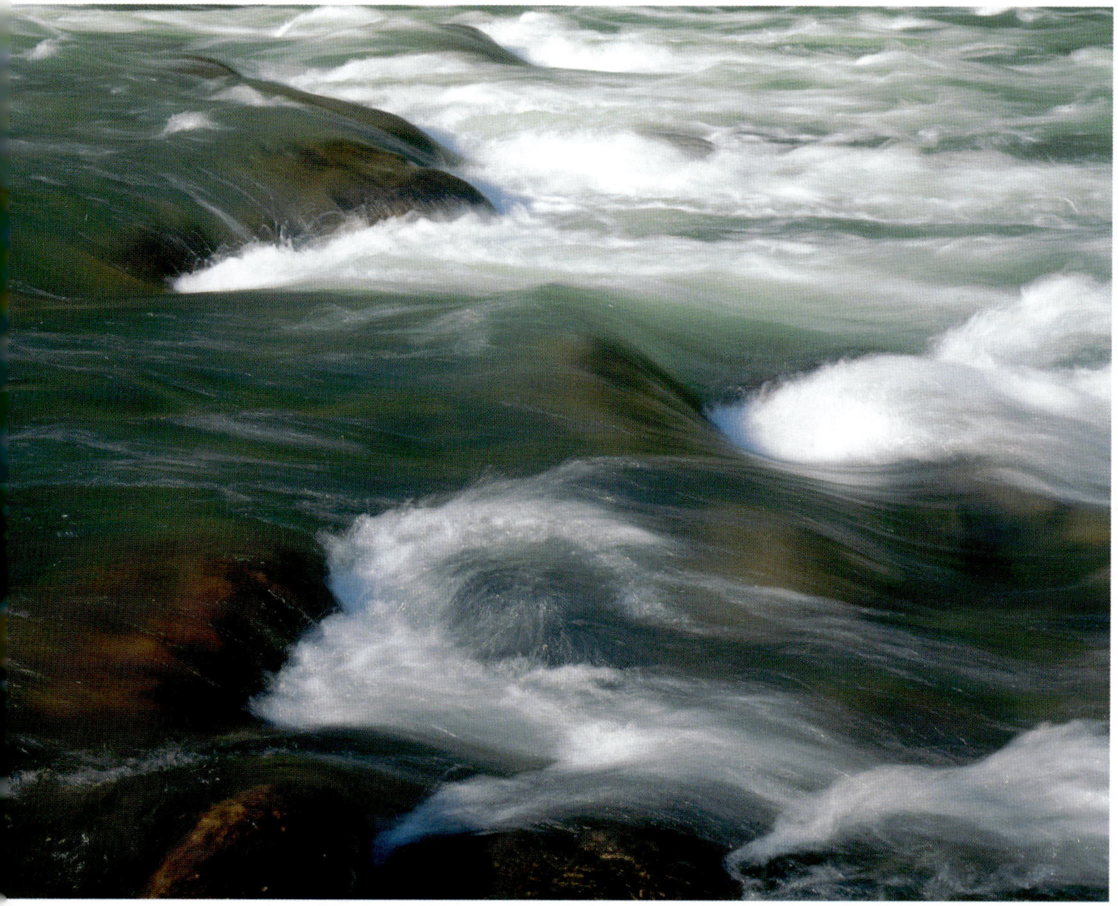

Rapids on the Tully River.

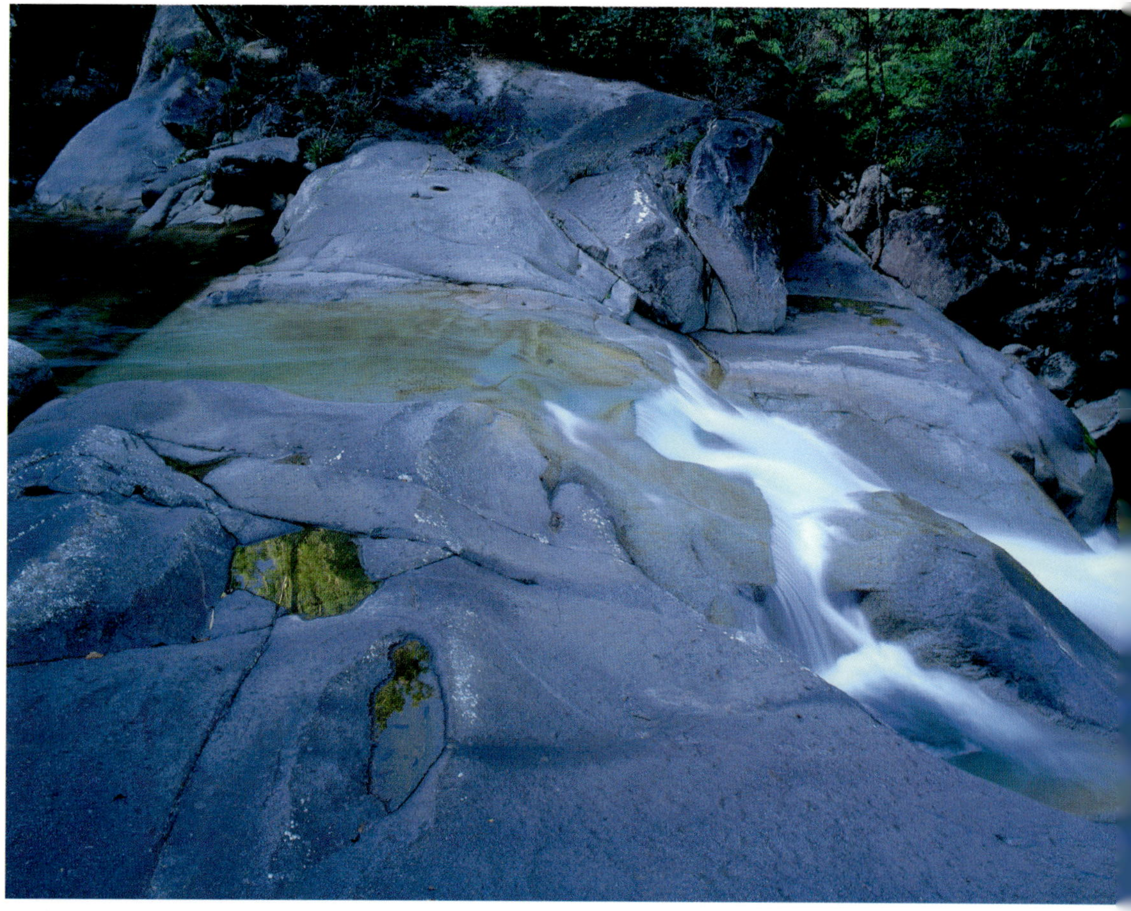

Water cascades over smooth granite rocks at Josephine Falls, at the base of Mt Bartle Frere.

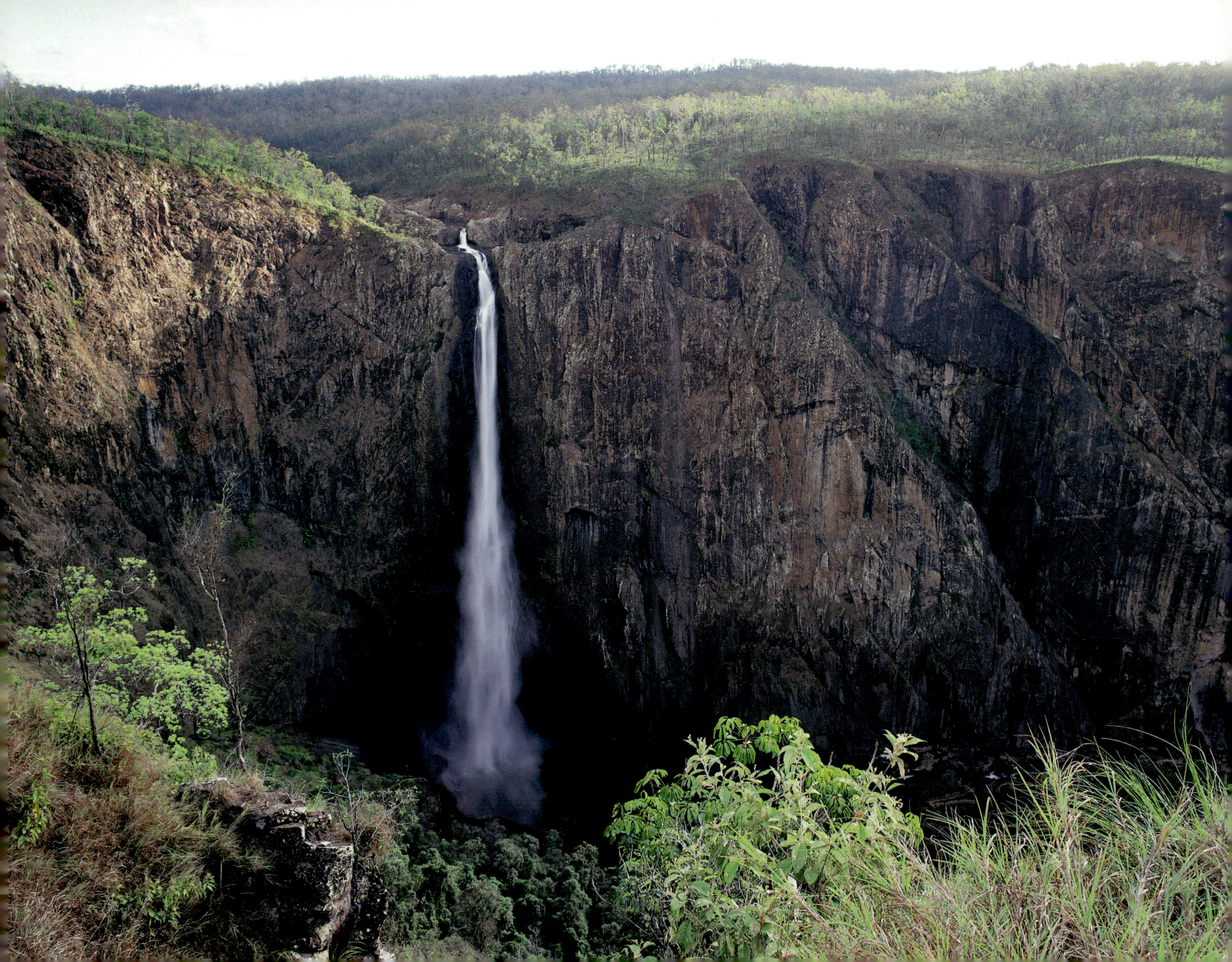

Wallaman Falls is the highest clear drop waterfall in Australia at 305 metres. The falls are protected in Lumholtz National Park, about 50 kilometres west of the town of Ingham in Far North Queensland, and are part of the Wet Tropics of Queensland World Heritage area. An annual rainfall of over two metres has scoured out a gorge below the falls up to 500 metres deep.

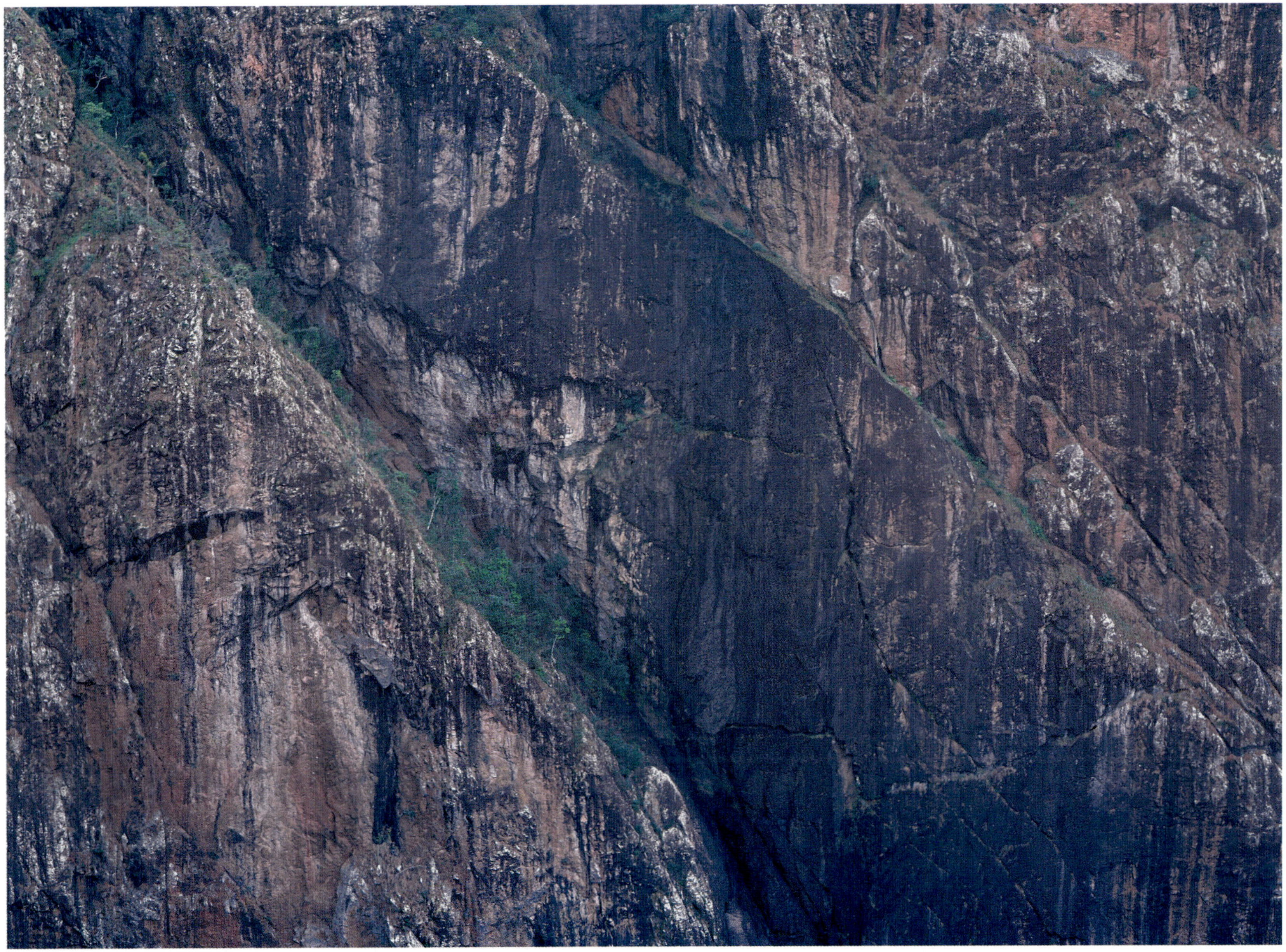

Top: Rain streaked rock walls at Wallaman Falls.

Opposite page: Stony Creek plunges off the Seaview Range to create the spectacular Wallaman Falls.

The Paluma Range National Park is the southernmost part of the Wet Tropics of Queensland World Heritage area, a group of rainforest reserves that have the highest concentration of primitive flowering plant families in the world. The national park includes the spectacular Jourama Falls and rainforest around Paluma, a mountain village an hour north west of Townsville lying at an altitude of 1000 metres. The Aboriginal name for the Paluma Range is Munan Gumburu, which means "misty mountain" – an apt name indeed.

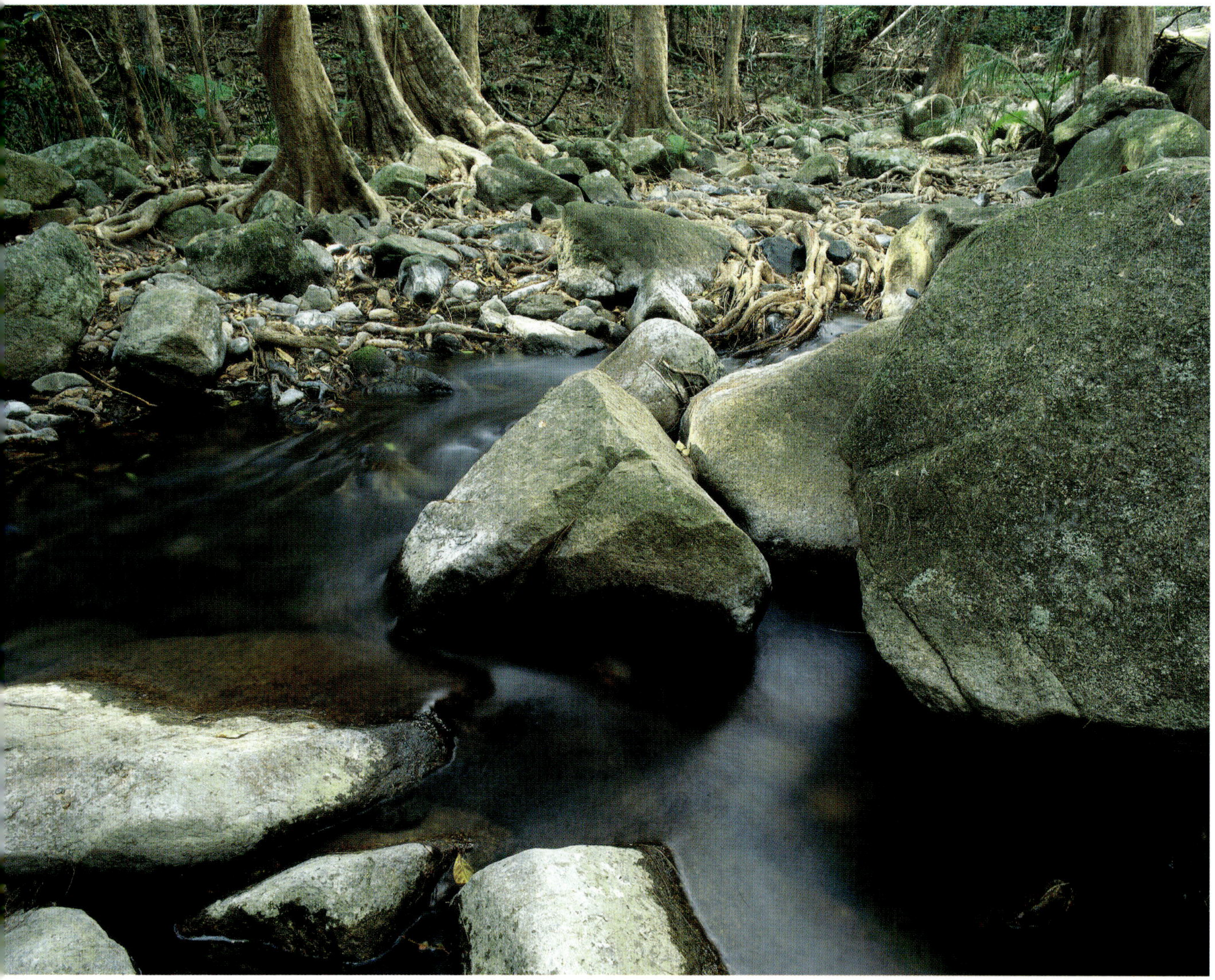

The rocky Waterview Creek and rainforest at Jourama Falls.

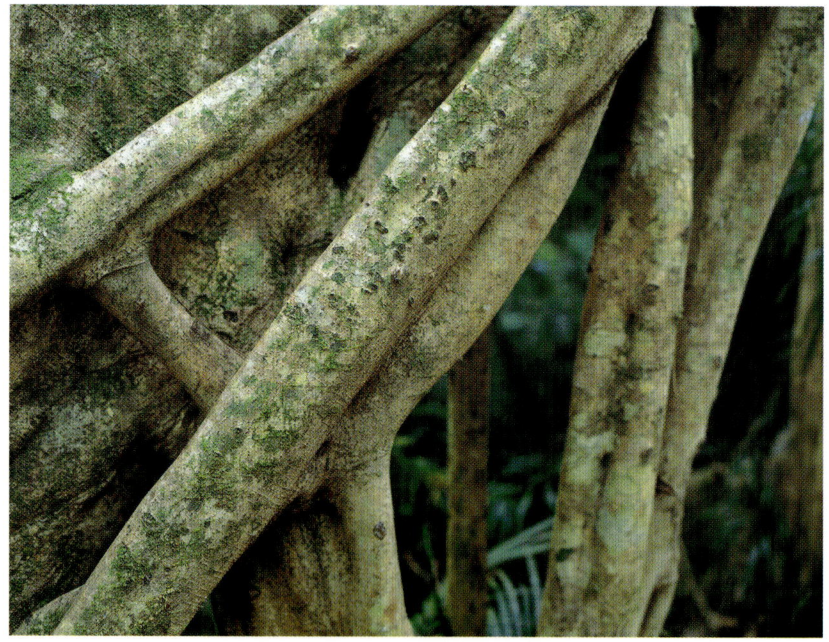

Top: The intricate trunk system of a giant strangler fig tree at Paluma.

Opposite page: Interesting "banded" rock at Jourama Falls, 91 kilometres north of Townsville.

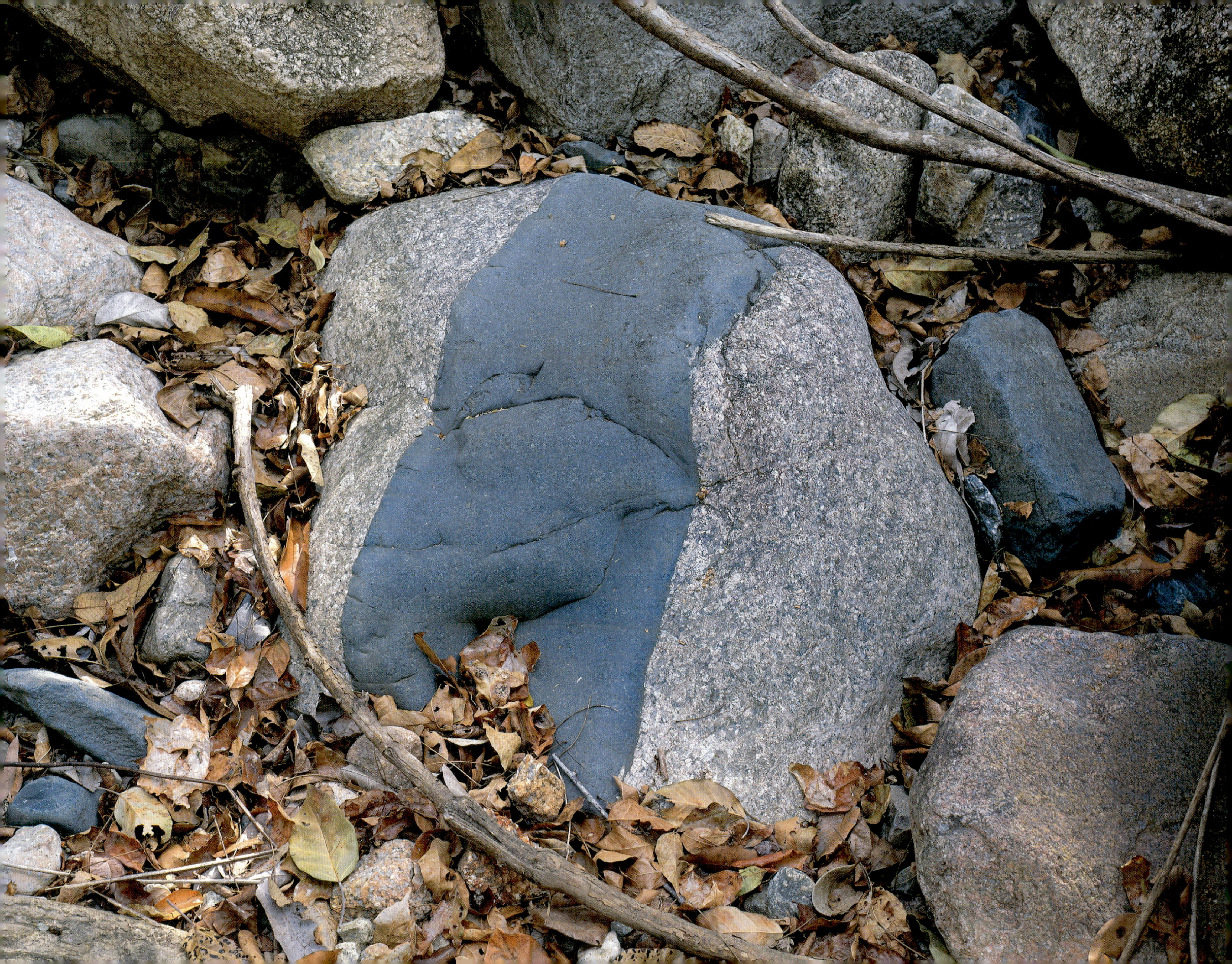

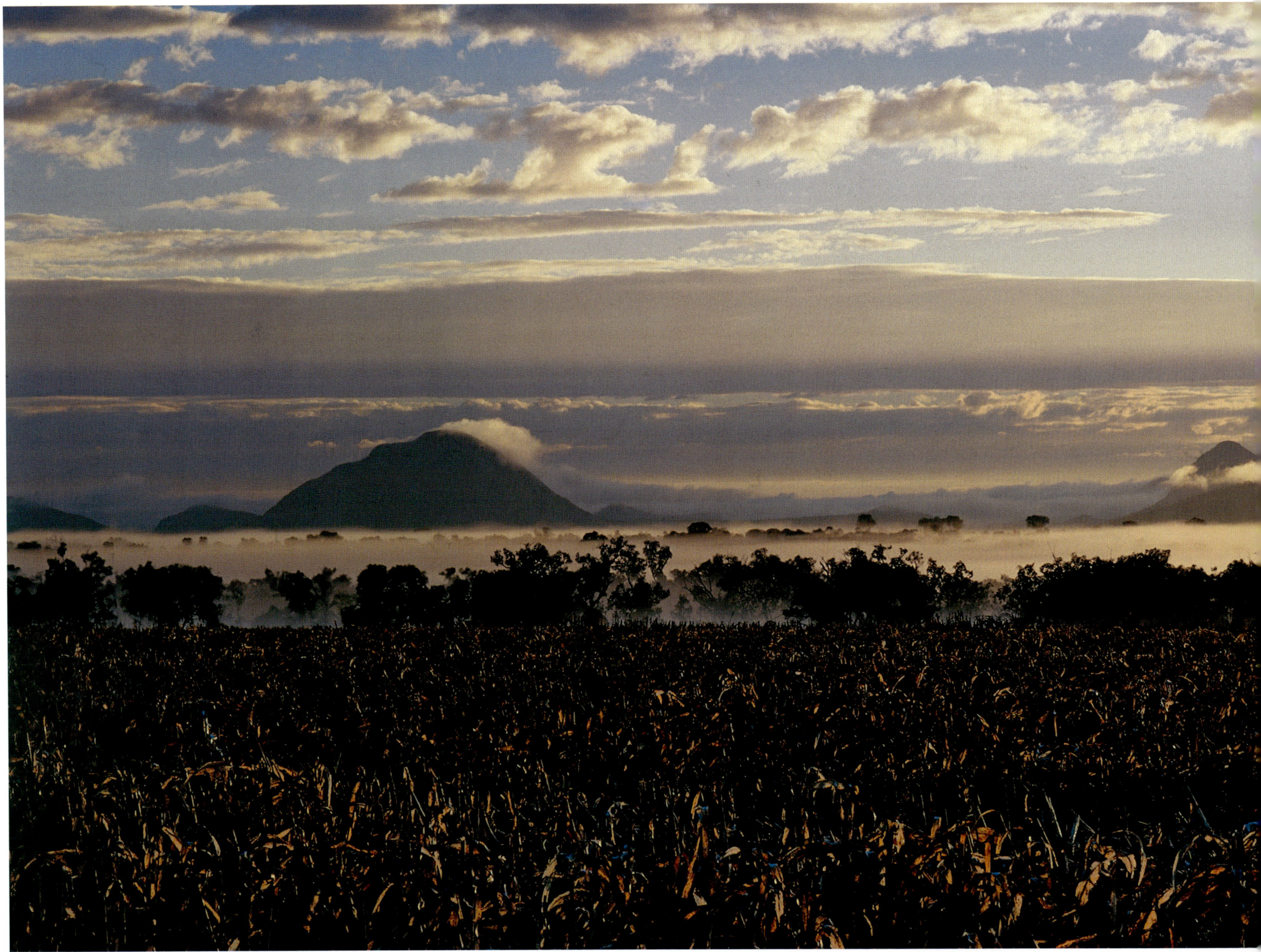

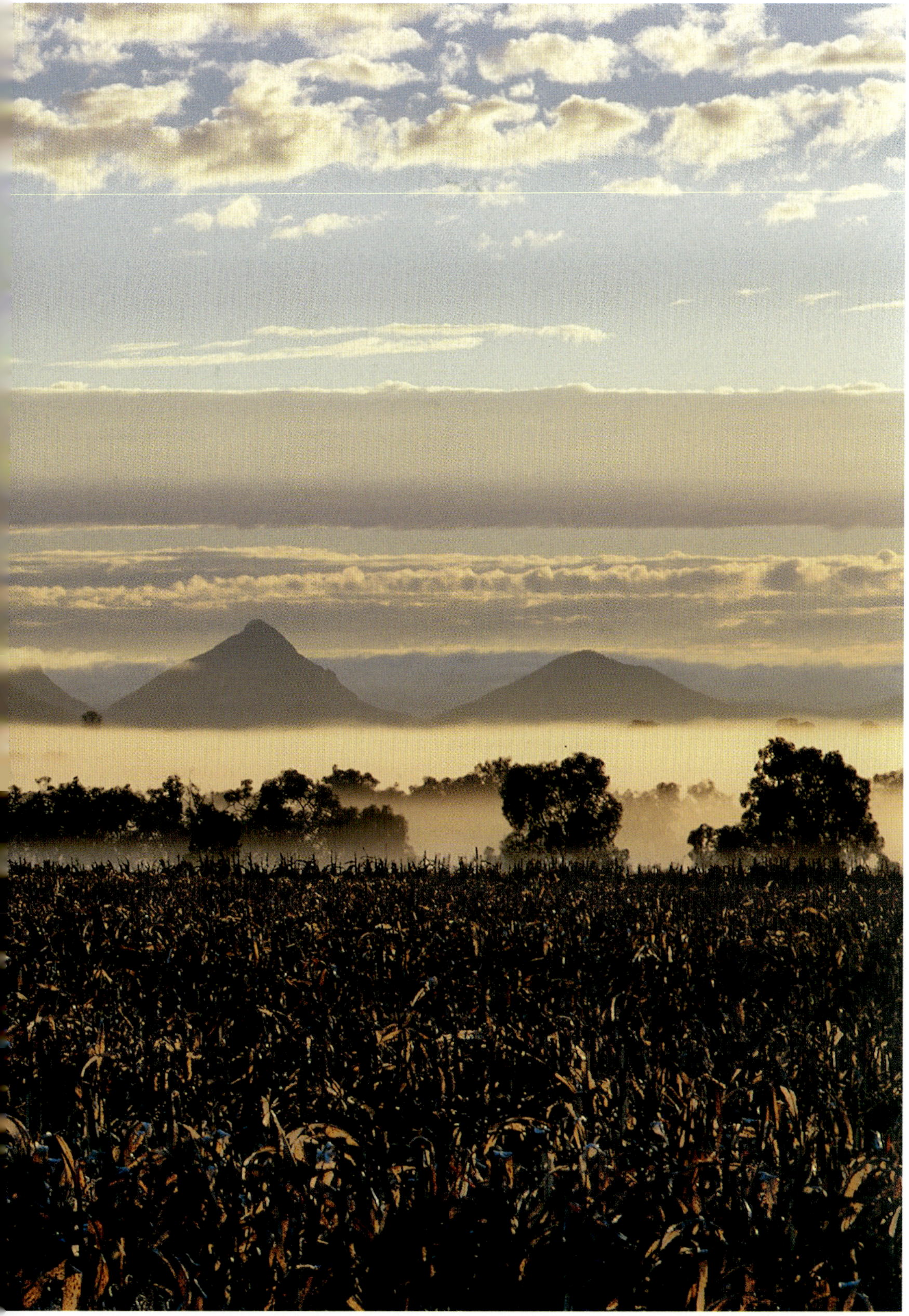

Dawn mists over the mysterious mountains of the Peak Range in central Queensland.

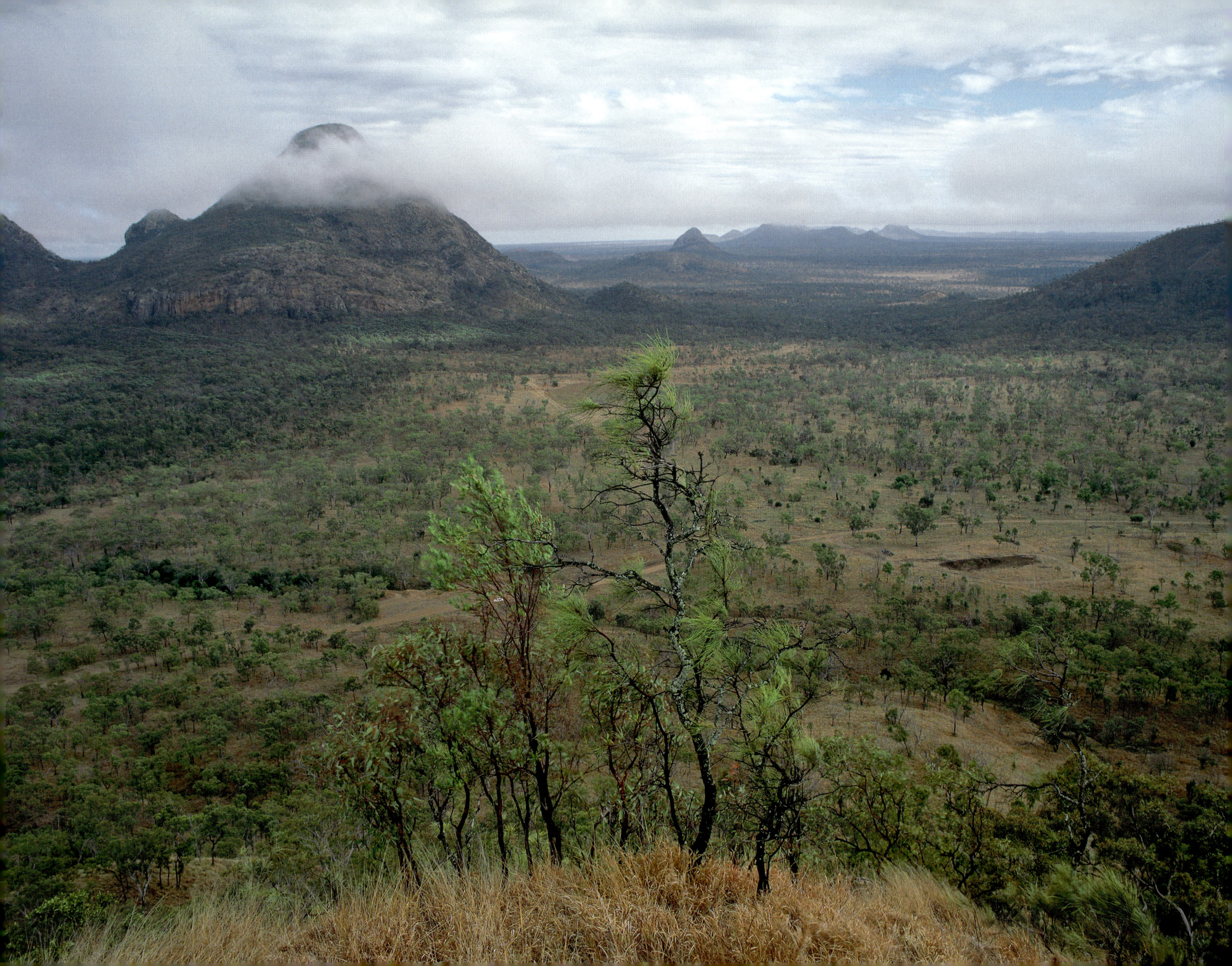

The Peak Range National Park protects a series of volcanic plugs, near the small towns of Clermont and Capella in central Queensland. I had wanted to explore them for many years and finally got the chance on my trip around Australia when I stayed at Capella for a couple of nights. I wrote *"they were spectacular isolated peaks rising out of a flat plain and all shapes and sizes. I got up at dawn and drove towards Dysart through early morning mist. After about 20 minutes I crested a rise and the peaks rose in front of me enveloped in clouds and mist."*

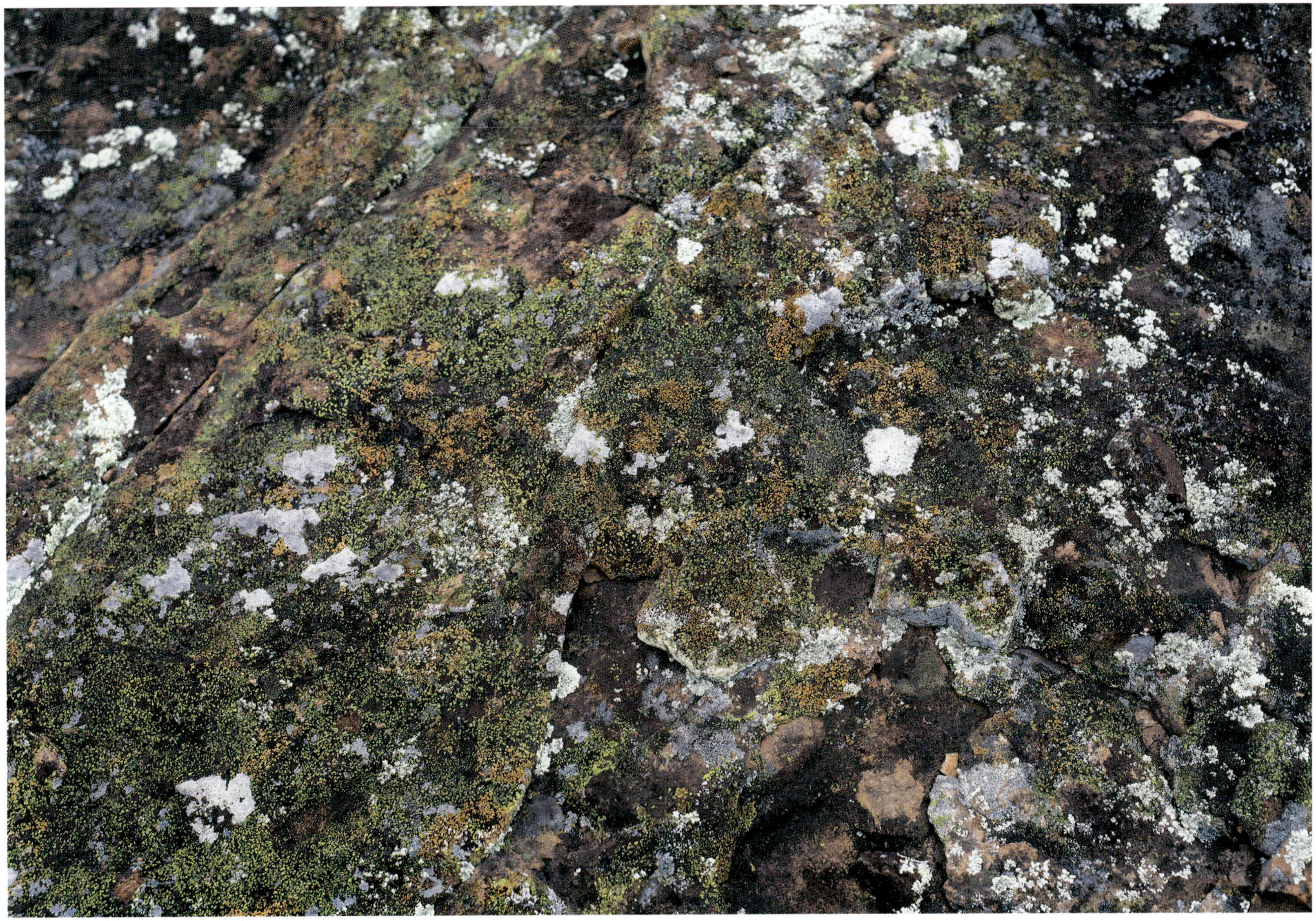

Top: Unusually coloured lichen on a volcanic rock, Peak Range.

Opposite page: Looking across to Scotts Peak (755m) from a small hill in the range. Note my Camry on a gravel road in the distance!

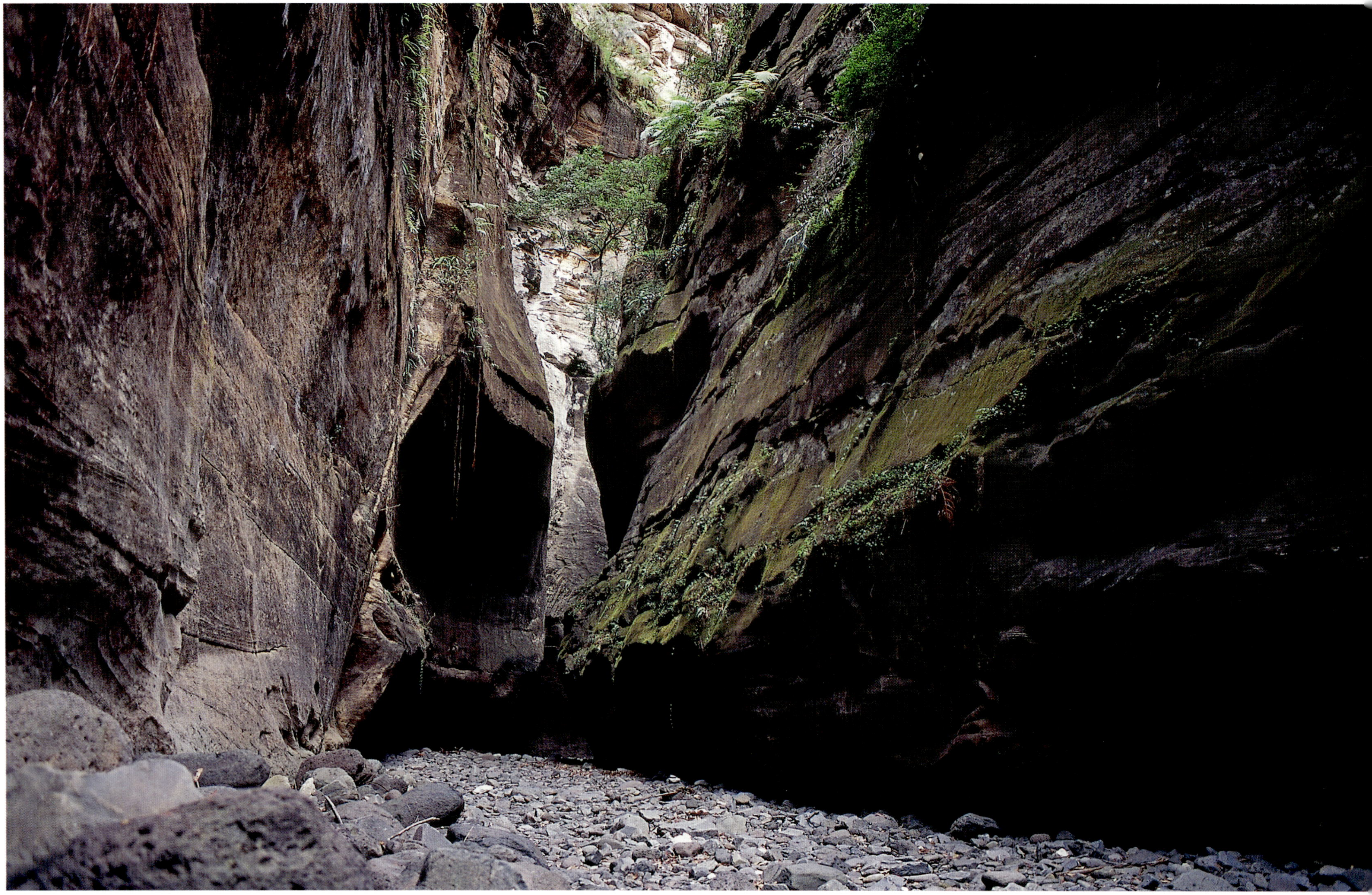

There are many side canyons from the main gorge, including basalt cobbled Boowinda Gorge.

Carnarvon National Park, in central Queensland, is one of Australia's great scenic reserves. Its most famous feature is Carnarvon Gorge, carved through white cliffs of Precipice sandstone dating back 190 to 135 million years ago. A higher tableland behind the cliffs is composed of basalt from a relatively recent lava flow of about 28 million years ago. The gorge has been occupied by Aboriginal people for almost 20,000 years, and their presence is recorded in engravings, paintings and hand stencils. I spent a few nights here and enjoyed exploring features like the Amphitheatre and the Moss Garden, and the ancient rock art galleries of the gorge.

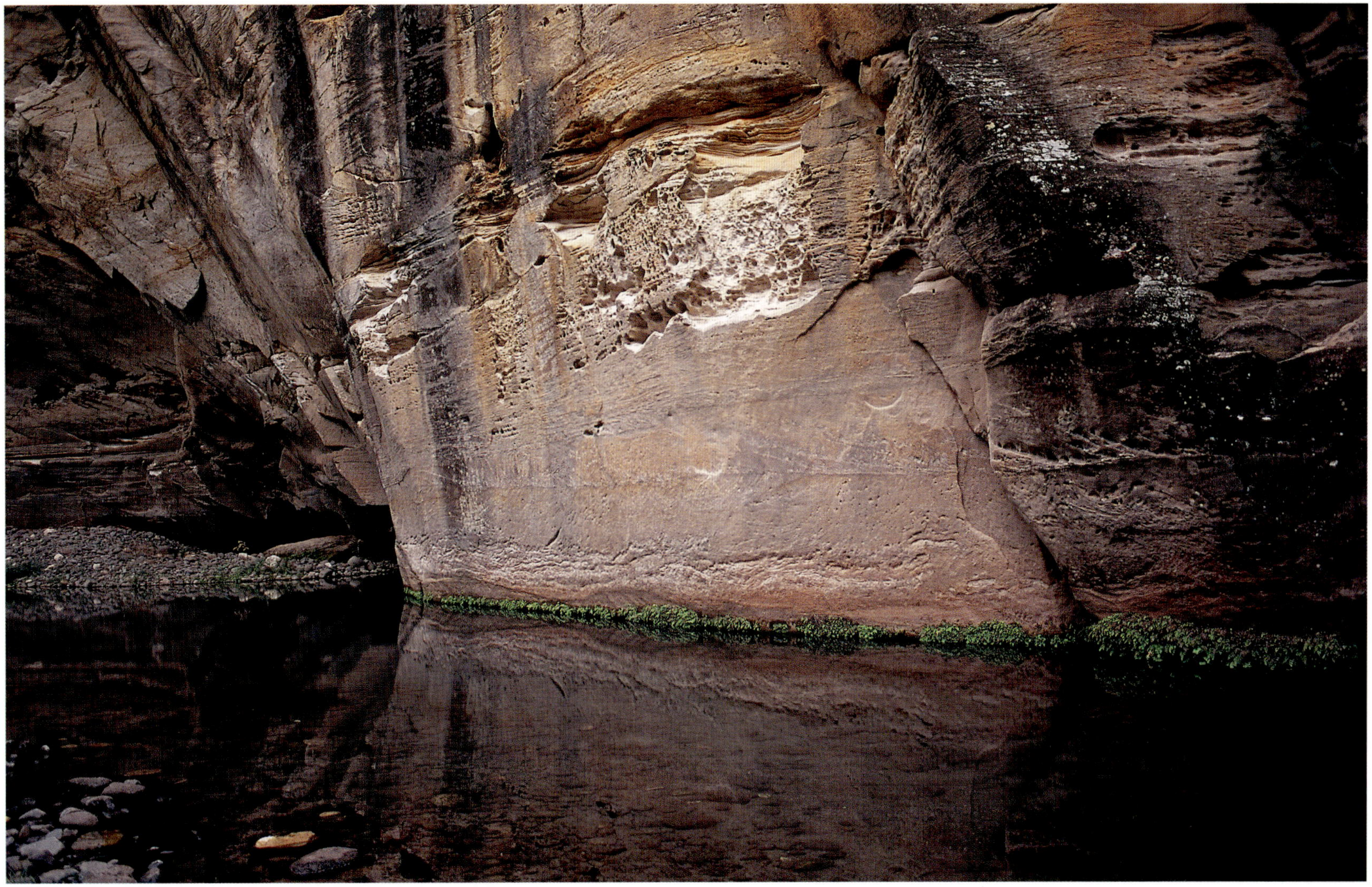

A sandstone wall and a pool at Big Bend near an overnight campsite for hikers, about nine kilometres from the park headquarters.

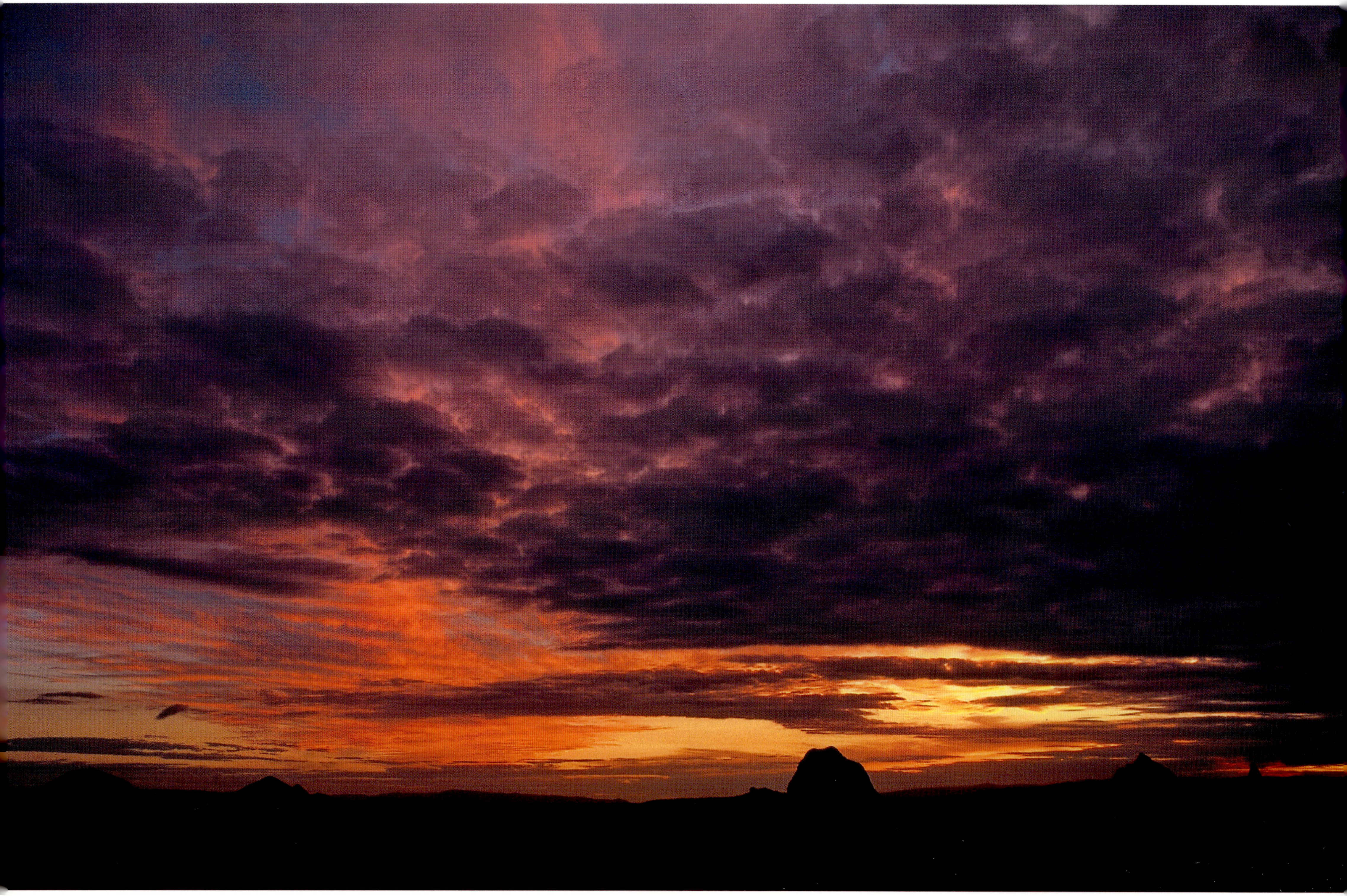

Sunset colours over the distinctive shapes of the Glasshouse Mountains. Tibrogargan (364m) is the prominent peak near the centre of the photograph.

The Sunshine Coast is a scenic stretch of coastline starting about 90 kilometres to the north of Brisbane. It is one of the most popular holiday destinations in Queensland, along with the Gold Coast south of Brisbane. The coast is backed by fertile farmland and ranges including spectacular volcanic plugs like the Glasshouse Mountains. A famous art, craft and produce market is held every Wednesday and Saturday at the town of Eumundi and includes live music and entertainment. There are other great markets throughout the region, like the Noosa Farmers Market, the Peregian Beach Market and the Caloundra Street Fair.

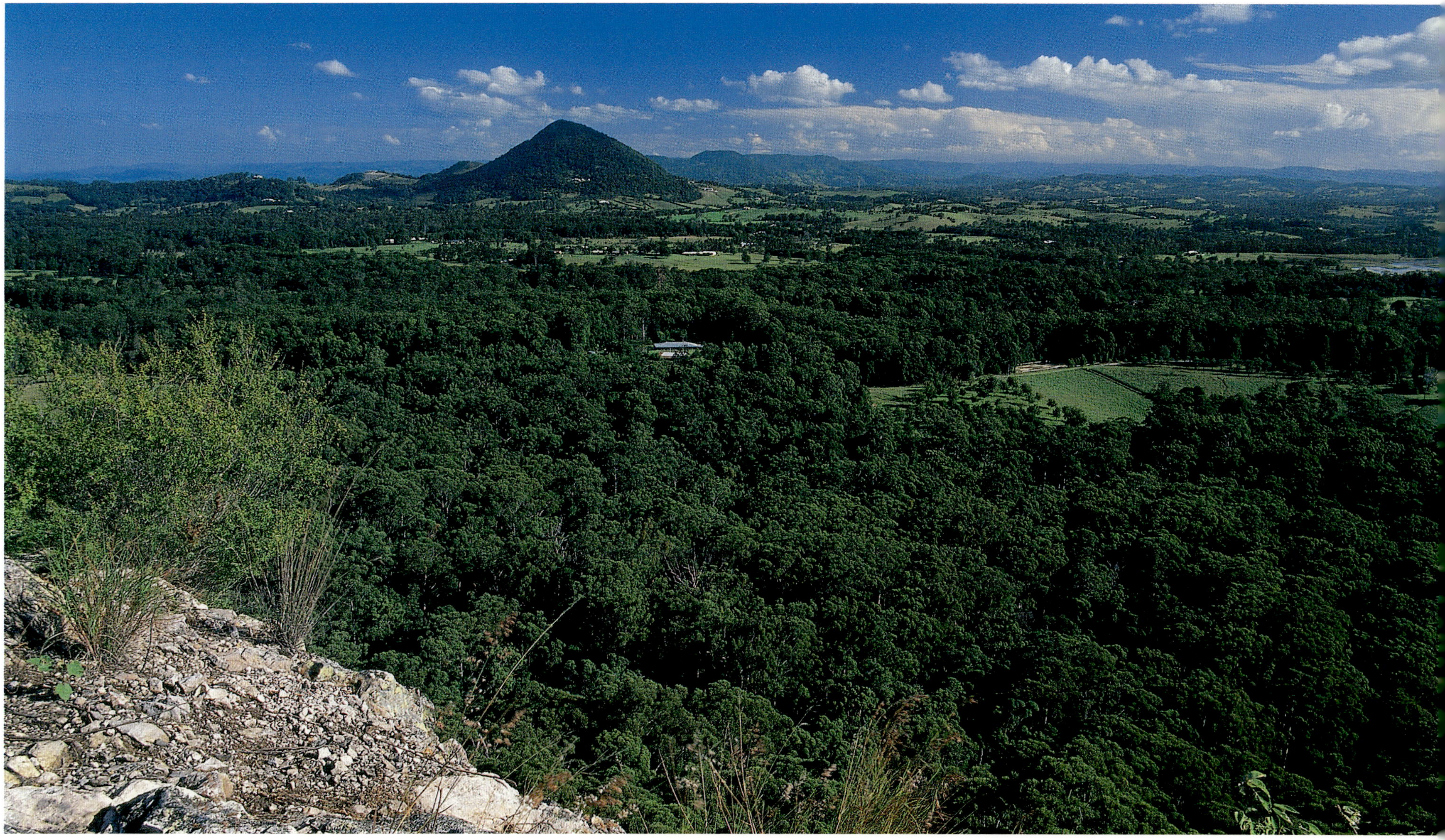

View over lush Sunshine Coast hinterland from the top of Tinbeerwah, a volcanic peak near Noosa.

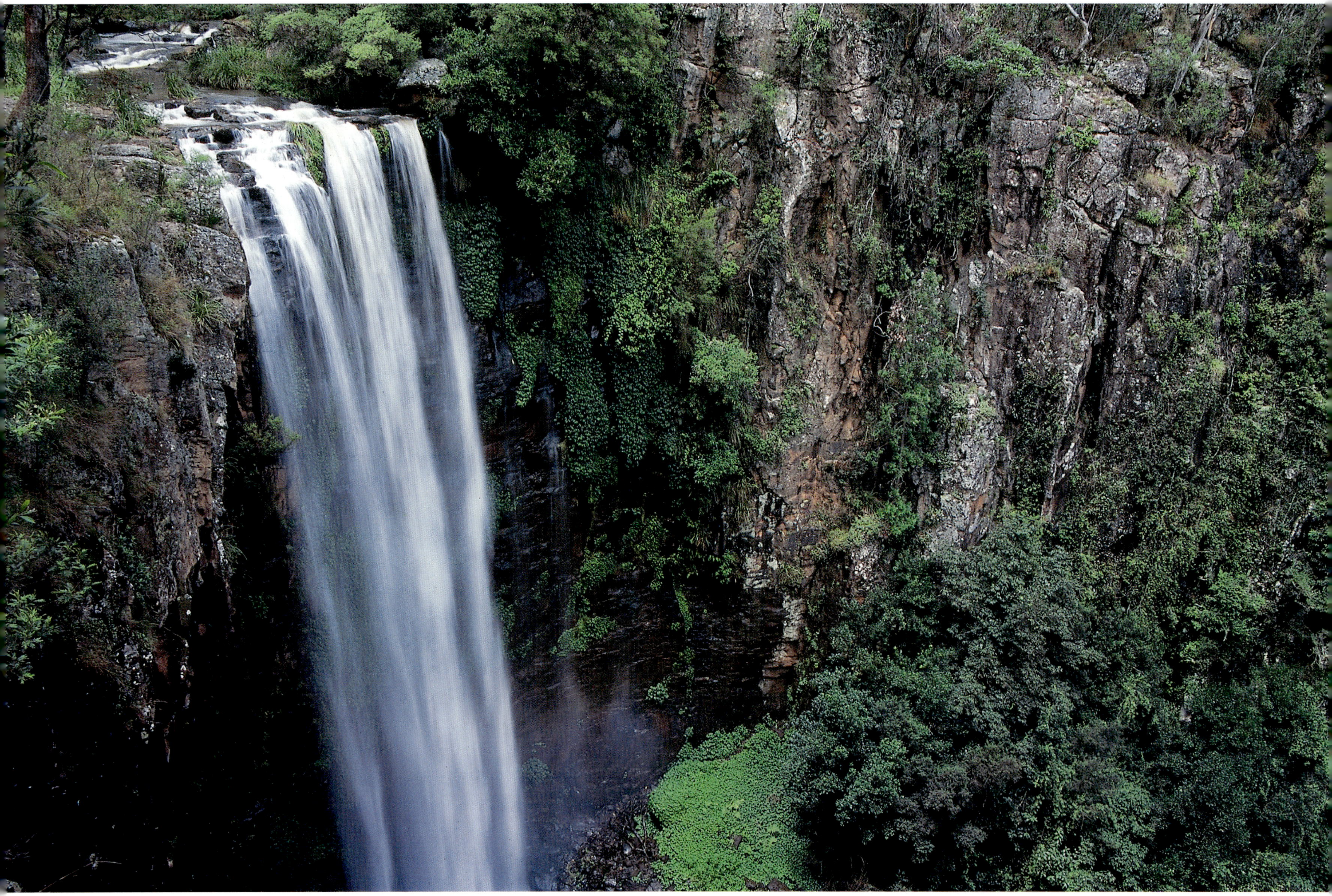

The beautiful 40 metre high Queen Mary Falls lies near the small town of Killarney.

South East Queensland is the most heavily populated part of Queensland, but also contains some of the finest wild areas in the state. A ring of mountains lies west of Brisbane and extends along the southern border with New South Wales, forming what is known as the Scenic Rim. The peaks originate from a series of ancient volcanoes. Along with my brother Stuart and other members of my family, I enjoy camping here and exploring spectacular areas like the Main Range, Mount Barney and Lamington National Park.

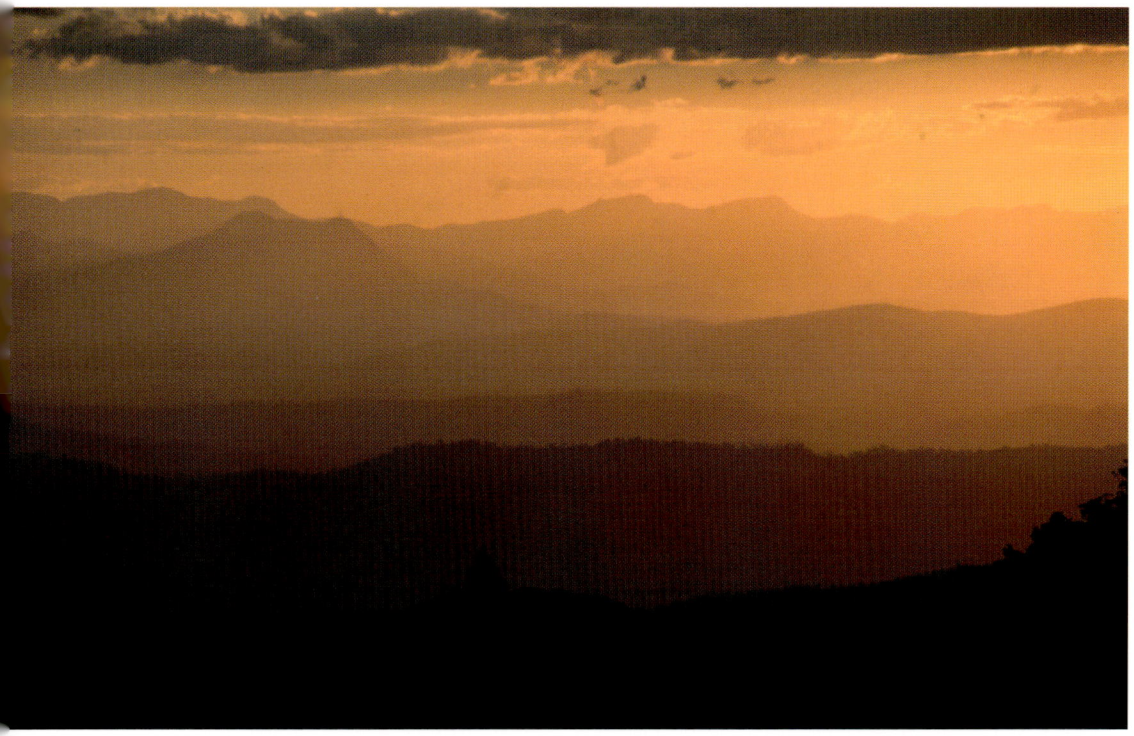

Sunset over the Main Range of South East Queensland, as seen from O'Reilly's Rainforest Guesthouse.

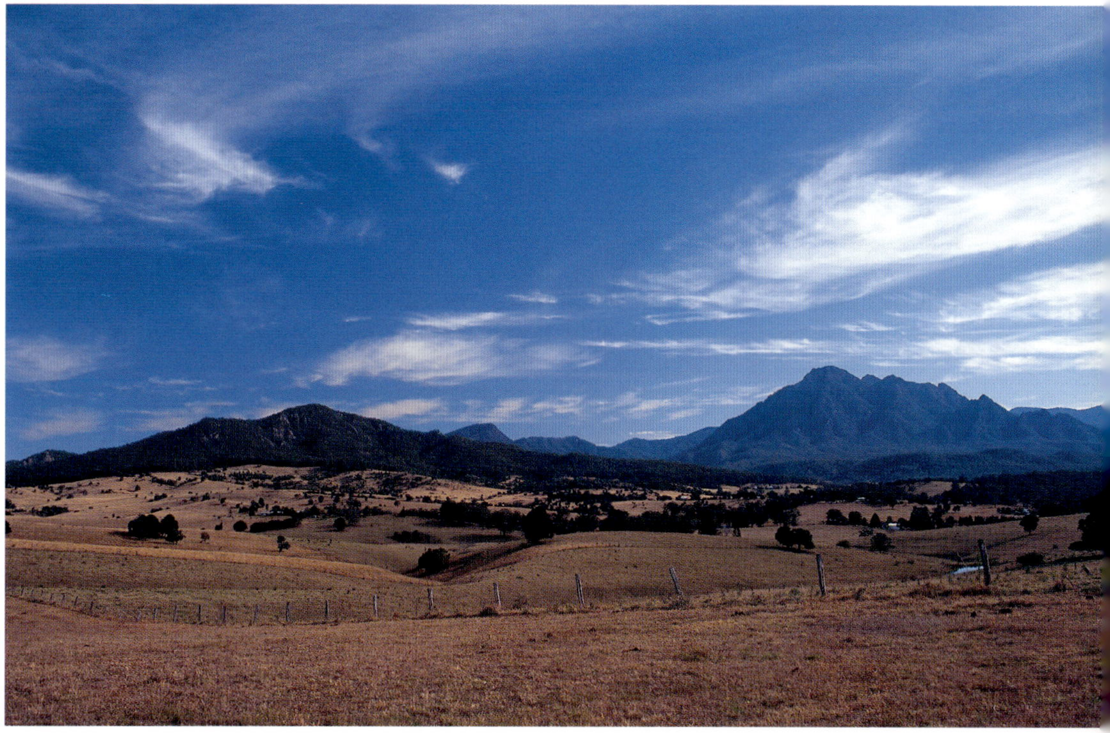

A view over rolling paddocks to Mount Barney (1359m), probably the most imposing peak in South East Queensland.

The Scenic Rim has extensive areas of rainforest that have been included in the Gondwana Rainforests of Australia World Heritage Area. These include the Main Range National Park, Mount Barney NP and Lamington NP. The latter has over 20,000 hectares of pristine wilderness; it was proclaimed in 1915 and is home to the famous Binna Burra Lodge and O'Reilly's Rainforest Guesthouse. I have stayed at both places and they are highly recommended! A network of walking tracks lead out from the guesthouses to waterfalls and scenic lookouts, through virgin rainforest alive with birdcalls.

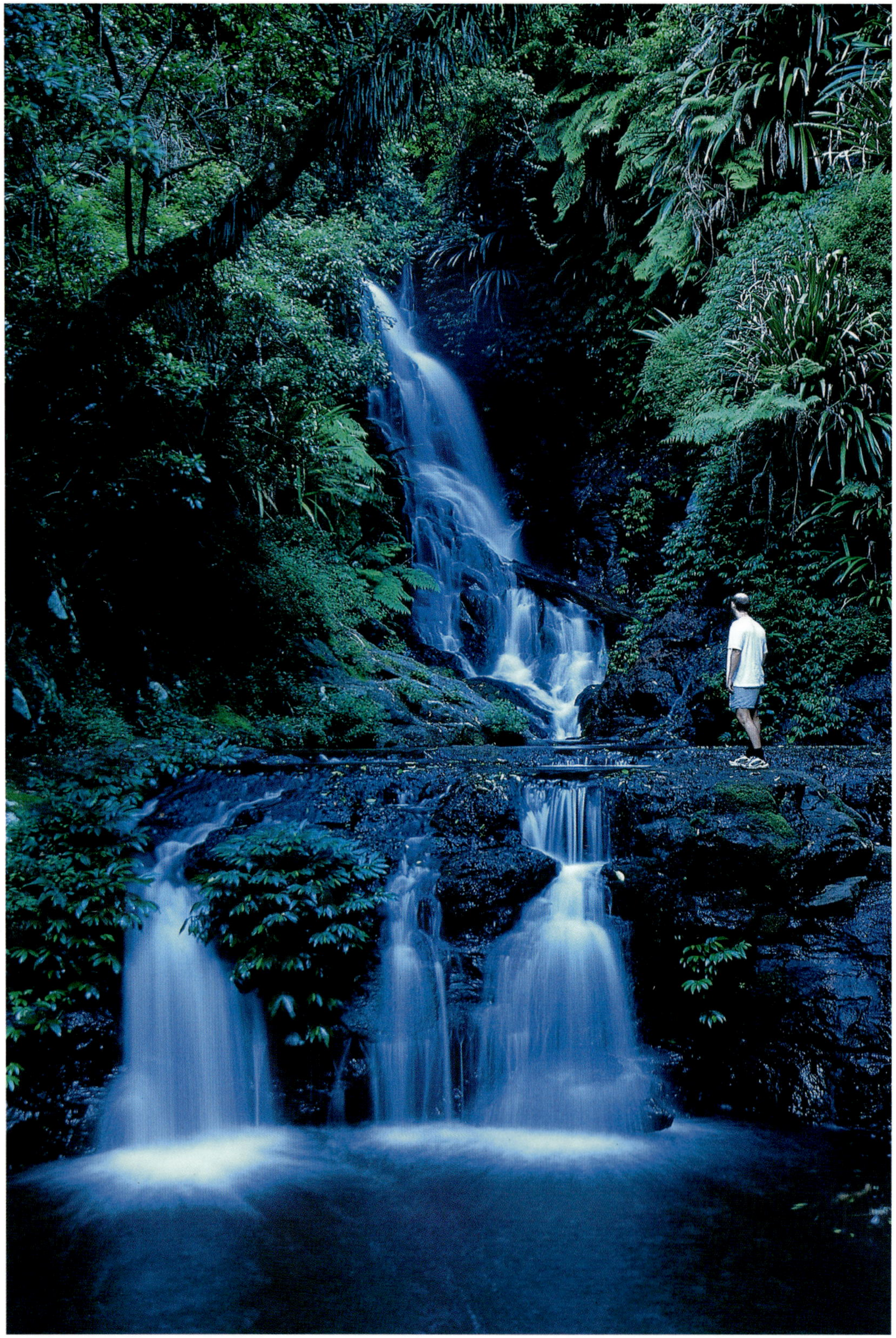

Elabana Falls is one of many beautiful waterfalls in Lamington NP.

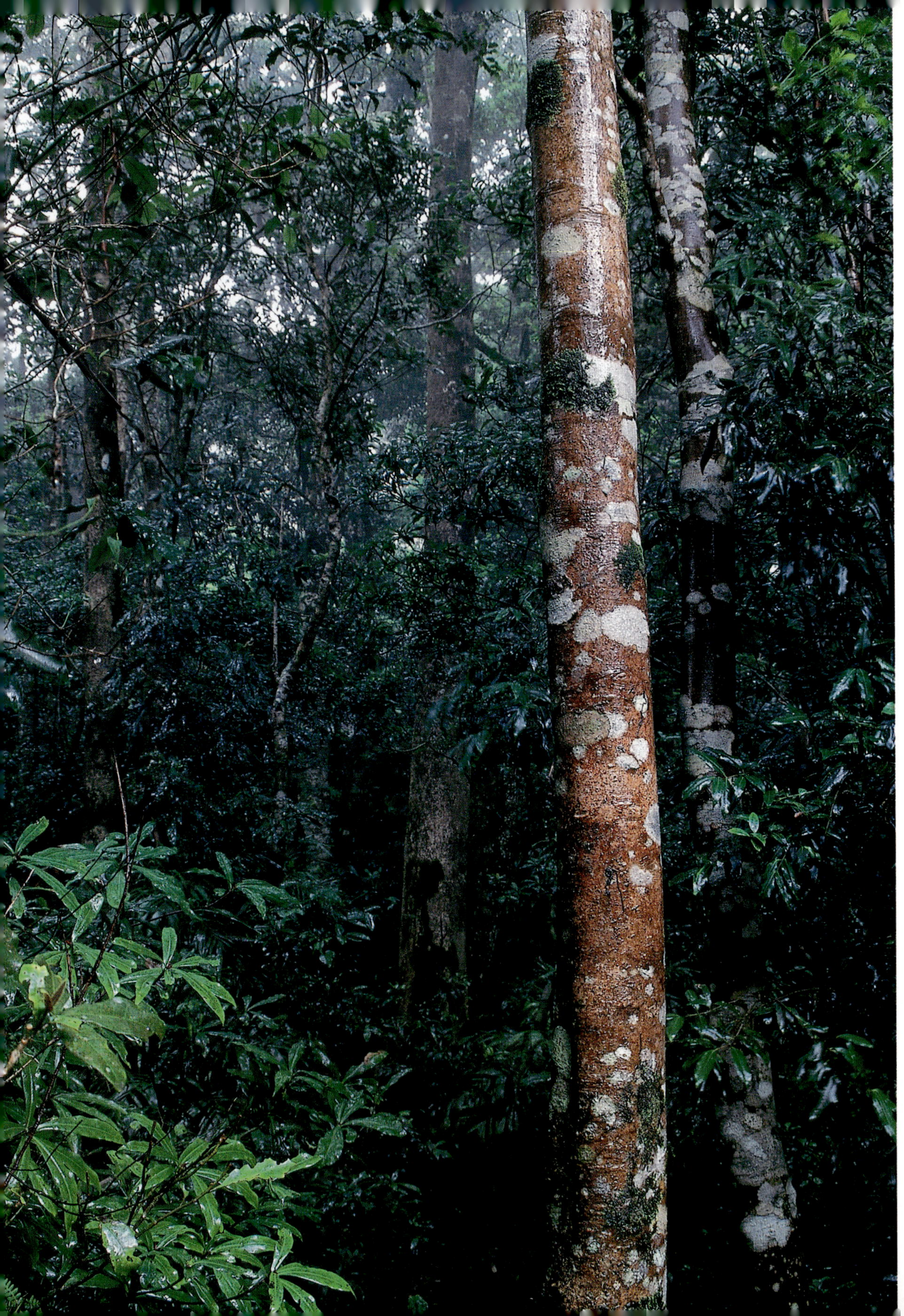

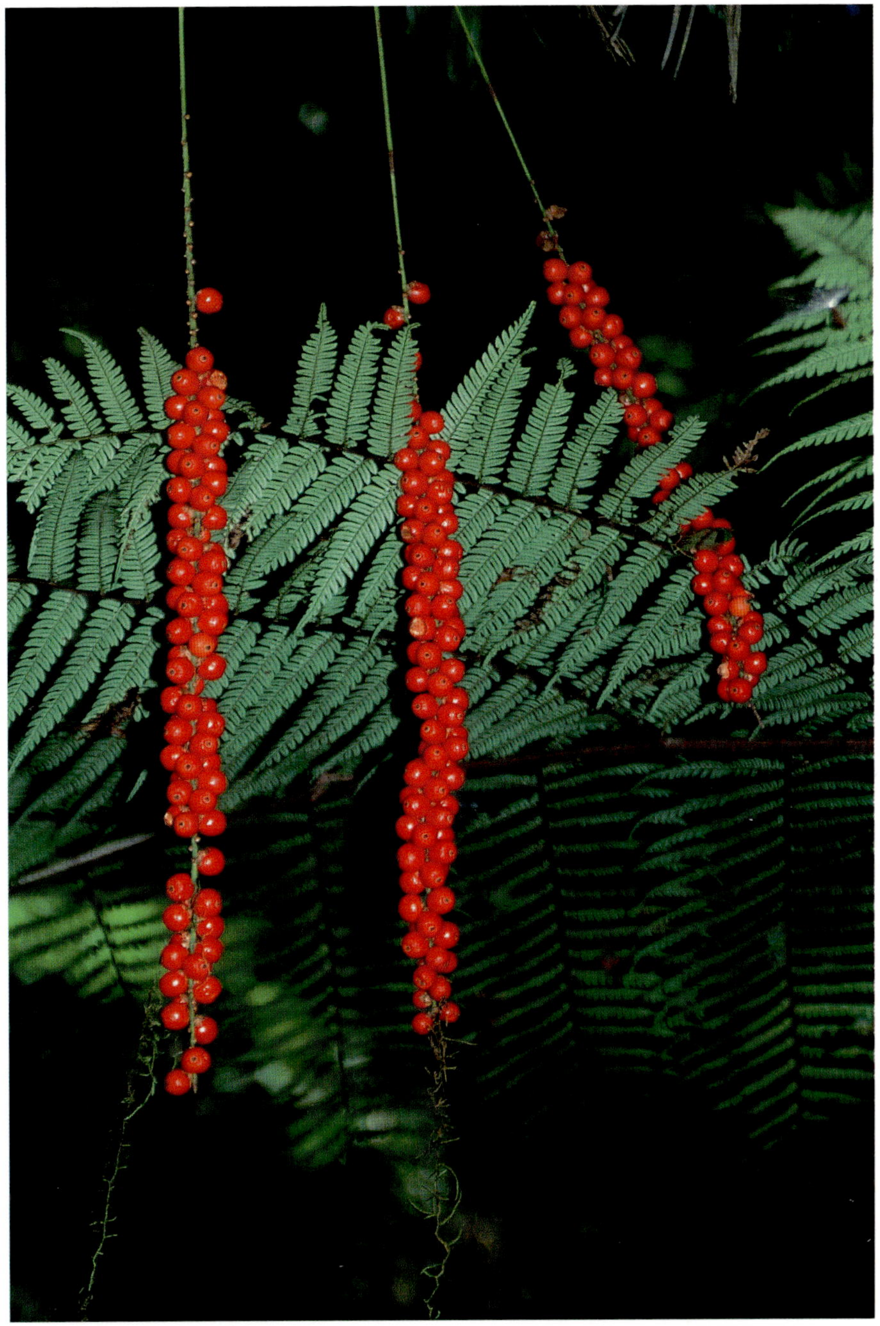

The brightly coloured berries of the walking stick palm, Lamington NP.

Left: Dripping rainforest at "Rum Jungle", on the east-west saddle of Mount Barney.

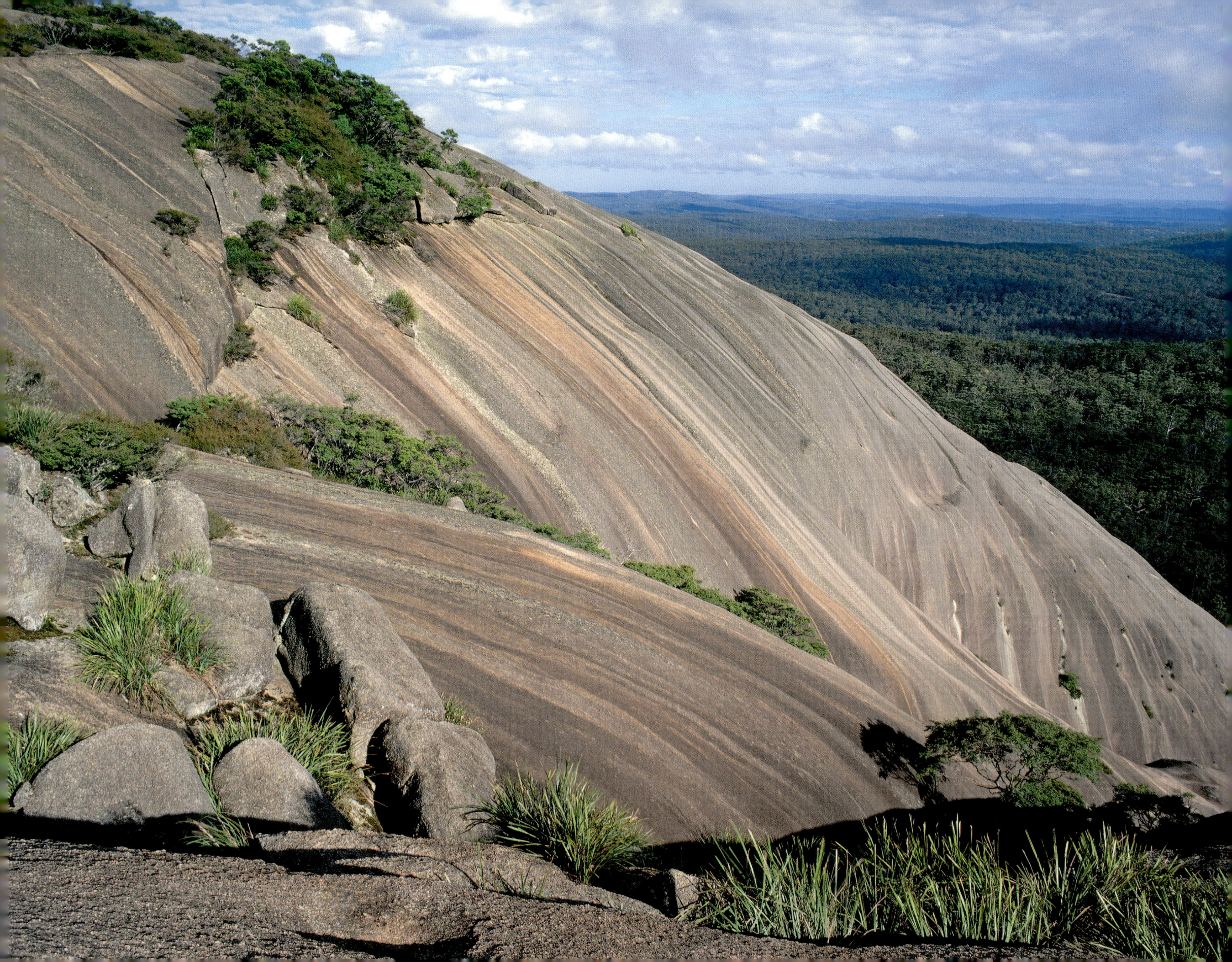

New South Wales

New South Wales is full of diversity and stunning scenery. There is true outback country to the west; the highest peaks in Australia in the Snowy Mountains; a spectacular and varied coastline; and rich farming regions like the Hunter Valley and Liverpool Plains. The climate varies from the subtropical north coast to temperate southern districts, the snowfields of the high country and the arid interior. The Great Dividing Range runs down the state as a series of high tablelands and peaks and has interesting variations in scenery due to changing geology. Much of the southern boundary with Victoria is defined by the Murray River, and towns along the border retain much of the history of the riverboat era.

In 1770 Captain Cook took possession for the British of all Australian territories east of the 135th meridian longitude, naming them New South Wales. The states of Queensland, Victoria and Tasmania were excised later, and the state now covers 801,428 square kilometres. Sydney is Australia's oldest and largest city with a population of over four and a half million and was established as a penal colony in 1788 under Governor Arthur Phillip. It is situated on one of the most beautiful natural harbours in the world and has famous ocean beaches like Manly, Bondi and Cronulla. Sydney is surrounded by many national parks and wild areas, including the Blue Mountains National Park to the west, Ku-ring-gai Chase NP to the north, and Royal NP to the south, the second oldest national park in the world, gazetted in 1879.

Australia's capital, Canberra, is the largest inland city in the country, with a population of over 370,000 people. It lies in land set aside for the seat of Federal Government – the 2,400 square kilometre Australian Capital Territory in south-eastern New South Wales. "Kamberra" is a Ngun(n)awal Aboriginal word meaning "a meeting place", either of rivers or of people joining together to feast on bogong moths in the nearby mountains. In 1911 a competition held for the city's design attracting 137 entries worldwide. The winners were the American architects Walter Burley Griffin and Marion Mahony Griffin, whose plan included a central artificial lake (now known as Lake Burley Griffin) and a parliamentary triangle in which the important national buildings would be sited, including the current Houses of Parliament opened in 1988. The ordered city has a series of circles and avenues, important buildings like the Australian War Memorial, the National Museum of Australia and the National Gallery of Australia, and many parks and areas of bushland.

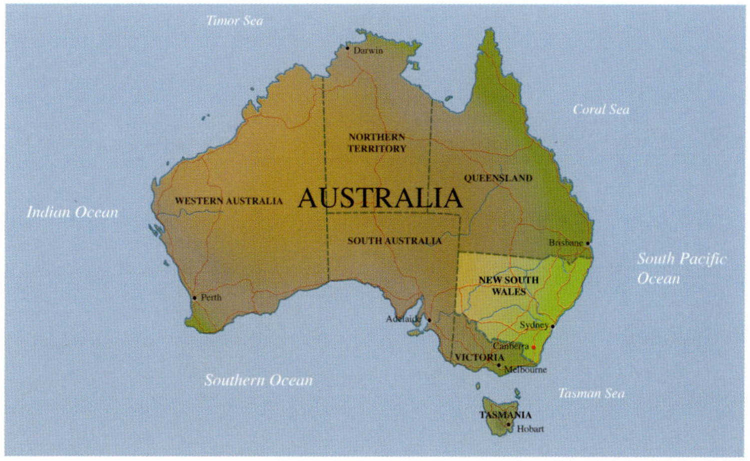

Opposite page: The rain-streaked dome of Bald Rock (1277m).

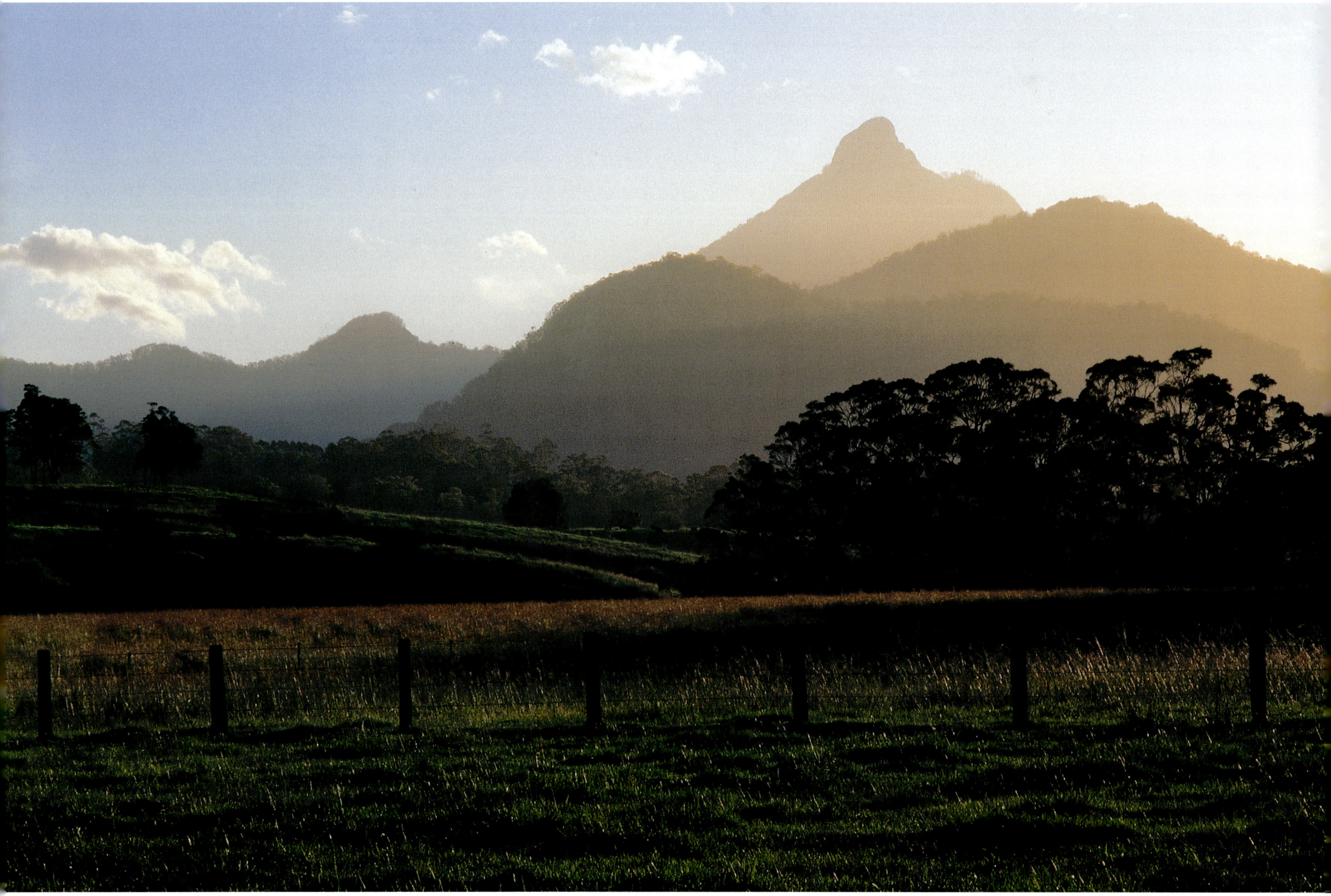

Late afternoon light on Wollumbin (1156m) rising over paddocks.

The Tweed Caldera is a remarkable example of the erosion of an ancient volcano in northern New South Wales. The Mount Warning Shield Volcano formed about 23 to 20 million years ago and was perhaps 2000 metres high before wind and rain carved out a huge bowl around the central vent. The remaining peak, made of erosion resistant rock, was named Mount Warning by Captain James Cook after he encountered dangerous reefs near Fingal Head in 1770. The local Bundjalung Aboriginal people call it Wollumbin, "cloud-catcher" or "fighting chief of the mountains." The name is appropriate, as the often mist-shrouded peak towers over the landscape, dominating other lesser summits.

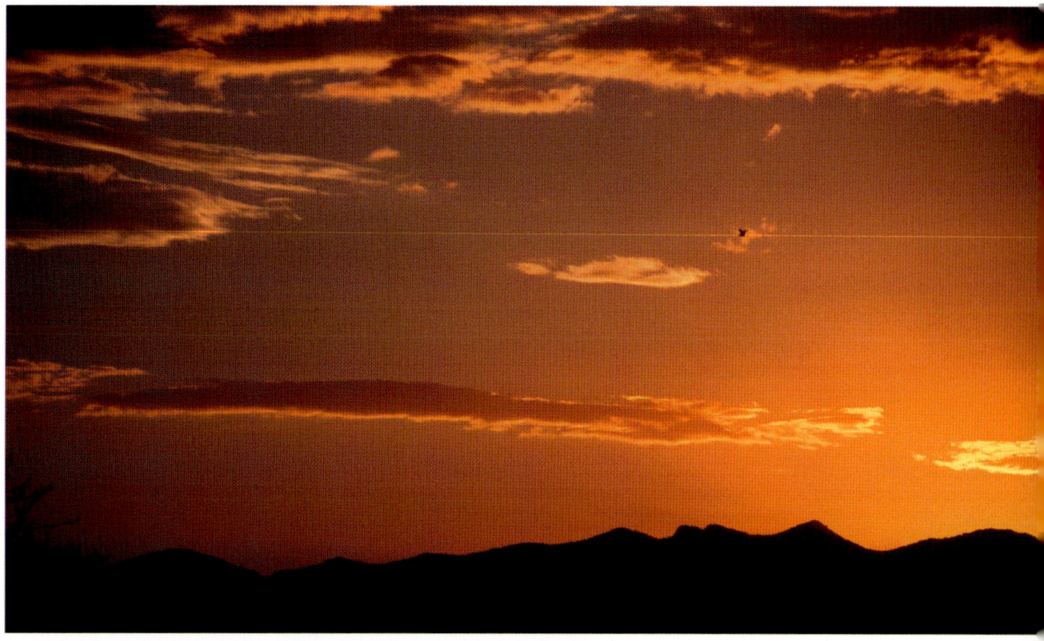

A bird wings its way across the sunset skies above the caldera rim or Border Range of Northern New South Wales.

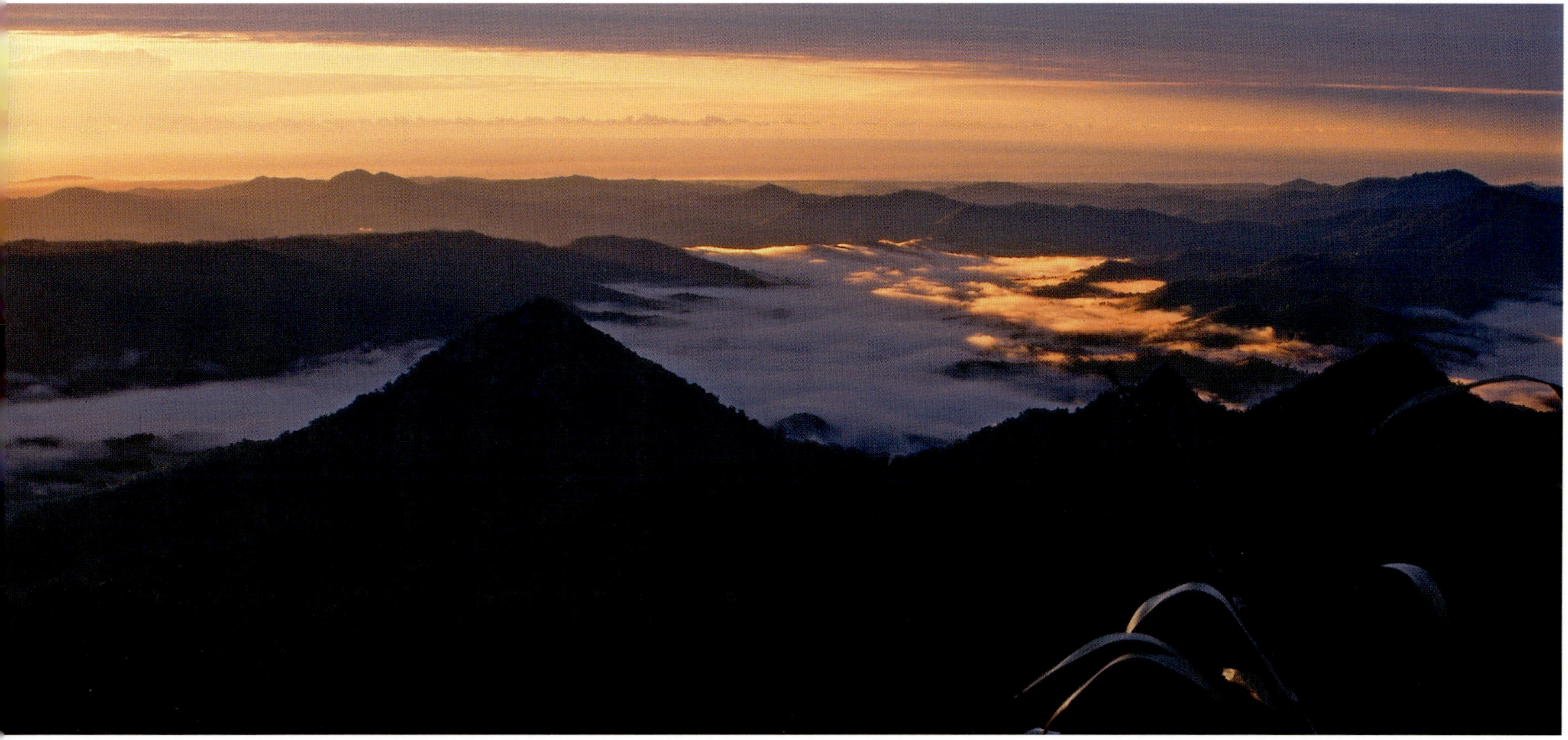

Dawn from near the summit of Wollumbin, reputedly the first place in mainland Australia to catch the sun's rays at the break of a new day.

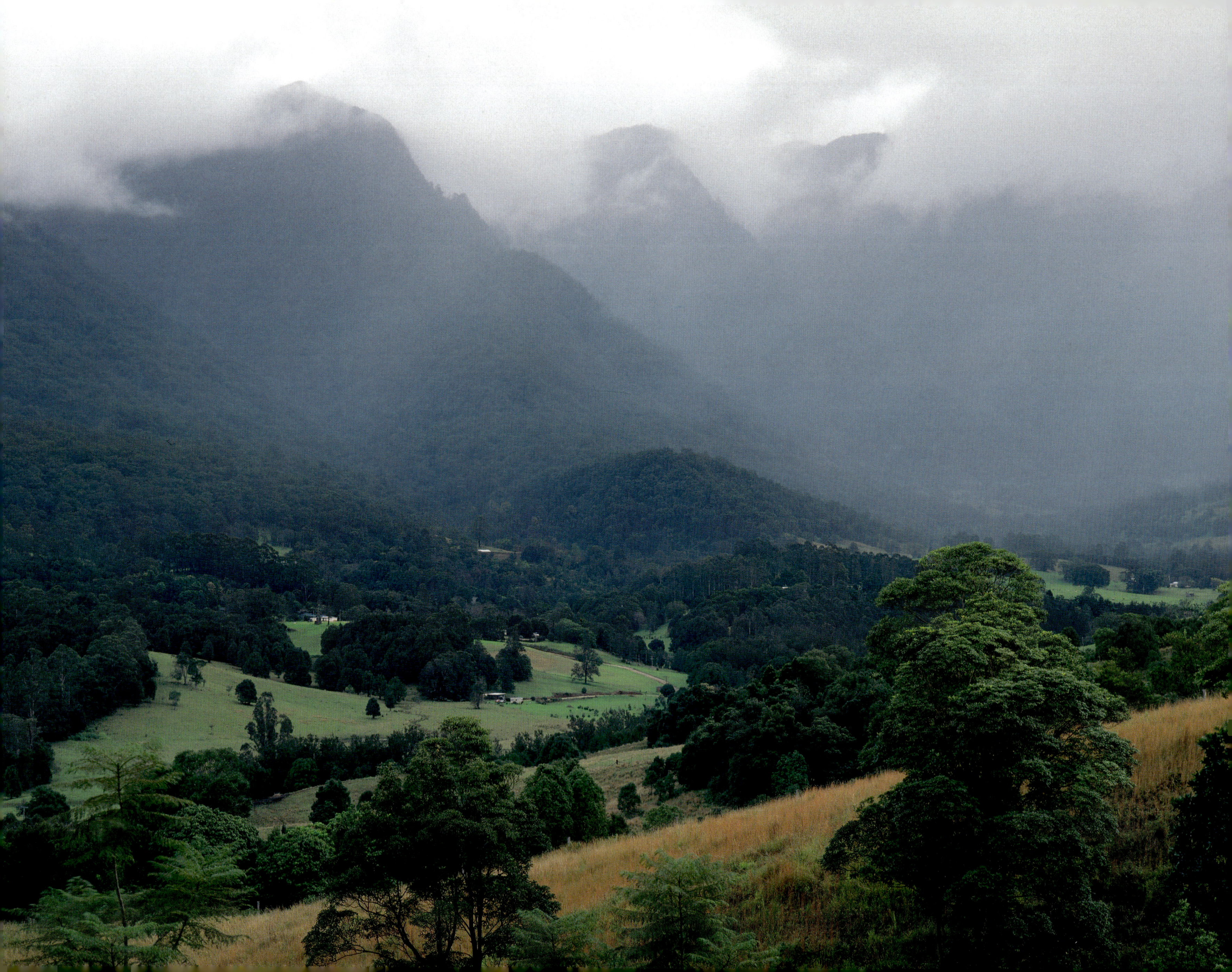

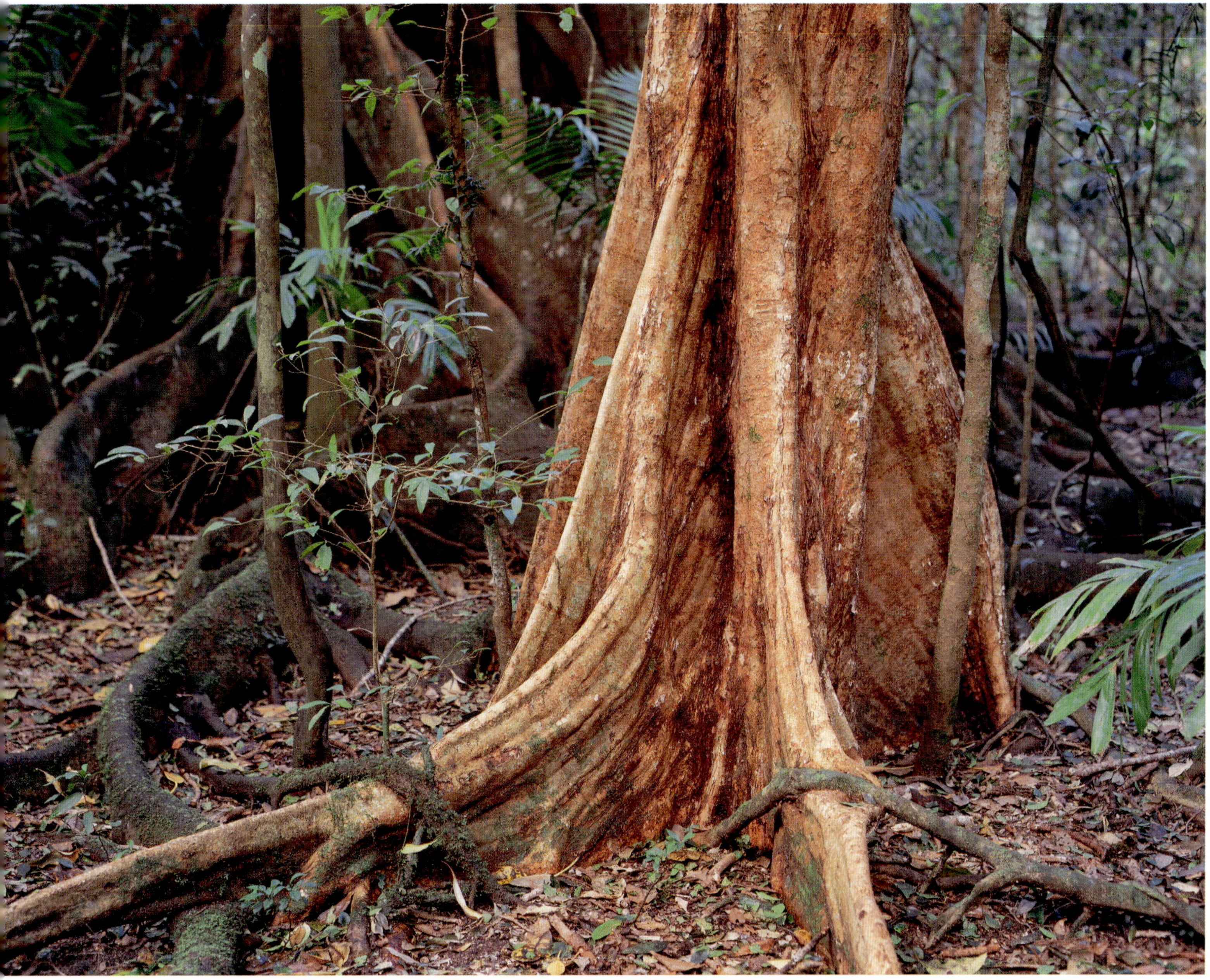

My home is now Murwillumbah, a town in northern New South Wales under the brooding mountain of Wollumbin. After sorting out my affairs in Western Australia, I moved interstate in October 2012, taking the Indian Pacific train from Perth to Adelaide and driving from there to Murwillumbah. I described the last day drive from Tenterfield thus; *"I was packed up ready to leave by 9am and headed out on the road – it turned out to be a scenic but windy and tiring drive. I got to Murwillumbah at noon and dropped into the real estate agent – she said I could go straight to the flat. Later on while unpacking I got caught in a huge thunderstorm – but it didn't matter, I got a bit wet but not cold and I sat for a while outside on my porch watching the rain."*

Top: World Heritage listed rainforest at Mebbin National Park in the Tweed Caldera. Note the giant strangler fig tree behind the smaller tree in front.

Opposite page: View of the lush Limpinwood valley below the mist-shrouded Border Ranges.

The far northern coastline of New South Wales boasts iconic surf beaches, rocky headlands and river estuaries. There are still a few patches of remnant coastal rainforest at places like Iluka. One of the common small trees of this coast is the distinctive pandanus, with its thick "prop" roots to anchor itself in the loose sand. Pandani often brave the worst of the wind and weather and cling to headland cliff faces and other exposed places.

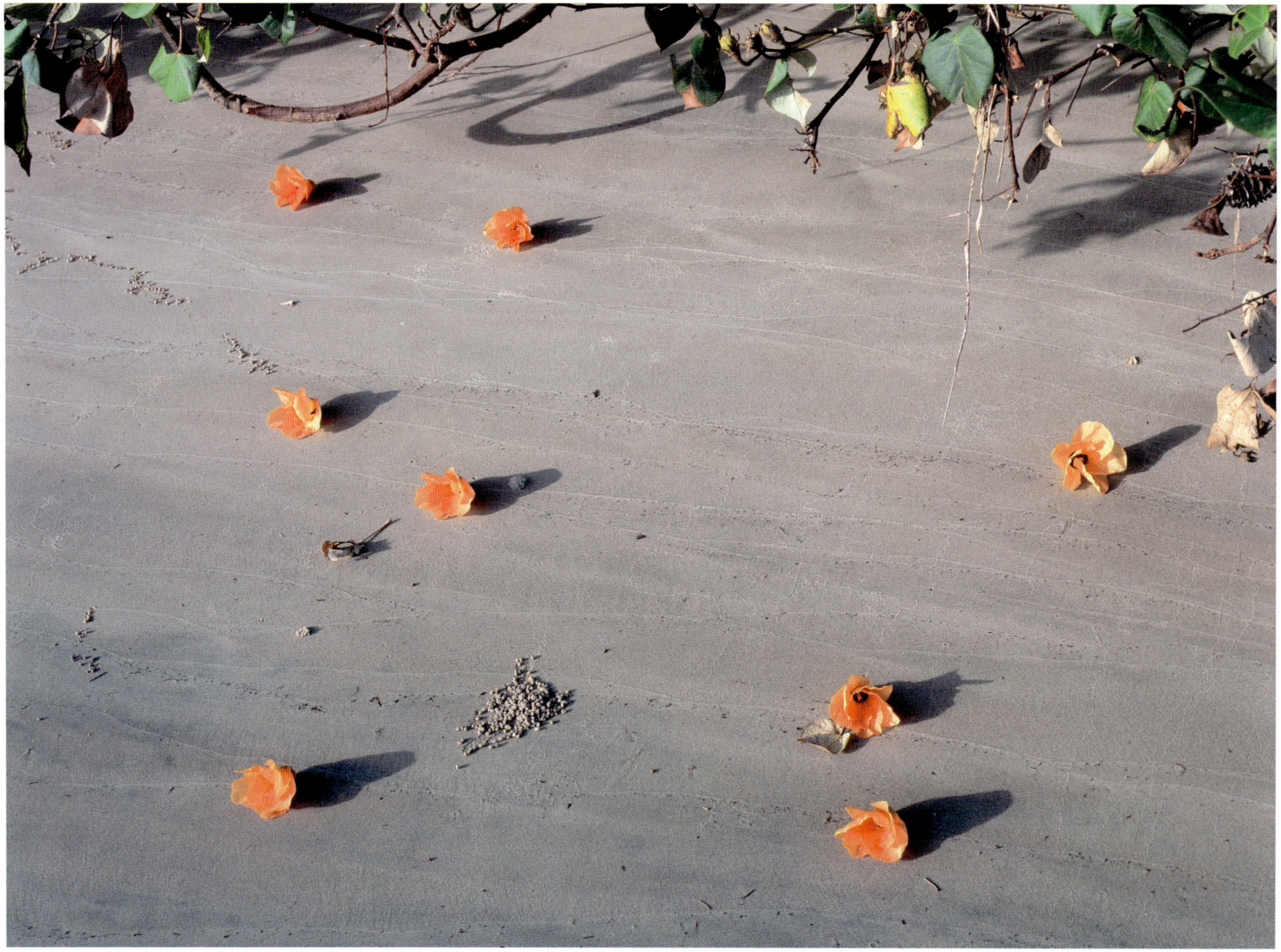

Top: Native hibiscus flowers on a north coast estuary beach.

Opposite page: View south over Cabarita Beach from Norries Head, Bogangar, northern New South Wales.

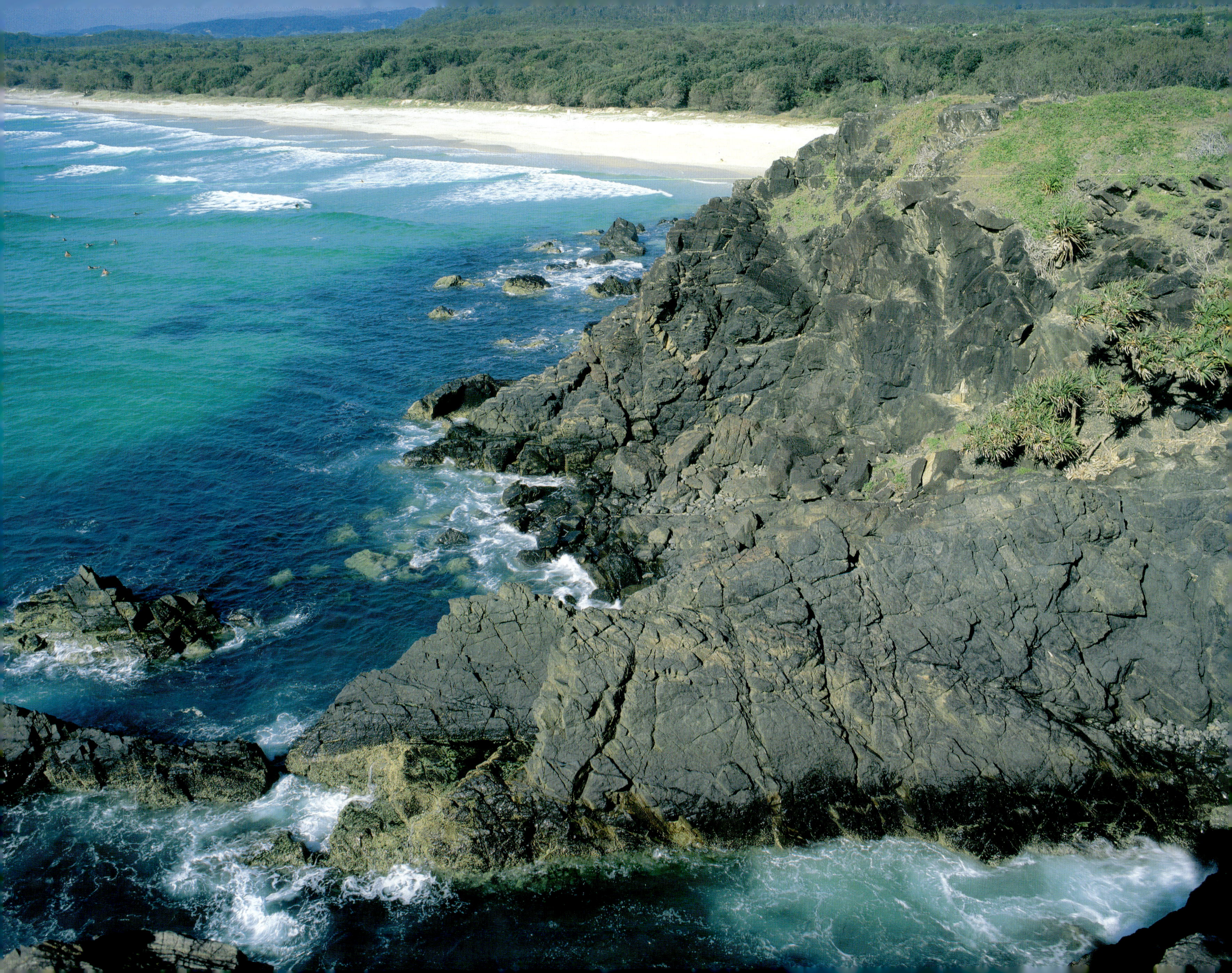

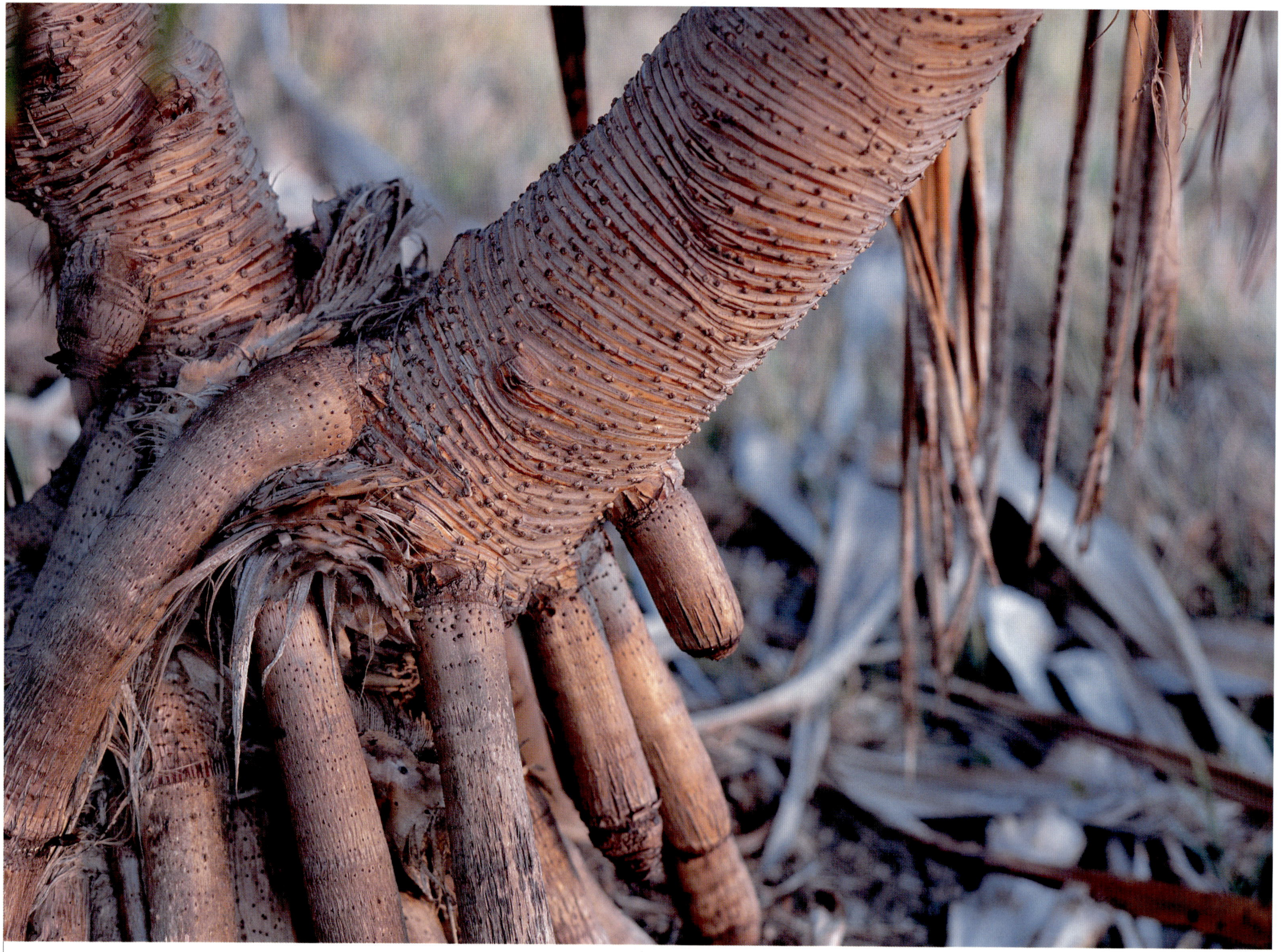

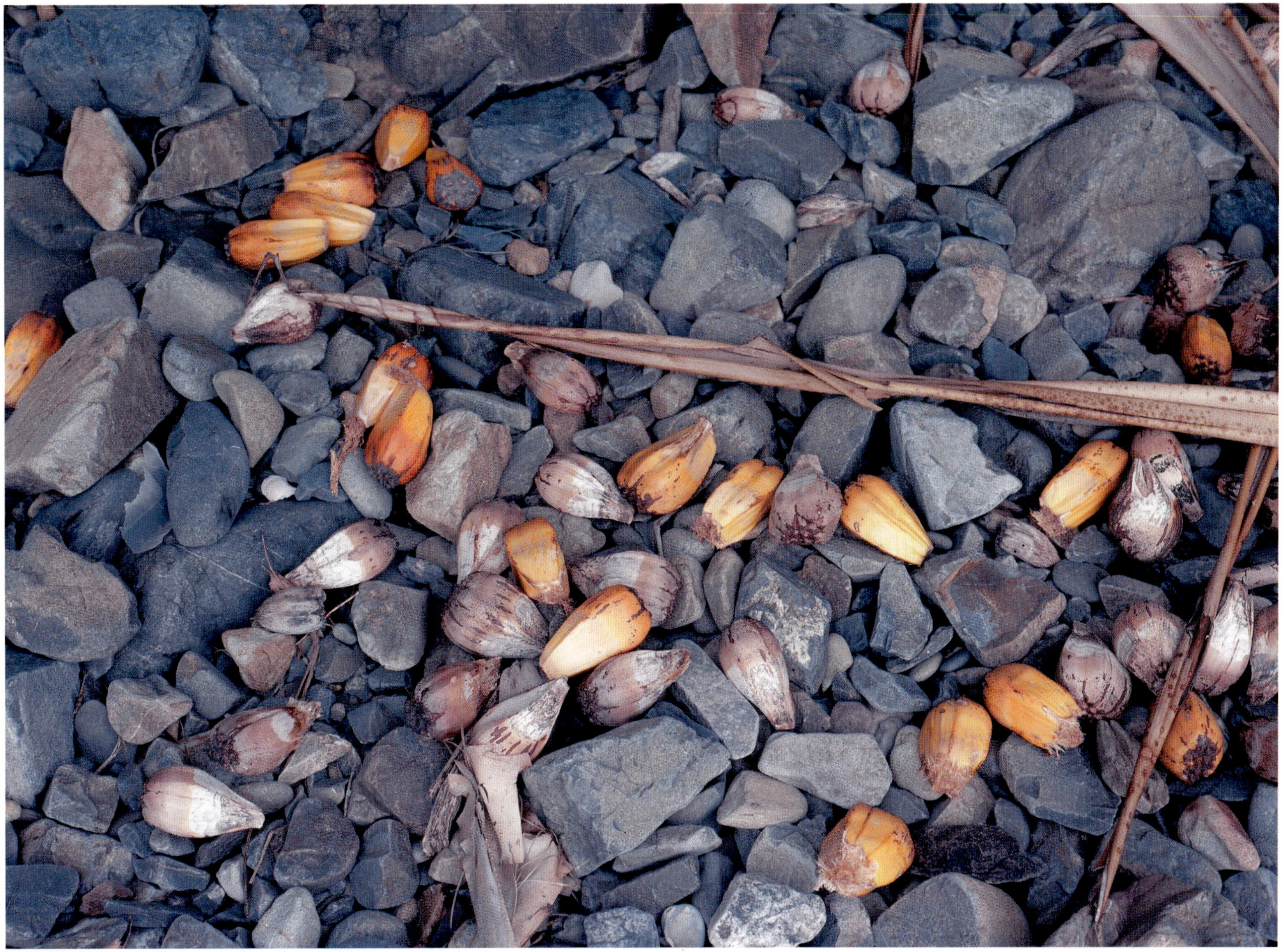

Top: Fallen pandanus seeds on a rocky headland. The seeds are brightly coloured when first released from the "woody pineapple" type fruit.

Opposite page: A small Pandani tree at Fingal Head.

The Gondwana Rainforest of Australia World Heritage Area protects the largest area of subtropical rainforest in the world and includes some 50 protected areas in northern New South Wales and South East Queensland. It is home to over 200 rare or threatened plant and animal species, including Antarctic beech trees and the giant barred frog. The New England National Park, 85 kilometres east of Armidale, is part of the World Heritage Area. Here you can drive to the summit of one of the highest mountains, Point Lookout (1564m), for stupendous views and excellent walks through the lush Gondwana rainforest.

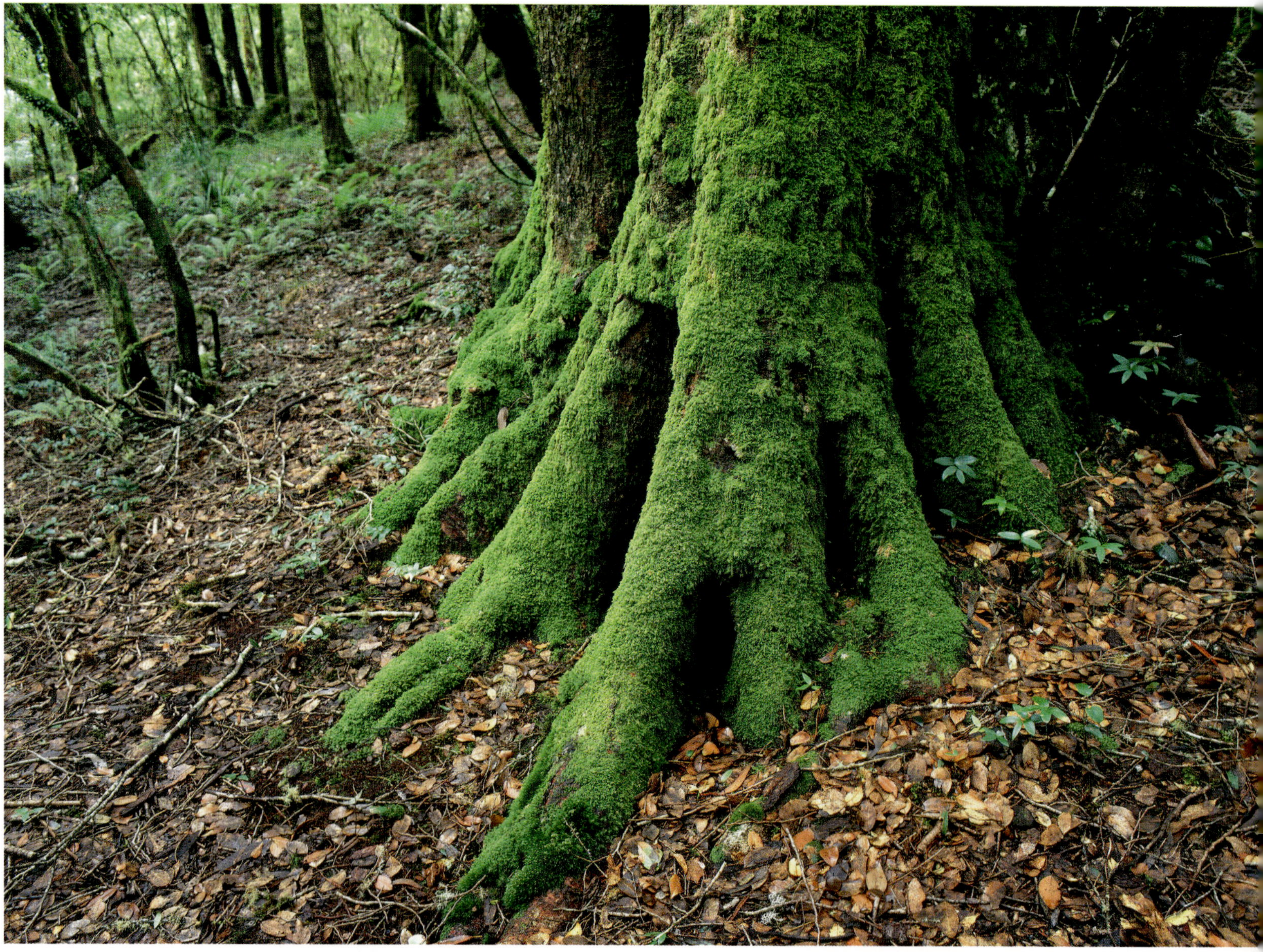

Top: Moss covered buttress roots of an ancient Antarctic beech tree at Point Lookout in the New England NP.

Opposite page: Looking up into the canopy of the beech forest.

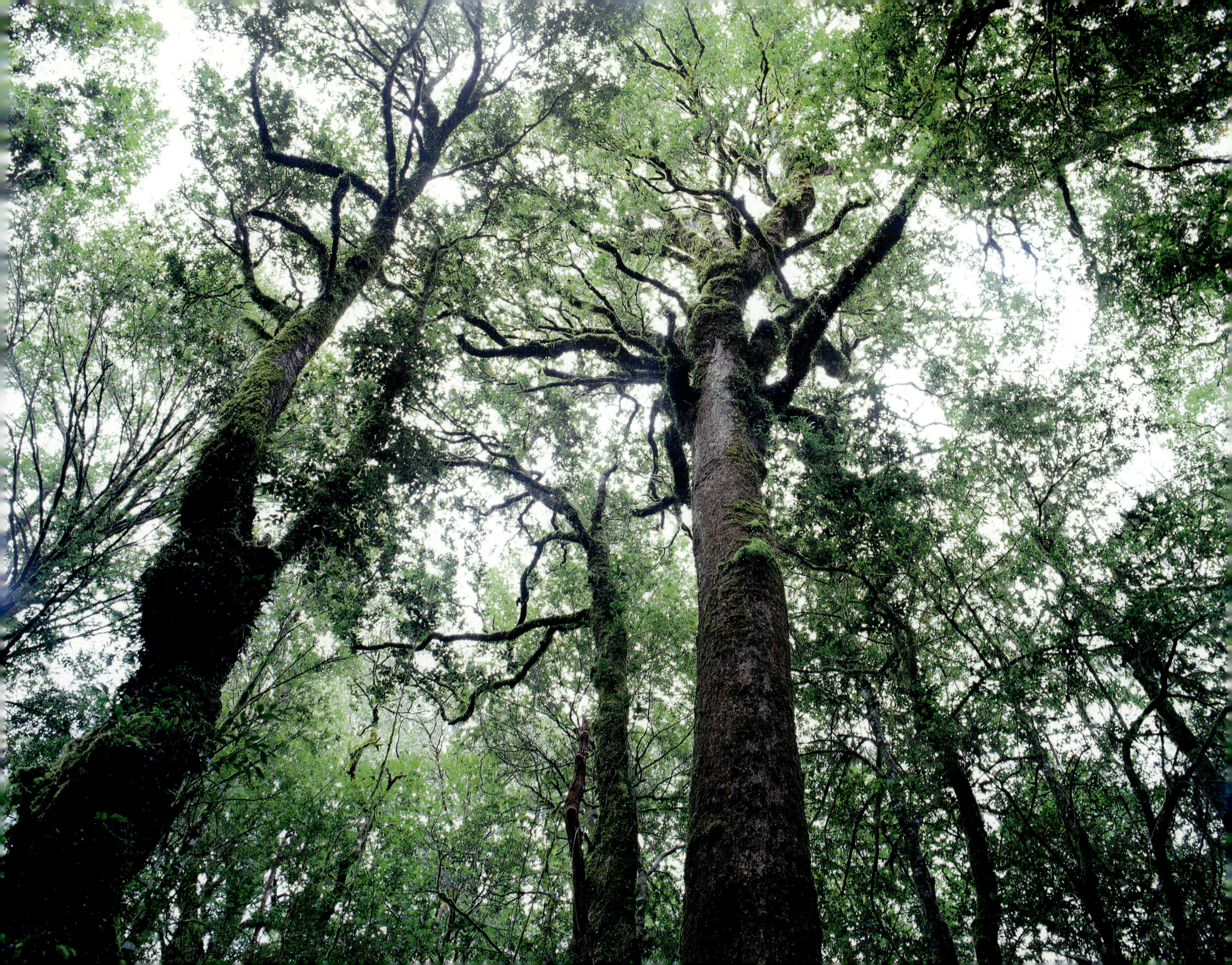

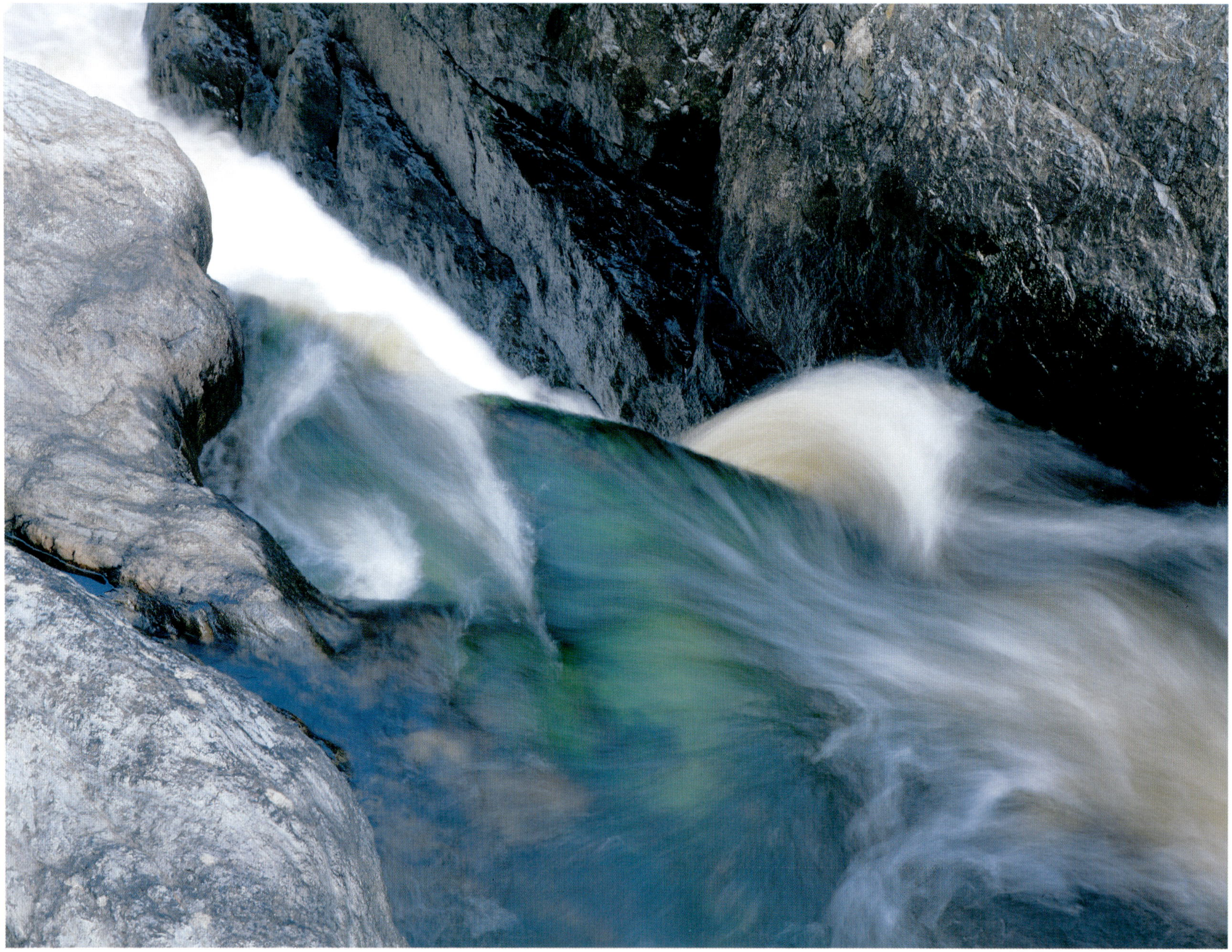

Rapids on the Wollomombi River above Wollomombi Falls, near Armidale.

Much of the Great Dividing Range in northern New South Wales is a high inland plateau or tableland dissected at its eastern edge by gorges and waterfalls. Granite belts occur throughout this area, resulting from ancient lavas that were intruded underground and later exposed by weathering of the surrounding land. Bald Rock, near Tenterfield (see page 122) is the largest granite monolith in Australia, and rises 200 metres above the surrounding plains. The summit can be reached by a three kilometre return walk which takes about two hours.

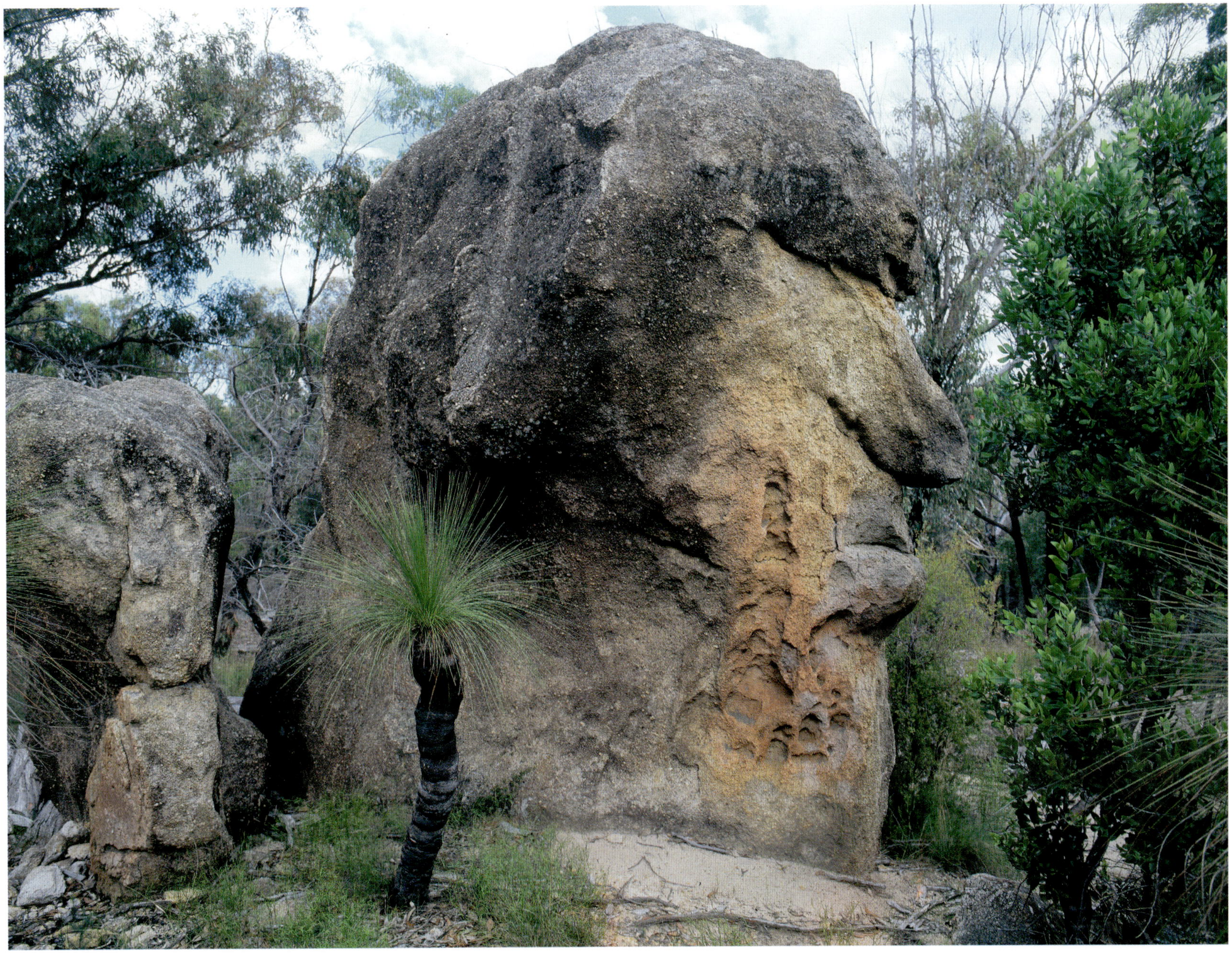

Torrington State Conservation area on the New England tablelands has some amazing granite rock formations including this one, known as "Mystery Face". The area is rich in plants, with over 750 species present.

I also headed further west during my travels to the Warrumbungle National Park near Coonabarabran in north central New South Wales. This area of 20,000 hectares protects a remarkable series of volcanic spires and trachyte plugs resulting from the weathering of an ancient shield volcano, active about 13 million years ago. The national park has large populations of koalas, eastern grey kangaroos, wallaroos and emus and boasts more than 42 kilometres of excellent walking tracks.

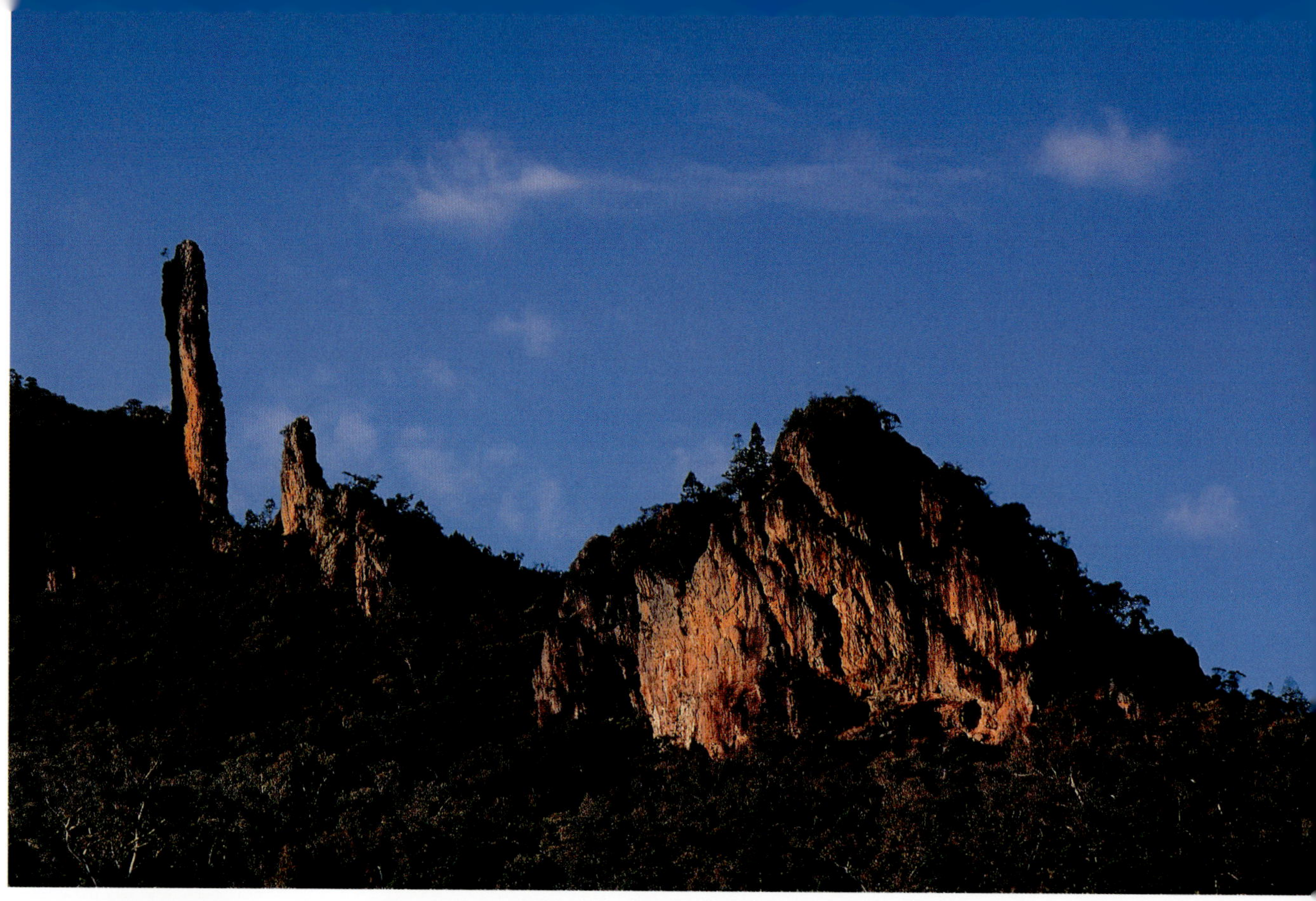

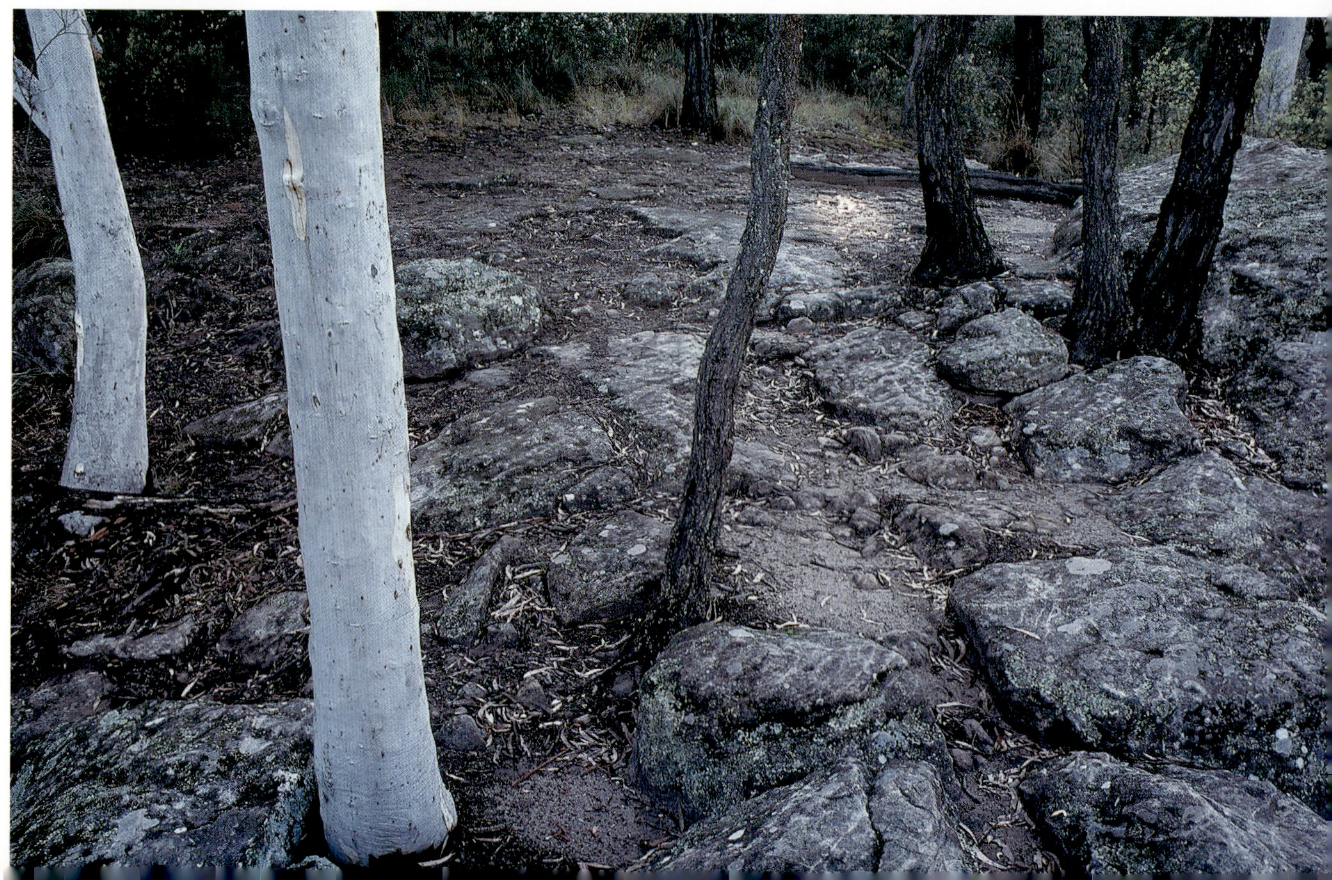

Top: The distinctive 90 metre high rock wall of the Breadknife is one of the most recognisable formations in the Warrumbungles.

Below: Tranquil dry sclerophyll woodland in the Warrumbungles.

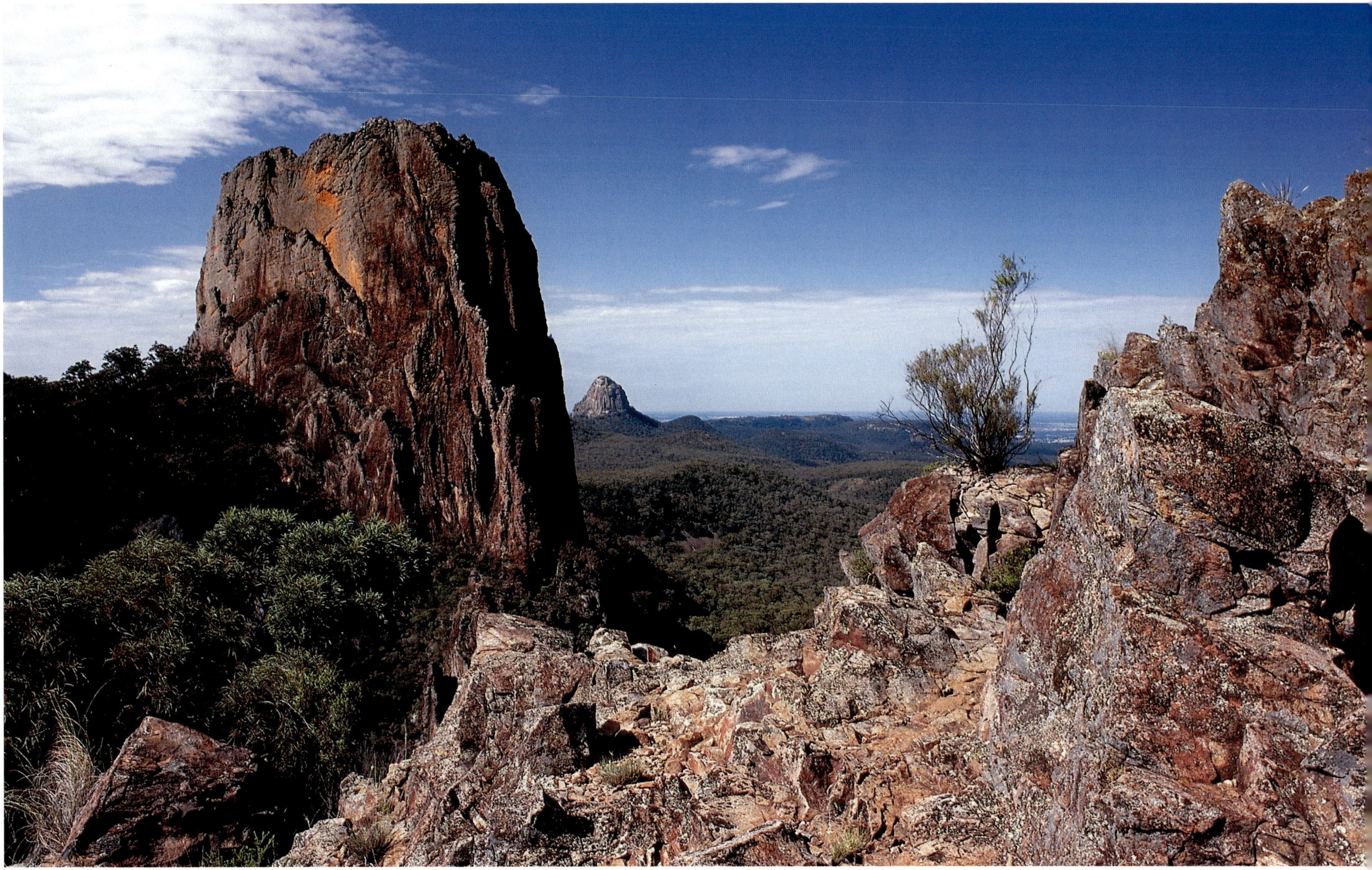

The sheer cliffs of Crater Bluff, seen here from the Grand High Tops walking track.

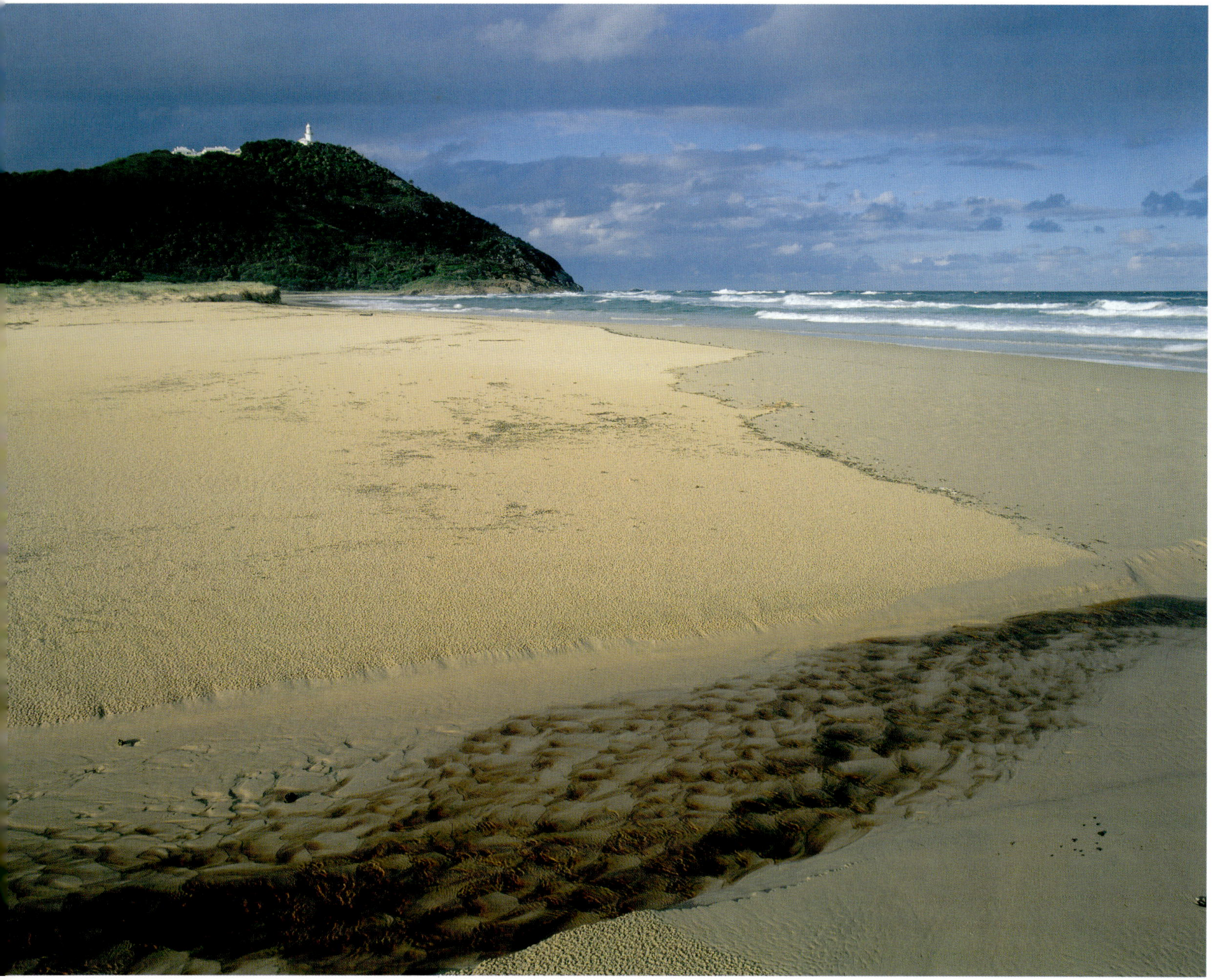

Continuing the journey south-east, you will find many wonderful places to visit on the mid north coast of New South Wales. Migrating southern right whales and humpbacks can be seen during winter and spring from the scenic headland of Smoky Cape and its operational lighthouse, near the small coastal town of South West Rocks. Further south lies the popular holiday destination of Port Stephens, a large inlet guarded at its mouth by two extinct volcanoes, Tomaree and Yacaaba Heads.

Left: A tannin stained stream makes its way to the sea at Smoky Cape.

Opposite page: View past the cliffs of Tomaree Head to Yacaaba Head. Cabbage Tree Island on the far right protects the only known breeding colony of one of the world's rarest birds, the Gould's petrel.

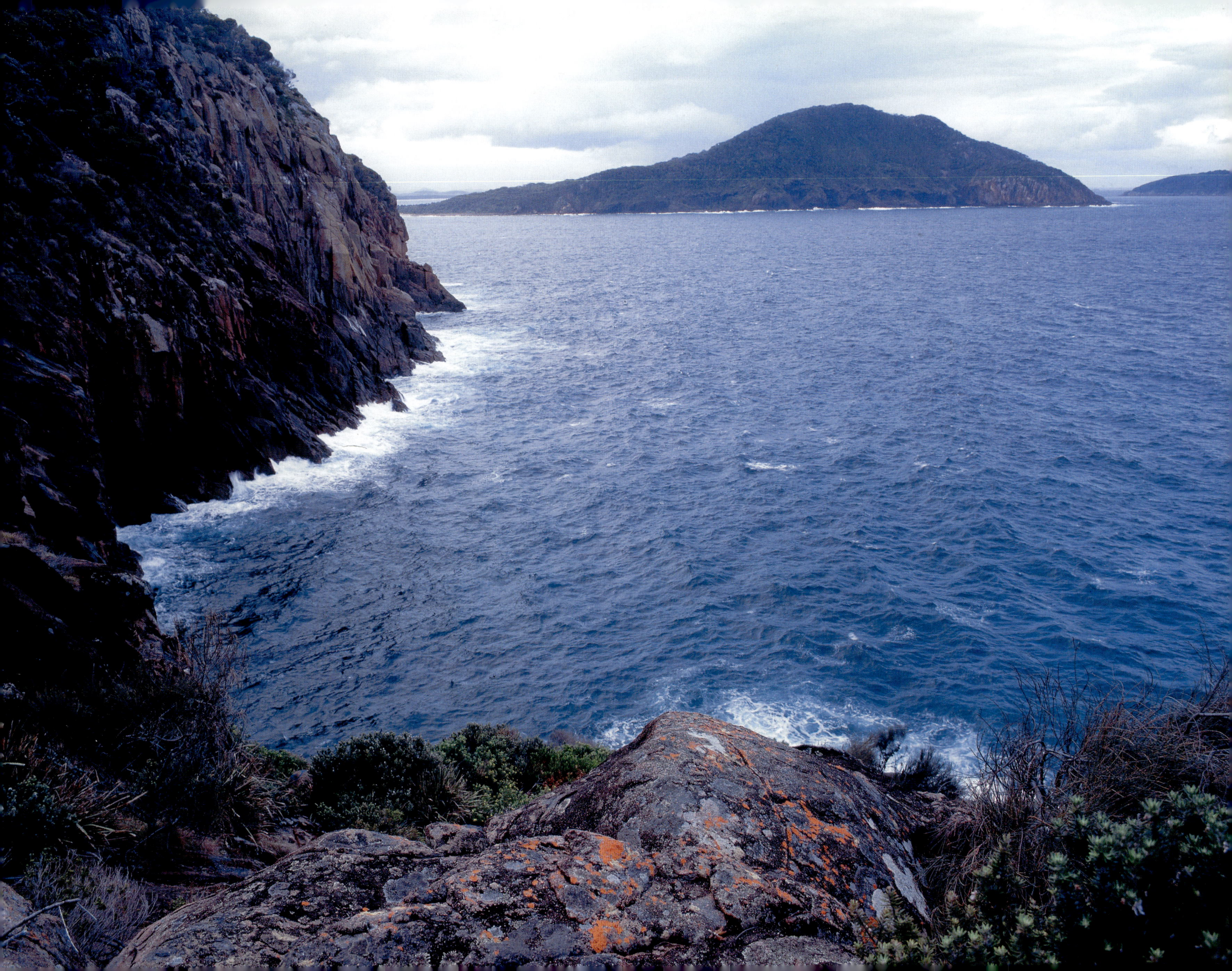

Heading west from the Sydney basin, the Blue Mountains are an iconic sandstone plateau cut by deep gorges, with abundant wildlife, forests and waterfalls. The World Heritage-listed mountains reach over 1000 metres and are so named because droplets of eucalyptus oil in the atmosphere lend a blue hue to the distant peaks. Katoomba is the major centre here and lies 110 kilometres to the west of Sydney. The mountains are the traditional territory of the Dharug Aboriginal people and were first crossed by Europeans in 1812, when explorers Gregory Blaxland, William Wentworth and William Lawson found a way through the maze of peaks and canyons to the western plains beyond. The mountains today are a mecca for bushwalkers, sightseers and rock climbers.

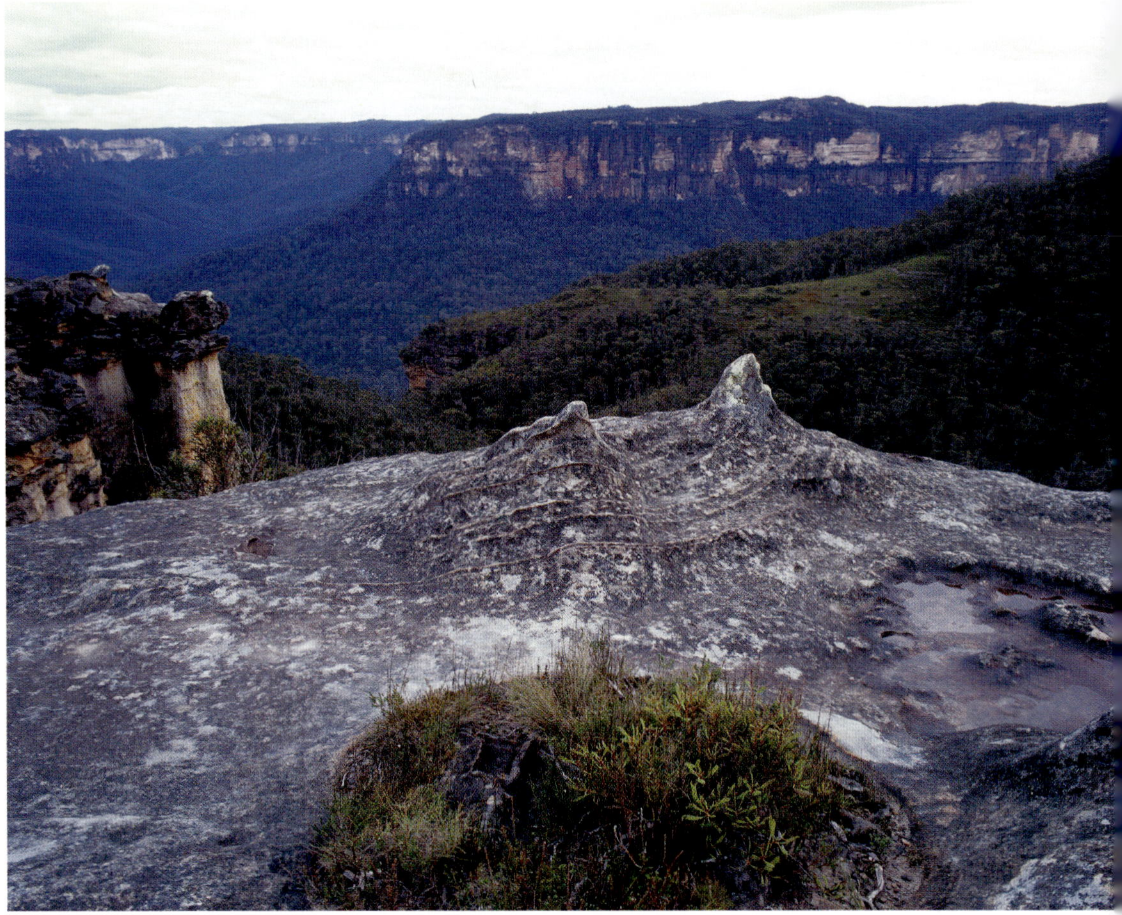

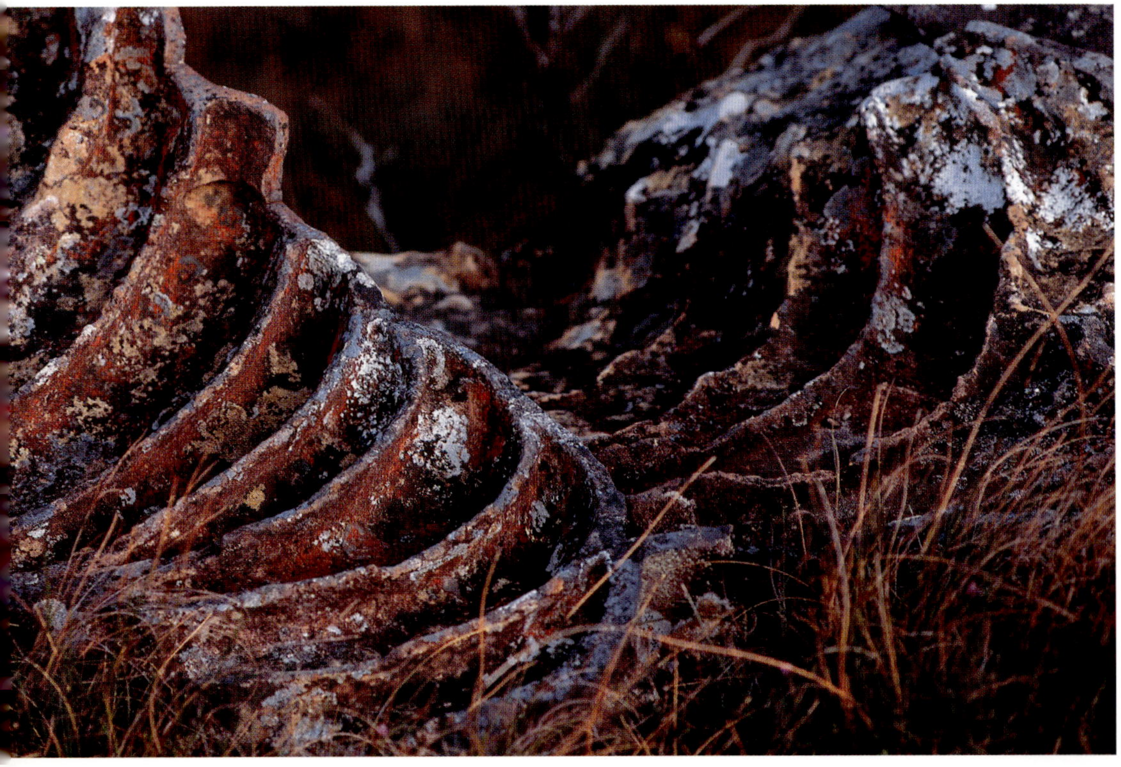

Top: Looking out over the Grose Valley from the rim of the escarpment.

Left: Lichen paints unusually shaped "ribbed" rocks in the Blue Mountains.

Opposite page: The golden light of dawn on sandstone cliffs in the Grose Valley, Blue Mountains.

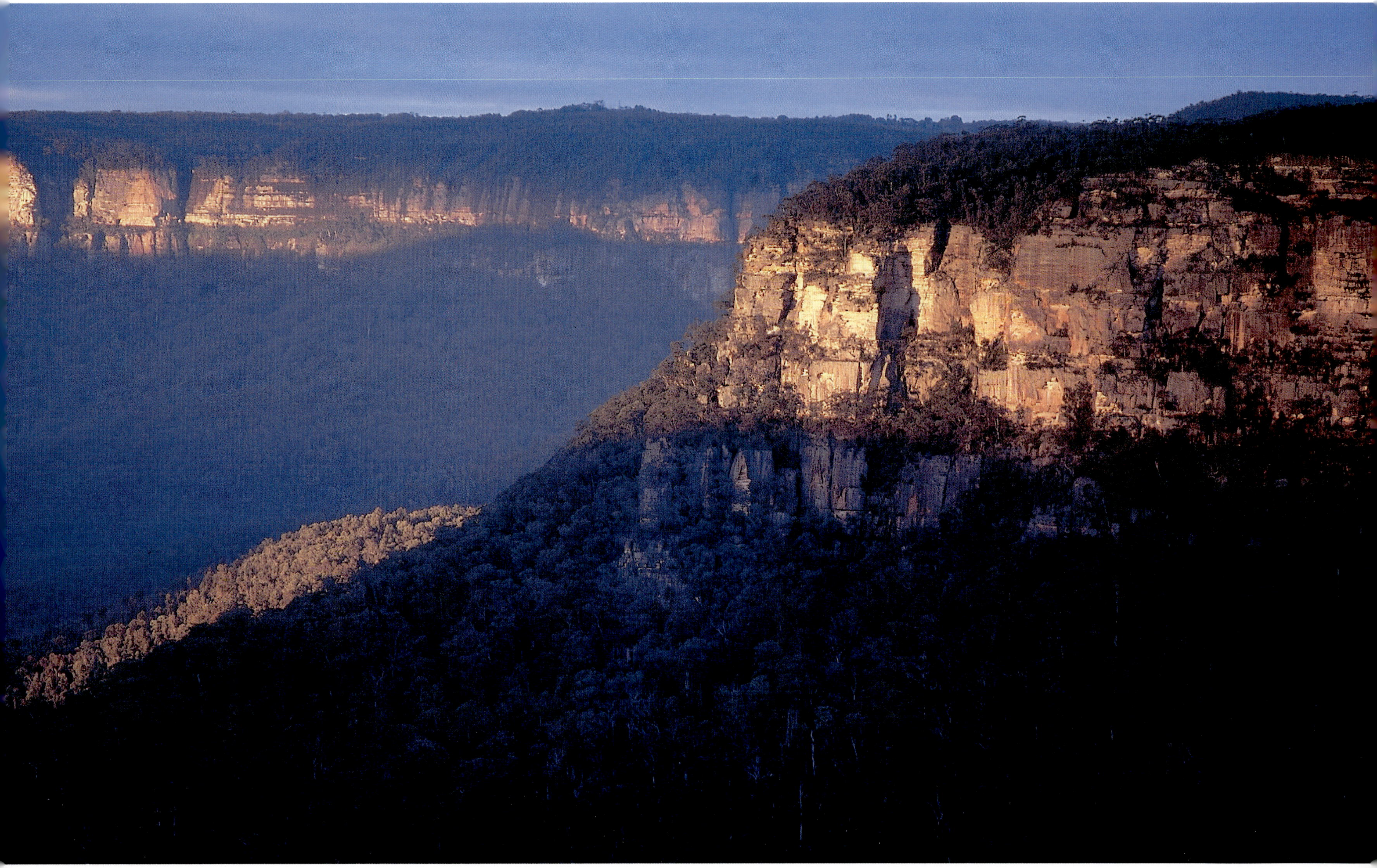

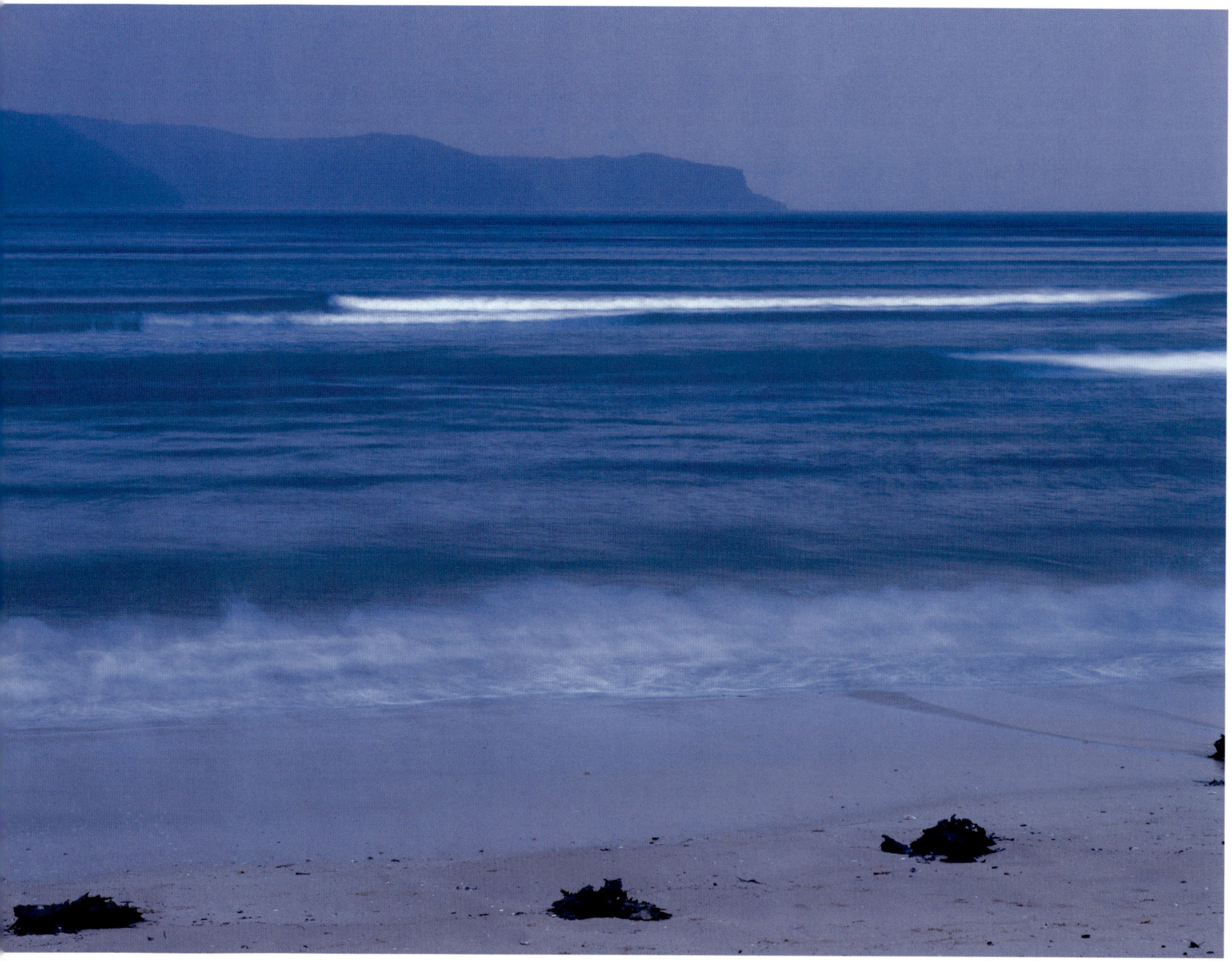

New South Wales has many wonderful scenic spots lying up and down the coast that entice holiday makers in their thousands. I stayed at Umina Beach, a coastal town 90 kilometres north of Sydney, and *"got up just after 7am and went for a walk to the beach. It was still ok then but I could see heavy storm clouds massing on the horizon. I should have packed up the tent straight away – my instinct was telling me to! Anyway I went to the beach and got one pic before the rain hit. It really bucketed down! I went back to the car, put on my rain jacket and packed the tent up wet."*

Left: A storm approaches Umina Beach. Box Head, part of Bouddi National Park, can be seen in the distance.

Opposite page: The colourful clay formation known as the Pinnacles has been exposed by natural erosion in Ben Boyd National Park on the New South Wales south coast.

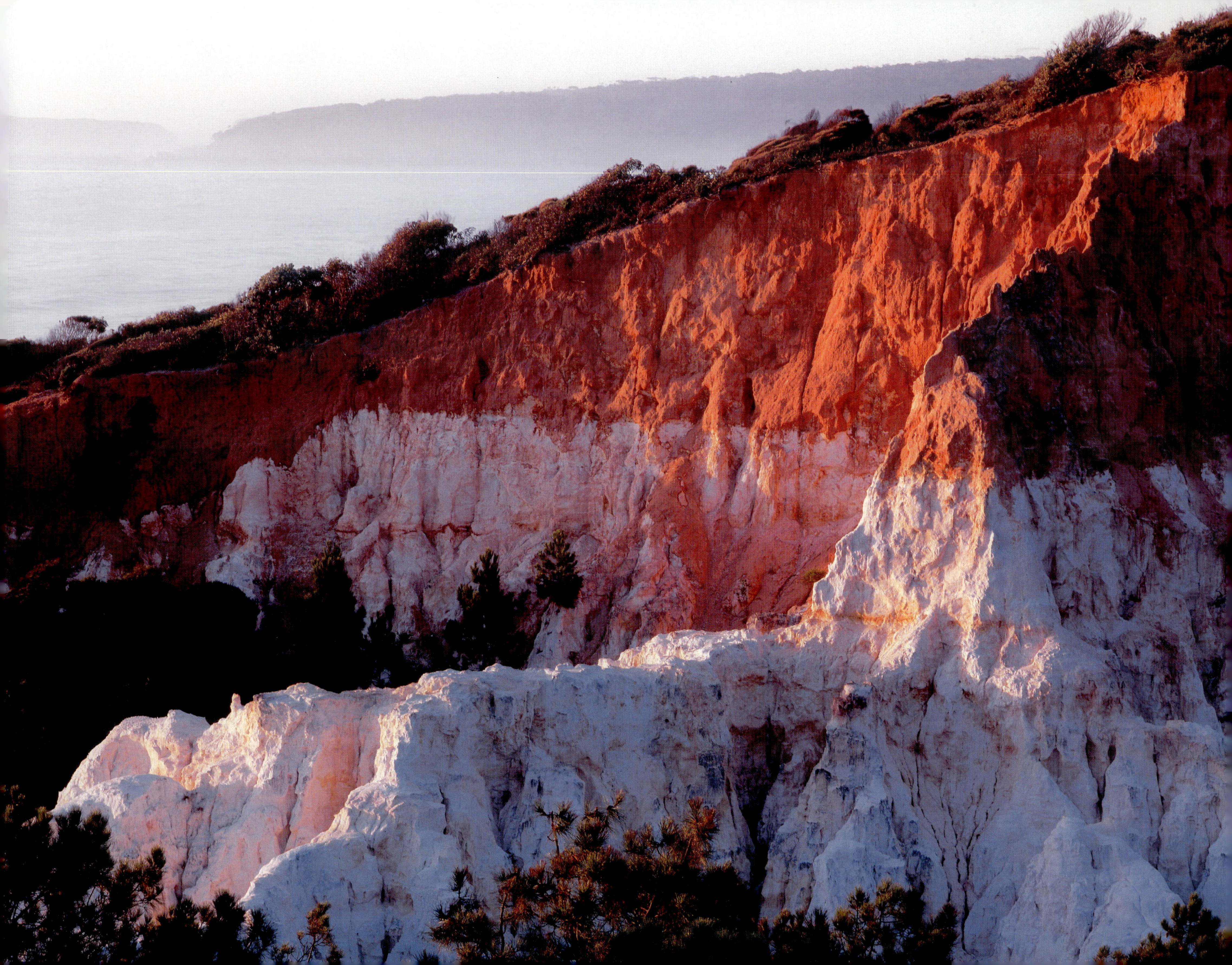

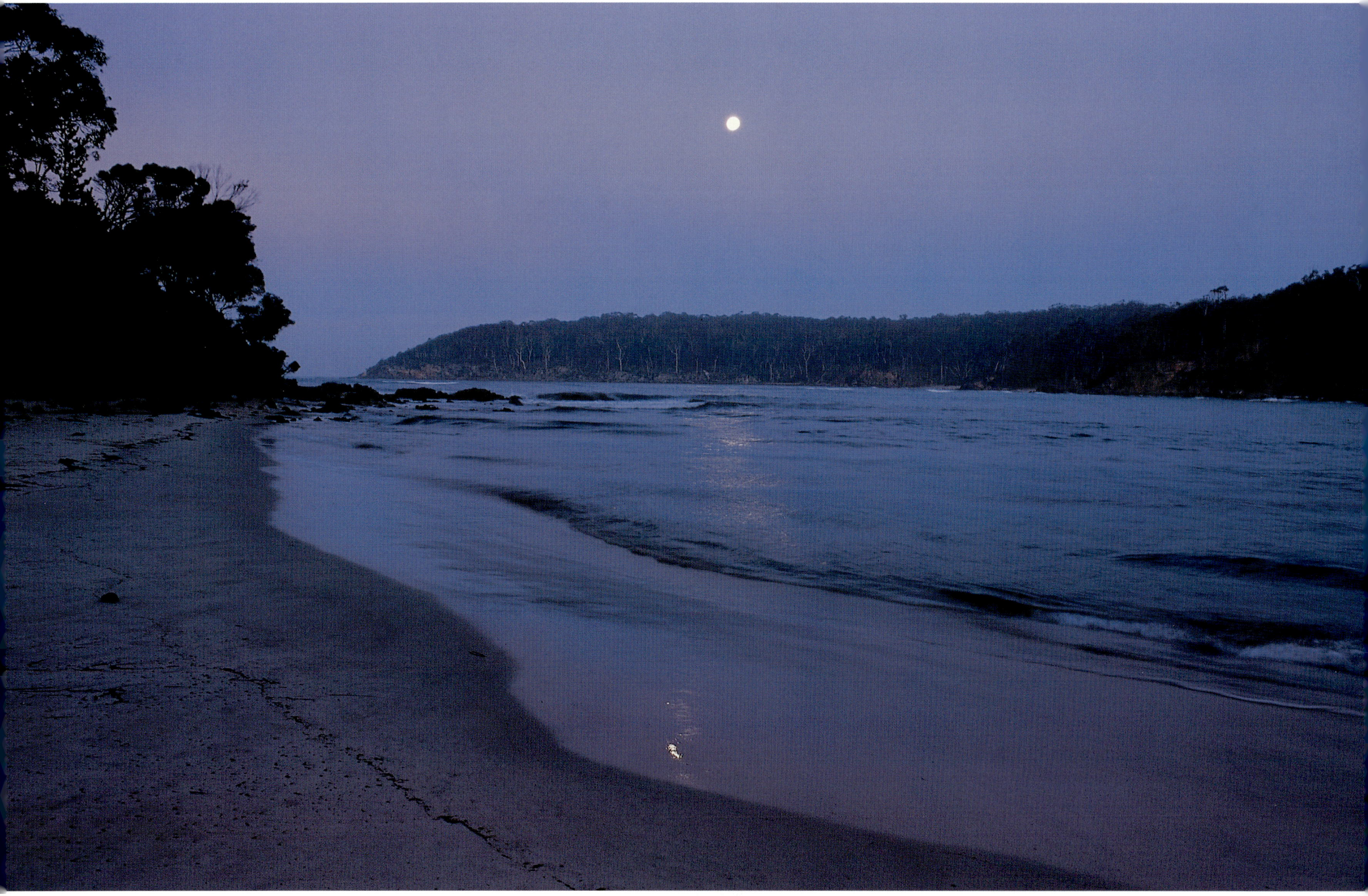

The southern coastline of New South Wales has picturesque headlands, rivers, beaches and charming holiday towns like Eden and Merimbula. Large stretches of coastline are protected in national parks, like Ben Boyd north of Eden and Bournda south of Tathra. I visited the Pambula River mouth in the Ben Boyd NP one evening. *"I noticed a large kangaroo on the other side hop in and swim across. The river was about 100 metres wide at this point! He jumped out upstream of where I sat and a few minutes later hopped past an astonished photographer (me) using the walking track. I finished writing that story in my writing pad and when I looked up I saw the most amazing moonrise over the river mouth."*

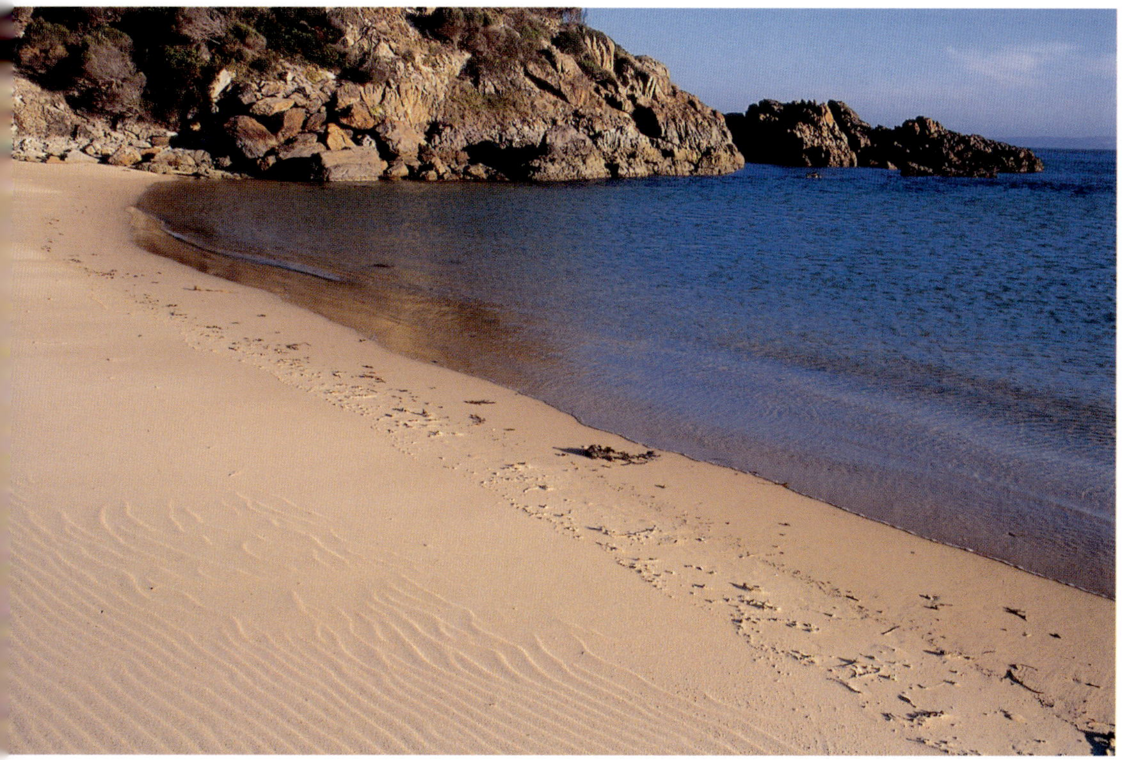

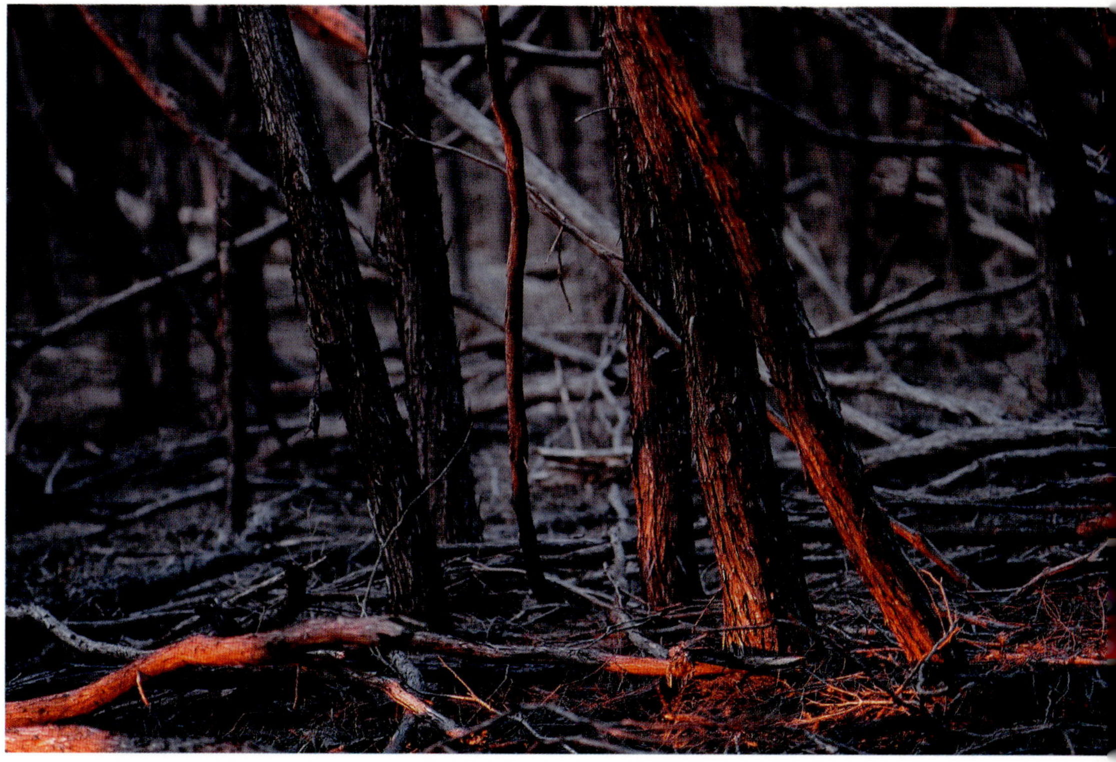

Top: Interesting sand patterns on Bournda Beach, with Turingal Head in Bournda NP behind.

Right: A dense woodland of Casuarina trees catch the last light in Bournda NP.

Opposite page: Moonrise over Pambula River mouth, a short distance south of the town of Merimbula in the Ben Boyd NP.

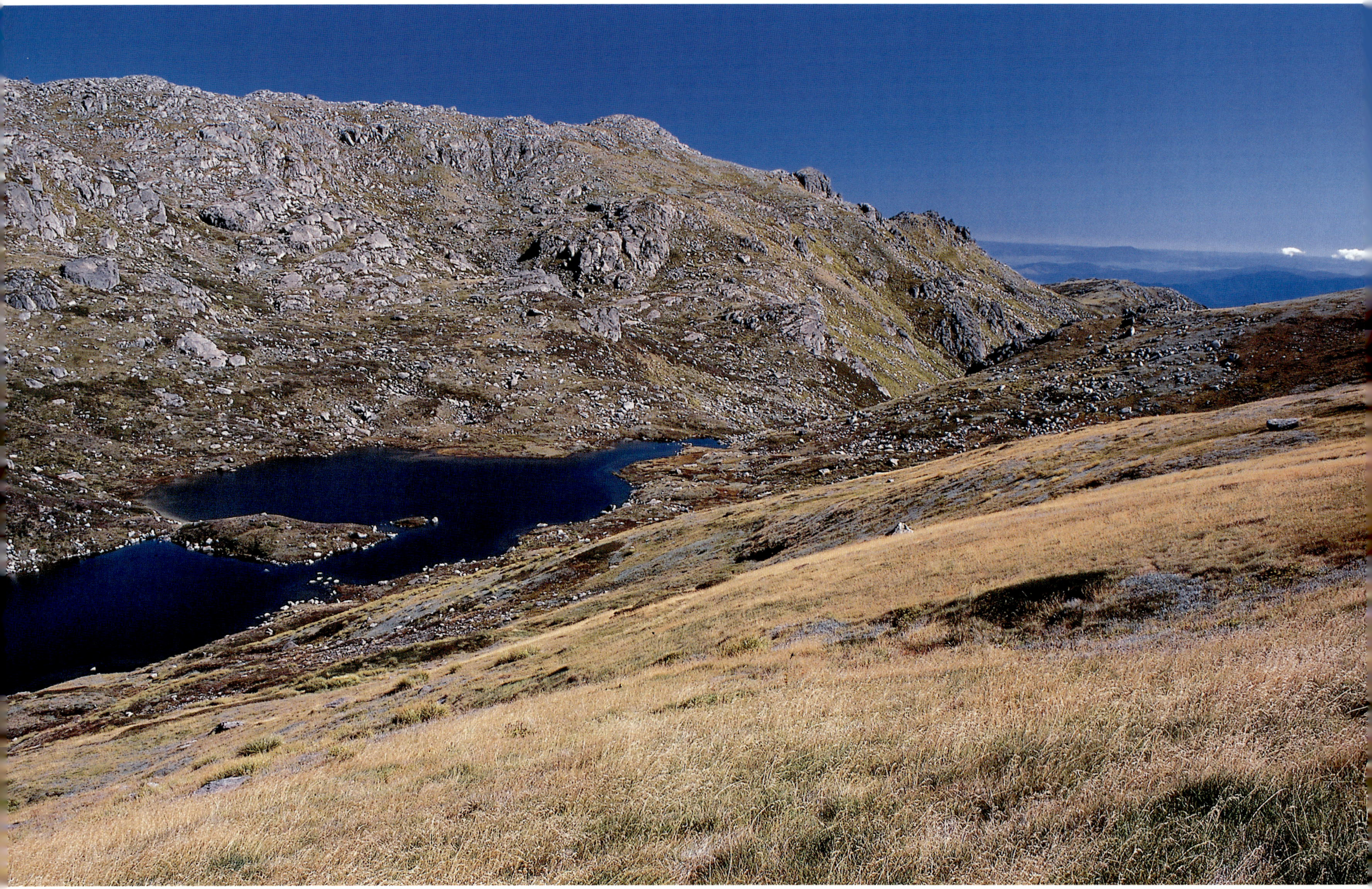

Inland from the south-eastern coastline, Kosciuszko National Park protects the highest peaks in the country and the headwaters of major rivers like the Murray, Murrumbidgee and Snowy. I did the Main Range Track in March 2013, a 21 kilometre circuit taking in Blue Lake, Carruther's Peak, Lake Albina and Mount Kosciuszko (Tar Gan Gil, 2228m), Australia's highest mountain. I wrote *"the whole area is just stunning – open alpine heathlands, rolling hills with areas of cliffs and glacial lakes. When you get to the summit ridge there is an awesome drop of a thousand metres or more to the western plains. I continued on and as I neared Kosciuszko it started to get really busy with people! I got to the top at 12.30pm and got some girls I had met on the way up to take a photo of me on the summit."*

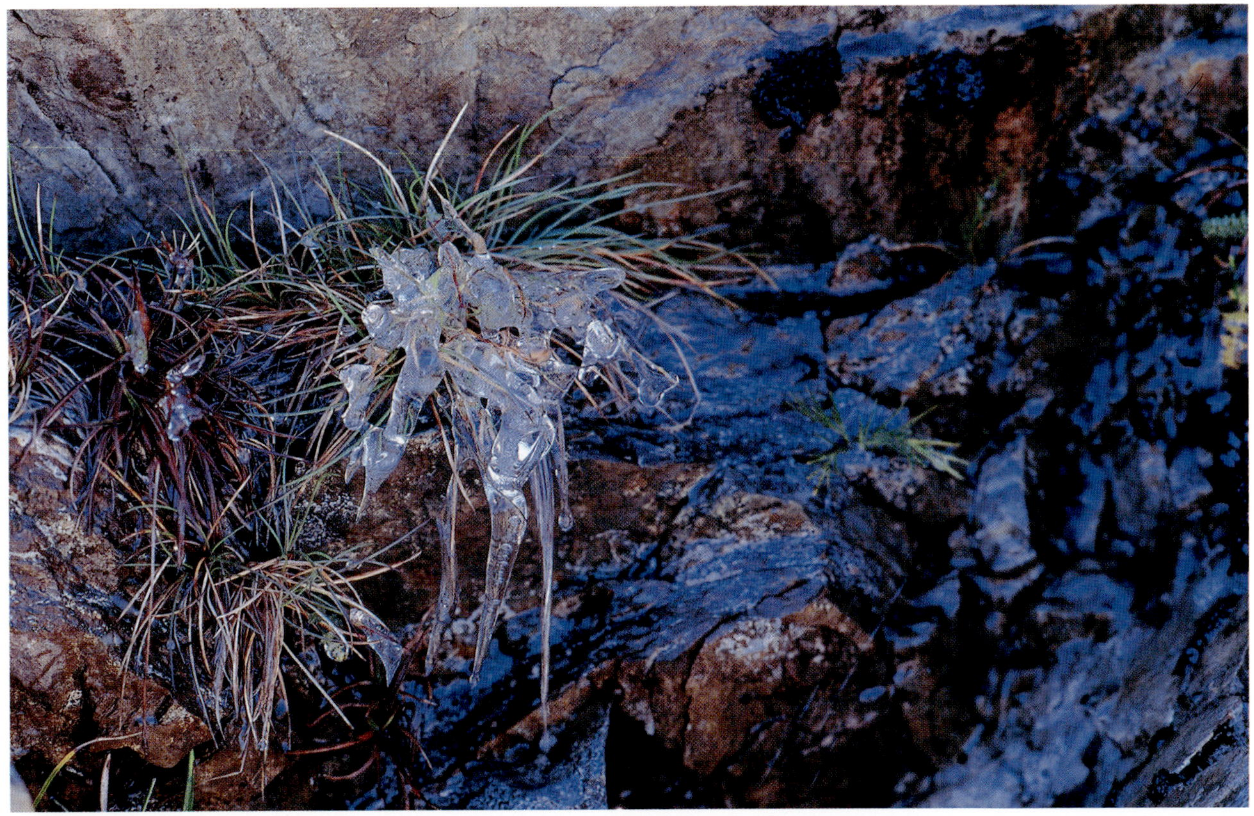

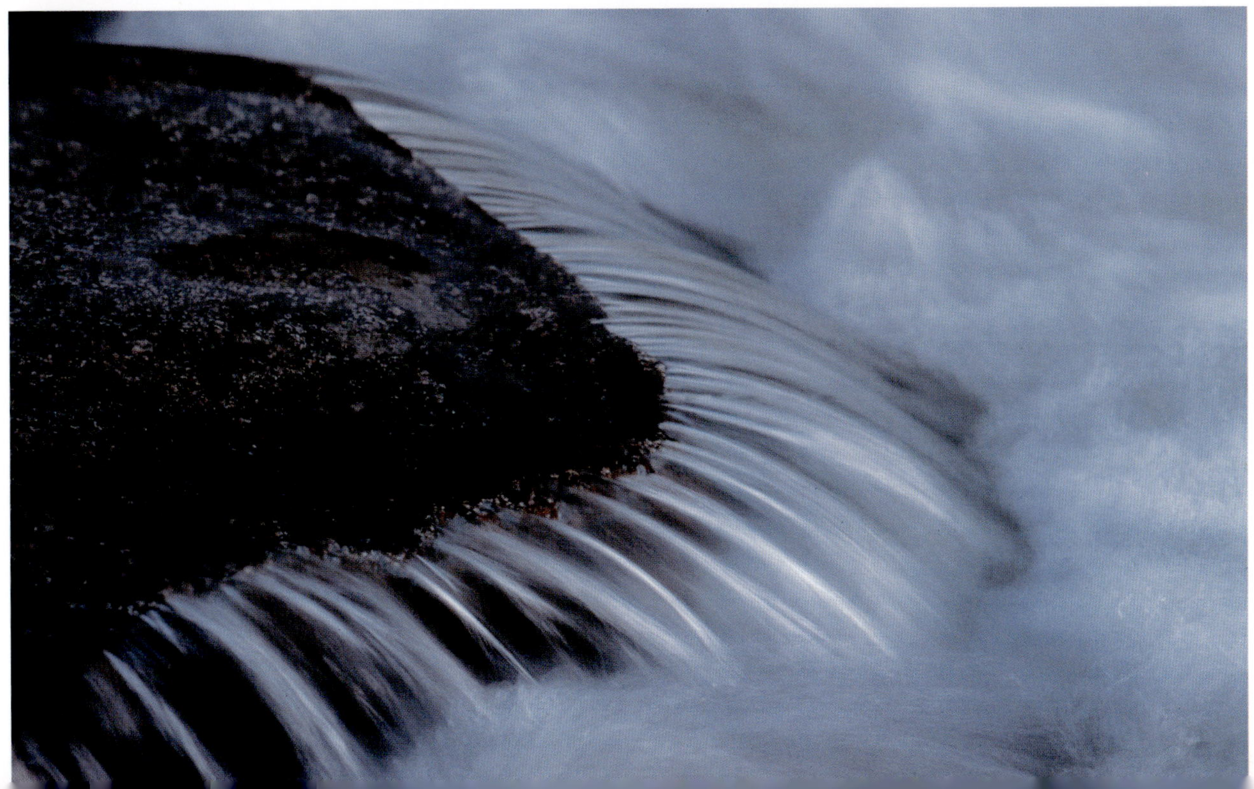

Top: Icicles cling to alpine grasses in a sheltered nook on the Main Range Track in early autumn.

Right: Pure mountain water pours over a rock in the Snowy River, Kosciuszko NP.

Opposite page: Alpine heathlands fall down to glacially carved Lake Albina with the rocky slopes of Mount Townsend (2210m), the second highest mountain in Australia, rising behind.

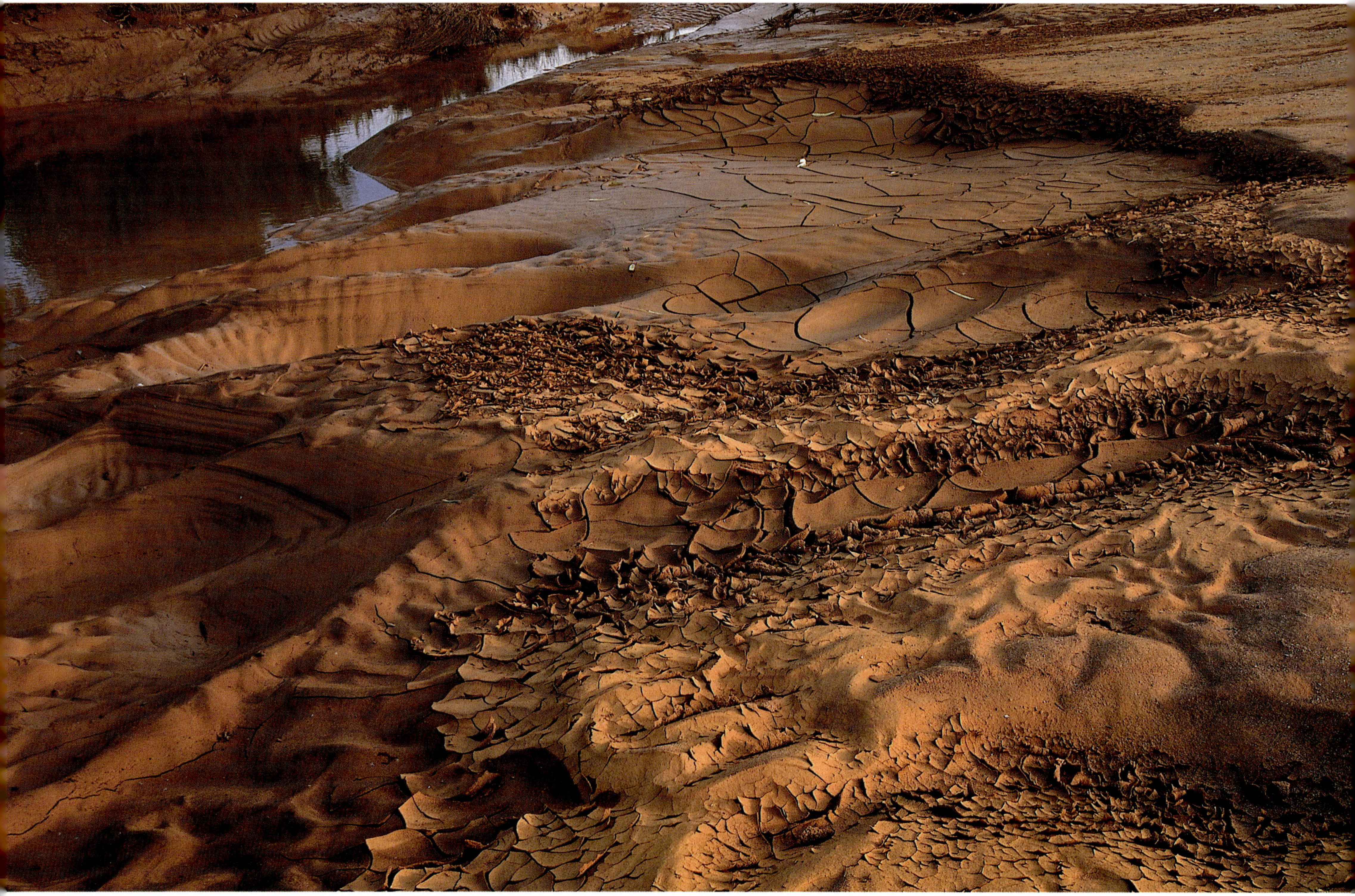

A dry riverbed at Silverton in outback New South Wales, five days after a significant rain event.

New South Wales has vast areas of outback in the west of the state, colloquially known as country to the "back o' Bourke" – Bourke being a town in the state's north west. These areas have a desolate beauty of their own and allow for silence and contemplation. There are endless flat plains around Hay in the south west and rugged outback ranges near Broken Hill, a mining town with large deposits of silver, lead and zinc. The river red gum-lined Darling, Lachlan and Murrumbidgee Rivers flow through this usually dry landscape, and occasionally flood vast areas of surrounding country after deluges of rain. These rivers are tributaries of the mighty Murray River, Australia's most important inland waterway.

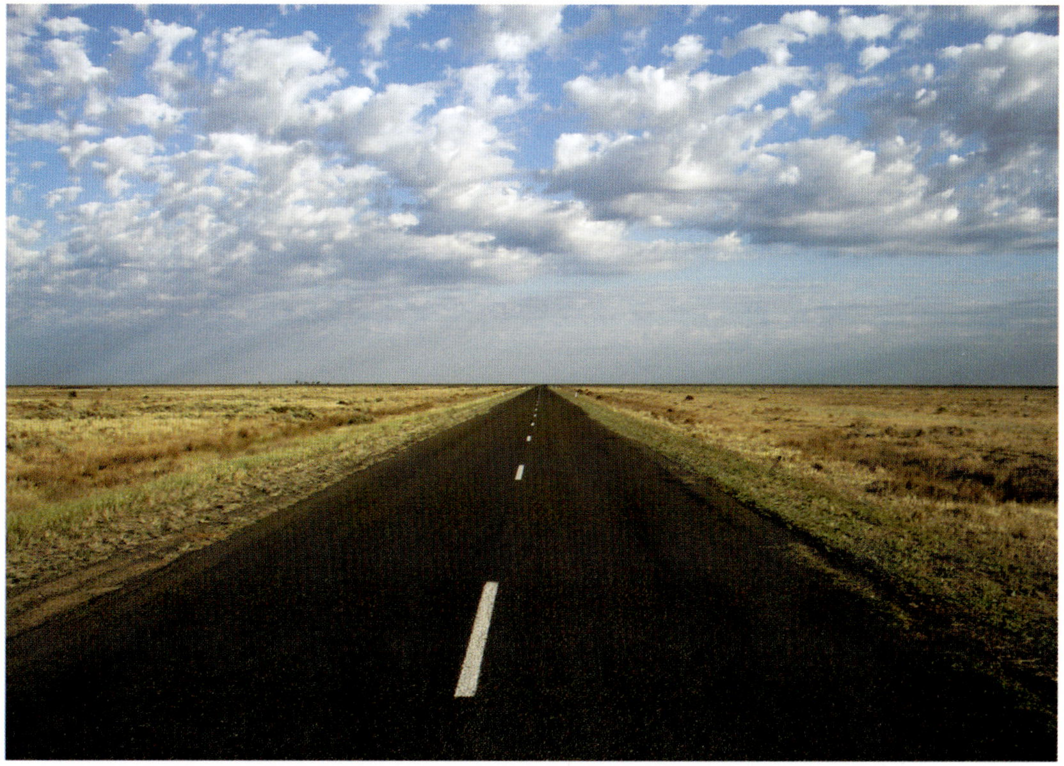

Lonely highway near Hay, south west New South Wales.

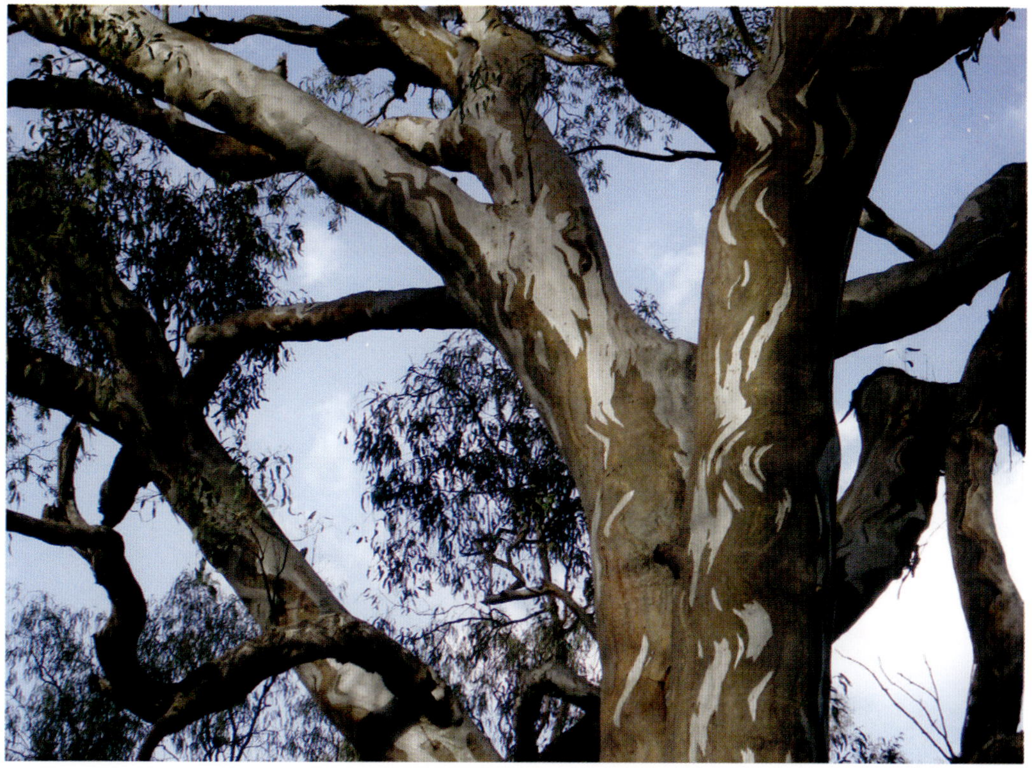

River red gum near the banks of the Murrumbidgee River, Hay.

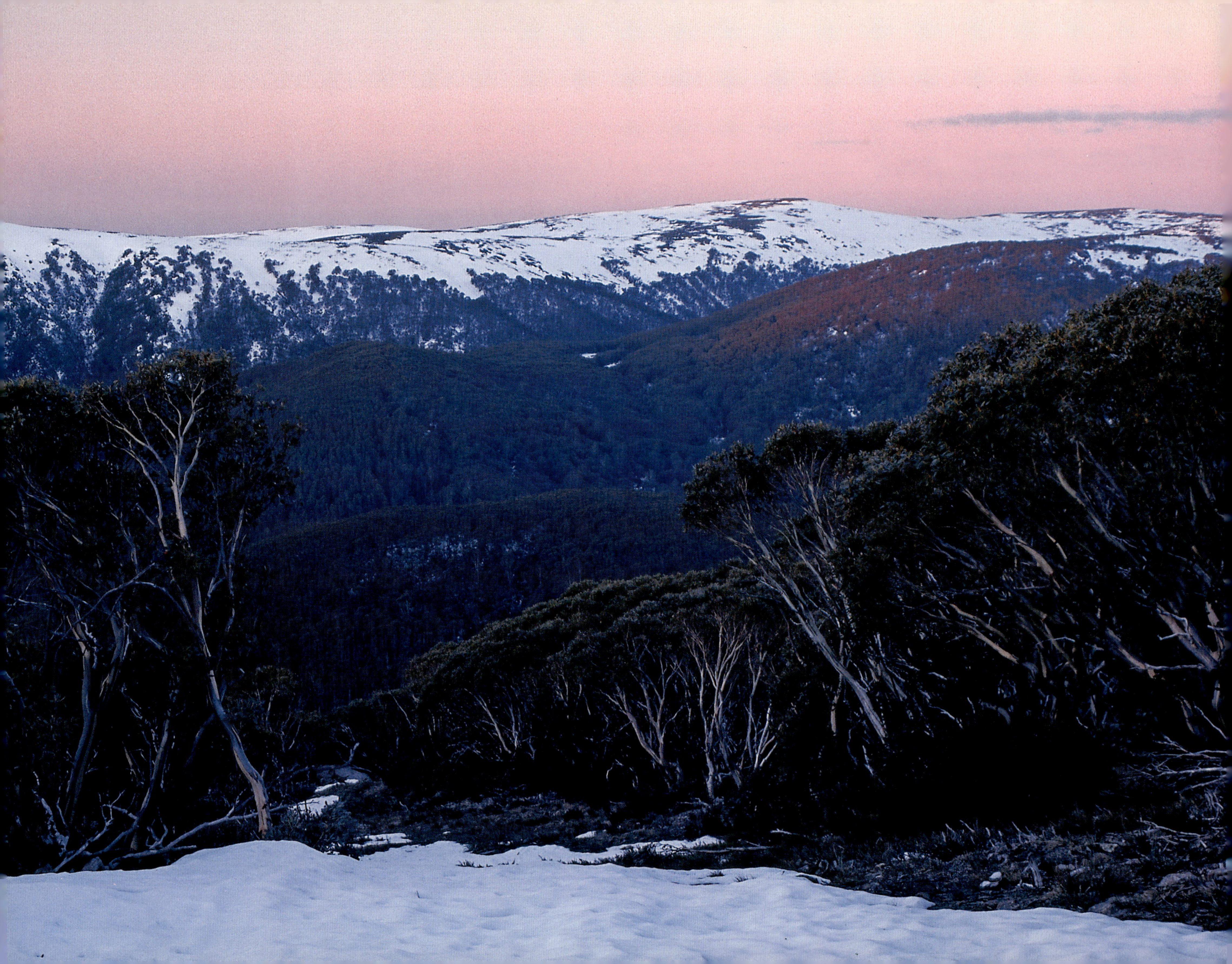

Victoria

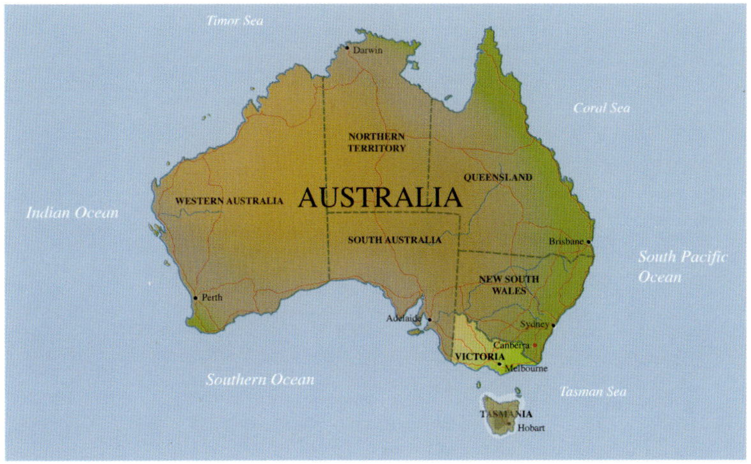

Victoria is the smallest and most densely populated mainland state, but packs a lot of scenery and variety into its borders. Its scenic coastline and productive farmland is backed by the high mountains of the Victorian Alps to the north-east and the Grampian Ranges and sweeping plains to the north-west, that lead eventually to the Murray River, the border with New South Wales. Before the arrival of Europeans, the river provided a bountiful food supply for Aboriginal groups, and it was a major paddle steamer trade route in the latter half of the 19th century. Since the 1880s the Murray has provided irrigation water for vast, intensive agriculture schemes.

Aboriginal people have been in Victoria for at least 40,000 years, the age of artefacts discovered at an ancient campsite at Keilor on Melbourne's north west outskirts. The first unsuccessful European settlement in Victoria was attempted in Port Phillip Bay in 1803. During this time the convict William Buckley escaped and lived with local Aboriginal tribes for more than 30 years. He was the only European living in Victoria until 1834, when parties from Tasmania, searching for arable land, settled along the south-west coast of Victoria. Their glowing reports prompted John Batman and John Fawkner to investigate the Port Phillip area and subsequently to purchase land on opposite sides of the Yarra River from local Aboriginal people, paying them with knives and blankets. A squatting town grew up rapidly, was named Melbourne after the British Prime Minister of the day, and is today the second largest city in Australia with a population of over four million.

Nervous of inheriting the penal system of settlement, in 1851 Victoria was granted separation from New South Wales. Soon afterwards, gold was discovered near Melbourne and further big discoveries at Ballarat and Bendigo triggered gold rushes and a massive increase in the population of the state. Many towns retain grand examples of architecture built during this era. In 1854, a dispute over miners' rights led to 10,000 miners burning their licences and swearing allegiance to a flag based on the Southern Cross. A stockade was built at the Eureka goldfield near Ballarat, and fighting between miners and troopers broke out in the early hours of 3 December 1854. About 5 troopers and 22 miners were slain. The leaders were tried and acquitted, and a government commission recommended the granting of many of the miners' demands. This incident is the only serious attempt at revolution Australia has ever seen. Victoria today boasts a vibrant arts and culture scene and Melbourne hosts many major sporting events like the Australian Tennis Open and the Australian Football League Grand Final.

Opposite page: Dusk falls over snowgum woodland and the snow covered slopes of Mount Bogong.

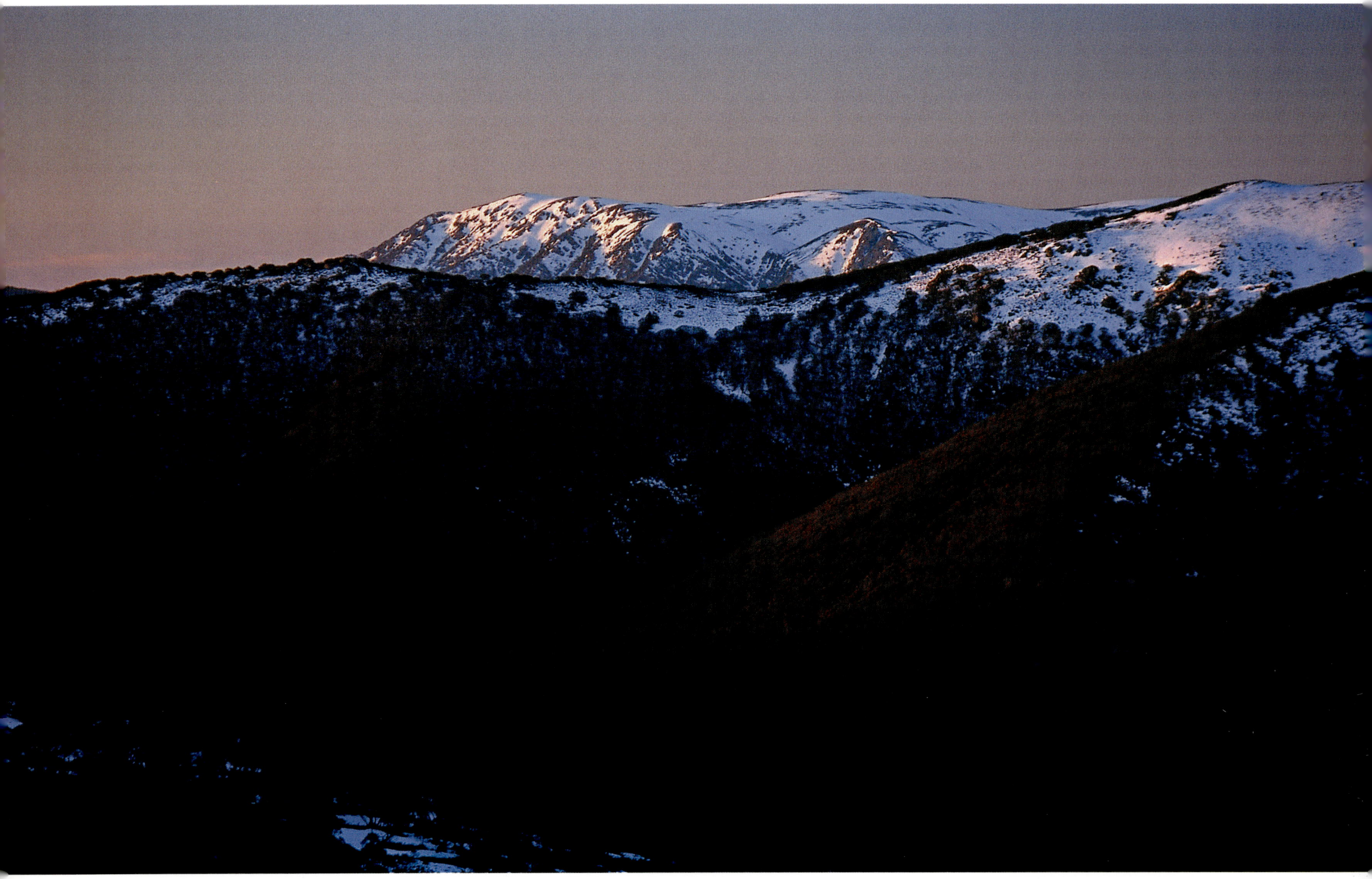

Sunset colours over Mount Bogong, viewed from Falls Creek.

Victoria's high country stretches from the New South Wales border to the outer suburbs of Melbourne in the Dandenong Ranges. The highest peak is Mount Bogong, an extensive undulating plateau rising to 1,986 metres at its highest point. The Alpine National Park protects most of the high country of the Great Dividing Range – some 6460 square kilometres. Winter sports are popular at resorts like Falls Creek, Mt Hotham, Mt Buller, Mt Buffalo and Mt Baw Baw. Fishing, horse riding, bushwalking and canoeing are also enjoyed in warmer weather.

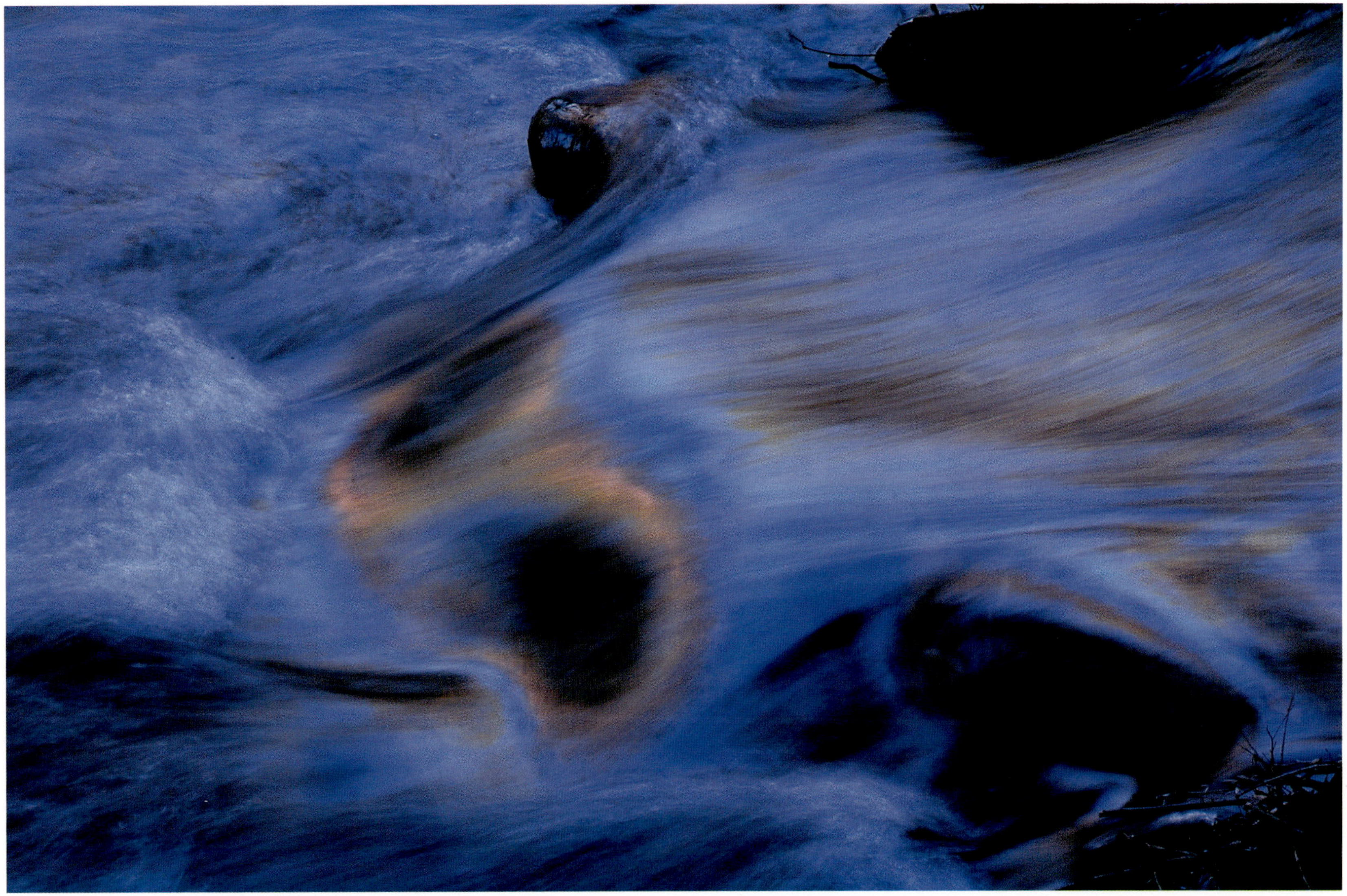

Reflections in a small rapid on Snowy Creek near the town of Mitta Mitta in the Victorian Alps.

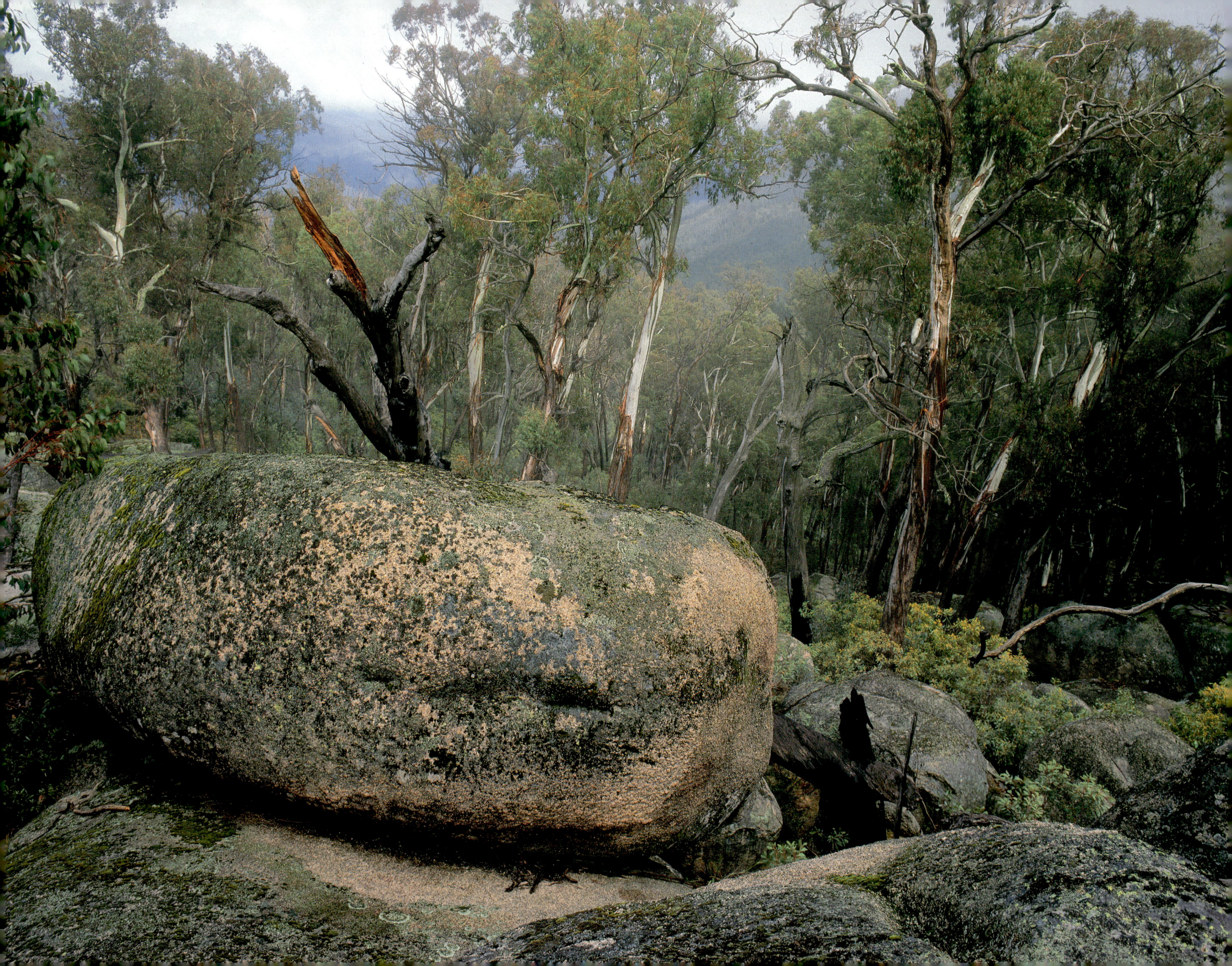

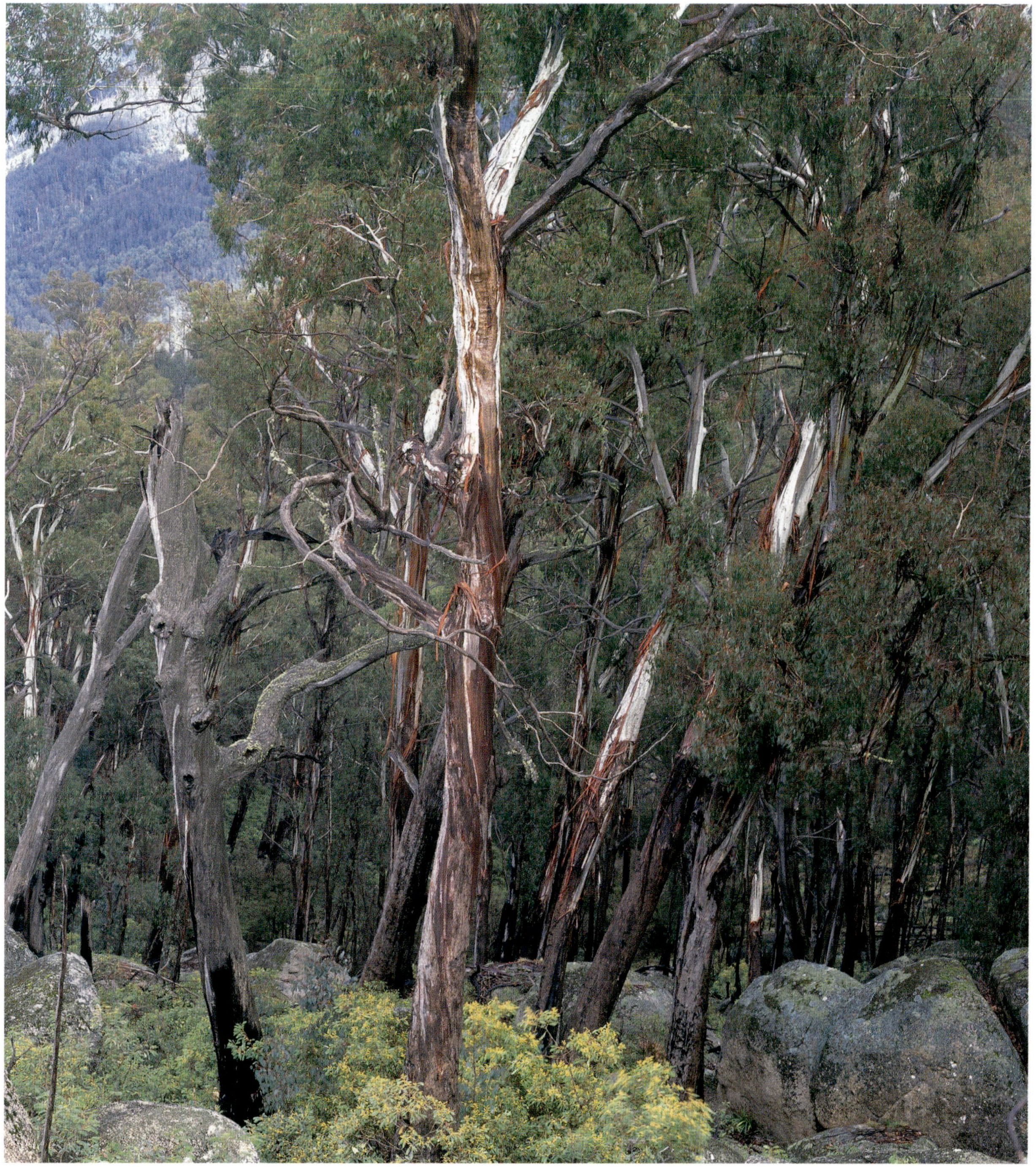

Mount Buffalo National Park is 325 kilometres north-east of Melbourne and protects a great granite slab of mountain, with its highest point known as the Horn (1723m). Mount Buffalo has cross country skiing and tobogganing in the winter season, and bushwalking, swimming, mountain biking and picnicking are also popular. The mountain is part of the traditional country of the Minjambuta Aboriginal people, who used to journey up the mountain in spring and summer to have ceremonies and feast on Bogong moths. The moths gathered in rock crevices to escape hot temperatures and were an important protein-rich food, which they cooked on hot stones or in hot ash.

Left: Bark peeling from tall eucalypt forest at Mount Buffalo NP. The mountain has snowgum woodlands and alpine heathlands at higher altitudes.

Opposite page: A large granite boulder at Mount Buffalo on the Old Galleries track, a one kilometre circuit through woodlands and narrow passages between giant rocks.

Cape Conran Coastal Park lies 420 kilometres east of Melbourne near the Gippsland town of Orbost. It is a quiet and peaceful spot, and for no particular reason it was the place where I reached an emotional crisis point, and released all the deep seated sadness resulting from the sale of my dream home in the Porongurups. I camped here one month into my second trip in March 2013 and wrote: *"I felt jaded and a bit depressed and uninspired. I went out to the beach and started walking along the sands. After a little while I just screamed out in agony – and suddenly I was crying and screaming and cursing. Yelling at the sea gods! I was wondering what I have to do to be happy in this life ... Anyway after letting out the angst and the anger I felt better."* I wrote later in my diary that this was a crux day – a turning point – for the trip and perhaps also for my life.

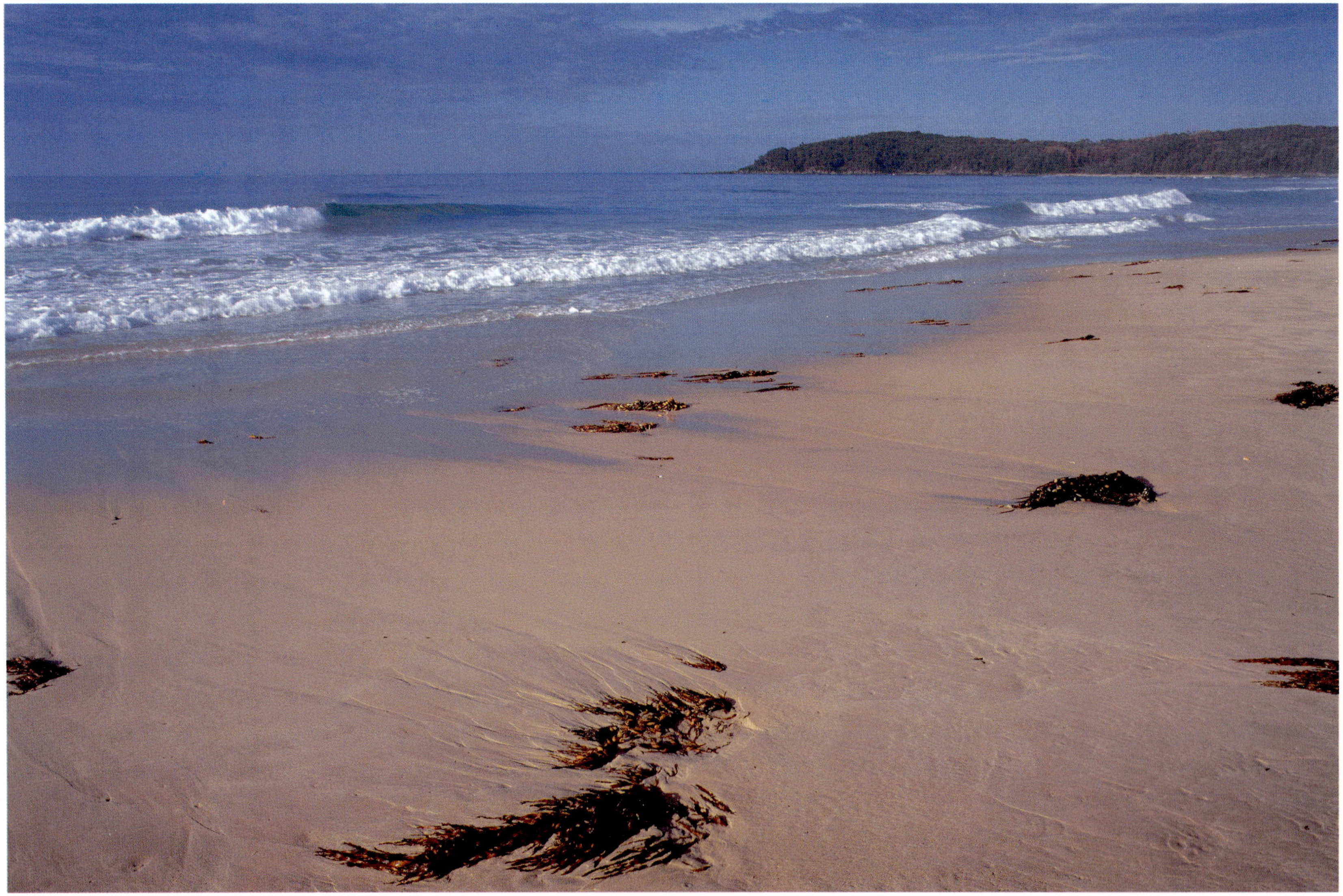

Washed up seaweed and sand patterns on East Cape Beach at Cape Conran.

Opposite page: Sunrise over East Cape Beach, Cape Conran.

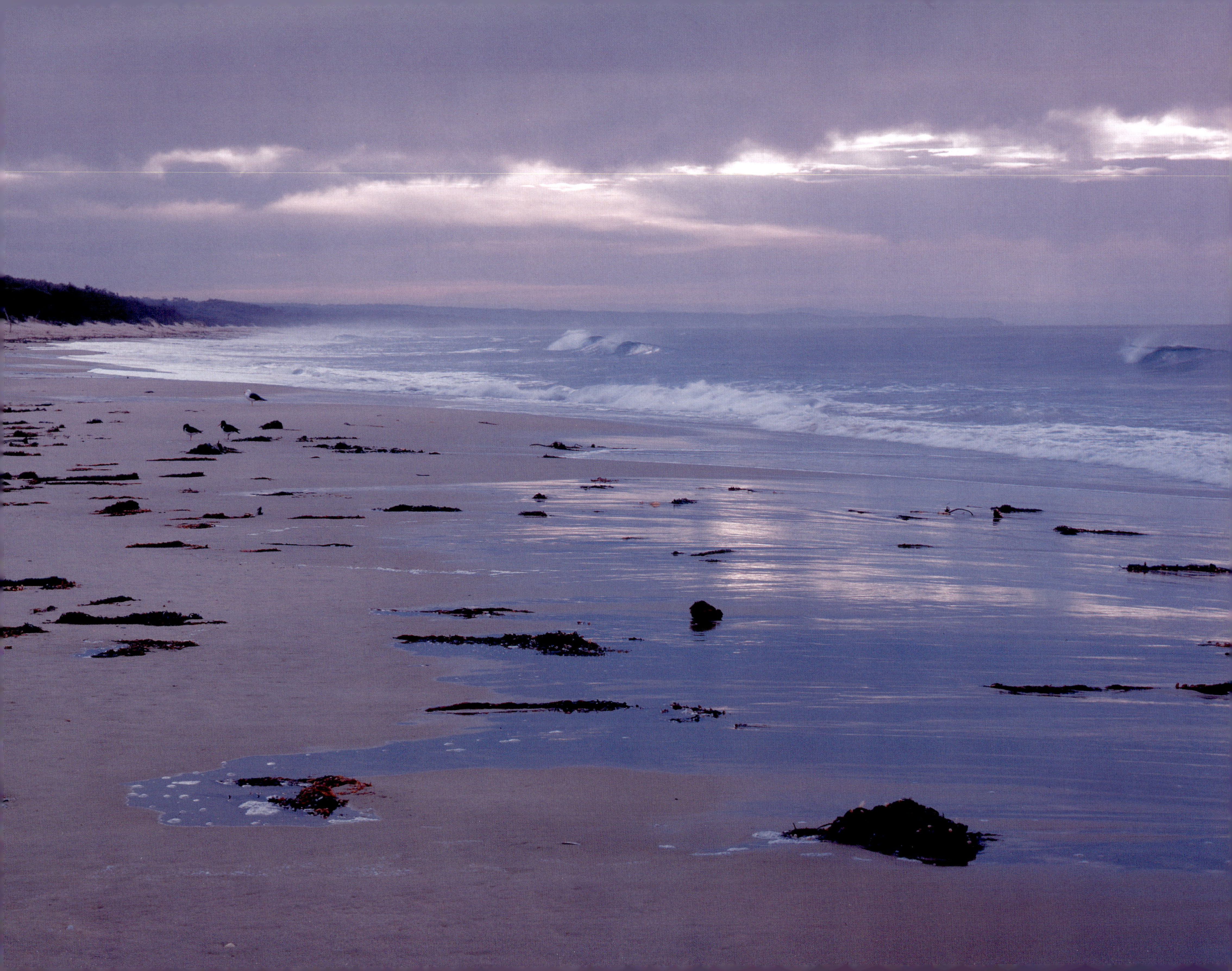

Wilsons Promontory National Park protects the southernmost tip of the Australian mainland, a hook-shaped peninsula of pristine beaches, rainforest patches, granite mountain peaks and offshore islands. It is one of Australia's best known national parks, and a popular destination for day-trippers, campers and hikers. Wildlife here includes potoroos, koalas and wombats.

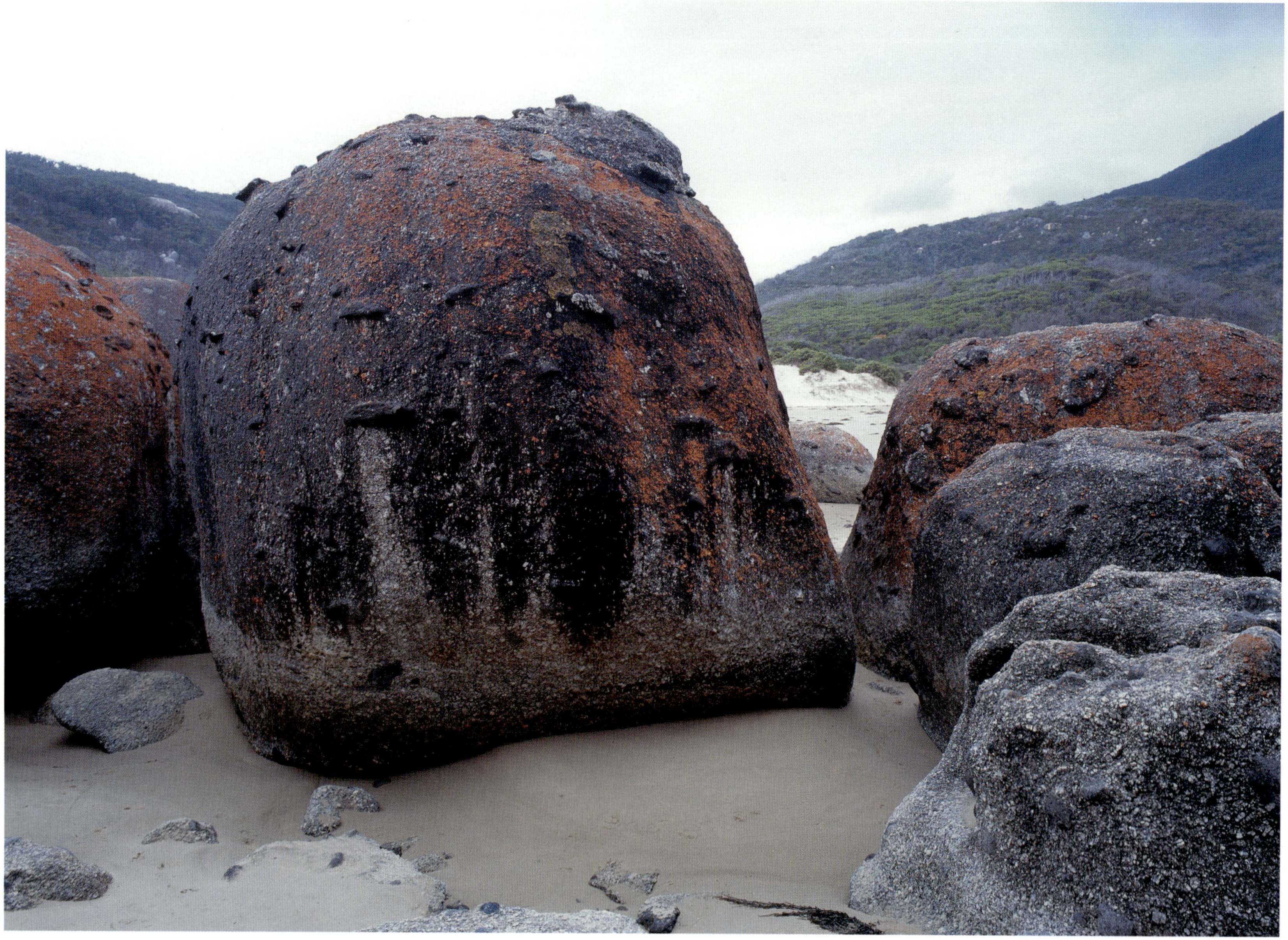

Red lichen colours boulders at Whisky Bay.

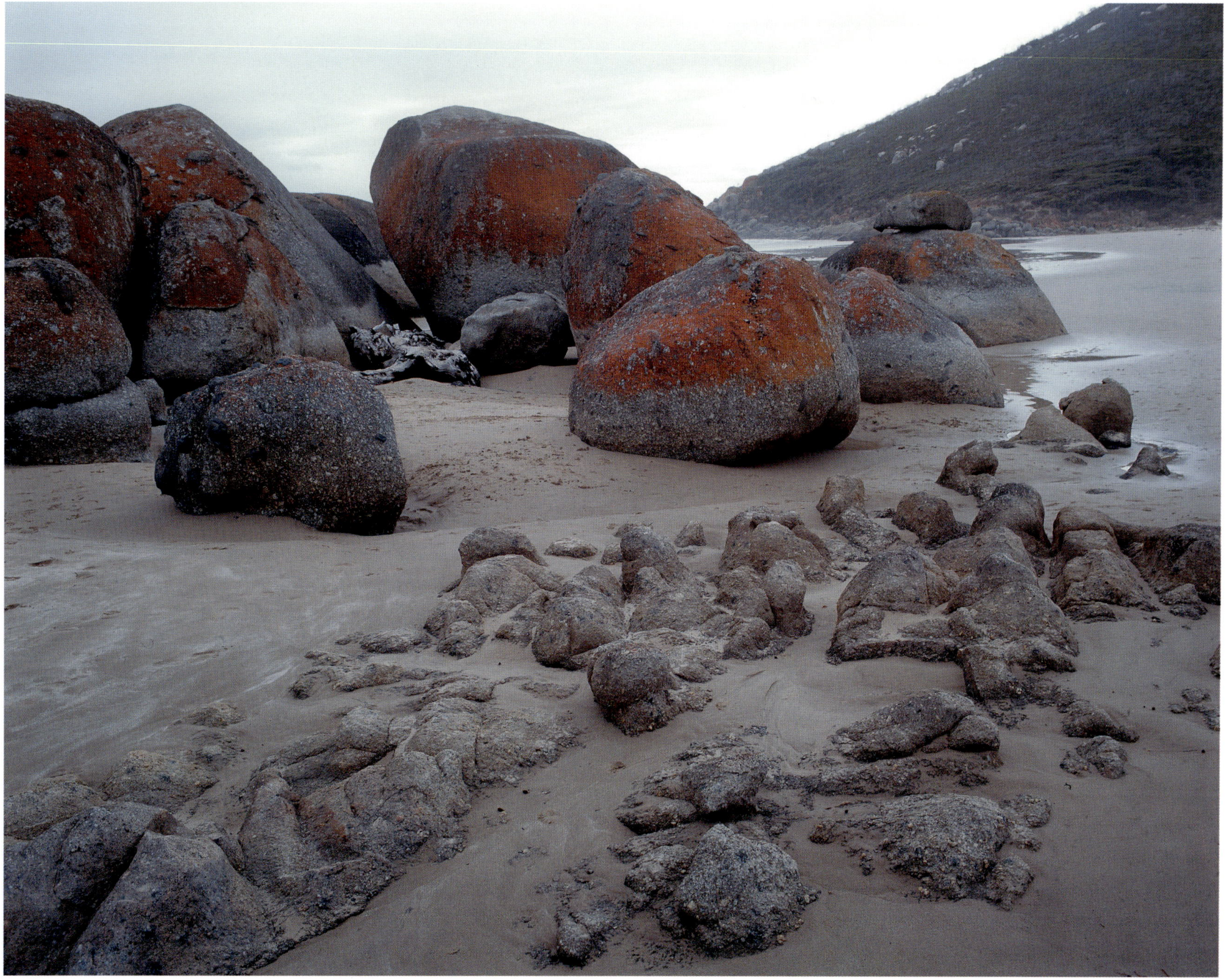

Giant granite boulders at Whisky Bay on the west side of Wilsons Promontory.

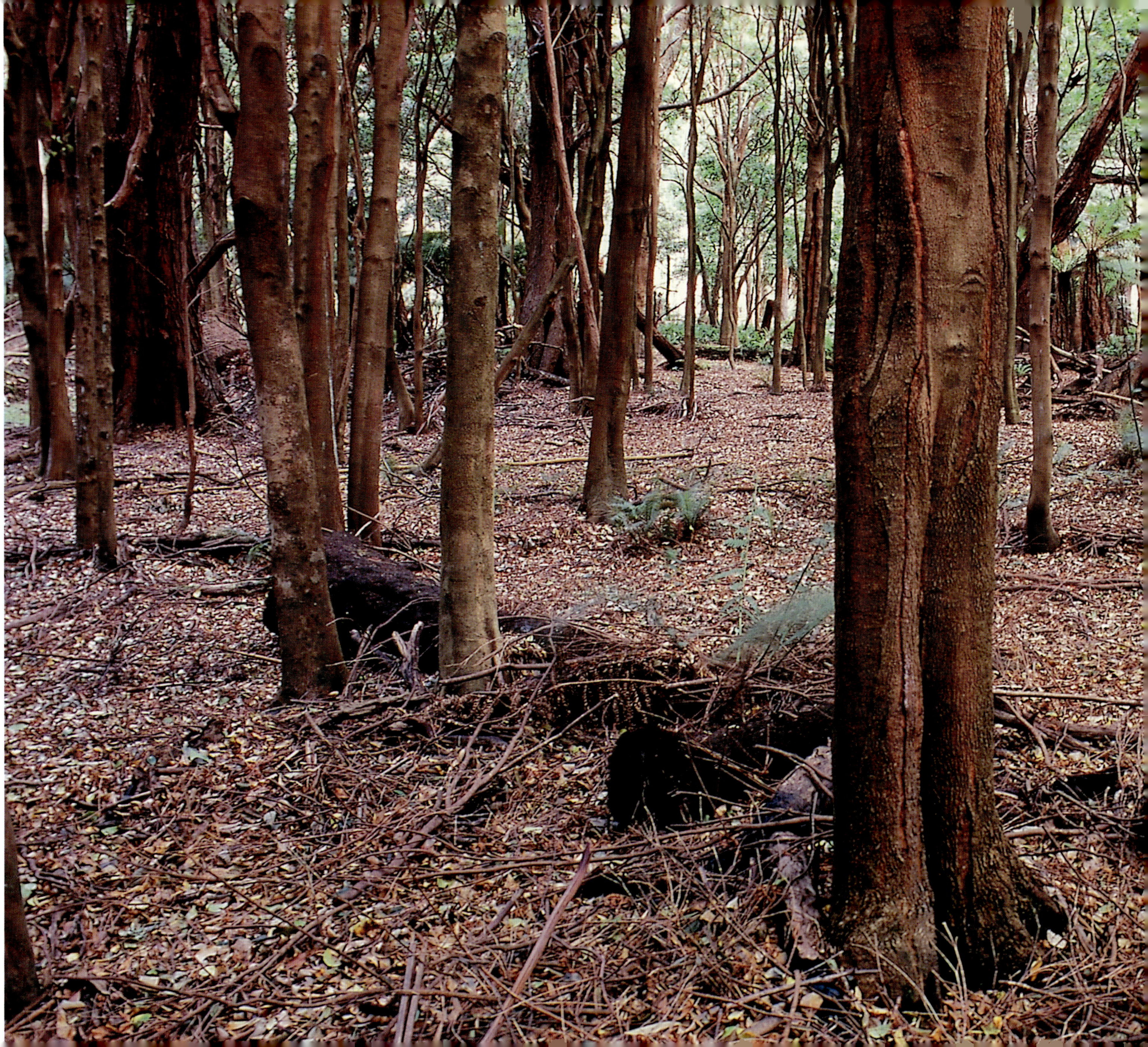

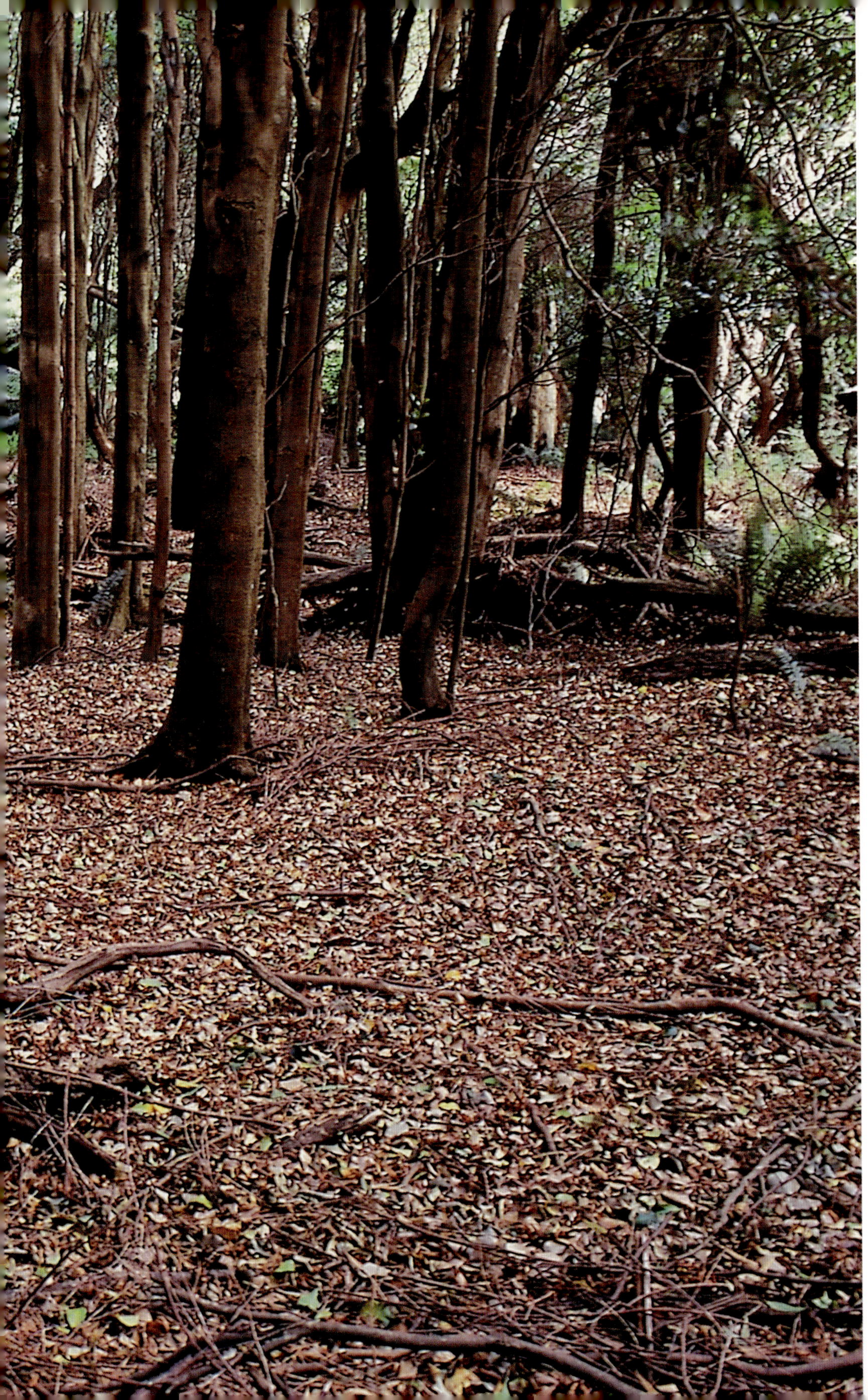

A five kilometre return walk through heathland and eucalypt forests leads to a relict patch of warm temperate rainforest at Lilly Pilly Gully, Wilsons Promontory.

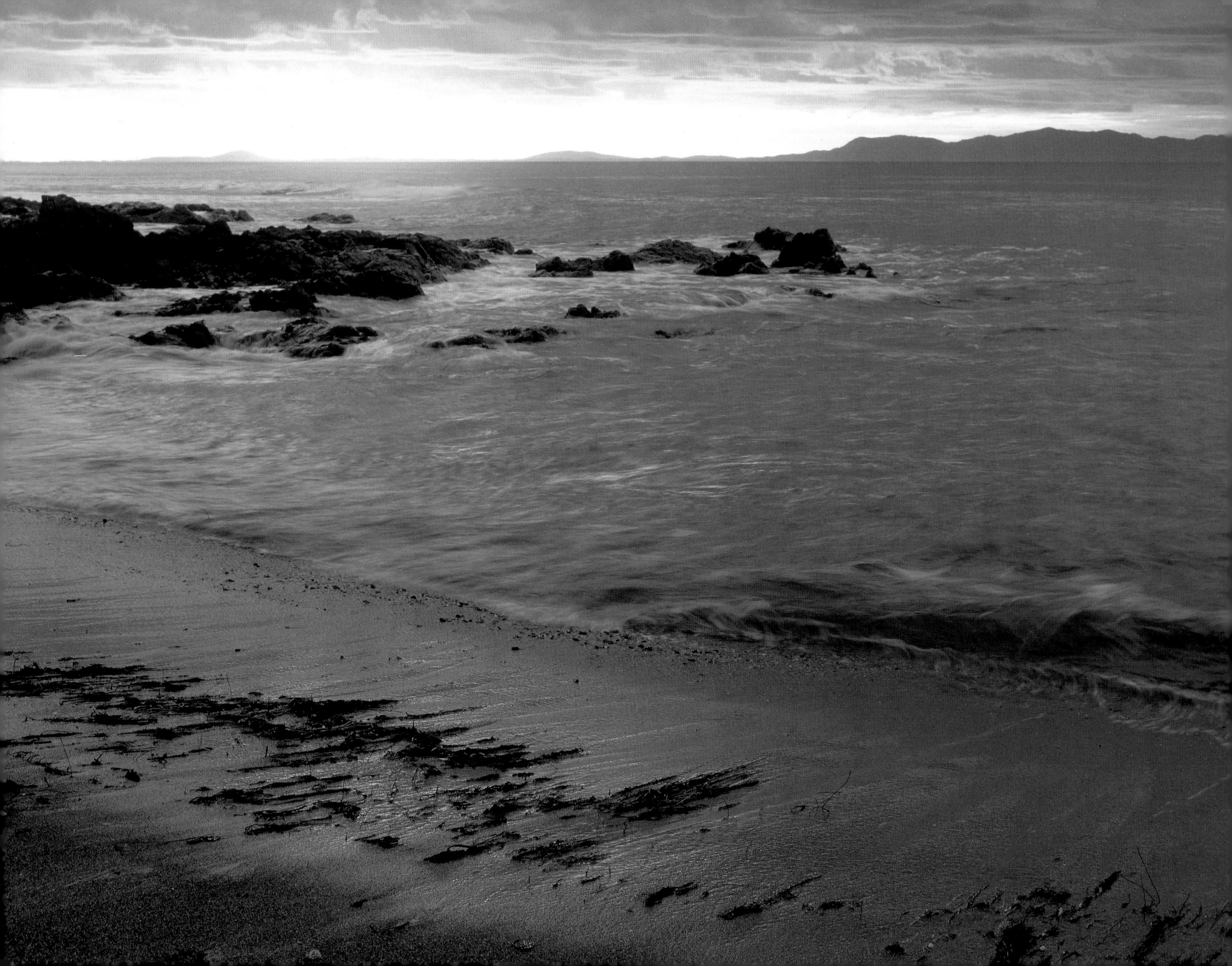

Cape Liptrap Coastal Park protects the headland directly to the west of Wilsons Promontory and is a worthy destination in itself. There are a number of accommodation options and a popular camping area at Bear Gully. I camped here in March 2013, a couple of days before reaching Cape Conran (see page 156) and found myself struggling with various long-standing issues. *"It seems like a nice spot, although I must admit I was feeling really down. After putting up the tent I slumped in a depressed state in the car. Eventually I dragged myself up and went and took some photographs of the late afternoon light on the beach and a small stream. I then cooked tea and watched a glorious sunset. You get a good view from here out across the bay to the mountains of Wilsons Promontory. I did feel a bit better after all this."*

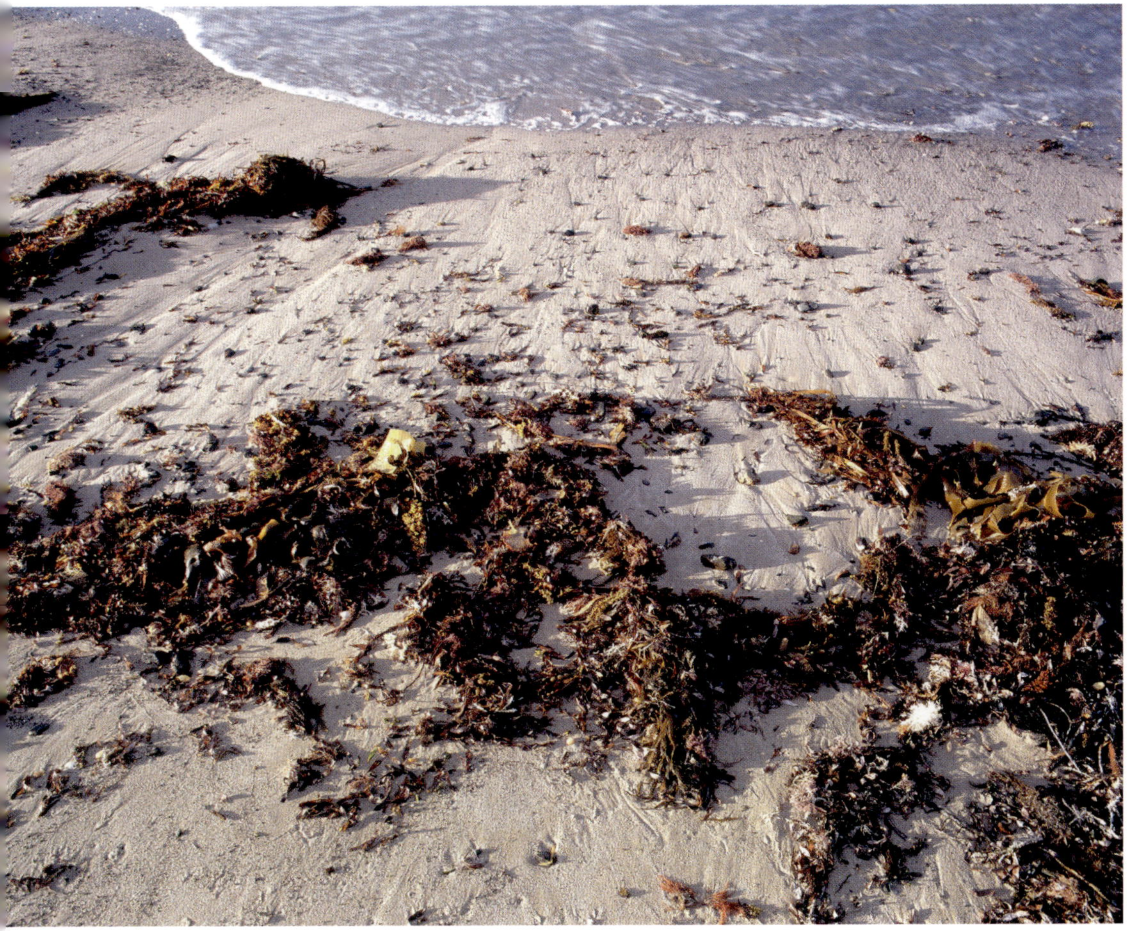

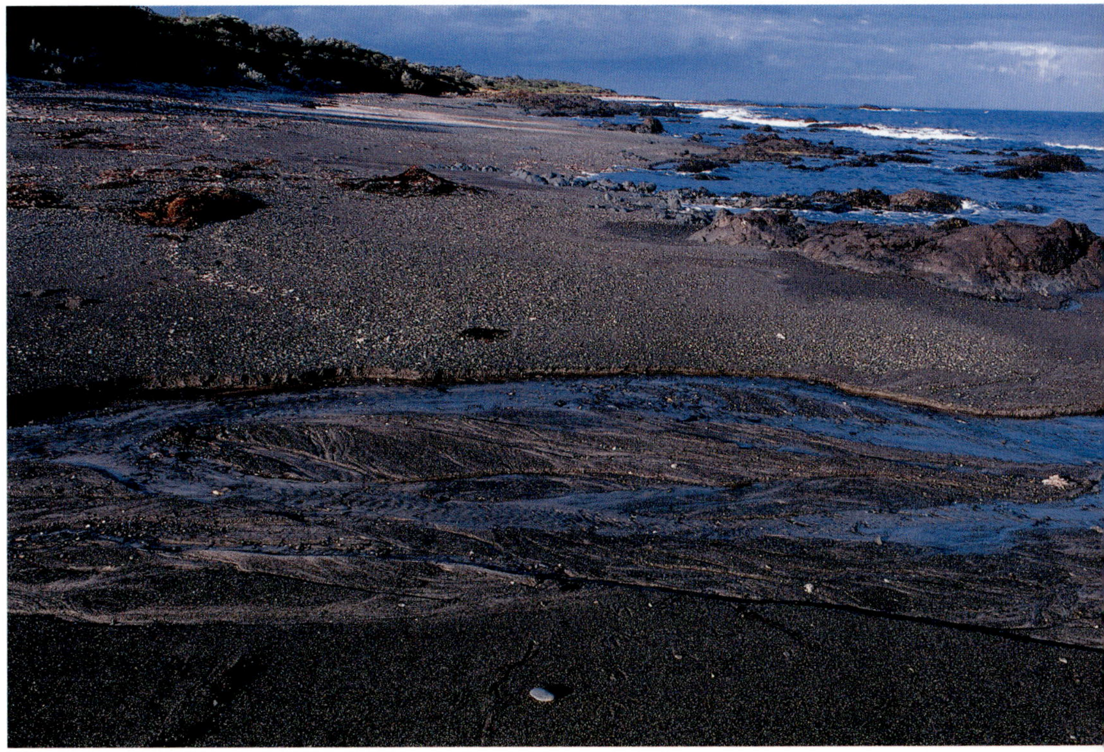

Top: Bear Gully stream finds its way over a gravel beach to the ocean.

Left: Sand and seaweed.

Opposite page: Sunrise from a beach near Bear Gully camping area, Cape Liptrap.

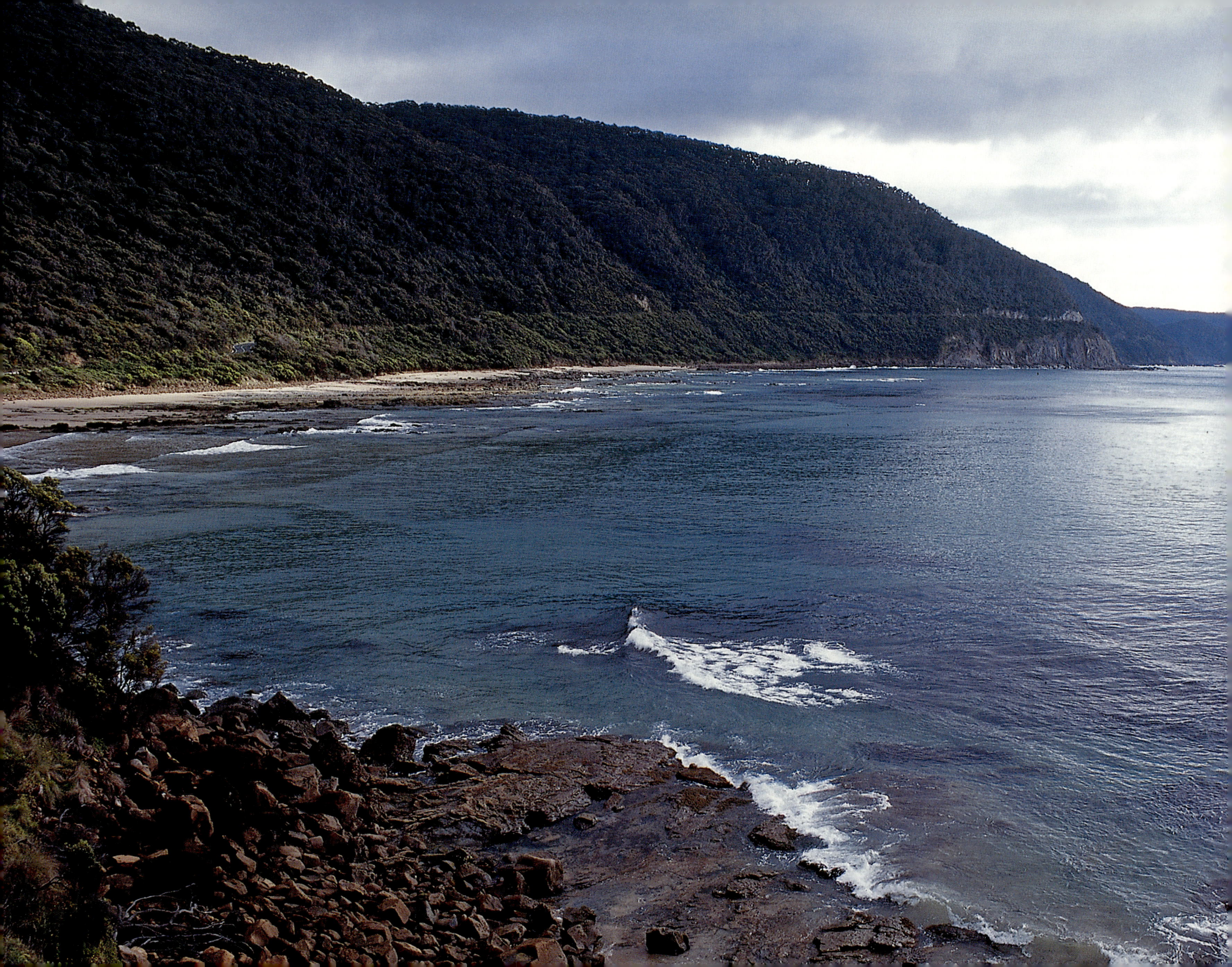

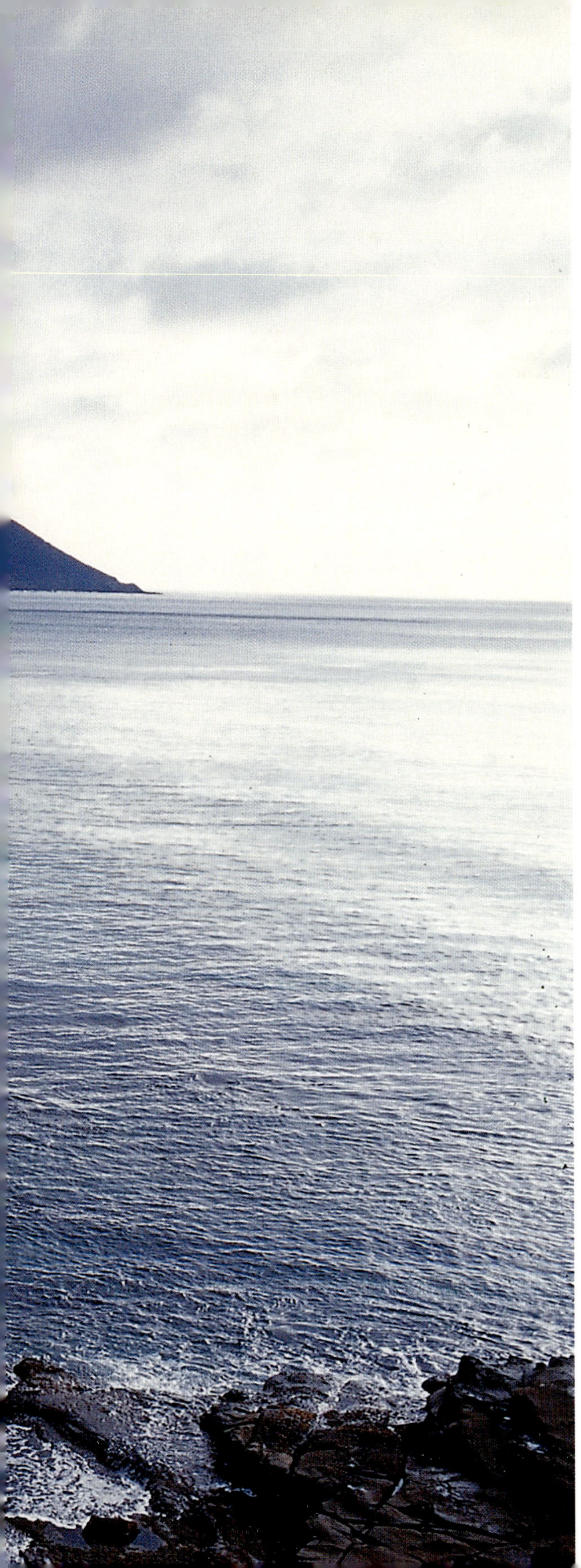

In October 2011, after staying with friends in Melbourne for a few days, I continued my trip around Australia by driving to Sorrento and catching a ferry across the mouth of Port Phillip Bay to Queenscliff. I stayed one night at Barwon Heads and the next day travelled the Great Ocean Road to Lorne. The road, one of Australia's most scenic drives, winds for 320 kilometres from Torquay to Warrnambool in south western Victoria, skirting the Otway Ranges in the eastern section and running above dramatic cliffs in the Port Campbell National Park after Cape Otway. The national park has spectacular features like the Twelve Apostles, limestone pillars left behind by coastal erosion.

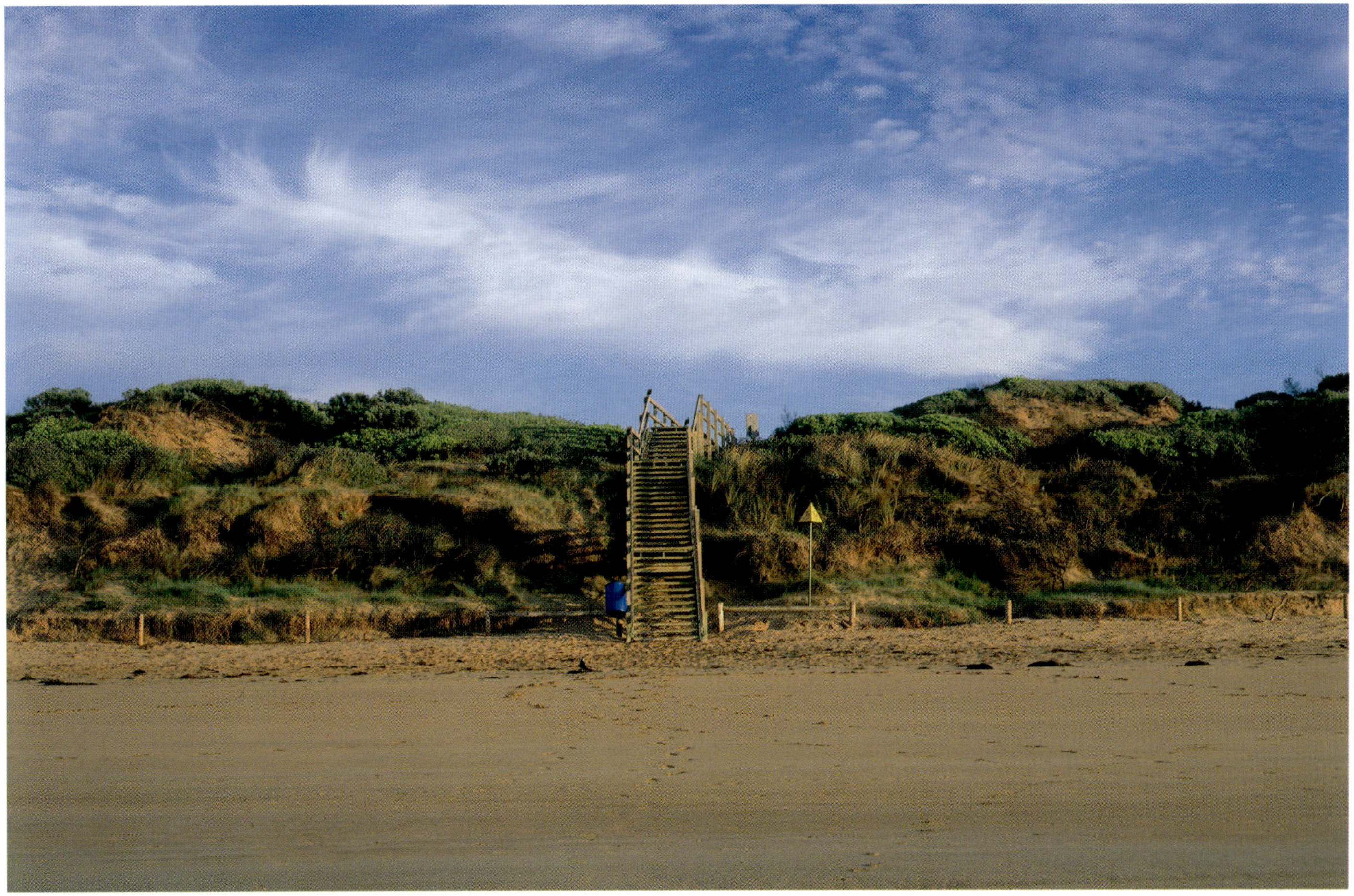

Top: Surf beach access at Barwon Heads.

Left: The Otway Range falls into the sea near Lorne with the line of the Great Ocean Road clearly visible on the hillsides.

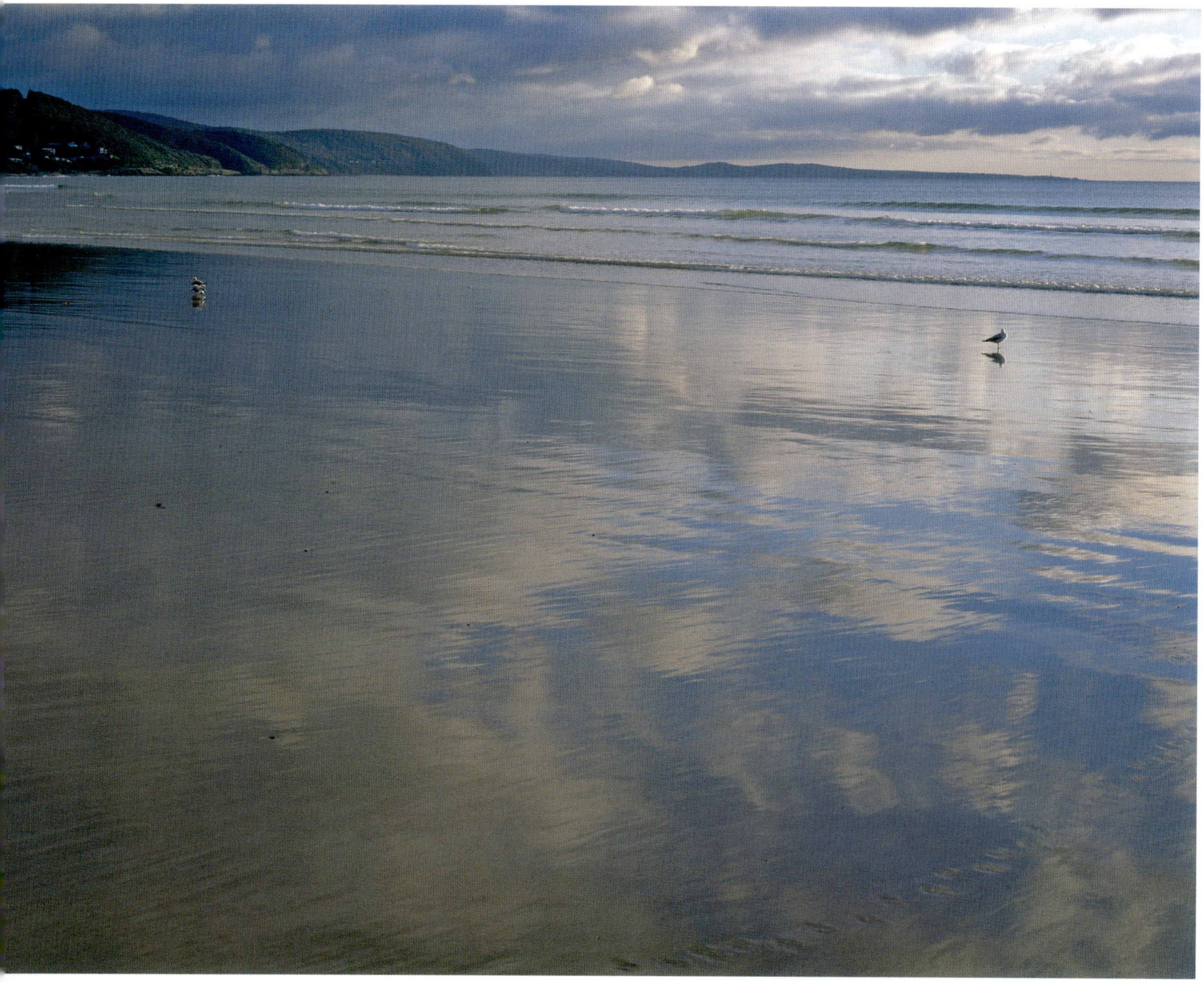

I stayed overnight at Lorne, a lovely town nestled in a bay on the Great Ocean Road, in October 2011. The next evening I wrote: *"It has been a long, tiring day but with a lovely start – sunshine and beautiful scenery at Lorne, and along the Great Ocean Road. I had bacon and eggs and a coffee at Apollo Bay and after that the weather turned with rain and wind buffeting me while I took photographs at the Twelve Apostles. I then headed inland slowly towards the Grampians, getting to Dunkeld eventually and watching some of the Rugby World Cup at a local pub."*

Left: Seagulls adorn the beautiful beach at Lorne soon after dawn.

Opposite page: The famous Twelve Apostles near Port Campbell.

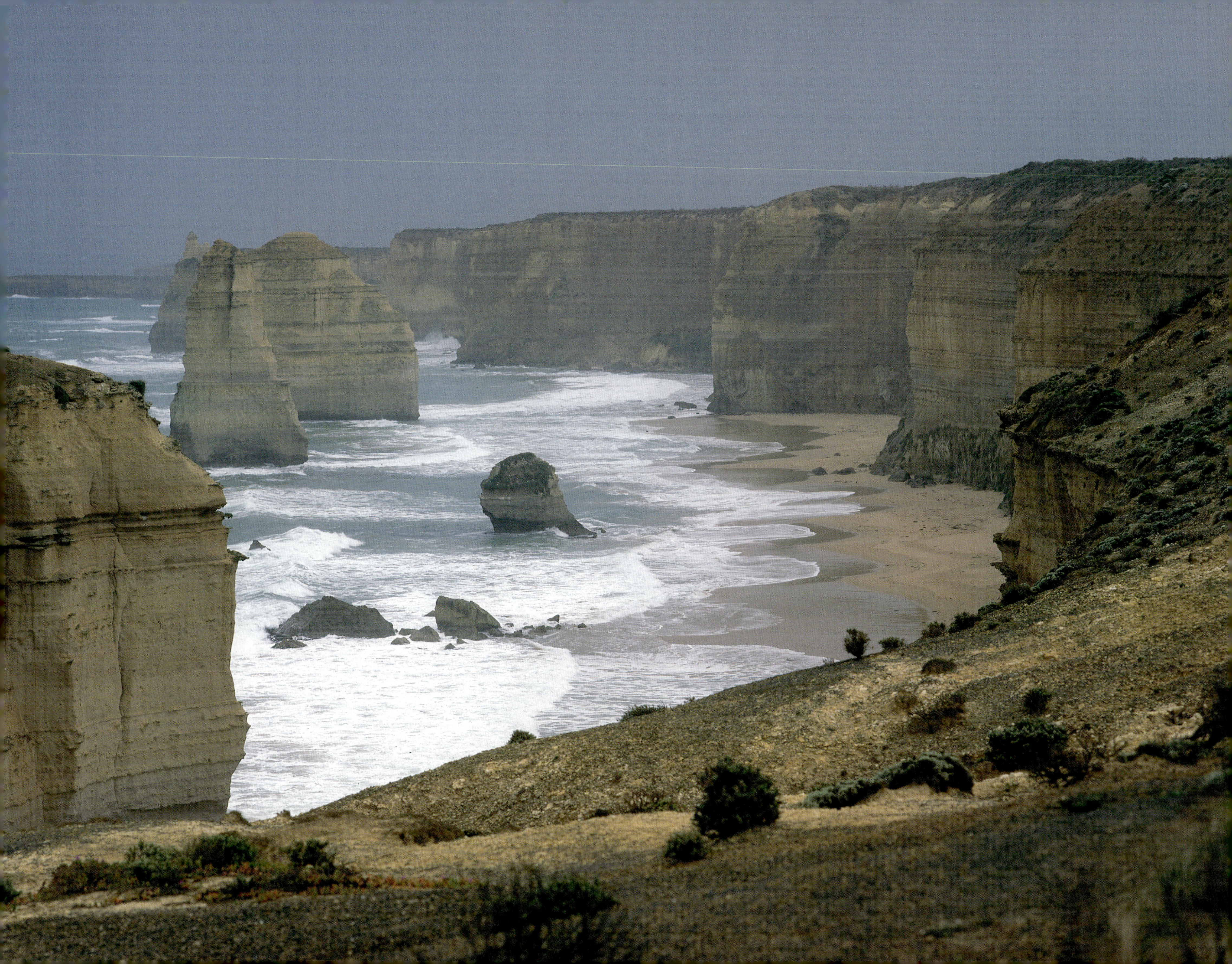

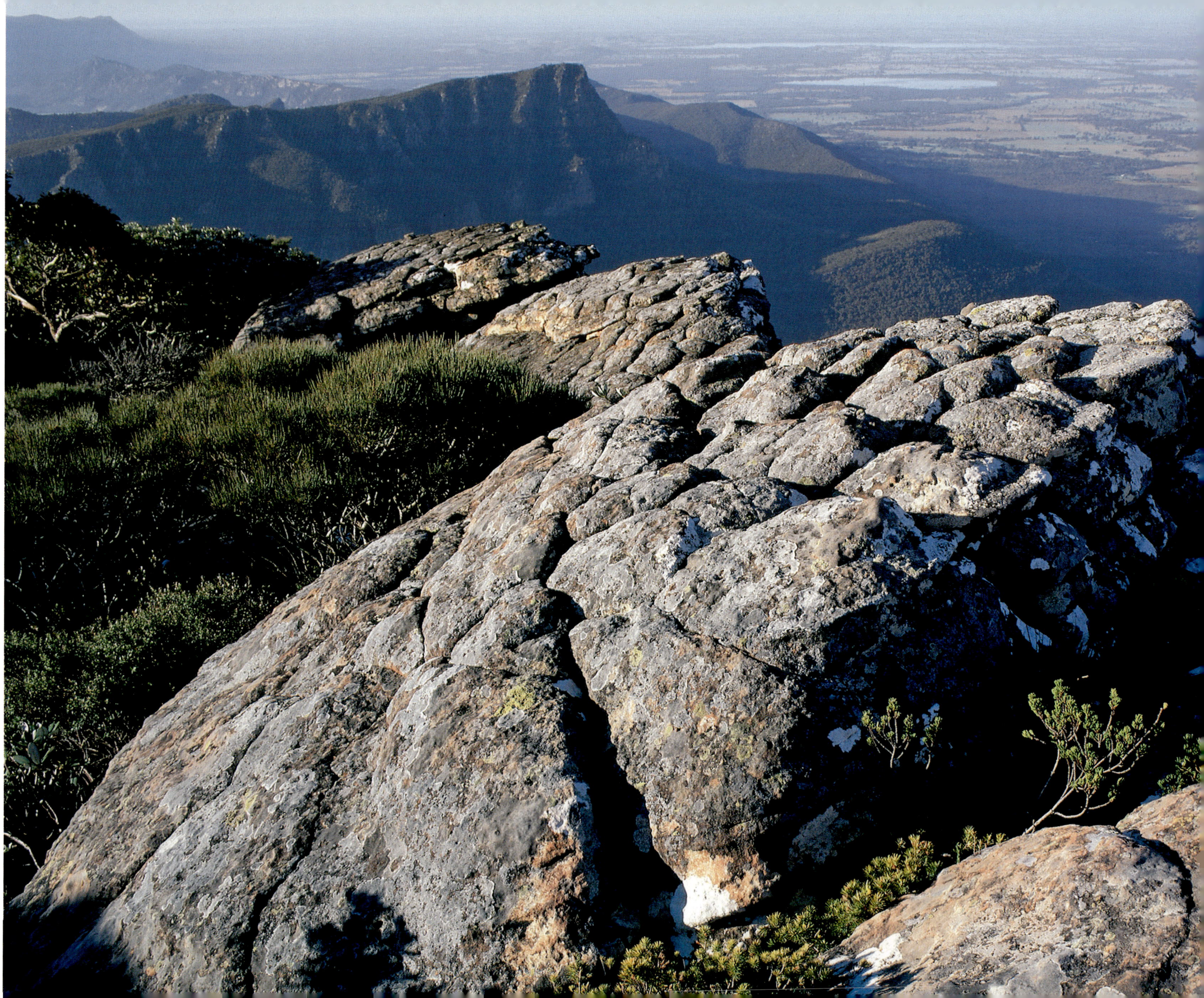

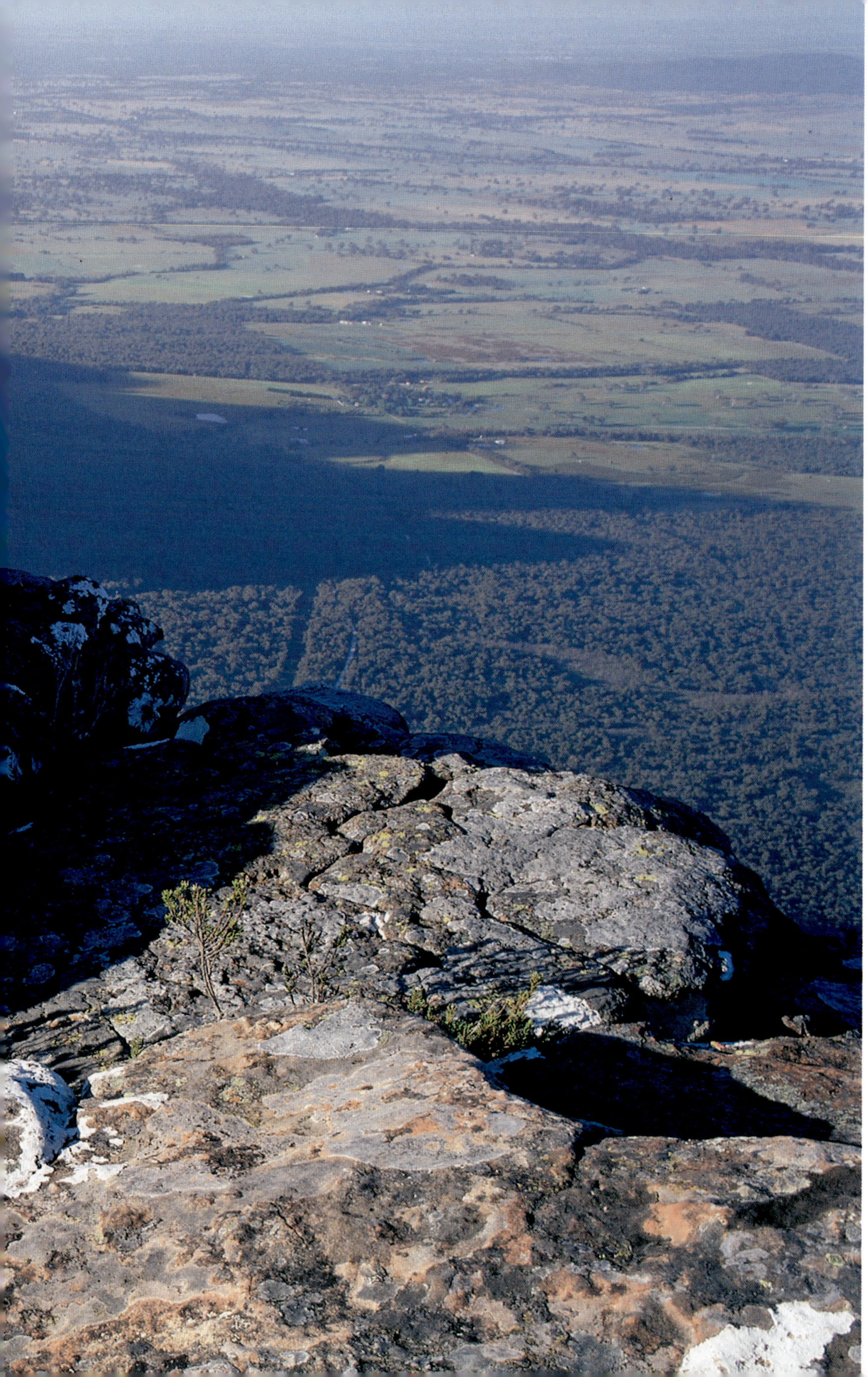

Moving inland in south western Victoria, the mountainous region known as Gariwerd to Jardwadjali and Djab Wurrung Aboriginal people is today known as the Grampians. The sandstone mountains, the most south-westerly extension of the Great Dividing Range, are protected in a 168,000 hectare national park about 260 kilometres west of Melbourne. The park boasts 970 plant species, with 20 found naturally nowhere else in the world, and is the richest area of Aboriginal rock art in Victoria, with over 100 sites. The Grampians are a popular tourist destination, renowned for colourful wildflowers, great bushwalking and challenging rock climbing.

View north to Redman Bluff from the top of Mount William (Duwil, 1167m), the highest point in the Grampian Range.

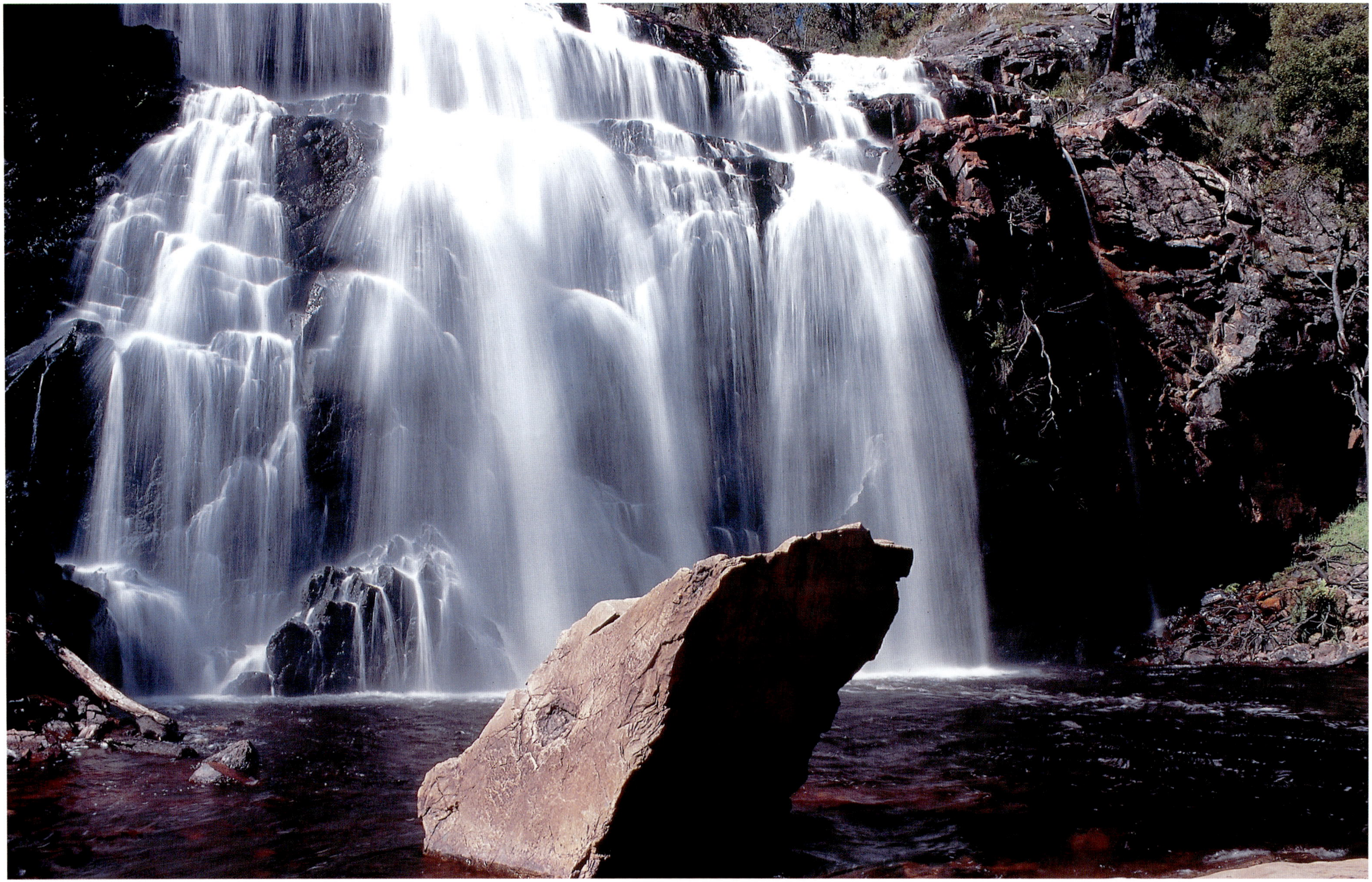

The bottom of McKenzie Falls can be reached via a two kilometre return walk in the western section of Grampians NP.

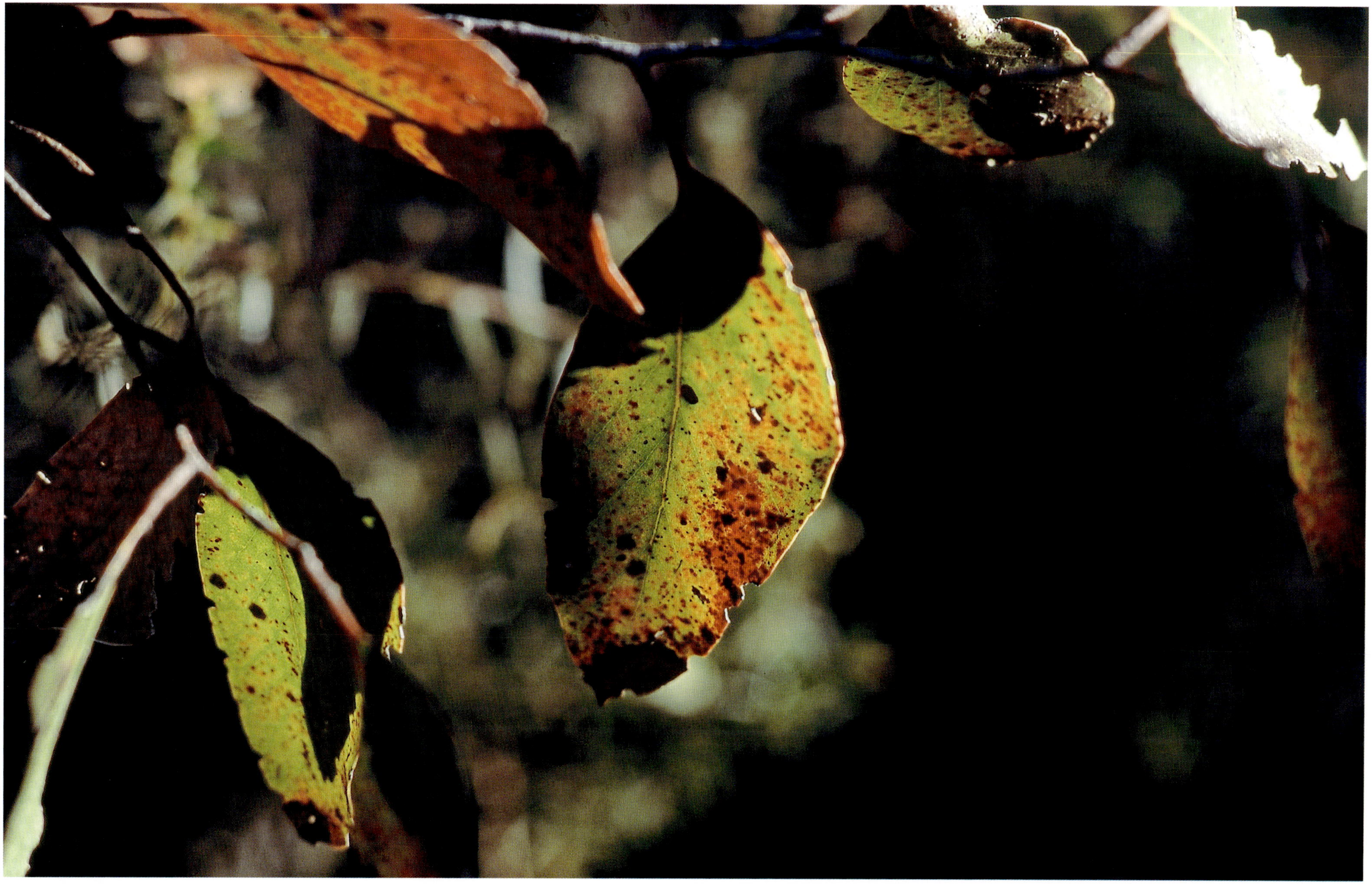

Backlit leaves on the walk to the Balconies, Grampian NP.

The region known as the Wimmera lies in the western districts of Victoria. This area has wheat and sheep farms and some large protected areas including the Little Desert National Park. The natural vegetation is wildflower rich mallee country, important for the protection of birds like the malleefowl. Mount Arapiles (369m), in Tooan State Park near the town of Natimuk is arguably the premier rock climbing venue in Australia and has over 2000 routes up its steep quartz and sandstone faces. The park protects 500 species of plants and 109 bird species, and provides nesting sites for the endangered peregrine falcon.

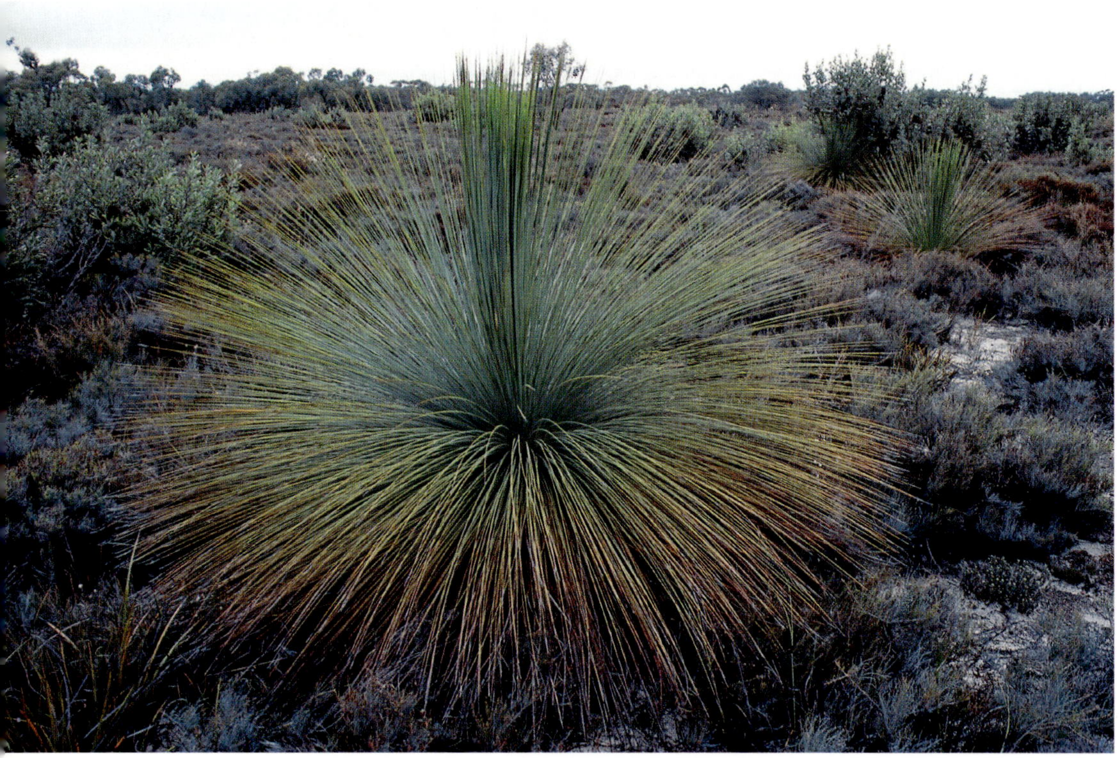

Grasstree and heathland in the Little Desert National Park.

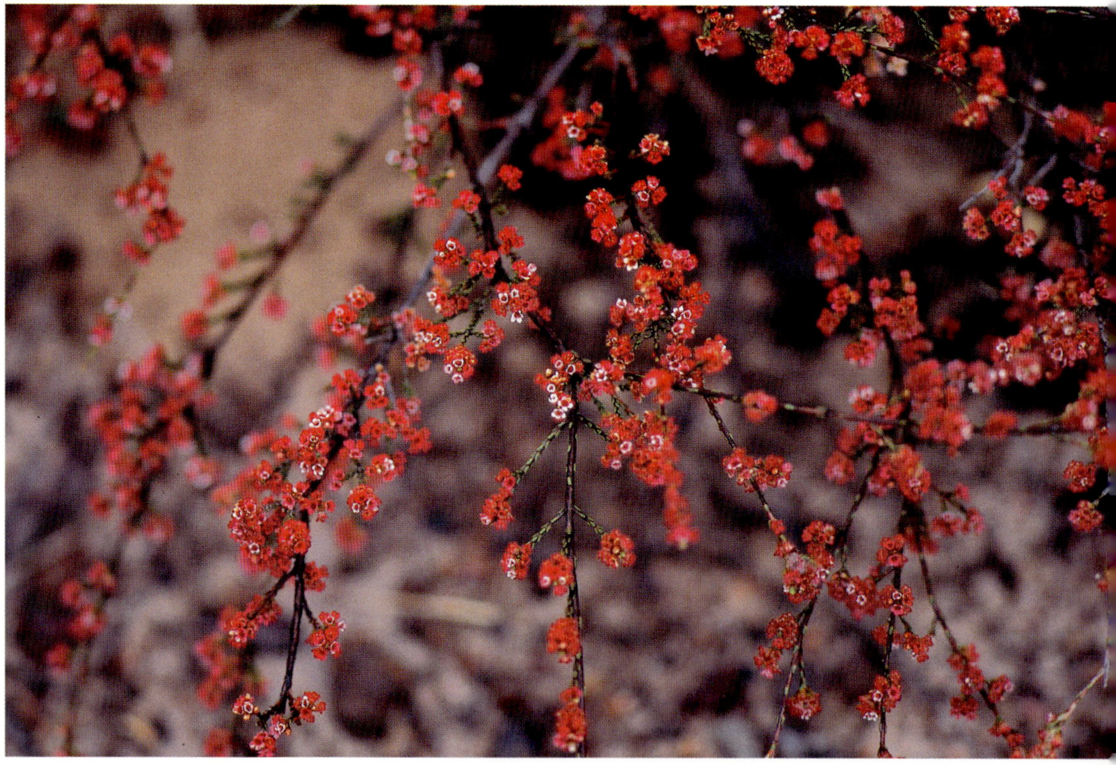

Top: Wildflowers, Little Desert NP.

Opposite page: Wildflowers and semi-arid woodland below Mount Arapiles.

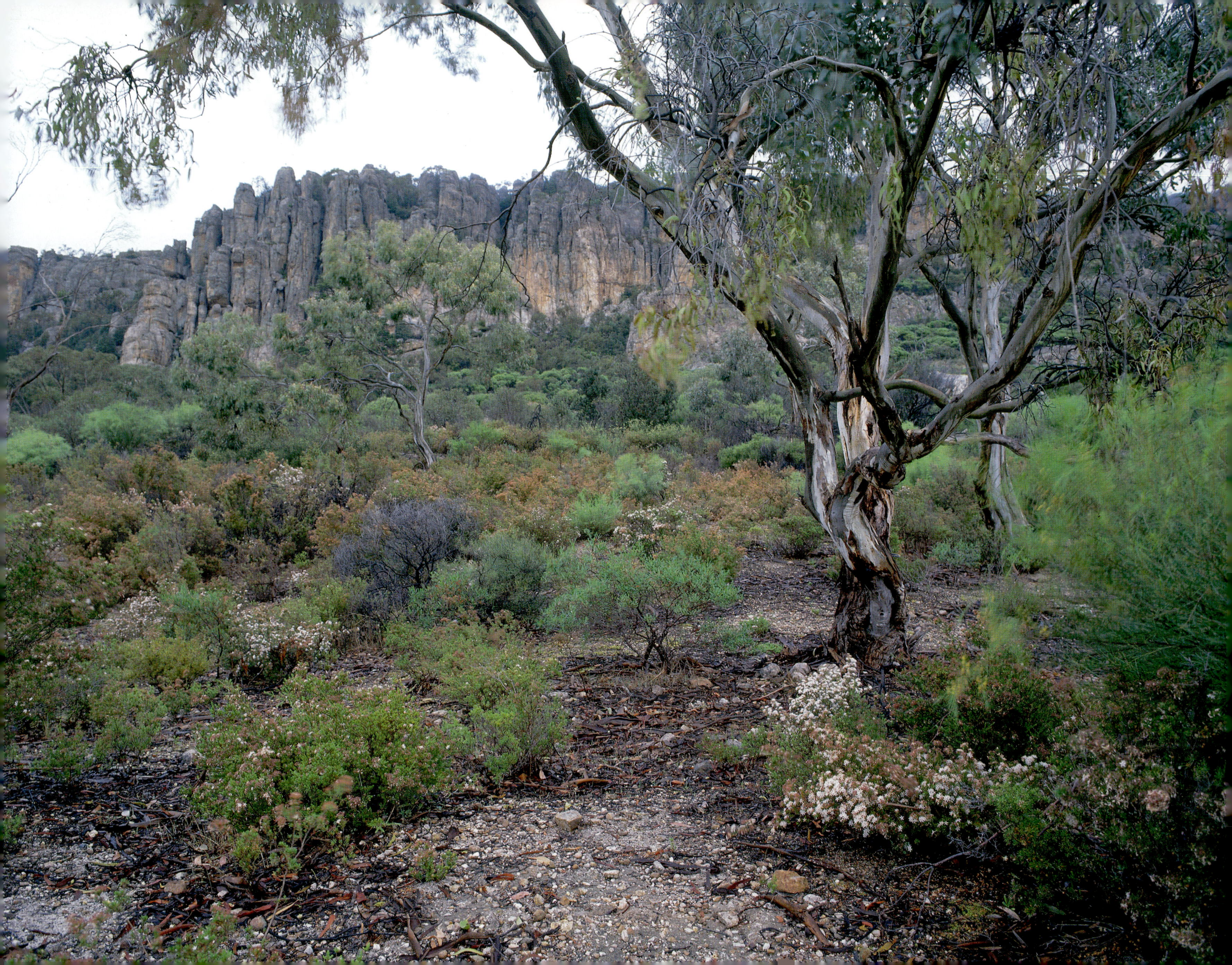

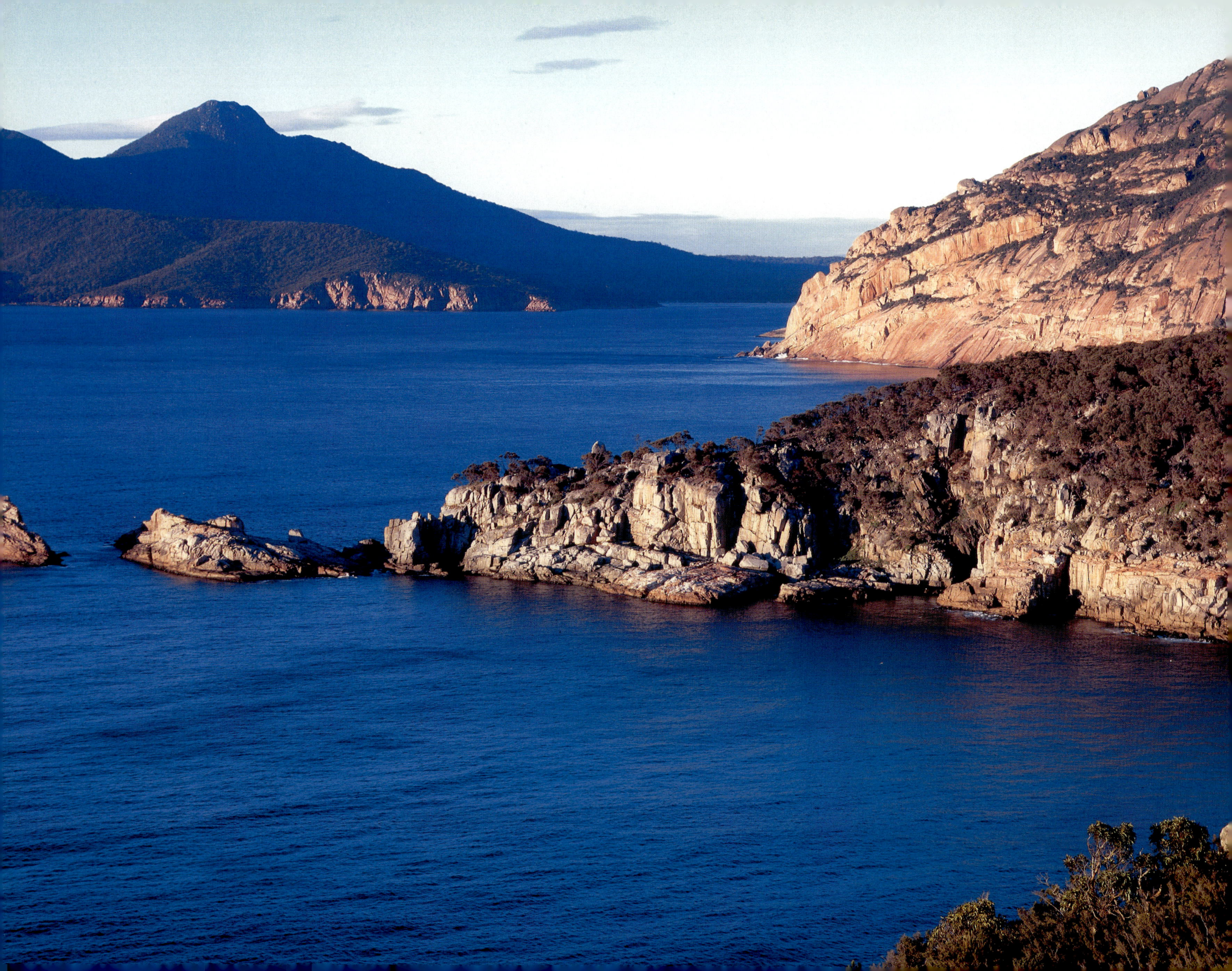

Tasmania

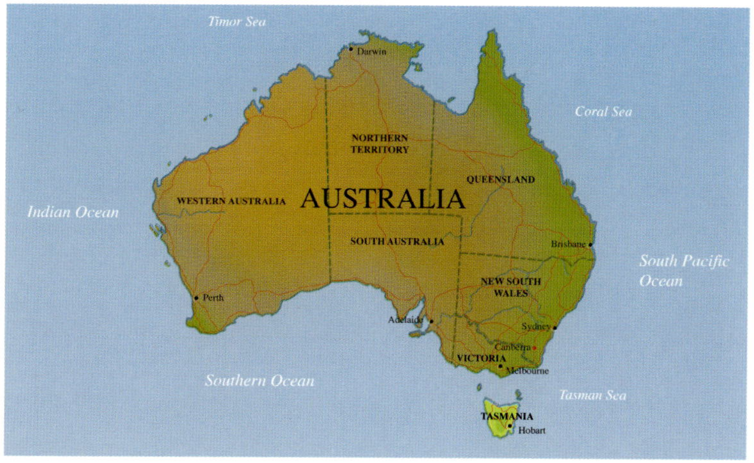

The scenic island state of Tasmania, of only 68,000 square kilometres, feels almost European in character, although the gum trees remind you that this is still Australia. It is mountain country sculpted by glacial action, resulting in jagged, impressive peaks and deep alpine lakes. The wild west coast rises to a central plateau and then descends over escarpments like the Great Western Tiers to the gentler northern and eastern coastal regions. The island has mild summers and cool winters, and snow can fall in the mountains year round. Tasmania has abundant wildlife, including Tasmanian devils and spotted-tailed quolls, and around 400 species of endemic plants. It has one of the largest remaining temperate wilderness areas left in the world in the Tasmanian Wilderness World Heritage Area, which covers 15,800 square kilometres, or almost the entire south-west region. Australia's modern day environmental movement began around 1972 when the beautiful original Lake Pedder, the jewel of south-west Tasmania, was flooded for a hydro-electric scheme.

More than 30,000 years ago Aboriginal people crossed into Tasmania from the mainland via a land bridge exposed by the last Ice Age. The rising waters of Bass Strait around 12,000 to 8000 years ago isolated Tasmanian Aborigines, and they subsequently developed a culture and languages that resembled but were not the same as mainland Aboriginal people. The first European to sight the island was Dutchman Abel Tasman in 1642. Tasmania was later claimed by Captain Cook for England, and a penal colony was established on the east side of the Derwent River in 1803. An alternative settlement on the west side of the river, begun in 1804, grew into Hobart, the second oldest city in Australia. Tasmania had some of the most notorious penal colonies in Australia at places like Port Arthur and Sarah Island in Macquarie Harbour. Political separation from NSW was granted in 1825, and transport of convicts ceased in 1853.

Tasmania's nickname is the "Apple Isle", and agriculture is the main industry here, producing abundant fresh produce from fertile farmlands. There are also many cottage and artisan industries and a thriving tourist industry that focuses on the lure of its wonderful outdoors. Tasmania has some of the most challenging bushwalking terrain in Australia, and cycling, rock climbing, rafting and fishing are also popular. The biggest town is Hobart on the Derwent River estuary, overlooked by Mount Wellington (1270m). Launceston and Devonport are the other large towns, located in the north-east and north-west of the state respectively.

Opposite page: View past Mount Parsons (right) to Mount Freycinet, at 620 metres the highest point on the Freycinet peninsular.

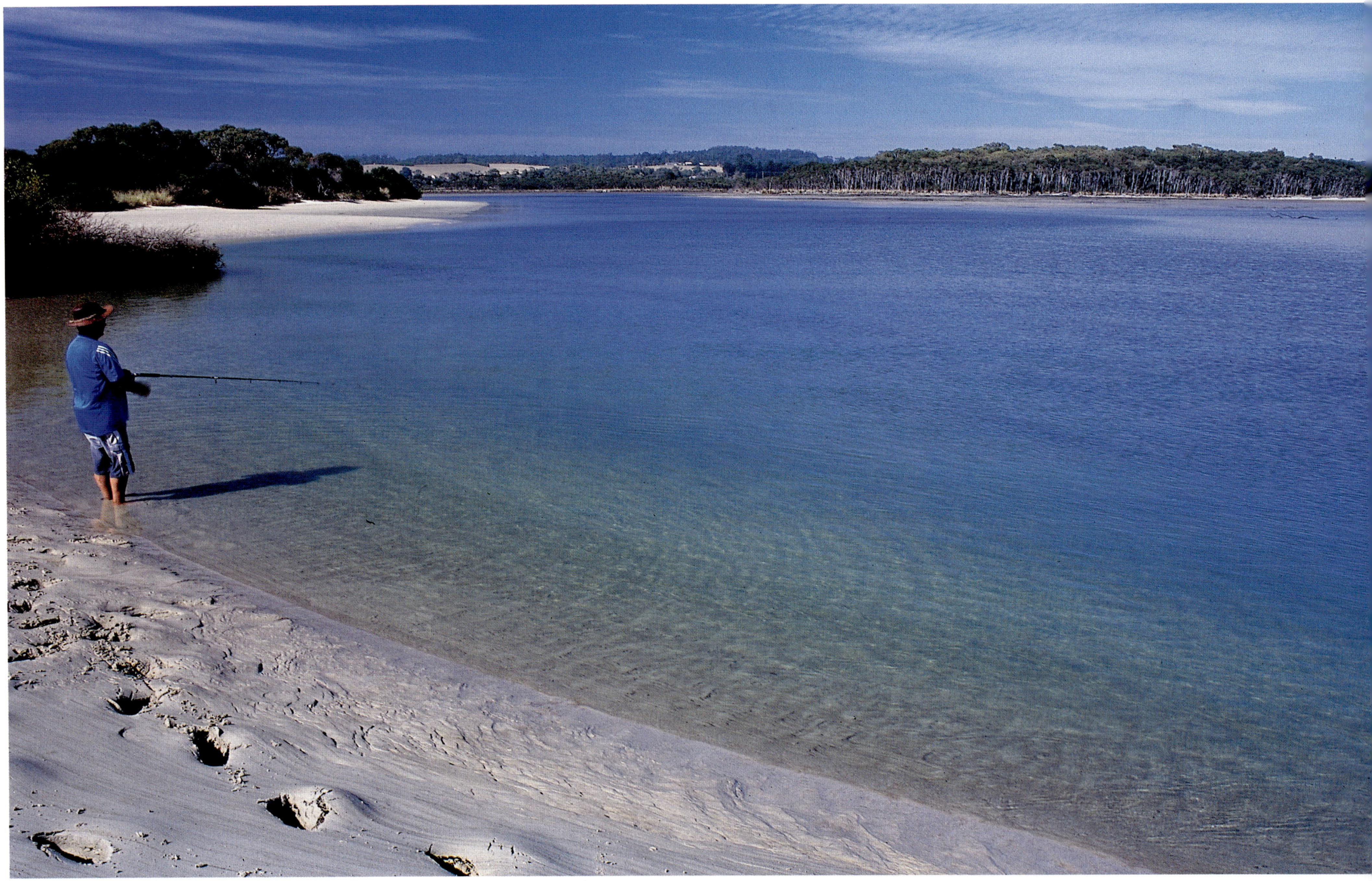

Fishing in the Black River estuary, North West Tasmania, near an idyllic camping area.

The north-west of Tasmania has spectacular coastal scenery and fertile farmland extending inland to the pristine rainforests and hills of the Tarkine region. I visited the area in March 2013. *"I took the road from Devonport out to Table Cape, a high scenic cliff over the blue ocean. The early morning fog had burned off eventually to a nice warm and sunny day. I did a short walk here and the colours in the sea were wonderful."* Later on I went for a stroll along the beach and took some photographs at the mouth of the Black River, near Stanley. I camped that night at Green Point campsite on the windy and scenic north-west coast.

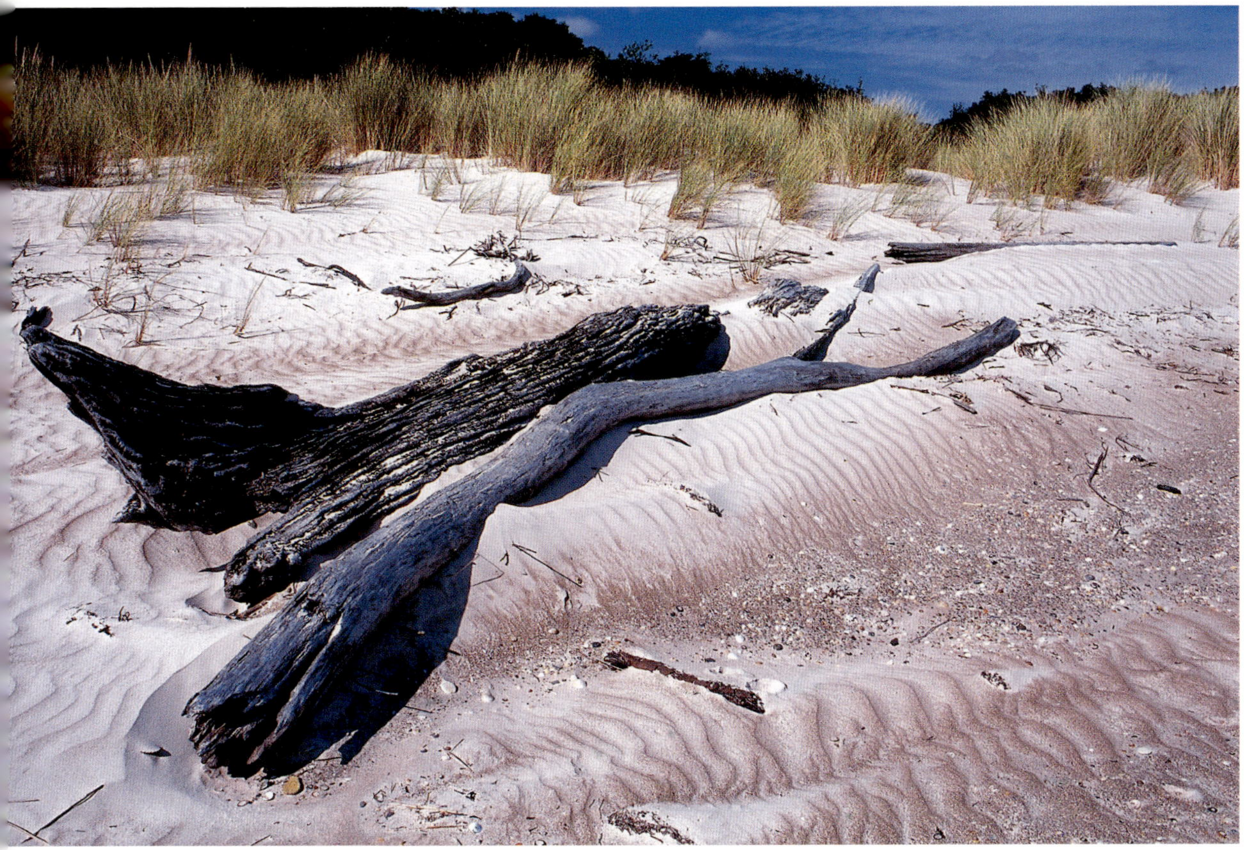

Driftwood and dunes at Black River mouth.

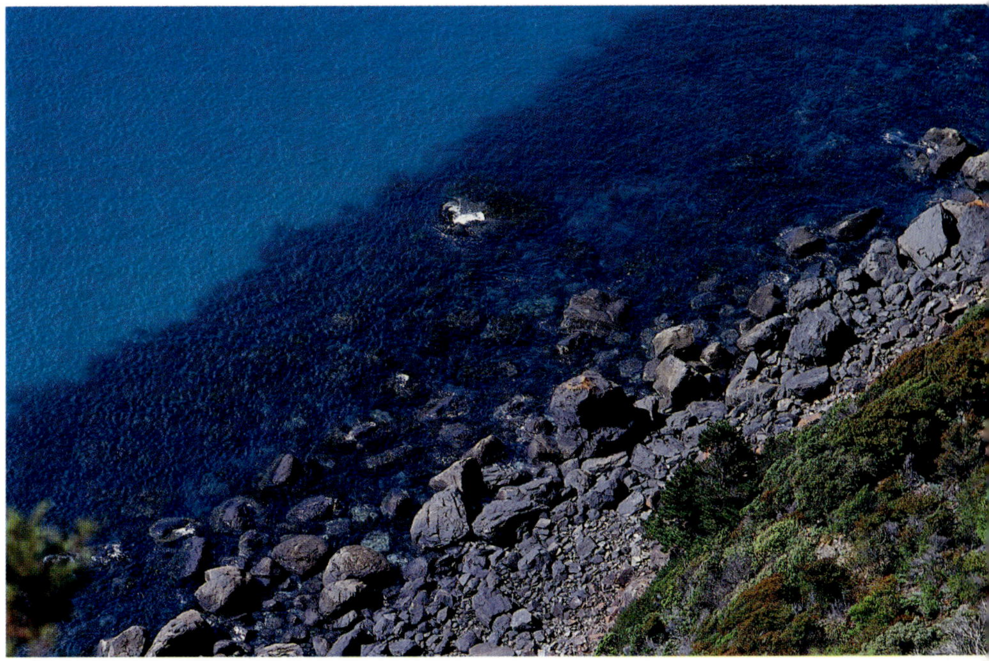

View of the ocean from the high headland of Table Cape, on the north coast of Tasmania.

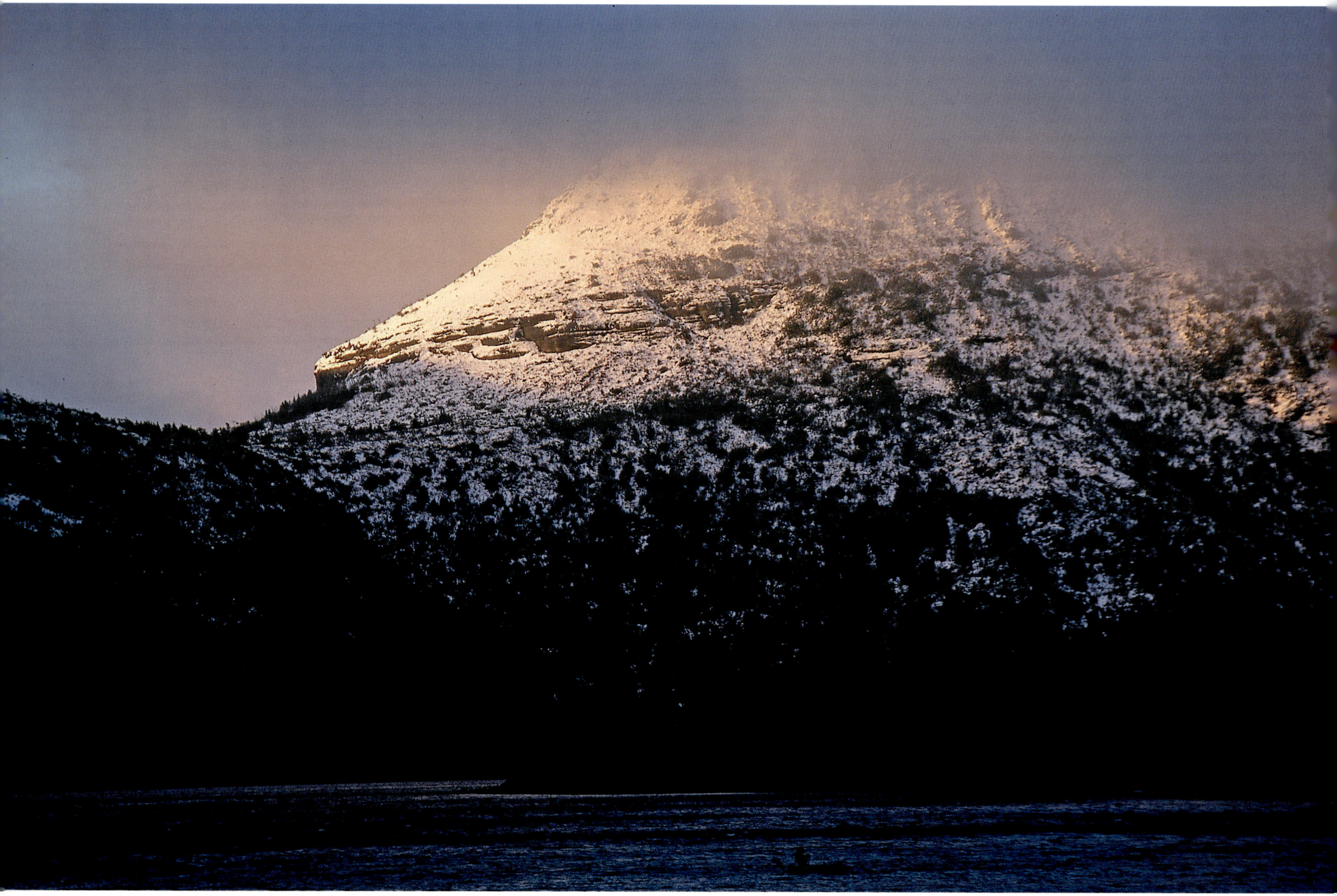

Snow and dawn mists shroud Little Horn (1355m) above Dove Lake. Cradle Mountain (1545m) lies to the right but is not visible.

Right: A twisted and colourful snowgum growing above Dove Lake.

Bottom: Moody light over Twisted Lakes, near Cradle Mountain, in midwinter.

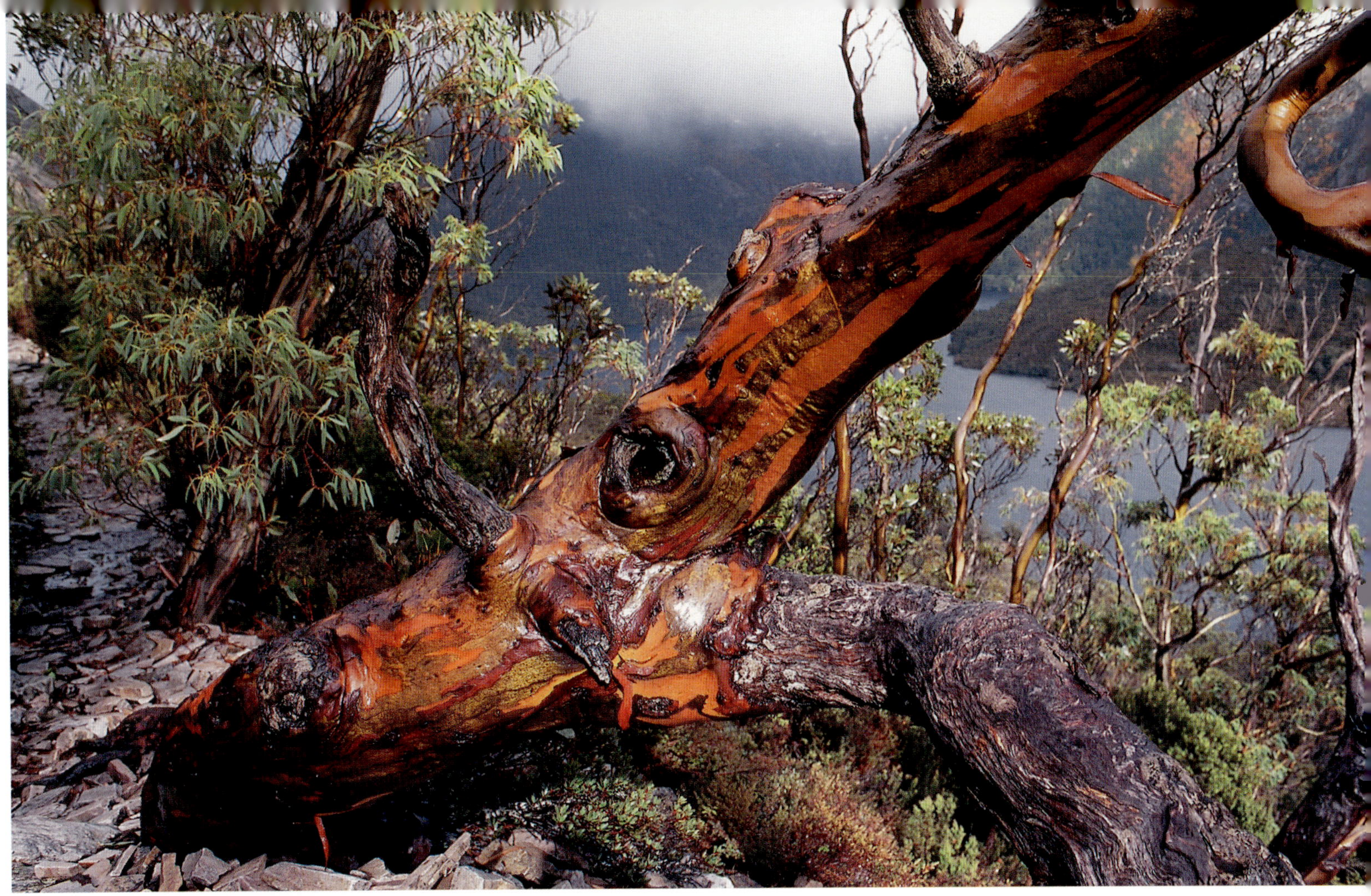

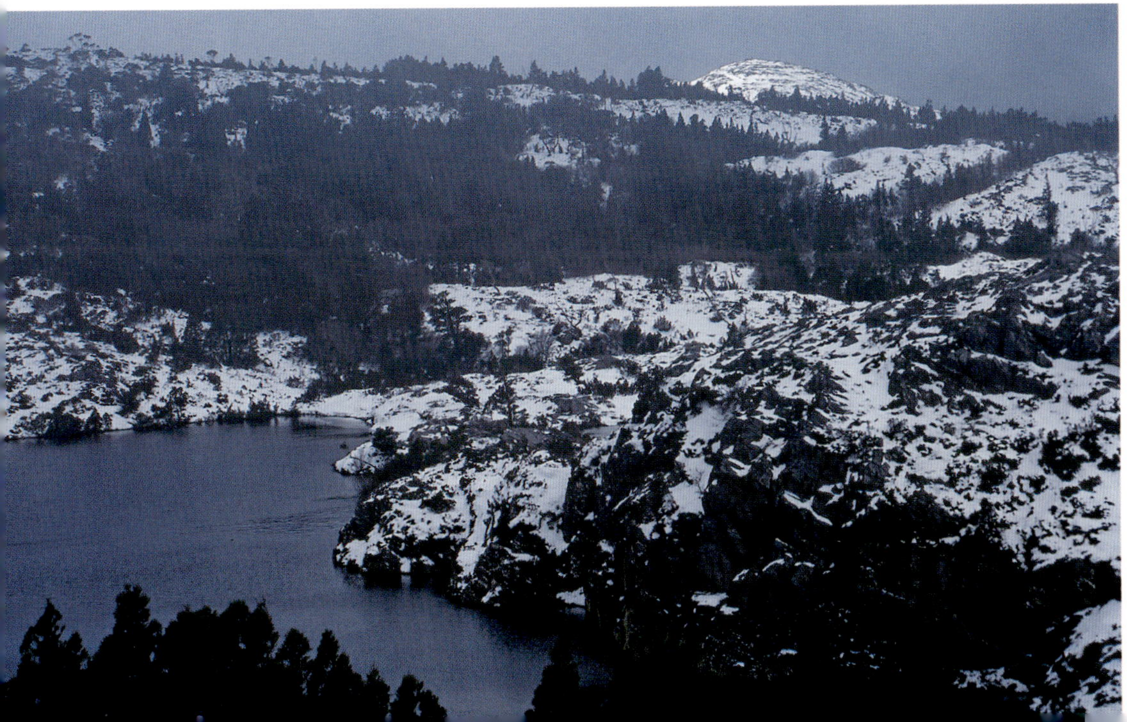

Cradle Mountain-Lake St Clair National Park is one of the icons of Australia. The park covers 161,000 hectares of glacially shaped dolerite mountains, interspersed with temperate rainforests, heathland and lakes. Along with the South West NP and Franklin-Lower Gordon Wild Rivers NP, the park is part of the Tasmanian Wilderness World Heritage area, one of the last great temperate wildernesses in the world. The WHA covers almost 20% of Tasmania!

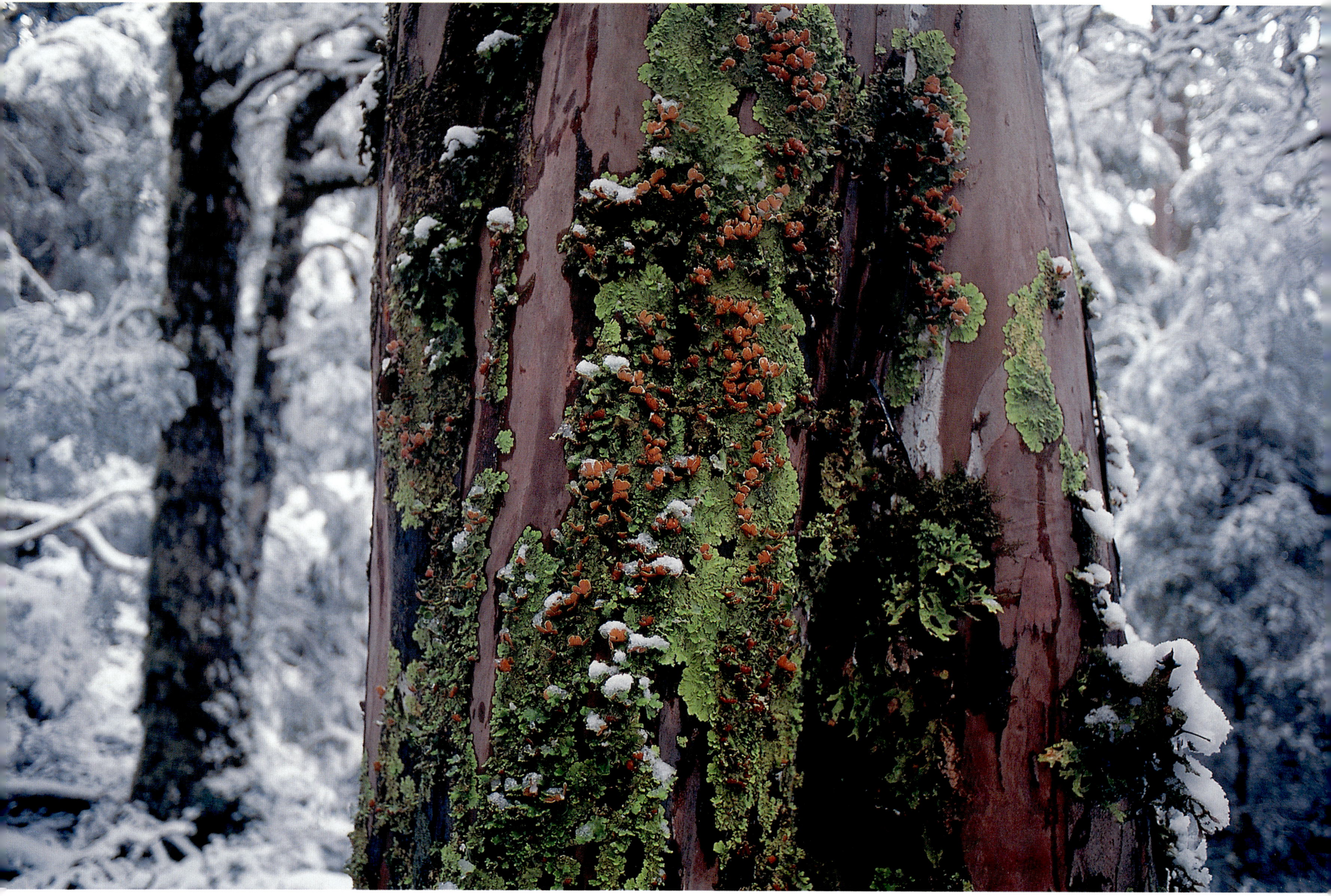

Moss and ice in a temperate rainforest on the Overland Track.

The Overland Track, between Cradle Mountain and Lake St Clair, is perhaps Australia's premier long distance walking track. The 83 kilometre track takes between five and eight days and many side trips are possible, including climbing Mount Ossa (1617m), the highest peak in Tasmania. The weather is notoriously fickle and blizzards are possible even in summer, but the beauty of the glaciated terrain and the magnificent beech forests, heathlands, lakes and mountains make it all worthwhile.

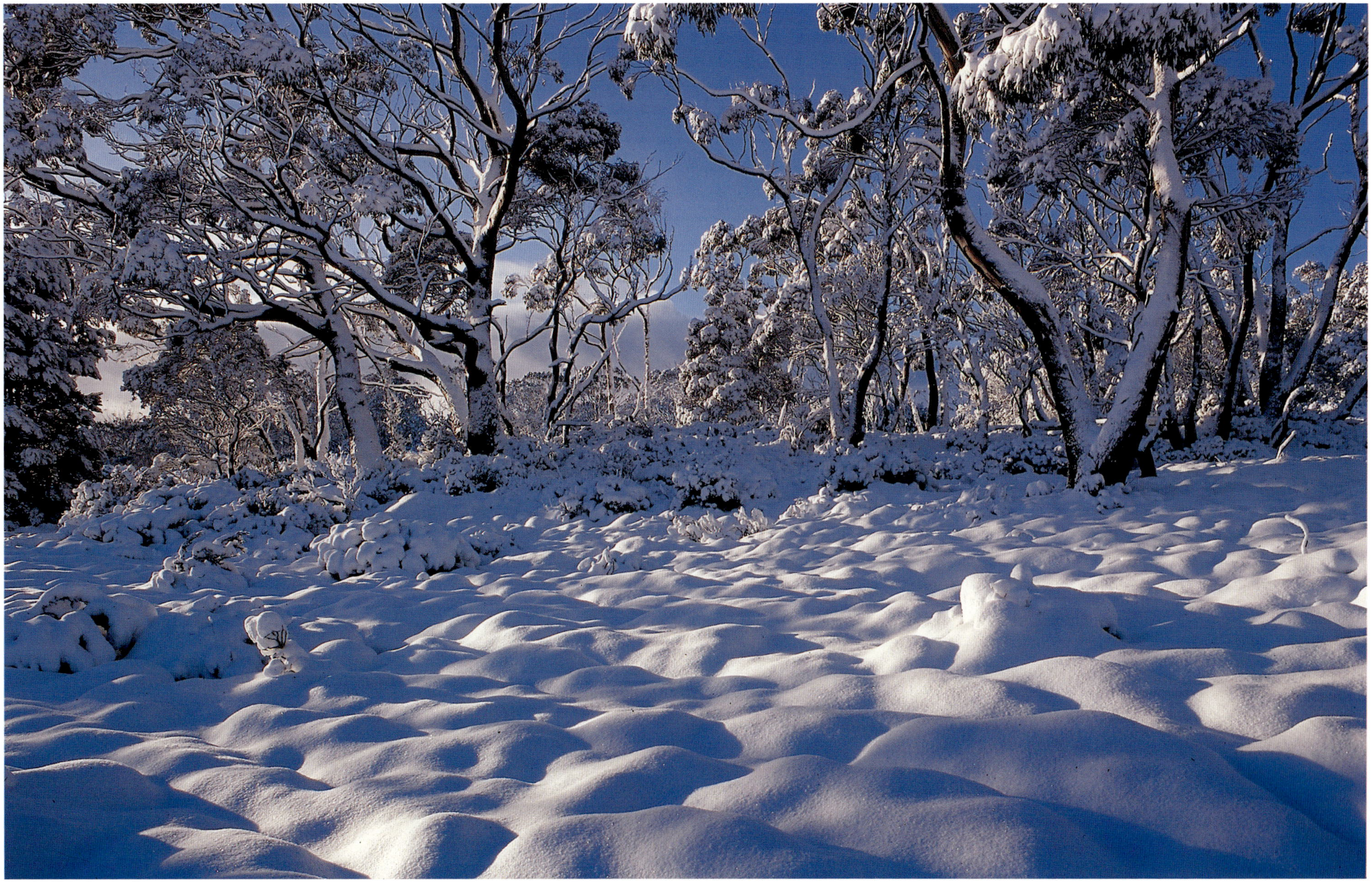

A heavy blanket of fresh snow covers woodland on the Overland Track in May.

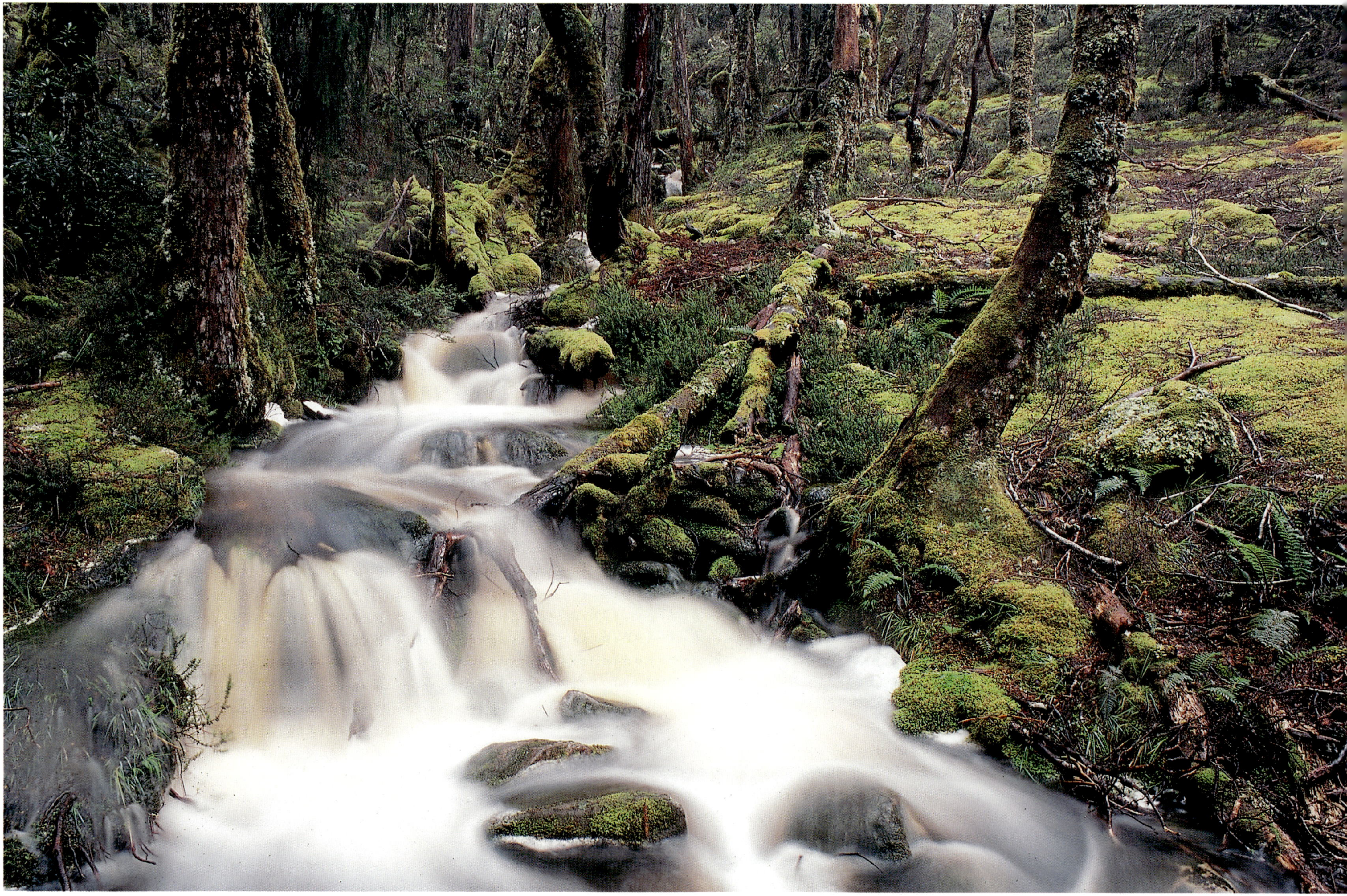

A small cascading stream amidst pristine rainforest.

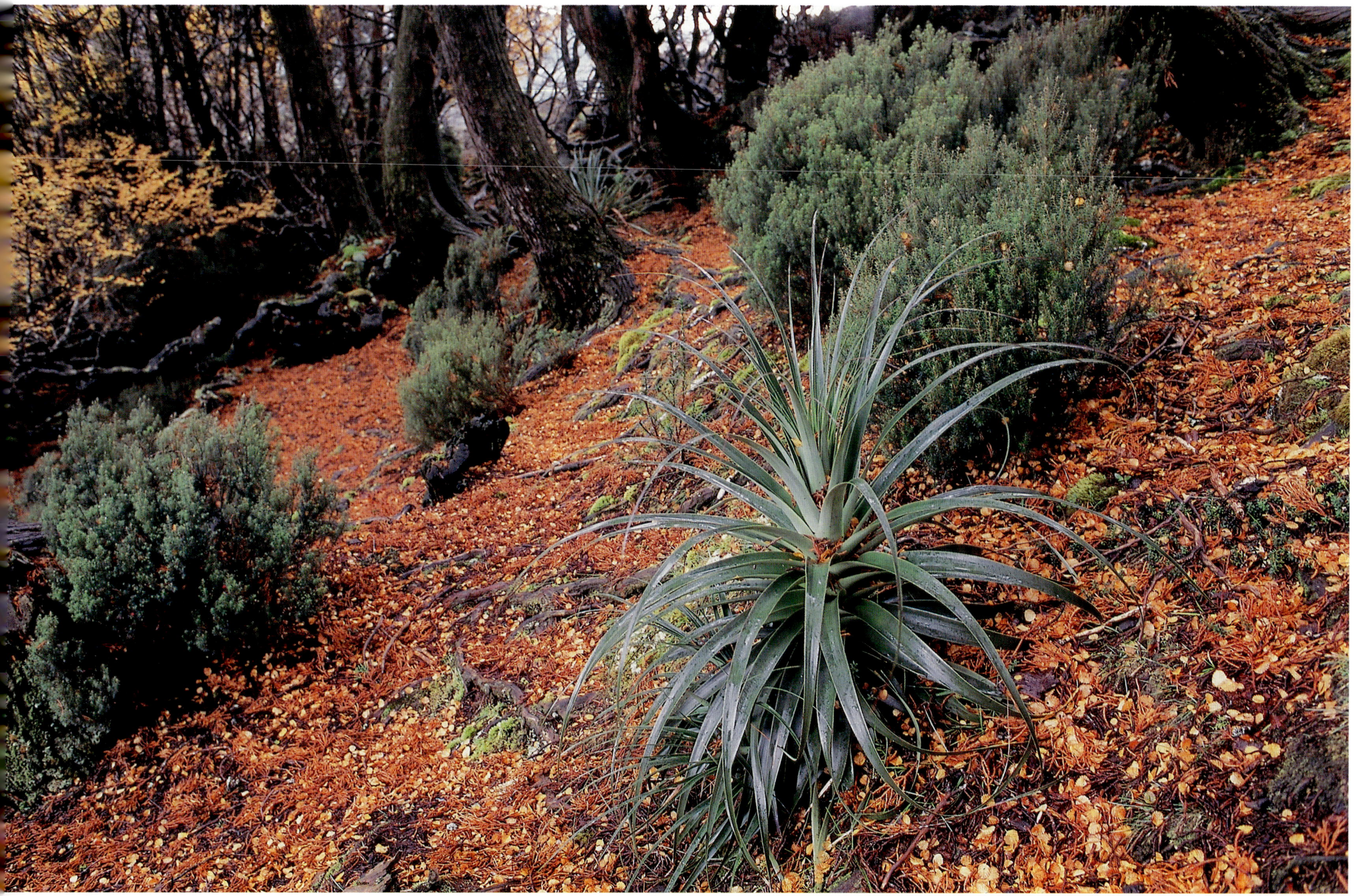

Pandani and fagus, Overland Track.

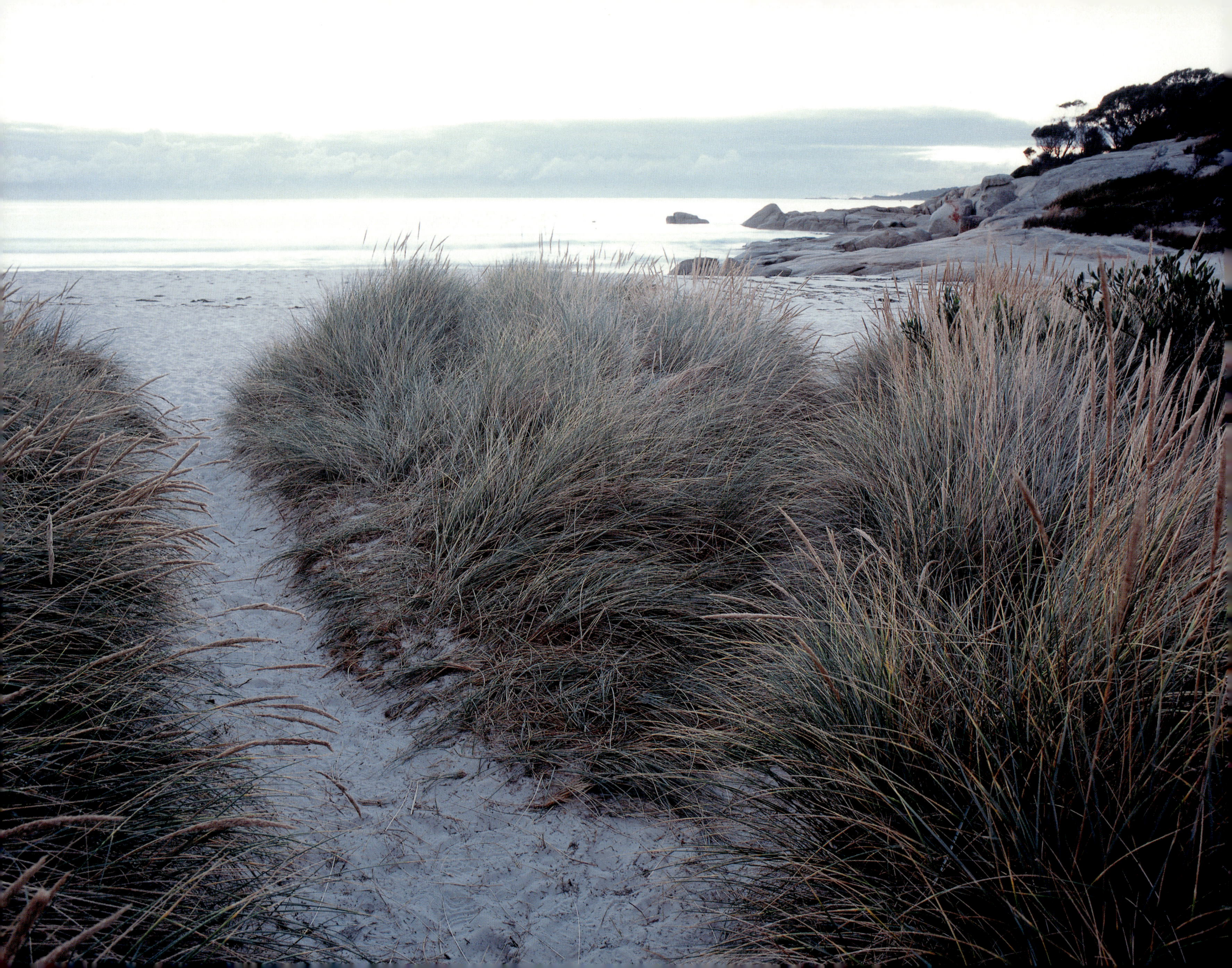

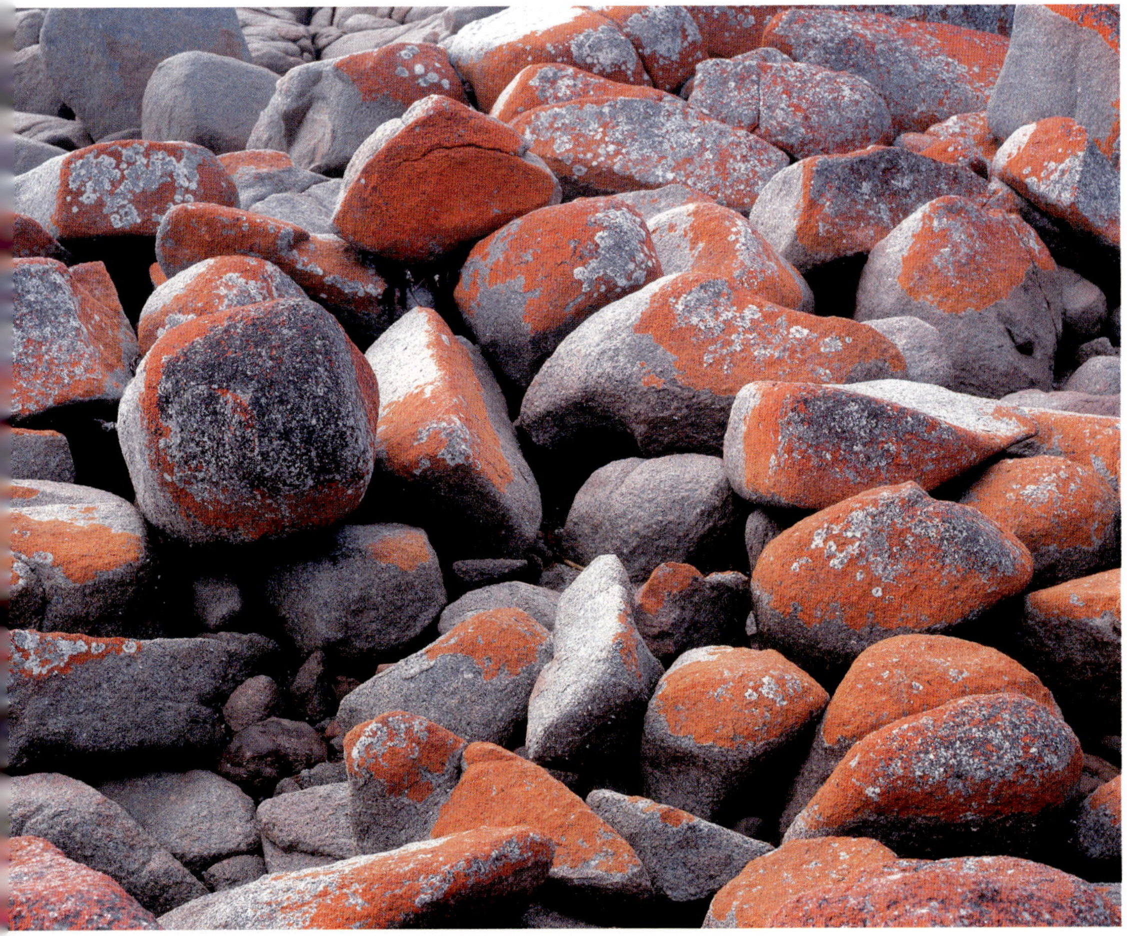

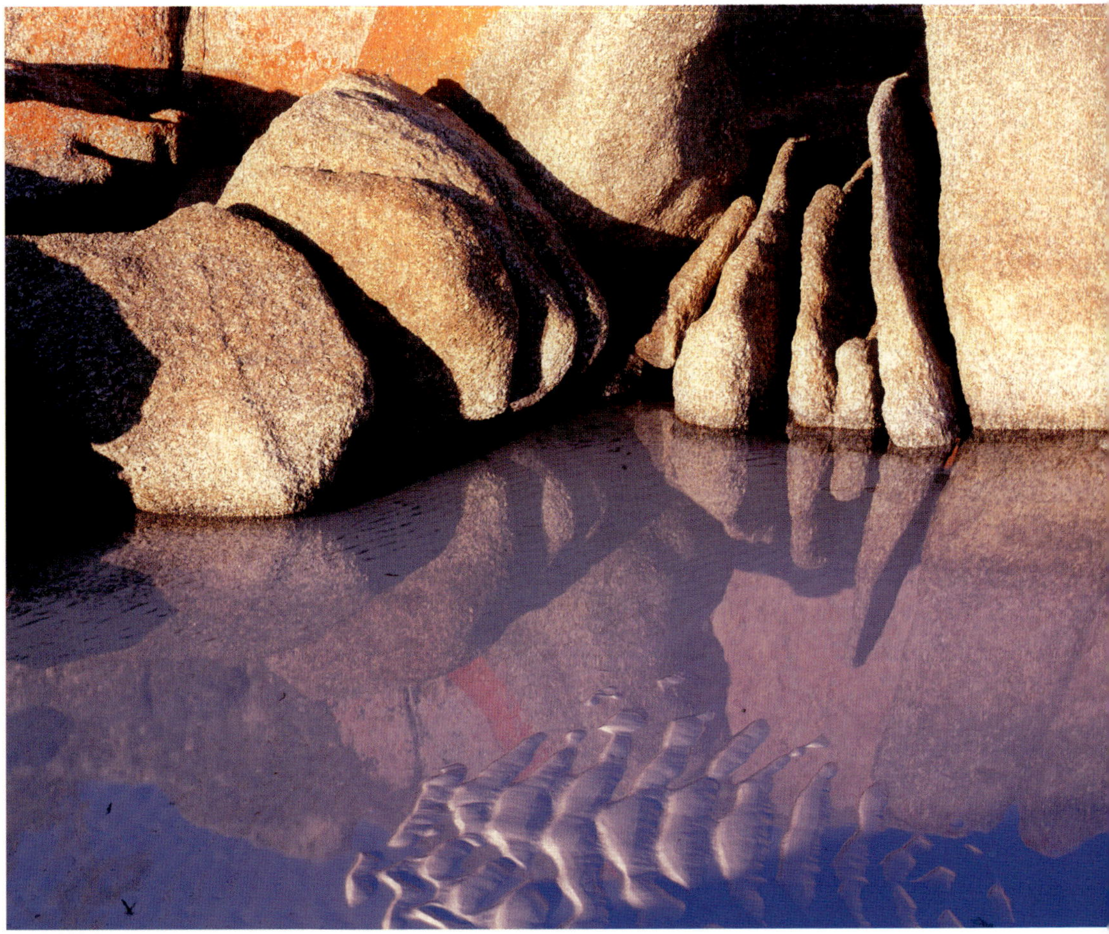

The evocative name of the Bay of Fires in north-east Tasmania was derived from Europeans seeing the campfires of many Aboriginal groups near the beaches and bays of this coast. The Bay of Fires Conservation Area is still a popular place to camp, and enjoys a relatively mild and dry climate compared to the rest of Tasmania. I wrote *"at around 4pm I drove into the Jeanneret Beach camping area, not far north of Binalong Bay, and set up the tent. It is a lovely spot on a small headland between two beaches… I had a short rest and then a great walk around the rocks before tea. I found a quiet spot where I was all alone and sat contemplating life for a while. I was quite content, if a little sad that I was alone."*

Top left: Bright orange lichen covers rocks at Binalong Bay.

Top right: Reflections and sand ripples in a tidal rock pool at Jeanneret Beach.

Opposite page: Subdued early morning light on the path to Jeanneret Beach.

One of the most popular tourist destinations in Tasmania is Freycinet National Park near Coles Bay on the east coast. The park protects a rugged and wild peninsula dominated by the pink granite peaks of the Hazards Range and offers great bushwalking and idyllic views. A famous walk here leads up to a viewpoint over the magnificent sweep of Wineglass Bay, and is a moderately steep climb of three kilometres return, taking about 1 – 1 ½ hours.

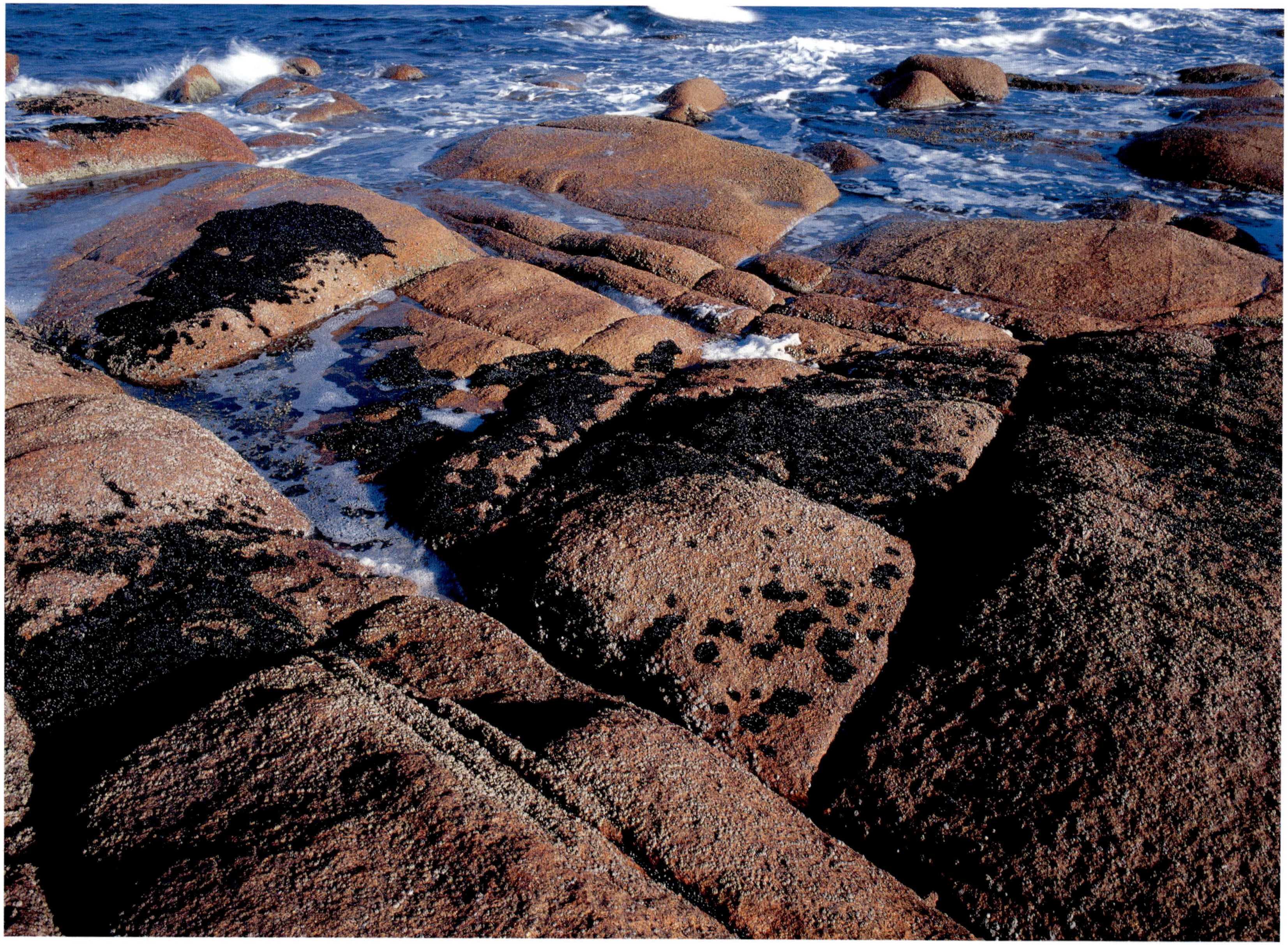

Top: Faulted granite rocks at Coles Bay.

Opposite page: The magic of pink granite and peaceful waters at Sleepy Bay, Freycinet National Park.

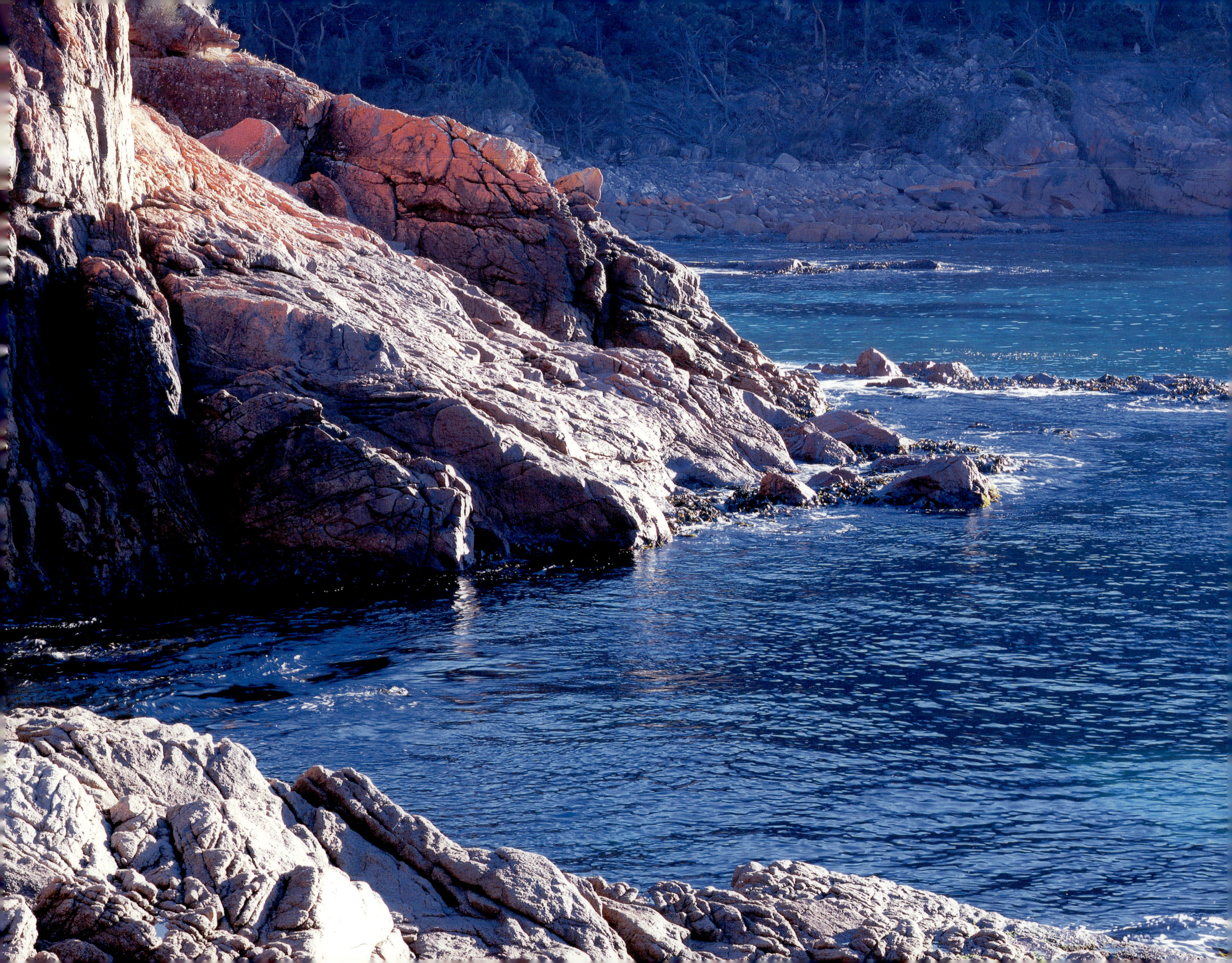

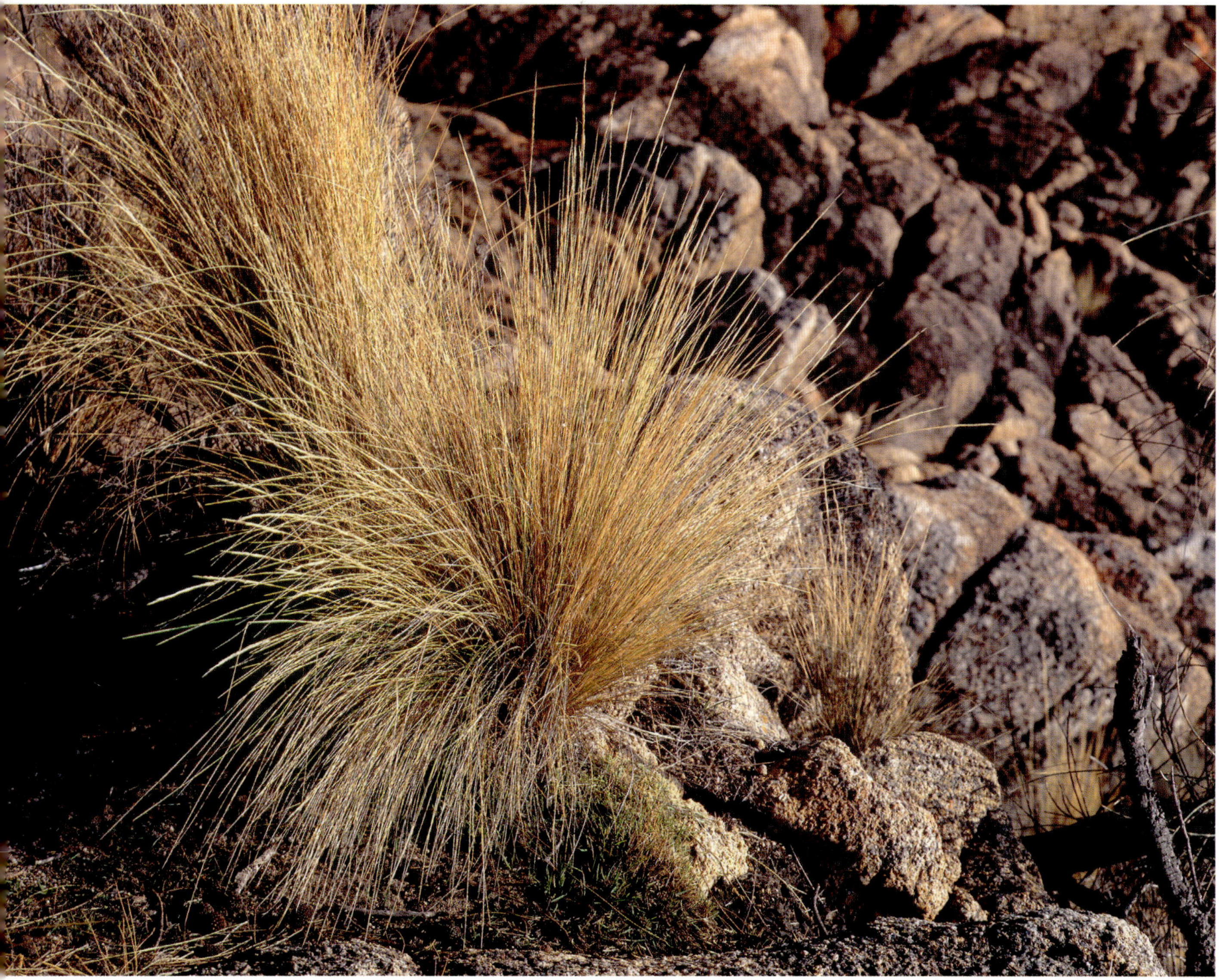

Wild grass on rocks at Sleepy Bay, Freycinet National Park.

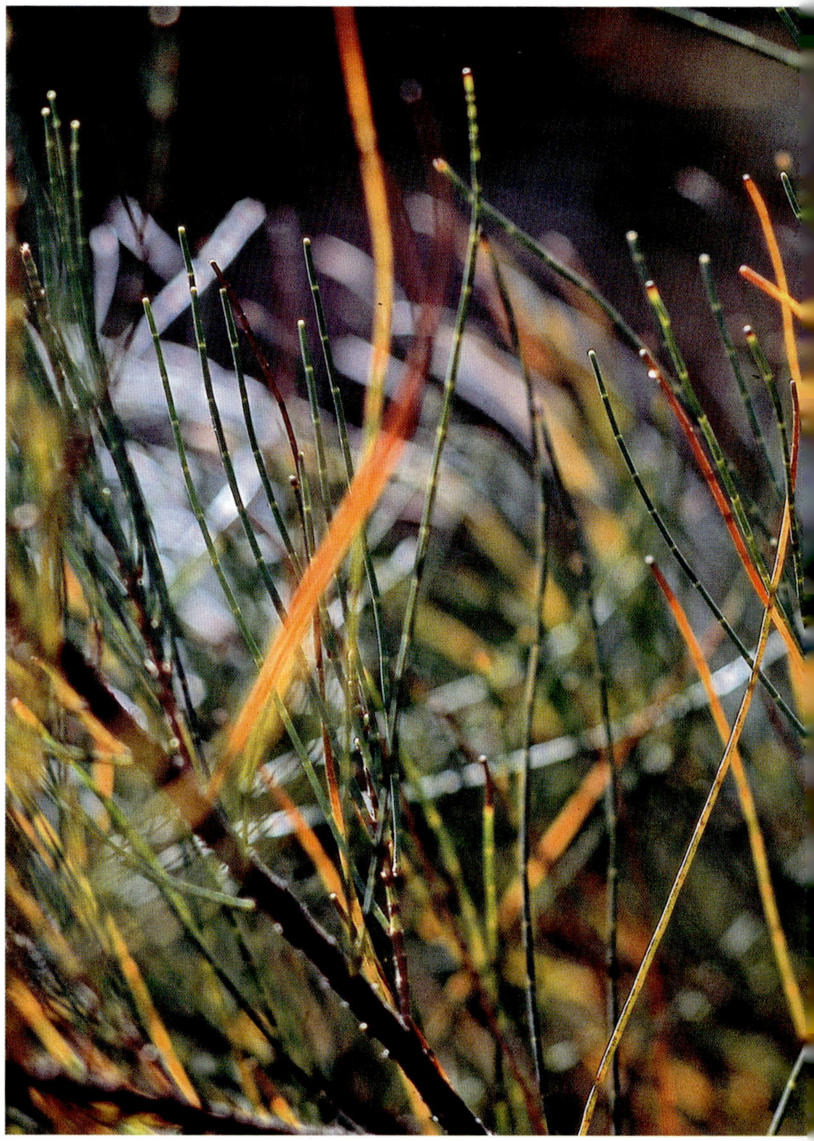

Sunlight through she-oak needles, Wineglass Bay walk.

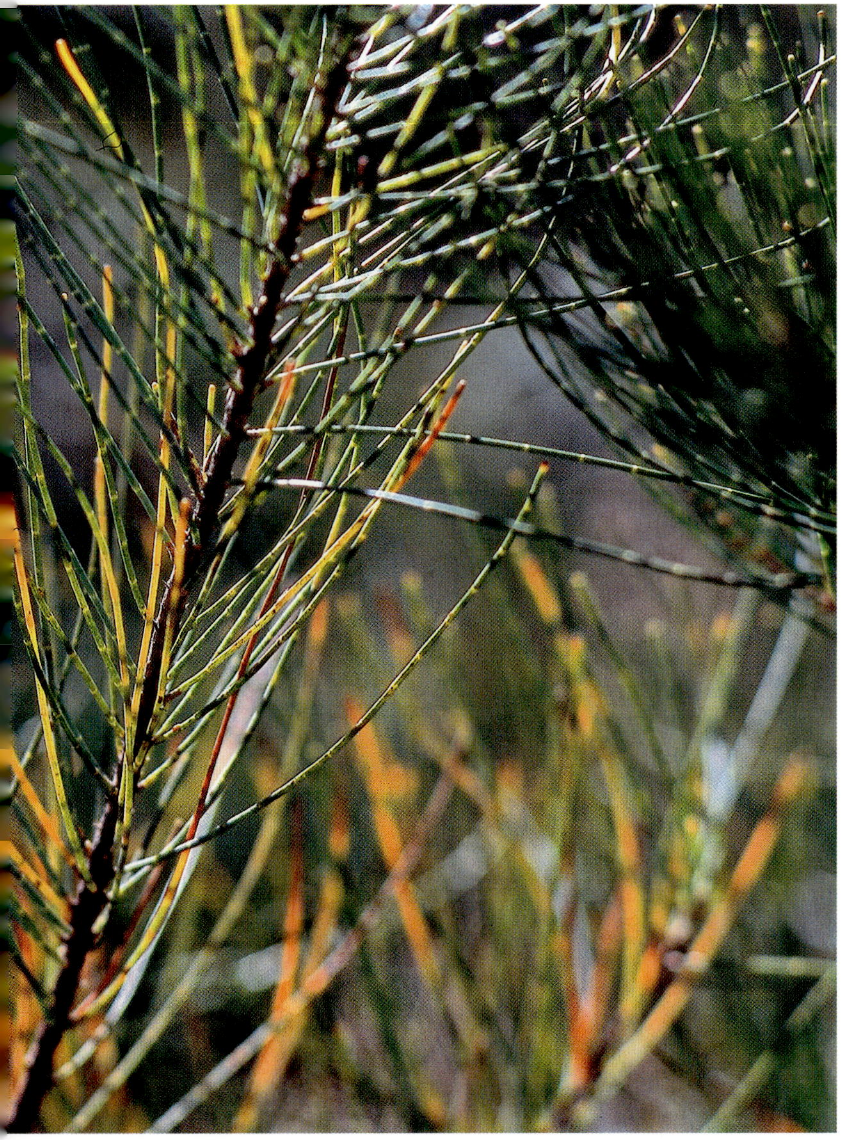

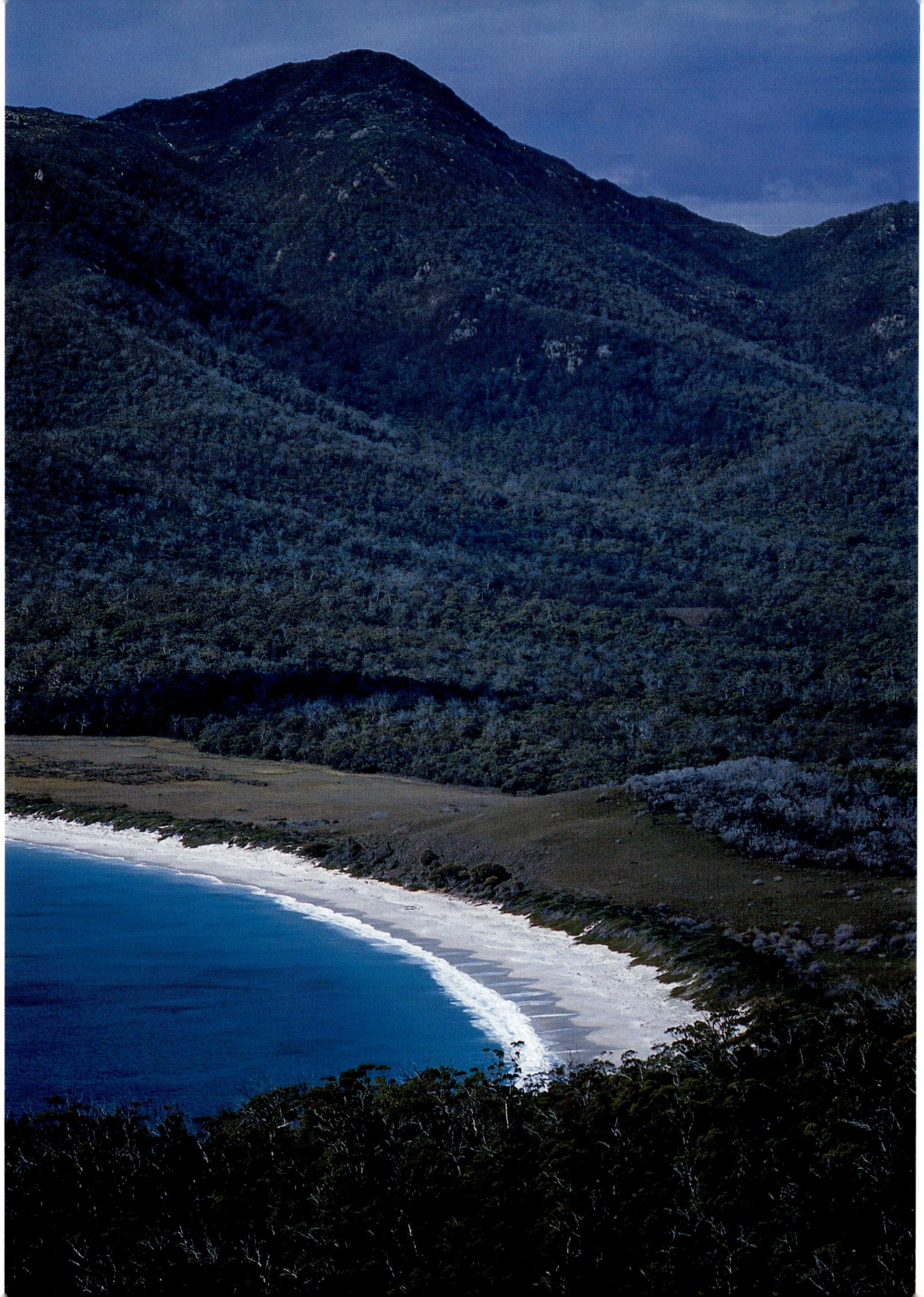

View over beautiful Wineglass Bay to Mount Graham (579m).

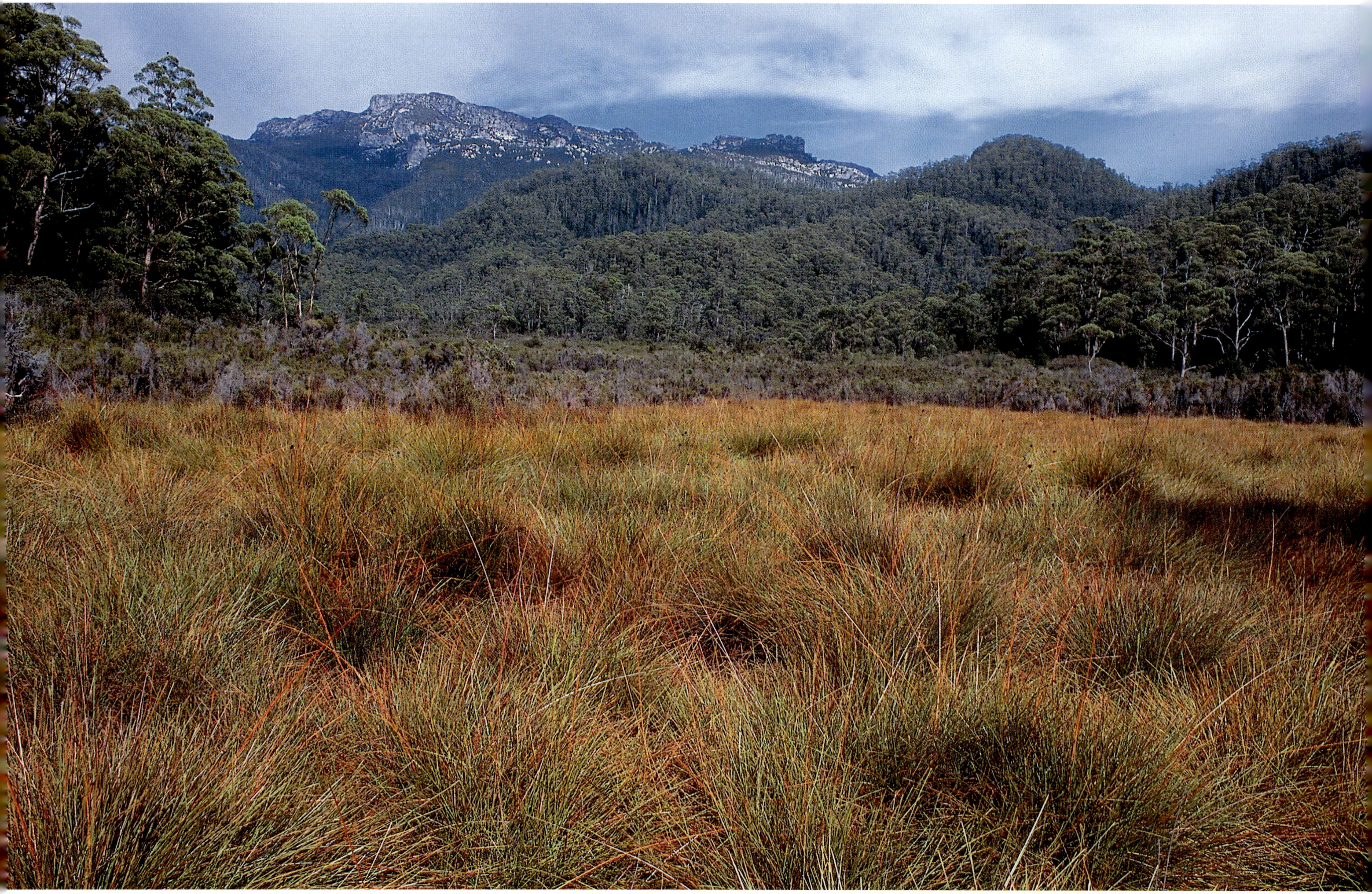

Buttongrass on the Loddon Plains on the walk in to Frenchmans Cap (not visible).

One of the most impressive mountains in Tasmania is Frenchman's Cap (1443m) in the Franklin-Lower Gordon Wild Rivers National Park. This isolated quartzitic mountain is surrounded broadly on three sides by the wild and broken country of the Franklin River gorge, and can be ascended over a challenging three to five day return hike from the Lyell Highway. The area was extensively shaped by ancient glaciers and there are many picturesque alpine lakes.

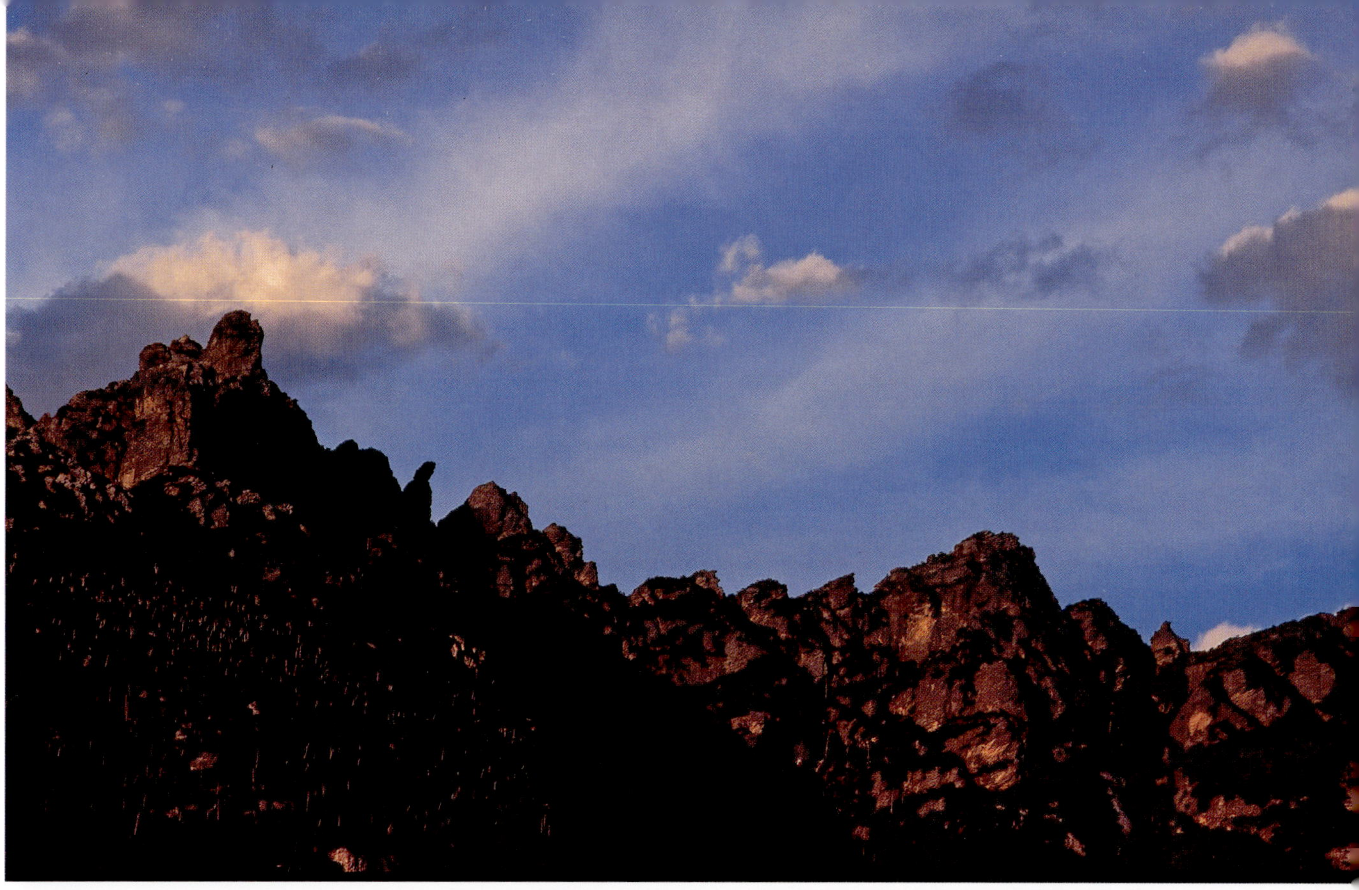

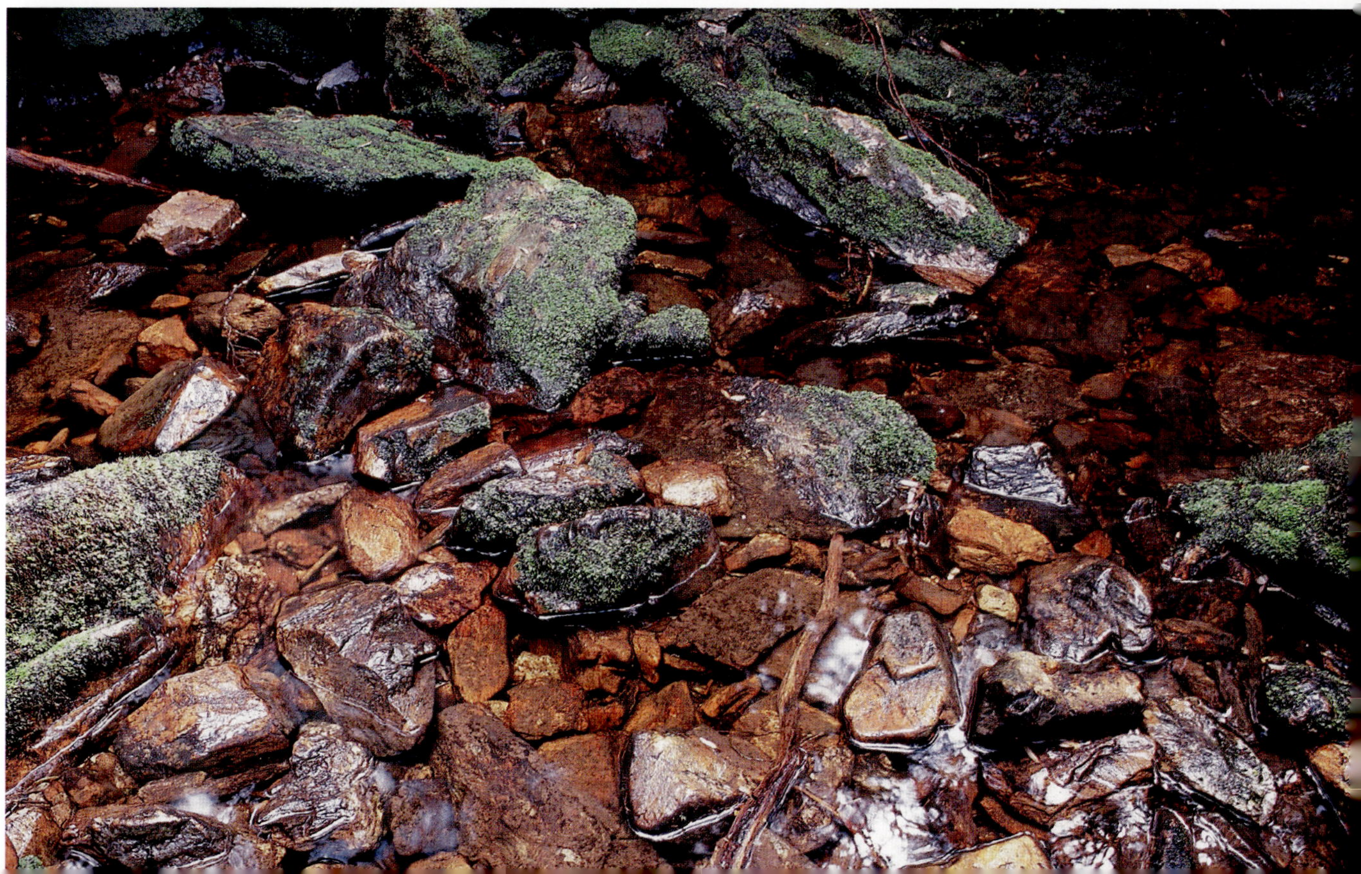

Top: Serrated mountains including Philps Peak and White Needle rise above Lake Vera at dawn.

Right: Moss covered rocks and tannin stained waters in a rainforest stream.

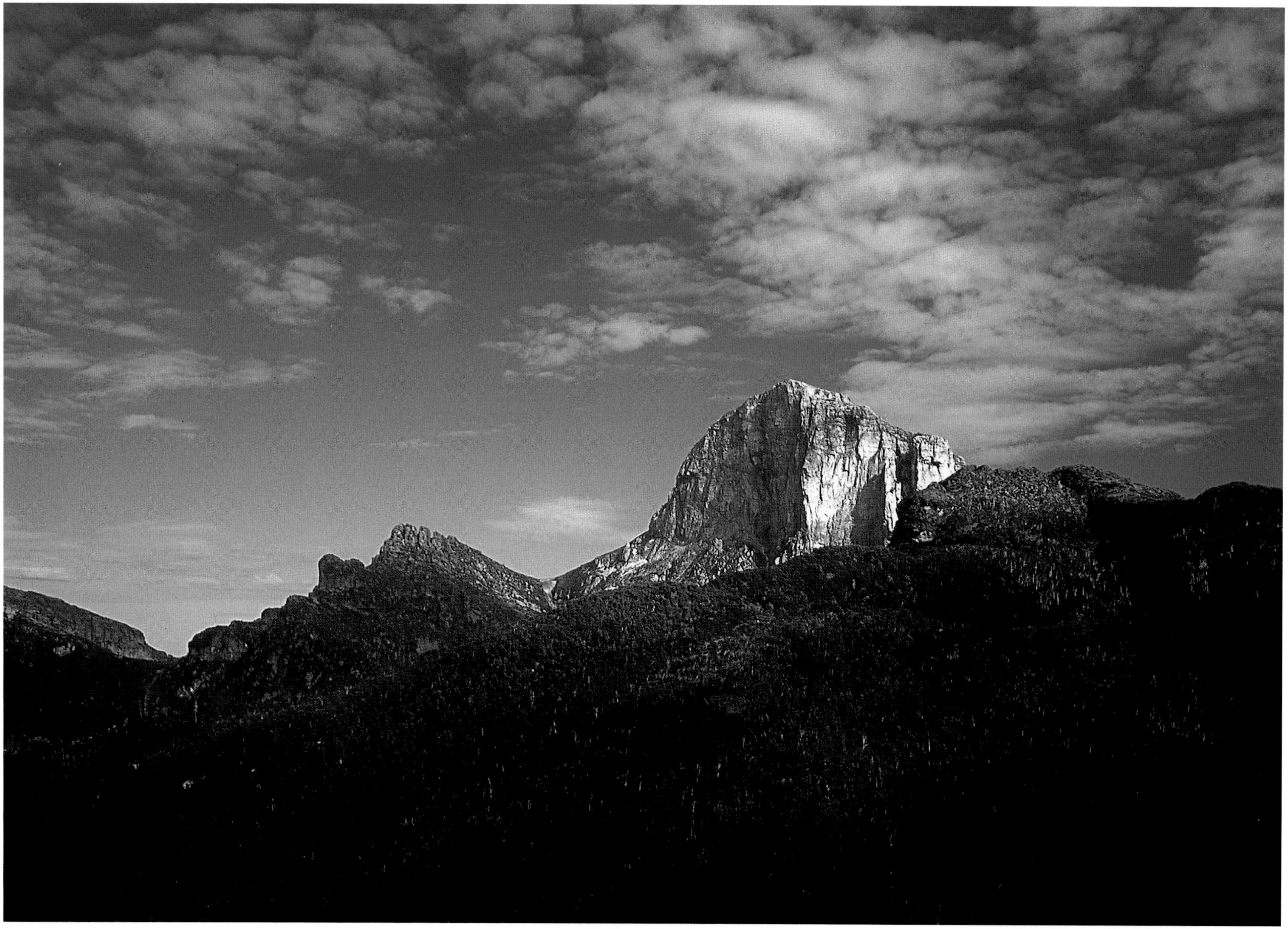

Frenchman's Cap from the Barron Pass, showing its sheer 300 metre high east face.

I climbed Frenchman's Cap over four days in March 2013 with two friends. I described the first part of day two thus: *"The track today was very rough. Even the flattish first section was over a tangle of roots and rocks and you constantly had to be careful about your footing. We skirted the lake edge and then started ascending, following a small stream with 2 or 3 small cascades. It was hot and I had a short shower fully clothed under a waterfall falling from the cliffs above – very refreshing! We continued on up very steeply, finally topping Barron Pass and looking across to Frenchman's Cap in all its glory."* We all returned safely to civilisation, although I did end up with badly blistered feet at the end of the hike!

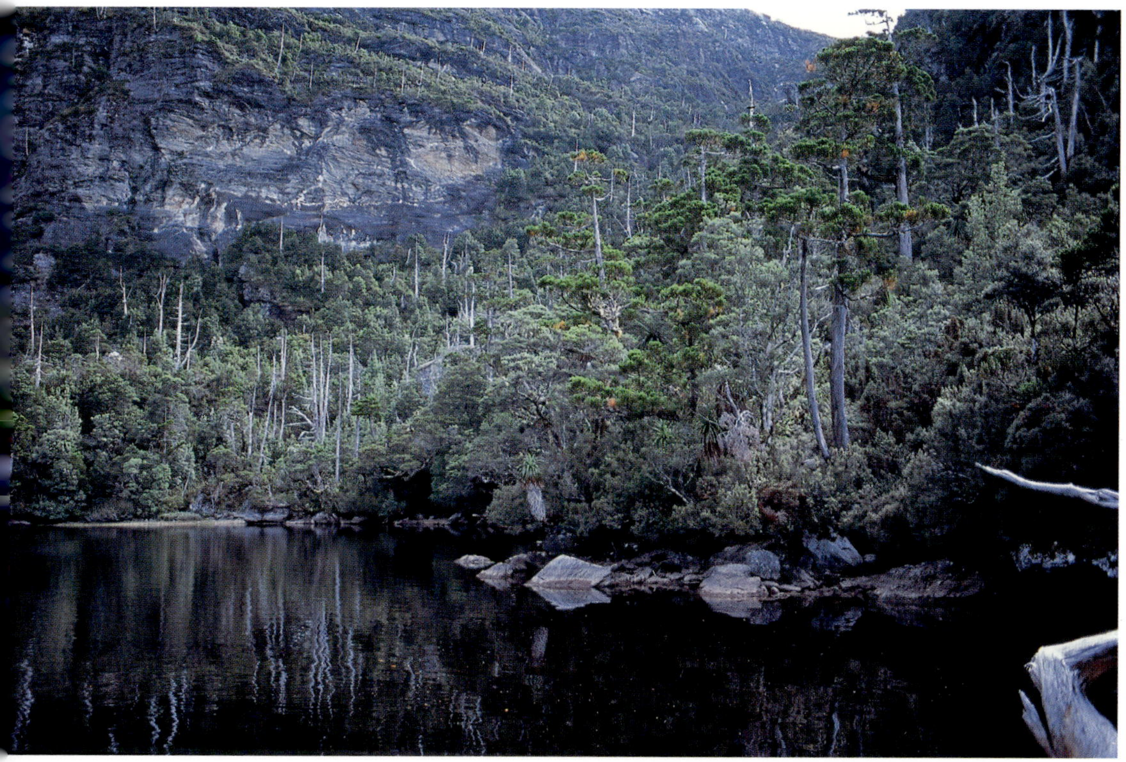

Pencil pines and pandani grow on steep slopes above the dark waters of Lake Tahune.

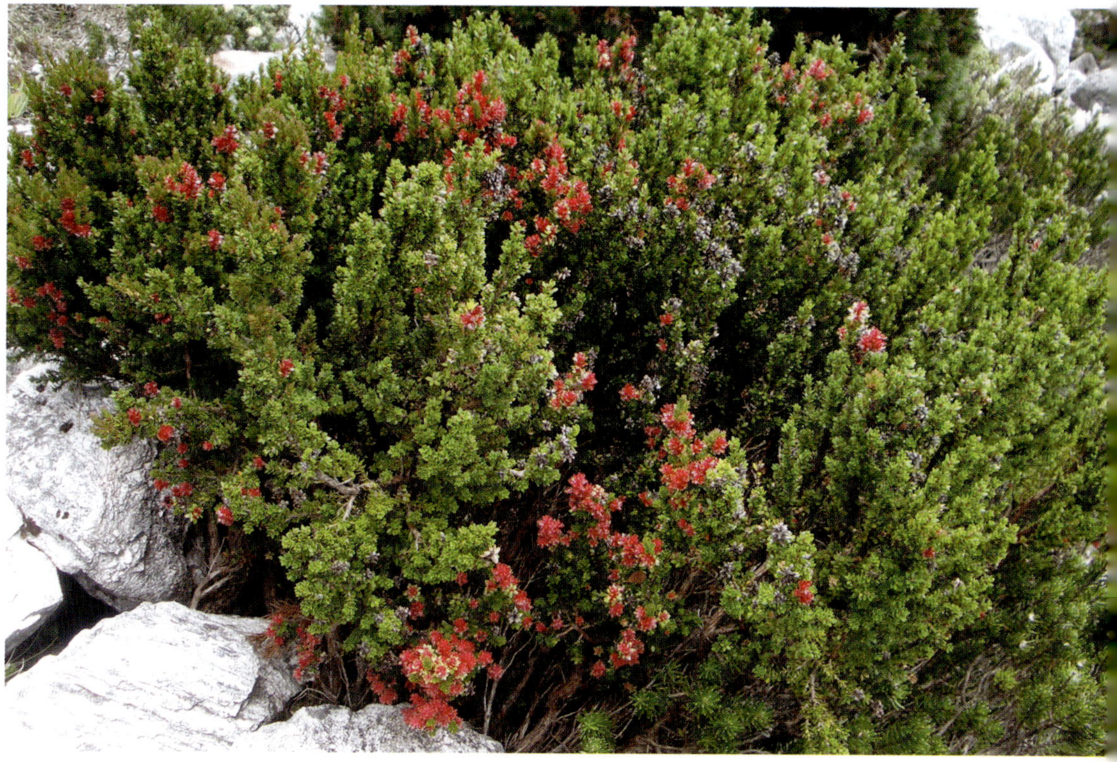

A colourful plant near the summit of Frenchmans Cap.

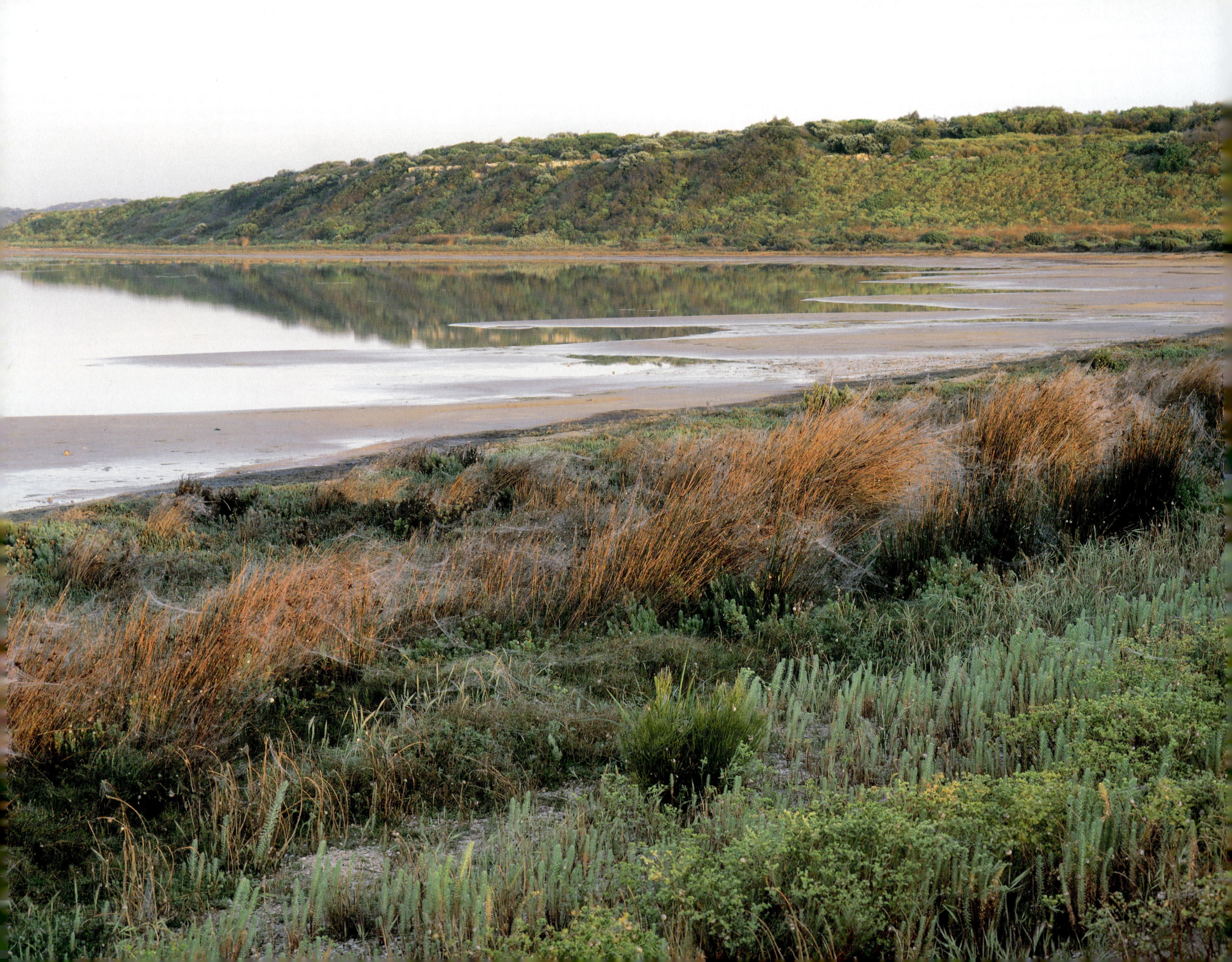

South Australia

South Australia is a land of vast plains, desert mountain ranges and usually dry salt lakes like Lake Eyre. It is the driest state; 83 per cent of the land receives less than 250mm of rain a year. But it also has productive farmland, especially in the south-east. South Australia produces about half of Australia's wine in famous regions like the Barossa Valley, Clare Valley, Coonawarra, McLaren Vale and the Riverland. The state's first vintage was bottled in 1841 in the Adelaide Hills. The hills are part of the Mount Lofty and Flinders Range system which runs for 800 kilometres from Cape Jervis in the south to the northern end of Lake Torrens. The mightiest river in Australia, the Murray, meanders through the south east corner of the state and down to Lake Alexandrina and the sea via the Coorong National Park. The Musgrave Range in the far north near the Northern Territory border boasts the highest mountain in the state, Mount Woodroffe (Ngarutjaranya, 1435m).

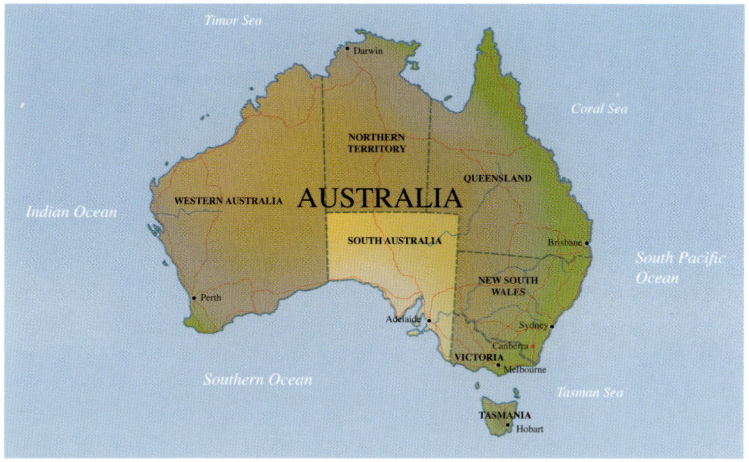

Aboriginal people have inhabited South Australia for possibly 50,000 years, and ceremonial sites and rock art abound at places like the Flinders Ranges. South Australia's initial European settlement began after Edward Gibbon Wakefield, an English politician, had an idea for creating a model economy. He thought that if land were sold at 2 pounds an acre so that only men of capital could buy, those who could not afford it would provide a source of labour, and the money generated would allow development. In January 1836 the South Australian Company was formed and the first European settlement was founded at Reeve's Point on Kangaroo Island in July 1836. A lack of fresh water and building materials forced them to abandon this settlement two years later.

Meanwhile, a permanent site for a colony had been selected on the banks of the Torrens River by Surveyor-General Colonel William Light, and 9 vessels with 636 people landed in December 1836. Light was responsible for the infant town of Adelaide's orderly and pleasant layout. In 1895 the colony of South Australia became the second place in the world after New Zealand to grant universal suffrage to women, although most Aboriginal women were excluded as they were not considered citizens at that time. Adelaide today is known as the "City of Churches" and has many well preserved heritage buildings and excellent parks. It is a culturally vibrant city and has many festivals, including the Adelaide Festival of Arts, the Fringe Festival and WOMADelaide, the world music, arts and dance festival.

Opposite page: Scenic view of the Coorong.

The Coorong National Park lies at the mouth of the mighty Murray River and contains freshwater lakes, saline estuaries, dune systems and lagoons. It is an internationally significant wetland for migrating birds, and has at least 160 resident and visiting bird species. *"I camped at Parnka Point, the narrowest part of the Coorong where it splits into northern and southern lagoons. The channel between the two is called Hells Gate. The northern lagoon is brackish as it is partly fed by the Murray River but the southern lagoon is always hypersaline. The birdlife was great and during a short walk I happened upon a bearded dragon lizard on a bush."*

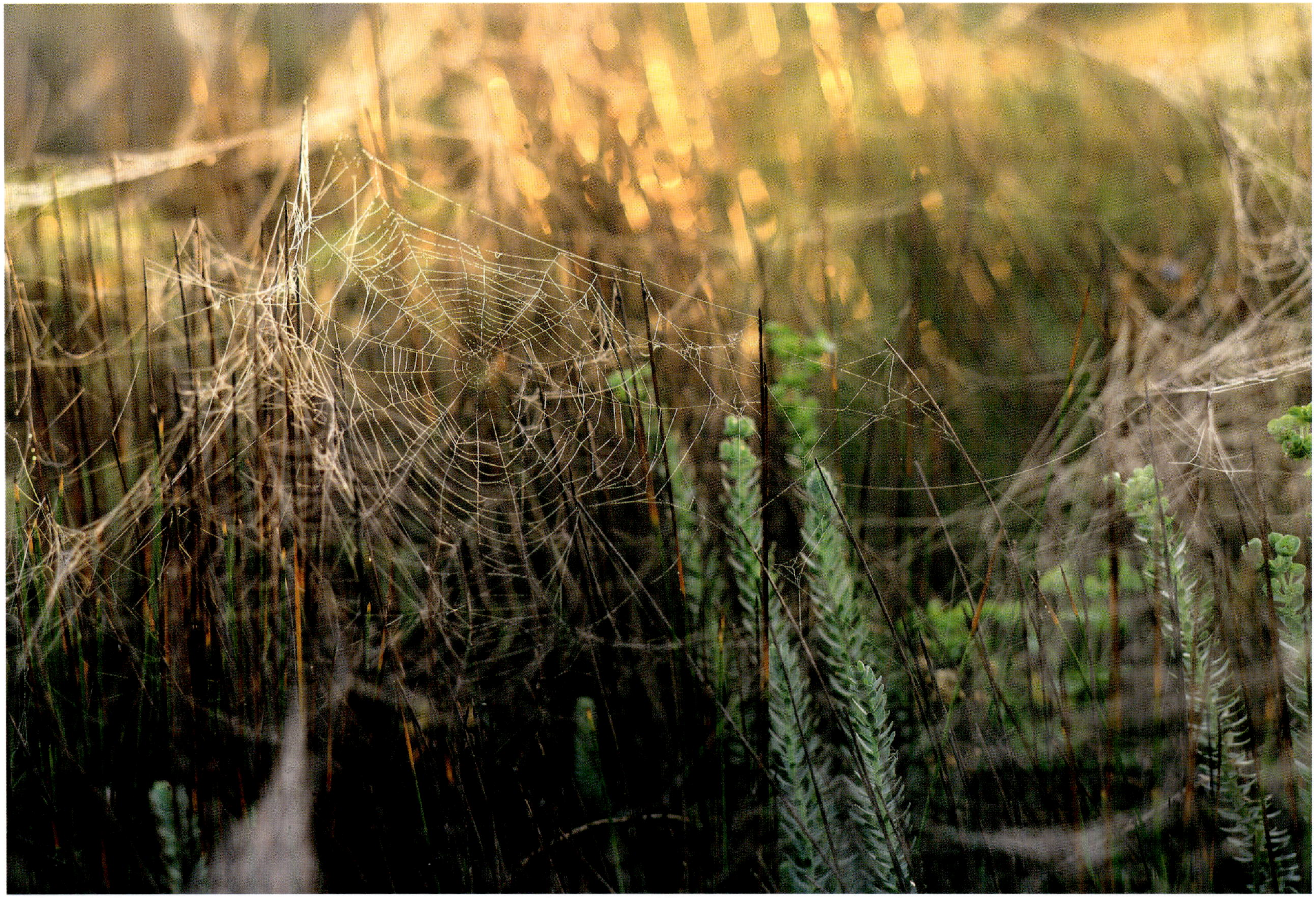

Cobwebs, Coorong NP.

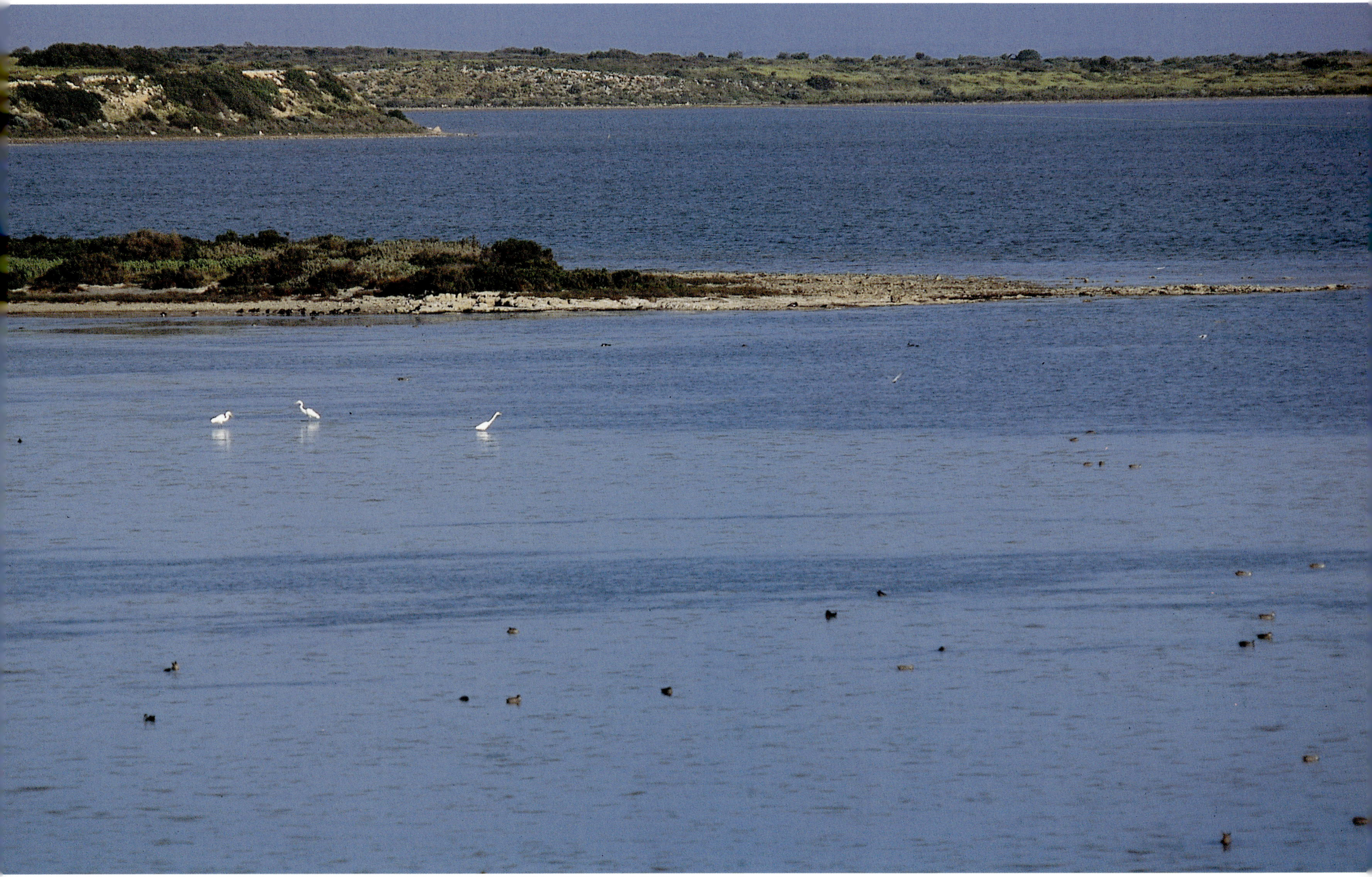

Egrets and other waterbirds, Coorong NP.

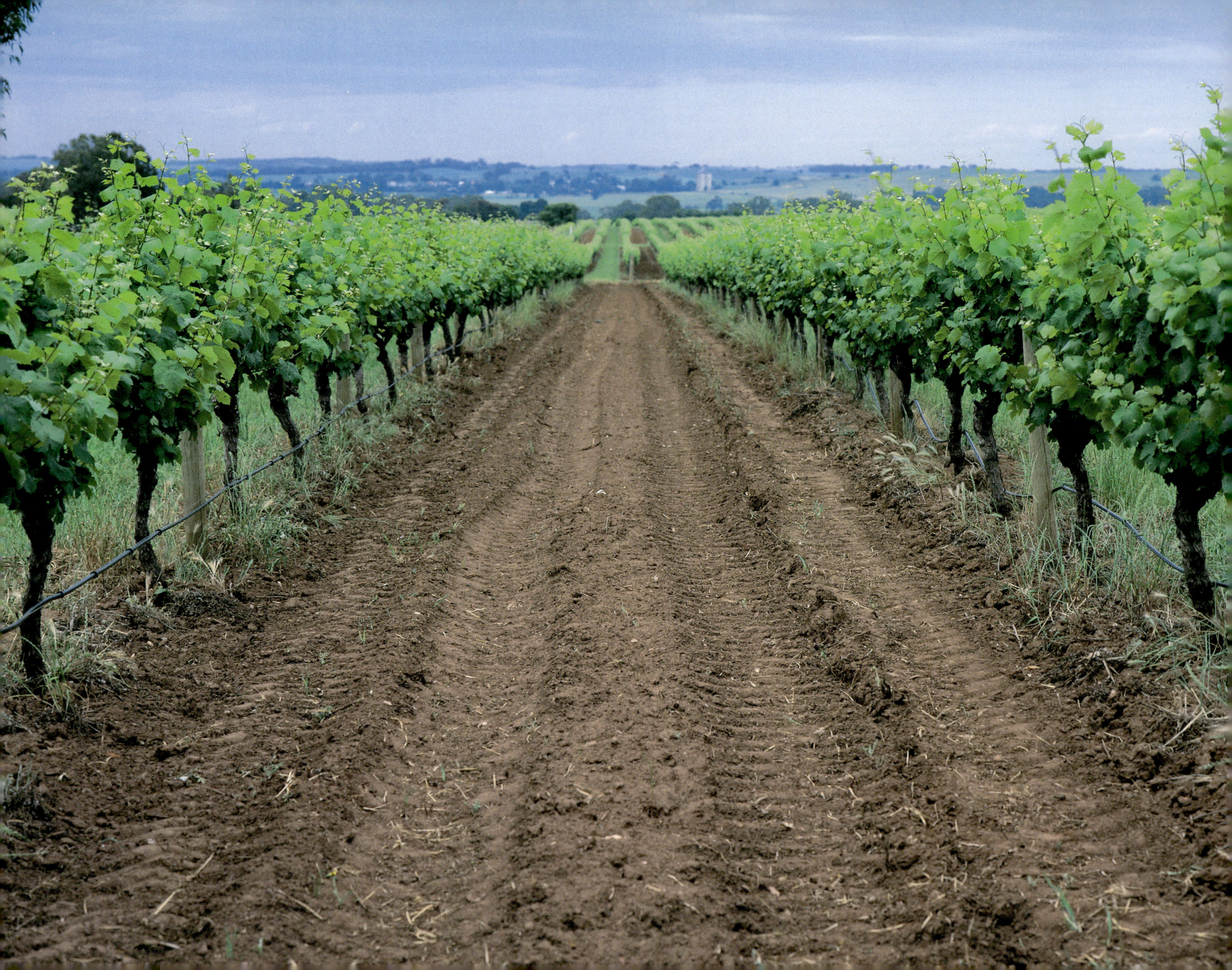

The Barossa Valley, 60 kilometres north east of Adelaide, was first settled in 1842 and is the most famous winery region of Australia. It also has well preserved European style heritage towns like Angaston and Tanunda, originally settled by German Lutherans who planted orchards, olive groves and vineyards. Other early settlers were Cornish miners and other Britons. The Barossa's first vineyard was planted by Johann Gramp on the banks of Jacobs Creek in 1847. The main varieties grown are Shiraz, Riesling, Semillon, Grenache and Cabernet Sauvignon.

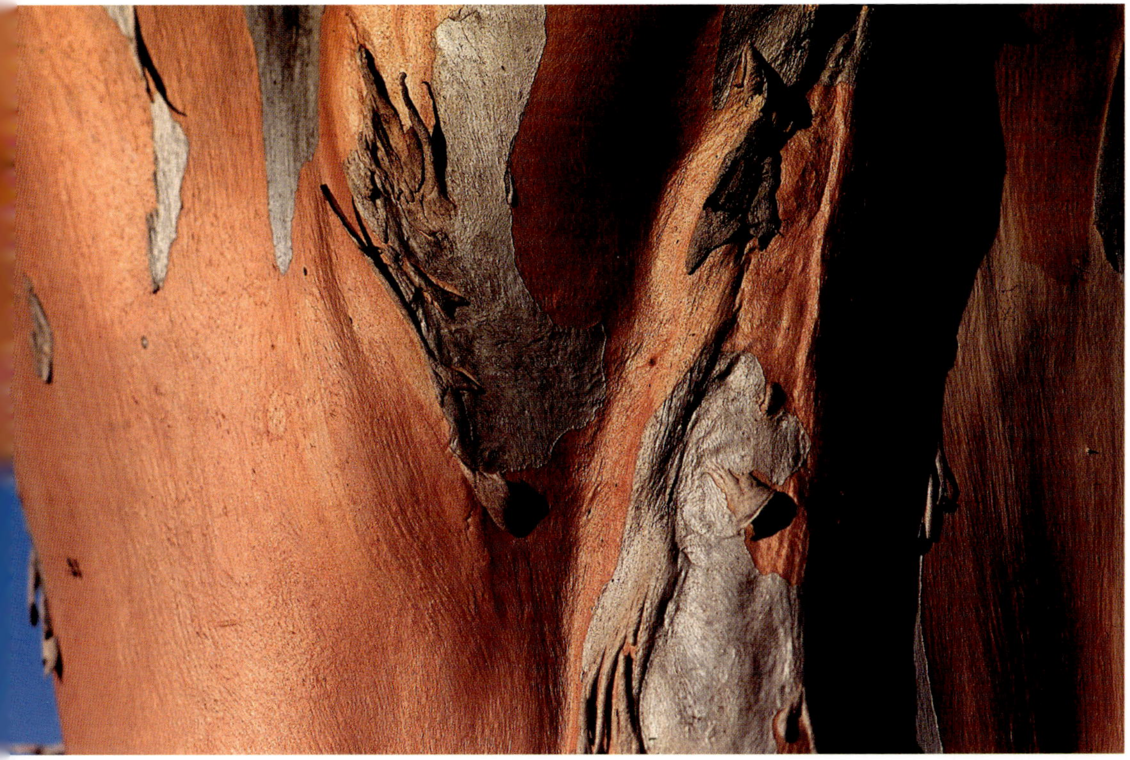

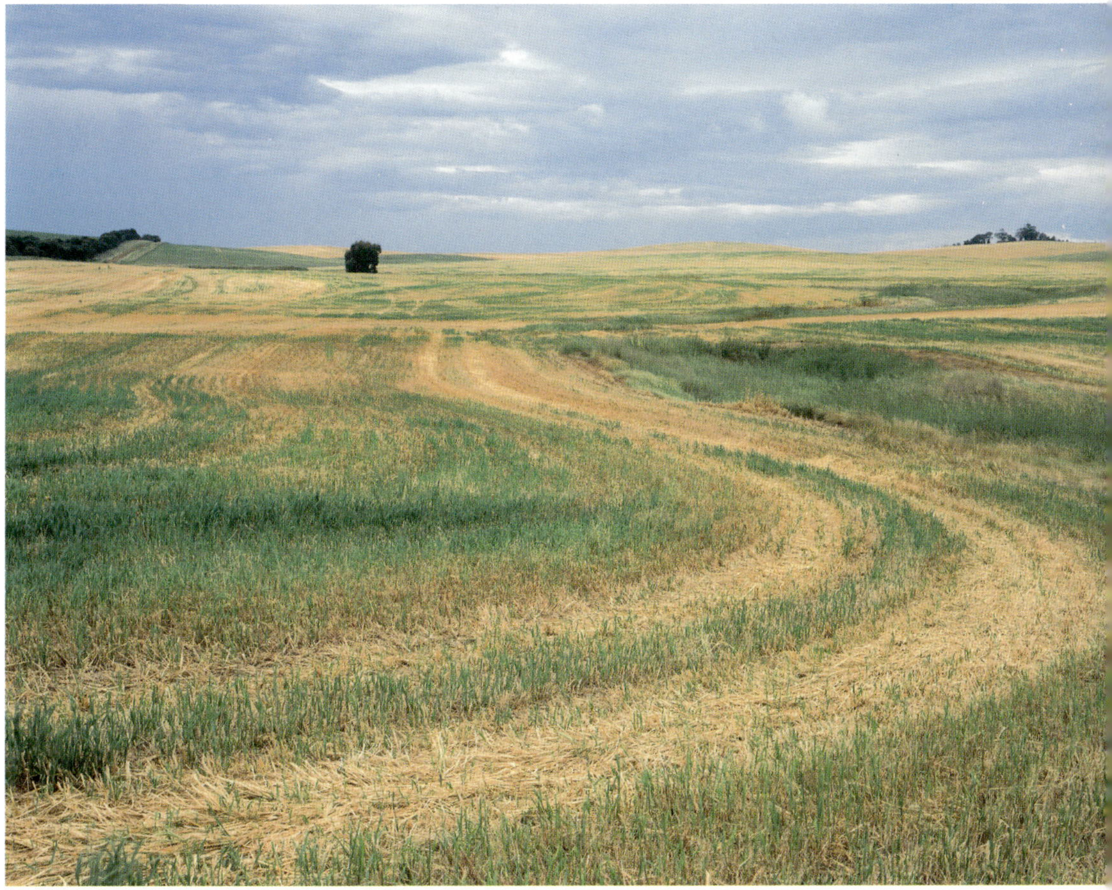

Top: Vivid coppery and silver bark of a gum tree near Orroroo.

Right: Plough patterns in a paddock, southern Flinders Ranges.

Opposite page: Barossa vineyard near Angaston.

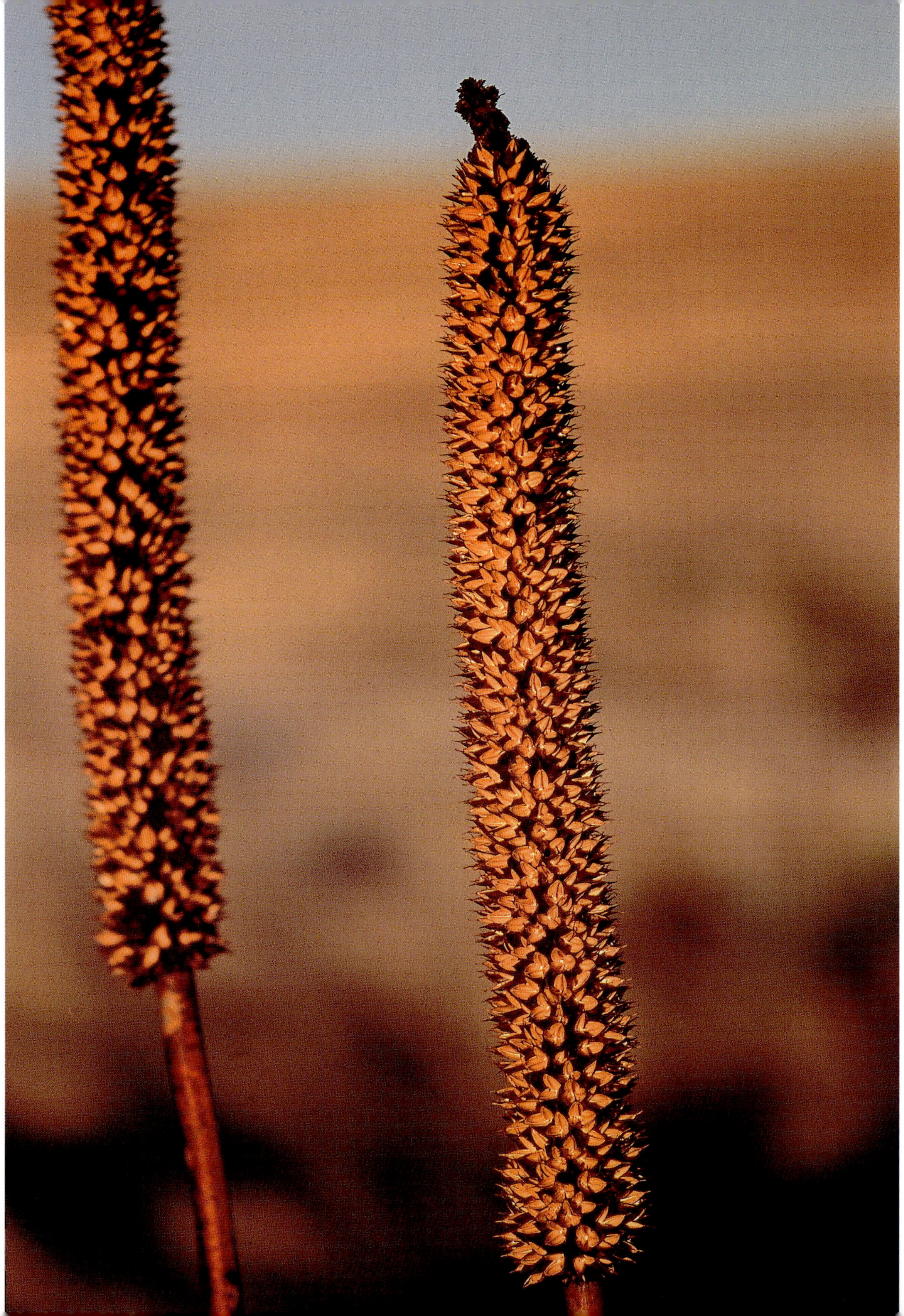

The iconic Flinders Ranges start in the desert country of the north and merge into the Mount Lofty Ranges north of Adelaide. I stayed at in an atmospheric camping area near Orroroo in the southern Flinders Ranges, *"by some low, grasstree studded ranges. I went up a hill at dusk to get some pics and while I was setting up the tripod a massive euro buck came hopping up. He was just as surprised to see me as I was to see him. Then a little joey came hopping right past me! The female was there too behind the dark, huge male. They hopped off after about 10 seconds and the joey took off too, around the other way."*

Left: Grass tree spikes.

Opposite page: The rolling, semi-arid landscape near Orroroo, seen here at dusk.

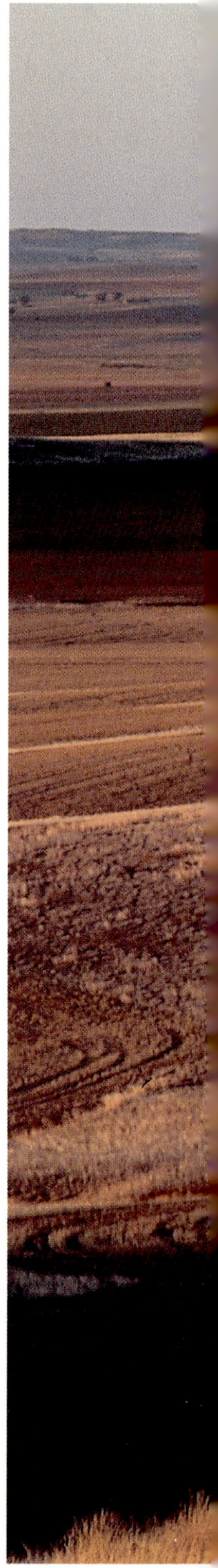

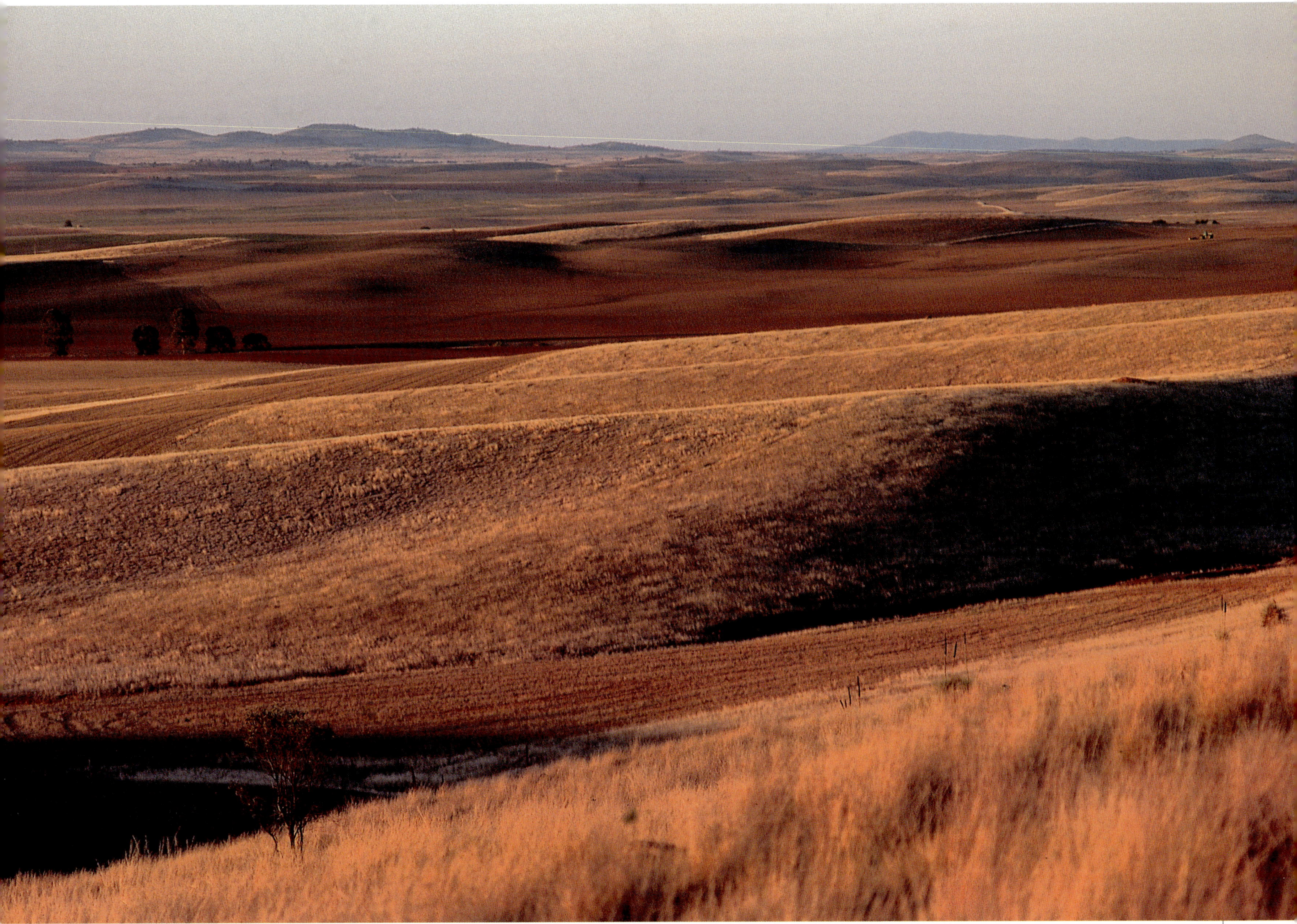

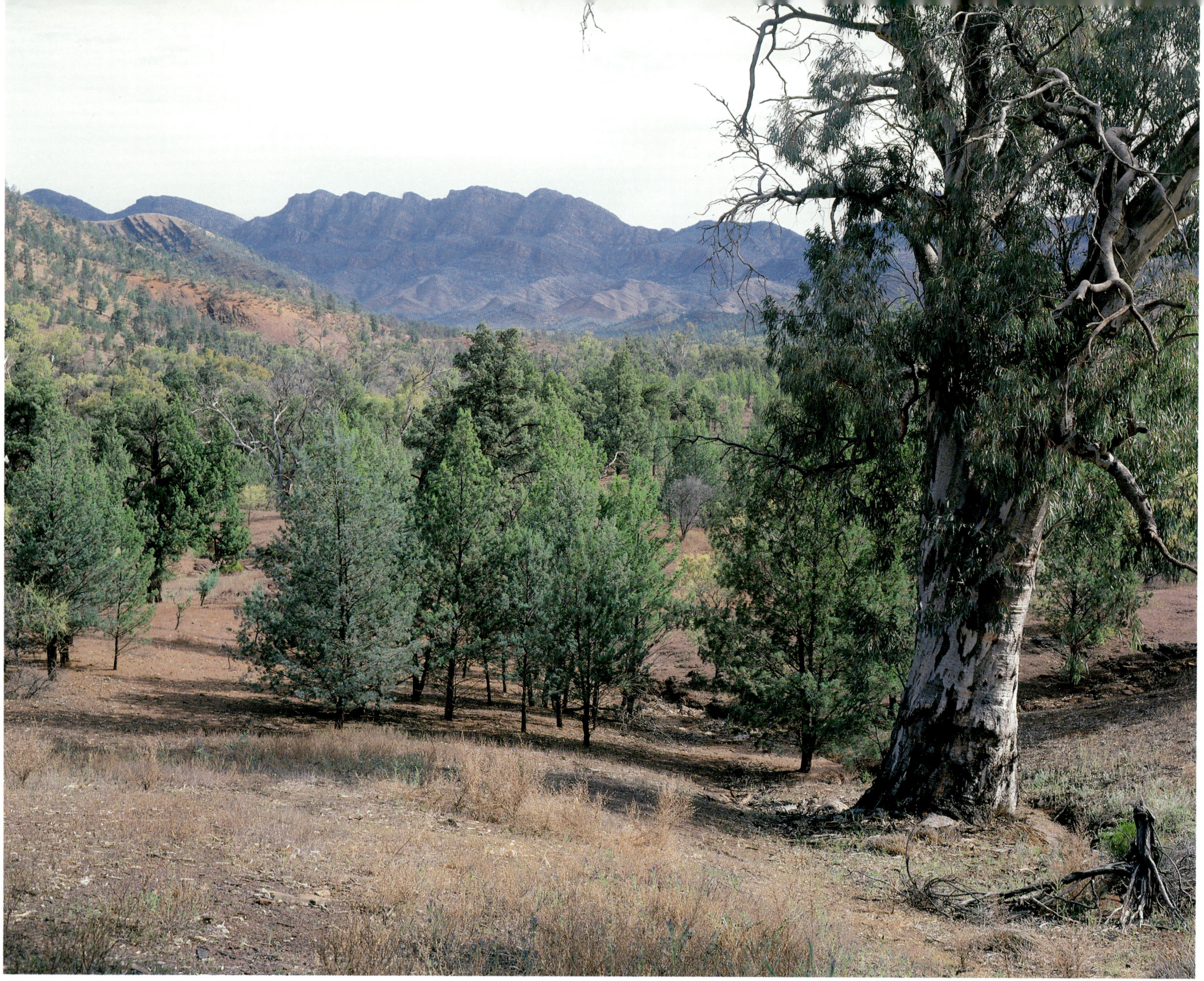

A classic view of Mount Sawtooth in the Flinders Ranges from the Bunyeroo Valley Scenic Drive.

The Flinders Ranges National Park lies 450 kilometres north of Adelaide and protects a semi-arid mountainous landscape that is quintessentially Australian. This area is the traditional land of the Adnyamathanha Aboriginal people. The ancient folded mountains were formed by plate movements and collisions more than 500 million years ago.

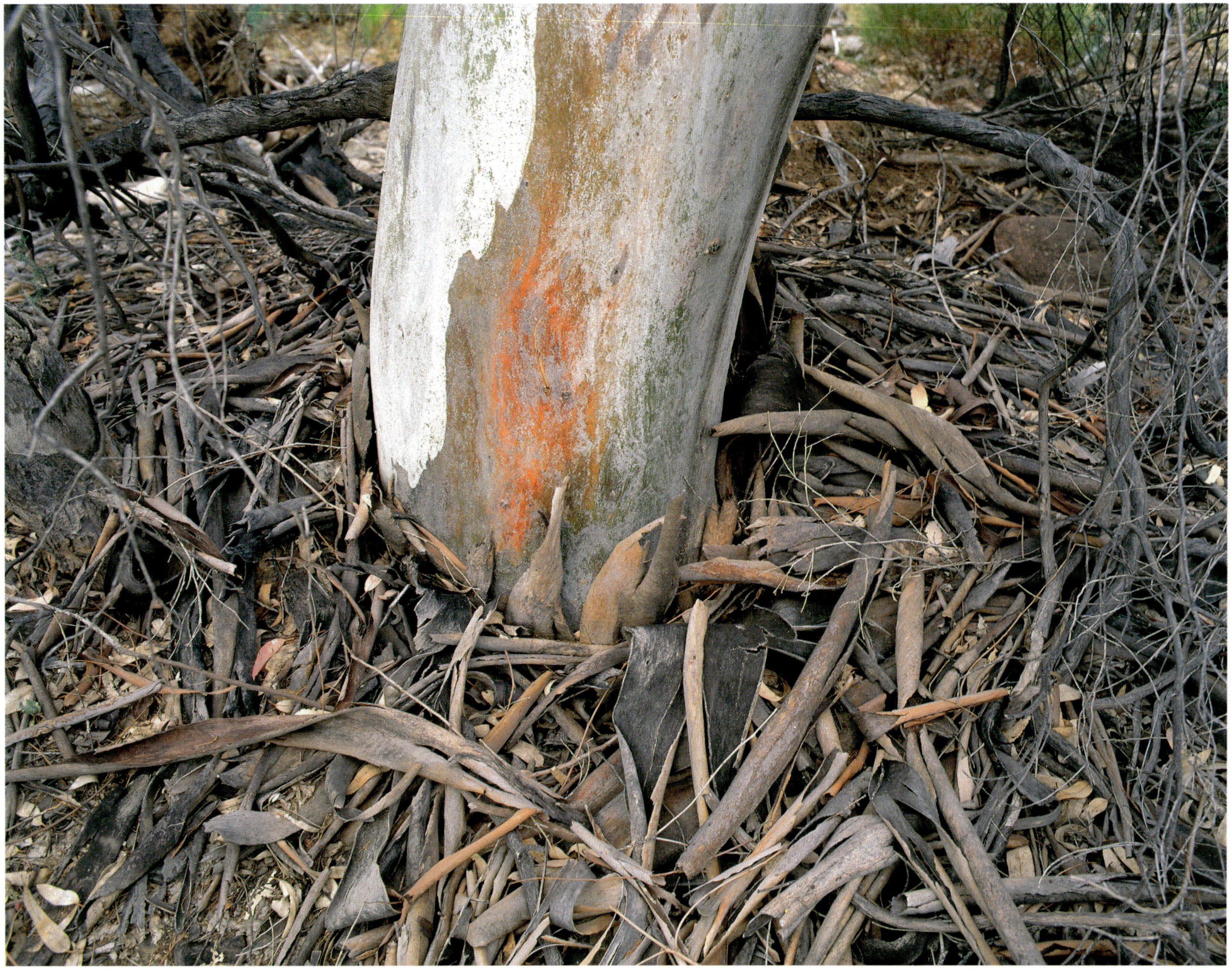

Peeled bark below a river red gum in the Bunyeroo Gorge.

Brachina Gorge, in the northern part of Flinders Ranges NP, has outstanding geological formations and a dramatic scenic drive that travels through geological time and amongst warped and tilted strata. The gorge shows off folded layers of quartzite, limestone, sandstones and shales and even has some rocks from an ancient meteorite. Fossils like soft bodied ancient jellyfish and trilobites have been found here, and the gorge is a mecca for wildlife such as emus and the yellow footed rock wallaby.

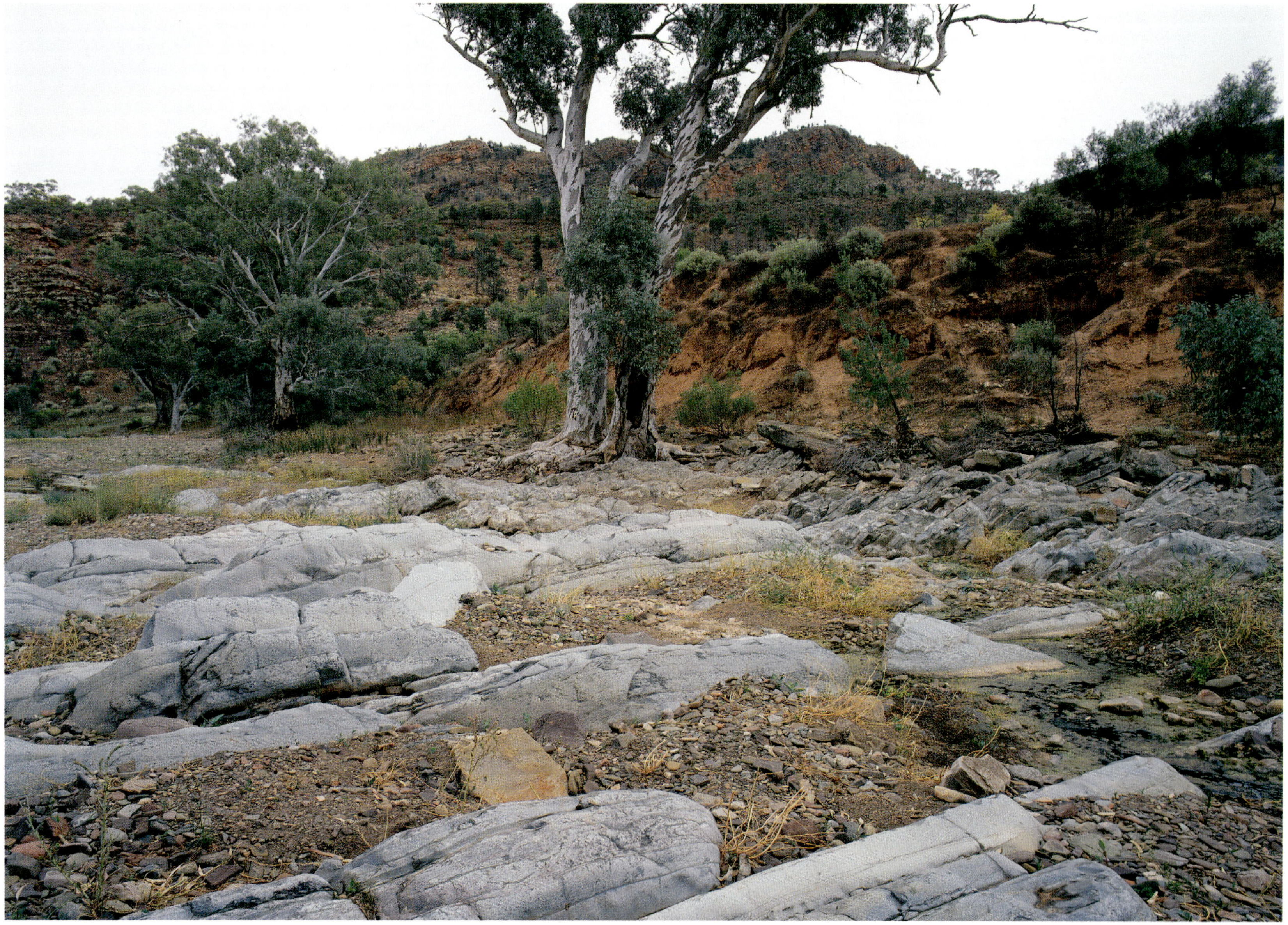

Rocks and river red gums in Brachina Gorge.

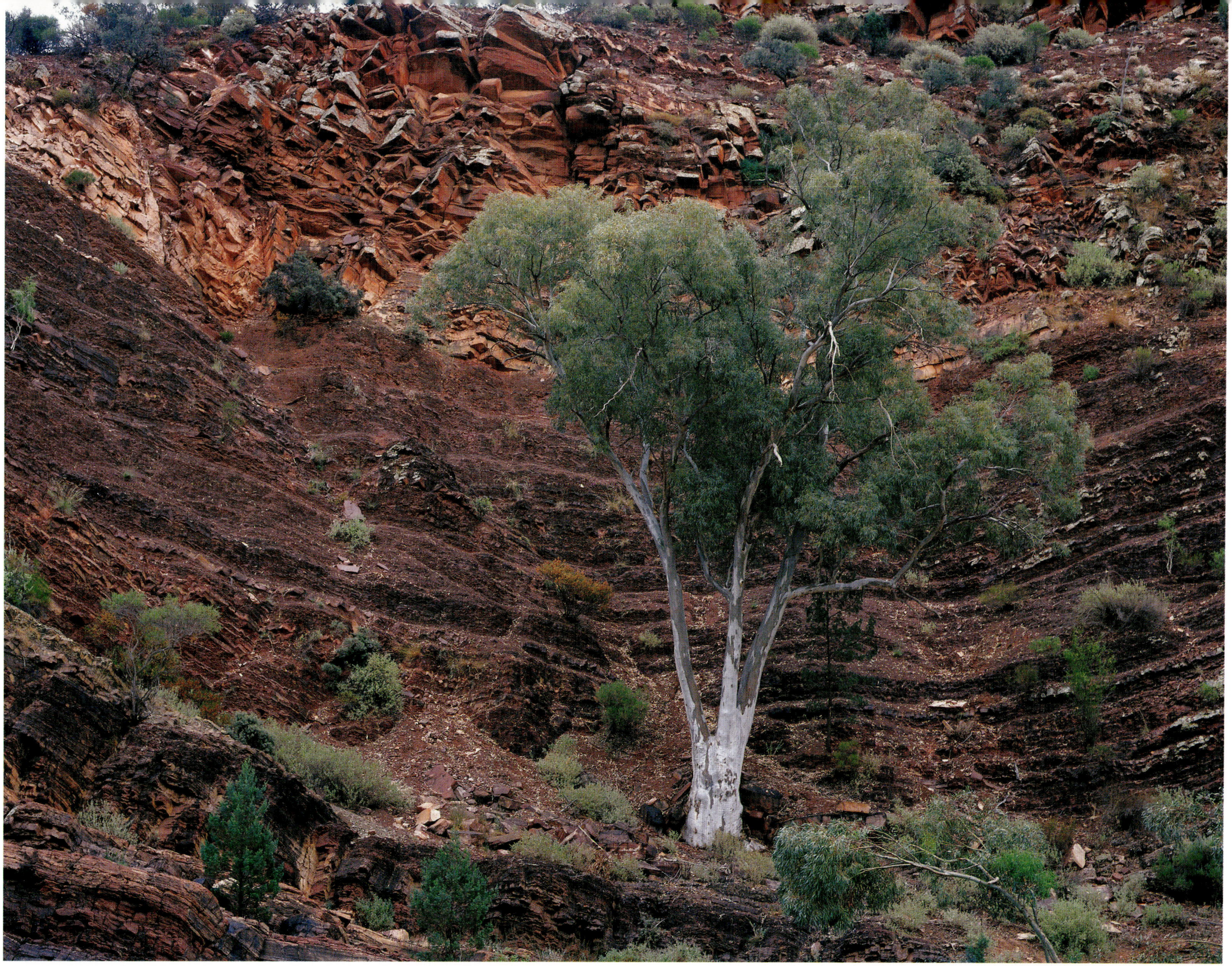

The join between two rock strata is shown clearly in this cliff face in Brachina Gorge.

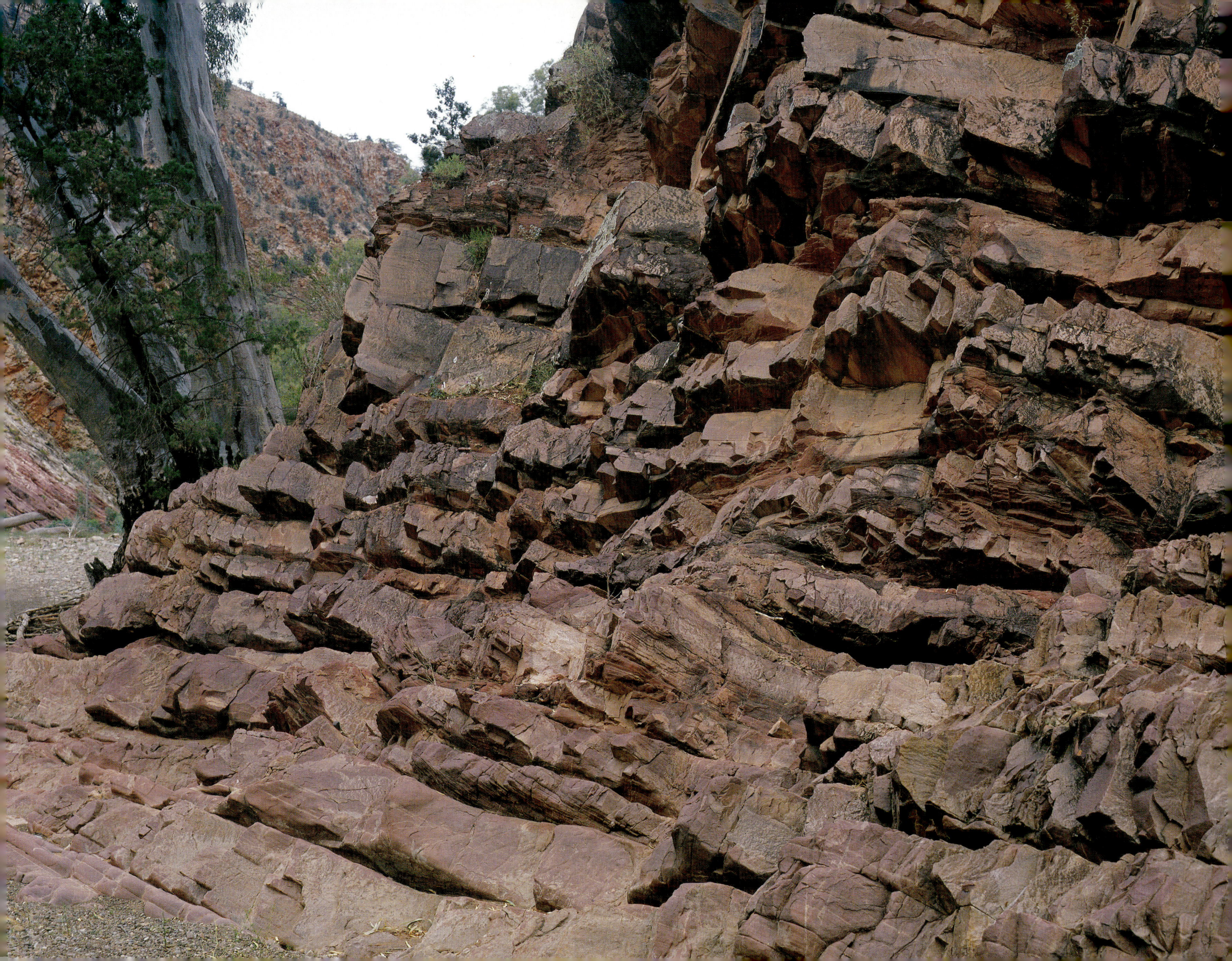

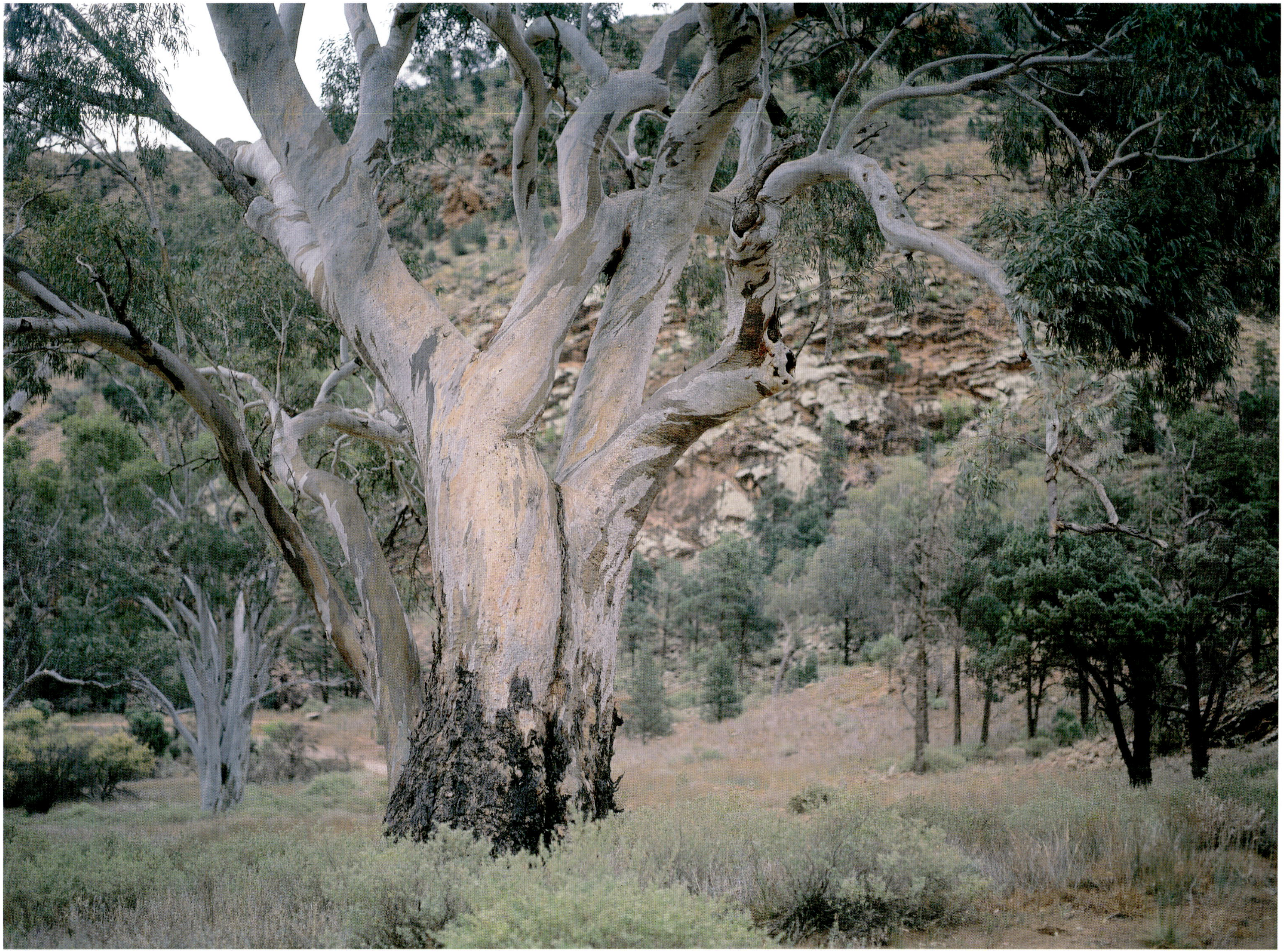

Top: Giant river red gum in Brachina Gorge.

Opposite page: Rock patterns in a cliff.

Wilpena Pound is the most famous area of the Flinders Ranges National Park and contains its highest mountain, St Mary's Peak or Ngarri Mudlanha (1168m). The Aboriginal word Wilpena means the place of bent fingers, referring to the way the pound resembles a cupped hand. I climbed St Mary's Peak in 2011 via a 21 kilometre long circular day walk from the Wilpena Pound Resort and wrote: *"A full on, but excellent day. I got up at 6 am and left shortly afterwards, getting back about 3pm. The views were great and I met some nice people – a lady from the UK and three young Kiwis. After the walk I had a swim, meeting up with the Kiwis a little later for drinks and chuckles. I had the best laughs of the whole trip with these three! Pretty tired now though."*

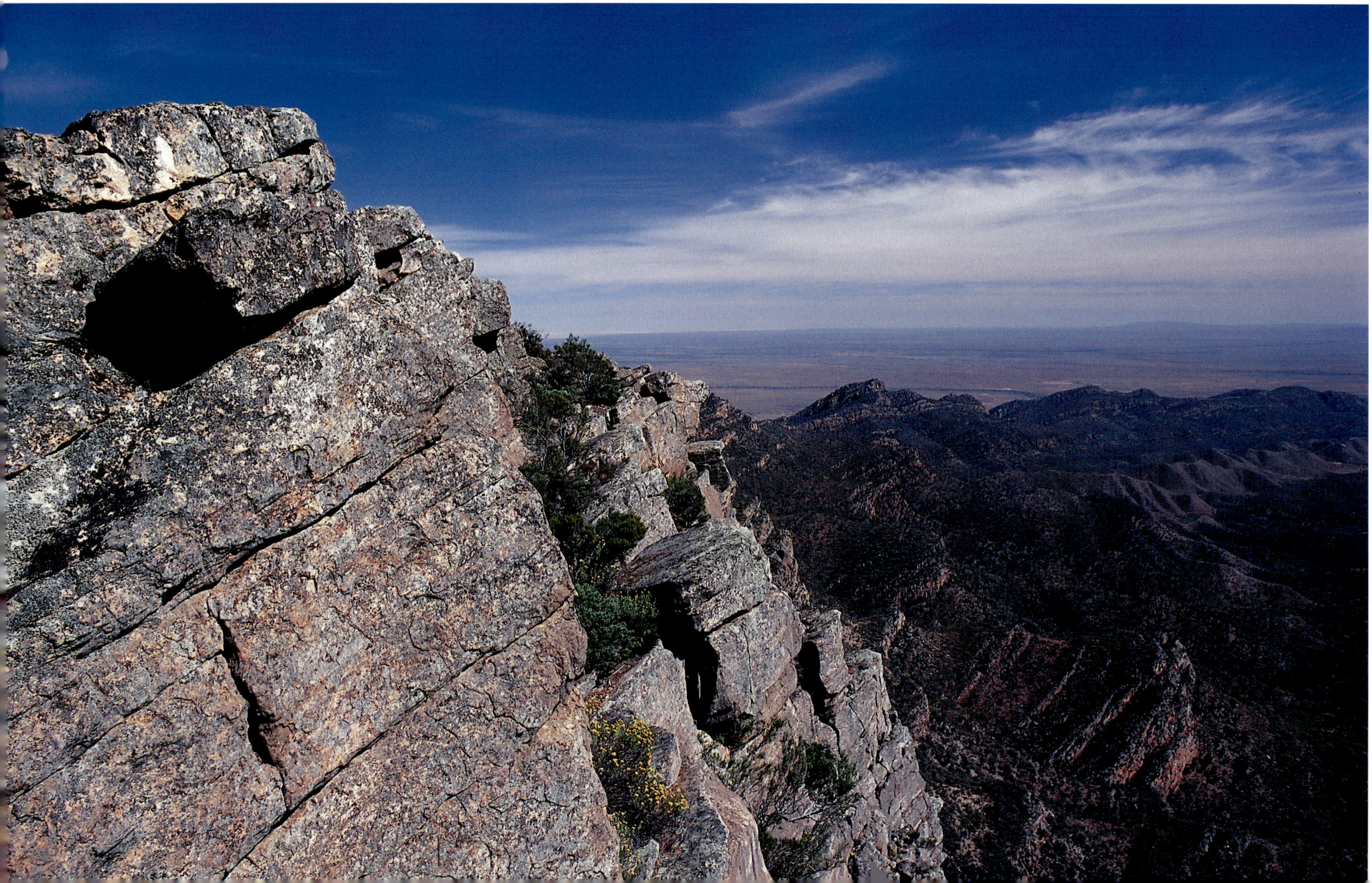

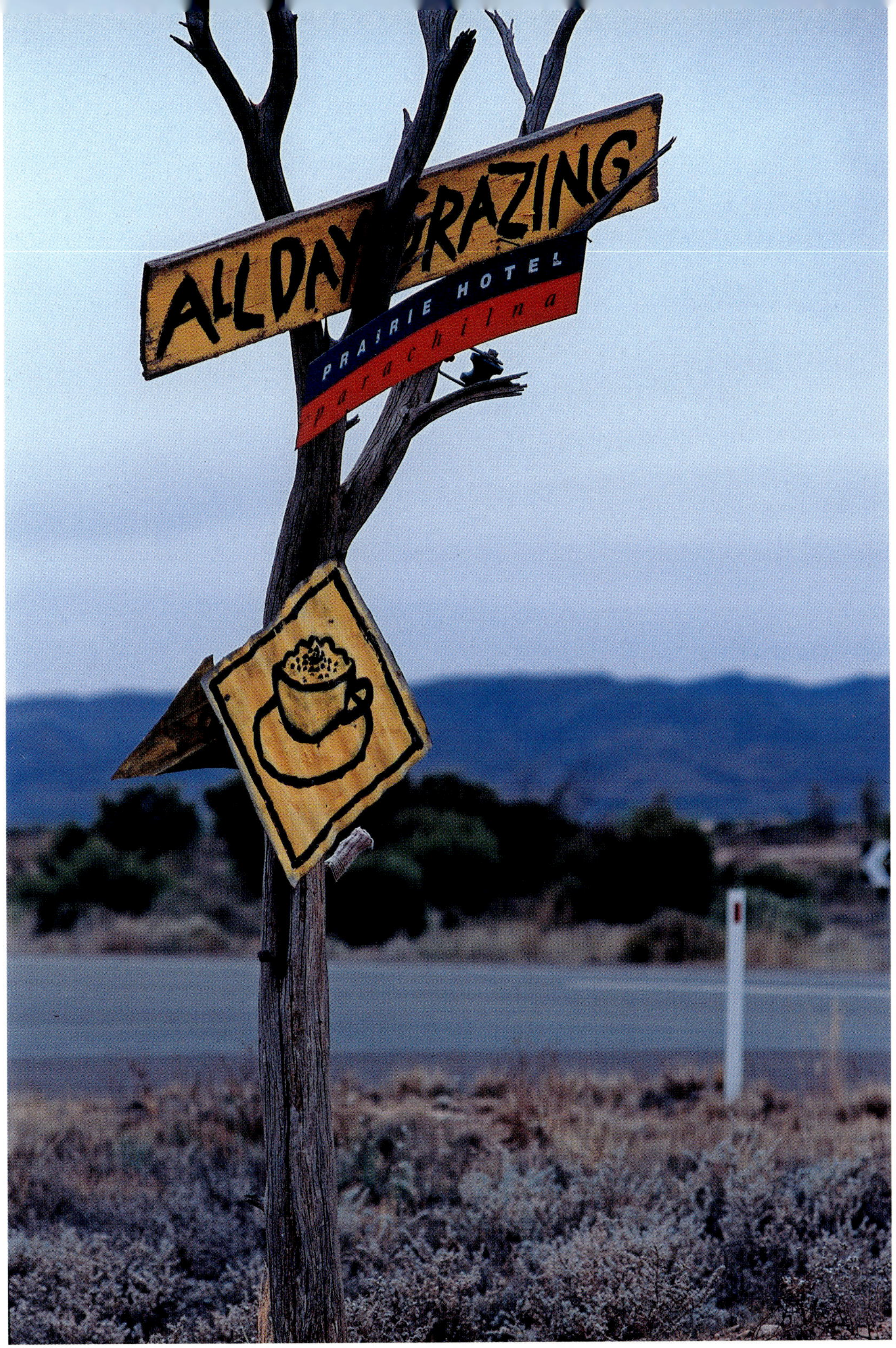

Top: The Prairie Hotel at Parachilna was first licensed in 1876.

Opposite page: View from St Mary's Peak.

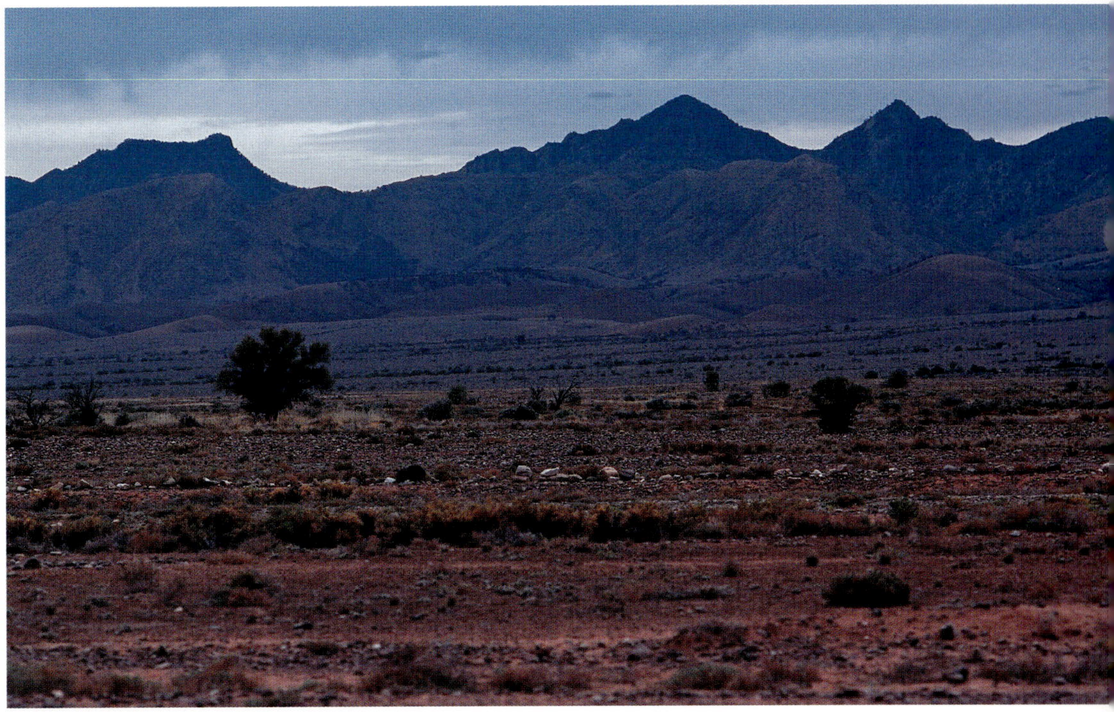

The rugged and arid hills of the Flinders Ranges north of Wilpena Pound.

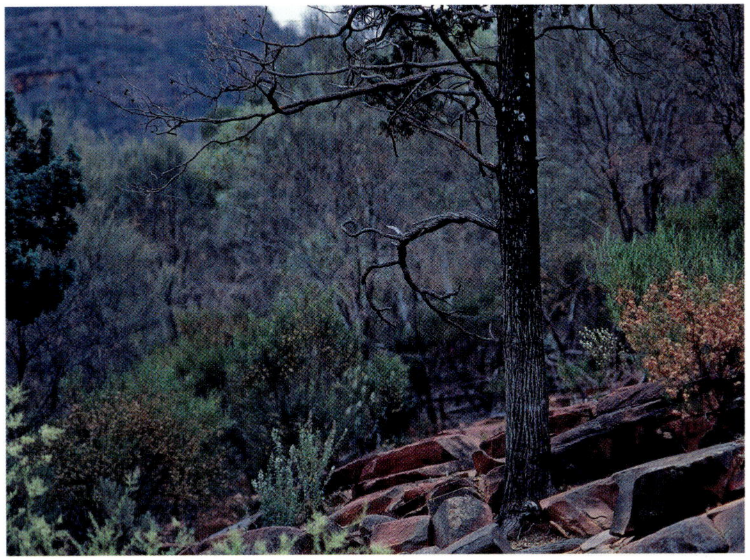

Black cypress pine at Wilpena Pound.

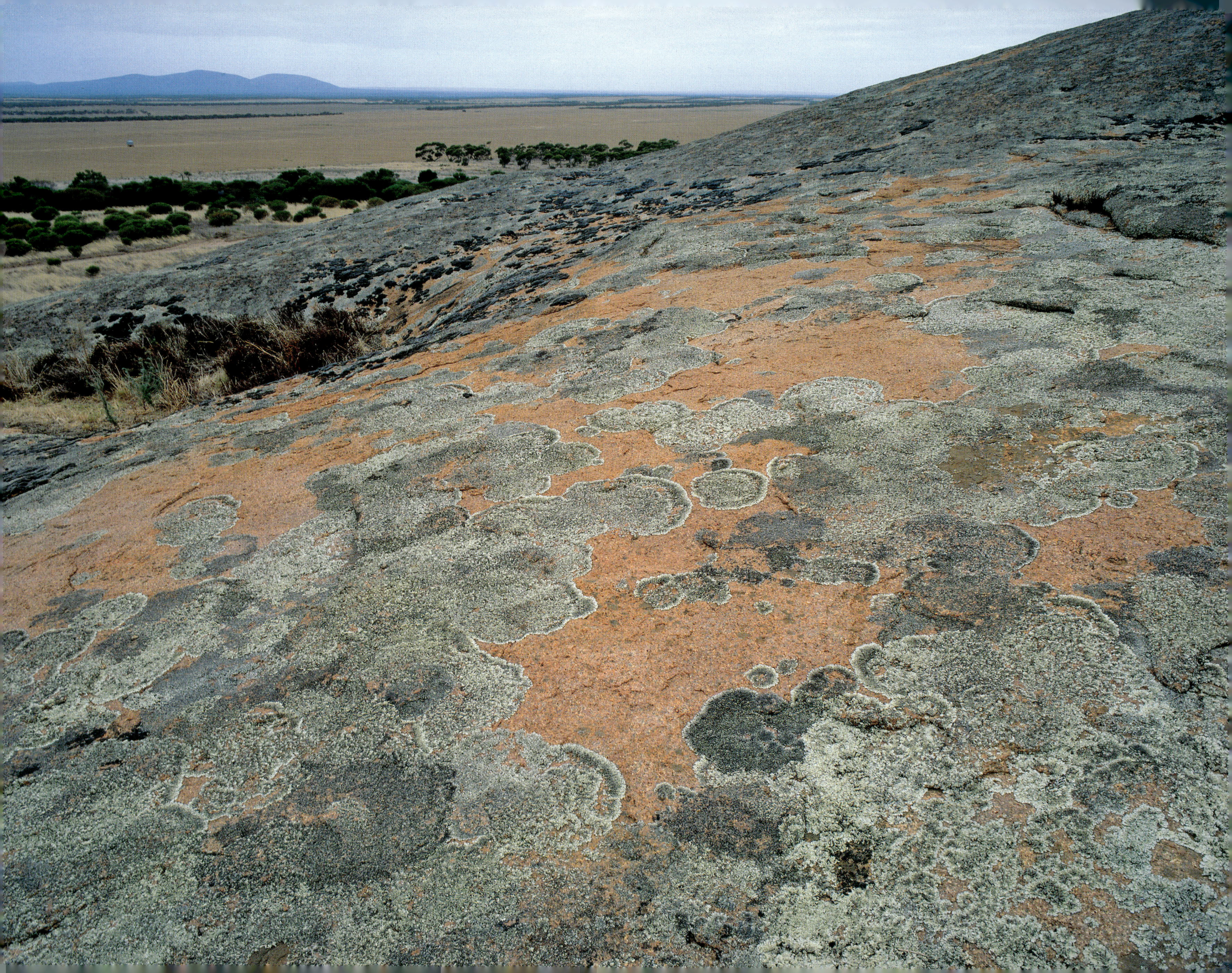

The Gawler Ranges are volcanic hills in south-west South Australia. A small granite outlier of this range is Pildappa Rock, 15 kilometres north east of the town of Minnipa. The rock has mini wave formations and deep gnamma holes, hollows eroded or indented in solid rock, which ensured an almost permanent water supply for Aboriginal people. A free camp site is available here for self sufficient campers.

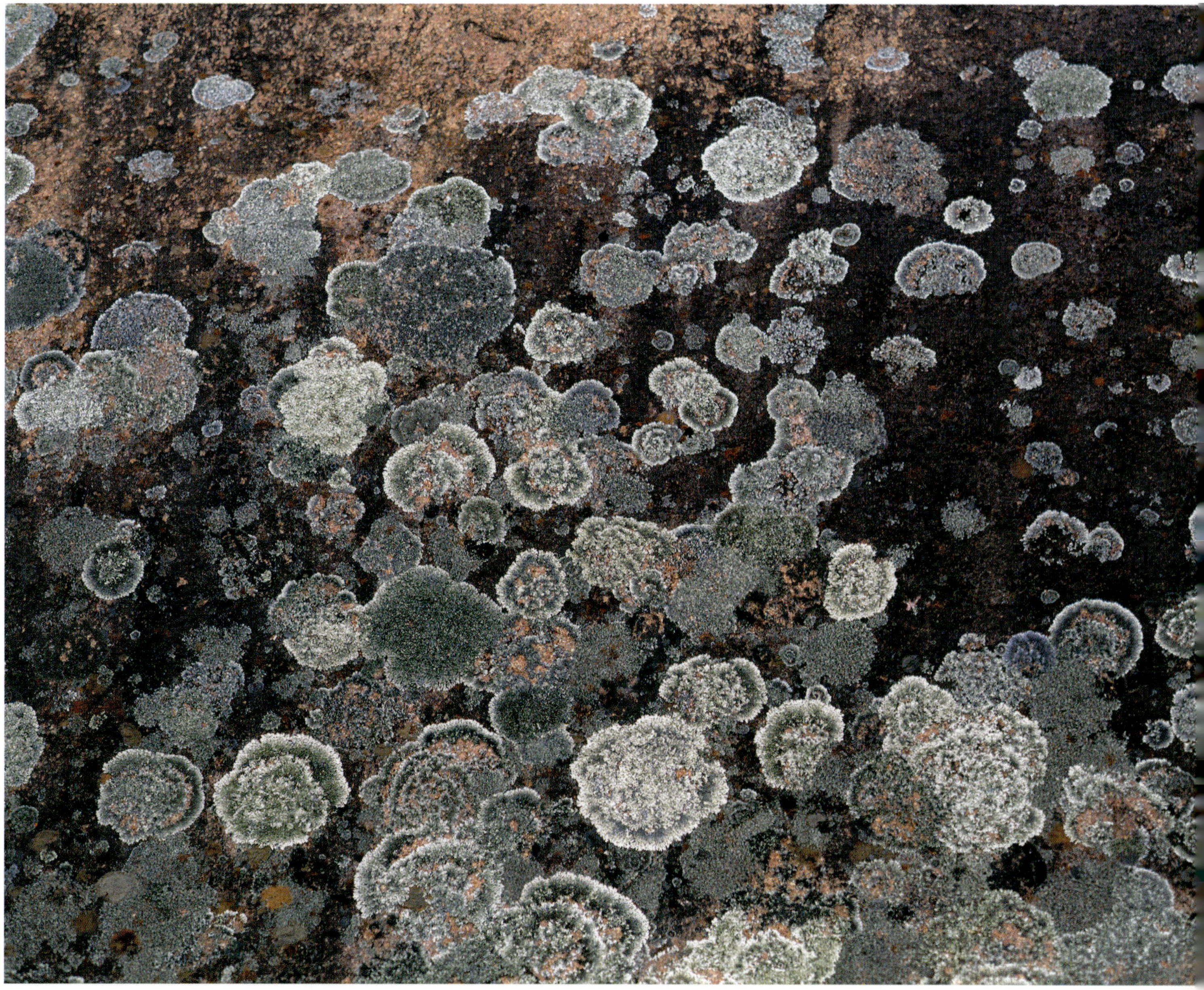

Right: Lichens make beautiful patterns on the granite faces of Pildappa Rock.

Opposite page: View to the north from Pildappa Rock over wheat fields to the distant Gawler ranges.

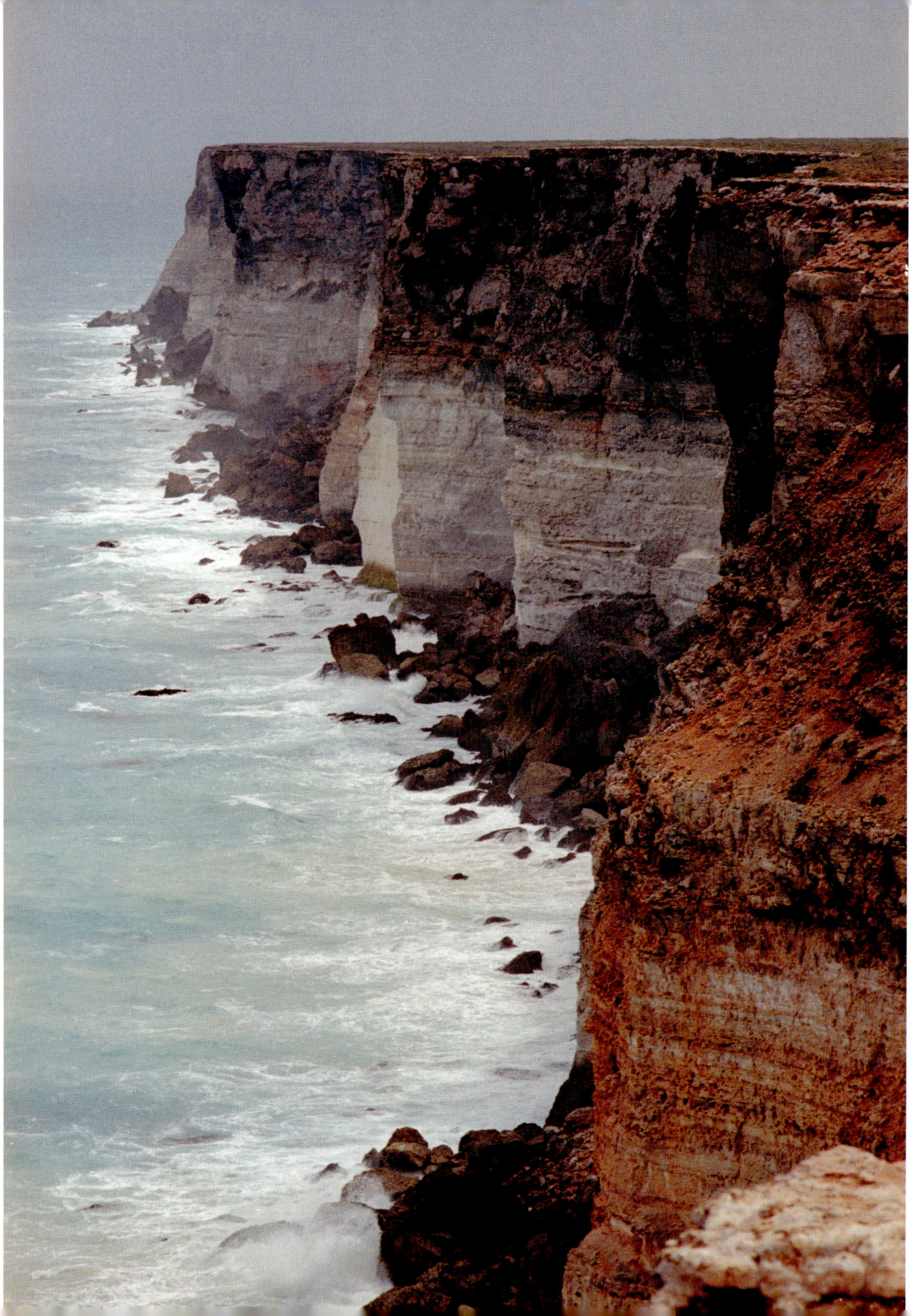

The Nullarbor (literally meaning "no trees" in Latin) is a vast limestone plain or plateau sprawling over 250,000 square kilometres and riddled with underground caves. In the north it merges into the mulga and bluebush covered dunes of the Great Victoria Desert, and in the south plunges sheer for 80 metres into the Southern Ocean at places like the spectacular Bunda Cliffs near the Western Australian border. In October 2011 I wrote: *"the Nullarbor is a great advert for trees – gee it can be bleak and windy! But everyone is on the same road (in the same boat so to speak) and there is great camaraderie at the cliff top lookouts and even sometimes in the roadhouses."*

Left: The Bunda Cliffs stretch for 200 kilometres along the Great Australian Bight. Southern right whales can often be seen from the cliffs between May and October.

Opposite page: Dirt track, Nullarbor.

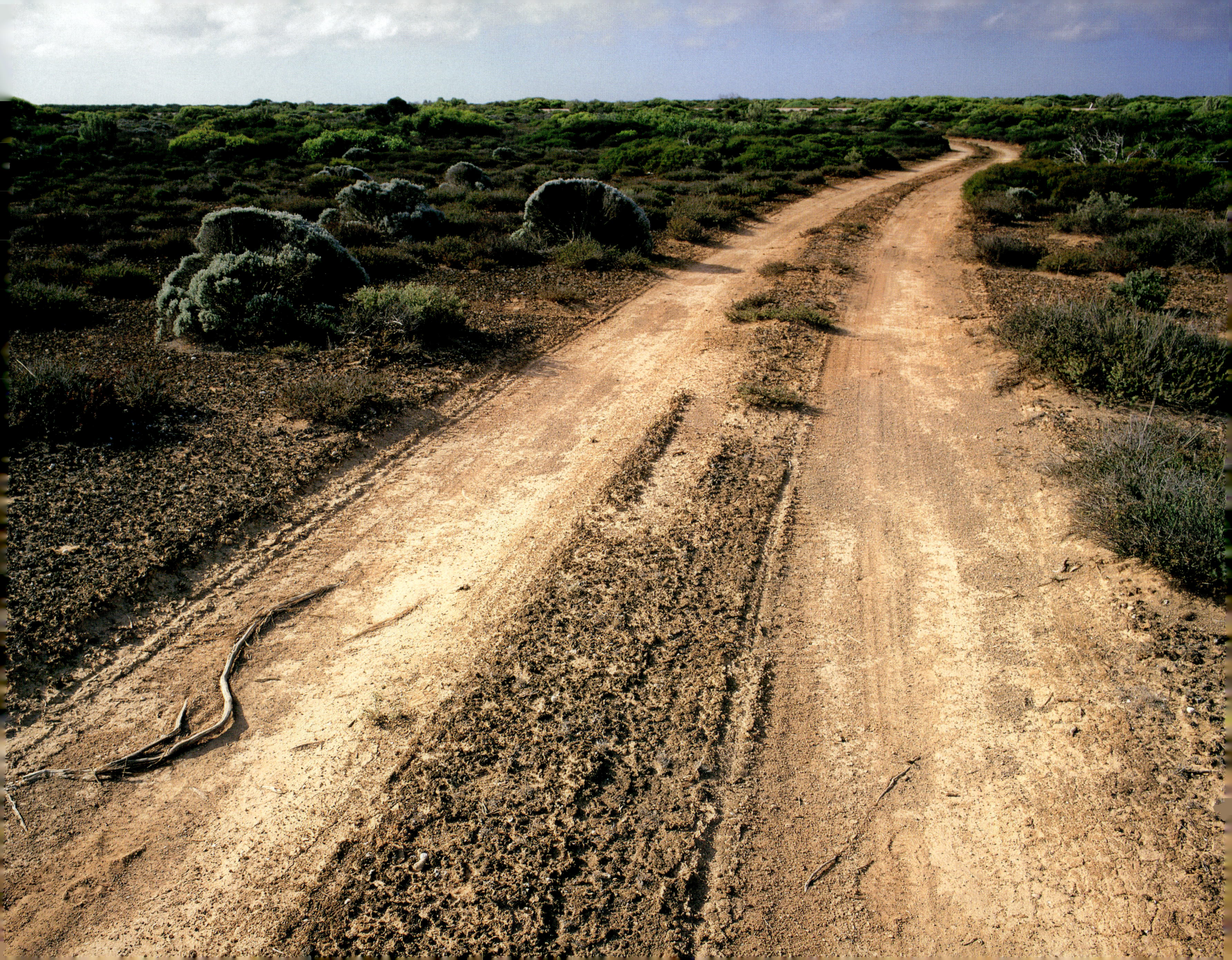

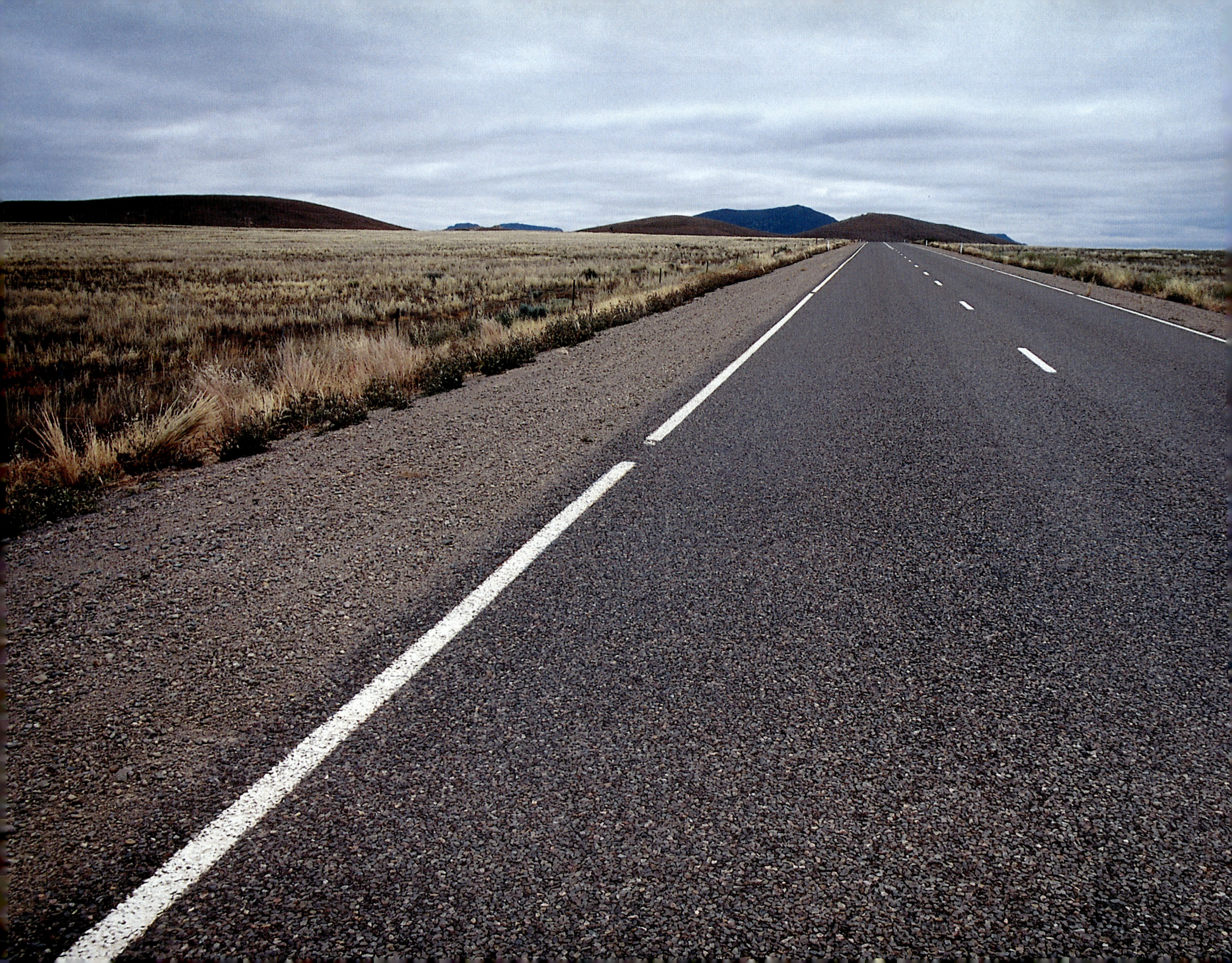

Journey's End

I travelled around the continent and back to Perth in about five months. It was the most special time of my life so far, full of adventure and discovery. Although I travelled alone I was rarely lonely and met many wonderful people on the journey, some of whom I still keep in touch with. I did have some difficult moments and times of reflection. In the Grampians in Victoria I had a long overdue rest *"and spent most of the day in a daze trying to work out whether I was Arthur or Martha! What to do? And the world is turning to s... while we speak. I think the key is love – true love, one for oneself, one for their partner, one for their family, one for humanity and one for the earth that sustains us. And that is the beginning and the end of it."*

During the journey I made the decision to relocate to the east coast of Australia and so in 2012 loaded up the mighty Camry and headed once more across the Nullarbor. After staying with my brother and his family in Brisbane for a short while, I drove to northern New South Wales to have a look at the towns there. I had decided that I would prefer to live in a country town with a genuine sense of community. I got to the town of Murwillumbah, in northern New South Wales, and the poor old car blew up! It was a serious breakdown and I was stuck in the town for over a week. During this time I stayed at a motel near the town centre and wandered around and explored. I was struck by the beauty of the area and thought it looked like a great place to settle. One day I chanced across a Sustainability Street meeting in a neighbouring road and sat down and joined in the lively discussion. At the end of the meeting I mentioned to one of the locals that I was interested in moving to the area. She said that she knew someone looking to rent out a studio flat in the street. I went and saw the flat that very day and moved in to "Sustainability Street" about a month later after another quick trip back to the west. I have been here ever since!

For the purposes of this book I did a shorter trip in March and April 2013 through New South Wales, Victoria and Tasmania to photograph the landscapes there. During this difficult and sometimes lonely trip I reached an emotional crisis point at Cape Conran in Victoria (see page 156), but after going through that felt more at peace with myself and more sure of my place in the world. After five weeks I arrived back in Murwillumbah and wrote *"well, what a trip. In many ways it has been one of my toughest ever. It had challenging hikes, foot injuries, changeable weather and difficult emotional issues to deal with. But I got through ok and had some sublime moments too. This morning I was reading a travel book by Bill Bryson and had a wonderful belly laugh – my first for a long time! I had a good night's sleep last night, an early morning walk, packed up and headed to Mullumbimby where I celebrated with a delicious omelette and coffee."*

Have I learnt anything from my travels? Well most importantly life is what we make it and we must "have a go"! I enjoyed exploring this breathtakingly beautiful country and had many memorable adventures, but at the same time realised that Australia can be an unforgiving land. I am still concerned about where we are headed as a society but am more optimistic about the future. I think this great land will sustain us if we make the difficult changes that are necessary. We will have to slow down the pace of our lives, reduce debt, grow, buy and eat local food and rebuild community. Globalisation, which relies on cheap and abundant fossil fuels, will run its course, but I believe the localisation movement, which includes farmers markets and community gardens, can save us from its aftermath. Above all Australians are good hearted, resilient and adaptable people and pull together in times of crises. Australia is a land of flood, fire and drought but also endless vistas, desert ranges and fragrant bush and remains my home. It is the best place in the world to live!

Rob Olver

www.robolver.com

Opposite page: Road, southern Flinders Ranges.

Selected References

Adelaide and South Australia, Lonely Planet Publications, 2005.

Chapman J & M, *Bushwalking in Australia*, John Chapman, Melbourne, 2003.

East Coast Australia, Lonely Planet Publications, 2011.

Goldrick C, ed. "Postcards from Australia: A pictorial journey", *Australian Geographic*, Bauer Media, Sydney, 2013.

Macintyre S, *A Concise History of Australia*, Cambridge University Press, Cambridge, 1999.

Rankin R, *Classic Wild Walks of Australia*, Rankin Publishers, Brisbane, 1995.

Smith M, *Bushwalking in the Rainbow Region*, self-published, 2010.

Smith R & Abell S, "Australia, Journey Through a Timeless Land", *National Geographic*, Washington D.C., 1999.

Thomas T & Close A, *Australia's Best Walks*, Explore Australia Publishing, Melbourne, 2008.

Walton P & Gaylard G, Landscape Australia: *Images of a colourful land*, PTN Australia, Port Melbourne 2005.

Welsh F, *Great Southern Land: A New History of Australia*, Allen Lane, Melbourne, 2004.